The Advertising and Consumer Culture Reader

Commercial breaks, radio spots, product placements, billboards, pop-up ads—we sometimes take for granted how much advertising surrounds us in our daily lives. We may find ads funny, odd, or even disturbing, but we rarely stop to consider their deeper meaning or function within society.

What, exactly, does advertising do? How and why do ads influence us? How does the advertising industry influence our media? These are just a few of the many important questions addressed in *The Advertising and Consumer Culture Reader*—an incisive, provocative collection that assembles twenty-seven of the most important scholarly writings on advertising and consumer culture to date.

The classic and contemporary essays gathered here explore the past, present, and future of advertising—from the early days of print to the World Wide Web and beyond. These selections offer historical, sociological, critical, cultural, and political-economic lenses to explore a wide range of topics—from consumer activism to globalization to the role of ads in the political process. Together, these key readings chart the past, present, and future of advertising, while also examining the effects of advertising and consumer culture upon individuals, society, cultures, and the world at large.

Designed for use in courses, the collection begins with a general introduction that encourages students to think critically about advertising and consumer culture. Section and chapter introductions offer valuable historical and critical context, while review questions after each reading will spark classroom debates and challenge students' understanding of key concepts.

CONTRIBUTORS:

Mark Andrejevic

Ben H. Bagdikian

Maitrayee Chaudhuri

Hong Cheng

Gary Cross

Greg Dickinson

Stuart Ewen

Katherine Frith

J. Matt Giglio

Robert Goldman

J. Robyn Goodman

Bruce W. Hardy

Christine Harold

Sut Jhally

Aidan Kelly

Naomi Klein

Katrina Lawlor

Devin Leonard

Ruth E. Malone

Matthew P. McAllister

John H. Murphy, II
Stephanie O'Donohoe
Mark P. Orbe
Stephen Papson
Jef I. Richards
Gary Ruskin
Juliet Schor
Michael Schudson
Ping Shaw

Elizabeth A. Smith
Inger L. Stole
Susan Strasser
Joseph Turow
James B. Twitchell
Jose Antonio Vargas
Eric King Watts
Raymond Williams

Joseph Turow is Robert Lewis Shayon Professor of Communication at the University of Pennsylvania's Annenberg School for Communication. He has authored eight books, edited five books, and written more than 100 articles on mass media industries. Most recently, he is author of the third edition of his textbook *Media Today: An Introduction to Mass Communication* and co-editor of the companion volume *Key Readings in Media Today: Mass Communication in Contexts*, both published by Routledge.

Matthew P. McAllister is Associate Professor of Communications at Pennsylvania State University. He is author of *The Commercialization of American Culture: New Advertising, Control and Democracy* and co-editor of *Comics and Ideology* and *Film and Comic Books*.

The Advertising and Consumer Culture Reader

Edited by

Joseph Turow and Matthew P. McAllister

Routledge
Taylor & Francis Group

NEW YORK AND LONDON

First published 2009
by Routledge
270 Madison Ave, New York, NY 10016

Simultaneously published in the UK
by Routledge
2 Park Square, Milton Park, Abingdon, Oxon OX14 4RN

Routledge is an imprint of the Taylor & Francis Group, an informa business

© 2009 Taylor & Francis

Typeset in Perpetua and Bell Gothic by
RefineCatch Limited, Bungay, Suffolk
Printed and bound in the United States of America on acid-free paper by
Sheridan Books, Inc.

Library of Congress Cataloging-in-Publication Data
The advertising and consumer culture reader / Joseph Turow and Matthew McAllister.
p. cm.
Includes bibliographical references and index.
1. Advertising—Social aspects.   I. Turow, Joseph.   II. McAllister, Matthew P.
HF5821.A284 2009
306.3—dc22
2008048806

ISBN10: 0–415–96329–X (hbk)
ISBN10: 0–415–96330–3 (pbk)

ISBN13: 978–0–415–96329–9 (hbk)
ISBN13: 978–0–415–96330–5 (pbk)

Contents

Acknowledgments   ix

Joseph Turow and Matthew P. McAllister   1
GENERAL INTRODUCTION: THINKING CRITICALLY ABOUT
ADVERTISING AND CONSUMER CULTURE

PART ONE
The Rise of Commercial and Consumer Culture   9

INTRODUCTION TO PART ONE   11

1   Raymond Williams   13
    ADVERTISING: THE MAGIC SYSTEM

2   Susan Strasser   25
    THE ALIEN PAST: CONSUMER CULTURE IN
    HISTORICAL PERSPECTIVE

3   Stuart Ewen   38
    "EDUCATE THE PUBLIC!"

PART TWO
The Political Economy of Advertising   55

INTRODUCTION TO PART TWO   57

4   Inger L. Stole   59
    TELEVISED CONSUMPTION: WOMEN, ADVERTISERS AND THE
    EARLY DAYTIME TELEVISION INDUSTRY

5   Ben H. Bagdikian   76
    DR. BRANDRETH HAS GONE TO HARVARD

6   Jef I. Richards and John H. Murphy, II   91
    ECONOMIC CENSORSHIP AND FREE SPEECH: THE CIRCLE OF
    COMMUNICATION BETWEEN ADVERTISERS, MEDIA, AND CONSUMERS

7   Matthew P. McAllister and J. Matt Giglio   110
    THE COMMODITY FLOW OF U.S. CHILDREN'S TELEVISION

PART THREE
Creating Advertising   **129**

    INTRODUCTION TO PART THREE   131

8   Aidan Kelly, Katrina Lawlor, and Stephanie O'Donohoe   133
    ENCODING ADVERTISEMENTS: THE CREATIVE PERSPECTIVE

9   Devin Leonard   150
    NIGHTMARE ON MADISON AVENUE: MEDIA FRAGMENTATION,
    RECESSION, FED-UP CLIENTS, TiVo—IT'S ALL TROUBLE,
    AND THE AD BUSINESS IS CAUGHT UP IN THE WAKE

10 Elizabeth A. Smith and Ruth E. Malone   159
    THE OUTING OF PHILIP MORRIS: ADVERTISING TOBACCO TO
    GAY MEN

PART FOUR
Ads and Globalization   **171**

    INTRODUCTION TO PART FOUR   173

11 Maitrayee Chaudhuri   175
    GENDER AND ADVERTISEMENTS: THE RHETORIC OF GLOBALISATION

12 Katherine Frith, Ping Shaw, and Hong Cheng   193
    THE CONSTRUCTION OF BEAUTY: A CROSS-CULTURAL
    ANALYSIS OF WOMEN'S MAGAZINE ADVERTISING

13 Robert Goldman and Stephen Papson   207
    "JUST DO IT," BUT NOT ON MY PLANET

PART FIVE
Ads and Cultural Meaning 223

INTRODUCTION TO PART FIVE 225

14 James B. Twitchell 227
REFLECTIONS AND REVIEWS: AN ENGLISH TEACHER
LOOKS AT BRANDING

15 Michael Schudson 237
ADVERTISING AS CAPITALIST REALISM

16 Eric King Watts and Mark P. Orbe 256
THE SPECTACULAR CONSUMPTION OF "TRUE"
AFRICAN AMERICAN CULTURE: "WHASSUP" WITH
THE BUDWEISER GUYS?

17 J. Robyn Goodman 275
FLABLESS IS FABULOUS: HOW LATINA AND ANGLO WOMEN
READ AND INCORPORATE THE EXCESSIVELY THIN BODY
IDEAL INTO EVERYDAY EXPERIENCE

PART SIX
Ads and Politics 291

INTRODUCTION TO PART SIX 293

18 Greg Dickinson 295
SELLING DEMOCRACY: CONSUMER CULTURE AND
CITIZENSHIP IN THE WAKE OF SEPTEMBER 11

19 Bruce W. Hardy 312
POLITICAL ADVERTISING IN US PRESIDENTIAL CAMPAIGNS:
MESSAGES, TARGETING, AND EFFECTS

20 Jose Antonio Vargas 328
CAMPAIGN. USA: WITH THE INTERNET COMES A NEW
POLITICAL "CLICKOCRACY"

PART SEVEN
Advertising and the Active Citizen 335

INTRODUCTION TO PART SEVEN 337

21 Gary Cross 339
A NEW CONSUMERISM, 1960–1980

22 Christine Harold   348
    PRANKING RHETORIC: "CULTURE JAMMING" AS
    MEDIA ACTIVISM

23 Naomi Klein   369
    LOCAL FOREIGN POLICY: STUDENTS AND COMMUNITIES
    JOIN THE FRAY

PART EIGHT
Ads and the Future   **381**

    INTRODUCTION TO PART EIGHT   383

24 Mark Andrejevic   385
    THE WORK OF BEING WATCHED: INTERACTIVE MEDIA
    AND THE EXPLOITATION OF SELF-DISCLOSURE

25 Joseph Turow   402
    ADVERTISERS AND AUDIENCE AUTONOMY AT THE END
    OF TELEVISION

26 Gary Ruskin and Juliet Schor   410
    EVERY NOOK AND CRANNY: THE DANGEROUS SPREAD OF
    COMMERCIALIZED CULTURE

27 Sut Jhally   416
    ADVERTISING AT THE EDGE OF THE APOCALYPSE

    Index   429

Acknowledgments

Joseph Turow would like to thank the following Penn-Annenberg doctoral students: Brooke Duffy and Joel Penney for their help with the chapter introductions and questions, Lokman Tsui for his help accessing and organizing material for the book, and Brett A. Bumgarner and Angela M. Lee for their help in copyediting the first half of this book. Matt McAllister would like to thank Penn State doctoral students Rafael R. Daz-Torres and Rachen Ruben for their help in copyediting the second half of this book.

Chapter 1: Williams, R. (1980). Advertising: The Magic System. In *Problems in Materialism and Culture*, 170–195. London: Verso. Reprinted with permission of Verso.

Chapter 2: Strasser, S. (2003). The Alien Past: Consumer Culture in Historical Perspective, *Journal of Consumer Policy*, 26(4), 375–393.

Chapter 3: Ewen, S. (1996). "Educate the Public!" In *PR!: A Social History of Spin*, 82–101, plus end notes. New York: Basic Books. Copyright © 1996 by Basic Books. Reprinted by permission of Basic Books, a member of Perseus Books Group. All rights reserved.

Chapter 4: Stole, I. L. (2003). Televised Consumption: Women, Advertisers and the Early Daytime Television Industry. *Consumption, Markets and Culture*, 6(1), 65–80. Reprinted by permission of Taylor & Francis Ltd, http://www.informaworld.com.

Chapter 5: Bagdikian, B. (2004). Dr. Brandreth Has Gone to Harvard. In *The New Media Monopoly*. Reprinted by permission of Beacon Press, Boston.

Chapter 6: Richards, J. I., and Murphy, J. H., II (1996). Economic Censorship and Free Speech: The Circle of Communication between Advertisers, Media, and Consumers. *Journal of Current Issues and Research in Advertising*, 18(1), 21–34. Reproduced by Permission of CtC Press. All Rights Reserved.

Chapter 7: McAllister, M. P., and Giglio, J. M. (2005). The Commodity Flow of U.S. Children's Television. *Critical Studies in Media Communication*, 22(1), 26–44. Reprinted by permission of Taylor & Francis Ltd, http://www.informaworld.com.

Chapter 8: Kelly, A., Lawlor, K., and O'Donohoe, S. (2005). Encoding Advertisements: The Creative Perspective. *Journal of Marketing Management*, 21, 505–528. Reproduced by permission of Westburn Publishers Ltd.

Chapter 9: Leonard, D. (2004, June 28). Nightmare on Madison Avenue. *Fortune*, 93–101. Reprinted with permission of *Fortune*.

Chapter 10: Smith, E. A., and Malone, R. E. (2003). The Outing of Philip Morris: Advertising Tobacco to Gay Men. *American Journal of Public Health, 93*(6), 988–993. Reprinted with permission from the American Public Health Association.

Chapter 11: Chaudhuri, M. (2001). Gender and Advertisements: The Rhetoric of Globalisation. *Women's Studies International Forum, 24*(3/4), 373–385. Reprinted with permission from Elsevier.

Chapter 12: Frith, K., Shaw, P., and Cheng, H. (2005). The Construction of Beauty: A Cross-cultural Analysis of Women's Magazine Advertising. *Journal of Communication, 55*(1), 56–70. Reprinted with permission from Blackwell.

Chapter 13: Goldman, R. and Papson, S. (1998). "'Just Do It,' but Not on my Planet." In *Nike Culture: The Sign of the Swoosh*, 169–186. London: Sage Publications Ltd. Reprinted with permission of Sage Publications Ltd.

Chapter 14: Twitchell, J. B. (2004). Reflections and Reviews: An English Teacher Looks at Branding. *Journal of Consumer Research, 31*(2), 484–489. © 2004 by Journal of Consumer Research, Inc. Reprinted with permission of the University of Chicago Press.

Chapter 15: Schudson, M. (1984). "Advertising as Capitalist Realism." In *Advertising, the Uneasy Persuasion* 209–233. New York: Basic Books. Copyright © 1984 by Michael Schudson. Reprinted by permission of Basic Books, a member of Perseus Books Group. All rights reserved.

Chapter 16: Watts, E. K., and Orbe, M. P. (2002). The Spectacular Consumption of "True" African American Culture: "Whassup" with the Budweiser Guys? *Critical Studies in Media Communication, 19*(1), 1–20. Reprinted by permission of Taylor & Francis Ltd, http://www.informaworld.com.

Chapter 17: Goodman, J. Robyn. (2002). Flabless is Fabulous: How Latina and Anglo Women Read and Incorporate the Excessively Thin Body Ideal into Everyday Experience. *Journalism & Mass Communication Quarterly, 79*(3), 712–727. Reprinted with permission of the *Journalism & Mass Communication Quarterly*.

Chapter 18: Dickinson, G. (2005). Selling Democracy: Consumer Culture and Citizenship in the Wake of September 11. *Southern Communication Journal, 70*(4), 271–284. Reprinted by permission of Taylor & Francis Ltd, http://www.informaworld.com.

Chapter 19: Hardy, B. W. (2009). Political Advertising in US Presidential Campaigns: Messages, Targeting and Effects. Reproduced with permission.

Chapter 20: Vargas, J. A. (2008, April 1). Campaign.USA: With the Internet Comes a New Political "Clickocracy." *The Washington Post*, C1. From *The Washington Post*, April 1 © 2008 *The Washington Post*. All rights reserved. Used by permission and protected by the Copyright Laws of the United States. "The printing, copying, redistribution, or retransmission of the Material without express written permission is prohibited."

Chapter 21: Cross, G. (2000). "A New Consumerism, 1960–1980." In *An All-Consuming Century: Why Commercialism Won in Modern America*, 146–155. Columbia University Press. Reprinted with permission of the publisher. © 2000.

Chapter 22: Harold, C. (2004). Pranking Rhetoric: "Culture Jamming" as Media Activism. *Critical Studies in Media Communication, 21*(3), 189–211. Reprinted by permission of Taylor & Francis Ltd, http://www.informaworld.com.

Chapter 23: Klein, N. (1999). "Local Foreign Policy: Students and Communities Join the

Fray." In *No Logo: Taking Aim at The Brand Bullies* 397–410. New York: Picador. Reprinted by permission of HarperCollins Publishers Ltd. © 1999.

Chapter 24: Andrejevic, M. (2002). The Work of Being Watched: Interactive Media and the Exploitation of Self-disclosure. *Critical Studies in Media Communication, 19*(2), 230–248. Reprinted by permission of Taylor & Francis Ltd, http://www. informaworld.com.

Chapter 25: Turow, J. (2009). Advertisers and Audience Autonomy at the End of Television. Reproduced with permission.

Chapter 26: Ruskin, G., and Schor, J. (2005, January/February). Every Nook and Cranny: The Dangerous Spread of Commercialized Culture. *Multinational Monitor*, 20–23. Reprinted with permission of the publisher.

Chapter 27: Jhally, S. (2000). "Advertising at the Edge of the Apocalypse." In R. Andersen and L. Strate (Eds.), *Critical Studies in Media Commercialism* 27–39. Oxford: Oxford University Press. By permission of Oxford University Press.

JOSEPH TUROW AND
MATTHEW P. McALLISTER

GENERAL INTRODUCTION
Thinking Critically about Advertising and Consumer Culture

JENNY WAKES AT 7:30am to the sounds of a radio commercial urging her to eat lunch at McDonald's. The next song played is "Pass the Courvoisier"; she remembers seeing the music video with that brand of liquor prominently displayed. She turns on NBC's *The Today Show* as she heads to the shower, and she hears a chef from a new reality show talking about the program and mentioning his Chicago restaurant. After the segment is over, a commercial break airs with several ads and a network promotional spot for that same reality show. As she eats her "Rice Krispies" cereal, she reads the box's recipes for cookies made of "Rice Krispies," "Gold Medal Flour," and "Sunkist" raisins. There is a coupon in the box for the "Sunkist" raisins. On her way to the bus stop, she passes several signs touting local businesses, store window displays with different fashions, and one large billboard announcing a new Honda. When the bus slides in, it carries an ad for another car, a Ford. Inside the bus, which is heading to her college, a number of the ads call out to her that the Princeton Review company can help her study for her law school, medical school, or business school entrance exams. She realizes that she had seen an amateur video on YouTube by an enthusiastic Princeton Review teacher who talks about the average score for Princeton Review students on the MCAT. An ad for Princeton appeared in one of the magazines to which she subscribes. And an ad for Princeton prep courses stared at her from the college newspaper two days ago. "Princeton keeps stalking me," she mutters to herself, almost out loud. And then she wonders, "Maybe I ought to think about a prep course . . ."

Although the particulars of Jenny's fictional experience may not have happened to you, you probably have experienced what she has: We live in a world filled with advertisements and other types of commercial messages. We take that world so much for granted that it seems perfectly natural that we move through it without paying special attention. We may acknowledge that certain ads can sometimes lead us to buy things. Every now and then, though, some ads do come at us that make us pay attention. These may be ads that we find funny or odd or particularly relevant at a point in our lives. They may be ads that are aimed at us based on the neighborhoods in which we live, the websites we visit, or an entire range of information about us that media firms (such as magazines) buy and use without our knowing it. They may be ads that show up once and are so memorable we keep them in our minds. Or they may be ads in a multi-pronged campaign that create a pincer movement around us so that we can't help but think about them. Rarely, though, do we give pause to think deeply about ads on the radio, commercial plugs on news-talk shows, and outdoor signs touting a variety of products. They are just part of the background of our lives. And even rarer do we think deeply about how the finances of advertising may affect us.

Well, the purpose of this Reader is to offer reasons, and some help, to think deeply about the commercial culture, including advertisements, that surrounds us. The writings in the following pages look at our world of commercialized images in a wide variety of ways from a broad gamut of political viewpoints. They are sometimes funny, sometimes sad, sometimes enraging, but we hope they are always provocative and smart. In putting this book together, our goal was to go beyond choosing pieces about "advertising and contemporary culture" that we think are interesting and varied. We also wanted to organize the articles in ways that would make sense in terms of their coverage of key subjects as well as in terms of the flow of the arguments in relation to one another. Our goal in this essay is to present an overview of this book that will introduce the topics and explain ways in which we see the readings relating to each other. It will be great if you disagree with us and find other ways of putting the pieces together that are more meaningful to your understanding of this territory. In fact, we welcome your emailing us about that.

Before presenting our bird's-eye view of the readings, it will be useful to share our understanding of the territory we are covering by explaining what we mean by advertising and commercial culture. Let's start with advertising. We can define advertising as the activity of explicitly paying for media space or time in order to direct favorable attention to certain goods or services. Three points about this definition deserve emphasis. First, advertisers (a local dry cleaner or an international company such as Kraft) pay for the space or time that they receive. Second, advertising clearly states its presence. When you see an ad, you know what it is for, and you often know quite easily who is sponsoring it. Third, advertising involves persuasion—the ability or power to induce an individual or group of individuals to undertake a course of action or embrace a point of view by means of argument, reasoning, or emotional plea.

This description of advertising implies an important point that needs to be made explicit: Advertising is typically carried out by several organizations working together in the process of creating, distributing, and exhibiting the persuasive messages contracted by the advertisers. In many countries, the several organizations are, in fact, part of a complex advertising industry made up of thousands of competing large and small companies. Specifics on how all of this takes place could fill up several books; you will get tastes of it in the chapters that follow. What we want to emphasize here is that the advertising industry's work involves two interconnected systems of activity that are crucial to Western society. These are a system of ideology and a system of media support.

By system of ideology we mean a body of beliefs about the values, needs, and aspirations that guide the behaviors of people and organizations in relation to one another. When people hear the word ideologies, they often think of sets of political ideas—for example, capitalism, communism, or socialism. That understanding of ideology certainly applies to advertising. People who create ads do start with a view of the political and economic values that guide the society. Advertising organizations in old communist Russia or China, for example, approached their work with very different ideas of governmental authority and economic competition than those in capitalist countries such as the United States or Canada. But the system of ideology that is part of advertising practitioners' activities is made up of more than straightforwardly political and economic ideas. It comprises their views of what will motivate people in the society to act favorably toward the product or service that is being advertised. It also involves their views of what types of people—even what particular individuals—to try to persuade, why, and—especially key—how.

How, for example, do workers in the ad agency for the upscale Saks Fifth Avenue department store think of the women it will target with its Fall Fashion ads? What categories about them are important to creating the message? Should they take into consideration age, income, education, profession, body shape, marital status, type of car, type of home—or all of these and/or other characteristics? What do these categories and others mean to the creators of advertising in terms of their creation of images? If they decide that their target Saks' customer is 40 years old, what ideas about lifestyles and attitudes would the ad practitioners link to that age in their creation of persuasive messages? How do they symbolically represent in the ads these lifestyles and attitudes? How do they make these symbols conform to, or even change, the image of the brand that already exists? How do they make sure they stand out from ads for the other products we see? The answers to these questions reflect the system of ideology that the advertising practitioners have learned as they work within their industry. The ad practitioners may have different views of the needs and aspirations that guide the behaviors of certain types of people depending on their economic status and maybe even their political values—conservative, liberal, Democrat, Republican, Independent. The ways they think Saks' customers will understand Fall Fashion ads is probably startlingly different from the way they think value-conscious Wal-Mart customers will understand such ads. And the ads they create may be very different as well. Although the goal of advertising is to sell a brand, the above system of the advertisement's creation means that the targeting of certain audiences in advertising, and the symbols used in ads, have cultural implications beyond this selling goal.

As the above argues, beliefs that ad practitioners develop about economic, political and social, psychological, attitudinal and physical characteristics of target customers become the basis for the advertisements that art personnel and writers create. Ideas about what customers like and where they can be reached also have profound implications for the advertising industry's second system of activity, its system of media support. Advertising is a major revenue source for much of our media. Advertisers pay media firms if they can reach the people these advertisers need to persuade. If Saks' ad people believe the most efficient way to reach their potential customers is by buying several pages in *Vogue* magazine rather than in *People* magazine, *Vogue* will get the cash, not *People*. *People* may get money from Wal-Mart advertising—if Wal-Mart's media planners decide that magazines are good ways to reach potential customers. If they decide that advertising on cable TV and the Internet are better at reaching Wal-Mart customers than is advertising in *People*, that magazine would not get the money and certain cable and Internet firms would. These types of media-buying decisions for advertisers take place all the time, and it is through them that certain types of media outlets do well and others do not. And if media outlets are not doing well—if they are losing advertising revenue to their competitors—not only are they in danger of disappearing, but they may decide to make themselves more "advertising-friendly." Media may try to attract adverting revenue by giving advertisers more influence over the media's content.

The impact of these decisions is particularly large because so many media in the United States and elsewhere depend on advertising for most of their funding. Consumer magazines, for example, draw more than half their revenue from advertising. Broadcast television draws almost all of it. The advertising industry's decisions regarding media support are major factors in shaping the audiences that media executives try to attract and the media that they use to do that. Some companies have more power than others over these decisions because of the amount of money they spend. Consumer packaged goods giant Procter & Gamble, for example, invested billions of dollars in advertising during 2007. And Mindshare, a media buying company with many clients, spent billions on select media based on certain perspectives of where audiences go and what they want. It is no exaggeration to say that media-support decisions by large advertisers and agencies help decide if and how media industries survive and, if they do survive, how they may behave toward advertising.

In view of what we have said about the advertising industry's systems of ideology and media support, it should be no surprise that the industry is deeply involved in creating consumer culture. By consumer culture, we mean the symbols and messages that surround people about products and services that they buy and use (that is, consume). Consumer culture also involves how people make meaning from these messages: how we understand ourselves and our lives through consumer messages. It might initially strike you that all of these sorts of messages come from advertising. But think of it a bit more and you will realize that although advertising is a widespread vehicle for consumer culture (with over $200 billion spent on it in 2007), there is more to consumer culture than advertising.

Think, for example, of Jenny's experiences and ruminations during her trek from her bed to her college. "Pass the Courvoisier" is not an ad; it's a hip-hop song. *The Today Show*'s chef appearance was billed as an interview, not an ad. The "Rice Krispies" recipe-with-coupon is less a standard advertisement than an incentive for cereal box readers to make cookies with a product they had already bought. The YouTube video for Princeton Review seems to be from a happy customer. The first might be called unpaid product integration; the second, publicity; the third, product promotion; and the fourth, buzz—either of the accidental kind (if it really was put up there by a happy camper) or the planned, stealth kind (if it was put there by Princeton Review to look amateurish and therefore more credible to college students than an ad). Add to these activities public relations, product licensing, and event marketing (which includes mall marketing, marketing at sports and entertainment events, and marketing at moveable "road shows"), and it becomes clear how so much of consumer culture comes to us in forms other than advertising. Not surprisingly, companies spend a lot of money on these activities; one research outfit estimated that spending on consumer event marketing in 2005 reached nearly $28 billion and valued TV product placements in the same year at almost $6 billion. Not surprisingly, too, industries separate from but interacting with the advertising industry have developed around these businesses.

But while the amounts of money that marketers are pouring into these activities are huge and growing, they are not the primary reason for our interest in these non-advertising engines of consumer culture. Rather, our interest centers on an awareness that, just like advertising, public relations, event marketing, and the other consumer-culture businesses are very much involved in a system of ideology and a system of media support. Like advertising, but without calling attention to the commercial purpose of their activity, they create messages based on, and perhaps influencing, beliefs about the values, needs, and aspirations that guide the behaviors of target audiences. And like advertising, they provide support to media—either directly (for example, by paying for product placement) or indirectly (by supplying "free" guests for talk shows and free products for programs).

One result is what Jenny and all of us see around us: a cavalcade of images that surround us with messages about who we are and how we fit into society as part of a business of continually encouraging us to buy products and services. Another result is what neither Jenny nor most of us see: a media support system based on the idea that the best media are those that help to sell products and services to advertising-desirable audiences. Put another way, the support system is not neutral. It affects what the media offer us. It ties media to the spread of consumer culture in the interests of marketers and the advertising, public relations, event-marketing, and other industries that help them.

"OK," you might ask. "I'll accept your description of the ideological and economic activities that are part of advertising and other aspects of consumer culture. But what real difference do those roles make to the way I live my life and think about the world? Should I be worried or happy that I see all these great offers? Is it a problem that advertisers try to get me to laugh at commercials or that product-placement experts try to understand my likes and dislikes? And if I can get magazines cheaply and Internet sites for free, why should I be worried that it comes along with ideas about what I should buy, particularly because I pay so little attention to them? In general, why shouldn't I accept that consumer culture has become part of my life and the life of my society?"

The Plan of the Book

These are important questions. The readings that follow present many answers, and they do it from a variety of political and social perspectives. You are about to dive into a world of competing ideas and sometimes-angry arguments about phenomena we typically consider once, and then not too deeply. You might not have thought very hard about the Bud ad where African Americans greet each other with "Whassup," about a "bumper" during a Nickelodeon television show, or about a Nike swoosh. Writers in this book have paid a lot of attention to these aspects of commercial culture, and they have very interesting things to say.

We have arranged their essays into eight parts. The first, logically enough, starts an exploration into the history of advertising and other aspects of commercial culture. Of course, to get a detailed understanding of how commercial culture grew in the West, in general, and in the United States, in particular, you would have to read many books. Our purpose here is to present three experts in this subject who ruminate on the roles that advertising and public relations have played in society, particularly as they became industries, not just activities by individuals. Part Two continues an interest in the social role of consumer-culture industries but turns the focus on the "support system" implications of advertising: also referred to as the political economy of the advertising business. That is, the articles look at ways in which economic relationships among advertisers and media firms have both reflected and shaped power of various segments of society. Two of the articles—by Stole and Bagdikian—are of an historical nature, while the two others—by Richards and Murphy and McAllister and Giglio—discuss more recent developments. All, however, raise topics about the impact that advertising money has on media "speech" in the broadest sense. Moreover, the very different perspective that Richards and Murphy take from the others can spark interesting conversation on why the political economy of advertising matters and what we ought to do about it.

Part Three retains concern with the industrial and economic power of advertising, but shifts emphasis from the industry's leverage on media images to a focus on the way the industry works to create and circulate its own images. The articles enter into quite different parts of the process. Smith and Malone's exploration of Philip Morris' attempt to target gays with cigarette commercials reveals the interconnection of creative strategies, media planning, and the rhetoric of political defense. Kelly, Lawlor, and O'Donohoe investigate broader relationships between advertisers and audiences, leading to a central claim about advertising's ability to watch us that "Advertising agencies can be seen to be operating in the engine room of a panoptic marketing system." Leonard delves into the tumultuous changes facing the ad business that are affecting the ad industry's creative practices and media planning. Far from being a legendary location for fun-loving eccentrics, he finds bitterness and a concern in the industries that the ad agency is becoming a "depressing place to work." At the same time, the power of a small number of firms over the creation and placement of commercial messages in the US and around the world is enormous.

Part Four moves to the worldwide impact of Western advertising from three perspectives. Goldman and Papson argue that sometimes an ad campaign can actually activate a worldwide dialog, as when Nike's self-creation through its campaigns bumped against the hard realities of news reports of its labor practices. Chaudhuri discusses the implications of global advertising for male and female images in India, while Frith, Shaw, and Cheng compare ideas of beauty in commercials of Singapore, Taiwan, and the US. Those writers suggest that we have to spend a fair amount of effort to draw out the political and social messages that may be specific to particular societies.

Part Five brings in five authors who help us do just that for American society. From a variety of perspectives, they explore ways to understand the meaning of advertising in general, and specific ad campaigns in particular. Twitchell and Schudson take the broad view, exploring ways to understand advertising as an extension of nineteenth-century poetics and twentieth-century realistic art, respectively. Goodman looks at the relationship of gender and promotional forms as she reflects on ways Latina and Anglo women understand ads that reflect on body types that are presumably American ideals. Watts and Orbe focus on a particular campaign, for Budweiser, using rhetorical analysis and interviews to reflect on how the campaign "works" for African Americans and non-African Americans.

By now you probably get the idea that all of the readings we have chosen make the case in one way or another that advertising does exercise power in the life of society. Some writers believe that advertising's impact is on balance benign, even helpful. Other commentators worry that the system of ideology and the system of media support raise problems that we cannot ignore. Many of these writers would undoubtedly agree that all aspects of advertising are political, in the broad sense of *political* as reflecting a struggle for power in society. When Schudson says that "advertising is capitalism's way of saying 'I love you' to itself," that is a statement that advertising is set up to make a politically important case for capitalism as an economic system. When Chaudhuri writes of the power of global advertising messages to shape agendas about how men and women should behave, she is saying that those messages have political implications—that is, they support people with certain views of gender over others who dispute those views.

Of course, there is a narrower understanding of political as standing for the process of participating in democracy through voting and other forms of influencing government actions. Parts Six and Seven take up this meaning in different ways. Part Six focuses on advertising's role in the democratic process. Bruce Hardy presents an historical and contemporary overview of political advertising. Picking up where Hardy leaves off, Vargas reviews concerns about the use and effect of the Internet for political campaigns. Dickinson steps back from the conceptions of politics and democracy that guide Hardy and Vargas to point out how a national tragedy—the 9/11 attacks—led companies to argue that commercial consumption and the work of a democratic society go hand in hand. Continuing to buy would send the message that the country is strong, that its people are united, that its political system is stable, and that terrorists will not win.

We suspect that the writers in Part Seven would, like Dickinson, question the ethical premise of merging commercialism and democracy as a sales approach, or even a patriotic statement. All three are concerned with how the democratic process has been or can be used to rein in alleged abuses of commercial culture. Gary Cross looks at this issue historically, from the standpoint of anti-commercialism crusades and "hippie" lifestyles of the 1950s and 1960s. Harold argues that contemporary ways in which advertising and media critics are drawing attention to what they consider the absurdities of commercial logic is to implement pranks that use media's incentives against themselves and that skewer marketers' logics. Not believing that these "pranking" activities are enough to eliminate the worst impact of commercialism (such as its reliance on cheap, virtually enslaved foreign labor), Naomi Klein encourages people to enter the political fray, to use their leverage (or their organization's leverage) as buyers of products to put pressure on local companies and governments and not to buy from marketers who are not good citizens of the world.

You might wonder (and well you should) whether and how people can agree that marketers are good citizens or bad citizens. While you do that, take a look at Part Eight, which presents a range of views about the future of advertisers' relationships to people and the planet. Gary Ruskin and Juliet Schor review many of the traditional complaints of advertising's critics and argue that the way things are going, the complaints will deserve to get louder. Joseph Turow and Mark Andrejevic separately consider new concerns that changing media and advertising strategies and technologies are raising, concerns that center on marketers' surveillance of their customers and the possibility that various forms of discrimination may arise as a result of new ways of thinking about audiences and consumers. Sut Jhally concludes this part, and the book, with a sad reflection on what we might call the ultimate concern about commercial culture: its encouragement to buy, throw away, and consume more, thereby despoiling the earth. Jhally presents no way out of this dilemma, and we hesitated to end the readings with a scenario this downbeat. We encourage you, though, to consider the readings in earlier sections as ways to further understand the problem Jhally raises and to develop possible political and industrial responses to it. In general, we hope that your movement though this book's worlds of advertising and consumer culture will make you think a bit differently about the world in which you live, about the media system that you use, and the marketing images that are all around.

PART ONE

The Rise of Commercial and Consumer Culture

INTRODUCTION TO PART ONE

THE THREE READINGS IN THIS PART all discuss historical developments in advertising and public relations. They highlight especially how modern trends in promotion and publicity have their roots in earlier times. As we will see from the readings, modern techniques such as two-way public relations, planned obsolescence of products, advertising "clutter" throughout our society, the integration of advertising campaigns with public relations efforts, and the advertising theme that buying branded products can solve our social and personal problems have their origins in earlier eras.

All three authors in this Part are also major scholars in advertising history and the broader fields of cultural studies and critical approaches to media. Raymond Williams was a central figure in the development of British Cultural Studies, which in turn has influenced much scholarly work on popular culture throughout the world. His chapter in this Part is one of the most widely cited critical assessments of advertising. Susan Strasser's earlier work, *Satisfaction Guaranteed*, is a detailed and well-read history of the development of modern advertising, and the later piece reproduced here highlights some of the major social and cultural shifts brought about by the introduction of consumer culture. Stuart Ewen has published several works that have greatly informed our understanding of the development of the persuasion industries. His earlier work, *Captains of Consciousness*, links the development of advertising to the larger social context of the development of industrial capitalism. Ewen's 1996 book, *PR!: A Social History of Spin*, from which this reading is drawn, was a much-needed and very well received critical history of the practice of public relations.

Chapter 1

RAYMOND WILLIAMS

ADVERTISING
The Magic System

THIS ESSAY WAS ORIGINALLY WRITTEN IN THE EARLY 1960s and reflects much on the British advertising experience. It is valuable in its insights about the historical development of advertising, but also amazingly timeless in its observations about modern advertising throughout the world, despite the essay's early publication date and British focus. In the first half of the essay, Williams delineates a few important themes in the development of modern advertising. These themes include (1) the use of "puffery," or exaggerated language to promote a product; (2) the influence of government policy and regulation on how advertising operates; (3) the degree to which advertising "clutter" may be present not just in individual media, but even in our social environments (such as Times Square); (4) the movement of advertising from primarily a "newspaper-style" classified and largely textual form to a more "display-ad style" and visual form; (5) the role of public relations as a complement to advertising campaigns; and (6) the constant complaint that "ads cannot get much worse," when history continues to prove this prediction wrong.

The second half of the essay develops one particular characteristic of modern advertising. In a famous observation, Williams writes that advertising, in its current form, is not persuasive to us because people are too materialistic, but rather it is effective because modern people are not materialistic enough. (We see this point echoed by James Twitchell in a later chapter.) If we were truly materialistic, then we would just want material goods for their pure material function, their inherent "use value." But just showing the product in an ad would not easily differentiate brands that are often exactly alike in substance and function. Ads, therefore, frequently say that buying the material product (the brand) will solve non-material problems: buying a car will provide family security; buying a medicated skin cream will offer peer admiration and romance. In this sense, advertising makes brands "magic." In ads, brands have the power to solve our problems. Williams notes that modern capitalistic society cannot truly solve many of our deeply human needs. In fact, he argues that capitalism creates many of our social and personal problems. But advertising, positioning us as individuals with plenty of consumer choice, helps to alleviate this. It tells us that we do have agency, or individual power, in our lives. The agency is that we can choose from among many, many brands! As a form that encourages individual agency, though, consumer choice is extremely limited in how it may solve larger problems of society. Williams' argument is similar to other critics who point to the "commodity fetishism" that advertising encourages; the celebration of brands and consumption, no matter what the specific product being advertised is, or how that product was made.

History

It is customary to begin even the shortest account of the history of advertising by recalling the three thousand year old papyrus from Thebes, offering a reward for a runaway slave, and to go on to such recollections as the crier in the streets of Athens, the paintings of gladiators, with sentences urging attendance at their combats, in ruined Pompeii, and the flybills on the pillars of the Forum in Rome. This pleasant little ritual can be quickly performed, and as quickly forgotten: it is, of course, altogether too modest. If by advertising we mean what was meant by Shakespeare and the translators of the Authorized Version—the processes of taking or giving notice of something—it is as old as human society, and some pleasant recollections from the Stone Age could be quite easily devised.

The real business of the historian of advertising is more difficult: to trace the development from processes of specific attention and information to an institutionalized system of commercial information and persuasion; to relate this to changes in society and in the economy: and to trace changes in method in the context of changing organizations and intentions.

The spreading of information, by the crier or by handwritten and printed broadsheets, is known from all periods of English society. The first signs of anything more organized come in the seventeenth century, with the development of newsbooks, mercuries and newspapers. Already certain places, such as St Paul's in London, were recognized as centres for the posting of specific bills, and the extension of such posting to the new printed publications was a natural development. The material of such advertisements ranged from offers and wants in personal service, notices of the publication of books, and details of runaway servants, apprentices, horses and dogs, to announcements of new commodities available at particular shops, enthusiastic announcements of remedies and specifics, and notices of the public showing of monsters, prodigies and freaks. While the majority were the simple, basically factual and specific notices we now call 'classified', there were also direct recommendations, as here, from 1658:

> That Excellent, and by all Physicians, approved China drink, called by the Chineans Tcha, by other nations *Tay* alias *Tee*, is sold at the Sultaness Head Cophee-House in Sweeting's Rents, by the Royal Exchange, London.

Mention of the physicians begins that process of extension from the conventional recommendations of books as 'excellent' or 'admirable' and the conventional adjectives which soon become part of the noun, in a given context (as in my native village, every dance is a Grand Dance). The most extravagant early extensions were in the field of medicines, and it was noted in 1652, of the writers of copy in news-books:

> There is never a mountebank who, either by professing of chymistry or any other art drains money from the people of the nation but these arch-cheats have a share in the booty—because the fellow cannot lye sufficiently himself he gets one of these to do't for him.

Looking up, in the 1950s, from the British Dental Association's complaints of misleading television advertising of toothpastes, we can recognize the advertisement, in 1660, of a 'most Excellent and Approved DENTIFRICE', which not only makes the teeth "white as Ivory", but

> being constantly used, the Parties using it are never troubled with the Tooth-ache. It fastens the Teeth, sweetens the Breath, and preserves the Gums and Mouth from Cankers and Imposthumes.

Moreover

> the right are onely to be had at Thomas Rookes, Stationer, at the Holy Lamb at the east end of St Paul's Church, near the School, in sealed papers at 12d the paper.

In the year of the Plague, London was full of

> SOVEREIGN Cordials against the Corruption of the Air.

These did not exactly succeed, but a long and profitable trade, and certain means of promoting it, were now firmly established.

With the major growth of newspapers, from the 1690s, the volume of advertisements notably increased. The great majority of them were still of the specific 'classified' kind, and were grouped in regular sections of the paper or magazine. Ordinary household goods were rarely advertised; people knew where to get these. But, apart from the wants and the runaways, new things, from the latest book or play to new kinds of luxury or 'cosmatick' made their way through these columns. By and large, it was still only in the pseudo-medical and toilet advertisements that persuasion methods were evident. The announcements were conventionally printed, and there was hardly any illustration. Devices of emphasis—the hand, the asterisk, the NB—can be found, and sailing announcements had small woodcuts of a ship, runaway notices similar cuts of a man looking back over his shoulder. But, in the early eighteenth century, these conventional figures became too numerous, and most newspapers banned them. The manufacturer of a 'Spring Truss' who illustrated his device, had few early imitators.

A more general tendency was noted by Johnson in 1758:

> Advertisements are now so numerous that they are very negligently perused, and it is therefore become necessary to gain attention by magnificence of promises and by eloquence sometimes sublime and sometimes pathetick. Promise, large promise, is the soul of an advertisement. I

remember a washball that had a quality truly wonderful—it gave *an exquis-ite edge to the razor*! The trade of advertising is now so near to perfection that it is not easy to propose any improvement.

This is one of the earliest of 'gone about as far as they can go' conclusions on advertisers, but Johnson, after all, was sane. Within the situation he knew, of newspapers directed to a small public largely centred on the coffee-houses, the natural range was from private notices (of service wanted and offered, of things lost, found, offered and needed) through shopkeepers' information (of actual goods in their establishments) to puffs for occasional and marginal products. In this last kind, and within the techniques open to them, the puffmen had indeed used, intensively, all the traditional forms of persuasion, and of cheating and lying. The mountebank and the huckster had got into print, and, while the majority of advertisements remained straightforward, the influence of this particular group was on its way to giving 'advertising' a more specialized meaning.

Development

There is no doubt that the Industrial Revolution, and the associated revolution in communications, fundamentally changed the nature of advertising. But the change was not simple, and must be understood in specific relation to particular developments. It is not true, for example, that with the coming of factory production large-scale advertis-ing became economically necessary. By the 1850s, a century after Johnson's comment, and with Britain already an industrial nation, the advertising pages of the newspapers, whether *The Times* or the *News of the World*, were still basically similar to those in eighteenth-century journals, except that there were more of them, that they were more closely printed, and that there were certain exclusions (lists of whores, for example, were no longer advertised in the *Morning Post*).

The general increase was mainly due to the general growth in trade, but was aided by the reduction and then abolition of a long-standing Advertisement Tax. First imposed in 1712, at one shilling an announcement, this had been a means, with the Stamp Duty, of hampering the growth of newspapers, which successive Governments had good reason to fear. By the time of the worst repression, after the Napoleonic Wars, Stamp Duty was at 4d a sheet, and Advertisement Tax at 3s 6d. In 1833, Stamp Duty was reduced to 1d, and Advertisement Tax to 1s 6d. A comparison of figures for 1830 and 1838 shows the effect of this reduction: the number of advertisements in papers on the British mainland in the former year was 877,972; by the later date is stood at 1,491,991. Then in 1853 the Advertisement Tax was abolished, and in 1855 the Stamp Duty. The rise in the circula-tion of newspapers, and in the number of advertisements, was then rapid.

Yet still in the 1850s advertising was mainly of a classified kind, in specified parts of the publication. It was still widely felt, in many kinds of trade, that (as a local newspaper summarized the argument in 1859)

it is not *respectable*. Advertising is resorted to for the purposes of intro-ducing inferior articles into the market.

Rejecting this argument, the newspaper (*The Eastbourne Gazette and Fashionable Intel-ligencer*) continued:

Competition is the soul of business, and what fairer or more legitimate means of competition can be adopted than the availing oneself of a channel to recommend goods to public notice which is open to all? Advertising is an open, fair, legitimate and respectable means of competition; bearing upon its face the impress of free-trade, and of as much advantage to the consumer as the producer.

The interesting thing is not so much the nature of this argument, but that, in 1859, it still had to be put in quite this way. Of course the article concluded by drawing attention to the paper's own advertising rates, but even then, to get the feel of the whole situation, we have to look at the actual advertisements flanking the article. Not only are they all from local tradesmen, but their tone is still eighteenth-century, as for example:

> To all who pay cash and can appreciate
> GOOD AND FINE TEAS
> CHARLES LEA
> Begs most respectfully to solicit a trial of his present stock which has been selected with the greatest care, and paid for before being cleared from the Bonded warehouses in London . . .

In all papers, this was still the usual tone, but, as in the eighteenth century, one class of product attracted different methods. Probably the first nationally advertised product was Warren's Shoe Blacking, closely followed by Rowland's Macassar Oil (which produced the counter-offensive of the antimacassar), Spencer's Chinese Liquid Hair Dye, and Morison's Universal Pill. In this familiar field, as in the eighteenth century, the new advertising was effectively shaped, while for selling cheap books the practice of including puffs in announcements was widely extended. Warren's Shoe Blacking had a drawing of a cat spitting at its own reflection, and hack verses were widely used:

> The goose that on our Ock's green shore
> Thrives to the size of Albatross
> Is twice the goose it was before
> When washed with Neighbour Goodman's sauce.

Commercial purple was another writing style, especially for pills:

> The spring and fall of the leaf has been always remarked as the periods when disease, if it be lurking in the system, is sure to show itself.
> (Parr's Life Pills, 1843).

The manner runs back to that of the eighteenth-century hucksters and mountebanks, but what is new is its scale. The crowned heads of Europe were being signed up for testimonials (the Tsar of all the Russias took and recommended Revalenta Arabica, while the Balm of Syriacum, a 'sovereign remedy for both bodily and mental decay', was advertised as used in Queen Victoria's household). Holloway, of course a 'Professor', spent £5,000 a year, in the 1840s, spreading his Universal Ointment, and in 1855 exceeded £30,000.

Moreover, with the newspaper public still limited, the puffmen were going on the streets. Fly-posting, on every available space, was now a large and organized trade, though made hazardous by rival gangs (paste for your own, blacking for the others). It was necessary in 1837 to pass a London act prohibiting posting without the owner's consent (it proved extremely difficult to enforce). In 1862 came the United Kingdom Billposters Association, with an organized system of special hoardings, which had become steadily more necessary as the flood of paste swelled. Handbills ('throwaways') were distributed in the streets of Victorian London with extraordinary intensity of coverage; in some areas a walk down one street would collect as many as two hundred different leaflets. Advertising vans and vehicles of all sorts, such as the seven-foot lath-and-plaster Hat in the Strand, on which Carlyle commented, crowded the streets until 1853, when they were forbidden. Hundreds of casual labourers were sent out with placards and sandwich boards, and again in 1853 had to be officially removed from pavement to gutter. Thus the streets of Victorian London bore increasingly upon their face 'the impress of free trade', yet still, with such methods largely reserved to the sellers of pills, adornments and sensational literature, the basic relation between adver-tising and production had only partly changed. Carlyle said of the hatter, whose 'whole industry is turned to *persuade* us that he has made' better hats, that "the quack has become God". But as yet, on the whole, it was only the quack.

The period between the 1850s and the end of the century saw a further expansion in advertising, but still mainly along the lines already established. After the 1855 abolition of Stamp Duty, the circulation of newspapers rapidly increased, and many new ones were successfully founded. But the attitude of the Press to advertising, throughout the second half of the century, remained cautious. In particular, editors were extremely resistant to any break-up in the column layout of their pages, and hence to any increase in size of display type. Advertisers tried in many ways to get round this, but with little success.

As for products mainly advertised, the way was still led by the makers of pills, soaps and similar articles. Beecham's and Pears are important by reason of their introduction of the catch-phrase on a really large scale; 'Worth a Guinea a Box' and 'Good morning! Have you used Pears' Soap?' passed into everyday language. Behind this familiar van-guard came two heavily advertised classes: the patent food, which belongs technically to this period, and which by the end of the century had made Bovril, Hovis, Nestlé, Cadbury, Fry and Kellogg into 'household names'; and new inventions of a more serious kind, such as the sewing-machine, the camera, the bicycle and the typewriter. If we add the new department-stores, towards the end of the century, we have the effective range of general advertising in the period, and need only note that in method the patent foods followed the patent medicines, while the new appliances varied between genuine information and the now familiar technique of slogan and association.

The pressure on newspapers to adapt to techniques drawn from the poster began to be successful from the 1880s. The change came first in the illustrated magazines, with a crop of purity nudes and similar figures; the Borax nude, for example, dispelling Disease and Decay; girls delighted by cigarettes or soap or shampoos. The poster industry, with its organized hoardings, was able from 1867 to use large lithographs, and Pears introduced the 'Bubbles' poster in 1887. A mail-order catalogue used the first colour advertisement, of a rug. Slowly, a familiar world was forming, and in the first years of the new century came the coloured electric sign. The newspapers, with Northcliffe's *Daily Mail* in the lead, dropped their columns rule, and allowed large type and illustrations. It was noted in 1897 that 'The Times itself' was permitting 'advertisements in type which three years ago would have been considered fit only for the street hoardings', while the front page of the Daily Mail already held rows of drawings of rather bashful women in combinations. Courtesy, Service and Integrity, as part of the same process, acquired the dignity of large-type abstractions. The draper, the grocer and their suppliers had followed the quack.

To many people, yet again, it seemed that the advertisers had 'gone about as far as they can go'. For many people, also, it was much too far. A society for Checking the Abuses of Public Advertising (SCAPA) had been formed in 1898, and of course had been described by the United Bill Posters Association as 'super-sensitive faddists'. SCAPA had local successes, in removing or checking some outdoor signs, and the 1890s saw other legislation: prohibiting uniform for sandwich-men (casual labourers, dressed as the Royal Marine Light Infantry or some other regiment, had been advertising soaps and pills); regulating skyline and balloon advertisements; restricting flashing electric signs, which had been blamed for street accidents. It is a familiar situation, this running fight between traditional standards (whether the familiar layout of newspapers or respect for building and landscape) and the vigorous inventiveness of advertisers (whether turning hoardings into the 'art-galleries of the people', or putting an eight-ton patent food sign halfway up the cliffs of Dover). Indeed ordinary public argument about advertising has stuck at this point, first clarified in the 1890s with 'taste' and 'the needs of commerce' as adversaries. In fact, however, even as this battle was raging, the whole situation was being transformed, by deep changes in the economy.

[. . .]

'Public Relations'

Advertising was developed to sell goods, in a particular kind of economy. Publicity has been developed to sell persons, in a particular kind of culture. The methods are often basically similar: the arranged incident, the 'mention', the advice on branding, packaging and a good 'selling line'. I remember being told by a man I knew at university (he had previously explained how useful, to his profession as an advertiser, had been his training in the practical criticism of advertisements) that advertisements you booked and paid for were really old stuff; the real thing was what got through as ordinary news. This seems to happen now with goods: 'product centenaries', for example. But with persons it is even more extensive. It began in entertainment, particularly with film actors, and it is still in this field that it does most of its work. It is very difficult to pin down, because the borderline between the item or photograph picked up in the ordinary course of journalism and broadcasting, and the similar item or photograph that has been arranged and paid for, either directly or through special hospitality by a publicity agent, is obviously difficult to draw. Enough stories get through, and are even boasted about, to indicate that the paid practice is extensive, though payment, except to the agent, is usually in hospitality (if that word can be used) or in kind. Certainly, readers of newspapers should be aware that the 'personality' items, presented as ordinary news stories or gossip, will often have been paid for, in one way or another, in a system that makes straightforward advertising, by comparison, look respectable. Nor is this confined to what is called 'show business'; it has certainly entered literature, and it has probably entered politics.

The extension is natural, in a society where selling, by any effective means, has become a primary ethic. The spectacular growth of advertising, and then its extension to apparently independent reporting, has behind it not a mere pressure-group, as in the days of the quacks, but the whole impetus of a society. It can then be agreed that we have come a long way from the papyrus of the runaway slave and the shouts of the town-crier: that what we have to look at is an organized and extending system, at the centre of our national life.

The System

In the last hundred years, then, advertising has developed from the simple announce-ments of shopkeepers and the persuasive arts of a few marginal dealers into a major part of capitalist business organization. This is important enough, but the place of advertising in society goes far beyond this commercial context. It is increasingly the source of finance for a whole range of general communication, to the extent that in 1960 our majority television service and almost all our newspapers and periodicals could not exist without it. Further, in the last forty years and now at an increasing rate, it has passed the frontier of the selling of goods and services and has become involved with the teaching of social and personal values; it is also rapidly entering the world of politics. Advertising is also, in a sense, the official art of modern capitalist society: it is what 'we' put up in 'our' streets and use to fill up to half of 'our' newspapers and magazines: and it commands the services of perhaps the largest organized body of writers and artists, with their attendant managers and advisers, in the whole society. Since this is the actual social status of advertising, we shall only understand it with any adequacy if we can develop a kind of total analysis in which the economic, social and cultural facts are visibly related. We may then also find, taking advertising as a major form of modern social communication, that we can understand our society itself in new ways.

It is often said that our society is too materialist, and that advertising reflects this. We are in the phase of a relatively rapid distribution of what are called 'consumer goods', and advertising, with its emphasis on 'bringing the good things of life', is taken as central for this reason. But it seems to me that in this respect our society is quite evidently not materialist enough, and that this, paradoxically, is the result of a failure in social meanings, values and ideals.

It is impossible to look at modern advertising without realising that the material object being sold is never enough: this indeed is the crucial cultural quality of its modern forms. If we were sensibly materialist, in that part of our living in which we use things, we should find most advertising to be of an insane irrelevance. Beer would be enough for us, without the additional promise that in drinking it we show ourselves to be manly, young in heart, or neighbourly. A washing-machine would be a useful machine to wash clothes, rather than an indication that we are forward-looking or an object of envy to our neighbours. But if these associations sell beer and washing-machines, as some of the evidence suggests, it is clear that we have a cultural pattern in which the objects are not enough but must be validated, if only in fantasy, by association with social and personal meanings which in a different cultural pattern might be more directly available. The short description of the pattern we have is *magic*: a highly organ-ized and professional system of magical inducements and satisfactions, functionally very similar to magical systems in simpler societies, but rather strangely coexistent with a highly developed scientific technology.

This contradiction is of the greatest importance in any analysis of modern capitalist society. The coming of large-scale industrial production necessarily raised critical problems of social organization, which in many fields we are still only struggling to solve. In the production of goods for personal use, the critical problem posed by the factory of advanced machines was that of the organization of the market. The modern factory requires not only smooth and steady distributive channels (without which it would suffocate under its own product) but also definite indications of demand without which the expensive processes of capitalization and equipment would be too great a risk. The historical choice posed by the development of industrial production is between different forms of organization and planning in the society to which it is central. In our own century, the choice has been and remains between some form of socialism and a new form of capitalism. In Britain, since the 1890s and with rapidly continuing emphasis, we have had the new capitalism, based on a series of devices for organizing and ensuring the market. Modern advertising, taking on its distinctive features in just this economic phase, is one of the most important of these devices, and it is perfectly true to say that modern capitalism could not function without it.

Yet the essence of capitalism is that the basic means of production are not socially but privately owned, and that decisions about production are therefore in the hands of a group occupying a minority position in the society and in no direct way responsible to it. Obviously, since the capitalist wishes to be successful, he is influenced in his decisions about production by what other members of the society need. But he is influenced also by considerations of industrial convenience and likely profit, and his decisions tend to be a balance of these varying factors. The challenge of socialism, still very powerful elsewhere but in Britain deeply confused by political immaturities and errors, is essentially that decisions about production should be in the hands of the society as a whole, in the sense that control of the means of production is made part of the general system of decision which the society as a whole creates. The conflict between capitalism and socialism is now commonly seen in terms of a competition in productive efficiency, and we need not doubt that much of our future history, on a world scale, will be determined by the results of this competition. Yet the conflict is really much deeper than this, and is also a conflict between different approaches to and forms of socialism. The fundamental choice that emerges, in the problems set to us by modern industrial production, is between man as consumer and man as user. The system of organized magic which is modern advertising is primarily important as a functional obscuring of this choice.

'Consumers'

The popularity of 'consumer', as a way of describing the ordinary member of modern capitalist society in a main part of his economic capacity, is very significant. The description is spreading very rapidly, and is now habitually used by people to whom it ought, logically, to be repugnant. It is not only that, at a simple level, 'consumption' is a very strange description of our ordinary use of goods and services. This metaphor drawn from the stomach or the furnace is only partially relevant even to our use of things. Yet we say 'consumer', rather than 'user', because in the form of society we now have, and in the forms of thinking which it almost imperceptibly fosters, it is as consumers that the majority of people are seen. We are the market, which the system of industrial production has organized. We are the channels along which the product flows and disappears. "In every aspect of social communication, and in every version of what we are as a community, the pressure of a system of industrial production is towards these impersonal forms.

Yet it is by no means necessary that these versions should prevail, just because we use advanced productive techniques. It is simply that once these have entered a society, new questions of structure and purpose in social organization are inevitably posed. One set of answers is the development of genuine democracy, in which the human needs of all the people in the society are taken as the central purpose of all social activity, so that politics is not a system of government but of self-government, and the systems of production and communication are rooted in the satisfaction of human needs and the development of human capacities. Another set of answers, of which we have had more experience, retains, often in very subtle forms, a more limited social purpose. In the first phase, loyal subjects, as they were previously seen, became the labour market of industrial 'hands'. Later, as the 'hands' reject this version of themselves, and claim a higher human status, the emphasis is changed. Any real concession of higher status would mean the end of class-society and the coming of socialist democracy. But inter-mediate concessions are possible, including material concessions. The 'subjects' become the 'electorate', and 'the mob' becomes 'public opinion'.

Decision is still a function of the minority, but a new system of decision, in which the majority can be organized to this end, has to be devised. The majority are seen as 'the masses', whose opinion, *as masses* but not as real individuals or groups, is a factor in the business of governing. In practical terms, this version can succeed for a long time, but it then becomes increasingly difficult to state the nature of the society, since there is a real gap between profession and fact. Moreover, as the governing minority changes in character, and increasingly rests for real power on a modern economic system, older social purposes become vestigial, and whether expressed or implied, the maintenance of the economic system becomes the main factual purpose of all social activity. Politics and culture become deeply affected by this dominant pattern, and ways of thinking derived from the economic market—political parties considering how to sell themselves to the electorate, to create a favourable brand image; education being primarily organized in terms of a graded supply of labour; culture being organized and even evaluated in terms of commercial profit—become increasingly evident.

Still, however, the purposes of the society have to be declared in terms that will command the effort of a majority of its people. It is here that the idea of the 'consumer' has proved so useful. Since consumption is within its limits a satisfactory activity, it can be plausibly offered as a commanding social purpose. At the same time, its ambiguity is such that it ratifies the subjection of society to the operations of the existing economic system. An irresponsible economic system can supply the 'consumption' market, whereas it could only meet the criterion of human use by becoming genuinely respon-sible: that is to say, shaped in its use of human labour and resources by general social decisions. The consumer asks for an adequate supply of personal 'consumer goods' at a tolerable price: over the last ten years, this has been the primary aim of British govern-ment. But users ask for more than this, necessarily. They ask for the satisfaction of human needs which consumption, as such, can never really supply. Since many of these needs are social—roads, hospitals, schools, quiet—they are not only not covered by the consumer ideal: they are even denied by it, because consumption tends always to materialize as an individual activity. And to satisfy this range of needs would involve questioning the autonomy of the economic system, in its actual setting of priorities. This is where the consumption ideal is not only misleading, as a form of defence of the system, but ultimately destructive to the broad general purposes of the society.

Advertising, in its modern forms, then operates to preserve the consumption ideal from the criticism inexorably made of it by experience. If the consumption of individual goods leaves that whole area of human need unsatisfied, the attempt is made, by magic, to associate this consumption with human desires to which it has no real reference. You do not only buy an object: you buy social respect, discrimination, health, beauty, success, power to control your environment. The magic obscures the real sources of general satisfaction because their discovery would involve radical change in the whole common way of life.

Of course, when a magical pattern has become established in a society, it is capable of some real if limited success. Many people will indeed look twice at you, upgrade you, upmarket you, respond to your displayed signals, if you have made the right purchases within a system of meanings to which you are all trained. Thus the fantasy seems to be validated, at a personal level, but only at the cost of preserving the general unreality which it obscures: the real failures of the society which however are not easily traced to this pattern.

It must not be assumed that magicians—in this case, advertising agents—disbelieve their own magic. They may have a limited professional cynicism about it, from knowing how some of the tricks are done. But fundamentally they are involved, with the rest of the society, in the confusion to which the magical gestures are a response. Magic is always an unsuccessful attempt to provide meanings and values, but it is often very difficult to distinguish magic from genuine knowledge and from art. The belief that high consumption is a high standard of living is a general belief of the society. The conversion of numerous objects into sources of sexual or pre-sexual satisfaction is evidently not only a process in the minds of advertisers, but also a deep and general confusion in which much energy is locked.

At one level, the advertisers are people using certain skills and knowledge, created by real art and science, against the public for commercial advantage. This hostile stance is rarely confessed in general propaganda for advertising, where the normal emphasis is the blind consumption ethic ('Advertising brings you the good things of life'), but it is common in advertisers' propaganda to their clients. 'Hunt with the mind of the hunter', one recent announcement begins, and another, under the heading 'Getting any honey from the hive industry?', is rich in the language of attack:

> One of the most important weapons used in successful marketing is adver-
> tising. Commando Sales Limited, steeped to the nerve ends in the skills of
> unarmed combat, are ready to move into battle on any sales front at the
> crack of an accepted estimate. These are the front line troops to call in
> when your own sales force is hopelessly outnumbered by the forces of
> sales resistance . . .

This is the structure of feeling in which 'impact' has become the normal description of the effect of successful communication, and 'impact' like 'consumer' is now habitually used by people to whom it ought to be repugnant. What sort of person really wants to 'make an impact' or create a 'smash hit', and what state is a society in when this can be its normal cultural language?

It is indeed monstrous that human advances in psychology, sociology and communication should be used or thought of as powerful techniques *against* people, just as it is rotten to try to reduce the faculty of human choice to 'sales resistance'. In these respects, the claim of advertising to be a service is not particularly plausible. But equally, much of this talk of weapons and impact is the jejune bravado of deeply confused men. It is in the end the language of frustration rather than of power. Most advertising is not the cool creation of skilled professionals, but the confused creation of bad thinkers and artists. If we look at the petrol with the huge clenched fist, the cigarette against loneliness in the deserted street, the puppet facing death with a life-insurance policy (the modern protection, unlike the magical symbols painstakingly listed from earlier societies), or the man in the cradle which is an aeroplane, we are looking at attempts to express and resolve real human tensions which may be crude but which also involve deep feelings of a personal and social kind.

The structural similarity between much advertising and much modern art is not simply copying by the advertisers. It is the result of comparable responses to the contemporary human condition, and the only distinction that matters is between the clarification achieved by some art and the displacement normal in bad art and most advertising. The skilled magicians, the masters of the masses, must be seen as ultimately involved in the general weakness which they not only exploit but are exploited by. If the meanings and values generally operative in the society give no answers to, no means of negotiating, problems of death, loneliness, frustration, the need for identity and respect, then the magical system must come, mixing its charms and expedients with reality in easily available forms, and binding the weakness to the condition which has created it. Advertising is then no longer merely a way of selling goods, it is a true part of the culture of a confused society.

Questions

1 What specific examples of policy changes encouraged or discouraged the growth of advertising?

2 How did posters and handbills encourage the development of advertising as a visual symbol system?

3 Why does Williams disagree with the criticism that "our society is too materialist," and does he use advertising to support his claim?

4 Why does Williams feel there is a difference between people being "users" versus "consumers," and what is the danger of a widespread use of the consumer metaphor?

5 What recent examples of advertisements attributed "magic" powers to brands?

Chapter 2

SUSAN STRASSER

THE ALIEN PAST
Consumer Culture in Historical Perspective[1]

SUSAN STRASSER, AN AMERICAN HISTORIAN, argues in this essay that the introduction of consumer culture was a radical shift in our society. It was so radical, in fact, that many elements of a pre-consumer society would seem extremely strange—even alien—to us. We have experienced a major shift not just in our society (how goods are produced and distributed), but also in our culture (how we think about products—how we interpret them), including shifts in our value systems, which is what Strasser emphasizes. Strasser notes that "common sense" modern values like efficiency, convenience, and obsolescence were greatly enhanced—if not created—by consumer culture. For example, in pre-industrial America, especially for the non-wealthy, people's work lives were often inseparable from their family and social lives. The idea of "convenience" made very little sense in this social context. As modern products and modern ways of selling these products developed, convenience became a major value in modern consumer culture. But it is not a neutral term; it assumes that time is valuable, that there is a separation of our labor and leisure time, that leisure time is desirable and often involves consumption of goods and services, that life does not mean labor, and that leisure is desirable. Through advertising, leisure becomes a *goal* of modern living, not just an attribute used to sell a product.

The same modern emphasis applies to the concept of obsolescence. Originally a concept only for fashion, obsolescence refers to replacing old goods with new goods even if the old goods are still functional: this year's latest fashion replaces last year's "old" fashion. Consumer culture applied obsolescence to nearly all product categories as a way to regulate market demand. And so we think of products beyond their material function, as a fashionable accessory. New lines of cars come out ever year, even if no new technological advance is implemented. Electronics like MP3 players are released in different colors and designs that do not enhance functioning, but instead are "fashionable electronics." Such value systems would be strange indeed to the average person living in pre-1850s America.

The perspective of historical change is intrinsically complicated, and the development of consumer society has proceeded unevenly. Even in a given city or region, there have been many kinds of consuming households at any historical moment, thanks to the multiplicity of personal tastes and of cultural and class lifestyles. Within households, generations understand consumption issues quite differently (and often come into conflict about them), for the new is normal to the young. Interacting with the many kinds of households and the many kinds of individual consumers have been many kinds of businesses, large and small, both making and distributing many kinds of goods, services, and marketing materials.

As if this multiplicity were not complication enough, new ways have coexisted with old ones. Rich people have usually bought new products before poor people did, people in the city before their country cousins, and teenagers before their grandmothers. People who have bought new products have also kept some of their old things and maintained some of their old ways. Early-twentieth-century American farmers both ordered from the Sears catalogue *and* bartered eggs at the crossroads general store; housewives kept chickens *and* lit their homes with electricity during the depression of the 1930s: children of the 1950s jumped rope *and* watched television; shoppers today use credit cards for internet shopping *and* bargain with cash at yard sales.

Even the most significant cultural shifts, then, happen piecemeal. People create historical change by living their lives, making decisions that they may consider trivial or wholly personal but that have critical effects in the aggregate. Individuals' lives transform incrementally, in response to new technologies, new opportunities, new attitudes formed in interaction with neighbors as well as with the popular media, and their own stages in the life cycle. Over the long run, bit by bit, seemingly unconnected and unprofound events in millions of lives form patterns, but new developments interact in complex ways and exhibit contradictions and incongruities that frustrate the historian's effort to tell a clear story of cause and effect or even to provide accurate generalizations. Nor may consumers perceive changes in production and distribution even as they help make them. Over the course of a long transition, they might recognize new practices and routines only in retrospect.

The Household and the Industrial Order

Even when they have discerned trends, consumers generally have not changed their ways in response to that awareness. More often, they made practical decisions. People chose plumbing to make their lives easier; they preferred electric lights to kerosene lamps because electricity gave more light with none of the dirty work; they bought ready-made clothing because they wanted to spend their time on other things besides sewing. Shorter hours and better working conditions – less hard physical labor, in safer and more comfortable circumstances – distinguish twentieth-century housework as they distinguish other twentieth-century labor in industrialized countries. Like other workers, the housewife lost control of her work process; manufacturers exerted their control on her through product design and advertising rather than through direct supervision. The clock and the calendar replaced the sun as arbiter of everyone's time. But, while other workers labored in groups, housewives lost the growing daughters and full-time servants who worked with them at home, the iceman and the street vendors who came to their houses, the sewing circle and the group of women around the well.

That isolation, combined with the illusory individualism of consumerism, intensified the notion that people could control their private lives at home, protected behind the portals of their houses from the domination of others.

That idea was a central legacy of the industrial order, which – in theory, at least – separated the home from the rest of society. Entrepreneurs gathered workers together in factories to produce goods for profit, equipping them with machines and raw materials, and supervising their labor to ensure peak production. At first, many people still made their livings from agriculture and home-based handcrafts, and by modern standards the early factories look small and inefficient. But working in a factory was different, indeed, from working at home, where women continued to supervise them-selves, isolated from the dominant trends of the new society in what American popular writers, around 1825, began to call their own "sphere." In its most extreme form, this doctrine of separate spheres conceptualized a private realm – the arena of consumption and of leisure, the domain of women – that stood apart from and even opposed a public sphere of men, work, and production.

But the distinctions between the sphere of the household and the world of industry were always blurry. Families had to adapt to industrial workers' new schedules; natural cycles of light and dark could not dictate routine when some family members lived by the clock. The very relationships of production and consumption presupposed some connections between homes and businesses. Factories produced goods that helped people adapt to urban industrial life: soap for urban dwellers who had no reserves of fat left from slaughtering, lamps and lamp oils to brighten the time left after work. Indeed, historians have amassed considerable evidence about topics that show the separate spheres idea to have been primarily ideological, describing the productive work women did both in factories and in homes, as well as public leisure activities at dance halls, saloons, and sporting events.

Toward a Consumer Culture

Eventually, mass production and mass distribution amplified industrialization and indus-trial culture, bringing large numbers of people many more new products and services: gas, electricity, running water, prepared foods, ready-made clothes, and factory-made furniture and utensils. The decisive changes happened between about 1890 and 1920 in the United States; the timing was different in other countries, and the process is still going on in some parts of the world. With these products, households became the direct beneficiaries of a profound economic transformation, led by large corporations that sold goods over long distances. Standardized, uniform products that cost money were manufactured in highly mechanized factories, organized for efficiency as defined by Frederick Winslow Taylor and Henry Ford. The new products transformed the texture of daily life. They replaced the various makeshifts that had constituted most people's subsistence, and began to substitute for much of the massive productive and maintenance work once done by housewives and servants. Mass communications brought information about the rest of the world, and new ideas about doing household work, as well as advertisements. Electric and telephone wires, water and gas pipes literally joined the private household to the public world.[2]

The foundation for the rapid cultural transformation that accompanied mass pro-duction had been laid throughout a long period of change. Beginning a century before with the textiles of the industrial revolution, new products had come sooner to the cities than to the countryside, while in both rural and urban environments, wealthy people enjoyed more benefits from economic growth than did the poor. Business cycles brought depressions regularly, each graver than the one before as more people depended on wages and manufactured products and as more businesses engaged in trade over longer distances. As production moved out of households and artisans' shops, an ever-expanding market for manufactured goods was not only an economic abstraction. Whether they bargained with rural peddlers or shopped at big-city department stores with fixed prices, customers traded in an environment of constant change. New products from new companies – indeed, new kinds of products from new kinds of companies – found their way into those stores, and into people's homes and daily routines.

Branded, standardized products came to represent and embody the new networks and systems of mass production and distribution, the social relationships that brought people the things they used. Household routines involved making fewer things and purchasing more; consumption became a major part of everyday life and of household work. Formerly customers – purchasing the objects of daily life from familiar crafts-people and storekeepers in networks of relationships based in villages, small towns, and big-city neighborhoods – people became consumers. They bought and used mass-produced goods as participants in a developing global market composed of masses of people associating with big, centrally organized companies. Decision-making at those companies was increasingly driven by marketing rather than production; they aimed to create markets, not merely to satisfy them. As consumers came to depend on complex goods from distant sources, they came to understand less about how things were made, how they worked, how they could be fixed.

New ways of relating to the objects of everyday life – the material culture of a developing consumer society – developed along with the new physical and economic landscape. Everyday objects are artifacts of culture; they represent and are embedded in human relationships. The plastic takeout food container is analogous to the Indian tiffin, the Japanese bento box, and the leaves that people in less industrialized cultures wrap food in. Everyday objects embody both the relationships and routines of private life and the social relationships of production and distribution. Though both will wash, a chunk of soap handmade from wood ashes and animal fat, to be used by its maker, is an artifact distinct from a bar of Ivory Soap, labeled with its Universal Product Code and sold at a supermarket. Chemically dissimilar and made with tools and processes from separate eras, the two soaps incorporate quantitatively different amounts of human labor in qualitatively different forms: the handmade soap produced for use, the factory-made manufactured in order to generate wages and profits. The uniformity of the modern soap hides the human involvement in its production. Its distribution depends on tele-phones, computers, refined fossil fuels, and the people who make those technologies possible. Cost accounting, corporate law, stock-market fluctuations, and the whole panoply of contemporary financial procedures and government policies regulate both production and distribution of every bar.

Many public events, then, coincided with the private behavior of consumers to create the shift from a production-driven to a consumption-driven culture. New needs surfaced in tandem with new products and with the new habits that characterized urban industrial society. Unprecedented changes in daily routines were entangled with new and old customs, ideas, attitudes, social organization, religion, environment, and economic organization – in short, the elements of culture. Markets *per se* were certainly not new; in America, even so-called subsistence farmers had always done some trading for goods such as salt and tools. But now the market came to be understood as the only way of satisfying needs, wants, and desires. As a global consumer culture developed, daily life underwent profound changes that truly rendered the past as alien, changing consumers' fundamental relationships with their bodies and with the material world.

The Ideal of Convenience

Convenience, for example, because a feature of products advertised as worth paying for, a value expounded by the advertising for a wide range of products.[3] Like efficiency in the factory, convenience in the home was intended to save time and reduce wasted effort, but the concept went further. Factory efficiency offered the "one best way" to do a job from the employer's point of view. It never promised freedom from work itself. The concept of convenience, on the other hand, was used in marketing to suggest that products could liberate housewives from troubles ranging from annoyance to hard labor. Modern products offered release from the responsibility of caring for material goods, the stewardship of objects and materials that characterized relationships to the material world throughout the nineteenth century, when even factory-made goods were cleaned, mended, sharpened, and used over and over. By the 1920s, advertising proposed that purchasing rust-free aluminium pans or throwaway paper handkerchiefs offered consumers the leisured lifestyles once accessible only to wealthy people with servants.

The American philosopher Thomas F. Tierney writes that convenience is central to "the hold which technology has on modernity . . . an integral part of the modern self." Assisted by technology, Tierney suggests, the modern household focuses not merely on satisfying the demands of the body for food, clothing, and shelter, but on satisfying them quickly. The needs of the body are understood as limits: "inconveniences, obstacles, or annoyances" that impinge on time. The products of modern technology appeal to consumers because they alleviate inconvenience by helping them satisfy their bodies' needs in as little time as possible, according to Tierney (1993, pp. 6, 30, 36).

Certainly time was central to convenience as it was interpreted by American advertising of the 1920s. "Women, whose time must not be wasted, value the simplicity and reliability of the Hotpoint Vacuum Cleaner," that company declared in a 1923 advertisement. Packaged food ads counted minutes. Wheatena cereal could be prepared in "just 2 minutes of boiling and bubbling"; consumers of Borden's condensed milk could whip up a snack of hot chocolate and macaroons "in just nineteen minutes." Grape Nuts cereal did not have to be cooked at all, a welcome solution for the special problem that breakfast posed in the modern household. A 1927 ad for the product depicted the chaos of morning with a Cubist-inspired drawing juxtaposing a frantic couple at the table with fragments of clock faces. "Is there no hope?" read the copy.[4]

One way to save time was by saving steps to make things accessible or handy, an approach suggested by industrial time and motion studies. This aspect of convenience sometimes had the particularly profitable feature of requiring that consumers purchase duplicates of a product. "Telephones near at hand," suggested an advertisement for the American Telephone and Telegraph Company in the late 1920s, "for Comfort and

Convenience." The company's campaign for extension phones sought to break down an attitude that the telephone was a utility, not to be used for frivolous conversation. The text of this ad recommended extra phones in rooms that most people didn't even have: the dressing-room, the library, and the sun porch. Like so many other advertisements for household products, this one showed a well dressed woman with a servant near at hand (Marchand, 1985, pp. 177–219).

Many advertisements used such upper-class imagery, implying that products could stand in for the servants that most American women could only wish for. The Edison Electric Appliance Company actually called its line of small appliances—iron, toaster, curling iron, chafing dish, and the like—"Hotpoint Servants." The naphtha in Pels-Naptha soap made it seem "as if you had hundreds of tiny helpers doing the rubbing for you." Procter and Gamble's laundry soap could be thought of "as a laundress—not merely as soap." Laundry product advertising promised emancipation from the care and responsibility that washing clothes had required in a previous era. Women whose mothers had made their own soap, and heated washwater on the stove after carrying it from wells or creeks, might well regard running water and commercial laundry products as liberating.[5]

Beyond efficiency, then, convenience was a synonym and a metaphor for freedom, a form of well-being that products could provide, an amalgam of luxury, comfort, and emancipation from worries. In this sense, convenience was much like the satisfaction that consumers were expected to derive from the service offered by the turn-of-the-century department store. "Give your home the convenience of Frigidaire," the refrigerator subsidiary of General Motors recommended in 1925. "It is entirely automatic – nothing to replenish, nothing to worry about." The Frigidaire offered "freedom from the possible annoyance of outside ice supply – automatic day-after-day, week-after-week operation, without any attention on your part."[6]

Indeed, convenience meant freedom from work itself. The general claim was applied to all kinds of products. "What a convenience electric light is," General Electric captioned a picture of an 18th century woman dipping candles in a 1925 ad. "The early settlers had to learn to make candles themselves – the most arduous of their women's tasks. *Your* light comes at a finger touch."[7] Candle-making had actually not been so arduous two centuries earlier as the ad implied – it was done infrequently, and many households purchased their candles. But this history lesson seemed credible because the readers of American women's magazines ran their households with a wide range of technology in the mid-1920s. Nobody dipped candles anymore, but everybody understood that most household tasks could be done with more or less labor. Floors might be swept with brooms, carpet sweepers, or vacuum cleaners. The advertising for laundry products made washday look easy and pleasant whether a woman labored over a washboard or used the hand-cranked machines of the day. Chipso, a flaked soap that Procter & Gamble introduced with considerable fanfare in 1925, "cuts work in half," bringing "washday relief" to women whether or not they used a washing machine. "Please don't make a mistake," one ad insisted. "CHIPSO is not a special soap for a *special* method. It doesn't say 'Change your method and I will help you.' It says, 'Wash as you like – I will make your work easier.' "[8]

The point of the ads was that every woman should have her work cut in half – indeed, that no woman should really have to work very hard, whatever her laundry technology. The fundamental assumptions about life and labor that had prevailed everywhere before the twentieth century, for all but the aristocracy, were now regarded as arguments for drudgery, a word repeated endlessly in the ads. "Free from the drudgery of 'oven watching,' " promised a company that made thermostats for gas ranges, as if checking the oven temperature had once been seriously burdensome or time-consuming. "The woman of today has far too much use for her time and strength to waste it watching an oven in a hot kitchen."[9]

The "convenience" of modern products took many forms; the word was used in advertising and in marketing literature to cover a multitude of positive attributes, especially savings in labor and time, and freedom from attention, care, and responsibility. Convenience was promoted as a potential benefit of so many products that it became one of the aims of modern living, an attribute of the modern lifestyle and of the entire panoply of consumer goods that modern life required. It joined cleanliness among the selling points for a wide variety of products that transformed Americans' relationship to the material world. In a few decades, the ideal of the durable and reusable was displaced by aspirations of leisure and luxury. A level of ease and cleanliness that had once been attainable only with many servants – if at all – could now be achieved by buying things, and even by throwing things away. With Kleenex, you could always have a clean handkerchief with no work.

Obsolescence as a Marketing Tool

"Convenience" was only one of the enticements for American consumers of the 1920s. Technological improvements made many new products work better than their predecessors. Radios provide a historical example of technological obsolescence that seems familiar to those of us who have by now owned and discarded several computers. In automobile sales, the technological advances symbolized by the Model T Ford were giving way to fashion – style changes made independent of utility – symbolized by the General Motors cars that eventually forced Ford, too, to change styles. Many other products as well brought fashion into their sales strategies during the period after World War I. More and more things were made and sold with an expectation that they would soon be worthless or obsolete.

The French social critic Gilles Lipovetsky calls contemporary consumer culture an "empire of the ephemeral."[10] He argues that its central feature is the extension of the principle of fashion – obsolescence on the basis of style – to material goods other than clothing and to a broad spectrum of people, "a society restructured from top to bottom by the attractive and the ephemeral." Fashion's "abbreviated time span and its systematic obsolescence have become characteristics inherent in mass production and consumption," he writes, and "consumers spontaneously hold that the new is by nature superior to the old." In Lipovetsky's view, this generalization of the fashion process defines consumer society, which depends on the expansion of needs and "reorganizes mass production and consumption according to the law of *obsolescence, seduction*, and *diversification*" (Lipovetsky, 1994, pp. 5, 134–135).

The expansion of fashion into new realms was part of a more general development in the history of marketing. In the decades before World War I, American manufacturers came to understand that markets were not shaped by pre-existing supply and demand, but could be developed and extended. In the pages of their trade journals, marketers spelled out the principles for selling more. Repositioning a product could increase the market; thus Carnation canned milk, once sold to mining expeditions, moved into the home. Markets could be expanded by suggesting more uses for products: Nearly every successful food company gave away recipe booklets full of ideas for using more of its product, while Procter and Gamble advertised that Ivory soap could be used both in the bath and the laundry. Year-round demand was created for products previously considered seasonal. And manufacturers found that they could sell more of products as different as phonographs and canned foods if they offered a range of options, different grades at different prices.[11]

Encouraging people to replace goods before the old ones were used up was another strategy for increasing markets, and fashion a means for doing so. A wide range of consumer goods could be sold according to the principles that French critic Roland Barthes describes as fundamental to fashion. "If the garment is replaced as soon as it is worn out," he explains, "there is no Fashion; . . . if the garment is worn beyond its natural replacement time, there is pauperization; . . . if a person buys more than he wears, there is Fashion, and the more the rhythm of purchase exceeds the rhythm of dilapidation, the stronger the submission to Fashion" (Barthes, 1983, pp. 297–298). Lipovetsky adds that manufacturers convince consumers to buy more of what they already have by offering more options. Products "are never offered in just one unique form; increasingly, the consumer is invited to choose between one variant and another, between one set of accessories, or gamuts, or programs, and another, and to combine the elements of each more or less freely. Like haute couture, mass consumption implies the increasing of models, the diversification of series, the production of optional differences, the stimulation of a personalized demand" (Lipovetsky, 1994, p. 80).

No Limits to Fashion

By the 1920s, American academic analysts of household life noted that modern fashion went well beyond the wardrobe. In his 1923 text *Economics of the Household*, Benjamin R. Andrews listed its characteristics: "(1) The immense number of objects to which it extends; (2) the uniformity of fashion, which knows no territorial or class limit; and (3) the maddening tempo of the changes of fashion" (p. 384). Economist Hazel Kyrk attributed the extension of fashion to technological change – decreasing production costs and new materials. Manufacturers could not be blamed for the maddening tempo or for their desire to change styles, she explained. Some innovated, evaluating the potential profits and risks that accrued from being the first to introduce new fashions. But others chose not to, fearful of failure or because postponing change allowed them to dispose of stock on hand or to utilize dies or patterns to their fullest (Kyrk, 1923, p. 267).

Historian Roland Marchand has shown that the process of extending fashion to a wide variety of objects was well under way in the 1920s, especially with respect to color, which could be varied without redesigning products or retooling factories. Marchand explains that color offered manufacturers a way of converting staple goods, purchased according to Barthes' "rhythm of dilapidation," into fashion goods, purchased on the basis of desire. Many products that had once come in standard black or white were now available in rainbow hues. Parker offered a pen with a red barrel: Willys-Overland pioneered the colored automobile during the early 1920s. By 1927, Marchand writes, "a writer in *Printers' Ink* had enthroned color as 'the sex appeal of business' " (1985, pp. 122, 123).

Color fashions were marketed for every room in the house, to people of all classes. The Montgomery Ward company – which served a rural and working class market with its mail order catalog and a few urban stores – advertised bathroom sinks, tubs, and toilets that met "the modern demand for COLOR in Bathroom Fixtures." So did the more expensive Crane company. To coordinate with the plumbing – or for those who wanted to spruce up their bathrooms but could not afford new fixtures – textile manufacturers introduced colored towels, previously available only in white. "The plain vanilla, so to speak, of the modern bathroom is turning pistachio and orange!" one of those manufacturers rejoiced in the *Ladies' Home Journal* in 1927, recommending towels to match the soap. "If you are fond of color schemes – and what woman is not? – try having the bathroom appear in towels bordered with blue and orange one week, lavender and green the next." The ad claimed that accommodating to seasonal and weekly rhythms in bathroom fashion "costs no more money," but of course it did.[12]

There were other voices besides those of the advertisers. Most women could never afford new bathroom fixtures, and many continued to equip their houses with hand-embroidered kitchen towels made out of flour sacks rather than colored bath towels from the department store. Academics still read the work of Thorstein Veblen, whose *Theory of the Leisure Class* (1899) had analyzed and satirized the rise of consumerism. Engineers promoted standardization, insisting that vast resources were being wasted because products came in too many styles and sizes. The American Society for Thrift, established in 1914 and active well into the 1920s, organized school lessons on saving (American Society for Thrift, 1915; Chamberlain, 1928). And in *Middletown*, their best-selling study of Muncie, Indiana, the sociologists Robert and Helen Merrell Lynd (1929) observed the emerging consumer culture with a critical eye.

A Cultural Juggernaut

But savings lessons represented an old ethic, and even the strongest advocates of stand-ardization and thrift had to make those concepts palatable to readers steeped in the new consumer culture. Nearly every discussion of standardization included an obligatory explanation that nobody was advocating standardized sofas or women's hats. In 1925, the editor of the *Journal of Home Economics* even redefined thrift to mean "wise spending of money" (Tucker, 1991, p. 69).[13] Despite the complaints of the critics, the develop-ment of a consumer culture was changing the relationships of the market, the activities of the household, and the meanings of work.

And they have continued to change. In the United States between the world wars, some clothes were made at home; most women bought coats, for example, but many made and mended their housedresses and their children's clothes. Canned food was widely available, but restaurants were for traveling and special occasions; most meals were prepared in private kitchens, from scratch. Except in the South, where African American women tended small children of both races, infants and toddlers were generally cared for by family members.

Since World War II, the production of clothing and food have become more public affairs, increasingly fulfilled by machines and systems designed by corporations for their own profit. Even childcare has taken on market overtones. Religious organizations and political parties employ marketing techniques developed for toothpaste. The services of doctors and educators are construed as commodities. Everyone is defined as a consumer; even presidents are not exempt, as the senior George Bush learned during his presidency when he was ridiculed for never having seen the automatic checkout scanners common in American supermarkets. Consumption is the reason people work, and equal opportunity to consume is entangled with concepts of citizenship. American consumption is shaped by persistent, well-crafted indoctrination, created in the interests of increasingly concentrated economic, political, and cultural power. For more than a century, advertisers, marketers, and the developers of retail space have diverted consumers from that reality by associating buying itself with leisure, pleasure and fantasy.

But we do our critique a disservice if we narrate history as a tale of conspiracy. The process that makes people into consumers amalgamates changing ideas, habits, technology, demographic trends, and many other facets of culture that even the most powerful marketers cannot control. Corporate managers did not necessarily set out to create needs, nor did they do so in any straightforward way. They made products in order to sell them. Their goal, in Thorstein Veblen's words, was the "quantity-production of customers," the making of consumer markets (1923, p. 305). The manipulative power of even the largest and most expensive marketing efforts was limited by ethnic, regional, and personal preferences. If marketing could turn consumer desire into necessity, so much the better, but if it could not, manufacturers generated more new products, and cultivated consumer desire for the next thing.

Critiques of Consumer Culture

In the United States, the historical study of consumption was at first a contribution to critical discussions of contemporary political issues as well as historical ones. Critiques of consumer culture were grounded in the multifaceted social and political movements of the 1960s and 1970s and the broad sense of "political" that prevailed at that time. Feminists plastered billboards with "this ad degrades women" stickers; they debated the importance of consumerism to women's oppression and, more generally, the relationship of consumption to women's unpaid household labor. Hippies promoted dropping out: working as little and spending as little as possible. Leftists sought to interpret Marx's writings on commodity fetishism and the analyses of the Frankfurt School.

In recent years, in my country, these political viewpoints have declined. Beyond the academy, an apolitical or celebratory stance towards consumer culture has been fortified by the fall of communism; among some intellectuals, cultural studies has dared to suggest that consumption may actually have liberatory potential. Yet after all these years, and despite substantial changes in women's lives, feminist analyses of marketing retain their vitality. Regionalist and aesthetic cases against homogenized culture have gone on the global stage. Social injustice becomes ever more compelling, and not simply because the rich have more stuff, or because private extravagance ties up money that could be given to charity or taxed for public use. In contemporary culture, consumption reproduces inequality, a task accomplished in traditional cultures by birth and caste. Individualism and the decline of social values and social space foster the idea that satisfying personal needs and desires takes precedence over the values of tribe, religion, or nature.

But of all the critiques of consumer culture, the environmental one is, I believe, the least debatable; as global warming becomes more obvious and oil wars proliferate, it becomes ever more potent. We are literally consumers: Few of us sew clothes, build houses, or make music. We don't know how to get clean water or how to make gasoline, and the systems that comprise daily life are too complex for most of us to comprehend at all, and for any of us to comprehend completely. Our dissociation from our bodies and the planet may be regarded as a function of widespread self-indulgence or as an understandable response to the pressures of modern and postmodern life. But even those who glorify first-world consumer culture must regard it as reasonable for people elsewhere to want an equivalent level of convenience and comfort, and must question whether the planet can provide sufficient resources.

An understanding of history does not contribute in any straightforward way to environmental solutions. Indeed, understanding and embracing the concept of change over time complicates the issues. But, like foreign travel, the historical perspective provides us with a viewpoint from which we may observe some other way to be human, and where we may ask heretical but important questions: Is everything a commodity? How might we go about reassociating ourselves with our bodies and the planet? What are the costs of commercial values framing all facets of life? What, to use the words of the organizers of this conference, do the economic and social well-being of consumers and families mean in light of the pressing issues of the global environment, the global labor force, and human rights?

Above all, the historical perspective tells us that things change. With it, we can regard artifacts and institutions as ephemeral. Transitory phenomena, they come and go; McDonald's is no more eternal than the Sears catalogue, which dominated American merchandising in its day. Like travel in distant lands, travel in the foreign country that is the past highlights both advantages and drawbacks of contemporary consumer culture. Keeping it in mind inevitably enriches our awareness of market behavior.

Questions

1. What does Strasser mean when she says that a pre-consumer culture seems alien to us now?
2. Why is the change from "customer" to "consumer" significant for the author?
3. How do a chunk of handmade soap and a bar of Ivory embody different social relationships?
4. How did "convenience" become a modern value, and what were its meanings?
5. What are some of the relationships of fashion, obsolescence, and consumer culture?
6. How do modern advertisements use convenience and fashionable obsolescence to sell brands?

Notes

1. This essay is a distillation of major points in Strasser (1992), Strasser (1989) and Strasser (1999).
2. Not all the new goods were, technically speaking, mass produced. Philip Scranton points out that "the seasonal styles that made department stores palaces of middle-class consumption, as well as the 'knock-offs' vended to working-class and rural purchasers" were not produced by mass production methods, nor were furniture or home decorations (1991, pp. 28, 32).
3. The following discussion of convenience and fashion is taken from Strasser (1999, pp. 181–199).
4. "To the Busy Mother who doesn't intend to let her Social Duties slide," Hotpoint advertisement, *The Ladies' Home Journal*, May, 1923, p. 138; other advertisements reproduced in Marchand (1985, pp. 57, 58, 143).
5. "Hundreds of extra helpers *under the suds*," Fels-Naptha advertisement, *Ladies' Home Journal*, November, 1927, p. 47; P&G advertisement, *Good Housekeeping*, October, 1916, p. 11, reproduced in Marchand (1985, p. 10).
6. "Give your home the convenience of Frigidaire," Delco-Light ad, *Good Housekeeping*, July, 1925, p. 132.
7. "What a convenience electric light is," *Good Housekeeping*, October, 1925, p. 227.
8. "Let CHIPSO bring you washday relief," *Good Housekeeping*, September, 1925, pp. 118–119. LaFrance bluing and cleansing agent used the same appeal. "Some women use a washing machine. Some women use a tub. Some women use a boiler," the ad was headlined. But every woman who redeemed the coupon for a free package "will save half her washday work." See "But every woman who uses this coupon." La France ad. *Good Housekeeping*, July, 1925, p. 130.
9. "Free from the drudgery of 'oven watching,' " Wilcolator advertisement, *Good Housekeeping*, September, 1925, p. 150.
10. "Empire of the ephemeral" is a literal translation of the title of Lipovetsky's book (1994).
11. For details on the argument in this paragraph, see Strasser (1989, Ch. 5, "Designing markets").
12. Cannon and Martex ads reproduced in Marchand (1985, pp. 125, 123).
13. For a typical standardization discussion, see Waite (1928, pp. 73–74); *JHE* editor quoted in Tucker (1991, p. 116).

References

American Society for Thrift (1915). *The thrift propaganda in America*. New York: The American Society for Thrift.

Andrews, B. R. (1923). *Economics of the household: Its administration and finance*. New York: Macmillan.

Barthes, R. (1983). *The fashion system* (M. Ward & R. Howard, Trans.). New York: Hill and Wang.

Chamberlain, A. H. (1928). *Thrift education: Course of study outline for use in Years One to Eight inclusive*. New York: The American Society for Thrift.

Kyrk, H. (1923). *A theory of consumption*. Boston: Houghton Mifflin.

Lipovetsky, G. (1994). *The empire of fashion: Dressing modern democracy* (C. Porter, Trans.). Princeton, NJ: Princeton University Press.

Lynd, R. S., & Lynd, H. M. (1929). *Middletown: A study in modern American culture*. New York: Harcourt, Brace & World.

Marchand, R. (1985). *Advertising the American dream: Making way for modernity, 1920–1940*. Berkeley, CA: University of California Press.

Scranton, P. (1991). Diversity in diversity: Flexible production and American industrialization. *Business History Review, 65*, 27–90.

Strasser, S. (1982). *Never done: A history of American housework*. New York: Pantheon Books.

Strasser, S. (1989). *Satisfaction guaranteed: The making of the American mass market*. New York: Pantheon Books.

Strasser, S. (1999). *Waste and want. A social history of trash*. New York: Metropolitan Books.

Tierney, T. F. (1993). *The value of convenience: A genealogy of technical culture*. Albany, NY: State University of New York Press.

Tucker, D. M. (1991). *The decline of thrift in America: Our cultural shift from saving to spending*. New York: Praeger.

Veblen, T. (1899). *Theory of the leisure class*. New York: Viking.

Veblen, T. (1923). *Absentee ownership and business enterprise in recent times*. New York: Viking.

Waite, W. C. (1928). *Economics of consumption*. New York: McGraw-Hill.

Chapter 3

STUART EWEN

"EDUCATE THE PUBLIC!"

IN THIS CHAPTER STUART EWEN FOCUSES on the story of how the major telephone company AT&T developed and enhanced many of the modern practices of public relations. One such practice was the move away from the earlier model of public relations as mere "press agentry." This original model was a "reactive" one where public relations efforts would only kick in when a scandal or image problem needed to be corrected. Modern PR involves a more proactive stance to aggressively mold the public's view of the company. Such a strategy required greater awareness of public opinion about the company, and institutionalized data collection of public views. Along these lines, the telephone giant also worked toward a "two-way street" approach to public relations, creating and publicizing policies that its executives believed would be especially well received. This effort foreshadowed the "two-way communication" view of public relations that is widely taught in classes today.

The chapter also illustrates the early use of advertising as part of public relations efforts. AT&T's advertising both helped "grease the wheel" for newspapers' friendliness to PR efforts by offering additional revenue to newspapers. Advertising also had a symbolic function by thematically complementing and reinforcing the messages in press releases and other PR efforts. These coordinated symbolic efforts of ads/press releases are reminiscent of much larger Integrated Marketing Communications (IMC) activities that are today used by large companies. The AT&T campaign also illustrates not just how companies may be symbolically constructed in persuasive materials ("Telephone service, a public trust"), but also how audiences may be similarly constructed (the public presented as dispersed but connected). In this sense Ewen's history resonates with other work in this book such as that of Greg Dickinson, who talks about how company rhetoric can symbolically create a public through modern advertising.

If Ivy Lee supposed that "the facts" he propagated would induce the public to see things through the Rockefellers' eyes, the response his press work received cast a dark shadow over this assumption. Lee's efforts did little to cleanse the reputation of the Rockefellers—or of Standard Oil—in the public mind. Even thirty years after the Rockefellers first hired Lee—in 1945—a high-level executive of Standard Oil of New Jersey (still a Rockefeller company) was forced to concede that the "history of Standard Oil in its relations with the public has not been too fortunate."

> Back in the days after the turn of the century, in the "trust busting" days of
> Teddy Roosevelt, Standard Oil was regarded as the prime example of a
> powerful, grasping, iniquitous business organization. . . . In the 30 years
> or more that followed, very little was done to offset this idea.[1]

On occasion Lee was able to convince John D. Rockefeller to partake in some minimal public relations schemes. In some of these instances, news coverage improved. An arranged golf match between the old man and a reporter for the *New York World*, for example, yielded a series of cheerful puff pieces presenting "the human side of the Rockefellers."[2] Such publicity stunts, however, misrepresent the normal cast of Lee's work—or of Rockefeller's public posture—during their long association. Standard Oil's policies toward the public changed little, and Lee was left, for the most part, with the formidable task of interpreting the Rockefeller family's oil and energy interests to an often critical press and public.

Lee's work for the Rockefellers embodied the limits faced by most of the journalists who crossed the line into corporate public relations work during the early years of the century. Unremitting corporate arrogance made their work extremely difficult. At best, their efforts bore mixed results. While some pliant publications provided an open forum for their pronouncements, countless others continued to portray corporations and their press agents in extremely negative terms.

Following the Ludlow Massacre, for example, despite the fact that Lee's press releases were intended to curry favorable news coverage for Rockefeller interests, the bulletins were widely dismissed as roguish prevarications.

"During the Colorado coal miners' strike," the *San Francisco Star* reported, "the Rockefellers hired Ivy L. Lee to present their side of the controversy to the public in a series of bulletins masquerading as 'Facts Concerning the Strike in Colorado for Industrial Freedom.' . . . The chief trouble with Ivy Lee," the article concluded, "is his disposition to wander from the fireside of truth. Testimony given before the Federal Commission on Industrial Relations—even that given by some of the mine owners—shows that Lee twisted facts, and invented some that he couldn't find outside of his imagination."[3]

The *Toledo Blade* reported that "throughout the Colorado troubles, pamphlets, circulars and letters fairly rained down upon the newspapers. It was a flood, a deluge. If it converted or influenced anyone, we have not heard of it. A broad reading of the American press indicated that the stuff went into the waste baskets throughout the country just as it did here. It swelled the postal receipts and added to the tonnage of houses that buy waste paper. But as for education, there was no result at all."[4]

Poet Carl Sandburg, writing in the *New York Call*, dismissed Lee as a "hired slanderer" and a "paid liar."[5] Meanwhile, in a two-part *Harper's Magazine* exposé presenting an itemized rebuttal of Lee's strike bulletins, the progressive journalist George Creel discredited the "entirely false view of the situation" presented in the pamphlets and accused Lee of being a would-be "poisoner of public opinion."[6] The sobriquet "Poison Ivy" would hound Lee for years.

Yet there was another—less apparent—facet of Lee that merits some consideration here. It emerged briefly during his testimony before the U.S. Commission on Industrial Relations. At one point in his long deposition, Lee made a suggestive excursion from an otherwise unscrupulous discourse on "the facts" concerning Ludlow. Responding to a question about his personal affiliation with the Rockefeller family, Lee began to speculate on the proper relationship that ought to exist between a public relations specialist and his corporate client.

"My idea," he started off, "is that the principal himself should be his own publicity agent; that the function for a person like myself . . . should be to advise with the man who is to take responsibility for the act itself as to what he should do and what he should say, and that he should do the same."[7] Commandeering the technocratic patois of his day, Lee explained that his paradigm of public relations was something that reached beyond the standard conventions—and mostly cosmetic habits—of press agentry.

> Publicity is not a game; it is a science. The difference between the two is as wide as the discrepancy between a press agent and a doctor of publicity. The function of a press agent is to put things across. The problem of a doctor of publicity is to induce his patient to behave in such a way as to commend himself unto the approval of a good city editor.[8]

In this conjecture, Lee's idealized vision of corporate public relations was hitching its wagon to Progressive ideas. Business leaders themselves, he speculated, must finally see the light and assume hands-on responsibility for making the institutions that they run more authentically responsive to the common good.

> Publicity in its ultimate sense means the actual relationship of a company to the people, and that relationship involves far more than saying—it involves doing. An elementary requisite of any sound publicity must be, therefore, the giving of the best possible service.[9]

A "doctor of publicity" would operate as an unfailing behind-the-scenes adviser—an invisible counsel—offering perpetual guidance on what to say, how best to behave, and even how to restructure a corporation for the purpose of securing public confidence. Intrinsic to this view was the insight that press releases alone could not generate a sympathetic climate of public opinion. The public must witness changed behavior—an altered deportment—on the part of a company and its leaders. Lee christened such unaccustomed intercourse between public interest and corporation policy a "two-way street," a self-congratulatory phrase that has persevered in canonical folktales of the public relations industry ever since.[10]

Lee's own career never came close to achieving the goal of a two-way street. Indeed, during the early years of the century, there were few captains of industry who yet felt obliged to move in this direction.

There was, however, one notable exception to this general rule: a man named Theodore Newton Vail, who, starting in 1907, was president of the American Telephone and Telegraph Company (AT&T). More than any other corporate chieftain of his era,

Vail approximated the vision of business leadership that Lee conjured up in his testimony before the U.S. Commission on Industrial Relations in 1915.

To some extent, the link between AT&T and public relations strategy predated Vail's presidency. From the beginning of the century—while most corporations paid little attention to the temperature of public opinion—unique exigencies impelled the Bell System, as it was called, to look upon "public relations" as a vital element of its corporate policy.

By the turn of the century, the AT&T leadership was already committed to establishing a privately owned, nationwide monopoly over an important new public service, the telephone.[11] This objective was set in the midst of a society in which anticorporate, antimonopoly sentiments—calls for governmental regulation and governmental ownership of public utilities—were approaching their zenith. To reach the objective of a Bell System monopoly over all wire communication in the United States, company leaders reasoned, the public had to be diverted—at least in respect to AT&T—from its general distrust of big business. With this, the wheels of an innovative public relations apparatus—one that continues to operate at full speed—began to turn.

The establishment of a Bell System monopoly faced acute challenges from two general directions. From one side, there were widespread calls for governmental ownership of telephone service, an approach that was taking hold in Europe and elsewhere. Many argued that phone service—drawing an analogy from the U.S. Post Office's jurisdiction over written and printed communications—should be "postalized," government run.

AT&T also faced headstrong competition from numerous localized independent phone companies. In a society in which huge national corporations were commonly despised and relatively few individuals yet required frequent access to long-distance phone services, a number of local telephone companies possessed "sentimental" advantages over AT&T and enjoyed a great deal of public support.

Confronted by these threats, AT&T, in 1903, engaged the services of a recently founded enterprise known as the Publicity Bureau, located in Boston. The Publicity Bureau, a partnership of experienced former newspaper men, was already achieving a reputation for being able to place prepackaged news items in papers around the country, and Frederick P. Fish, president of AT&T, believed that this know-how might be serviceable in the defense of the Bell System's corporate game plan.[12]

James T. Ellsworth, a seasoned journalist with the Bureau, was given the job of steering the AT&T account. One of the first things to happen under Ellsworth's guidance was the decision to jettison all corporate use of the expression "Bell System." "It seemed injudicious to use the term Bell System," he would later explain, because this phraseology "suggested a trust." With this, a new public identity was ushered in—"the Bell Companies"—a designation more in tune with the anticorporate spirit of the time, one that suggested a loose federation of localized businesses.[13]

Beyond this early example of corporate image management, Ellsworth methodically generated public relations pieces—crafted to read like impartial feature articles—for syndication to newspapers around the country. He also assumed the task of promoting friendly relationships with editors and publishers around the country, particularly in those territories where competition from "the independents" or antitrust sentiments posed particular problems for AT&T interests.

In 1903, for example, regional phone companies posed a problem for AT&T in Kansas City, which had recently granted a franchise to an independent, and in Milwaukee, which seemed to be on the brink of doing so. "These two cities being considered in a critical condition at the time the publicity work started," Ellsworth later recalled, he "was sent to survey the ground."

What he found was daunting. AT&T interests were under fire, and the corporation had few opportunities to defend itself. "At Kansas City," Ellsworth remembered, "the newspaper situation was so antagonistic that the local Bell Company—the Missouri and Kansas Telephone Company—had no means of presenting its facts to the public." Adding to this problem, there was little practical PR wisdom for him to fall back on during those early years; "organized publicity was little more than a theory and practically no one knew how to practice it."

Developing a strategy out of his firsthand journalistic experience, Ellsworth took a first step, which was based on his understanding of newspaper economics. By 1900, advertising—not circulation—was already the prime source of income for most news-papers, and Ellsworth fully comprehended the unspoken power that advertisers could exert over editorial policy and content. AT&T's publicity work in Kansas City, there-fore, began by directing significant advertising revenues toward a number of local newspapers.

These economic seedlings soon bore fruit. With the lubricant of advertising dollars, Ellsworth was soon providing suddenly compliant editors with a diverse range of packaged articles, already typeset and ready to be placed. Ad revenues, Ellsworth recounted, "broke the ice" with these newspapers, and the Missouri and Kansas Bell company was "given access to the news columns of the several papers in Kansas City and had an opportunity to make itself better understood."[14]

In a 1904 memorandum to AT&T executives, the Publicity Bureau was already boasting that it had "disabused the public mind" of the "Twenty Million Dollar Trust Myth" that had surrounded the Missouri and Kansas Bell company. Milwaukee, the Bureau reported, would soon be theirs.

Internally, AT&T was pleased with the Bureau's work. Walter S. Allen, AT&T's corporate liaison with the Publicity Bureau, reported to President Fish that it should become increasingly easy to get pro-AT&T articles published. In a memo that reflected the increasingly sophisticated sensitivity of the newspaper as a communications environment, Allen asserted that the key to maintaining friendly relations with news-papers was to continue paying for advertising. Publicity articles, he cautioned, must appear to remain on the "news" side of the stylistic border that separates journalism from overt salesmanship. Though articles might be promotions for AT&T, they should not appear to be so. "Each new story presented," Allen explained, "can be made more and more frankly a Bell advertisement, but it can not be allowed to degenerate into material which will be considered by the editors of such a nature as to justify them in charging for it as paid reading matter at the standard rate of one dollar per line." To maintain this fine distinction, he continued, AT&T must ensure that publicity articles would be written only by experienced "newspaper writers."[15]

In time, Allen believed, these crack news writers would be skillful enough to translate the long-range intention of AT&T—to establish unchallenged control of all telephone communications in the United States—into a journalistic idiom that would be acceptable to a public that was generally hostile to monopoly. In a July 1904 letter to Fish, Allen elaborated:

> The objective point of the policy of this company, as I understand it, is . . . to secure as complete a system throughout the country as is possible, and to that end everything which educates the public in the use of the telephone is of ultimate advantage to this company. The work of this Bureau seems to me well adapted to interest the public, and as the foothold becomes more secure in newspaper circles it will in all probability be possible to lead many of them to the point we desire to reach, namely, the education of the public to the belief that the telephone system is necessarily national in character.[16]

While these documents reveal that AT&T's corporate leadership was, early on, paying exceptional attention to public relations concerns, the particular PR strategy being described was not that exceptional. Though on a grander and more credible scale than that employed by other companies, it was still predominantly press agentry. Farmed out to an independent contractor, public relations was not yet a part of the corporate fabric.

Initial enthusiasm for the Publicity Bureau's work soon proved premature. Despite the agency's earlier proclamations of triumph, by 1906 "the state of public opinion concerning large corporations" had deteriorated considerably, as had AT&T's public reputation in relation to independent regional phone companies. Writing again to Fish, in October of 1906, Allen complained that "much talk of the independents as to the Bell methods and the Bell theories passes muster with the mass of people . . . as being true."

In an ambience of escalating crisis, AT&T's leaders began to entertain the need for "radical change" in their effort to generate more amicable public relations. "It seems to me essential," wrote Allen to Fish, "that if this company is to secure the co-operation of the public, a more aggressive position as regards the presentation of its claims to the consideration of the public must be taken."[17]

It was at this decisive moment, that AT&T moved toward Lee's fantasy of proper public relations. In 1907, AT&T took its public relations activities out of the hands of the Publicity Bureau and placed them under the direct supervision of a new chief executive, Theodore Newton Vail, a man who had been employed by the Bell System in years past. To assist him, Vail hired Ellsworth away from the Publicity Bureau and placed him at the head of the newly created AT&T Information Department.[18]

Vail was, for his era, an unusual kind of corporate chief. Unlike most business leaders of the time—who kept a deliberate distance from public view—Vail saw public relations as a key ingredient of corporate leadership in the twentieth century. In this sense, his elevation to the presidency of AT&T constituted a dramatic rejoinder to the philosophy of men like John D. Rockefeller and others who rated the appellation robber baron. Vail was a quintessential "corporate liberal."[19] In his desire to curry favorable public opinion and in his multilevel campaign to project and nurture an altruistic corporate identity, he embodied a business-oriented variant of the Progressive impulse.

As president of a privately held public utility, Vail was in a unique position to appreciate the delicate balance between the interests of a large corporation and a middle-class public that was expected to purchase its services or invest in its stock. From this vantage point, Vail demonstrated a business class consciousness that was rare among his peers. Within an often bitter anticorporate milieu, he cultivated a conciliatory style of leadership, predicated on the belief that conventional business practices—unless modified—posed a threat not only to the interests of privately owned utilities, but to the viability of corporate capitalism in general.

There was "danger, grave danger," Vail forecast, if business continued to choose the incentive of short-term profit over the more strategic question of long-term survival.[20]

> Our personal rights will not amount to much if they come in conflict with public greed or selfishness, or with public prejudice. For this reason and these reasons, and for the preservation of society such as we can live under, it is necessary that we subordinate our personal and selfish desires to what is best for all, and keep alive in the minds of the public the necessity of this subordination.[21]

In its sense of imminent peril, Vail's worldview was remarkably close to that of Walter Lippmann in *Drift and Mastery*. Like Lippmann, Vail believed that the flammable alliance of corporate arrogance from above and radical forces from below was propelling society toward chaos. Echoing familiar middle-class anxieties, Vail was troubled by a vast population of impoverished immigrants who, as they transfigured American society, presented a mounting threat to the social order.

> Millions of immigrants . . . with no realization of any difference between liberty and license, were cut loose from the restraint imposed upon them by custom and tradition, and without education or ideas of public obligations were put on a political equality in every respect with those who by experience and generations of education were prepared for all the rights of higher citizenship.

These "discontented forces," Vail continued, were being incited by agitators who were forging them into "an influence in the politics of this country that must be reckoned with."[22] Decrying a distending tide of democracy, Vail asserted that social progress could not be achieved at the expense of social distinction.

> No matter what may be the future of "uplift" or development some conditions will never change. . . . [S]ome must bear the physical burden, some the mental, and some the financial. There must be mutual concession and subordination of the individual to the comfort of all. There must be leaders and followers, for without organization there can only be chaos.[23]

Like Lippmann, Vail also believed that the middle-class public was being misguided by "utopian" theorists and the general ambience of recrimination they were fomenting. Persisting habits of corporate greed, he allowed, contributed a kernel of truth to the accusations.

> The public have been educated entirely by those whose entire capital is in exciting class prejudice and class feeling. Mismanagement and unprincipled promotion and combination have furnished the agitators with some material, which freely coupled with misstatements, misinformation and misinterpretation of rightful things . . . have produced deplorable results.

Against these false prophets and their teachings, Vail contended, corporations must furnish an alternative truth. "The only thing to bring about a millennium, is to be as active in giving correct information, and in upsetting of heresies and delusions, as others have been in cultivating them."[24] As the "private rights" of corporations are dependent on "public acquiescence," the public must be "educated" toward a greater understanding of these rights.[25]

Vail's commitment to "educating" the public was a critical piece within a sophisticated political outlook. Consistent with the thinking of the Progressives, his notion of "the public" was emphatically middle class; Vail's commitment to the practice of corporate public relations was rooted in the conviction that if educated to be more sympathetic toward business, this public might serve as a buffer against the greater threats that lurked below.

Against the danger of chaos from below and to nullify public "delusions," Vail formulated a far-ranging public relations strategy aimed at convincing the middle class that their interests and the interests of the Bell Companies were congenial. More than press agentry, Vail's PR policy was planned to provide middle-class phone subscribers with tangible proof that AT&T's corporate policies were responsive to the needs of an anxious public.

Phone rates were established to project this priority. At a time when long-distance service was used, for the most part, by businesses, AT&T regional companies inflated long-distance telephone costs to subsidize their local phone rates. With the Bell Companies offering the only comprehensive national telephone service, businesses engaged in interstate commerce had little choice but to go with AT&T. Meanwhile, the surcharge levied on business users permitted AT&T to provide local service at a price that was affordable to most middle-class subscribers, people who only rarely relied on long-distance lines.

Other policies were more semiotic in nature. Though AT&T was controlled exclusively by a male hierarchy, a conscious decision was made to give the direct link between the public and the corporation—the telephone operator—a woman's voice. The employment of female operators, who would begin each phone transaction with a courteous "Number please?" established AT&T as a prescient innovator of the "user-friendly interface."

At a time when there was widespread middle-class unease over exploitative working conditions, AT&T advertised internal labor policies designed to encourage "esprit de corps . . . morale" among employees. For AT&T's primarily Anglo-Saxon workforce, Vail promised wages scaled to match "the very highest that are paid for any similar class of work" and an unprecedented employee health program to provide "benefits for sickness and disability."

Ultimately, AT&T's success rested on its ability to project a sympathetic corporate personality. Vail insisted that this required a sure understanding of the public mind; the "whole question of public relations" was increasingly conceived in terms of the company's ability to present itself "through the eyes of the public." This objective demanded new ways of thinking. As never before, company executives were encouraged to become students of public attitudes and opinions, to familiarize themselves with the public's point of view on a range of relevant issues. Though this idea is a cliché of public relations today, at the time it constituted a dramatic break from the disdainful short-sightedness of the past, a move toward a more socially conscious style of corporate behavior.

"Get the public's view point," said E. K. Hall, Vail's vice president, to a meeting of his New England managers; "see if you can work out the problem from that basis."

> Don't bristle at the man who makes a complaint, but make him feel that he is doing you a favor. Most people are reasonable, and if you take this point of view you can make him not only reform his opinion of your company, but respect you as an individual.[26]

All these strategies—cut-rate local phone bills, the friendly greetings of Ma Bell, employee esprit de corps programs, presenting things through the public's eyes—were essentials in Vail's innovative effort to defend AT&T against a "curse of bigness." Yet it was his effort to place an altruistic spin on the idea of an AT&T telephone monopoly that occupied the core of his PR endeavors. This was the company's underlying corporate objective, and a contentious political climate required that it be adroitly pursued.

Vail's campaign to ennoble the concept of an AT&T telephone monopoly confronted difficult obstacles. In a nation in which the fear of "bigness" was widespread and most people still lived a more or less localized existence, provincialism had buttressed public loyalty to regional phone companies. In the face of this hurdle, AT&T's Information Department worked to advance the oracle of a different America, an America to come, in which people's lives—following the lead of the modern business system—would take on an increasingly national and cosmopolitan character: Within such a world, the limits of regional phone service would become clear.

It was the nervous public that provided Vail with the basic ingredient of his PR strategy. In a world where rapid change and a sense of drift were often dismaying facts of life, Vail's public relations was calculated to provide Americans with a consoling picture of the people they were in the process of becoming. Remarkably attuned to the nationalization of social and economic life that was rapidly taking place, his platform was founded on the majestic promise of "universal service."

People would be more dispersed yet more connected. Beyond claims of high-quality phone service, Bell public relations continually portrayed the ordinary phone subscriber as a person requiring contact with a wider world. "When you lift the Bell receiver," the company repeatedly announced, "you are in contact with the world."[27]

As president, Vail dramatically increased corporate funding for publicity matters and launched—for the first time in the company's history—an illustrated institutional advertising campaign, touting the "Bell System" as a service benefiting "all the people all the time." Vail personally approved "every piece of copy and made many suggestions."[28]

Proclaiming that "every Bell Telephone is the Center of the System," these ads encouraged telephone users to view the company not as a dark monopolistic leviathan, but as a beneficent mother figure who would make each and every one of them the center of her attentions. At the bottom of each ad stood AT&T's oath of infinite and equitable access: "One System, One Policy, Universal Service." The deftness of this strategy was its unprecedented openness. Rather than hide from AT&T's conspicuous size or its monopolistic ambitions, Vail energetically transformed these often maligned characteristics into pure and simple virtues.

Building on preexisting patterns of publicity, AT&T, under Vail's leadership, also expanded the bulk of materials produced and sent out to news services and newspapers. Beyond articles responding directly or implicitly to those hostile to an AT&T monopoly, many of these pieces were of a human-interest variety, designed to portray the telephone in general, and AT&T in particular, as the glue that holds a modern society together.

Vail personally prepared "a syllabus on the life history of the telephone" for publication in magazines, and other articles featured telephone etiquette; "girl" switchboard operators; and the role of the telephone in suburban life, in church life, in the wilderness, in the law, in the army, and so forth. In each story the telephone was the star; the Bell System supplied the mise-en-scène that made the drama possible.

While magazine and newspaper publishers criticized many companies for attempts to secure "free publicity" in their pages, AT&T's self-conscious mix of paid advertising and packaged news items gained publishers' approval and often their active collaboration with AT&T's corporate goals.

This collaboration is apparent in a 1909 letter from H. W. Pool, advertising manager of *Moody's Magazine*, to Ellsworth. Pool was writing to offer the company advertising space on "the outside back cover" of an upcoming issue of the magazine for a fee of seventy-five dollars. "This issue," Pool continued, "will contain an exhaustive article of your company written by Mr. John Moody which is highly complimentary to your company." The exchange between favorable editorial coverage and advertising revenues was unabashedly affirmed as Pool inserted: "We believe that support from you from an advertising standpoint would prove mutually advantageous."[29]

The amalgam of syndicated public relations articles and paid institutional advertising—a mix that was cementing relations with editors even before Vail took over—continued to reap benefits for AT&T. In confidential meetings, regional directors of Bell Companies would swap detailed stories of how they had secured desirable press connections.

At a June 1914 meeting of the Bell Companies, Mr. Fortier, of Bell of Canada, reported to his corporate associates that "the relations of our Local Manager with the newspapers are such I think that any news story that is deserving of insertion, they will find no difficulty having it published in the papers. There are papers that we are on such exceptional terms with," Fortier continued, "that they will print practically anything within reason."

On the same occasion Mr. Sullivan, of Southwestern Bell, painted a graphic picture of friendships being cultivated to serve corporate interests. He explained:

> We have in each General Manager's division a publicity agent. . . . [I]t is his business to know personally and intimately every newspaper reporter, newspaper man, and newspaper owner personally. One man in particular has succeeded in being intimately acquainted and being a friend of 98% of the editors and owners in his State. That friendship is played up in different ways; by calling on them once, twice, three or four times a year, by meeting with them at their conventions, and by assisting to entertain them. . . .[30]

These activities, however, do not fully reveal the nature of AT&T's Information Department (or, as it was later renamed, the Public Relations Bureau). More than simply producing and disseminating materials for publication, Vail's public relations operation also engaged in a continuous and detailed analysis of public opinion insofar as it related to AT&T's far-flung interests. Proceeding along terrain mapped—at least

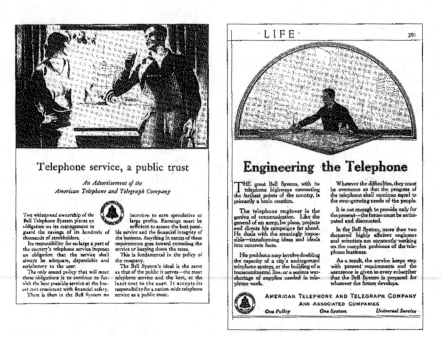

Figure 3.1 Three print advertisements for AT&T: 1909, 1916, 1928. All follow Vail's public relations lead, emphasizing the idea of AT&T's public service. AUTHOR'S COLLECTION.

theoretically—by Gabriel Tarde, Vail intuited that the grooves of borrowed thought embraced complex networks of human interaction.

Beyond the authority of journalistic materials, there was a diverse range of other opinion shapers that influenced attitudes, that shaped conversations, in America. To be fully informed about relevant currents of popular thought, Vail surmised, it was essential to keep a corporate ear close to the ground. Toward this purpose, the Information Department, and later the Public Relations Bureau, deployed an intricate intelligence-gathering-and-surveillance apparatus, designed to provide the corporation with an ongoing profile of its adversaries.

AT&T's reconnaissance chores included the methodical collecting and clipping of newspapers, magazines, books, and "ephemeral pamphlets" from around the country on anything that appertained to the Bell System's corporate situation. Proposed legislation, as well, and even the spoken utterances of college professors, students, "radical politicians and progressive editors" were painstakingly monitored, to pinpoint potential sources of opposition and to provide an up-to-the-minute picture of "the general trend of public sentiment."[31]

Assembled from the findings of field operatives, weekly intelligence summaries were distributed to all AT&T executive officers and to executives and attorneys in the field. The purpose behind these exhaustive activities was simple: to permit AT&T to prepare for and "meet actual situations as they arise in advance of general public clamor."[32] Transcending the ex post facto strategies of "damage control" that marked most corporate PR of the period, AT&T's operations were designed to forecast and defuse problems before they arose.

At times this meant shadowing people whose public statements were felt to endanger company interests. In 1913, for example, David J. Lewis, a Democratic congressman from Maryland, was barnstorming local organizations, calling for a government takeover of telephone service. To AT&T's Public Relations Bureau, Lewis's "speeches before economic, civic and business societies throughout the country, and particularly before the Granges . . . constituted an appreciable form of publicity," one that demanded a corporate response.[33]

Ellsworth, speaking at a confidential public relations meeting in 1914, addressed the Lewis problem directly. "We have had the occasion to sort of keep tab on him and follow him around," he reported. This gumshoe behavior, he explained, was enacted to undermine Lewis before he could arrive to deliver a speech.

> It has been our idea that it was a good thing to find out where he was going, and if possible to secure a list of the people or members of the Grange or Association or Society he was going to speak before, and circularize them before he got there. In some instances we found this was impossible because they would smell a rat and would not let us have the list of names till after he came around, but in every instance we have found we could get to people either before or after.[34]

To offset the impact of men like Lewis, the company also arranged public debates on the question of governmental ownership or other thorny issues. Pro-AT&T speakers—drawn ideally from the community—were furnished with debating kits, indexes of relevant issues, and other ammunition with which to mount an effective response.[35] As never before, local forums of public discussion were being infused with scripted lines.

Guiding these activities was Vail, a new breed of businessman who—more than any corporate leader of the period—appreciated the importance that public relations would assume in twentieth-century American life. Along the way, Vail catapulted the telephone giant toward the forefront of modern public relations thinking and toward achieving the monopoly it so forcibly pursued.

At the center of Vail's managerial vision was his commitment to the idea of "education," his obsessional quest to convince Americans that the AT&T catechism of "One System, One Policy, Universal Service" would provide them with an interconnected future and a quality and efficiency of service that no other system could match.

Amid the often intense pandemonium of antimonopoly sentiment, Vail—an unflinching proponent of corporate progressivism—was convinced that proving AT&T's case was simply a matter of appealing to people's common sense through the presentation of facts, assisted by the agency of public reason. "Educate the public," he exhorted his executive corps in 1913. Their job, he continued was to present the public with those facts and arguments necessary for them to see AT&T's ambitions as conforming to their sense of their own best interests.

> It is you who must do it. . . . If you can impress upon . . . the public, the fact that we can give them better service than could be obtained under government ownership, and that a monopoly does not necessarily mean public disadvantage, the time will come. Before we can accomplish our plan for a universal . . . system, the public mind must be thoroughly inbued with its economies and advantages.[36]

Responding to an onrush of social agitation in 1909, Theodore Roosevelt had cautioned that "unless there is a readjustment" in the conduct of business in the United States, "there will come a riotous wicked, murderous day of atonement." The survival of capitalism, he believed, demanded a more comprehensive social vision on the part of businessmen. While most corporate leaders ignored this admonition, Vail was articulating a new vision of publicly engaged corporate management. The hidebound secrecy that had escorted earlier industrial development was now being challenged by a public relations-oriented conception of enlightened self-interest—an approach to corporate leadership that, in years to come, would gain a widening circle of disciples.

The distinction between a man like Vail and a man like Rockefeller cannot be understood simply in the terms provided by muckrakers' morality plays, dramas pitting the forces of good against the forces of evil. Neither can the differences between the two men be reduced to a matter of different temperaments. Whatever personal genius stood behind Vail's innovations, they were also framed by the particular exigencies of the industry over which he presided: telephone service.

Rockefeller had been part of a generation of industrialists and financiers who had assembled America's industrial base. Barons of finance, transportation, capital-goods production, coal, and petroleum, these men controlled large-scale industries in which direct contact with the public or the need for public approval had seemed relatively minimal. Their activities were, for the most part, shielded from the middle-class public by a vast layer of local middlemen who had little power to influence the policies of large-scale industry and finance. Only on rare occasions, usually at moments of crisis, had these early captains of industry felt obliged to explain themselves.

Vail, on the other hand, oversaw a corporation that dealt directly with middle-class Americans. Its product—person-to-person telephone communication—was a fundamental component in the evolution and assembling of a modern public of consumers.

This historical proximity to the emerging consumer culture demanded that Vail's vision move beyond that of preceding industrial barons. The public and its problems stood unavoidably at the center of AT&T's long-term ability to achieve its corporate goals.[37]

There is another factor that may have contributed to Vail's aptitude for public relations. It emanates from the changing choreography of public life itself and from Vail's particular vantage point on those changes.

In 1898 Tarde had depicted his contemporary "public" as "one which never ceases to grow and whose indefinite extension is one of the most clearly marked traits of our period." Just as newspapers had abetted a mode of public life that could "extend indefinitely," telephones were also inseminating that indefinite extension into the realm of people's private existence. Complementing the development of newspapers and other mass media as the connective tissue of public life in the modern age, AT&T—in its vision of One System, One Policy, Universal Service—was engaged in the development of a pervasive network that would help connect private existence to that increasingly vaporous public realm.

When Edward A. Ross wrote of newspapers that "mental touch is no longer bound up with physical proximity" and that in the modern era "remote people are brought, as it were, into one another's presence," he might just as well have been describing the telephone. Both the newspaper and the telephone were engaged in reshaping the terms of public interaction.

Vail's insights into the architecture of a modern public and the importance of public relations echoed the perception of contemporary social thinkers, journalists, and others who were in positions that permitted them to witness a new consumerist way of life unfolding. All had an understanding that a "different public," as Tarde had described it, was in the process of being formed. This public consisted of individual consumers bound together not by the tendrils of kinship and community, but by modern instruments of communication. Vail's recognition of this new public's existence and the pathways by which it was informed also suggested the means by which those outlooks might be influenced. While many businessmen continued to disregard the terms of their world, public relations was an idea whose time had come.

Questions

1   How were Ivy Lee's efforts to insert pro-Standard Oil views in the press received by newspapers and other writers?
2   What is the "two-way street" view of public relations?
3   How was advertising used to complement public relations efforts by AT&T?
4   How did AT&T use customer pricing, hiring and labor practices to win the public over?
5   How did the different conceptualizations of the public and customer encourage AT&T to think of the public differently than earlier large corporations like Standard Oil had?
6   When you watch local TV news, can you spot stories that may have originated from press releases?

Notes

1. F. M. Surface, "A Review of Public Opinion Particularly Affecting Standard Oil Company," in Standard Oil (New Jersey) and Affliated Companies, 1945 Public Relations Conference *Proceedings* (Rye, N.Y., November 19–20, 1945), p. 8.
2. Ray E. Hiebert, "Ivy Lee and the Development of Press Relations," *Public Relations Journal* 21 (March 1965), p. 9.
3. Clipping from the *San Francisco Star*, January 9, 1915. Packet 1, Box 4, Folder 1 of the Ivy L. Lee Collection, Seeley G. Mudd Manuscript Library, Princeton University.
4. Clipping from *Toledo Ohio Blade*, May 18, 1915. Ivy L. Lee Collection, Packet 1.
5. Clipping, Carl Sandberg, "Ivy L. Lee, Paid Liar," *New York Call*, March 15. Ivy L. Lee Collection, Packet 1.
6. George Creel, "Poisoners of Public Opinion: Part II," *Harper's Magazine* (November 14, 1914), pp. 465–66.
7. Lee's typewritten testimony before the U.S. Commission on Industrial Relations, City Hall (New York, April 1915). Ivy L. Lee Collection, Packet 1, pp. 31–32.
8. "House of Rockefeller Learns to Talk," *New York Press*, April 11, 1915. Lee's personal clipping file, Ivy L. Lee Collection, Packet 1.
9. Eric F. Goldman, *Two Way Street: The Emergence of the Public Relations Counsel* (Boston, 1948), p. 9.
10. Goldman's *Two Way Street* is a stunning example of such a gloss over. This brief volume was a promotion for the public relations industry and, for the most part, parroted the industry's PR for itself.
11. The company sought to consolidate control of telegraphy, as well. This goal would be accomplished within a decade when AT&T took over Western Union.
12. Alfred McClung Lee, *The Daily Newspaper in America: The Evolution of a Social Instrument* (New York, 1937), p. 442.
13. James Ellsworth, "Introduction to Historical Memoranda on Bell System Publicity," January 17, 1929. AT&T Corporate Archive, Box 1066, p. 4.
14. Ibid., pp. 4–5.
15. Walter S. Allen, letter to Mr. Frederick P. Fish, regarding renewal of contract with the Publicity Bureau, July 22, 1904. AT&T Corporate Archive, Box 1398, Item 14663, pp. 1–2.
16. Ibid., p. 3.
17. James D. Ellsworth, Memos to President Fish regarding news placement, October 3, 1906. AT&T Corporate Archive, Box 1317, Folder, Item No. 16634.
18. Ellsworth, "Introduction to Historical Memoranda on Bell Systems Publicity," p. 6.
19. The emergence of corporate liberalism in the National Civic Federation and Vail's place within it are discussed by James Weinstein, *The Corporate Ideal in the Liberal State, 1900–1918* (Boston, 1968).
20. "Speech to Railroad Commissioners, San Francisco, October, 1915," in Theodore Vail, *Views on Public Questions: A Collection of Papers and Addresses, 1907–1917* (privately printed, 1917), p. 241.
21. Ibid., p. 246.
22. Ibid., p. 248.
23. Ibid., p. 249.
24. "Speech to Annual Conference of Bell Systems, October 1913," in Vail, *Views on Public Questions*, p. 143.
25. Ibid., pp. 143–44.
26. American Telephone and Telegraph, "General Policy" memorandum. AT&T Corporate Archive, Box 56, File on Public Relations-Securities-Competition–1920, p. 2.
27. Morton E. Long, "Public Relations of the Bell Systems," *Public Opinion Quarterly* 1 (October 1937), p. 19.
28. James D. Ellsworth, "Start of General Magazine Advertising," memorandum, January 17, 1929. AT&T Corporate Archive, Box 1066.
29. H. W. Pool, letter to James D. Ellsworth, September 7, 1909. AT&T Corporate Archive, Box 1317, Folder 2, Item 664278.

30. American Telephone and Telegraph, "Confidential" minutes of a "Meeting of Publicity Men of the American Telephone and Telegraph Companies," June 26, 1914. AT&T Corporate Archive, Corporate Box 1310, pp. 16–17, 21.

31. American Telephone and Telegraph, memorandum of September 19, 1912, from Walter S. Allen to Vice President N. C. Kingsbury, establishing a Publicity Bureau for the corporation. AT&T Corporate Archive, Box B–20. A slightly revised version of this memo exists under the following entry: Walter S. Allen, Public Relations, "Plan for Establishing a Public Relations Department, July 23, 1913," Corporate Box 2035.

32. Ibid.

33. The Grange, a national network of farmers' organizations, was of particular interest to At&T because it was seen to "exert a powerful influence throughout the country."

34. American Telephone and Telegraph Company, "Confidential" minutes of a "Meeting of Publicity Men," June 26, 1914.

35. American Telephone and Telegraph Company, Minutes of Advertising Conference Bell Telephone systems, Philadelphia, June 28, 1916. AT&T Corporate Archive, Box 1310, p. 14.

36. "Address at the Opening of the Annual Conference of the Bell Telephone System in New York, October 1913," in Vail, *Views on Public Questions*, p. 155.

37. Other companies dependent on individual consumption also moved to the forefront of corporate public relations thinking. Advertising men were among the first to see the need for PR. See also, David E. Nye, *Image Worlds: Corporate Identities at General Electric, 1890–1930* (Cambridge, 1985), on General Electric's PR-photography activities that commenced as the electric giant moved toward producing and selling home appliances.

PART TWO

The Political Economy of Advertising

INTRODUCTION TO PART TWO

ADVERTISEMENTS ARE AMONG THE MOST VISIBLE forms of our media culture. But, despite this symbolic presence, the ad itself may not be the most influential aspect of advertising. Advertising also serves as a major funding system for our media. Ben Bagdikian observes in his contribution to this Part that the print media (newspapers and magazines) receive, on average, the majority of their funding from advertisers, and electronic media forms (especially broadcast television and radio, and certain websites) receive virtually 100 per cent of their funding from advertising. Even media that we believe to be "ad-free," such as theatrical movies or public television, often receive revenue from advertisers through such promotional forms as product placement and sponsorship.

This Part discusses the implications of advertising as a source of revenue for media. The chapters here critically engage the economic aspects of advertising and media, a perspective regarding the financial dynamics of media that is often labeled a "political economic" approach. A major assumption of such work is that, as a financial source for media, advertising shapes not just the ads appearing in these media, but even the non-advertising content. Advertisers do not just randomly place ads on media. They want the media "environment" to be especially welcoming for the ad message that delivers the right kind of audiences/consumers. This does not just mean reaching those demographic groups that match up with a marketers' consumer base (although this is important). It also means content that encourages an appropriate "buying mindset" to make the ads more effective. Because of these interests, advertising can have a profound and long-term effect on the pace, tone, and meanings of media content.

The four readings in this Part approach the political economy of advertising-funded media from different angles. Inger Stole takes an historical perspective by looking at the consumption orientation of early television, especially in the form of daytime TV targeted at women consumers. Ben Bagdikian offers a broader view by explaining the various ways that advertising as a funding source may negatively affect media content and especially subvert media's democratic mission. Jef Richards and John Murphy take an alternative perspective to Bagdikian, arguing that advertisers are often unfairly blamed for their influence upon content. Finally, Matthew McAllister and Matt Giglio contend that children's television is being dominated by new forms of promotion that often exploit loopholes in regulation designed to curtail excessive commercial influence.

Chapter 4

INGER L. STOLE

TELEVISED CONSUMPTION
Women, Advertisers and the Early Daytime Television Industry

STOLE'S CHAPTER FOCUSES ON THE COMMERCIAL IMPERATIVE of early television, in particular the interplay of gender and consumption of the 1950's NBC program *Home*. She observes that the role of advertising as a funding system for television was virtually unquestioned, unlike in the early days of radio. In her case study, she focuses on women as a key market and the role the desire for this market played in the development of early daytime television.

The network TV series *Home*, although ultimately not an enduring success, foreshadowed many of the current characteristics of advertising-supported programming. The show helped to establish a "magazine-style" advertising placement strategy, in which an advertiser buys one commercial spot rather than sponsoring an entire program. *Home*'s attempt to attract "upscale" women—an audience particularly attractive to advertisers—is similar to cable networks' focus on niche audiences today. The mentioning of the program in magazine stories and other media is now a common technique known as cross-promotion. And of course the integration of products into the program itself (via cooking and other household demonstrations) is routine today on television and other media. Cable networks such as Home and Garden and the Food Network are built on such advertising-friendly programming.

Introduction

When Betty Friedan published her seminal work *The Feminine Mystique* in the early 1960s, she quickly dispelled some of the romantic notions surrounding the immediate postwar era. Specifically, Friedan identified advertising and the commercial mass media among the leading social institutions holding on to an antiquated, but for them quite profitable, construct of gender. "Somehow, somewhere," she speculated, "someone must have figured out that women will buy more things if they are kept in the underused, nameless-yearnings easy-to-get-rid-of state of being housewives" (Friedan 1983: 207).

Starting from Friedan's by now famous arguments, this article traces the emergence of daytime television in the late 1940s and early 1950s. In pursuit of this goal, the study uses a qualitative research approach and relies on standard historical methods. In addition to archival material from the National Broadcasting Corporation's (NBC) papers, housed at the State Historical Society in Madison, Wisconsin, the article draws on trade journals, newspapers and accounts from the popular press. It discusses how the early television industry, through programming and scheduling practices, hoped to appeal to white, middle-class homemakers and to influence their consumption habits. What emerges is a picture in which a sexist construct fused (and, at times, collided) with the overwhelming commercial logic of the new medium's attempt to develop a composite notion of the American woman at mid-century. What is striking—and somewhat in contrast to Friedan's argument—is how difficult this proved to be for the early daytime television industry.

Unlike early television soap operas which, much like their radio counterparts, portrayed women in a variety of roles and life situations (Allen 1985; Cantor and Pingree 1983), daytime variety shows had their own agenda. Designed primarily as sales vehicles for their sponsors' products, these programs were aimed at white middle-class women and most often addressed their viewers as mothers, homemakers, and consumers.

This targeting was not entirely novel, of course. Ever since the early 1900s, when it had been "established" that 85 percent of all consumer purchases were made by female consumers, advertisers had directed most of their sales-appeals towards women (Lears 1994; Marchand 1985; Pollay 1994). When introduced immediately after the Second World War, television only accentuated these tendencies. In many cases, and this was especially prevalent on shows intended for the predominantly female daytime audience, the editorial content served primarily as an accommodating backdrop for demonstration of the sponsors' products. Few places is this more evident than in the case of *Home*, a daytime show broadcast by the National Broadcasting Corporation (NBC) every weekday between 1954 and 1957. Launched as the first-network produced program targeted specifically for a female daytime audience, *Home* provides an interesting look at how NBC conceptualized its first daytime viewers.

In this article, I first look at advertisers' conceptualization of the female consumer in the period following the end of the Second World War. I then turn to an exploration of the emergence of daytime television, including broadcasters' views on their predominantly female audience and their desire to sell this audience to advertisers. I conclude with a discussion of how these concerns were played out on NBC's *Home*. I argue that by grasping the underlying network principles behind the show, one can gain an understanding, not only of the manner in which female audiences were addressed in the 1950s, but also of the ways in which mass media addresses women today (Stole 1997).

Advertisers and the Female Consumer

When television was introduced to the American public in the late 1940s, few of the concerns regarding advertising and commercialization that had surrounded radio some twenty years earlier could be heard (Boddy 1990; McChesney 1993). Whereas in the 1920s, concerns about turning radio into a purely commercial medium could be detected even in advertising circles (Marchand 1985), television's commercial potential was celebrated enthusiastically, not only among advertisers, but in government circles as well. A commonly expressed postwar fear was that the economy might revert to its prewar depression standards without the impetus of wartime spending to stimulate production (Lipsitz 1990). More than a mere entertainment medium, America's manu-facturers therefore looked to television as a means of jump-starting the economy and increasing their sales (Schofield 1950).

Judging from consumers' interest in postwar consumer durables, however, manu-factures seemed to have little reason to worry. Wartime savings had enabled many Americans to participate in a postwar consumer boom and to enjoy a new, and higher, standard of living. Between 1946 and 1950, for example, Americans purchased 21.4 million automobiles, more than 20 million refrigerators, 5.5 million electric stoves, and 11.6 million television sets (Hartmann 1982: 8). Although it was considered unfortunate for a wife to have to work outside the home, it was considered even more unfortunate for a family not to be able to afford items considered necessary for the postwar home (May 1988). Many couples found it difficult to fulfill their dreams of a higher standard of living on one income alone, and by 1955 more women held jobs outside the home than at any time in the nation's history (Douglas 1995: 55).

Interestingly, however, the mass media and advertisers tended to ignore this fact, insisting instead on addressing women in roles as homemakers, mothers, and consumers. Women's magazines of the postwar era tended to promote their readers as young, married, and in charge of an expanding family budget (Advertisement for *Modern Romances* 1950a, b; Advertisement for *Today's Woman* 1952). "Concentrate your advertising on young mothers," advised *Parents' Magazine*, "they buy the most." From a commercial perspective, the woman with young, growing children was considered especially desirable. "Her home and family needs are large and constantly increasing making her the definitely biggest buyer of most products," stressed *Parent Magazine* (Advertisement for *Parent Magazine* 1953). Single women, married women without children, and older women, according to the same publication, "failed" to live up to the ideal of family-oriented consumption and were deemed to be of lesser interest to advertisers. The exception, according to *Seventeen* and *Modern Bride*, was the young woman about to marry (Advertisement for *Seventeen* 1953; Advertisement for *Modern Bride* 1953). Once married, *McCall's* helped define the couple's division of labor. "Sharing plans and problems and personal interests—their lives are linked closer together than ever," stated the magazine. "And even buying is part of their pattern— for the woman buys what the family eyes, from dishwashers to dungarees, from detergents to desks" (Advertisement for *McCall's* 1956).

America's postwar consumer culture "was predicated on the notion that women were the major consumers of most goods—that was their job after all—and that, to sell to them, you had to emphasize their roles as wives and mothers, because it was in these capacities, not in their capacities as secretaries or nurses, that women bought" (Douglas 1995: 56). The middle-class homemaker became "an important basis of the social economy—so much that it was necessary to define her in contradictions which held her in her limited social place" (Haralovich 1989: 66). Her role as homemaker was marginalized in the sense that her labor within the home was kept outside the market-place for commodity production. Yet, at the same time, her role and function in the home made her the focus of a large consumer industry (Haralovich 1989). While the entire advertising industry seemed gripped by the notion that all women identified themselves primarily as wives and mothers (Douglas 1995), it was also conscious of the fact that women did not always view themselves in this role. "The manufacturer wants to intrigue her back into the kitchen—and we show him how to do it the right way," explained an advertising strategist in the early 1960s. "If he tells her that all she can be is a wife and mother, she will spit in his face. But we show him how to tell her that it is creative to be in the kitchen" (Friedan 1983: 227). In designing programming and commercial structures for their daytime operations during the late 1940s and early 1950s, television broadcasters based much of their strategies on such theories.

The development of commercial television, modeled to a large degree on experiences with radio broadcasting two decades earlier, was largely based on widespread sale of television sets to private homes (Baughman 1987). The success of programming supported by direct advertising was seen to depend on the housewife as the "household purchasing agent" and the attentive target of advertising messages. Those most involved in planning television's commercial development—the electronic manufacturers and the commercial broadcasters—defined television as both a consumer product for the home and an "audio-visual showroom for the advertiser's consumer goods" (Boddy 1990: 20).

In the early days of television comedies, for example, comic impetus was often drawn from consumption-related situations. Frequently, the plot revolved around women's shopping habits and their use of commodities in order to "get ahead" socially. In many of these comedies, the working-class male, opposing his wife's consumption and choice of upwardly mobile strategy, was made "the butt of the joke" (Ewen 1977: 209). Also in terms of programming the early television industry borrowed from radio. Frequently, however, television producers demanded that radio scripts undergo changes. *I Remember Mama*, a long-running radio program adapted to the television screen in 1949, is one example. The televised version of the show transformed the Hansen family from an ethnic working-class family, able to solve its problems through collective efforts and personal ingenuity, into a modern nuclear family highly dependent on consumer products and commercial solutions. The transition from radio to television also changed the Hansen family's view on gender roles, including the "appropriate" career choice for women. For example, while one daughter, in the 1930s radio version, was encouraged to seek a career as a writer, the televised counterpart discouraged this goal, suggesting instead that she apply herself to finding a husband (Lipsitz 1990). Such programming attempted to mask social contradictions and naturalize (white) middle-class life where the woman's place was in the home because it was within the domestic sphere that the postwar consumer industry could best address the female consumer (Haralovich 1989).

Daytime Television

It is through an understanding of the rather fluid interconnection between leisure and labor within the home that representations of the early daytime audience best can be understood. By offering daytime programming that emphasized cooking, sewing, shopping, as well as tips on beauty and fashion, broadcasters hoped that women would regard daytime television as instrumental in making housekeeping more efficient and as an aid in bringing about a more "gracious" standard of living for their families (Stasheff and Bretz 1956). Suggesting that women's leisure time was conterminous with their work time, the television industry "addressed the woman as a housewife and presented her with a notion of spectatorship that was inextricably intertwined with her useful labor at home" (Spigel 1992: 75).

Television executives hoped that daytime television would follow the introductory pattern of previous entertainment media. Both the phonograph and radio had rapidly overcome initial suspicions regarding their disruptive presence in the work routine within the home. However, while radio quickly developed programming formats that served successfully as "background activity" for the working homemaker, broadcasters feared that television's visual component might represent a problem. In order to avoid interference with the efficient functioning of the household, the early daytime industry was warned against the production of programs which demanded constant and undivided audience attention (Boddy 1990; Spigel 1992).

In November 1948, WABD, Du Mont's flagship station in New York, became the first television station to offer daytime programming on a regular basis. WABD's move was first and foremost based on a desire to attract a growing group of advertisers who considered prime-time television to be too expensive. The task of locating an audience for the new medium was more of a challenge, however (*Broadcasting* 1948). After overcoming some initial concerns about women's ability to operate television sets because they were "a piece of engineering equipment, not an item of household furniture" (Horton 1946: 16), broadcasters decided that their most pressing task was to design television programming that complemented rather than disrupted the daily routine within the home. Through abstractions and speculations as to what a "typical housewife" would find interesting, the industry hoped to capture women's attention. Not only did broadcasters try to develop schedules that mimicked the patterns of the homemaker's daily activities; they also aspired to make television viewing part of her daily routine (Spigel 1992; *Newsweek* 1948b).

The early television "soaps", a carryover from radio, were perfect in this regard. With their minimum amount of action and limited visual interest, they enabled the housewife to follow the storyline while working away from the television set. Also, the soap opera's segmented storylines (usually two a day), combined with their constant synopsizing of previous episodes, allowed women to combine television watching with household work. The television "magazine" was another flexible format. Consisting of various, and often unrelated, programming segments strung together by a television host or hostess, magazine shows allowed the busy housewife to tune in and out of a program while losing little in terms of narrative plots (Spigel 1992).

Not all broadcasters were convinced, however. "Many observers," noted *Business Week*, "feel that the housewife is not going to be able to watch a television screen while she washes, peels potatoes and cooks the evening meal. Will she be able, they ask, to transfer her radio-listening habits to video?" (*Business Week* 1948). Set on overcoming the attention-getting problem, WABD broadcast an audible signal whenever a programming segment it believed to be of special interest to homemakers was aired. As *Newsweek* explained, "When a shot of the latest fashion (from Manhattan show windows) or a particularly difficult stitch (on the daily sewing class) turns up something that must be seen to be appreciated, then Du Mont will sound an audio come-on to bring mother running to the set" (*Newsweek* 1948b).

In the spring of 1949, a marketing outfit called Advertest Research published its first—and among broadcasters and advertisers, eagerly awaited—report on daytime television. One of the more significant findings in the report was that women were rather selective in their choice of television programs. If the daytime audience found a program to be of particular interest, time for watching would be found. If, on the other hand, women did not like the programming, they would not watch even if they had ample time to do so (e.g. during a break from housework and children's demands). "Thus," concluded the report, "it is possible for broadcasters to overcome the inconvenience factor by causing the housewife to rearrange her work schedule so that she finds time to watch a program she likes" (Advertest Research 1949: 2). Much to the television industry's concern, however, a majority of respondents admitted to not be watching television in the daytime. They stated lack of time and a general disappointment with the programming as their main reasons.

As research into television audiences, their attitudes, product preferences, lifestyles and spending habits had expanded, it became increasingly clear that advertisers should not only be concerned with the size of a program's audience. Programming preference among different population groups was important as well. Sponsors of daytime television were not alone in wanting to reach people who were consumers, or potential consumers, of their products (Leiss *et al.* 1990). Prior to the late 1950s, however, broadcasters did not always have access to reliable data about their audiences. The task of reaching a specific audience involved a good deal of speculation and sheer guesswork (Beville 1985; Christopher 1953; *Advertising Age* 1954).

In 1951, a research organization called Social Research claimed to have found an answer to some of the television industry's problems. The outfit pointed to distinct differences between the daytime viewing preferences of the upper-middle class and those of the lower-middle class or "middle majority." "The upper-middle class," stated the report, "look for sophistication, cosmopolitan poise and individuality in character and taste in their entertainment. They feel it genteel to devaluate their possessions and are likely to become hostile when exposed to long sales talks." Social Research used *Kukla, Fran & Ollie*, a popular, and among critics, highly acclaimed children's show with an integrated commercial pitch, as an example of programming with upper-middle class appeal. *The Kate Smith Hour*, according to the same outfit, appealed to middle majority women because of its sincere, successful, and motherly aura. Social Research stressed that these two types of programming represented different worlds both in terms of entertainment appeal and the social structure of their audiences. "We find that commercials, unless carefully attuned to the different audiences, will be ignored," cautioned the report (*Advertising Age* 1951).

These concerns did not deter Du Mont's enthusiasm for daytime television. On the contrary, its bold daytime move had attracted a wide range of advertisers and many viewers seemed to prefer WABD's daytime shows over popular radio programs (*Time* 1948). So encouraged was Du Mont, that it began to offer regular daytime television programming to its other affiliates. The first program broadcast on a network-wide basis was an audience-participation show called *Okay Mother*. The fact that Sterling Drugs, one of the pioneer sponsors of daytime radio back in the 1930s, agreed to a lengthy sponsorship of the show and started to move its advertising allocations from radio to daytime television, did not escape the other networks' attention. Slightly worried, they began to explore their own daytime TV options.

It was not until late 1950 or early 1951 that the other networks began to offer daytime programming to their affiliates on a regular basis. With evening schedules close to fully booked, however, a daytime expansion made financial sense. It did not take long before NBC and Columbia Broadcasting Systems (CBS), the leading networks at the time, began to realize the importance of developing reliable daytime schedules and programming that would appeal to audiences and sponsors alike (*Newsweek* 1951; *Sponsor* 1951a; Spigel 1992). In the fall of 1950, NBC launched a daytime package which included *The Kate Smith Hour*, hosted by the popular singer Kate Smith, to 31 of its affiliates. At approximately the same time, 51 CBS-affiliated stations could offer *The Garry Moore Show* to their viewers. The commercial structure of *The Kate Smith Hour* represented a dramatic departure from established practices handed down to the television industry via radio. Whereas prime-time shows and television soap operas adhered to the established system of allowing one single advertiser to sponsor (and produce) an entire program, *The Kate Smith Hour* sought one sponsor for every fifteen-minute interval of programming. While publicly claiming that increased network control would lead to better programming for its audiences, NBC's real motives could not have been more obvious: it was mainly about putting the network in a position to maximize the commercial potential of television (Boddy 1987; Jaffee 1954; Stole 2000; Wilson 1995). While greatly reducing sponsors' financial risk, the new format also introduced competition between program segments for viewers' attention during the same show. High ratings on *The Kate Smith Hour* helped put sponsors at ease. After three months, the show commanded an ARB rating of 22.3, which translated into an audience of close to 2 million homes with over 4.5 million viewers. No wonder that NBC declared the show "one of the best bargains in TV" (McFadyen 1950). One month later, in January 1951, an overly optimistic trade journal predicted a "virtual sellout for daytime network television within a year" (*Sponsor* 1951a).

Unlike local daytime programming, which to a large degree devoted their service programs to cooking, beauty, and household tips, network shows tried to set themselves apart. *The Kate Smith Hour*, for example, devoted only 30 percent of the content to such topics. Likewise, most segments of *The Garry Moore Show* consisted of interviews and entertainment (*Sponsor* 1951a). This programming trend was completely in tune with surveys conducted by Advertest Research in the summer of 1950. When asked, close to six in ten respondents mentioned entertainment as the main reason for watching television during the daytime. Only one in ten admitted to watching daytime television in order to obtain information. The survey concluded that much like prime time audiences, those who watched TV during the day preferred variety shows, audience participation programs, and dramas (Advertest Research 1950). "Women's service programs on network television," predicted *Sponsor* in late 1951, would soon be replaced by "escapist television programming for the housewife" (*Sponsor* 1951b).

Television producers were somewhat frustrated by these findings. On the one hand, they wanted to develop programs that commanded high ratings and massive sponsor demand. On the other hand, they wanted to accommodate advertisers' desire for programming that would serve as a great backdrop for their products. Homemaking shows exemplified this dilemma. While these provided great vehicles for the integration of sponsors' products, they failed to attract large audiences. "Our expertise to date," noted one NBC executive in 1952, "indicate [that] as soon as you start to televise to women about home service exclusively you are no longer televising to them. They switch the dial over to the charms of Francis X. Bushman in a 1912 thriller rather than look at a 1952 kitchen range in action" (*Journal of Practical Home Economics* 1952). Because "the realities of domestic routine," according to the same spokesman, discouraged the housewife from viewing home service programs on the screen, the best use of home economics programming was to fold it into small segments on shows like *Kate Smith* (*Journal of Practical Home Economics* 1952: 46).

On the local level, however, industry leaders considered the blurring of programming with commercial messages to be one of daytime TV's strongest attributes. Cooking shows, for example, were popular among broadcasters and advertisers alike. In addition to being relatively inexpensive to produce, the editorial format of these programs allowed for perfect integration of sponsors' products. "It is as natural as baking a biscuit for the show's star to switch from talking about cooking to a commercial for a flour product, or a food brand," enthused one supporter (*Sponsor* 1951a: 43). Other shows stressed shopping as home entertainment. The basic ingredient for the standard "shopping program" was a charming "femcee" backed up by an organization of shoppers bringing new products and "good values" back to the television studio for "on-air" presentations. "In one sense, the whole show is commercial," proclaimed the trade journal *Sponsor* in a piece celebrating daytime television's commercial attributes. "It is virtually impossible to determine where the commercial starts and leaves off. The commercial pitch is indirect and completely interwoven with the program" (*Sponsor* 1950).

Not only did these programming formats provide excellent opportunities for commercial display and promotion, they also introduced audiences to the concept of consumption as home entertainment. In addition to practically bringing the store to the audiences' living rooms, some daytime programs transformed their studio settings into stages resembling domestic settings where selling could take place. *Your Television Shopper*, for instance, featured two different sets, one resembling a living room and the other a kitchen, where clothes, toys, and gadgets could be demonstrated to potential buyers who watched the show from their own kitchens and living rooms. Producers claimed enthusiastically that most newcomers to the show would have a difficult time telling which items on the show were advertised and which were not (Robertson 1949).

In line with traditional gender stereotyping, most homemaking shows featured a woman in charge of the kitchen. Men's roles on these shows were most often as "general-taste-testers," as on WADF-TV's *Kitchen Klub* (Advertisement for WDAF-TV 1954) or as "next door neighbor" types informing homemakers about new products, news, and human interest happenings, as on *Let Skinner Do It* (Advertisement for WTPZ 1952). Frequently, however, daytime shows used male show-business personalities to "educate" women about the superiority of the sponsors' products. In 1950, for example, television station WABD in Kansas City credited show personality Johnny Olson with "showing women how to use Sauce Arthuro successfully" (*Broadcasting* 1950). And *A Trick in Time* had "Uncle Allie" dole out helpful household hints to "the average young housewife" played by the show's female star (*Broadcasting* 1952). The notion that these shows provided their predominantly female audiences with needed services was reflected on a regulatory level as well. In 1952, for example, the National Association of Radio and Television Broadcasters (NARTB) asserted that these "announcement programs" provided a special service to the public. Stating that the commercial contents of daytime television held particular information value to its viewers, the NARTB allowed more advertising on these programs than it did during prime-time broadcasts (Head 1982: 201).

Home

In 1954, after a few years of experience in the daytime television field, NBC claimed to have invented a perfect programming concept for the daytime crowd. Intended as NBC's flagship program during the daytime, *Home* was broadcast between 1954 and 1957 as a component of the network's non-prime time programming along with *The Today Show* and *The Tonight Show*. In contrast to the latter two, which have enjoyed close to fifty years of success, *Home*'s reign on the air was relatively short-lived.

Much like "women's service" programs had already done on local television, *Home* offered its viewers a staple menu of cooking, beauty, gardening, home-making, child-rearing and shopping. Unlike its local cohorts, however, the network-produced show set out to attract a new group of potential daytime television viewers. Asserting that the existing daytime fare tended to draw a lowbrow, and for advertisers not-so-attractive audience, NBC wanted to attract an audience that was able to identify itself with the lifestyle, interests, and, most importantly, the consumption pattern of up-scale women.

NBC's belief that *Home* would appeal to this class of women was based on two major assumptions. Not only did the network declare a general lack of daytime television programs with appeal to up-scale-minded women. It predicted that once such daytime programming became available, the desired audience would flock to their television screens. To lay out the stark contrast between *Home* and other forms of daytime TV, NBC determined that the best time-slot for *Home* would be in the early afternoon when CBS offered its television soap operas (NBC papers n.d.b).

Much like copy-writers in the 1920s and 1930s, broadcasters during the early 1950s experienced difficulties when it came to "keeping the audience in focus" (Marchand 1985). Just like copy-writers, NBC executives in charge of *Home* revealed their own programming biases against soap operas and game shows and projected these onto the audience. Soaps and guessing games may be acceptable to "the masses" but the upper-middle class of women, which quite probably counted the executives' wives as its members, were not supposed to be attracted to this kind of programming. "Cultural up-lift" in the form of upscale hints and household tips were regarded as more appropriate.

In terms of commercial structure, *Home* further expanded the sponsor-participation format it had developed on *The Kate Smith Hour* a few years earlier. While the latter had required advertisers to sponsor at least a fifteen-minute segment of a show, the new concept, called "magazine advertising," offered them short, and relatively affordable, segments of commercial time. This, according to NBC, gave advertisers the "flexibility to move in and out of shows at will, to put pressure in peak seasons, and to get maximum results at minimum cost" (NBC papers 1954a). By the late 1950s, and certainly by the 1960s, this would become the dominant form of television advertising. In order to get advertisers' commitment, NBC promised discounts and special deals to those signing up for a minimum of fifty-two weeks of weekly one-minute participations on *Home*. Sponsors signing up as Charter Members were assured a prominent role in the show's editorial features and were told that once a year, an entire show would be devoted to them and their products. On this day, promised the network, "the difference between service features and commercials would be as imperceptible as possible." It would, in fact, be "difficult to tell where the commercial begins and information leaves off" (Mills 1953b). *Home*'s audience, bragged the show's producers, would consist of "women preconditioned to buy" (Pinkham 1953).

As part of an elaborate branding strategy, NBC intended to capitalize upon *Home*'s merchandising potential. It was speculated that the show, through "exploitative" devices such as magazines bearing its imprint and featuring *Home* personalities and experts, could bring in as much as half a million dollars a year in additional revenues. *Home* test kitchens *à la Good Housekeeping* as well as establishing a *Home* seal of approval to adorn *Home* sponsors' products were considered as well. Other plans included the creation of a dress line based on the outfits worn by the show's femcee and sale of special boxes for collection of recipes demonstrated on the program (NBC papers n.d.a). In order to present *Home*'s various segments, the network constructed an innovative $200,000 set for the show's premiere. The studio featured gadgets to revolve, lift and tilt consumer goods, promoting and demonstrating their every feature. It was also equipped with a special-effects area to portray the effects of rain, fog, and sleet on various kinds of merchandise. The set, in NBC's own words, was built to accommodate *Home*'s function as a "machine for selling" (NBC papers 1954d). Perhaps best of all, speculated the network, "We will be consciously creating an atmosphere, a mood, an editorial background against which the advertiser's sales job can be at its maximum effectiveness. The audience will be in a buying frame of mind" (Pinkham 1953).

Much consideration went into the planning of a central personality or "editor-in-chief" to lead the show. NBC did not consider a glamour girl to be the ideal hostess. It wanted "a pleasingly attractive, middle-aged woman—Hollywood's answer to the home economics teacher" (Spigel 1992: 84). The network's final choice fell on Arlene Francis, a "self declared anti-feminist" and "ordinary housewife" who held decidedly traditional opinions about gender roles and women's place in society. "A girl's job is to be a girl," stated Francis. "Once she takes over a man's position, she loses her femininity and her place in society" (*TV Guide* 1954). As hostess on *Home*, Ms Francis strung together a wide range of departments designed with the up-scale-oriented woman in mind. *Home* offered fashion tips, recipes, interior decoration and gardening, child rearing and, not coincidentally, information on shopping and consumption (Spigel 1992). Determined to maintain its up-scale profile, the network tried hard, though not always successfully, to reflect these aspirations in its programming. On August 8, 1954, for example, Arlene Francis welcomed the ballerina Alexandra Danilova, performer of Tchaikovsky's *Swan Lake* and *Sleeping Beauty* ballets. Francis also introduced Dr Ashley Montagu, an "outstanding authority on human behavior," who discussed "the baby" (NBC papers 1954b). Only four days later the show's hostess interviewed "a famous time-and-motion-engineer" whose function was to estimate the number of miles an average housewife might walk in the kitchen during the year and suggest how the amount of walking could be reduced by as much as one-half. "While Arlene bakes a gingerbread cake, the efficiency expert will trace her steps [and] after the cake pops from the oven, the engineer shows Arlene how she could have saved herself half the time" (Marshall 1954). Later that week, *Home* introduced Dick Satterfield, a man who had brought beauty aid to "a million women." Dick's purpose on the show was to instruct the audience on how to combine weight-reducing exercise with garden work. This was the same day Arlene Francis introduced Jim, a gentleman with a penchant for "doing anything," including hatching an ostrich egg by himself and selling an icebox to an Eskimo (NBC papers 1954c).

The Response to *Home* and its Demise

NBC had high expectations for *Home*. Even before the show was aired, network executives predicted that it would score a minimum Nielsen rating of 10.0 within six to nine months of its premiere, which would translate into an estimated audience of 4.4 million viewers (Mills 1953a,b). Although the first Trendex ratings placed *Home* behind both of its direct network competitors (*Strike It Rich* and *Arthur Godfrey* on CBS), NBC was very optimistic about the show's ability to eventually capture the time slot (Beville 1954; Cornell 1954). By early April, however, the show's ratings had leveled off to a little over 3.0, leaving NBC to concede that the network was in for "several months of very bitter fighting" (Culligan 1954; NBC papers 1954e). Trendex ratings for the early part of June carried more bad news: *Home*'s ratings had fallen to 1.9 (Dauenspeck 1954). Network executives were quite bewildered as to why the show was not catching on.

Critics provided some clues. *Home*'s difficulty, suggested one, was that, even for a woman's program, it consisted of too much straight talk. "Almost everything is a demonstration or a discussion and after several mornings the pace begins to drag, at least for masculine ears" (Gould 1954). Paying close attention, one network producer proposed more entertainment on the show. "As long as *Home* must be fundamentally about 'things', it can never be endowed with identification, spirit, warmth, and the rest of the things that goes with the fundamental human relationships that makes most successful television (emphasis on daytime television in particular)," he concluded (Parks 1954).

Conceding some of its lofty aspirations, *Home* producers started to create segments they hoped would reflect the concerns and interests of "the average gal in Suburbia" (Barry 1954). "*Home* Story of the Day," with its "steady heart and human interest appeal" was one new addition. "Dish of the Day" represented another attempt at improving the show. This particular segment provided daily answers to what the show's producers believed was a nagging question for housewives: "What in the world can I give the old boy tonight?" Other changes competed with *Strike It Rich* and other game shows. *Home*, which during its planning stages, had denounced such fare as too low-brow for its audience, suddenly featured guessing games around food products and retail prices (Linkreum 1954). Another criticism, which NBC appeared less eager to address, was *Home*'s failure to engage the daytime viewers' intellect. "Won't you men ever give us women, some of us anyway, credit for wanting to think about the larger issues of our lives, rather than the things most of us can learn by ourself?" wrote one disenchanted *Home* viewer in a letter to the network (Rogers 1954). Others felt likewise: "There may be some women in the audience," concurred a critic, "who would not be adverse to being respected for their brain rather than their pocketbook" (Gould 1954).

The network's hopes of establishing *Home* as a "machine for selling" were fading. "We know," insisted a defensive network, "that the basic concept of *Home* . . . providing demonstrable service information for America's housewives . . . is one which is long overdue for both audiences and advertisers" (NBC papers 1954e). Unfortunately for NBC, however, the daytime audience did not think so.

In August 1957, after more than three years with poor ratings, NBC realized that *Home*, which had been accorded one of the largest staffs and budgets of any program in the NBC stable, had proven a resounding failure. The network attributed the show's cancellation to low ratings, high programming costs and, most important, declining advertising revenues (*Newsweek* 1957; *Variety* 1957).

In analyzing what went wrong with *Home*, much suggests that NBC was hurt by its producers' arrogant attitude towards daytime viewers. For example, while fully aware of the fact that women preferred entertainment over instruction, the network insisted on airing a show instructing viewers on how to run up-scale households and use the advertisers' products. It more or less assumed that socially aspiring housewives from the middle classes wanted up-scale household and shopping tips as much as advertisers wanted their dollars. The overwhelming "product propaganda" worked neither in the audiences' nor the advertisers' interests. In order to sell products, advertisers must be in tune with, and reflect the concerns of their desired audiences. This did not happen on NBC's *Home*. Largely to blame may be the network's insistence on programming that easily lends itself to showcasing sponsored products. The magazine format of programming "turned out to be first and last to accommodate advertising. At its worst the format amounted to little more than commercials in search of a program" (Bergreen 1980: 173).

If given a choice, women may have chosen programming which more accurately reflected their interests. What these interests were, we have no accurate way of knowing. In spite of broadcasters' claim of "giving the audience what they want," this only holds within the range of what is considered financially profitable. Within the narrow range of programs which are produced because they complement advertisers' sales objectives, (female) viewers have a choice. Outside the established boundaries, however, may lurk an interest in programs that challenge, or are at direct odds with, the advertisers' immediate or long-term goals (McChesney 1999). Such programming, even if it might attract a large audience, is generally avoided. This is true for the television industry in general but, as the close to fifty-year-old case of *Home* shows us, is particularly true when it comes to programming targeted to women.

Epilogue

Given the more than fifty years that have passed since the introduction of daytime television and the unsuccessful tenure of programming concepts like *Home*'s, one might think that the television industry had learned a lesson. Add to this that during the last half-century, society has undergone a drastic turn-around regarding its views on "acceptable" roles and professions for women. Consequently, one might assume that the advertising community, which prides itself on being a step ahead of new trends, and the media industry, which is joined at the hip to the advertising industry, would be reflecting these changes.

Although contemporary broadcasters are willing to discuss a wider range of topics with their female viewers, it would be inaccurate to claim that these changes reflect a new, and radically wider, acceptance of women and their lived experiences. *Home*'s legacy to the television industry is its commercial structure. By exercising control over editorial as well as commercial content, broadcasters are able to create synergy between the two. Judging from the manner in which contemporary mass media address their female audiences, this becomes very obvious. Directly and indirectly, news and entertainment segments on the individual shows reinforce the need for products that are advertised. The secret behind successful advertising is to make consumers aware of their shortfalls and to offer them products with which to redeem the problems.

Given the synergy between editorial and commercial content on programming targeted at women, it should come as no surprise that these shows rarely tell their audiences to be happy with their current consumption patterns. Self-improvement in all shapes and forms is constantly promoted. Ironically, as women have gained more rights and personal freedom, the commercial mass media has responded by pointing to new sets of female shortcomings. Striving for the kind of domestic perfection promoted on *Home* is no longer enough. Today's women are told that they also need a perfect body, a flawless appearance, and a successful career in order to have "made it" (Faludi 1991). Frequently, however, mass media makes the pretense of representing "the average woman."

Lifetime, a cable television channel established in 1984, is a good example. Lifetime claims to operate on behalf of women and has successfully promoted itself to the public as a network with a mission to "serve women's interests" (Bronstein 1994–1995: 214). Instead of catering to the diverse needs and interests of its viewers, however, Lifetime has spent most of its time and effort in designing commercial strategies that tend to maximize corporate profits. Issues and topics are presented on the show, not because of their usefulness to viewers, but because of their tie-in value with advertised products and services. Lifetime was among the first networks to create an area for its viewers on the Internet. Innovative thinking does not always extend to its programming, however. Dominating its line-up are programs on homemaking, celebrities, and personal appearance (Bronstein 1994–1995).

Oxygen, a competitor to Lifetime, which proudly labels itself "the antidote to traditional women's television," started as a joint cable and on-line channel in 1999 (*Vanity Fair* 2001: 101). Examples from Oxygen's programming include a segment where three female panelists competed about making themselves look the "most cheap and tarty in 20 seconds." The same women were later asked to ponder the tough question of "whether their friends would rather have one million zits or one million moles" (*Vanity Fair* 2001: 104). On another Oxygen show called *Pajama Party*, viewers could watch a segment called "Surgery Scars." Here, host Katie Puckric and guest Lisa Kushell sipped frothy fruit drinks and compared scars from their spinal operation and nose-job, respectively.

But in all fairness, television for women has overcome some taboos. It is difficult, for example, to imagine *Home*'s Arlene Francis interviewing mothers about raising gay children. This, however, this was a recent topic on one of Oxygen's shows (*Vanity Fair* 2001). Such changes, however, are clearly among the exceptions (Prose 2000). This is evident even on the Internet, a medium that did not come of age until the latter part of the 1990s. Take ivillage, a website created specifically for women, for example. In an eerie throwback to the manner in which television executives promoted daytime television in the 1950s, iVillage.com entices its users with "relaxation and distraction, solitude and community," during "a few precious moments stolen—just for [women]— from [their] families and jobs" (Prose 2000, Spigel 1992). The online magazine offers hints on self-improvement and reasons why chocolate may be beneficial to one's health. "Not interested in football?" asks an article, then—"Cook up a 'Souper' Bowl and other tasty snacks for your favorite football fans!" (Prose 2000: 66). Arlene Francis could not have said it better.

The manner in which advertisers and mass media continue to address women suggests that instead of escaping the postwar "gender prison" described by many scholars (Chafe 1972; Douglas 1995; Miller and Nowak 1977), women have ended up

72 INGER L. STOLE

with what Francine Prose terms "A Wasteland of One's Own" (Prose 2000: 66). Exactly how and why this happened, and what we can do about it short of breaking mass media's dependence on advertising dollars, continues to be an area that is ripe for future study.

Questions

1 Why would television and advertisers have an incentive to emphasize women's roles as homemaker or mother over their role in the workforce?
2 How did *Home* attempt to position itself as more upscale, and why?
3 How did *Home* serve as a "machine for selling"?
4 What are the legacies of *Home* for the future of television and advertising? What programs on cable TV are modern versions of *Home*?

References

Advertest Research
1949 *The Television Audience of Today; Study of Daytime Television*, Box 193, Folder 10, National Broadcasting Corporation papers, the State Historical Society of Wisconsin, Madison [hereafter: NBC papers] 1, No. 1 (March 1949).
Advertest Research
1950 *The Television Audience of Today; Study of Daytime Television*, Box 193, Folder 10, NBC papers 2, No. 2 (June 1950).
Advertisement for *McCall's*
1956 *Advertising Age*, 20 February, 90.
Advertisement for *Modern Bride*
1953 *Advertising Age*, 26 October, 25.
Advertisement for *Modern Romances*
1950a *Advertising Age*, 13 March, 49.
Advertisement for *Modern Romances*
1950b *Advertising Age*, 10 April, 43.
Advertisement for *Parents' Magazine*
1953 *Advertising Age*, 26 October, 39.
Advertisement for *Seventeen*
1953 *Advertising Age*, 17 April, 35.
Advertisement for *Today's Woman*
1952 *Advertising Age*, 10 November, 68.
Advertisement for WDAF-TV *Kitchen Klub*
1954 *Broadcasting*, 5 July, 47.
Advertisement for WPTZ's *Let Skinner Do It*
1952 *Broadcasting*, 1 September, 61.
Advertising Age
1951 Social Research Issues First of Six TV Reports, 15 January, 66.
Advertising Age
1954 Who's Looking, 16 November, 92.
Allen, Robert C.
1985 *Speaking of Soap Operas* (University of North Carolina Press, Chapel Hill, NC).

Barry, Charles C.
  1954 "To Richard Pinkham." Letter. Box 123, Folder 17, *NBC Papers* (3 March 1954).
Baughman, James L.
  1987 The Promise of American Television, *Prospects*, **11**, 119–133.
Bergreen, Laurence
  1980 *Look Now, Pay Later* (Doubleday & Company Inc., Garden City, NY).
Beville, Hugh M. Jr.
  1954 "To Robert Sarnoff." Memo. Box 567C, Box 17, *NBC Papers* (9 March 1954).
Beville, Hugh Malcolm Jr.
  1985 *Audience Ratings: Radio, Television, and Cable* (Lawrence Erlbaum Associates, Hillsdale, NJ).
Boddy, William
  1990 *Fifties Television: The Industry and Its Critics* (University of Illinois Press, Urbana and Chicago).
Boddy, William
  1987 Operation Frontal Lobes Versus the Living Room Toy: The Battle Over Programme Control
      in Early Television, *Media, Culture, and Society*, **9**(3) (July), 347–368.
Broadcasting
  1948 WABD Delays Launching Full Daytime Schedule, 18 October, 63.
Broadcasting
  1950 Rumpus Room, 13 November, 63.
Broadcasting
  1952 Household Hint Shows, 24 November, 94.
Bronstein, Carolyn
  1994–1995 Mission Accomplished? Profits and Programming at the Network for Women, *camera
      obscura*, 33–34 (May-September-January), 213–241.
Business Week
  1948 Television Reaches Stage of Big-Volume, 10 January, 26.
Cantor, Muriel G. and Pingree, Suzanne
  1983 *The Soap Opera* (Sage Publications, Beverly Hills, CA).
Chafe, William H.
  1983 *The American Woman: Her Changing Social, Economic, and Political Roles, 1920–1970* (Oxford
      University Press, New York).
Christopher, Maureen
  1953 "Ratings. Raidings and Rebates Are Broadcasting's Bugaboos: Sarnoff", *Advertising Age*, 21
      September, 3.
Cornell, Jim
  1954 "To NBC executives." Memo. Box 123, Folder 26, *NBC papers* (March 2 1954).
Culligan, Joe
  1954 "To Jake Evans and Fred Dodge." Memo. Box 567C, Folder 17, *NBC papers* (14 April 1954).
Dauenspeck, Robert D.
  1954 "To all Trendex Pocketpiece Receivers." Memo. Box 374, Folder 58, *NBC papers* (14 July 1954).
Douglas, Susan J.
  1995 *Where the Girls Are: Growing Up Female with the Mass Media* (Times Books, New York).
Ewen, Stuart
  1977 *Captains of Consciousness* (McGraw-Hill Book Company, New York).
Faludi, Susan
  1992 *Backlash: The Undeclared War Against America's Women* (Doubleday, New York) [first published
      in 1991].
Friedan, Betty
  1983 *The Feminine Mystique* (W.W. Norton & Company, New York) [first published in 1963].
Gould, Jack
  1954 *Home*, Daytime Show for Women on N.B.C. Starts Ambitiously, *The New York Times*, Box 280,
      Folder 21, NBC papers (5 March 1954).
Haralovich, Mary Beth
  1989 Sitcoms and Suburbs: Positioning the 1950s Homemaker, *Quarterly Review of Film and Video*,
      11, 61–83.

Hartmann, Susan M.
   1982 *The Homefront and Beyond: American Women in the 1940s* (Twayne Publishers, Boston).
Head, Sydney W.
   1982 *Broadcasting in America* (Houghton Mifflin Company, Boston).
Horton, Donald
   1946 They Like Video But Look to Future, *Broadcasting*, 7 October, 16.
Jaffee, Alfred J.
   1954 What are Your "Rights" to a Timeslot? *Sponsor*, 5 April, 31.
Journal of Practical Home Economics
   1952 The Network's View of Homemaker Shows, 15 October, 15+.
Lears, Jackson
   1994 *Fables of Abundance* (Basic Books, New York).
Leiss, William, Kline, Stephen and Jhally, Sut
   1990 *Social Communication in Advertising* (Routledge, New York).
Linkreum, Richard
   1954 "To Davidson Taylor." Memo. Box 123, Folder 26, *NBC papers* (19 April, 1954).
Lipsitz, George
   1990 *Time Passages* (University of Minnesota Press, Minneapolis).
Marchand, Roland
   1985 *Advertising: the American Dream* (University of California Press, Berkeley and Los Angeles).
Marshall, Jack
   1954 "To Harry Trigg." Telegram. Box 133, Folder 68, *NBC papers* (10 August 1954).
May, Elaine Tyler
   1988 *Homeward Bound* (Basic Books, New York).
McChesney, Robert W.
   1993 *Telecommunications, Mass Media and Democracy: The Struggle for Control of U.S. Broadcasting, 1928–1935* (Oxford University Press, New York).
McChesney, Robert W.
   1999 *Rich Media, Poor Democracy: Communication Politics in Dubious Times* (University of Illinois Press, Urbana and Chicago).
McFadyen, Robert W.
   1950 "To Sales Staff." Memo. Box 567B, Folder 2, *NBC papers* (29 December 1950).
Miller, Douglas and Nowak, Marion
   1977 *The Fifties: The Way We Really Were* (Doubleday & Company Inc., Garden City).
Mills, Ted
   1953a "To John K. Herbert." Memo. Box 397, Folder 44, *NBC papers* (10 June 1953).
Mills, Ted
   1953b "To Sylvester L. Weaver." Memo. Box 377, Folder 6, *NBC papers* (11 September 1953).
NBC papers
   n.d.a Some facts about *Home*, Box 397, Folder 44.
NBC papers
   n.d.b Today's *Home*: A Preliminary Report on Two Audiences, Box 279, Folder 48.
NBC papers
   1954a Broadcasting—as you need it, Box 142, Folder 17.
NBC papers
   1954b *Home* promotion on A Time To Live, Box 133, Folder 68 (13 August 1954).
NBC papers
   1954c *Home* promotion on Three Steps to Heaven, Box 133, Folder 68 (17 August 1954).
NBC papers
   1954d Promotional material for *Home*, Box 374, Folder 58 (12 April 1954).
NBC papers
   1954e Report on *Home* to NBC affiliated stations, Box 123, Folder 26 (9 April 1954).
Newsweek
   1948 All-Day Television, 4 October, 52.

Newsweek
 1951 All Day Long, 24 September, 57.
Newsweek
 1957 No Place for *Home*, 10 June, 98.
Parks, Ben
 1954 "To Sylvester L. Weaver." Memo. Box 123, Folder 26, *NBC papers* (30 April 1954).
Pinkham, Richard A.H.
 1953 "To John K, Herbert." Memo. Box 567C, Folder 17, *NBC papers* (8 December 1953).
Pollay, Richard W.
 1994 Thanks the Editors for the Buy-ological Urge! American Magazines, Advertising, and the
   Promotion of the Consumer Culture, 1920–1980, In: Sheth, Jagdish N, and Fullerton,
   Ronald, eds, *Research in Marketing* (Supplement 6) (JAI Press, Westport, CT), pp. 221–235.
Prose, Francine
 2000 A Wasteland of One's Own, *The New York Time Magazine*, 13 February, 66–71.
Robertson, Bruce
 1949 Kathy's Daytime Success, *Broadcasting*, 7 November, 6.
Rogers, Mrs. Harris J.
 1954 "To Sylvester L. Weaver." Letter. Box 123, Folder 26, *NBC papers* (8 March 1954).
Schofield, Arthur
 1950 Selling Advertisers on Video, *Televiser*, February, 105.
Spigel, Lynn
 1992 *Make Room for TV: Television and the Family Ideal in Postwar America* (University of Chicago Press.
   Chicago).
Sponsor
 1950 Department Store TV, 24 April, 31.
Sponsor
 1951a Daytime TV: Network Programming, 29 Januray, 36 +.
Sponsor
 1951b Don't Lose Out on Daytime TV, 8 October, 37.
Stasheff, Edward and Rudy Bretz
 1956 *The Television Program* (Hill and Wang Inc., New York).
Stole, Inger L.
 1997 There Is No Place Like *Home*: NBC's Search for a Daytime Audience, 1954–1957, *The
   Communication Review* 2(2), 135–161.
Stole, Inger L.
 2000 The Kate Smith Hour and the Struggle for Control of Television Programming in the Early
   1950s, *Historical Journal of Film, Radio and Television*, **20**(4), 549–564.
Time
 1948 All-Day Looker, 22 November, 46.
TV Guide
 1954 What is Her Line, 9–18 July, 4.
Vanity Fair
 2001 Wanting to Exhale, January, 100–104.
Variety
 1957 Ratings, Biz Dip, *Home* Gets Boot; New Arlene Show, 29 May, 26.
Wilson, Pamela
 1995 NBC Television's "operation frontal lobes": Cultural hegemony and fifties' programming,
   Historical Journal of Film and Television, **15**(1), 83–104.

Chapter 5

BEN H. BAGDIKIAN

DR. BRANDRETH HAS GONE TO HARVARD

THIS CHAPTER FROM BEN BAGDIKIAN'S FAMOUS BOOK *The New Media Monopoly* discusses how advertising can affect media content in anti-democratic ways. He maintains that advertising "conspiracies"—cases where an individual advertiser successfully coerces media producers to censor ad criticism—are rare (although not unheard of). Instead, the ways that advertising shapes media are more enduring and often subtle. Ad-supported media make themselves more advertising friendly in a long-term process of media creators adjusting to financial incentives. Controversial ideas tend to be downplayed, whereas pro-corporate ideas, as well as entertainment and amusement, are emphasized. The chapter ends with an extended discussion of the influence of tobacco that for many years was one of the most advertised product categories in the media. He argues that the heavy revenue stream to media that tobacco companies offered may have seriously compromised earnest reporting about the dangers of tobacco use.

> I would rather be the man who bought the Brooklyn Bridge than the man who sold it.
>
> (Will Rogers)

James Gordon Bennett, founder of the *New York Herald*, is one of American journalism's bad boys. In August of 1835 his Ann Street plant suffered a disastrous fire, but the *Herald* was back on the street nineteen days later with this pronouncement:

> We are again in the field . . . more independent than ever. The Ann Street conflagration consumed types, presses, manuscripts, paper, some bad poetry, subscription books—all the outward appearance of the *Herald*, but its soul was saved.[1]

The *Herald* was "again in the field" but not "more independent than ever." After the fire, Bennett was saved by a large advertising contract from a "Doctor Brandreth," a quack who sold phony cure-all pills. After the *Herald* was back in circulation, the Brandreth ads appeared in profusion. But so did a steady diet of "news" stories, presuming to be straight reporting, "more independent than ever," recounting heroic cures effected by none other than Dr. Brandreth's pills. While other pill makers complained that Brandreth was getting front-page news accounts as well as ads, Bennett replied in his news columns:

> Send us more advertisements than Dr. Brandreth does—give us higher prices—we'll cut Dr. Brandreth dead—or at least curtail his space. Business is business—money is money—and Dr. Brandreth is no more to us than "Mr. Money Broker."[2]

Nine months later, when Brandreth canceled his advertising contract, Bennett, in print, called the good doctor a "most impudent charlatan" who "deceived and cheated."

In the new dignity of modern American journalism, this kind of corruption in the news is a thing of the past, having occurred only in the bad old days before the turn of the century. Modern media, it is said, are immunized by professional ethics from letting advertising influence editorial content.

Contemporary news and entertainment are, to use Bennett's phrase, "more independent than ever." Newspapers make 80 percent of their revenues from ads and devote about 65 percent of their daily space to them. Magazines, similarly clothed in virtue, make roughly half their money from ads, though they used to make more, and they usually insist that their advertising departments never shape the articles, stories, and columns produced by professional editors and writers. Radio and television, the most pervasive media in American life, have varied nonadvertising content like game shows, situation comedies, cops-and-robbers serials, news, talk shows, documentaries, and musical recordings.

Broadcasters vary in their separation of commercials and programs. Some, no longer satisfied with a brand name product simply appearing in the background of a scene, now have the commercial product integrated into the dialogue of the program itself. The whole idea is to escape the viewer's mute button. This new insidious technique has been given the name of its predecessor, "infotainment," "a repellent word that is alleged to be in the English language."[3]

In short, nineteenth-century money changers of advertisers have not been invited into the temple, they have been given the deed to the temple.

Present-day Brandreths have changed their technique. So have the contemporary Bennetts. The advertiser does not barge through the front door announcing. "I am Dr. Brandreth. I pay money to this network (newspaper, magazine, radio station) and I am pleased to introduce to you the producer (reporter, editor, writer) who, with all the powers vested by society in independent journalism, will proclaim the wonder of my pills." Except for a few clumsy operators, such a tactic is much too crude for the twenty-first century.

Today Dr. Brandreth makes his proper appearance in his ads. He then leaves politely by the front door, goes to the back of the television station (radio studio, newspaper newsroom, magazine editorial offices), and puts on the costume of a professional producer (reporter, editor, writer) whom you have been told to trust: "Through professional research and critical analysis, it is my independent judgment that Dr. Brandreth's pills, politics, ideology, and industry are the salvation of our national soul."

The Subtle Corruption

Modern corruption is more subtle. Today, or in recent times, advertisers have *successfully* demanded that the following ideas appear in programs around their ads.

All businessmen are good or, if not, are always condemned by other businessmen. All wars are humane. The status quo is wonderful. Also wonderful are all grocery stores, bakeries, drug companies, restaurants, and laundries. Religionists, especially clergy, are perfect. All users of cigarettes are gentle, graceful, healthy, youthful people. In fact, anyone who uses a tobacco product is a hero. People who commit suicide never do it with pills. All financial institutions are always in good shape. The American way of life is beyond criticism.

The above messages, to cite only a few, have not been vague inferences. Major advertisers have insisted that these specific ideas be expressed not in the ads but in the ostensibly "independent" news reporting, editorial content, or entertainment programs of newspapers, magazines, radio, and television. The readers, listeners, and viewers did not know that these messages were planted by advertisers. They were not supposed to know. They were supposed to think that these ideas were the independent work of professional journalists and playwrights detached from anything commercial. If the audiences were told that the ideas represented explicit demands of corporations who advertised, the messages would lose their impact.

But for too long, the taboo against criticism of the system of contemporary enterprise, in its subtle way, was almost as complete within mainstream journalism and broadcast programming in the United States as criticism of communism was explicitly in the Soviet Union. The forbidden criticism of the system of free enterprise that experienced spectacular explosions of Enron, Tyco, and other giants of the free market economy in 2001 can be better appreciated by considering what used to be inflexible demands once made and obeyed by broadcasters in, for example, the case of Procter & Gamble and, of course, tobacco products.

The entry of pro-corporate ideas into news and entertainment was specific. Procter & Gamble, once the largest advertiser in television, is now the fourth largest. For years it has been one of the leaders in creating promotions in all media, including commercials inserted into television programs. It has always appreciated the power of advertising. The company was created in 1837 with a soap called, simply, White Soap.[4] But in 1879 Harley Procter, a descendant of the founder, read in the Forty-fifth Psalm, "All thy garments smell of myrrh and aloes and cassia out of the ivory palaces. . . ." Ivory Soap was born and with it the first of the full-page ads for the product. Within a decade Procter & Gamble was selling 30 million cakes of the soap a day. Since then, the company has been spectacularly successful, combining soap, detergent, Christian religion, patriotism, and profit making. After World War II it projected its ideas to television programs in the form of advertising.

They, like most major advertisers, do not merely buy a certain number of commercials, deliver the tapes to the networks and local stations, and let the commercials fall where they may. Some television and radio ads are bought on that basis but not, usually, those of major advertisers. Big advertisers in particular want to know what time of day their commercials will be shown, since that helps define the makeup and size of the audience they are buying. And they want to know the nature of the program into which their commercials will be inserted.

In the early years of television, advertisers sponsored and produced entire news and entertainment programs. This gave them direct control over the nonadvertising part of the program and they inserted or deleted whatever suited their commercial and ideological purposes. NBC's news program in the early 1950s was called *Camel News Caravan* after its sponsor, Camel cigarettes, which banned all film of news that happened to take place where a No Smoking sign could be seen in the background.[5]

After the 1950s, networks produced their own shows and advertisers bought commercials of varying lengths for insertion during the networks' programming. Advertising was allotted six, then twelve, and now almost unlimited minutes per hour of prime-time evening hours and longer periods at other times of the day. But no network produces a program without considering whether sponsors will like it. Prospective shows usually are discussed with major advertisers, who look at plans or tentative scenes and reject, approve, or suggest changes.

Major advertisers like Procter & Gamble do not leave their desires in doubt.

Wars without Horror

The Federal Communications Commission (FCC) held hearings in 1965 to determine how much influence advertisers had on noncommercial content of television and radio. Albert N. Halverstadt, general advertising manager of Procter & Gamble, testified that the company established directives for programs in which Procter & Gamble would advertise. These policies were to create standards of "decency and common sense. . . . I do not think it constitutes control."[6] He then gave the FCC the formal requirements for television programs, as established by the medium's largest advertiser in their memorandums of instruction to their advertising agency:

> Where it seems fitting, the characters in Procter & Gamble dramas should reflect recognition and acceptance of the world situation in their thoughts and actions, although in dealing with war, our writers should minimize the "horror" aspects. The writers should be guided by the fact that any scene that contributes negatively to public morale is not acceptable. Men in uniform shall not be cast as heavy villains or portrayed as engaging in any criminal activity.[7]

Procter & Gamble was particularly interested in the image of business and business people on television programs:

> There will be no material on any of our programs which could in any way further the concept of business as cold, ruthless, and lacking all sentiment or spiritual motivation.
>
> If a businessman is cast in the role of villain, it must be made clear that he is not typical but is as much despised by his fellow businessmen as he is by other members of society.
>
> Special attention shall be given to any mention, however innocuous, of the grocery and drug business as well as any other group of customers of the company. This includes industrial users of the company's products, such as bakeries, restaurants, and laundries.

The company view of religion and patriotism is built into programs. If, in a drama or documentary, a character attacks what the memo called "some basic conception of the American way of life," then a rejoinder "must be completely and convincingly made someplace in the same broadcast."

The same is true of what Procter & Gamble called "positive social forces": "Ministers, priests and similar representatives of positive social forces shall not be cast as villains or represented as committing a crime or be placed in any unsympathetic antisocial role."

The memo specifies, "If there is any question whatever about such material, it should be deleted."

Halverstadt testified that these policies were applied both to entertainment programs in which Procter & Gamble commercials appeared and to news and public affairs documentaries.[8]

Thus, corporate ideology was built into entertainment and documentary programming that the audience believes is presented independent of thirty-second and sixty-second commercials that happen to appear in the program. It is sobering that these demands are made of a medium reaching 100 million homes for seven and a half hours every day.

But insertion of corporate ideology and commercial themes in the nonadvertising portion of television programming is not limited to Procter & Gamble. An executive of Brown & Williamson Tobacco Corporation placed into evidence before the FCC the company's policy on programs carrying cigarette commercials, directives that prevailed until the end of televised cigarette commercials in 1970:

> Tobacco products should not be used in a derogatory or harmful way. And no reference or gesture of disgust, dissatisfaction or distaste be made in connection with them. Example, cigarettes should not be ground out violently in an ashtray or stamped out underfoot.
>
> Whenever cigarettes are used by antagonists or questionable characters, they should be regular size, plain ends and unidentifiable.
>
> But no cigarette should be used as a prop to depict an undesirable character. Cigarettes used by meritorious characters should be Brown & Williamson brands and they may be identifiable or not.

A vice president of an advertiser of headache tablets, Whitehall Laboratories, told the FCC that the company demanded of networks that "if a scene depicted somebody committing suicide by taking a bottle of tablets, we would not want this to be on the air."

A vice president of Prudential Insurance Company, sponsor of public affairs programs, said that a positive image of business and finance was important to sustain on the air. The company rejected the idea for a program on the bank holiday during the Depression because "it cast a little doubt on all financial institutions."

All major advertisers, it seems, would concur with a statement made by a Procter & Gamble vice president for advertising in 1979: "We're in programming first to assure a good environment for our advertising."[9]

Corporate demands on television programs underlie what many consider the most grievous weakness of American television—superficiality, materialism, blandness, and escapism. The television industry invariably responds that the networks are only giving people what the people demand. But it is not what the public says it wants: It is what the advertisers demand.

The Best Atmosphere for Selling

At one time the Bell & Howell Company attempted to break the pattern of escapist, superficial prime-time programs by sponsoring news documentaries.[10] The president of the company told the FCC that this was tried to help counter the standards applied by most advertisers, which he described, disapprovingly, as consisting of the following requirements:

> One should not associate with controversy; one should always reach for the highest ratings; one should never forget that there is safety in numbers; one should always remember that comedy, adventure and escapism provide the best atmosphere for selling.

Even if a nonescapist program becomes a commercial success, it is likely to be canceled by the networks or major local stations. In the early days of television, there were outstanding serious programs, including live, original drama: *Kraft Television Theatre*, *Goodyear Playhouse*, *Studio One*, *Robert Montgomery Presents*, *U.S. Steel Hour*, *Revlon Theater*, *Omnibus*, *Motorola TV Hour*, *The Elgin Hour*, *Matinee Theater*, and *Playhouse 90*. It was the era of striking television plays by playwrights such as Paddy Chayefsky, who said he had discovered "the marvelous world" of drama in the lives of ordinary people.

Erik Barnouw in his definitive history of American broadcasting writes:

> That this "marvelous world" fascinated millions is abundantly clear from statistics. These plays—akin to the genre pointings—held consistently high ratings. But one group hated them; the advertising profession . . . Most advertisers were selling magic. Their commercials posed the same problems that Chayefsky drama dealt with: people who feared failure in love and in business. But in the commercials there was always a solution as clear-cut as the snap of a finger: the problem could be solved by a new pill, deodorant, toothpaste, shampoo, shaving lotion, hair tonic, car, girdle, coffee, muffin recipe, or floor wax.[11]

That was a generation ago. Today's audience is more jaded and sophisticated. So commercials are more insidious and clever. They use humor, self-deprecation, even satire of the product in such a way to leave the viewer with a sympathetic, warm smile that becomes associated with the brand name product.

There is another reason networks and advertising agencies resist serious or nonescapist programs. Networks make most of their money between the hours of 8:00 and 11:00 P.M.—prime time. They wish to keep the audience tuned from one half-hour segment to the next and they prefer the "buying mood" sustained as well. A serious half-hour program in that period that has high ratings may, nevertheless, be questioned because it will interrupt the evening's flow of lightness and fantasy. In that sense, the whole evening is a single block of atmosphere—a selling atmosphere.

Programs like *Roots* on the origins of American black slavery had very large audiences but no comparable commercial support at the level an audience that size ordinarily receives. The forcible seizure of West African men and women and their shackled boat trip on the Atlantic Ocean with dumping sick ones overboard did not create "a buying mood."

The printed media have not escaped the pressure, or the desire, to shape their nonadvertising content to support the mood and sometimes the explicit ideas of advertisers. Magazines were the first medium to carry sophisticated, artistic advertisements.[12] Magazines had graphic capabilities superior to newspapers, with better printing and color illustrations (the first successful national magazine, *Godey's Lady Book*, begun in 1830, hired 150 women to tint the magazine's illustrations by hand). Until late in the 1800s, ads were a minor part of magazine publishing, but once national merchandizing organizations grew, this national medium responded. By 1900, *Harper's*, for example, was carrying more ads in one year than it had in its previous twenty-two years.

"Bait the Editorial Pages . . ."

Before television emerged in the 1950s, successful magazines were 65 percent ads. By that time, most magazines were fundamentally designed for advertising rather than editorial matter. The philosophy of Condé Nast had triumphed. Nast, who had created *Vogue, Vanity Fair, Glamour, Mademoiselle*, and *House and Garden*, regarded his mission "to bait the editorial pages in such a way to lift out of all the millions of Americans just the hundred thousand cultivated persons who can buy these quality goods."[13]

The role of most magazines, as seen by their owners, was to act as a broker in bringing together the buyers and sellers of goods. There was, and still is, a significant difference among magazines in how far they go to sell their readers to advertisers. But the influence of advertisers on magazine content continues.

A 1940 *Esquire* article declared that the guitar is a better accompaniment to singing than a piano. A few months later the magazine ran an apology, "We lost all our piano ads . . . We can and do beg the pardon of the piano manufacturers." By then the fiery owners of the magazine had already been tamed. Two years earlier they had started *Ken*, a magazine of liberal idealism that seemed to start with great promise. Advertisers disliked the liberal ideas in its articles and not only refused to advertise in the new publication but threatened to pull out their ads from *Esquire* as well. So the owners of *Esquire* killed *Ken*, even though it met its circulation plans.[14]

In 1962 Paul Willis, president of the Grocery Manufacturers Association, warned television operators that they had better run more programs boosting the food industry. He boasted that a similar warning had worked with national magazines.

> We suggested to the publishers that the day was here when their editorial department and business department might better understand their interdependent relationships . . . as their operations may affect the advertiser—their bread and butter.[15]

The periodical *Advertising Age* said Willis "pointed with pride" to favorable food articles printed thereafter by "*Look, Reader's Digest, American Weekly, This Week, Saturday Evening Post, Good Housekeeping, Ladies' Home Journal, Family Circle*, and *Woman's Day*, among others."

If, like Bennett's *Herald*, this was merely the bad old days, there has been little evidence to give comfort in recent years. Condé Nast could create *Vogue* in 1909 with his philosophy of using his articles to get "the cultivated person who can buy these quality goods." In 1972, with *Vogue* under a new owner (S. I. Newhouse, the newspaper chain, which bought the Condé Nast magazines in 1959), it seemed to make no difference. Richard Shortway, publisher of *Vogue*, sixty-three years after Nast's candid statement, made his own candid statement: "The cold, hard facts of magazine publishing mean that those who advertise get editorial coverage."[16]

Magazines have been the Achilles' heel of corporations who also own book houses. The New York Times Company is a conglomerate involved in magazines, books, and broadcasting, as well as newspapers. In 1976 the *New York Times* published a series of articles on medical malpractice.[17] The news series angered the medical industry, including pharmaceutical firms. They could not retaliate effectively against the *New York Times*, which does not carry much medical advertising. But medicine-related advertisers were crucial to magazines published by the New York Times Company, including a periodical called *Modern Medicine*. Pharmaceutical firms threatened to withdraw 260 pages of their ads from *Modern Medicine*, a loss of half a million dollars, and the Times Company sold its medical magazines to Harcourt Brace Jovanovich.

The Permissible Lies

Reader's Digest Association owns the magazine *Reader's Digest* and Funk & Wagnalls book publishing.[18] In 1968 Funk & Wagnalls prepared to publish a book, *The Permissible Lie*, which criticized the advertising industry. A month before publication date, Reader's Digest ordered its book subsidiary to cancel the book. Reader's Digest advertising revenues in its magazine, at that date, were $50 million a year and the association presumably felt threatened by loss of advertising from its magazine if its book subsidiary offended the advertising agency.

Newspapers are considered the most scrupulous of all the media subsidized by advertising. It had been a sacred edict in official newspaper ethics that church and state—news and advertising—are separate and that when there is any doubt each is clearly labeled. This is a relatively recent change. Thirty years ago it was common for newspapers to resist any news that offended a major advertiser. Department store fires, safety violations in stores, public health actions against restaurants that advertised, and lawsuits against car dealers seldom made their way into print. The average paper printed stories about some advertiser or prospective advertiser that were solely promotional propaganda. A standard fixture in almost every newspaper was the memorandum from the business office—B.O.M., or "business office must," meaning that the news department was ordered to run a story for purposes of pleasing an advertiser.

Over the years, in most newspapers—but not all—those blatant corruptions of news had diminished. But censoring of information offensive to advertisers continues. News that might damage an advertiser generally must pass a higher threshold of drama and documentation than other kinds of news. But as more papers become properties of large media conglomerates where profit levels are dictated by Wall Street and distant CEOs, pressure has increased to subdue news that might offend an important advertisers. More common in contemporary papers is the large quantity of "fluff"—material that is not news in any real sense but is nonadvertising material supporting of advertisers.

A 1978 study by the Housing Research Group of the Center for Responsive Law found that

most newspaper real estate sections serve the real estate industry far
better than they serve consumers and general readers . . . Articles that
appear as "news" frequently are promotional pieces for developers, real
estate agents, or industry associations. [19]

Examples in the study included the following: the *Birmingham* (Alabama) *News*
printed four industry press releases without more than cosmetic rewriting on the front
page of its real estate section; one issue of the *Sacramento Union* had more than a dozen
articles promoting new subdivisions; press releases were substituted for news articles in
the *Baltimore Sun, Birmingham News, Boston Herald American, New York Post, Philadelphia
Evening Bulletin*, and *Washington Star*.

Bigger papers, including some of the country's most prestigious, often printed
more real estate propaganda than did some smaller papers. The reports said:

We were surprised to discover half a dozen smaller newspapers . . . that
had a small but respectable real estate section. Their success in presenting
real estate news in an objective, informative fashion compared quite favorably with some much larger newspapers.

These smaller papers were *Indianapolis Star, New Orleans Times-Picayune, Memphis
Commercial Appeal*, and *St. Petersburg* (Florida) *Times*.

The study seemed to have little influence. A year later a number of newspapers not
only kept up the flood of industry promotional material masquerading as news but
actually took real estate reporting out of the hands of reporters and gave it directly to
the advertising department. These papers include the *Van Nuys* (California) *Valley News,
Los Angeles Herald Examiner, Houston Chronicle*, and *Dallas Morning News*. Mainly because so
many newspaper readers are world travelers for pleasure and business, a few notes of
realism are found in travel columns. A description of a lovely white-sanded tropical
beach may add "Take your DEET to ward off the sand fleas."

The bulk of "news" in the newspaper is contained in similar special sections. The
fashion section, for example, is almost always either taken from press releases submitted
by designers and fashion houses or written by fashion editors who attend the fashion
shows with all expenses paid by the fashion houses. The result is an annual flood of
gushy promotion of exotic garments, all in a "news" section. The contamination
becomes more blatant with time. In 1980 John Brooks, director of communications for
the *Toronto Star*, said that when the paper created a new fashion section,

all market research was turned over to the editorial department so that
planning of editorial content would be consistent with the wants and
needs of readers and prospective readers. The Family Editor, under whose
jurisdiction Fashion/80 would fall, spent a lot of time with advertising
department personnel in meetings with advertisers. [20]

The same is true of travel and usually food sections. A survey in 1977 showed
that 94 percent of food editors use food company releases for recipes and 38 percent
attend food events at the expense of food companies. This, too, has not changed in the
twenty-first century. [21]

Nothing Controversial

The growing trend among newspapers to turn over sections of the "news" to the advertising department usually produces copy that is not marked "advertising" but is full of promotional material under the guise of news. The advertising department of the *Houston Chronicle*, for example, provided all the "news" for the following sections of the paper: home, townhouse, apartments, travel, technology, livestock, and swimming pools. The vice president of sales and marketing of the *Chronicle* said: "We do nothing controversial. We're not in the investigative business. Our only concern is giving editorial support to our ad projects."[22]

One of the most compelling needs for readers in the dramatic inflation of the 1970s was reliable information about comparative shopping, yet it is one of the weakest elements in American newspapers. The consumer information most needed by families concerns industries with control over the advertising income of newspapers—food, transportation, and clothing. A feature that has always been extremely popular with readers during its spasmodic and brief appearances is the market basket survey. A reporter periodically buys the items on a typical family shopping list and writes a story about price changes in major supermarkets. It is not a story that grocery store advertisers like, so it has practically disappeared in American papers precisely when it is most needed. Even when the market basket surveys are conducted by university researchers, as at Purdue University, most papers refuse to carry the reports, one admitting it bent to advertisers' pressure.[23]

In 1980 the *Washington Star* announced a five-part series on the pros and cons of shopping coupons that have become common in newspapers, but the series was killed after the first story for fear of discouraging advertisers who bought space in the *Star* for shopping coupons.[24]

Given the eagerness with which newspapers protect major advertisers, it is understandable that by now advertisers expect that when the interests of readers are in competition with the interests of advertisers, the newspapers will protect the advertisers.

A senior vice president of MGM told newspaper executives in 1981 that he had seen too many negative reviews of movies and warned newspapers that the $500 million worth of movie ads

> cannot be taken for granted and you've got to get this word to your editorial counterparts . . . Today the daily newspaper does not always create a climate that is supportive and favorable to the motion picture industry . . . gratuitous and hateful reviews threaten to cause the romance between newspapers and the motion picture industry to wither on the vine.[25]

Death for Sale

The most shameful conspiracy in the history of American news and a major advertiser was the prolonged complicity of the news and advertising media in suppressing or neutralizing the irrefutable evidence that smoking cigarettes kills. According to the British medical journal *Lancet*, as late as the 1990s, in the United States, Europe, Canada, Japan, Australia, and New Zealand, 21 million people died tobacco-related deaths, usually after pain and suffering. The World Health Organization estimated that 3 million people die each year from tobacco.[26]

For decades, newspapers, with rare exceptions, kept smoking deaths out of the news, even after a 1927 definitive study in England made it inexcusable. As late as fourteen years after the Surgeon General of the United States cited serious health risks from smoking, and seven years after the Surgeon General declared that even second-hand smoke may cause lung cancer, 64 million Americans, obviously already addicted, smoked an average of twenty-six cigarettes a day.[27]

But for years newspapers (for whom the top three or four advertisers were always tobacco companies) faithfully reprinted the reports of the tobacco industry public relations operation, the Tobacco Institute, that there was no proven cause-and-effect between smoking and cancer. It seemed that the science of epidemiology that solved the problem of the bubonic plague, typhoid fever, and many other notorious killers of human beings was not applicable to tobacco. Perhaps only after the chromosomes of the cancer cell under the microscope spelled out the name "Brown & Williamson" would the Tobacco Institute at most say that it required "more research" and the major news media obediently report it with a straight face.

The prolonged behavior of newspapers was worse, given their ability to be unambiguous about mass deaths based on mounting scientific evidence. In 1971 tobacco advertising was banned from television—or television networks "voluntarily" banned it when it became clear that it was going to be made into communications law anyway. Significantly, thereafter, television was much more willing to highlight antismoking research than was the printed press.[28]

If there is a date beyond which there appears to be the obstinate suppression of the link between tobacco and widespread death, it is 1954. In 1953, the year the AMA banned tobacco ads from its journals, the *New York Times Index*, reflecting probably the best newspaper reporting on the tobacco-cancer link, had 248 entries under "Cancer" and "Smoking" and "Tobacco." Ninety-two percent said nothing about the link; of the 8 percent that did, only 2 percent were articles mainly about the tobacco-disease connection; the other 6 percent were mostly denials of this from the tobacco industry. In 1954, the year of the American Cancer Society's study, the *New York Times Index* had 302 entries under the same titles. Of the stories dealing mainly with tobacco's link to disease, 32 percent were about the tobacco industry's denials and only 20 percent dealt with medical evidence.

In 1980, sixteen years later, there were still more stories in the daily press about the causes of influenza, polio, and tuberculosis than about the cause of one of every seven deaths in the United States.

A Media Disease

There began to be suspicions of a strictly media disease: a strange paralysis whenever solid news pointed at tobacco as a definitive cause of disease and death. For years, up to the present, medical evidence on tobacco and disease has been treated differently than any other information about carriers of disease that do not advertise. The print and broadcast media might make page 1 drama of a junior researcher's paper about a rare disease. But if it involves the 300,000 annual deaths from tobacco-related illness, the media either do not report it or they report it as a controversial item subject to rebuttal by the tobacco industry.

It is a history filled with curious events. In 1963, for example, Hudson Vitamin Products produced Smokurb, a substitute for cigarettes. The company had trouble getting its ads in newspapers and magazines and on the air. Eli Schonberger, president of Hudson's ad agency, said, "We didn't create this campaign to get into a fight with anyone, but some media just stall and put us off in the hope that we'll go away."[29]

This was, of course, strange behavior for media that are anxious for as much advertising as they can get. One major magazine told the company its product was "unacceptable."

The tobacco industry once spent $4 a year for every American man, woman, and child for its cigarette advertising. At the same time, the government's primary agency for educating the public about the dangers of cigarettes, the Department of Health and Human Services, spent one-third of a cent a year for every citizen.

National publications, especially the news magazines, are notorious for publishing dramatic stories about health and disease. *Time* and *Newsweek* have both had cover stories on cancer. *Newsweek*, for example, had a cover story January 26, 1978, entitled "What Causes Cancer?" The article was six pages long. On the third page it whispered about the leading cause—in a phrase it said that tobacco is the least disputed "carcinogen of all." The article said no more about the statistics or the medical findings of the tobacco-cancer link, except in a table, which listed the ten most suspected carcinogens—alphabetically, putting tobacco in a next-to-last place. A week later, *Time*, in a common competitive duplication between the two magazines, ran a two-column article on the causes of cancer. The only reference it made to tobacco was that "smoking and drinking alcohol have been linked to cancer." A few weeks earlier, a *Time* essay urged smokers to organize to defeat antismoking legislation.

When R. C. Smith of *Columbia Journalism Review* studied seven years of magazine content after 1970, when cigarette ads were banned from television, he found:

> In magazines that accept cigarette advertising I was unable to find a single article, in several years of publication, that would have given readers any clear notion of the nature and extent of the medical and social havoc wreaked by the cigarette-smoking habit. [30]

The few magazines that refused cigarette ads did much better at their reporting, he said. (The most prominent magazines that refused cigarette ads were *Reader's Digest* and *The New Yorker*.)

The magazines that carried accurate articles on the tobacco-disease link suffered for it. In July 1957 *Reader's Digest* ran a strong article on medical evidence against tobacco. Later that month, the advertising agency the magazine used for twenty-eight years said it no longer wanted the *Digest* as a client. The agency, Batten, Barton, Durstine and Osborn, had $1.3 million in business a year from the magazine. But another client, the American Tobacco Company, which spent $22 million a year with the agency, had asked the agency to choose between it and *Reader's Digest*.

In 1980 a liberal-left magazine, *Mother Jones*, ran a series of articles on the link between tobacco and cancer and heart disease, after which tobacco companies canceled their ads with the magazine.[31]

Elizabeth Whelan reported, "I frequently wrote on health topics for women's magazines, and have been told repeatedly by editors to stay away from the subject of tobacco."[32] Whelan, on a campaign to counter the silence, worked with the American Council on Science and Health to ask the ten leading women's magazines to run articles on the growing incidence of smoking-induced disease among women, just as they had done to promote the Equal Rights Amendment. None of the ten magazines— *Cosmopolitan, Harper's Bazaar, Ladies' Home Journal, Mademoiselle, Ms., McCall's, Redbook, Seventeen, Vogue,* or *Working Woman*—would run such an article.

The Seven Oath-Takers

Television, confronted with FCC moves to make it run antismoking commercials to counter what the FCC considered misleading cigarette ads, aired a few documentaries, most of them emphasizing the uncertainty of the tobacco link. The best of them was by CBS in 1965. But Howard K. Smith, of ABC, speaking on a public-television panel, expressed what many have seen as the media's treatment of tobacco and disease:

> To me that documentary was a casebook example of balance that drained a hot issue of its meaning. On that program there were doctors who had every reason to be objective, who maintained that cigarettes have a causal relation to cancer. On the other side, there were representatives of the tobacco industry, who have no reason to be objective, who state persuasively the opposite. The public was left with a blurred impression that the truth lay between whereas, as far as I am concerned, we have everything but a signed confession from a cigarette that smoking has a causal relation to cancer.[33]

If magazines and broadcasting had been muffled on the national plague, newspapers had been no better. According to medical and other researchers, as well as the editors who produced it, the only lengthy in-depth special feature on tobacco and disease in a standard American daily newspaper was published by the *Charlotte* (North Carolina) *Observer* on March 25, 1979.

The answer lies in a simple statistic: Tobacco was the most heavily advertised product in America, and for a good reason. As the publishing trade journal *Printer's Ink* reported in 1937, "The growth of cigarette consumption has . . . been due largely to heavy advertising expenditure. . . ." In 1954—the year beyond which any reasonable doubt of the link should have disappeared among the media—the trade journal of newspapers, *Editor & Publisher*, criticizing the American Cancer Society and Surgeon General's reports as "scare news," complained that it had cost newspapers "much lineage and many dollars to some whose business it is to promote the sale of cigarettes through advertising—newspaper and advertising agencies."[34]

It is not surprising that surveys in 1980 by Gallup, Roper, and Chilton found that 30 percent of the public was unaware of the relationship between smoking and heart disease, 50 percent of women did not know that smoking during pregnancy increases the risk of stillbirth and miscarriage, 40 percent of men and women had no idea that smoking causes 80 percent of the 98,000 lung cancer deaths per year, and 50 percent of teenagers did not know that smoking may be addictive.[35]

In 1994 researcher Dr. Stan Glance of the University of California at San Francisco released internal documents from Brown & Williamson on nicotine. Brown &

Williamson general counsel Addison Yeaman noted in a confidential memo to his superiors, "Nicotine is addictive. We are then in the business of selling nicotine, an addictive drug."[36]

There was, of course, the famous photograph and television scene of seven leaders of the tobacco industry called before Representative Henry Waxman of California and his committee testifying about the habit-forming character of nicotine. The seven splendidly suited tobacco executives stood behind the witness table, right hands upraised, swearing under oath that they believed that "nicotine is not addictive." They had taken the oath, "so help me God."

They did indeed require the help of the Deity, but He or She must have been listening to a different channel.

Questions

1   Who was Dr. Brandreth, why does the author say he has "gone to Harvard," and what is the lesson to be learned from him?

2   How does Proctor & Gamble reflect an influence of advertising upon messages in the media?

3   What happened to the original theatrical dramas in early television, and why?

4   What does the author conclude about the historical relationship of tobacco to advertising-supported media?

5   When you watch TV now, what are the ways that you see—both blatant and subtle—that advertising influences content?

Notes

1.   *American Journalism* (New York: Macmillan, 1972), 231.

2.   Alfred McClung Lee, *The Daily Newspaper in America* (New York: Macmillan, 1937), 317.

3.   *San Francisco Chronicle*, 3 January 2003, C3.

4.   Frank Presbery, *The History and Development of Advertising* (New York: Doubleday, Doran, 1929), 396.

5.   Erik Barnouw, *Tube of Plenty* (New York: Oxford University Press, 1975), 170.

6.   Federal Communications Commission, *Second Interim Report by the Office of Network Study, Television Network Program Procurement* (Washington, D.C., 1965).

7.   Senate Committee on Interstate and Foreign Commerce, *Report* (Washington, D.C., 1963), 446–53.

8.   Individual verbatim testimony in FCC hearing is from *New York Times*, 27 September 1961, 28 September 1961, 29 September 1961, 30 September 1961, 3 October 1961, 4 October 1961, 5 October 1961, 7 October 1961, 8 October 1961.

9.   *Fortune*, 31 December 1979, 70.

10.   *New York Times*, 28 September 1961, 163.

11.   Barnouw, *Tube of Plenty*, 163.

12.   Theodore Peterson, *Magazines in the Twentieth Century* (Urbana: University of Illinois Press, 1975), 5.

13.   *Time*, 28 September 1942, 51–52.

14.   Peterson, *Magazines in the Twentieth Century*, 279.

15. "Look, Reader's Digest," *Advertising Age*, 19 November 1962, 1.
16. *Advertising Age*, 17 April 1972, 85.
17. Ben H. Bagdikian, "Newspaper Mergers," *Columbia Journalism Review*, March/April 1977, 19–20.
18. *Publishers Weekly*, 17 June 1968, 49.
19. Housing Research Group, *For Sale or for Rent* (Washington, D.C.: Center for Responsive Law, 1978).
20. *Editor & Publisher*, 18 October 1980, 20.
21. "Food Section Survey," Food Editors Conference. Chicago, October 1977.
22. *Editor & Publisher*, 31 March 1979, 11.
23. *Editor & Publisher*, 29 March 1980, 15. Joseph N. Uhl. director of the project, said that papers stopped carrying the reports after complaints from grocers.
24. *Washington Journalism Review*, October 1980, 46–47.
25. *Editor & Publisher*, 31 January 1981, 7, 44
26. http://users.erols.com/mwhite28/waisat8.atm#smokers.
27. Moskowitz et al., *Everybody's Business Almanac*.
28. *Frontline*, www.pbs.org/wgbh/pages/frontline/shows/settlement/timelines/criminal.html.
29. *New York Times*, 22 July 1963, 35.
30. R. C. Smith, "The Magazines' Smoking Habit," *Columbia Journalism Review*, January/February 1978, 29–31.
31. *Mother Jones* carried articles on smoking hazards in its issues of April 1979 and January 1980, after which all its advertisements from tobacco companies were canceled. From interviews with publisher of *Mother Jones*.
32. Press release of American Council on Science and Health, San Francisco, 29 January 1980.
33. "The Deadly Balance," *Columbia Journalism Review*, Fall 1965, 13.
34. *Editor & Publisher*, 24 July 1954.
35. Meyers, Iscoe, Jennings, Lenox, Minsky, and Sacks, *Staff Report of the Cigarette Advertising Investigation* (Washington, D.C.: Federal Trade Commission, May 1981), 5.
36. *Frontline*, www.pbs.org/wgbh/pages/frontline/shows/settlement/timelines/criminal.html

Chapter 6

JEF I. RICHARDS AND JOHN H. MURPHY, II

ECONOMIC CENSORSHIP AND FREE SPEECH

The Circle of Communication Between Advertisers, Media, and Consumers

RICHARDS AND MURPHY ARE AWARE THAT ECONOMIC censorship occurs in media, and that much of this comes from advertisers. However, they attempt to counter the conclusions of critics such as Bagdikian by arguing that consumers and media companies have significant influence in this process. Consumers, for example, can complain if they feel advertising is exerting influence, or can reject media content that does not meet their needs. Other arguments made by the authors center on the influence of special interest groups upon the media, and the resistance to advertiser influence that the media themselves exert. They discuss cases of advertisements being rejected by media as evidence for such influence.

> Private economic censorship occurs when an advertiser formally or functionally dictates to the mass media what the public shall or shall not hear.
>
> (Collins 1992a)

Advertising and its practitioners are criticized for causing a multitude of society's ills. Critics suggest advertisements manipulate consumers, make them materialistic, and encourage them to abandon traditional values, along with a litany of other unattractive effects (Pollay 1986). Recently, the ad industry has been characterized as a serious threat to our "free press," using its financial leverage to dictate media content and censor the information received by the populace.

The purpose of this article is to assess the advertising industry's responsibility in "economic censorship" (EC). We will begin by reviewing the relationship between advertising and the media vehicles in which it appears.

Using Money to Censor

Pressure from Advertisers

Advertising provides the primary source of revenue for most news and entertainment media in this country (Bagdikian 1992, p. 115). This is both the blessing and the bane of modern media management. Because it is advertising that pays the bills, managers of newspapers, magazines, television, and radio stations must keep their advertisers happy: a task not unlike feeding crocodiles. The inherent danger is that advertisers might use their economic influence to act as unofficial censors of "the press," thereby barring media from publishing or broadcasting certain material.

An illustration of this problem is found in an article by Wolf (1992), in which he describes a hypothetical fact situation:

> An explosion rocks a clinic that performs abortions. A reporter from the Los Angeles Times is sent to the scene, where pickets from both pro-choice and pro-life groups are present. He interviews both sides, determined to come up with a story that is both objective and thought-provoking.
>
> As the reporter is writing the article, the paper's publisher receives a call from not one, not two, but six of the paper's largest advertisers saying that they are pulling their advertising from tomorrow's edition if any story about the abortion clinic bombing, no matter how objective, appears. Their attitude is polite but firm — they do not wish to be associated with such an issue.
>
> (Wolf 1992)

The publisher has two options: (1) run the story and risk losing a large percent of the paper's revenue, or (2) accede to the advertisers' wishes and risk the possibility that many readers will never learn about this bombing.

While this particular situation is fictional, similar circumstances are relatively common. Wolf points out that when his television show, NBC's "Law and Order," ran an episode about the bombing of an abortion clinic, $500,000 worth of advertising was pulled from the show, and an episode about assisted suicide for AIDS victims resulted in a $350,000 pullout (Wolf 1992). All three of the major television networks have experienced advertiser pull-outs of this sort. Exhibit 1 includes a few of the situations, publicly attributed to advertiser pull-outs, where networks incurred financial losses.

Although the evidence is primarily anecdotal, and it is conceivable that in some cases the losses result from poor management rather than advertiser withdrawals. However, the sheer number of losses and the circumstances surrounding each are strongly suggestive of EC.

That EC is behind these losses is particularly likely in light of modern media buying practices. It is well established that advertisers now systematically avoid shows that deal with certain "hot-button issues," such as abortion and homosexuality (Silverman 1991; Du Brow 1991). In fact, many major advertisers employ outside firms to pre-screen advance tapes of programs in which their commercials are scheduled to appear (Carter 1990; Wolf 1992). One screener explains, "Basically, we look for what we call the Big Six: sex, violence, profanity, drugs, alcohol and religion" (Carter 1990).

Some of those companies maintain "hit lists" of programs they advise clients to avoid. One screening firm, Telerep, reportedly had a 36-page hit list in 1990, that included some of the most popular shows on television (Mahler 1990). For example, one of the most popular syndicated shows in America, "A Current Affair," appeared on Telerep's list and was avoided by 94 potential sponsors (Mahler 1990). Today, advertisers have contract stipulations that allow them to back out of a media purchase if, after pre-screening a network show, they are uncomfortable with its content (Wolf 1992).

While the most publicized advertiser withdrawals revolve around programs with controversial subject matter, pull-outs are not limited to controversies. They commonly result from stories or television scripts that reflect poorly on the advertiser. For example, a "Saturday Night Live" script, co-written by Phil Hartman and guest host Tom Arnold, poked fun at Ford and General Motors (GM) executives. When a GM subsidiary reviewed the script and balked, references to Ford and GM were replaced with fictitious names (Piccoli 1992). Reflecting similar corporate concerns, one media buyer admitted, "We had a problem with an episode of 'Little House on the Prairie' because wild dogs were chasing a girl and we had a Puppy-Chow ad. We have to pull cat food commercials out of 'Alf' because Alf is constantly trying to eat the cat" (Kleinfield 1989).

Neither are advertiser pull-outs (or threats to pull-out) limited to television. Exhibit 2 provides a list of some known advertiser defections from newspapers and magazines.

Again, many of these offer only circumstantial evidence of EC, and some advertisers deny punative intent. However, some of these cases leave little room for doubt. For example, Proctor & Gamble reportedly warned it would pull ads from any newspaper or magazine — as well as broadcast stations — to run stories that singled out its products in what it considered to be an unfair manner (Ramirez 1990). And when the Vice President of Advertising for Radio Shack became upset by a story that appeared in *InfoWorld*, he ordered his Media Department to cancel all contracts for ad placement in that magazine and 60 other publications owned by the same company. His letter of complaint, announcing that decision, was published in the magazine (Beckerman 1985).

There is little question that a great deal of pressure is being placed on media managers to modify (or eliminate) programming and editorial content that advertisers find objectionable. Whether media are obliging these requests is somewhat more difficult to determine, since they are unlikely to publicize such facts.

Media Acquiescence

Robert N. O'Neil, director of the Thomas Jefferson Center for the Protection of Free Expression, acknowledges, "There is increased evidence" that the media do censor news stories about advertisers (Riley 1992). Gloria Steinem states, "I don't think anyone questions whether or not advertisers influence the editorial content of most women's magazines. It's already taken for granted that they do" (Enrico 1990). And Richard Kipling, of the Los Angeles Times, admits:

> I get calls from reporters across the country who are fearful . . . about the increasing pressure to do stories pleasing to advertisers. They've questioned the journalistic value of these "stories" and have been told simply to

find a way to make the "stories" work. They're panicked that their careers are in jeopardy, that they have only once choice — do the advertiser-friendly stories or join the burgeoning ranks of the journalistic unemployed.

(Collins 1992b)

These allegations are supported by a recent survey of 147 daily newspapers that found more than 90% of editors have been pressured by advertisers and more than one-third of them claimed advertisers had succeeded in influencing news at their papers (Soley and Craig 1992). A recent study of almost 100 magazines, covering a span of 25 years, found that magazines relying heavily on cigarette advertising are far less likely than others to publish stories about the health hazards associated with smoking (Lipman 1992). And some of the examples in Exhibits 6.1 and 6.2 strongly suggest that media do, indeed, acquiesce to advertiser demands on occasion.

Exhibit 6.1 Examples of Economic Censorship — Television

- In 1973, CBS re-ran an episode of "Maude," in which the leading character obtained an abortion. No national sponsors purchased ad time, and approximately 39 CBS affiliates even refused to run the episode (Hoffman 1992).
- When "Jesus of Nazareth" was broadcast by NBC in 1977, General Motors withdrew its ads after fundamentalist religious groups — that had not even seen the program — protested. However, the program turned out to be a big hit (Rosenberg 1987).
- ABC claims its series "Soap," which ran from 1977 to 1981, lost $3 million per year as the result of advertisers refusing to sponsor it. "Soap" was subject to pickets, threatened boycotts, and a letter-writing campaign, mostly inspired by several religious organizations upset at early reports of sexual content in the series (Margulies 1985).
- McDonald's restaurant chain sent a memo to its franchise holders advising them to keep ad spots out of ABC's mini-series, "The Thorn Birds," in 1983. The series dealt with a Catholic priest involved in a love affair with a girl he had practically raised from childhood (Clark 1983).
- The ABC mini-series "Amerika," in 1987, depicted an America ruled by the Kremlin. It was subjected to heavy criticism by a variety of special-interest groups. Chrysler Corporation, while denying it was motivated by those criticisms, withdrew $5,000,000 worth of advertising from the show (Rosenberg 1987).
- In 1989, ABC's "Thirtysomething" lost over $1 million when an episode depicted two gay men in bed together, and lost another $500,000 when the gay couple appeared in a later episode (Weinstein 1990).
- ABC's "Geraldo" talk show, which frequently dealt with controversial issues, also met with advertising losses (Mahler 1990).
- Mennen Company withdrew advertising from ABC's "Heartbeat" medical drama because the show included a lesbian nurse (Blau 1989).
- IBM, Acura, Anheuser-Busch, Toyota, Sharp Electronics, and Spalding all decided to withdraw or reduce their advertising commitments to ABC and/or ESPN telecasts of the 1990 PGA Championship golf tournament when the founder of an Alabama country club announced that his club would not be pressured into admitting blacks (McManus 1990).
- A few years ago Domino's Pizza Inc. pulled advertising from NBC's "Saturday Night Live" because of its allegedly "offensive" skits (Blau 1989).
- More recently Mazda pulled its advertising from "Saturday Night Live" for ostensibly the same reasons (Du Brow 1991).
- Ralston Purina backed out of the same show because in one skit the word "penis" was mentioned several times (Carton 1989).

- A made-for-TV movie about a Chicago lawyer who dies of AIDS, "An Early Frost," cost NBC $600,000 worth of advertising revenue when it first ran in 1985, even though it garnered respectable ratings, and lost another $1 million when it was rerun about six months later (McDougal 1991b).
- NBC's "Quantum Leap," a show that has won many awards, also faced advertiser withdrawals amounting to $500,000 when an episode dealt with homosexuality in a military school (Rosenberg 1992).
- NBC incurred a similar loss when it aired an episode of "Lifestories" that discussed gay television reporter and his battle against AIDS (Weinstein 1990).
- NBC also lost advertisers when it ran a movie about the controversial "Roe v. Wade" Supreme Court decision on abortion (Rosenberg 1992).
- CBS, too, has lost advertisers as the result of "controversial" programming. For example, advertisers have pulled out of two of the network's most popular series: "Murphy Brown" and "Northern Exposure" (Du Brow 1991).
- An episode of "China Beach" that dealt with abortion also experienced advertiser pull-outs, and was not rerun (Carman 1990).
- Robert Iger, president of ABC Entertainment, claimed that research showed ABC lost $14 million in the 1989–90 season, $9 million of which was attributable to controversial programming. He claimed that ABC lost over $1 million in one movie about Rock Hudson that dealt with his homosexuality (Carman 1990).
- In 1994, "NYPD Blue" won more Emmy nominations than any series in history (Pergament), won both People's Choice and Golden Globe awards, and consistently ranked in the "top 20" shows on television. But, because of controversy surrounding the show's occasional depictions of nude rear-ends and use of salty language, ABC was unable to attract major advertisers and consequently lost money on the show (Miller 1994).

Exhibit 6.2 Examples of Economic Censorship — Print Media

- A few years ago R.H. Macy & Co., one of *The New York Times'* three biggest advertisers, told the *Times* to remove a reporter from Macy's beat after the reporter published a book critical of the retailer (Dorfman 1989).
- The *Seattle Times* experienced a sharp reduction in advertising for Nordstrom stores after it published a series of articles about the retailer's labor problems (Zachary 1992).
- *Ms.* magazine closed its doors for failure to attract sufficient advertising. One reason: Advertisers were concerned about appearing in a magazine that took a strong stand on issues like abortion and sexual preference (Enrico 1990).
- After a bad review of "Patriot Games" appeared in *Daily Variety*, and a series of articles questioning exploitative marketing for "Juice" ran in the *Hollywood Reporter*, Paramount Pictures decided not to place its traditional congratulatory ads for "Patriot Games" in those publications (Welkos 1992).
- The *Arkansas Democrat* was chided for telling a columnist not to criticize advertisers. John Robert Star, managing editor of that paper, declared, "Our policy is no different from every other paper I know about: People hired as columnists by the paper don't trash advertisers" (Horowitz 1992).
- *Omni* magazine lost two of its top editors in 1990. They quit because the magazine's management acquiesced to the desires of an advertiser and ran an ad on the front cover of the publication (Donaton 1990).
- In 1993, Mercedes-Benz of North American warned 30 magazines not to print its ads in any issue containing an article that portrayed Germany or Mercedes-Benz in a negative light (Associated Press 1993).

- In the late 1980s, Reverend Donald Wildmon's American Family Association began a campaign against *Playboy* magazine — because of what Wildmon felt was obscene content — encouraging a boycott and letter-writing campaign targeted at the magazine's advertisers. Chrysler received hundreds of letters, and subsequently pulled its ads from *Playboy* (Farhi 1991).
- In the early 1980s, a major advertiser insisted that a press release concerning its financial problems be published exactly as written in the *Trenton Times.* A reporter who re-wrote the release was subsequently fired (Shaw 1987).
- Several years ago the *Atlanta Journal* published a story about Eastern Airline's baggage handling system at the Atlanta airport. The paper lost an estimated $100,000 in advertising by Eastern as a result (Shaw 1987).
- In the mid-1980s the *Wall Street Journal* ran a some stories about Mobil Oil Company and its executives. The company stopped advertising in the *Journal,* even though it had run $500,000 worth of ads in the paper the prior year (Shaw 1987).
- The *UmpquaWeekly Examiner*, in Oregon, was forced out of business after running a series of stories critical of the timber industry and others. The publisher blamed ad withdrawals, resulting from the efforts of Douglas Timber Operators urging advertisers to pull their ads dollars from the paper (Robertson 1993).
- WFLD-Channel 32 general manager Stacey Marks-Bronner was the subject of a critical article that appeared in the *Chicago Tribune* in 1994. The station pulled $42,000 worth of ads in protest (Feder 1994).
- In 1992, the Duluth, Minnesota, *News-Tribune* published a column that advised readers how to sell their home without using a real estate agent. As a result, the paper lost nearly half of its real estate agency advertising (Cox 1992).
- More than 40 automobile dealers cancelled their ads in the *San Jose Mercury News* when an article titled "A car buyer's guide to sanity" appeared in the paper. The dealers objected to the tone of the article, which they felt implied car sellers should be considered unethical adversaries in the negotiation process (Simon 1994).
- When the Hartford *Courant* newspaper ran an article that urged "buyer wariness" of car dealers, local dealers began an advertising boycott (Zachary 1992).
- When the Ogden, Utah, *Evening Standard* ran a full-page story that featured an auto dealer in another city, dealers in the Ogden area were outraged and withdrew their advertising(Stein 1992).
- In December 1985, the Federal Trade Commission charged 105 automobile dealerships, including some in the Detroit area, with antitrust violations. When the *Detroit Free Press* reported the story, several local dealerships cancelled their ads (*Washington Post* 1986).

Advertising can, of course, be used as a vehicle for free speech. Businesses and citizens, alike, can use it to voice opinions and convey information that the editorial content of media omits, assuming these same media will publish the ad. In years past, such ads were called "advertorials" (Rotzoll, Haefner and Sandage 1976, p. 134). But today the term "advertorials" represents yet another sign that advertiser influence is growing, because the word has taken on a new meaning: commercial advertisements that masquerade as editorial content (Fahri 1992). Media companies seem to have no objection to advertisers disguising promotional messages as "news." "Informercials," "documercials," product placement in television shows, and commercial video news releases all represent instances where media allow advertisers to hide a marketing message in the clothing of non-advertising content (Collins and Skover 1993, p. 718).

It also has become commonplace to find special advertising sections of newspapers and magazines: automotive, real estate and travel sections of newspapers that run only "positive" stories about those products and services (Topping 1992). For example, the *advertising* department of the *Houston Chronicle* reportedly provides all the "news" for the following sections of the paper: home, townhouse, apartments, travel, technology, livestock, and swimming pools (Bagdikian 1992, p. 165).

This is not to suggest that all vehicles do advertisers' bidding. Indeed, when Macy's confronted *The New York Times* (see Exhibit 2), the *Times* refused to give-in (Dorfman 1989). NBC went forward with its made-for-TV movie, "Roe vs. Wade," in spite of anticipated advertiser pull-outs (Graham 1989). In fact, most of the television series episodes mentioned in Exhibit 1 were run, even though the networks incurred significant losses. Undoubtedly many, if not most, media vehicles resist all or most attempts by advertisers to dictate news and entertainment content.

To date, it appears that television networks and magazines are more prone to such EC than newspapers (Goerne 1992), and women's magazines are especially susceptible (Henry 1979). However, even where there are no tangible signs that media are giving-in, pressure from advertisers may be resulting in a less visible form of censorship: a chilling effect (Baker 1992; Baker 1994; Kurtz 1991). That is, reporters and producers may avoid stories critical of advertisers or about controversial topics — consciously or subconsciously — even where media owners and managers make no such demands on them. One producer remarked, "This kind of climate alters the way you think. You find yourself censoring yourself. You start to edit yourself around controversial areas you might want to be examining" (Silverman 1991).

Whether because of direct pressure from advertisers, or as a result of self-censorship by editors, reporters, and producers, clearly some editorial and entertainment content in today's media has been filtered or even biased. The ultimate consequence is that consumers of those media are receiving limited information.

The Danger

The impact of pocketbook censorship on the citizenry is no less pernicious than government censorship. As Baker recognized:

> Anything preventing the press from effectively providing information and commentary that the public would want or that an "independent" press would conclude the public needs, is a serious threat to sound social policy and a properly functioning democracy.
>
> (Baker 1992, p. 2153)

While the First Amendment holds no sway over non-governmental censorship, any practice restricting public viewing, listening, or reading options — regardless of who initiated that policy — directly conflicts with the fundamental democratic principle on which that Amendment is predicated: to encourage public debate and diversity of ideas. This is evident in judicial recognition of "a profound national commitment to the principle that debate on public issues should be uninhibited, robust and wideopen" (*New York Times v. Sullivan* 1964). Our democracy is predicated on the idea that objective "truth" can be found only through the exposition of an unhindered variety of subjective opinions (*United States v. Associated Press* 1943; Mill 1859).

This principle may be especially important where, as is frequently the case with EC, controversial matter is screened from public consideration. The Supreme Court has noted that "a function of free speech . . . is to invite dispute. It may indeed best serve its high purpose when it induces a condition of unrest, creates dissatisfaction with conditions as they are, or even stirs people to anger" (*Terminiello v. Chicago* 1949).

EC, therefore, is a serious threat to this cornerstone of our society, and should not be taken lightly. An obvious solution, of course, would be to prohibit such activity just as the First Amendment forbids government-instituted censorship. In fact, some commentators recently have suggested that regulatory response is needed, and that the primary target of those regulations should be advertisers (Collins 1992a; Baker 1992; Baker 1994). The remainder of this article will discuss the propriety of this approach.

Regulating Economic Censorship

Placing the Blame

There is a tendency to blame much of this censorship on advertisers. A renowned observer of advertising, Sid Bernstein, once commented that there are people "who are absolutely certain that advertisers, individually and collectively, have a strangle-hold on the neck of all advertising media, both print and broadcast" (Bernstein 1991). If advertisers are in control, clearly they are to blame for this EC.

Television producer Richard Kramer decried, "I'm really sickened by this and feel we're being censored by advertisers who are not equipped to make this judgment. At this point in history, it's up to organizations like ABC to show they will not be victims of advertisers' whims" (Rosenberg 1990). Radio Moscow commentator Vladimir Posner criticized American media for lack of diversity in its news broadcasts, concluding that the sponsors ultimately were responsible for this "political and social desert" (Colford 1990).

Law professor C. Edwin Baker also pins most of the blame on advertisers. He declares, "[P]rivate entities in general and advertisers in particular constitute the most consistent and the most pernicious 'censors' of media content" (Baker 1992). As a solution he recommends a special tax on advertising, designed to shift the power from advertisers to readers.

Communication professors Soley and Craig (1992) seem to agree that the ad industry is responsible. They note, "The assertion that advertisers attempt to influence what the public sees, hears, and reads in the mass media is perhaps the most damning of all criticisms of advertising, but this criticism isn't acknowledged in most advertising textbooks." They suggest this is an ethical issue that should be taught to advertising students.

Even reports that do not explicitly name the guilty tend to imply the ad industry is the root of the problem. One news story refers to "the taint of advertiser influence" (Topping 1992), one discusses TV network attempts to "withstand advertiser pressures" (Silverman 1991), and yet another talks about it being counterproductive for networks to "knuckle under to the pressure of sponsor defections" (Weinstein 1990). And one media ethics book refers to the "advertiser onslaught" facing the press (Day 1991, p. 184). The clear message is that advertisers are in control, and consequently bear the responsibility.

A recent report published by the Center for the Study of Commercialism (CSC) placed this blame more squarely on the shoulders of advertisers (Collins 1992a). That report stated:

> Who controls the press? The answer should be apparent — ultimately, those who control the purse . . . . In contemporary America, advertisers wield much of this monetary might, meaning that much press independence is potentially surrendered in their name. (p. 1)

It concluded that "[s]elf-censorship represents a victory of advertising influence over editorial integrity, of commercialism over content" (p. 31), and recommended several actions to rectify this problem, including laws aimed at (1) prohibiting advertisers from exerting influence, and (2) protecting journalists who blow the whistle on such influence. That report received considerable media attention (e.g., Goerne 1992; Horovitz 1992; Collins 1992b), leading to additional negative publicity for the advertising industry.

Most of these commentators, including the CSC report, acknowledge that advertising is not solely responsible. After all, advertisers would have no power if the media refused to cooperate. Yet the picture being painted is that economic realities are placing media at the mercy of advertisers, if they are to survive (e.g., Silverman 1991; Rosenberg 1990).

The model implied by this process is top-down and linear, from advertisers to consumers (see Exhibit 6.3). Under this model it is consumers who are the victims of advertiser force and media acquiescence. Advertisers are seen as imposing their collective will upon media, thereby infringing on the "freedom of the press," and limiting the free flow of information to consumers. This viewpoint, however, idealizes media as an altruistic endeavor to provide citizens with news, art, and entertainment, without respect to its free-market nature.

The relationship between these three parties is much more symbiotic than suggested in Exhibit 6.3. To the contrary, each party has the power (whether or not that power is exercised) to influence the other two, as illustrated by the "circle of communication" in Exhibit 6.4. Communication, in this model, encompasses all means of persuasion, by which the three parties influence the actions of the others. This includes,

Exhibit 6.3 Top-down Model of the Communication Process

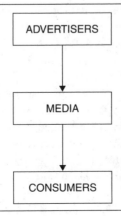

Exhibit 6.4 Circle of Communication Model of Influences on Media Content

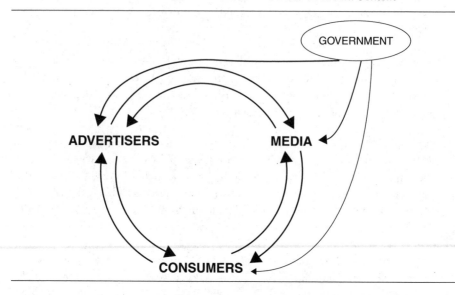

among others, the choice of editorial and entertainment matter in the media, the advertisements, the products sold by the advertisers, consumer complaints, and consumers' actions when buying or refusing to buy products.

The role that each of these parties plays in so-called "economic censorship" is discussed below. We will begin by considering the alleged victims of this censorship: consumers.

Vocal Consumers

It is indisputable that consumers often receive sterilized, biased, information from some media. But, in large part, this is a condition of their own making. Advertiser withdrawal from, or avoidance of, media virtually always results from feared consumer response to those media. And in many cases, consumers are actively petitioning advertisers to avoid certain media content.

Conservative consumer groups, collectively dubbed the "New Puritans," have bombarded advertisers with threats and complaints (Elliott 1989). "I call it advertising terrorism," says Jack Trout, of Trout & Ries. "A lot of folks have realized they can get their point of view across by jumping on the phones and threatening a boycott [of advertised products]" (Farhi 1989).

One conservative consumer group, Christian Leaders for Responsible Television [CLeaR-TV], was established by a Methodist minister named Donald Wildmon in 1986. Since then CLeaR-TV has spear-headed numerous boycotts — or threats of boycotts — against advertisers that sponsor television programs the organization identified as "un-Christian," sinful, or otherwise objectionable (Mahler 1990; Cox 1989). Wildmon says, for example, that he does not want to see homosexuality on television (Enrico 1991).

Another group, the National Coalition on Television Violence [NCTV], likewise has been involved in writing to advertisers about sponsorship of shows its members feel contain excessive violence, gratuitous sex, and Satanistic overtones (Mahler 1990). Americans for Responsible Television (Silverman 1991) and Concerned Citizens for Quality Television (McDougal 1991a) are yet two more such organizations. Each of these groups claims many victories in convincing advertisers to avoid buying time on certain shows (e.g., Fahey 1991, p. 657).

Conservative groups are not the only vocal consumers. There are, for instance, a variety of special interest groups that champion "politically correct" media content (Kurtz 1991). One example, the Nurses Association, successfully took on Chrysler and Sears for advertising on the show "Nightingales," because of its depiction of nurses as "boy-toys" (Clark 1989). Peter Tortorici, executive vice president of CBS Entertainment, admits that some things "All in the Family" used to do — especially the racist and sexist comments of its main character, Archie Bunker — might not get on the air today (Du Brow 1991).

In at least one instance an entire industry threatened an advertiser. Stroh Brewery withdrew sponsorship of an environmental program, *Ancient Forests: Rage Over Trees*, when the timber industry planned to boycott the company (Fahey 1991).

This proactive approach of consumers is not a new phenomenon, but has become more popular in recent years. In the distant past consumers relied heavily on government regulation to block "offensive" communication content, but a series of First Amendment cases have placed limits on government's ability to restrict material that offends some people (Schechter 1992). The result has been an increased popularity of advertiser boycotts. Reagan Administration deregulation of broadcast media may have been an additional catalyst for groups feeling they must rely on their own initiative rather than on government action (Hill and Beaver 1991).

Even where consumers are not *actively* trying to affect media content, they may well play a *passive* role. Advertisers, like politicians, want to alienate no one. Where they suspect consumers will be offended by media content, advertisers will avoid placing their ads in that context, even if no one threatens a boycott.

Consumers clearly do have a voice in EC, by expressing their desires to advertisers. They also have the power to actively voice those preferences directly to the media, but that approach is rare (Hill and Beaver 1991). They tend to declare their opinions to media passively, through rating points. If they dislike a program or a vehicle, they simply choose a different one.

The reason why consumers reserve active protests for advertisers rather than media is subject to speculation. It has been suggested this is because advertisers hold the purse strings (Collins 1992a), but this ignores the fact that an effective boycott of the medium or program would reduce ratings and therefore make the medium less attractive to advertisers. Consequently, the same effect could be realized by communicating directly with media rather than advertisers.

A more logical explanation is that boycotters are not trying to change the media *they* use, but rather to restrict what *other people* see and hear in the media (Fahey 1991, p. 654). After all, if boycotters are bothered by the content of media they use, they have the option of simply changing media. But if those protesters are not regular viewers of a particular program, their refusal to watch that program will have no measurable effect on program ratings. In this case, they have no leverage with which to control media content. Boycotting the advertisers, on the other hand, permits them leverage over such content.

Of course, these vocal consumers do not represent all consumers. So one might argue that the silent majority has no voice in this circle of communication, and that it is these silent consumers who are victimized by EC. In reality, if they were to take a more active role and collectively demand that media address controversial issues, both advertisers and media would readily comply. Alternatively, if these "victims" are sufficiently upset about the lack of information caused by EC, they can send a message to advertisers and media by giving preference to those media that accept no advertising. If they neither protest nor switch to alternative media, we can assume that most consumers are willing to accept the limitations of their current media.

Contrary to representations of advertiser-as-dictator, consumers command significant power in this process. Indeed, much of the recent EC is a direct result of consumers exercising that power. But it would be unfair to place the full blame for EC on consumers, because media also hold a share of power.

Free-Market Media

Collins (1992a; 1992b) and Baker (1992; 1994) claim that, as a result of advertiser pressure, the press is no longer "free." But the press *is* free. It is free to sell to advertisers, or solely to consumers. If a medium wishes to avoid advertiser influence, it could avoid selling ad space and finance its efforts strictly through consumer subscriptions. A "free press" refers to the rights of the press, not the rights of the audience. These commentators seem to confuse the right of the press to publish what it wants with the right of consumers to get untarnished information. To think these two rights coterminous is to romanticize media. What most media want to publish is whatever will make the most money.

Media companies are businesses. Most contemporary media have chosen to finance their businesses by selling ad space or time. And that space or time is worthless without readers, listeners, or viewers, which means these businesses serve two groups of customers: advertisers and consumers. While individual vehicles have complete freedom to print or broadcast whatever they desire, and to refuse the requests of advertisers and consumers, the principles of business require that they serve the wants and needs of those customers. This may not be what many envision as the ideal "free press," but it is good business.

In their efforts to remain fiscally strong, media sometimes find it advantageous to avoid certain content. But advertisers' demands are not their only concern. At times media alter content for the benefit of their other customers, the readers or viewers. In fact, even advertisers — who pay the bills — sometimes find their interests subjugated to those of the readers and viewers, when media choose to censor *ad* content. Quintessence, for example, recently ran afoul of NBC and CBS with an ad for its Jovan fragrance. The ad was a spoof of network censors, and the networks saw little humor in it (Hume 1992). Such content could reflect poorly on viewers' attitudes toward the networks.

Benetton Services, which has built a reputation for controversial advertising, recently had similar problems with *The New Yorker*. A Benetton ad scheduled to run in an issue of the magazine depicted an albino Zulu woman among a large group of other Zulu women. The albino woman looks embarrassed, and the others seem to be shunning her. Tina Brown, editor of *The New Yorker*, rejected the ad for the issue in which it was to appear: an issue containing an article about Malcolm X. She explained, "This ad is seeming to address the same issue, but obviously in a very punchy, advertising way. We wanted to make sure we didn't seem to be mixing advertising and editorial" (Elliott 1992). Again, it was readers rather than the advertiser that Tina Brown felt compelled to keep happy.

In 1991, Fox became the first and only network to accept condom advertising. In spite of national concerns about AIDS, other social diseases, and teenage pregnancy, the three established networks held fast to a universal policy against accepting these ads. The reason, of course, was a fear that the public would be offended and, hence, stop watching that network (Kitman 1991).

Another, particularly notable, instance of advertising being censored was the recent flurry of debate over whether or not college newspapers should publish advertisements by Bradley R. Smith (Bishop 1991). What makes this case especially important is that the ads in question were not "commercial" in nature, but rather were paid "editorial" or "opinion" ads. In late 1991 and early 1992 two full-page ads were sent by Smith to college newspapers around the country, in an attempt to publish them. The first ad was entitled, "The Holocaust Controversy: The Case For Open Debate," and the second was labelled, "Falsus in Uno, Falsus in Omnibus . . . The "Human Soap" Holocaust Myth." Both ads argued that popular historical accounts of Jews being executed en masse during World War II are exaggerated. On virtually all college campuses where the ads were considered, heated disputes resulted. In the end, several campus accepted the ad and several rejected it (Oshinskky and Curtis 1991; Warlick 1992; UPI 1992; Brooks 1992).

The debate at the University of Texas was particularly heated. Following a series of decisions that went back and forth, regarding whether to run the ads, students and faculty associated with the newspaper were called names, received death threats, and warned of potential lawsuits. Clearly, many readers did not want the ad published. Leaders of the campus Student Association even threatened to withhold the newspaper's funding if it should run the ad (Brooks 1992).

Further evidence that media business decisions adversely affect advertising — rather than just news and entertainment — content is the existence of advertising acceptability departments at many newspapers, magazines, and broadcast companies. Though some of these acceptability standards reflect legal concerns, many are designed to avoid offending readers or viewers.

Like consumers, the press clearly shares the power in this triad. That power is used to determine how best to serve all its customers, which sometimes requires limiting content desired by either consumers or advertisers. It has been suggested that advertisers have disproportionate power in this relationship, but the fact that ad content is also subject to EC seems to disconfirm that hypothesis. To substantiate this disproportionate power, critics point to such things as the special ad sections (e.g., real estate) that are commonplace in newspapers and magazines. But these special sections are not the result of advertiser demands; media offer them to create new opportunities for ad sales.

These are all reasonable (if not sound) business decisions, and media companies are businesses. Since advertisers are also subject to the rules of the marketplace, their decisions are very much like those of the press.

Advertisers

Baker (1992; 1994) argues there is an imbalance of power. He contends, "Of course, the medium's attempt to obtain advertising revenue leads it to tilt media content toward what advertisers, not readers or viewers, want" (p. 2180). However, these two wants are not mutually exclusive. A medium is only beneficial to advertisers if consumers use it, and consumers will not use a medium if they are unhappy with its content. Consequently, a smart advertiser will never make demands of a medium that will reduce audience satisfaction.

Quite the contrary, advertisers seek to attract the largest possible numbers of consumers. In addition, they want those consumers to like their brands. A Coca-Cola spokesperson explains, "We are in the business to make friends" (Hill and Beaver 1991). Consequently, it is not surprising that advertisers tend to avoid content that might cause some consumers to either change vehicles or develop negative attitudes toward the sponsor. Betsy Frank, of the Saatchi & Saatchi advertising agency, explains:

> When we use TV, we're not using it to support First Amendment rights or artistic freedoms, we're using it because it's a good business decision for our client, and nobody wants the result of a business decision to be loss of customers rather than gains.
>
> (Silverman 1991)

If placing their ad in a vehicle will cause them to lose money, it makes no sense for them to buy that particular ad space. Consumers are not forced to buy products they do not want, and neither should advertisers be coerced to buy undesired ad space. But that is precisely what would happen if, as Collins (1992a; 1992b) suggests, advertisers were prohibited from engaging in pull-outs or expressing their likes/dislikes to publishers and producers.

Media purchases frequently are made before content is known, based on expected ratings. When the content is known, the advertiser may anticipate a loss of value and decide to pull out. This is no different than consumers agreeing to buy an automobile on the basis of an inspection, then when they go to pick it up they discover the engine has been removed. Advertisers should have the same right to back out of a deal that individual consumers enjoy.

Normally, there are literally thousands of media buys that can fulfill their needs, so if one vehicle becomes unattractive it is both easy and sensible to switch to another (Baker 1992, p. 2161). Because advertisers seldom sponsor an entire television show the way they did 40 years ago, but simply purchase time, they have no commitment to the shows (or magazines, etc.) in which they place their ads (Hill and Beaver 1991).

There are two types of content that may reduce the value of a vehicle: (1) material that is offensive to viewers and therefore indirectly reflects on the sponsors, and (2) stories that directly, negatively, reflect on the company or product. In both cases the obvious fear is bad publicity, which can quickly damage a product's reputation (Schechter 1992). Since advertising is an investment in a positive reputation, the potential costs outweigh the minimal benefits offered by any specific vehicle.

And consumer boycotts have made advertisers feel that consumers will desert them if they support certain content. John McNulty, General Motors' vice president of public relations, claims that even a single offended viewer may represent a loss of car sales for years to come (Mahler 1990). In 1989 a lone housewife, by writing letters to sponsors, convinced several advertisers to pull out of the Fox network's "Married . . . With Children." She complained the show was replete with "soft-core pornography" (Stein 1989; Clark 1990). It appears advertisers fear that if one viewer is sufficiently upset to write, there probably are many more who were equally angry but did not act on those feelings.

This places advertisers in a precarious position, since attack can come from groups of consumers with conflicting agendas. For instance, it is not inconceivable for a television show to be boycotted by the gay community for negatively portraying homosexuals, and by conservative forces for any positive aspects of that portrayal (Fahey 1991, p. 678). Advertisers are in jeopardy no matter how homosexuals are depicted. They seem to be in a "no win" situation.

For many advertisers the benefits offered by a particular vehicle are few. They see the vehicle as simply an audience, and rarely is that audience unique. However, the potential costs, whether real or imagined, are great. Under those circumstances, it is easy to understand why advertisers might readily engage in EC. When consumers refuse to buy an advertiser's product it is called an economic *boycott*, but when advertisers refuse to buy a media vehicle's product it is deemed economic *censorship*.

Like the press, advertisers have the freedom to ignore the other two parties, but that would not be a good business decision. Advertisers are merely trying to operate at a profit. But, as compared to consumers, neither advertisers nor press are completely free to engage in unrestricted expression, because both are subject to some governmental intervention.

Government Restrictions on Advertisers and Media

All participants in this society — individuals and businesses, alike — are subject to some limitations on their expressive freedom. For example, "obscene" programming can be prohibited even if consumers, advertisers, and media want it broadcast (*Miller v. California* 1973). But businesses are generally subject to regulations not imposed on individuals, and those restrictions can make their ability to communicate less "free" than individuals.

Advertisers communicate with consumers through their advertising, sales promotions, sales force, packaging, product instructions, and even the product itself. Yet all of these are subject to varying degrees of government control. Unlike the expression of the consumers, who are free to write what they desire in letters of complaint and to engage in boycotts, "commercial speech" by advertisers receives limited protection under the First Amendment (*Central Hudson Gas v. Public Service Commission of New York* 1980). Indeed, advertisers' marketing communications are scrutinized, and frequently regulated, by the Federal Trade Commission, the Food and Drug Administration, the Securities Exchange Commission, and others. In addition, in response to the threat of regulation, many of those communications are reviewed and altered by the advertiser's legal counsel.

The advertised product, too, is subject to some limits imposed by government. State and federal authorities dictate safety and environmental standards for products and their manufacture. Toys must be safe for children to put in their mouths and must not be flamable, wireless transmitters must be licensed for a given radio frequency, insecticides must not poison their users, bedding materials must meet several composition standards, etc. Thus, the ability of advertisers to communicate through the medium of their products is severely constrained by government.

Media are somewhat less encumbered by regulation, because their product is communication and their speech generally is not considered "commercial speech." Quite the contrary, information flowing from the media typically is considered to fall squarely under the protection of the "press" clause of the First Amendment (e.g., *Miami Herald Publishing v. Tornillo* 1974). However, broadcast media are subject to several restrictions, under the auspices of the Federal Communications Commission. For example, bearing directly on the "controversial issues" involved in EC, "indecent" language that is not "obscene" is nonetheless subject to limitation by that agency (*F.C.C. v. Pacifica Foundation* 1978). And even print media are restrainted in ways individuals are not, including regulation of the ink and paper on which they print, the employees they hire, and distribution through the mails.

Although within the circle of communication each of the three parties is free to express themselves, in their own best interests, that freedom is neither absolute nor equal. Consumers are subject to far fewer limitations than either media or advertisers. Indeed, among these parties, the most consistently and heavily regulated are the advertisers.

Conclusions

That EC occurs is beyond dispute. The question is where to lay the blame. Advertisers are popular targets of social critics, so it should come as no surprise that advertisers are charged with responsibility for EC. In fact, two of the most vocal commentators who blame advertisers for EC also have criticized the ad industry for other societal ills. Collins (1992a) is a co-founder of the CSC, an advocacy group that explicitly "exposes and opposes commercialism" (Ibid.), and has charged advertising with subjugating rational consumer decisionmaking to the service of selling (Collins and Skover 1993). Baker (1994) elsewhere has argued that the profit motive behind advertising makes it unworthy of First Amendment protection (Baker 1976).

If one starts from the premise that the chain-of-events leading to EC begins with advertisers, the conclusion that advertisers bear primary responsibility is a *fait accompli*. But it is equally arguable that this process starts with consumers or with media. As with any circle, the process of EC has no definite beginning or end; it is a continuing and complex dynamic among all the participants. Consequently, they all bear some blame for EC.

But is EC really a cause for *serious* concern? Today consumers have a wide choice of media vehicles, and the number is expanding at a breath-taking rate. Since not all advertisers and media vehicles engage in EC, and probably none of them use it frequently, it is doubtful that great collective harm results from this process. Especially in light of new electronic data communication technologies, it is hard to imagine that a newspaper or broadcast station decision to avoid a topic will severely handicap an audience member's ability to obtain that information.

Finally, EC should never become too pervasive. When currently passive consumers become sufficiently unhappy about EC and more actively exercise their rights (e.g., change vehicles or boycott advertisers), media bias should be diminished. In short, the dangers of EC seem somewhat overstated.

Questions

1   Where do the authors feel that blame for EC (Economic Censorship) is usually unfairly placed?

2   What are the differences between the Top-down and Circle Models of Influence, and how do they reflect the different views of advertiser influence?

3   What influences do the authors feel that media companies, interest groups, and consumers have upon media content?

4   Are there additional advertising influences upon the nature of media content that the authors do not address in this chapter? For example, how might some audiences be given more influence than others by ad-supported media, and why?

Bibliography

Associated Press (1993), "Mercedes magazine request raises censorship questions," *Austin American-Statesman*, (September 17), E3.

Bagdikian, Ben H. (1992), *The Media Monopoly* (4th Ed.), Boston: Beacon Press.

Baker, C. Edwin (1976), "Commercial Speech: A Problem in the Theory of Freedom," *Iowa Law Review*, 62, 1–56.

—— (1994), *Advertising and a Democratic Press*, Princeton, NJ: Princeton University Press.

—— (1992), "Advertising and a Democratic Press," *University of Pennsylvania Law Review*, 140, 2097–2243.

Beckerman, David M. (1985), "Tandy Pulls Its Ads," *InfoWorld*, (August 5), 6.

Bernstein, Sid (1991), "Who's afraid of advertisers?" *Advertising Age*, (March 11), 17.

Bishop, Katherine (1991), "Ads on Holocaust 'Hoax' Inspire Campus Debates," *The New York Times*, (December 23), A12.

Blau, Eleanor (1989), "Domino's Pizza Cancels Ads on 'Saturday Night,'" *New York Times*, (April 11), Y45.

Brooks, A. Phillips (1992), "Free speech, responsible journalism at odds in bitter Holocaust ad debate," *Austin American-Statesman*, (May 10), B1.

Carman, John (1990), "Topics That Cost ABC Big Bucks," *The San Francisco Chronicle*, (July 25), E1.

Carter, Bill (1990), "Screeners Help Advertisers Avoid Prime-Time Trouble," *The New York Times*, (January 29), D1.

Carton, Barbara (1989), "Lashing back at TV sleaze; Outraged viewers gird to boycott advertisers," *The Boston Globe*, (April 23), A1.

Central Hudson Gas v. Public Service Commission of New York, 447 U.S. 557 (1980).

Clark, Kenneth R. (1989), "Will boycott fever affect television's disposition for fall?" *Chicago Tribune*, (May 4), Tempo section, 1.

—— (1990), "Housewife/lobbyist eyes TV 'raunch hour,'" *Chicago Tribune*, (August 2), Tempo section, 1.

—— (1983), "Church, advertisers criticize 'The Thorn Birds,'" United Press International, (March 23), wire story.

Colford, Steven W. (1990), "A Soviet view of U.S. advertising," *Advertising Age*, (May 7), 62.

Collins, Ronald K.L. (1992a), *Dictating Content: How Advertising Pressure Can Corrupt a Free Press*, Washington, D.C.: The Center for the Study of Commercialism.

—— (1992b), "Press Freedom vs. Advertising Pressure," *The Seattle Times*, (April 4), A19.

—— and David M. Skover (1993), "Commerce & Communication," *Texas Law Review*, 71, 697–746.

Cox, James (1992), " 'Herald' controversy flares, Cuban exile leaders doubt bomb threats," *USA Today*, (February 5), 2B.

—— (1989), "Rev. Donald Wildmon; Mississippi minister takes on TV networks," *USA Today*, (July 17), 6B.

Danzig, Fred (1990), "This wall must stay; Editors shouldn't be censors of ads," *Advertising Age*, (January 8), 22.

Day, Louis A. (1991), *Ethics in Media Communications: Cases and Controversies*, Belmont, CA: Wadsworth, Inc.

Donaton, Scott (1990), "Two editors quit over 'Omni' ad flap," *Advertising Age*, (October 22), 54.

Dorfman, Dan (1989), "Macy's ad clout fails to sway 'N.Y. Times,' " *USA Today*, (February 13), 2B.

Du Brow, Rick (1991), "When Does TV Cross the Line?; Censorship vs. Good Taste—The debate continues as the networks get pressed tigher in the Iron Triangle of viewers, advertisers and the folks who create those prime-time shows," *Los Angeles Times*, (November 3), 7.

Elliott, Stuart (1992), "Group Seeks to Curb Advertisers' Power," *The New York Times*, (March 13), D6.

Enrico, Dottie (1990), "Ms., Minus Ads, Makes Debut Today," *Newsday*, (July 30), 2.

Fahey, Patrick M. (1991), "Advocacy Group Boycotting of Network Television Advertisers and Its Effects on Programming Content," *University of Pennsylvania Law Review*, 140, 647–709.

Farhi, Paul (1991), "Chrysler to Halt Ads in Playboy: Auto Firm Acts After Getting Complaints," *Washington Post*, (February 22), C1.

—— (1989), "Pan Am Grounds an Ad after Listener Complaint," *The Washington Post*, (April 14), F1.

F.C.C. v. Pacifica Foundation, 438 U.S. 726 (1978).

Feder, Robert (1994), "Channel 32 Pulls Newspaper's Ads," *Chicago Sun-Times*, (August 29), 31.

Goerne, Carrie (1992), "Study blasts advertisers, fearful media for suppressing news," *Marketing News*, (April 27), 8.

Graham, Judith (1989), "NBC's 'Roe' may turn off advertisers," *Advertising Age*, (May 1), 1.

Henry, Nancy (1979), "Women's Mags: The Chic Sell," in *The Commercial Connection: Advertising & the American Mass Media*, John W. Wright, ed., New York: Dell Publishing Company, 251–255.

Hill, Ronald Paul and Andrea L. Beaver (1991), "Advocacy Groups and Television Advertisers," *Journal of Advertising*, 20(1), 18–27.

Hoffman, Jan (1992), "TV Shouts 'Baby' (and Barely Whispers 'Abortion')," *The New York Times*, (May 31), Sect. 2, 1.

Horovitz, Bruce (1992), "Advertisers Influence Media More, Report says," *Los Angeles Times*, (March 12), D2.

Hume, Scott (1992), "What is censored? Quintessence won't change Jovan ad," *Advertising Age*, (February 17), 58.

Kitman, Marvin (1991), "Advertising as a Fact of Life," *Newsday*, (November 21), 81.

Kleinfield, N.R. (1989), "Television That Makes Advertisers Dive for Cover," *The New York Times*, (March 6), D8.

Kurtz, Howard (1991), "Our Politically Correct Press; More and More Stories Seem Too Touchy For Journalists," *The Washington Post*, (January 20), B1.

Lipman, Joanne (1992), "Media Content is Linked to Cigarette Ads," *The Wall Street Journal*, (January 30), B5.

Mahler, Richard (1990), "The New Power of TV Advertisers; The increasing clout of sponsors has been seen more and more this season as 'objectionable' shows make some hit lists," *Los Angeles Times*, (May 6), 4.

Margulies, Lee (1985), " 'Hail to the Chief' Goes to a Quiet Death on ABC," *Los Angeles Times*, (May 21), Part 6, 1.

McDougal, Dennis (1991), "Hitting TV With the Off Switch," *Los Angeles Times*, (October 28), F1.

—— (1991b), "AIDS and airwaves: It's still a hard sell," *The Toronto Star*, (November 19), D4.

McManus, John (1990), "Furor over PGA cite sinks golf sponsors," *Advertising Age*, (July 30), 2.

Miami Herald Publishing v. Tornillo, 418 U.S. 241 (1974).

Mill, John Stuart (1859), *On Liberty*, Baltimore, MD: Penguin, (reprint 1974).

Miller, Cyndee (1994), "Advertisers in middle of the battle over 'Blue': 'Quality TV' counterattacks 'American Family,' " *Marketing News*, 28(10), 1.

Miller v. California, 413 U.S. 15 (1973).

New York Times v. Sullivan, 376 U.S. 254 (1964).

Oshinsky, David M. and Michael Curtis (1991), "The truth appears to be, with regard to the alleged extermination of the European Jews, that there was no order, no plan, no budget, no weapon . . .—From advertisements in college newspapers," *The New York Times*, (December 11), A27.

Pergament, Alan (1994), " 'NYPD Blue's' 26 Nominations Leave Others Green with Envy," *The Buffalo News*, (July 22), Lifestyles Section, 10.

Piccoli, Sean (1992), "Taming the TV Watch Dog; Once-mighty censors give in to nervous admen, competition," *The Washington Times*, (May 3), D1.

Pollay, Richard W. (1986), "The Distorted Mirror: Reflections on the Unintended Consequences of Advertising," *Journal of Marketing*, 50 (April), 18–36.

Ramirez, Anthony (1990), "Procter & Gamble Pulls Some TV Ads Over Slur to Coffee," *The New York Times*, (May 12), 1.

Riley, Karen (1992), "Media back down from advertisers, critics say," *The Washington Times*, (March 12), C1.

Robertson, Lance (1993), "Timber group ruined paper, publisher says," *Eugene Register-Guard*, (March 18), Business.

Rosenberg, Howard (1992), "NBC Takes Hit Over Gay Issue on 'Leap' Show," *Los Angeles Times*, (January 17), F1.

—— (1990), "ABC Pulls Plug on a Rerun of 'Thirtysomething,' " *Los Angeles Times*, (July 19), F1.

—— (1987), "Howard Rosenberg: The 'Amerika' Controversy: Let America Decide," *Los Angeles Times*, (January 30), Part 6, 1.

Rotzoll, Kim B., James E. Haefner, and Charles H. Sandage (1976), *Advertising in Contemporary Society: Perspectives Toward Understanding*, Columbus, OH: Grid, Inc.

Shaw, David (1987), "Credibility vs. Sensitivity: High, Thick Wall Divides Editors and Advertisers," *Los Angeles Times*, (February 16), 1.

Silverman, Jeff (1991), "TV's Creators Face a New Caution," *The New York Times*, (December 8), Sect. 2, 1.

Simon, Mark (1994), "Mercury News Ad Dispute Cooling Off: Advertisers return while reporters stew," *San Francisco Chronicle*, (July 15), B1.

Soley, Lawrence C. and Robert L. Craig (1992), "Advertising Pressure on Newspapers: A Survey," *Journal of Advertising*, 21 (December), 1.

Stein, M.L. (1992), "Dinner ends boycott: Auto dealers pull ads from Utah daily; publisher buys them dinner, they come back," *Editor & Publisher Magazine*, (Oct. 10), 38.

Stein, Sharman (1989), "And Now, a Few More Words to the Sponsors," *Newsday*, (March 6), 2.

Terminiello v. Chicago, 337 U.S. 1 (1949).

Topping, Seymour (1992), "Another wall crumbles; Editors 'taint of advertiser influence,' " *Advertising Age*, (May 11), 32.

United States v. Associated Press, 52 F.Supp. 362 (S.D.N.Y. 1943).

UPI (1992), "Ohio State refuses controverial ad," United Press International, (January 23), wire story.

Valentine v. Chrestensen, 316 U.S. 52 (1942).

Virginia State Board of Pharmacy v. Virginia Citizens Consumer Council, 425 U.S. 748 (1976).

Warlick, Debra (1992), "ETC," *The Atlanta Journal and Constitution* (February 29), E6.

Washington Post (1986), " Car Dealers Pull Ads in Protest," (May 28), G1.

Weinstein, Steve (1990), "When Gay Means Loss of Revenue," *Los Angeles Times*, (December 22), F1.

Welkos, Robert W. (1992), "Paramount Pulls Ads in Dispute with Trade Papers," *Los Angeles Times*, (June 10), F2.

Wolf, Dick (1992), "Hot Topics Get Chilly Ad Reception," *Los Angeles Times*, (September 1), F1.

Zachary, G. Pascal (1992), "Many Journalists See a Growing Reluctance To Criticize Advertisers," *The Wall Street Journal*, (February 6), A1.

Chapter 7

MATTHEW P. McALLISTER AND J. MATT GIGLIO

THE COMMODITY FLOW OF U.S. CHILDREN'S TELEVISION

THIS CHAPTER ARGUES THAT NEWLY CONSTRUCTED forms and sequences of brand images dominate both cable and broadcast television targeted at children in the United States. It highlights these new forms and "flows" of commercialization in light of corporate media ownership that characterizes children's media, advertising's aggressiveness to reach desirable audiences, digital media such as the internet and televisual graphics, and loopholes in children's media legislation. The resulting new forms of cross-promotion, branding, and licensing shape children's television as a continuous stream of commodity images rather than a series of discrete commercial and non-commercial units. In addition, the multiple-network ownership of media conglomerates makes the connection of commodity images a multi-channel—and with the integration of the Internet, a multi-media—flow experience. "Program separators" and network identifiers—legislated as a way to separate the commercial from the non-commercial—actually serve to enforce the commodity nature of children's television given their integration into corporate branding strategies. The chapter calls for more flexible legislative mechanisms that may keep pace with the quickly changing economic and technological contexts of children's media and the vulnerability of this audience.

Viewers watching the 8:30 am telecast of *Rocket Power*, a program on the children's cable network Nickelodeon on Saturday, January 26, 2002, may have noticed at its conclusion (at 8:55 am) a common technique called "living end credits." Also called "squeezed credits," these occur when the closing credits are reduced to a small portion of the television screen while the bulk of the screen is used to promote an upcoming program. In this case, however, the promotional space is not used to tout a future Nick show, but features a music video by heartthrob singer Aaron Carter. The song is part of the soundtrack for the film *Jimmy Neutron, Boy Genius*, at that time still in theatrical release. The Nick logo and the web address nick.com also appear on the bottom of the screen. Four minutes later, at 9:00, a government-mandated "program separator" (or "bumper") signals that a commercial break is about to start or end. In this case, the program separator airing before *Rugrats* features the character of Jimmy Neutron controlling an orange robotic monster with a Nickelodeon logo on its head.

At 9:10 am a video "bug" appears for several seconds during the *Rugrats* program. A bug is a small video icon in the screen's bottom corner; often this identifies the network being watched. In this case, the bug is quite elaborate. Appearing on the screen are the words, "Grab a pencil and paper. Nickelodeon Milk Mustache. Coming up." True to its word, at 9:12 a minute-long spot promotes a contest co-sponsored by Nickelodeon and the dairy industry. The spot states that the winner, along with a Nickelodeon character, will be featured in a "Got Milk?" advertisement in *Nickelodeon* magazine. When a copy of the magazine is displayed on screen, Jimmy Neutron is pictured on the cover.

Fifteen minutes later (9:27 am), a traditional spot commercial for the *Jimmy Neutron* movie airs. A promotion for a Jimmy Neutron computer game available at nick.com airs at 9:44. At 9:56 and 10:26, different versions of the commercial and squeezed credits for *Jimmy Neutron* air. At 10:58, a milk mustache commercial featuring the video-game character Mario completes the commercial circuit: the ad portrays live-action children interacting with a licensed property, just as promised to potential winners of the Nickelodeon contest.

The Jimmy Neutron example from Nickelodeon, although particularly licensing-oriented (Pecora, 2004), is not uncharacteristic of the often-seamless movement of product images and corporate branding that is increasingly a defining element of U.S. children's television. It thus illustrates "commodity flow," a concept that highlights the embeddedness of promotional and commercial techniques throughout television generally but especially in children's television. To explore how the phenomenon applies to commercial programming aimed at children, we first discuss commodity flow as a construct, including its establishment in the work of Raymond Williams (1975). The concept is valuable for deconstructing children's television, given the genre's long-established roots in commercial culture and more current role in media corporate synergy. The existence of different manifestations of commodity flow—including intra-channel, inter-channel, and synergistic flow—will then be demonstrated by an analysis of specific commodity flow patterns in several hours of children's programming. The analysis shows how the flow of commodities on children's television often blurs the distinction between content and promotional forms, dramatically illustrating the intense level of commercialism targeted at this audience.

From Television Flow to Commodity Flow

Television executives have probably understood the idea of flow, especially as manifested in audience viewing patterns and programming strategies, since the beginnings of commercial broadcasting. Raymond Williams is largely credited with introducing the scholarly concept of television flow, now one of the most commonly used concepts in television studies (Corner, 1999). Williams argued that television is a technological and cultural experience that brings together discrete phenomena (events that occur outside of the medium in different locales and contexts) by framing them in a continuous stream of images and sound channeled through television. Specific techniques such as television program promotions, cliffhangers in programs timed before a commercial break, and strategic program scheduling combine with television's characteristics as a medium to decrease the incongruence between images on the screen and enhance their ability to flow into one other. Content categories such as different program genres and product commercials therefore are enacted not as fragmented and isolated forms but more as the experience of "watching TV." The ease of channel switching (even in the pre-remote control 1970s, when Williams developed the concept), the similarity of program structure, and uniform scheduling on nearly all stations and networks render flow an inter-channel experience, "perhaps the defining characteristic of broadcasting" (Williams, 1975, p. 86).

The idea of television flow has been critiqued and transformed. Modleski (1983), for example, argues that flow does not adequately explain all television genres and "dayparts" (an industry term for sections of the broadcasting day), especially daytime television, which she contends is characterized by repetition and interruptability, to match the reception context of stay-at-home wives and mothers. Similarly, Corner (1999) regards Williams' concept as undertheorized and often misapplied. He concludes that over-zealous use of flow essentializes the medium and masks fundamental differences in its programming forms.

Revisionists also contend that Williams attributed too much agency to the technology of television in his explanation of flow, therefore downplaying the influence of economic factors (Corner, 1999). The "product" of commercial television is, after all, the audience, which the television industry sells to advertisers (an idea first attributed to Smythe, 1977). Viewers who switch channels or turn the television off can no longer be sold to advertisers. It is in the best economic interests of television, then, to reduce the disjointed nature of the transition between "switchable" moments, such as when a program breaks to a series of commercials, and thus keep viewers in their television place.

Budd, Craig, and Steinman (1999) point out another increasingly important way that advertisers influence television flow. They argue that the "flow of commodities," characterized by the similarity of specific elements in product commercials, promotional spots, and programs, is intended not just to keep an audience in front of the television, but also uses all possible televisual forms to sell, including but not limited to the traditional 30-second spot commercial. Their analysis of one night's broadcast of CBS, for instance, identifies such commodity-flow characteristics as the presence of one actor both as a character in a program and as a narrator for a commercial that airs during the program, and product placements.

Budd et al.'s (1999) emphasis on the pervasiveness of commodity flow is well aligned with other critiques of the increased level of commercialism in broadcasting (Andersen, 1995; Jacobson & Mazur, 1995; McAllister, 1996). These scholars argue that, beginning in the mid-1980s, television advertising was plunged into crisis as several developments unfolded. These included: (1) dissemination of technologies like the remote control and personal recording devices that facilitate viewers' avoidance of discrete commercial spot advertisements; (2) increased competition for viewers from cable, video games, and other sources that eroded traditional television network viewership; and (3) the large number of television commercials/promotions ("clutter") that may undermine the effectiveness of any single television spot ad. The result was an increased aggressiveness on the part of advertisers. In this context, television's commodity flow is cultivated when advertisers try to prevent viewer zapping, enhance the promotional power of ad campaigns with the help of increasingly accommodating television networks, and create connections between ads and beloved programs to help campaigns stand out from the clutter. Resulting examples of commodity flow on prime-time television include college football bowl sponsorships, "long-form" advertisements like infomercials, and aggressive product placement in such genres as reality-based programs.

Adding to the increased influence of commercial product flow on television are the synergistic strategies of many key corporations involved with the television industry. The increased emphasis on media promotion is one side-effect of the growth of large media entertainment conglomerates (see, for example, Bagdikian, 2004; McChesney, 1999). Corporations owning different media outlets often exploit promotional and licensing linkages between the properties to create corporate efficiencies. Television holdings, then, may be used to promote (and be promoted by) music, book, film, and other media subsidiaries. As manifested by such synergistically driven companies as Time Warner, Disney, Viacom, and News Corp., the temptation to create a "promotional flow" among different programming and commercial elements may be as great as—and complementary to—commodity flow driven by advertisers (McAllister, 2000).

A more salient example of this phenomenon is found in children's television, an especially commercialized genre of television, both historically and in the current hyper-promotional environment. The next section briefly discusses traditional connections between advertising and children's programming, as well as recent trends in synergistic ownership of children's media.

Children's Commercial Television in Historical and Corporate Contexts

Early children's programming was in many ways more crassly (if less strategically) influenced by advertising's influence than later versions. Advertisers began aggressively using the medium to sell directly to kids at least by the mid-1950s with the success of the Mickey Mouse Club to promote Disney and other brands (Kline, 1993).

Many early TV ads targeted at children in retrospect were highly "flow oriented." Sponsorship of programs by one dominant advertiser was common. In the late 1950s, for example, Kellogg Company owned the syndicated *Huckleberry Hound* (Mittell, 2003). Over 60% of children's programs sampled from the 1950s contained sales pitches by the program's host for sponsored products. These programs routinely used "integral ads" (seamless commercial messages in the program featuring established program characters) and "segue ads" (touting of products by program actors, but often in a neutral setting and conducted between program segments or before a more circumscribed commercial break) (Alexander, Benjamin, Hoerrner, & Roe, 1998).

Legislation eventually banned practices such as explicit host-selling. Nonetheless, other commercial and promotional techniques encouraged commodity flow. Fastfood restaurants, breakfast cereals, and other products are sold on children's television, but it is perhaps the toy industry that is the most integrated in the programming mix. Describing the relationship as symbiotic, Pecora (1998) says the "programs offer the toy industry advertisements for characters, and the toys present the entertainment industry with readily identifiable characters" (p. 40). Creating toys that feature licensed characters—characters that appear in a variety of program and commodity forms—

allows advertisers to grab the child viewers' attention and break out of commercial clutter (Seiter, 1993). In 1997, approximately half of all toys were based on licenses from television or movies (Kapur, 1999). This also works in the other direction: beginning in the 1980s programming based upon toy and game characters became common (Pecora, 1998). Significant money is at stake. In 2000–2001, advertising on children's network television earned $700–750 million a year for the cable and broadcast networks (Larson, 2001). This figure actually underestimates the value of children's television programming, given the promotional benefits this provides its corporate owners. As a market, children in the 4–12 age group directly control as much as $29 billion a year, and influence family purchases in the $290 billion range (McDonald & Lavelle, 2001), including media products such as DVDs.

Four corporate giants have been especially involved in producing and distributing children's television to tap the advertising and media-product purchasing potential of this market. Typically owning both a broadcast and cable outlet for their programming, these corporations use a synergistic philosophy to build multi-media brand identity. These four are briefly profiled below.

- News Corp, via its Fox Kids Network programming block, was a dominant player in the 1990s, triggered by its embrace of the Power Rangers franchise earlier that decade (Kinder, 1999; Pecora, 1998). Fox's audience share dwindled in the early 2000s and the network's sale of the Fox Family Channel to Disney in 2001 left it without the potential for all-important cable/broadcast "cross-platform promotions" (quoted in Bernstein, 2001, p. 30).
- Viacom, through its Nickelodeon cable network and franchise, was the ratings leader after the Fox drop-off, and is one of the top-rated U.S. cable networks of any type (Sandler, 2004). Nickelodeon often uses its corporate siblings such as Paramount to carry and promote licensing. CBS, also owned by Viacom, typically programs an abbreviated block of children's shows on Saturday morning, most of it heavily influenced by the Nickelodeon brand.
- Disney is, of course, a visible force in children's television, using ABC to reach younger child viewers early in its schedule, and its cable networks The Disney Channel and ABC Family (bought from Fox) to attract the slightly older "tween" market (Dempsey, 2001a). Although the Disney Channel is "commercial-free," it is hardly promotion-free: It generates revenue from cable license fees, licensing/merchandising activity, and sponsorship deals (Schmuckler, 2002).
- Time Warner uses both its cable-based Cartoon Network and its broadcasting subsidiary Kids WB to compete for the market. Each of these TW outlets is a separate entity with its own organizational culture, but the goal is to develop synergistic projects and approach advertisers as a combined unit (Bernstein, 2001; Schmuckler, 2002). In fact, the two networks frequently share or "repurpose" each other's programs (Sandler, 2003, p. 102).

Commodity flow in children's television is not wholly without constraints. Applying to both broadcast and cable (Kunkel & McIlrath, 2003), the Children's Television Act of 1990 established restrictions on the amount of "commercial time" during children's television (10.5 minutes per hour on weekends; 12 minutes per hour on weekdays) and broad requirements for the airing of children's educational programming. Host-selling and program-length commercials are prohibited; bumpers between programs and commercials are required. However, several loopholes in this Act, as well as recent media developments, leave much room for the cultivation of commodity flow, as will be illustrated. For example, the ambiguities embedded in the definitions of both commercial time and educational programming problematize the effectiveness of such measures (Kinder, 1999; Kunkel, 2001). Public service announcements (PSAs) and program promotions—both of which can incorporate commodity imagery—are not considered advertising by the Act (Kunkel & McIlrath, 2003). In addition, the definition of program-length commercial used by the Act, a result of policy compromise, essentially restates the definition of host-selling: "a program associated with a product in which commercials for that product are aired" (quoted in Kunkel, 2001). Programs based upon toys and media licenses, then, are perfectly legal, as long as ads for those same products do not air during the program on that same channel. *On that same channel*, it will be argued, becomes a significant factor in the modern multi-channel environment. Although their existence is mandated, bumpers can become tools for, rather than against, "connected selling" in a medium dominated by corporate branding.

Method

To capture the possibilities for commodity flow in children's television, several hours of programming from five different networks were taped and analyzed on two separate dates. Three continuous hours of programming (from 8 am to 11 am, EST) were collected on Saturday, July 29, 2000, and Saturday, January 26, 2002, for a total of 30 hours. Two different time periods were chosen to prevent analyzing an atypical historical moment, such as the highly commodified Pokémon craze in the late 1990s. In addition, two seasons, summer (from 2000) and winter (2002), were selected to avoid a sample skewed by calendar-based promotions or contests. The five networks (three cable and two broadcast) videotaped were ABC, Cartoon Network, FOX, Nickelodeon, and the WB. These five networks were chosen for study, given their uninterrupted three-hour block of children's programming (unlike NBC or CBS), their stable nature (unlike the troubled Family Channel, see Dempsey, 2001b), and their acceptance of product advertising (unlike PBS or The Disney Channel).

Tapings were coordinated so that analysis began at exactly 8 am, to enable cross-channel comparisons of images and content types. The authors took detailed notes about iconography, sounds, language, and other textual characteristics. They also noted the beginning and ending time of the discrete units of content types found on children's television: program credits, program segment beginning and endings, program separators, product commercials, promotional spots for programs, network and station IDs, and PSAs. The resulting 131 pages of single-spaced notes were then extensively re-read and compared to uncover points of convergence and emerging themes and groupings. Moreover, video tape segments were often viewed again to expand the analysis.[1]

Guiding the analysis of the programming and the subsequent notes was the idea of commodity flow, the main "sensitized concept" of the study. Sensitized concepts are "taxonomical systems that discover an integrating scheme within the data themselves" and facilitate analytical focus in qualitative research (Christians & Carey, 1989, p. 370). Using commodity flow as a significant sensitized concept enabled a focus on connections between content categories, especially when these connections involved commercial and promotional forms. These connections were then used to generate styles and categories of commodity flow. Various forms in the enhanced commercial and synergistically promotional environment of children's television often blur the distinctions among traditional content types, different networks, and even different media. The remainder of this article analyzes three kinds of commodity flow emerging from the programming: intra-channel commodity flow, inter-channel commodity flow, and synergistic commodity flow.

Intra-Channel Commodity Flow

Among the most common of the commodity flow categories found during the telecasts was intra-channel commodity flow, where commodity images are interwoven throughout the line-up of one network. The researchers found several sub-categories of intra-channel commodity flow.

Shared Textual Elements Between Programs and Commercials

Seiter (1993) notes that children's television commercials are "rapidly paced, musical, and filled with special effects and animation. Children behave raucously, outsmarting adults and escaping the dull restrictions of home and school" (p. 3). This, of course, also describes much of the children's programming that airs between the commercials. The visual styles and sounds of commercials and children's programs are strikingly similar.

Animation, obviously, is a common modality found throughout children's television. Often, the specific style of the animation of commercials matches that of other content types such as programs, program promos, and program separators. For example, in the 2002 ABC sample, similar visual styles mark the 8:00 am cartoon program *Mary Kate and Ashley in Action!* This program features the animated adventures of the Olsen twin sisters as secret agents, but the beginning and end of the program are live action segments featuring the actors Mary Kate and Ashley Olsen. This mix of live action and animation continue in a program separator at 8:27:35, which presents a live-action small girl (about the same age as Mary Kate and Ashley) dancing with an animated "1" (as in "Disney's 1 Saturday Morning," the network's branding slogan at the time). Immediately following, at 8:27:41, a commercial for Honeycombs cereal airs, with a plot involving a live-action snowboarder morphing into the animated Honeycomb "Craver." This is followed at 8:28:11 by a Three Musketeers candy bar ad, where the animated Musketeers accept a "Chocolately Award" at a live-action ceremony. Following this is a 15-second promotion for *Disney's Teacher's Pet* (all animated), back to the girl-dancing program separator, and then finally the life-action epilogue with Mary Kate and Ashley. Similar matching of styles continues throughout Saturday morning.

Sounds between commercials and other program types also match. In primetime television, the sound difference between programs and commercials is often significant. Adult television programs tend to be fairly sedate in terms of music and sound effects; the ads feature such elements more prominently. However, jarring sound effects and loud rock or hip-hop music are much more common in children's programming, matching the surrounding commercials. Sounds of conflict and strident music may be found in action-adventure cartoons and commercials for toys, such as a sequence on FOX 2002 that featured violent conflict and action music in a *Power Rangers Time Force* episode (8:31), a Lego commercial featuring Star Wars characters (8:34) and a promo for the spin-off *Power Rangers Wild Force* (8:35).

Similarly, the role of laughter varies more widely in primetime content forms than in children's television. Most primetime situation comedies feature a laugh-track or live audience reactions, an audio characteristic missing in most commercials. Alternatively, laugh tracks from real or virtual audiences are absent from children's programming, matching their absence in the ads. Tellingly, though, children's laughter itself (emanating from characters) is found in nearly all content forms, including programs and ads, depending upon the target demographic. One such example was a two-minute stretch on ABC 2002 that featured similar sounds of children laughing/playing on the opening credits of the *Recess* program, and the subsequent ABC program separator and Kool-Aid commercial.

Programming Featuring Licensed Characters

Virtually all Saturday morning programming involves licensing to some degree. Even a commercially sedate program like *Doug* (aired in 2000 on ABC at 8:30 and 9:00 am) has been available in video games (for Game Boy), theatrical film (with the franchise-hopeful title *Doug's 1st Movie*), video tapes, and books (well over 20 different titles).

Much Saturday morning programming is more definitively embedded in ancillary licensing. Many of these programs have their roots in video games, toys, or other merchandise. The WB and Fox in particular aired programming spun off from licensed commodities (see Tables 7.1 and 7.2). Nearly 80% of programs aired or promoted during the period sampled were based upon characters with strong ties to other media or commodities, including comic books (*Batman/Superman Adventures, Static Shock, X-Men*), movies (*The Mummy, Alienators: Evolution Continues, Jackie Chan Adventures*), book series (*R. L Stine's The Nightmare Room*), and toys (*Transformers, Action Man, Dinozaurs*).

Strikingly commodified are *Pokémon* and variations of this model, such as *Digimon, Monster Rancher, Medabot, Cubix, Mon Colle Knights, Yu-Gi-Oh!*, and *Card Captors*. *Pokémon*, a dominating brand in the child market from 1996 to 2001 (Tobin, 2004), represents the genre; plots ask characters to collect items such as cards or small creatures (*Pokémon* is an abbreviation of "Pocket Monster"), with the outcome of a key competition or even the fate of the world often hanging in the balance. In the programs these items are magical; in real life they are for sale. Specific plot points often emphasized the importance of amassing large collections (à la the Pokémon brand slogan "Gotta Catch 'Em All"). In a *Pokémon* episode on the WB 2000, one character states explicitly, "The more Pokémon you have, the better position you are in to win battles." Given the emphasis on collecting implied in nearly all of the above listed cartoons, the programs function as virtual commercials for the licensed collectables featured in the cartoons and related subsidiary properties.

One commodity flow element driving this point home was the use of multiple content forms to create a flow of licensed programming icons on a given network. As promoted programs *and* advertised products *and* cross-promoted/cross-mediated characters, images from licensed properties are sprinkled throughout the lineup. An example of this is seen in Table 7.3, which lists the promotional and commercial moments aired between 8:13 and 10:58 am for *Digimon*, which in July 2000 was Fox's highest rated children's program (Hall, 2000). The promotions and product commercials

Table 7.1 List of Children's Morning Programs Shown or Promoted on FOX during the Time Sampled (in order of first appearance)

July 29, 2000

Power Rangers LightSpeed Rescue[a]
Action Man[a] (based upon a Hasbro property[c])
Beast Machine[a]
Digimon[ab]
Angela Anaconda
NASCAR Racers[a]
Cybersix
X-Men[ab]
Dinozaurs[a] (based on action figures created by Bondai[c])
Flint the Time Detective
Escaflowne
Pokémon[ab] (syndicated version: local promo)
Histeria!
Monster Rancher[a]

January 26, 2002

Transformers: Robots in Disguise[a]
Digimon[ab]
Power Rangers Wild Force[a]
Galidor[a] (a "Lego-collaboration action show"[d])
Medabots[a]
Power Rangers Time Force[a]
Ripping Friends
Mon Colle Knights[a] (stands for "Monster Collector Knights")
Alienators: Evolution Continues[a] (based on the movie *Evolution*)

a A program that is heavily commodity-oriented through licensing activities in the U.S.
b A program with specific characters also used in commercials or other forms to promote product licensing during telecast.
c From Hall (2000).
d From Finnigan (2002).

create a steady flow of licensed images that connect the *Digimon* program with the Digimon website, the then-upcoming *Digimon the Movie*, Digimon video games, the brand identity of FoxKids, its website, and the various programs that Digimon promotions are connected to through "bug" symbols. Although only promotions for the Digimon television program aired during the Digimon program (i.e., no product commercials, thus fulfilling the letter of the Children's Television Act of 1990), the multi-licensed commodity orientation of the Digimon brand makes such distinctions irrelevant. Indeed, some forms, such as a "promotion" for the FoxKids *Digimon the Movie* tie-in contest, are difficult to classify. It could be legitimately labeled both a promotion for *Digimon* on FoxKids and an advertisement for the *Digimon* movie.

Programming Icons in Commercials

While the above practice integrates the commercial function into programs, another strategy creates "camouflaged ads" (McAllister, 1996) by making product commercials

Table 7.2 List of Saturday Morning Programs Shown or Promoted on the WB during the Time Sampled (in order of first appearance)

July 29, 2000
Batman/Superman Adventures[a]
Pokémon[ab]
Men in Black[a]
Cardcaptors[a]
Batman Beyond[a]
Detention

January 26, 2002
Cubix[a]
Jackie Chan Adventures[a]
Pokémon[a]
Static Shock[a]
Scooby-Doo[a]
Magic Schoolbus (local promo for a program on a competitor station)
The Mummy[a]
X-Men:Evolution[a]
R.L. Stine's The Nightmare Room[a]
Yu-Gi-Oh![a]

a A program that is heavily commodity-oriented through licensing activities in the U.S.
b A program with specific characters also used in commercials or other forms to promote product licensing during telecast.

look like programs. A primary mechanism for this is integrating television program characters into these product commercials.

For example, an ad for "The New Rugrats Edition Gateway Astro PC" (at 10:43:29) that aired on Nickelodeon during a 2000 installment of *Spongebob Squarepants*—and one that is part of a larger cross-promotional campaign between network and advertiser (Sandler, 2004)—uses clips and sounds from *Rugrats*. Although the commercial itself combines animation and live action, it begins with animation directly lifted from a *Rugrats* episode; the first sounds heard are the title music that also begins the program. The ad uses seven different clips from *Rugrats*, all intercut between live-action clips of a little girl laughingly using her *Rugrats*-branded personal computer. An episode of *Rugrats* had concluded on the network just 43 minutes earlier. Similarly, in 2000 a cross-promotional ad for Pokémon toys at Burger King featuring Pokémon animation aired on the WB in 2000—also carrying *Pokémon* the network program—and on the local FOX affiliate that also carried *Pokémon* the syndicated program. At 9:12 am in 2000, the Cartoon Network characters Cow and Chicken appear in a Got Milk ad on that network.

Kunkel & McIlrath (2003) argue that some product advertising may mask selling intentions by resembling the more benign public service announcement (PSA). PSAs likewise can be integrated into the larger licensed promotional flow of children's television. Resembling both the Fox cartoon *NASCAR Racer* and promotions for the program, a "wear your seatbelt" PSA aired on Fox 2000 (10:33 am, 90 minutes after the program ended) integrates icons, footage, music, and sounds of the cartoon with a message from real-life NASCAR racer Jeff Gordon and stock footage of a NASCAR race. Gordon is visually framed by a FoxKids graphic and wears his racing outfit, which

Table 7.3 Flow of *Digimon* Images, Fox, July 29, 2000

Time	Image
8:13:02	Promotion for *Digimon* summer reruns, framed with FoxKids logo (:20 seconds)
8:23:58	Promotion for *Digimon* summer reruns
8:34:36	Product commercial for Digimon website, which shows Digimon-licensed merchandise available in eight different product categories (:25 seconds)
8:41:51	Promotion for *Digimon* summer reruns
8:49:20	Promotion for FoxKids *Digimon The Movie* tie-in contest (:40 seconds); winners receive "Digimon Game Guide"
8:50:20	Promotion for *Digimon* summer reruns
8:57:27	Promotion in bug: Digimon character appears in bottom corner during the program *NASCAR Racer* (:10 seconds)
9:00:01	Program: *Digimon* first episode begins (:30 minutes)
9:14:37	Promotion for *Digimon* upcoming season (:20 seconds)
9:17:34	Promotion: Digimon character appears in promo for foxkids.com website
9:28:27	Promotion during credits, for *Digimon* summer reruns
9:43:17	Promotion for *Digimon* summer reruns
9:43:37	Promotion: Digimon character appears in promo for foxkids.com website
9:51:16	Promotion of FoxKids *Digimon The Movie* tie-in contest
10:10:05	Promotion for *Digimon* summer reruns
10:20:50	Promotion of FoxKids *Digimon The Movie* tie-in contest
10:27:10	Promotion in Bug: Digimon character appears in bottom corner during the program *Monster Rancher* (:10 seconds)
10:30:39	Program: *Digimon* second episode begins (:30 minutes)
10:43:30	Promotion for *Digimon* upcoming season
10:57:57	Promotion: narrator promotes *Digimon* upcoming season during closing credits

prominently displays sponsor logos such as Pepsi and GMAC. The PSA—essentially a promotion for the cartoon, NASCAR, and its merchandise and sponsors—ends with the same group voice from the cartoon's opening credits that shouts "NASCAR!" As a PSA, it is not counted toward the commercial limits imposed by the Children's Television Act of 1990.

Inter-Channel Commodity Flow

Although a significant part of television scheduling and advertising placement is still premised on the idea of the "lazy viewer," the remote control and channel surfing that results has nevertheless affected much programming placement strategy (Bellamy & Walker, 1996). Channel surfing by potentially short-attention-span child viewers is assumed to occur especially frequently. The same commercial is sometimes placed on different channels at the same time to try to "roadblock" those trying to escape ads via the remote control (McAllister, 1996).

With children's television, it is unclear how much inter-channel placement results from strategy, and how much is a matter of sheer redundancy. Many advertising and merchandising campaigns purchase multiple placements on the networks, so that even active channel surfers cannot avoid these ads. One common advertisement found during the 2002 sample, for instance, was for *MVP2: Most Vertical Primate*, a direct-to-DVD movie about a skateboarding chimpanzee (and sequel to *Most Valuable Primate*, about a hockey-playing chimpanzee). This advertisement aired 21 times during the three-hour sample across the five networks: ABC (six times), Cartoon (two), FOX (six), Nickelodeon (two), and WB (five). Inevitably, then, a roadblock, whether intentional or not, occurred on four of the six networks during one four-minute stretch: This ad appeared at 8:47:16 on WB; 8:50:09 on ABC; 8:51:07 on FOX; and 8:51:10 on the Cartoon Network.

This inter-channel commodity flow across networks was also true not just for one ad placed many times, but also for licenses that appear in many promotional forms. In 2002, 15 minutes before a promotion for *The Flintstones* program on the Cartoon Network, its sibling the WB aired a Fruity Pebbles cereal ad featuring Fred and Barney in a commercial mock-up of another program, *Survivor*. More extensive was Pokémon, still a hot property during the 2000 sample. Commercials for Pokémon products and for cross-promotional activities with fast-food restaurants as well as promotions for movies and TV were ubiquitous on the five-channel schedule of the sample. Table 7.4 focuses on 12 minutes when an active channel surfer could view promotional iconography of Pokémon on all five cable networks. Forms include ads for Pokémon products (a trading card league) and media extensions (the movie version), a promotional spot for the program, and tie-ins in advertisements for Burger King and the snack food Fruit by the Foot. Perhaps exploiting the potential for these multi-channel lead-in promotions, *Pokémon* the program begins a half-hour later on the WB.

Synergistic Commodity Flow

Besides the encroachment of product advertisements on other content categories in children's television, another influence on commodity flow is the corporate interests of the network's conglomerate owner. As noted earlier, all five networks studied are owned by entertainment media corporations. These corporations advocate promotional synergies, whereby any given property is used to promote other properties or an overarching corporate brand. Such activity adds a layer of media product promotion upon the traditional toy, cereal, and snack food product commodity flow in children's television. This strategy was especially evident for the corporations with significant multi-media branding targeted at children: Disney, Viacom, and Time Warner.

Table 7.4 *Pokémon* Iconography "Roadblock" on Five Networks, July 29, 2000

8:21:42, ABC	Commercial with cross-promotion (Burger King ad with a *Pokémon the Movie* tie-in)
8:27:40, WB	Program promotion (*Pokémon* mentioned as part of summer line-up)
8:28:15, NICK	Commercial for licensed product (Pokémon Trading Card League)
8:28:52, CN	Commercial for licensed product (Pokémon Trading Card League)
8:29:10, WB	Commercial for cross-promotion and licensed product (Pokémon video game shown in a Fruit-by-the-Foot tie-in with Nintendo)
8:33:36, FOX	Commercial with cross-promotion (Burger King ad with a *Pokémon the Movie* tie-in)

Disney has been especially aggressive in using its broadcasting and cable outlets to create a corporate brand. Many critics accuse Disney of appropriating culturally rich stories through corporate ownership and then transforming these texts into ideological visions of life that connect to the interests of corporate capitalism and patriarchy (see, for example, Giroux, 2001). Often the specific texts that Disney is accused of appropriating are classic fairy tales, such as Snow White and Cinderella. However, Disney stamps its identity on more recent cultural materials as well. As Table 7.5 shows, most of the ABC programs shown during the sample have a possessive modifier in their title: "Disney's——." This title characteristic explicitly signals Disney's owner-ship and connects the brand identity of the corporation with the specific program. This is true even for a program like *Doug*, which originally aired on Nickelodeon in 1991. Disney's name in the altered official title of the program, the result of a production company purchase in 1996, may be legally correct. However, the title *Disney's Doug* symbolically overwhelms the important role and original authorship of the program's creator, Jim Jinkins.

Even the other non-"Disney's" programs on ABC's Saturday morning schedule ultimately have their own synergistic purpose. *Sabrina, the Animated Series* (the title of which connotes "spin-off") in 2000 helped to plug the primetime *Sabrina, the Teenage Witch*, at that time still airing on ABC. In 2002, *Mary Kate and Ashley in Action!* helped create an inter-channel flow, as other Olsen programs like *Two of a Kind* and *So Little Time* were shown on the ABC Family Channel. *Two of a Kind* on ABC Family aired at 7:30 am, immediately before its cartoon equivalent on ABC, creating a quasi-interchannel lead-in. *Lizzie McGuire* and *Even Stevens* are "Powered by Zoog," as ABC program separators and other promotions informed viewers. "Zoog" was a "tween-targeted" programming brand strongly tied with The Disney's Channel's lineup. Both *Lizzie* and *Stevens* were shown on ABC and The Disney Channel during this time. One ABC promotional spot (10:54) tells viewers that *Lizzie McGuire* may also be found on The Disney Channel: this promotion aired about a half-hour after the ABC version of the program ended. Thus, a paradox in the new synergistic media environment is the promotion of a cable network by a broadcast network owned by the same corporate owner, essentially urging viewers to switch channels.

Other content forms besides the programs tout the Disney brand on ABC Saturday mornings. In 2000, the interstitial programming "Disney's One Saturday Morning" promoted Disney and featured Disney characters like Timon and Pumbaa from *The Lion King* in short skits. In a very similar manner, the shorter program separators (with a narrator saying "Disney's One Saturday Morning will be right back" and

Table 7.5 ABC's Program Line-Up, 8–11 am, July 29, 2000 and January 26, 2002

2000[a]	2002
Disney's Recess	*Mary Kate and Ashley in Action!*
Disney's Doug	*Disney's Teacher's Pet*
Disney's Recess	*Disney's Recess*
Disney's The Weekenders	*Disney's Recess*
Sabrina, The Animated Series	*Lizzie McGuire*
	Even Stevens

a Interstitial programming ("One Saturday Morning") filled the remainder half-hour.

the word Disney prominently displayed) do not separate Disney content from the Disney ads and Disney promotions at all. Instead, they become modern versions of "segue ads" from the 1950s, playing up the Disney brand and connecting programs to more conventional forms of commercial culture. ABC telecasts commercials for Disney products (*Atlantis* on DVD, 2002, for example) and promotions for Disney programs (*Disney's Mickey Mouse Works* on ABC, which aired after 11 am that day and therefore not part of the sample) to fill any potential void in the flow of Disney branding. As Table 7.6 illustrates, in the 2002 broadcast nearly all content types (with the exception of the few PSAs) mentioned or showed Disney, often quite extensively. This, then, creates a promotional flow whereby Disney's name is displayed or uttered 178 times during the three-hour span, nearly once a minute in ads, promotions, and programs. ABC essentially becomes, at least on Saturday mornings, a Disney branding channel.

Other networks also use their children's daypart to promote synergistic holdings. The Nickelodeon/Jimmy Neutron example cited earlier highlights the influence of synergy in that venue. For Time Warner holdings, an ad for *Pokémon the Movie 2000* airs on the Cartoon Network 2000 (9:26) at the same time that the *Pokémon* program is shown on the WB. This strategy subverts restrictions against program-length commercials and host-selling by using two different channels to link product (the movie) to the program. In addition, synergy was at the heart of the Pokémon property for Time Warner, creating an added incentive. Warner Brothers Pictures and Nintendo were involved with the production/distribution of *Pokémon the Movie 2000*. Meanwhile, Atlantic Records, a subsidiary of Time Warner, produced the sound track, which is also touted on the commercial for the movie.

The Internet is a large part of the synergistic strategy, encouraging an "inter-media" commodity flow, or an "overflow" (Brooker, 2001). The major children's programming players all have websites aimed at children (disney.com, foxkids.com, kidswb.com, cartoonnetwork.com, nick.com), and sometimes more than one; toonami.com, a Time Warner website hyped by both WB and Cartoon Network, for example, is devoted to action cartoons and anime. These sites are promoted through bugs (that often transform from the corporate name to the website address), squeezed credits, and their own promotional spots.

Such sites help to extend the brand, create sites to sell merchandise, and further encourage the flow of audiences through corporate programming. In a promotional spot for both *The Mummy* and kidswb.com that was shown on WB 2002, a contest is touted

Table 7.6 Instances of Visual Appearance and Vocal Mentions of "Disney" on ABC, 8–11 am, January 26, 2002

Content type	Visual appearance	Vocal mention
Program title/opening credits	9	0
Program ending credits	16	6
Program separators	43	43
Product advertisements	8	4
Program promotions	32	11
Network/station ID	6	0
Public service announcements	0	0
Totals	114	64

called "Ask Imhotep." The spot is shown at 9:52, during *The Mummy*, and repeated at 10:17. The narrator says, "Kids WB is giving you a chance to ask Imhotep [the Mummy's name] anything you want to know . . . Go to kidswb.com and ask your question. And then watch Kids WB on Saturday, February 9th, and Imhotep might read your question on TV." This spot, then, directs audiences from the TV to the Internet (where on-line shopping opportunities exist) and back to the TV. A similar tactic is used by the Cartoon Network in its 2002 Batman/Superman voting competition where viewers can "go to toonami.com, choose your favorite [character], and play them in a new on-line game . . . The winner is announced at 5 [on Cartoon Network]." One difference, as the narrator in a later version of the spot informs us, is that this network/Internet promotion is also a type of product ad, because it is "Brought to you by Gatorade . . . Is it in You?" In fact, the narrator for this promotion, although of course uncredited, sounds very much like Kevin Conroy, the actor who is the voice for Batman and has narrated earlier, stand-alone Gatorade commercials. This promotional spot pulls extra duty, plugging with the same images and sounds: (1) Cartoon Network; (2) Batman licenses; (3) Superman licenses; (4) DC Comics (owned by Time Warner); (5) the toonami brand and website; and (6) Gatorade.

Conclusion

This analysis of commodity flow on children's television shows the intrusion of selling and branding strategies across many content forms, and the erosion of distinctions between these forms that this intrusion fosters. The heavy commercialism found throughout the history of U.S. children's television notwithstanding, the increasingly strategic nature of commodity flow and the promotional synergy of entertainment corporations add levels of integration. Specific forms of flow subvert policy restrictions designed to decrease commercialism. Program separators and PSAs, for instance, become part of the branding mix rather than barriers to commercial blurring.

Both samples showed strong indicators of flow. However, even in the modest time that elapsed between 2000 and 2002, increases in promotional flows may be seen. Although the 2000 sample featured the visibility of collector programs like Pokémon and Digimon that were nearing the end of their reign, the 2002 sample offered more systematic integration of cross-promotion between corporate holdings, such as the multi-licensed promotion of Jimmy Neutron and the repurposing (Sandler, 2003, 2004) of programs like *Lizzie McGuire* from the Disney Channel to ABC, promoting and branding the former while decreasing production costs for the latter. Web addresses and promotions of websites were frequent in 2000, but the strategic movement of children to commercially friendly sites—such as the Mummy and Superman/Batman "contests" mentioned above—indicates that new techniques are evolving to fully integrate the Internet.

As noted earlier, some critics of the concept of television flow claim that it essentializes television and masks key distinctions among content categories found on television (discussed in Corner, 1999). In fact, there were moments of *disjunction* in the sample. Many PSAs were more sedate, shorter, and less sales-oriented than many of the forms around them, such as a 10-second PSA for the music-oriented website playmusic.org (ABC, 2002, 9:51, repeated at 10:31). Especially on the cable networks, an occasional "old school" commercial featured a traditional authoritarian male narrator discussing an educational product targeted more to parents than children, such as a two-minute long Zoobooks commercial on the Cartoon Network, at 8:41 am in 2002. But these differences were rare in the larger promotional environment, which featured other forms that were more synergistically and stylistically a part of the flow.

Another criticism of flow research is that it is typically "source-biased," and does not take into account the variability in reception contexts and interpretative frameworks that audiences bring to bear (see Budd et al., 1999). In particular, Seiter (1993) argues that children are perhaps more sophisticated television viewers than many researchers assume. It is true that this study did not analyze audience reception of flow, and no doubt children vary in how they view the images targeted to them.

Yet implied by this analysis is a concern about differences in social power between sources and audiences in children's television. Through collective ownership, media corporations are increasingly joined; audience members are isolated from each other. Corporations have collected much proprietary research about audience behavior, research that they are not compelled to make public. Children collectively have significant purchasing influence, but little political influence. Perhaps more significantly, children's self-concept is still being formed, while advertising and media brands have been solidly formed through a torrent of marketing research and branding messages. Children face waves of images of themselves and things they love that are increasingly connected together by a dominant message: "You should buy/watch this as part of being a kid." What, then, does this power difference between sources and audiences lead to? Although more research is needed, evidence exists that children's advertising may cultivate materialistic values among young viewers (Smith & Atkin, 2003). As media synergy and branding have come to dominate children's television as much if not more than more traditional toy and cereal advertising, the message of "you are what you watch" may contribute to the historically commodified ethos of product advertising by encouraging the purchasing and consuming of media products that connect so many different content forms.

More precise and assertive policy may help considerably. So may the viewing context. Parents as mediators—watching television with their children, for example—can blunt the cultivation of material values with children's television viewing (Smith & Atkin, 2003). But constantly evolving forms of promotion challenge the effectiveness of slow-moving policy development and the role of adult mediators. Much of the research about the effects of children's television examines the extent to which children can distinguish between commercials, which primarily have a selling function, and programs, which primarily have entertainment or educational function (Smith & Atkin, 2003). How do parents respond when there is little distinction? What happens when devices that were mandated to circumscribe the selling function (like program separators and PSAs discussed earlier) actually enhance it through their integration with branding strategies? How may regulation deal with new, more subtle forms of selling and promotion that are difficult to separate from other television forms, and that seem designed to undermine existing policy? Children may be at risk of growing up in a world with fewer "ad-free" cultural zones, zones that can serve as important high ground above commodity tidal waves.

Questions

1   What factors have led to the increased commercialization of children's television in the late 1990s, early 2000s?
2   What are the three main types of commodity flow on children's television, and what are their characteristics?
3   In what ways has current FCC policy failed to contain promotion on children's television?
4   How does Disney create a "branded, synergistic" flow on ABC?
5   Are there new forms of "commodity flow" in television, or between television and the Internet, that we see now?

Note

1.   One author analyzed all of the programming from the 2000 tapes, and the 2002 programming was divided up for analysis by the two authors (with one author taking ABC, Cartoon Network, and the WB; and the other taking FOX and Nickelodeon). Although the primary method is not a quantitative content analysis per se, training and double checks were conducted to increase the validity of the analysis. The researchers discussed their notes and analysis of textual characteristics. In addition, one stretch of programming was viewed by both researchers to check for similarities in uncovering textual nuances and similarities. Finally, the separate notes of the two researchers were compared for agreement when the same commercial or other program type was analyzed by both researchers, a common occurrence given the repetition found in children's television.

References

Alexander, A., Benjamin, L. M., Hoerrner, K., & Roe, D. (1998). "We'll be back in a moment": A content analysis of advertisements in children's television in the 1950s. *Journal of Advertising, 27*, 3, 1–9.

Andersen, R. (1995). *Consumer culture and TV programming*. Boulder, CO: Westview Press.

Bagdikian, B. (2004). *The new media monopoly* (7th ed.). Boston: Beacon.

Bellamy, R. V., & Walker, J. R. (1996). *Television and the remote control: Grazing on a vast wasteland*. New York: Guilford.

Bernstein, P. (2001, December 17). Ayem kid biz losing fizz. *Variety*, pp. 30–31.

Brooker, W. (2001). Living on Dawson's Creek: Teen viewers, cultural convergence, and television overflow. *International Journal of Cultural Studies, 4*, 456–472.

Budd, M., Craig, S., & Steinman, C. (1999). *Consuming environments: Television and commercial culture*. New Brunswick, NJ: Rutgers University Press.

Christians, C. G., & Carey, J. W. (1989). The logic and aims of qualitative research. In G. H. Stempel III, & B. H. Westley (Eds.), *Research methods in mass communication* (2nd ed., pp. 354–374). Englewood Cliffs, NJ: Prentice-Hall.

Corner, J. (1999). *Critical ideas in television studies*. Oxford: Clarendon Press.

Dempsey, J. (2001a, September 3). Disney Channel primo with tweens. *Variety*, p. 24.

Dempsey, J. (2001b, May 28–June 3). Fox Family put up for adoption. *Variety*, pp. 13–14.

Finnigan, D. (2002, June 17). When it comes to pitching properties almost everything old is new again. *Brandweek*, pp. 10–11.

Giroux, H. A. (2001). *The mouse that roared: Disney and the end of innocence.* New York: Rowman and Littlefield.

Hall, W. J. (2000, April 10). The toys are back in town. *Variety,* p. 55.

Jacobson, N. F., & Mazur, L. A. (1995). *Marketing madness: A survival guide for a consumer society.* Boulder, CO: Westview.

Kapur, J. (1999). Out of control: Television and the transformation of childhood in late capitalism. In M. Kinder (Ed.), *Kids' media culture* (pp. 122–128). Raleigh, NC: Duke University Press.

Kinder, M. (1999). Ranging with power on the Fox Kids Network: Or, where on earth is children's educational television? In M. Kinder (Ed.), *Kids' media culture* (pp. 177–203). Raleigh, NC: Duke University Press.

Kline, S. (1993). *Out of the garden: Toys and children's culture in the age of TV marketing.* London: Verso.

Kunkel, D. (2001). Children and television advertising. In D. G. Singer, & J. L. Singer (Eds.), *Handbook of children and the media* (pp. 375–393). Thousand Oaks, CA: Sage.

Kunkel, D., & McIlrath, M. (2003). Message content in advertising to children. In E. L. Palmer & B. M. Young (Eds.), *The faces of televisual media: Teaching, violence, selling to children* (2nd ed., pp. 287–300). Mahwah, NJ: Erlbaum.

Larson, M. (2001, August 13). Kids anticlimax: Upfront is a dud. *Mediaweek,* p. 4.

McAllister, M. P. (1996). *The commercialization of American culture: New advertising, control and democracy.* Thousand Oaks, CA: Sage.

McAllister, M. P. (2000). From flick to flack: The increased emphasis on marketing by media entertainment corporations. In R. Andersen, & L. A. Strate (Eds.), *Critical studies in media commercialism* (pp. 101–122). New York: Oxford University Press.

McChesney, R. W. (1999). *Rich media, poor democracy: Communication politics in dubious times.* Urbana, IL: University of Illinois Press.

McDonald, M., & Lavelle, M. (2001, July 30). Call it "kid-fluence.". *U.S. News and World Report,* p. 32.

Mittell, J. (2003). The great Saturday morning exile: Scheduling cartoons on television's periphery in the 1960s. In C. A. Stabile, & M. Harrison (Eds.), *Prime time animation: Television animation and American culture* (pp. 33–54). New York: Routledge.

Modleski, T. (1983). The rhythms of reception: Daytime television and women's work. In E. A. Kaplan (Ed.), *Regarding television: Critical approaches—an anthology* (pp. 67–75). Los Angeles: The American Film Institute.

Pecora, N. (1998). *The business of children's entertainment.* New York: Guilford.

Pecora, N. (2004). Nickelodeon grows up: The economic evolution of a network. In H. Hendershot (Ed.), *Nickelodeon nation: The history, politics, and economics of America's only TV channel for kids* (pp. 15–44). New York: New York University Press.

Sandler, K. S. (2003). Synergy nirvana: Brand equity, television animation, and Cartoon Network. In C. A. Stabile, & M. Harrison (Eds.), *Prime time animation: Television animation and American culture* (pp. 89–109). New York: Routledge.

Sandler, K. S. (2004). "A kid's gotta do what a kid's gotta do": Branding the Nickelodeon experience. In H. Hendershot (Ed.), *Nickelodeon nation: The history, politics, and economics of America's only TV channel for kids* (pp. 45–68). New York: New York University Press.

Schmuckler, E. (2002, April 1). Looking for a fight. *Mediaweek,* pp. 23–26.

Seiter, E. (1993). *Sold separately: Children and parents in consumer culture.* New Brunswick, NJ: Rutgers University Press.

Smith, S. L., & Atkin, C. (2003). Television advertising and children: Examining the intended and unintended effects. In E. L. Palmer, & B. M. Young (Eds.), *The faces of televisual media: Teaching, violence, selling to children* (2nd ed., pp. 301–325). Mahwah, NJ: Erlbaum.

Smythe, D. (1977). Communications: Blindspot of western Marxism. *Canadian Journal of Political and Social Theory, 1,* 3, 1–27.

Tobin, J. (2004). Introduction. In J. Tobin (Ed.), *Pikachu's global adventure: The rise and fall of Pokémon* (pp. 3–11). Durham, NC: Duke University Press.

Williams, R. (1975). *Television: Technology and cultural form.* New York: Schocken.

PART THREE

Creating Advertising

INTRODUCTION TO PART THREE

ASIDE FROM MEDIA AND ADVERTISERS, another key player in the advertising industry is the advertising agency. Although ad agencies are among the least well-known organizations to the general public, they play a central role in advertising activities. For example, they often are responsible for creating the advertising campaigns and the specific ads that are a part of the campaigns. The slogans, jingles, commercial actors, premises, and other elements involved in the symbolic makeup of advertisements are commonly turned out by the creative talent at agencies. But agencies also engage in other marketing activities. Large ad agencies are involved in marketing research, for instance. They gather information concerning awareness of and opinions about brand image, competitors, and potential and current ad campaigns. One of the most important activities they carry out is "media planning," a process in which decisions are made about the placement of ads. This involves choosing the particular media mix (such as radio, television, print, online), as well as the frequency of the ads' placement in the various media. In addition, agencies often work with media buying firms to purchase the ads, making the agencies an especially powerful group in the relationship between advertisers and media companies. With the rise of Integrated Marketing Communications (IMC), major advertising agencies may coordinate the various publicity, sales, promotion, public relations, and advertising activities of a brand to maximize the cultural volume that a consistent sales message may achieve.

The three readings focus on important processes in modern advertising agencies. The chapter by Kelly, Lawlor and O'Donohoe highlights the dilemmas of modern creative workers in the advertising industry. They ask, what are some of the peculiar tensions that those who create modern ad campaigns face? The contribution by Leonard argues that major changes are occurring in the ad agencies as they deal with the rise of online media and such viewing technologies as digital video recorders (DVR). Leonard posits that the power in agencies is shifting from the creative departments to media planning/buying as the media landscape becomes more complicated. Our last chapter in this Part is a case study involving a major advertiser, Philip Morris, targeting a gay market with a campaign for a dangerous product, tobacco. The story involves a collision of social issues regarding public health, corporate brand marketing, and homophobia.

Chapter 8

AIDAN KELLY, KATRINA LAWLOR, AND STEPHANIE O'DONOHOE

ENCODING ADVERTISEMENTS
The Creative Perspective

THE AUTHORS EXPLORE THE "CULTURE" OF advertising agencies using interviews and ethnography. Ethnography is a research methodology often employed by anthropologists to understand a culture, in this case the mini-culture of organizations. They explore the tensions that creative workers in agencies experience in their role as "cultural intermediaries," or those who translate cultural trends given their unique and often privileged place in society. As people who create advertisements—often influenced by marketing research about the latest trends—advertising creators are influential cultural intermediaries.

The authors note that ad creatives are often very aware of the "intertextual" nature of their work, where advertising refers to—and assumes that consumers know about—the latest thing in popular culture such as hit songs, TV programs, and movies. The chapter also highlights the work tensions that advertising creatives face, including tensions with other divisions such as research or media planning. This point fore-shadows ideas in the next chapter by Leonard. A key "battleground" is with the client, who frequently may express dissatisfaction with the creative ideas for an ad campaign generated by the agency.

Introduction

Advertising is a potent form of mass communication which is instrumental in providing products with symbolic meaning and developing symbolic associations for brands within consumer culture (Elliott 1999). However the work of advertising agencies and adver-tising practitioners as cultural intermediaries within this process remains relatively under-explored and under-theorised within the advertising and marketing disciplines. This paper considers the work of copywriters and art directors within advertising agencies, both in terms of critical perspectives on advertising as cultural and social production (Elliott and Ritson 1997; Goldman and Papson 1996; Jhally 1987), and in terms of recent ethnographic studies outside of the advertising and marketing literature which have explored the work of these cultural intermediaries from anthropological, cultural studies, and sociological perspectives (Cronin 2004a; Dewaal Malefyt and Moeran 2003; Lien 1997; Moeran 2005).

[. . .]

Advertising and the Cultural and Social World

[. . .] Advertisements work through the appropriation and incorporation of social discourses and the meaning structures of the cultural world through what McCracken (1986:74) has labelled as "meaning transfer", and by drawing upon the meanings which reside within the cultural and social world advertising works as a conduit streaming system to transfer these meanings to consumer goods. Advertising has an acknowledged dialogical and intertextual structure (Cook 1992; Fowles 1996; O'Donohoe 1997), which draws upon a multitude of cultural codes, ideologies, and discourses, such as music, books, movies, art, politics, current affairs, and celebrities to construct meaning (McCracken 1989; Scott 1990). Within the context of consumer culture advertising can be seen to "shape and reflect" social reality, by drawing upon patterns of meaning within the cultural and social world to construct symbolic associations for consumer goods, and these commodity discourses become ingrained within popular psyche and shape consumer experiences of social reality (Sherry 1987). Advertisements have become an integrated part of the popular culture which they parody (Olsen 2003), and by drawing upon socially situated codes, myths, cultural discourses, and national ideologies to develop resonant associations for consumer goods, advertisements both constitute prevailing ideologies and construct new mythologies and ideologies for commodities through these dialogical and intertextual relationships (Holt 2004; 2005; Randazzo 1993; Stern 1995; Thompson 2004). Tharp and Scott (1990) propose that advertising does not produce meaning in a top-down ideological fashion proposed by Marxian thought and commodity fetishism (Goldman 1992), or create meaning for the commodity form as Williamson (1978) suggests, but through the interactive flow between marketing institutions and the cultural world meaning is produced through a culturally determined and socially mediated process which is shared and negotiated between producers and consumers (Hall 1980; O'Donohoe 1999; Ritson and Elliott 1999). Interpretive developments in advertising research, such as Mick and Buhl's (1992) "meaning based model" of advertising experience, consumer "uses and gratifications" of advertising (O'Donohoe 1994), and the "social uses" of advertising meanings (Ritson and Elliott 1999) have challenged the hegemonic assumption that advertising "does things" to people, and have demonstrated how consumers are not only advertising literate and competent decoders of advertising, but use the meanings of advertising within social contexts in binding and ritualistic ways which are often unconnected to product consumption (Elliott and Ritson 1995). So while advertising discourse is unquestionably a prominent form of integrated social communication that has ideological effects, the text is not all-powerful or all-encompassing in its reach, and consumers are not merely passive receivers of advertising messages who process intended meanings in the exact fashion intended by advertisers and marketers (Buttle 1991). Indeed, interpretive advertising research has illustrated how consumers often resist the latent meanings that advertisers and marketers seek to impose upon the commodity form, and subvert marketing messages in both distorting and creative ways (Hirschman and Thompson 1997; Ritson et al. 1996). . . .

Advertising Agencies as Cultural Intermediaries: Linking Corporations to Culture

Advertising practitioners as an occupational group have been labelled "cultural intermediaries" (Bourdieu 1984; Featherstone 1991), as individuals who possess the appropriate cultural, social, and educational capital to construct symbolic meaning and utility for commodities. This group provide the critical link between corporations and the world of culture through the implicit knowledge and symbolic capital they possess about the discourses of culture and society (Thompson and Haytko 1997). Cultural knowledge thus has a central role in the production of advertising meaning (Hackley 2003a), and is instrumental in developing what Lien (2003:173) has described as a "shared cultural repertoire" between producers and consumers. Advertising agencies are immersed within the discourses of consumer culture from which situated cultural knowledge is extracted, and the close links and similarities between the work of advertising practitioners and cultural anthropologists has been explored within advertising literature (Dewaal Malefyt and Moeran 2003; Hirota 1995; Jackall and Hirota 2000; Moeran 2005). These discourses are extracted through both the formal knowledge frameworks of the marketing research and cultural discovery systems of marketing and advertising, and informal knowledge frameworks such as the dispositions and cultural identifications of advertising practitioners which are crucial to the development of commercial linkages between production and consumption within the advertising process (Nixon 2003). Research into advertising production has illustrated how advertising creatives draw extensively upon their personal experiences within the cultural world, and other forms of cultural text such as movies, music, books, and other advertisements with which they have contact in the construction of meaning for an advertisement, and circulating cultural discourses become the raw material for the construction of an advertising message (Cronin 2004b; du Gay 1997; Hackley 2003c; Miller 1997; Soar 2000). Hirota (1995:340) has emphasised how advertising creatives incorporate everyday life into advertisements through their observations of the social world:

> In their attentiveness to social activity, and perhaps in their willingness to enter new social worlds, creatives are commercial urban ethnographers of a sort whose subjects are the demeanour, idioms, interplay and foibles of other people. Whatever one's own viewpoint, one learns to discern the settled, taken for granted expectations of particular audiences, the commonplace cultural narratives that provide their frameworks of meaning and the familiar details that symbolise shared assumptions.

The conception of advertising creatives as "commercial urban ethnographers" illustrates how this occupational group attentively observe everyday social activity and incorporate these observations into symbols of mass consumption by weaving cultural narratives and shared meaning frameworks through the stories of consumer goods. Soar (2000:434) has emphasised how cultural intermediaries occupy "front row seats" in both the production and consumption and the encoding and decoding of meaning, and this dual situated positioning enables advertising creatives to selectively reflect social worlds and cultural values through advertisements, in what Marchand (1985:165) has described as advertising's "social tableau". Consumer research knowledge, codified by advertising agencies and constructed with a commercial imperative through qualitative research techniques also has an important function in the production of an advertising campaign. Hackley (2002) has argued that the cultural knowledge gathered by advertising agencies through consumer research is a major dynamic in the production of advertising's ideological power within consumer culture, and has elsewhere described how "advertising agencies can be seen to be operating in the engine room of a panoptic marketing system" (Hackley 2000:246). Hackley draws the panoptic metaphor for advertising agency practice from the work of Foucault (1979:204), who described how the panopticon functioned as a laboratory of experimentation and power within a society which through mechanisms of observation was able to penetrate into human behaviour and exercise disciplinary power and control over individuals. The metaphor of the panopticon applied to advertising agencies illustrates how they operate as laboratories of power and observation within culture and society, and through the mechanisms of consumer research knowledge exercise power and control over situated consumers (Hackley 2002). Cronin (2004a; 2004b; 2004c) adopts a different perspective, and contends that knowledge within advertising agencies is constituted through the "circuits of belief" that circulate and flow between advertising practitioners, clients, consumers, regulators, and academics. Her perspective draws upon Foucault's (1980) analysis of the production of knowledge and power within society, and explores how knowledge circulates and flows between these different groups. Cronin argues that this knowledge does not solely reside within the locale of any specific group or set of "experts" such as an advertising agency, and therefore consumer research knowledge does not necessarily provide an advertising agency with power over consumers. While knowledge may circulate and flow between these different groups within society as Cronin's insightful analysis highlights, advertising agencies have a pivotal role in channelling and directing this knowledge for the purposes of developing culturally based consumption meanings (Thompson 2004), and consumer research knowledge can be seen to have a formational role in the construction of advertising's ideological power and resonance. The production of an advertisement is a socially constructed and mediated process which is developed through the discursive interactions of a large group of individuals such as account planners, copywriters, art directors, clients, photographers, commercial directors, and consumers (Whose voices are represented through research findings), which coalesce in the development of an advertising campaign (Hackley 1999a 2001; Shankar 1999). The discourses of these different groups complexly intertwine in the campaign development process, and the social interactions and negotiations between these various groups impact upon the content and structure of the advertising texts produced (Clarkin 2005; Moeran 2005). The imperatives of clients are often dominant within this process as advertising agencies are often highly economically dependent upon the business of their clients, which creates asymmetrical power relations between advertising agencies and corporate clients as various studies have explored (Alvesson 1994; Hogg and Scoggins 2001; Lury and Warde 1997). Advertising agencies therefore hold a pivotal position of mediation between corporate clients and the cultural world, and have an instrumental role in connecting and fusing corporate ideologies to the cultural discourses and national ideologies that circulate and flow within consumer culture (Cronin 2004a; Holt 2005).

Research Methodology

The research reported in this paper adopted an interpretive approach to advertising production (Hudson and Ozanne 1988), and an ethnographic study of seven weeks duration was undertaken within an Irish advertising agency during which the first researcher conducted non-participant observation. The use of ethnography has gained much popularity within the social sciences (Hammersley and Atkinson 1995; Schwartzman 1993), and has also been widely embraced by marketing and consumer research studies (Arnould 1998; Elliott and Jankel-Elliott 2003; Kozinets 2002; Ritson and Elliott 1999). This particular paper will focus on one segment of the overall study and develops an analysis of five ethnographic interviews which were conducted with copywriters and art directors during the course of the ethnography. Three interviews were conducted with paired teams of copywriter and art director, who worked together in developing concepts for advertising campaigns, and two interviews were conducted with a copywriter and an art director separately. A total of eight creative advertising practitioner's responses are analysed and reported upon. The interviews varied in length from 45 minutes to over one hour, and were subsequently transcribed into over 40,000 words of interview text. This paper adopts a discourse analysis approach to the interview texts, drawing upon approaches within discursive psychology (Hackley 2000; Potter and Wetherell 1987; Potter 2003; Wetherell 1998; Wood and Kroger 2000). Discourse analysis is a theoretical development within social psychology which involves the close study of language in use (Taylor 2001). This perspective proposes that social worlds are constituted and constructed through the talk and language that people use, and discourse analysis explores patterns and recurring features across language. As advertising is an institutional practice which is constituted and constructed through language, it is a particularly rich site to excavate through discourse analysis (Cook 1992; Hackley 1999b). The discourse analysis approach has a commitment to studying social texts for their structure, such as how arguments are built within the texts and the features and recurring themes, metaphors, and tropes that seem to recur; their function, such as the purpose that these versions of events serve and the consequences they have; and their variability, such as variations that are present both within the same account and between different accounts, which can often give some insights into the function of the text (Elliott 1996; Hackley 2003b; Maclaren 2002; Wood and Kroger 2000). The discourse approach seeks to explore how accounts are built and how patterns are operating within the discourse at hand by focussing upon the categories of the participants as they orient to them within the interaction as opposed to the pre-conceived categories of the analyst. A central feature of the discourse approach is the identification of the "interpretative repertoires" that are used by informants to describe and account for particular actions, events, or ideas (Hackley 2003b). Potter and Wetherell (1987:138) define an interpretative repertoire as:

> . . . a lexicon or register of terms and metaphors drawn upon to characterise actions or events.

This paper explores the interview texts generated during the ethnography for their structure, function and variation and identifies the interpretative repertoires, or ways of talking about their work and the metaphors and sets of terms which are drawn upon by advertising copywriters and art directors to describe the processes and practices in which they engage. Guidelines for analysis and interpretation from within the consumer research tradition were used in the development of the analysis of the interview texts (Spiggle 1994), which are broadly commensurable with analytical approaches and conventions within discursive psychology (Potter and Wetherell 1987). The interviews were coded and interpretative repertoires identified and developed from the interview transcripts.

Feeding the Cultural Brain: Creatives' Appropriation of Cultural and Social Discourses

As the theoretical framework highlighted, advertising discourse is dialogical and intertextual in structure (Cook 1992; Fowles 1996), and it was interesting to explore within the interviews how creatives worked other areas of cultural discourse into advertisements. These intertextual discourses are bound up with the ideologies of the culture and society which they embody through their "social lives" (Appadurai 1986), and encoding these cultural fragments within an advertisement constructs cultural ideologies and values for a consumer good. One of the creative teams, P and M, described how they would develop advertising ideas from cultural referents and used the metaphor of a plant to describe how their brains would "soak up" research information and nutrients from other areas of cultural and social life. In this extract, M, the copywriter, describes how other areas of cultural discourse aid the development of creative ideas:

> M: I'd watch . . . not as many movies as I'd like to really but definitely watch as many as I can and listen to music and just try not necessarily stay kind of on the edge of things or like relevant or keep up to date with what's kind of happening but just kind of try and keep feeding that kind of creative part of your brain with like kind of new stuff you know? New kind of innovative movies and good music. I mean often I'd just locate and I'd hear a piece of music that I just think has the right atmosphere or something if I'm working on something like a brief and I'm not really getting anywhere with it and I hear a piece of music that to me just has the right atmosphere I think well I don't even know what the commercial is going to be or I don't have the idea but I just think that piece of music somehow seems to . . . has the right tone for that product and what we're trying to do with it I sit in a room and listen to it and try and put images to it you know what I mean and see if that helps you kind of think of something. So definitely yeah other areas of creative work can help. And again it's like I was saying about whether it's research material of whatever it's all information to feed your brain with that will hopefully help you produce something.

M's account provides a rich conception how advertising creatives develop ideas through their contact with the discourses that circulate within consumer culture. He describes how he watches movies and listens to music, and while he denies that it is necessary to "stay on the edge" of things within culture, he acknowledges that it was important to keep "up to date", and he draws upon a metaphor that was commonly used by creative teams of how it was important to "feed your brain" with new cultural material to develop advertising ideas. Another art director, A, described how it was important in her job to listen to music and watch a lot of television to know what was "out there", and this material was pivotal to the development of ideas within the creative process. Other studies of advertising producers have explored how cultural discourses are used as raw material to develop advertising meanings (Clarkin 2005; Grant 2004; Hirota 1995; Soar 2000), and the creatives interviewed within this agency described how this cultural material provided inspiration for the production of advertising. Interestingly, M acknowledges the formational role that consumer research can play in the development of advertising ideas, which illustrates the usefulness and relevance of Hackley's (2002) "panoptic" metaphor to the theoretical conception of advertising agency practice. M's account gives an example of how creatives intertextually weave these cultural sources, in describing how he will listen to music which he thinks has the right atmosphere, and how he puts images to the music to develop the advertising idea. It was particularly interesting that M was the copywriter within this team, who was primarily responsible for developing the words and dialogue in the production of advertisements, yet talked of putting images to music to develop advertising ideas. It became apparent within the interviews with creative teams that the lines of demarcation between the tasks of copywriter and art director often became blurred within the creative process, and copywriters and art directors would work interchangeably on different aspects of image and text to develop the initial advertising idea, and having accomplished this task would then bring their individual copywriting and art directing skills to bear upon developing and producing the finished advertisement. M's account demonstrates how cultural resources such as movies and music are fed into the creative development process through the personal and cultural identifications of copywriters and art directors (Nixon 2003). Another creative team, R and C, provided an insightful account of the ways in which they drew upon these cultural resources in their work, and how they appropriated other areas of culture for advertising messages:

> R: Like I flick around the TV channels all the time . . . I'll watch anything . . . and stuff that shouldn't necessarily interest me but I do . . . again it just helps . . . it's incredible, particularly when you're working on concepts it's amazing how often something you watch two weeks ago . . . you know? . . . Kind of . . . can certainly be the inspiration . . . or if it's a book you read or . . .

> C: Or just flicking through magazines . . . [R: Magazines yeah] . . . or photography books or anything that kind of gives you different ways of looking at the world or people. It's not necessarily that you'll find the perfect image in a photography book and you'll be able to stick your logo on that . . . [R: But it's usually the thinking behind it] . . . exactly yeah . . . if we were looking at a pint of Black Beer[1] in that way you know what would come out of it? What would we have to say about it? So that kind of thing can help even like reading a novel some kind of phrase can stick with you that sums up the moment or sums up the person and you realise what's going on with him . . . So you just have to constantly be kind of on the lookout for things . . . it's quite . . . it's much harder to come by it on purpose then it is by accident you know? Like when you've got a deadline and you know you're running out of time and you're flicking through all these books and you're going "There's nothing happening!" . . . and then

another time you might be on a bus just not even thinking about it and you
see something that's kind of interesting.

This account offers some insights into the cultural dispositions of advertising creatives,
and the implicit and idiosyncratic methods with which they approach their work. All of
the creative teams interviewed, as "cultural intermediaries" (Featherstone 1991), had
high levels of interest in all aspects of cultural discourse, such as movies, music, books,
and television, and through their work they filtered these cultural interests and identifications into the generation of symbolic ideas for advertising campaigns. R describes how
he will "flick around the TV channels" and "watch anything" as it helps him when he is
working on developing advertising concepts. C's account explains that while creatives
do have engagement with other cultural forms, they do not simply seek to "find the
perfect image in a photography book" and "stick your logo" on that. R interjects by
stating how the creative teams are interested in "the thinking behind" other forms of
cultural discourse, which was also drawn upon by other creative teams in describing
how this cultural material was utilised within the creative process. Interestingly, C
describes how as a creative "you have to constantly be kind of on the lookout for things",
and this description of the work of creatives positions them as cultural "magpies"
(Clarkin 2005:70), on the look out for shiny cultural signifiers with which to develop
their work and incorporate into advertising messages. C describes how the process of
finding these cultural signifiers is harder to come by on purpose than by accident, and he
describes how he can be "on a bus" and see something interesting. Another copywriter,
R, described how he would "hang around" a hairdresser's shop when writing ads for that
client, and would watch the ways in which consumers would interact with the hair-
dressers in the shop and the rituals in which the consumers would engage in having their
hair cut and then fed these observations into the development of advertisements, which
was a good example of how cultural creatives idiosyncratically adopted the methods of
the anthropologist to produce advertising ideas (Dewaal Malefyt and Moeran 2003;
Moeran 2005). These accounts demonstrate how creatives incorporate the raw material
of the everyday cultural and social world into advertising concepts, developing advertising ideas through a reflexive awareness of other cultural forms and the situations they
encounter within the course of their everyday lives (Clarkin 2005; Hirota 1995; Miller
1997; Soar 2000).

"Fighting" and "Battling" in the Advertising "Game"

The metaphors of "fighting" and "battling" were often drawn upon in interviews with
creative teams in describing the struggles they would encounter in trying to have their
ideas accepted, and many talked about the advertising process in terms of a game which
they played with both clients and other advertising practitioners within the agency. M,
a copywriter, provides a particularly rich example of how the fighting and battling
repertoires were drawn upon by creative teams:

> M: From a creative point of view you should be looking to try . . . not do
> an award winning ad every time cause you'd just drive yourself bonkers
> then but to always try and make sure there's something in that ad you
> think "Well that's quite good . . . . that's a different way of looking at it . . .

there's some element of originality in there" . . . And the best ad people are all the time pushing themselves kind of for that which then hopefully carries all the way through because if you do believe this piece of work is good then you kind of fight for it along the way and there is in this game a lot of fighting for your work. Other people have other priorities and in some ways they'd like the easy answer because the Marketing Manager's got the Marketing Director to answer to who's got an MD to answer to and if they do something kind of different they might have to go up and explain themselves and they mightn't want to or they mightn't feel comfortable about doing that . . . you know? . . . But often the best ideas are the ones you're not entirely comfortable with and so you have to be prepared to kind of go and do battle for your work.

Within this account, M emphasises the importance for creatives to have an "element of originality" in their advertising ideas, and how the best advertising people continually "push" themselves to achieve this. This was a common pattern across the data, as copywriters and art directors talked of their high levels of personal investment and involvement in their work, and described how they pushed themselves hard to develop original and exciting advertising ideas. M describes how if he believed a piece of work was good he would "fight" along the way for it, and uses the metaphor of a game to describe the advertising process. He then describes how "other" people within the advertising process have "other priorities", and uses the example of how the marketing manager of a client firm may not be willing to "go up" and "explain themselves" to a marketing director higher up the chain of command, and would prefer to have the "easy answer" in developing a campaign as opposed to taking a chance on a challenging or innovative new idea. He describes how as an advertising creative, you have to be prepared to "do battle" for your work. Other studies into advertising production have similarly identified battles and power struggles within the creative advertising process, both between different practitioners groups (Hackley 2000; Hirschman 1989), and between advertising agencies and their clients (Alvesson 1994; Lury and Warde 1997). Within these interviews, creative teams drew upon the battle and fight metaphors to describe how they strove to have their ideas and creative visions for advertising campaigns accepted by both the client and other practitioner groups within the advertising agency, and continually pushed for the development of advertising ideas which they perceived to be original and challenging. The creative teams reported how innovative or new ideas within the creative process could be met with resistance, often because clients or other practitioners were unfamiliar with a particular concept or were uncomfortable in experimenting with new concepts. While these battles were occasionally but not consistently described in volatile terms, they indicated how advertising creative teams struggled to have their creative visions for advertising campaigns realised by clients and other practitioners within the advertising process, and the barriers they would encounter to innovative or challenging advertising ideas.

The Ideology of Science in the Advertising Process

The prevalence of scientific and managerial ideologies to measure and evaluate advertising through scientific means has historically been an integral part of the advertising process (Frank 1997; Holt 2002). This process is often laced with uncertainty for clients (Lury and Warde 1997), and measuring and pre-testing audience reactions to advertising are often mechanisms which are used to reduce risk and uncertainty. However, as advertising is a process which is highly dependent upon the ingenuity of human creativity (El-Murad and West 2003; Hackley 1999b), the use of techniques for the objective measurement and evaluation of advertising can be a source of frustration for creative teams, and the clash between creative and managerial ideologies has been observed both historically and within contemporary advertising practice (Frank 1997; Hackley 2003c). In interviews with creative teams, they constructed clients as sub-scribers to the ideology of science, by seeking to evaluate and test advertising and make the process more measurable and safe for managerial purposes. This was particularly evident when creative teams talked about evaluation processes such as advertising copytesting (when advertisements are pre-tested with audiences to gauge the likely consumer response to the commercial), as D, an art director, described

> D: A mountain of research comes back about that thick on what they thought of your commercial and it's even got a joystick thing like where . . . pull back when you think it's really good . . . which part of it you think is crap . . . so you get a graph . . . You see 25 seconds . . . yes . . . look you've hit the . . . fu**ing . . . like . . . now that is just taking research to the point of . . . it's just . . . God like! . . . Does anybody believe in their gut anymore? . . . You know like? . . . You can't . . . it's not a science . . . it's advertising. Clients would like to think there is some way you can process it and turn it into a science but if you were to do that where would the creativity go? I think the danger with a lot of research to my mind and I can't really find anybody who can disprove it to me is you end up doing middle of the road stuff to keep everybody happy and that's the danger of research and creatives I think all over the world are pretty scared of research because . . . what's it going to do to our ad?

In this account, D describes how a "mountain" of research comes back from copytesting sessions on what consumers thought of "your" commercial. It was interesting that D uses the metaphor of the "mountain" to describe this research, illustrating how he perceived the magnitude of the research process. He describes the process through which audiences are shown the commercial and evaluate it through the use of a "joystick thing", and he rhetorically asks during his account in frustration "Does anybody believe in their gut anymore?" He then draws upon a common pattern across the interviews with the creative teams, in describing how advertising was "not a science" but that clients would like to turn it into a science. This was a particularly good example of how the creative teams constructed the clients as subscribers to scientific ideologies which they felt removed the creativity from advertising campaign ideas and sought to make the advertising process less uncertain and more predictable and measurable. This was a dilemma for the creative teams, and D describes how the danger with research is that the team end up compromising and producing "middle of the road" campaigns to keep all the participants within the process satisfied. Other creative teams metaphorically described how advertising would enter a "tunnel of mediocrity" once processes of evaluation and testing of advertising began, in which any element of risk or uncertainty was removed from the advertising campaign. The concept of risk within the advertising process has been explored by El-Murad and West (2003), who found that creative teams felt freer to take creative risks with less important clients, and from this they hypothesised that larger clients probably received less creative advertising. The interviews conducted within this study also revealed a similar pattern, in which creative teams described the advertising process for larger clients as having rigid structures and research filters in place, which could often lead to what they regarded as a dilution of the creative product. The teams described how ideas in the creative process for larger clients would be "eaten away" by research with the result that the end-product would become unrecognisable to the original idea conceived by the creative team, and the advertising would become bland and predictable under the paralysis of copytesting and research. Another copywriter, B, drew upon the analogy of poetry to describe the process through which client's copytested creative advertising work:

> B: They analyse it and analyse it and analyse it . . . like a poem that is over-analysed . . . eventually it's not a poem anymore.

This pattern was drawn upon frequently in interviews with creative teams. It was a dilemma for these cultural practitioners as the research tools used by clients within the advertising process "killed" advertising ideas as they perceived it, yet clients sought to engage consumers with these advertising messages. For creative teams, the processes of copytesting sapped the creativity and spark from advertising ideas, yet these processes of scientific evaluation were a dominant and modernist ideology which prevailed within the advertising process. Some of the informants conceded that clients would be spending vast amounts of money on advertising campaigns, which were essentially intangible processes, and had a necessity to try to eliminate risks and uncertainties. However, paradoxically from the creative perspective these processes of testing and evaluation often resulted in the production of advertising campaigns which were "middle of the road" that did not offend consumers yet did not engage them on any level either. These processes often caused much frustration for creative teams, who felt their work was destroyed by these scientific and managerial ideologies, and one creative team described the "heartbreaking" process in which their work would enter the evaluation process. This was a clear example of the symbolic capital of creatives clashing with the economic capital of clients, a distinction drawn from the work of Bourdieu (1993) in his analysis of the field of cultural production for literary and artistic works, which has also been applied to advertising agency practice (Moeran 2005). In his account, D describes how creatives all over the world are "pretty scared" of research, and asks rhetorically "What's it going to do to our ad?" This was an interesting comment, as it implied the creative team had ownership of the advertisement, and other studies into advertising production have similarly explored how ownership of the advertising idea was an issue of contention within the advertising process (Hirschman 1989; Hogg and Scoggins 2001). The ideology of science repertoire that creative teams drew upon demonstrated the prevalence that the managerial processes and strategic imperatives of clients have within the advertising production process, and how the creative imperatives of copywriters and art directors are often eclipsed and silenced as a result.

Clients in Control: The Holders of the Purse Strings

A repertoire that was commonly drawn upon by creative teams was that clients were the sponsors of the advertising campaign, and ultimately had control of the development of the process. The asymmetrical power relationship between advertising agencies and large corporate clients is a topic that has been explored within advertising literature (Hogg and Scoggins 2001; Lury and Warde 1997), and this power relationship was particularly evident in interviews with creative teams. Some of the teams described a sense of responsibility to the client, as it was the client's money which was at stake in the development of a campaign, and these creatives described how they would want to do their best for the clients concerned ("Good clients get the advertising they deserve" was a set of terms used by one art director to describe this relationship). However, there was considerable variation in how the relationship between the advertising agency and the client was described. While some creatives appreciated the client's money was at stake in the process, others resisted the control that clients often exercised, as one copywriter R explained:

> R: There's always like tales of the golden years of advertising where advertisers had a say and they'd more money and you know you hear tales of agencies in London who still do it like . . . "If you don't like what we're saying then go somewhere else!" . . . You know what I mean? Saatchi's used to do it like "We're right and if you don't think we're right then f**k off because this is what we do best" . . . And there's a certain amount of that with clients as well you'd like to think "Look we don't tell you how to run your bank or what interest rates to cut so don't tell us how to write ads". But you have to understand it's their money . . . they're the ones in control . . . they're the ones who say yes or no.

In this account R describes the "tales of the golden years of advertising" drawing upon the folklore of the stories of the advertising industry, when advertising agencies had more power within the agency-client relationship. He then offers the example of a bank, and how the agency does not tell the bank how to run their operations or what interest rates to cut, so the bank should not tell the advertising agency how to write ads. However, he concedes within his account that it's "their money" which funds the process, and that "they're the ones in control" and "the ones who say yes or no". In this sentence, R concedes to the power that the client has within this relationship. There was variation in how creative teams described the power relationship between the advertising agency and corporate clients. Some creatives expressed frustration at the rigidity that this relationship often imposed upon their work, such as R, while others described a more fluid and open relationship with the personnel of large clients that they had worked with for a long period of time. However, there was a common acknowledgement across the interview texts that larger clients in particular had a controlling and dominant influence upon the creative process. This power relationship was manifested within the practices of the advertising agency, and the teams described how client processes and ideologies for developing and evaluating advertising ideas, such as "Idea Understanding Tools" and "Ways of Brand Building", were dominant mechanisms for developing campaigns within the advertising process, which illustrated the extent to which the advertising agency was subservient to and economically dependent upon the larger corporate client.

Discussion and Conclusions

This paper has provided some empirical insights into the work practices of copywriters and art directors within an Irish advertising agency and the processes of advertising production in which they engage. Advertising creatives clearly draw from their cultural knowledge to construct advertisements in the fashion proposed by Hackley (2002) and Soar (2000), and the discourses of the cultural and social world become the raw material for the social construction and cultural constitution of advertising meaning. These cultural and social discourses embody the ideologies and values of the culture and society from which they are extracted, and when appropriated by advertising creatives these meanings become encoded and embedded within the structure of advertisements for commodities. Copywriters and art directors perform the role of what Lévi-Strauss (1966) described as "bricoleurs", weaving different and unrelated threads of cultural text together within a commercial tapestry. These commercial tapestries are constructed through the cultural and social capital of cultural intermediaries, who are dually situated as both producers and consumers of meaning within consumer culture, and they employ this situated knowledge to construct culturally resonant advertising (Cronin 2004a; Soar 2000). . . . The production of an advertising campaign is a socially constructed process, which is developed through the discursive interactions of a wide variety of different groups, each with their own set of ideologies and agendas. Advertising as an institutional practice provides a fascinating point of intersection between the creative and managerial ideologies of different practitioner groups within the advertising process, as anthropological based accounts of advertising practice have explored in-depth (Dewaal Malefyt and Moeran 2003; Moeran 1996, 2005). Lien (1997:51) for example has noted how latent conflicts between clients and creative teams and between aesthetics and commerce are embedded within the social structure of advertising agencies. The findings reported in this paper provide some empirical support for this proposition. Creative practitioners in advertising agencies occupy a cultural industry which is driven by the economic capital and strategic imperatives of their corporate clients, and have to try to negotiate their symbolic capital within the advertising process. However, they find they are often constrained in their work by the scientific ideologies of larger clients and by the power relations of economic dependency that exist between the advertising agency and the corporate client, which often results in a frustrating creative dilemma for these occupational groups (Hackley 2003c; Hirschman 1989). The advertising field could therefore not be considered an "art world" (Becker 1984) in the conventional sense of artistic production and aesthetic expression, as it is a form of sponsored creativity which is primarily motivated by the commercial agendas and strategic marketing objectives of corporate clients. So while advertising is often considered to be a culturally creative and socially expressive form of discourse, it is sponsored, shaped, and constituted through multinational corporate ideologies which can have a dominant influence upon the finished advertisement that is produced. The research reported in this paper has focussed upon the perspectives of Irish creative practitioners within one advertising agency. Future research could explore the perspectives of cultural creatives in other research sites across different cultural contexts, or examine the perspectives of different practitioner groupings within advertising agencies such as account planners, account handlers, creative directors, and media planners to understand the practices and processes in which they engage. Another possible route for future research would be to ethnographically follow the campaign development process for a particular product or brand in order to investigate how campaign ideas evolve and how advertisements come to constitute particular cultural meanings, ideologies, and mythologies through the development of this process. The wealth of new ethnographic and anthropological perspectives on advertising and marketing production has demonstrated the value of ethnographic insights into advertising and marketing based phenomena (Dewaal Malefyt and Moeran 2003; Lien 1997; Mazzarella 2003; Moeran 2005), which make this a particularly fruitful and exciting avenue for future research studies within the advertising and marketing disciplines. While the research reported in this paper has relied primarily upon interview data with copywriters and art directors, it is hoped these findings will contribute to a deeper understanding of the role and work of cultural intermediaries within consumer culture and the processes of advertising production in which these creative practitioners engage.

Questions

1   How are creative advertising workers a form of "cultural intermediaries"?
2   How do creative workers search for and use the "raw data" of culture in advertising?
3   Why might the creation of advertising be considered "battles" or "games"?
4   How does the ideology of science create tensions in the creation of advertising?
5   In what ways are the latest cultural trends—visual styles, cultural icons, songs—used in recent advertisements?

Note

1.   The name of the product mentioned in this account has been changed for the purposes of confidentiality and anonymity which was agreed between the first researcher and the advertising agency prior to conducting the research.

References

Alvesson, M. (1994). "Talking in Organisations: Managing Identity and Impressions in an Advertising Agency", *Organisation Studies*, **15**, (4), pp. 535–563.

Appadurai, A. (1986). *The Social Life of Things: Commodities in Cultural Perspective*, Cambridge, Cambridge University Press.

Arnould, E. J. (1998). "Daring Consumer-Orientated Ethnography", In: Brown, S. and Stern, B. B. (Eds.), *Representing Consumers: Voices and Visions*, London, Routledge, pp. 85–126.

Becker, H. (1984). *Art Worlds*, Berkeley and Los Angeles, University of California Press.

Bourdieu, P. (1984). *Distinction: A Social Critique of the Judgement of Taste*, London, Routledge.

Bourdieu, P. (1993). *The Field of Cultural Production: Essays on Art and Literature*, Cambridge, Polity Press.

Buttle, F. (1991). "What do People do with Advertising?" *International Journal of Advertising*, **10**, (2), pp. 95–110.

Clarkin, E. (2005). *"Who Makes the Laws that the Advertising Style-Police Enforce? An Insider's Ethnographic Account of the Social Process of Advertising Development and its Effects on the Texts it Produces"*, Unpublished MA thesis, Open University, Milton Keynes.

Cook, G. (1992). *The Discourse of Advertising*, London, Routledge.

Cronin, A. M. (2004a). *Advertising Myths: The Strange Half-Lives of Images and Commodities*, London, Routledge.

Cronin, A. M. (2004b). "Regimes of Mediation: Advertising Practitioners as Cultural Intermediaries?" *Consumption, Markets and Culture*, **7**, (4), pp. 349–369.

Cronin, A. M. (2004c). "Currencies of Commercial Exchange: Advertising Agencies and the Promotional Imperative", *Journal of Consumer Culture*, **4**, (3), pp. 339–360.

Dewaal Malefyt, T. and Moeran, B. (Eds.), (2003). *Advertising Cultures*, Oxford, Berg Publishing.

du Gay, P. (Ed.), (1997). *Production of Culture/Cultures of Production*. London: Sage Publications/Open University.

Elliott, R. (1996). "Discourse Analysis: Exploring Action, Function and Conflict in Social Texts", *Marketing Intelligence and Planning*, **14**, (6), pp. 65–68.

Elliott, R. (1999). "Symbolic Meaning and Postmodern Consumer Culture", In: Brownlie, D., Saren, M., Wensley, R. and Whittington, R. (Eds.), *Rethinking Marketing: Toward Critical Marketing Accountings*, London, Sage Publications, pp. 112–125.

Elliott, R. and Jankel-Elliott, N. (2003). "Using Ethnography in Strategic Consumer Research", *Qualitative Market Research: An International Journal*, **6**, (4), pp. 215–223.

Elliott, R. and Ritson, M. (1995). "Practicing Existential Consumption and the Lived Meaning of Sexuality in Advertising", In: Sujan, M. and Kardes, F. (Eds.), *Advances in Consumer Research*, Vol. 22, Provo, UT, Association for Consumer Research, pp. 740–745.

Elliott, R. and Ritson, M. (1997). "Post-Structuralism and the Dialectics of Advertising: Discourse, Ideology, Resistance", In: Brown, S. and Turley, D. (Eds.), *Consumer Research: Postcards from the Edge*, New York, Routledge, pp. 190–219.

El-Murad, J. and West, D. (2003). "Risk and Creativity in Advertising", *Journal of Marketing Management* 19, (5/6), pp. 657–673.

Featherstone, M. (1991). *Consumer Culture and Postmodernism*, London, Sage Publications.

Foucault, M. (1979). *Discipline and Punish: The Birth of the Prison*, New York, Vintage Books.

Foucault, M. (1980). *Power/Knowledge: Selected Interviews and Other Writings: 1972–1977*, Brighton, Harvester.

Fowles, J. (1996). *Advertising and Popular Culture*, London, Sage Publications.

Frank, T. (1997). *The Conquest of Cool: Business Culture, Counterculture, and the Rise of Hip Consumerism*, Chicago, The University of Chicago Press.

Goldman, R. (1992). *Reading Ads Socially*, New York, Routledge.

Goldman, R. and Papson, S. (1996). *Sign Wars: The Cluttered Landscape of Advertising*, New York, Guilford Press.

Grant, I. (2004). "Communicating with Young People through the Eyes of Practitioners", *Journal of Marketing Management* 20, (5/6), pp. 591–606.

Hackley, C. (1999a). "An Epistemological Odyssey: Towards Social Construction of the Advertising Process", *Journal of Marketing Communications*, **5**, (3), pp. 157–168.

Hackley, C. (1999b). "*The Social Construction of Advertising: A Discourse Analytic Approach to Creative Advertising Development as a Feature of Marketing Communications Management*", Unpublished Ph.D. thesis, University of Strathclyde, Strathclyde.

Hackley, C. (2000). "Silent Running: Tacit, Discursive and Psychological Aspects of Management in a Top UK Advertising Agency", *British Journal of Management*, **11**, (3), pp. 239–254.

Hackley, C. (2001). "Looking at me, Looking at you: Qualitative Research and the Politics of Knowledge Representations in Advertising and Academia", *Qualitative Market Research: An International Journal*, **4**, (1), pp. 42–51.

Hackley, C. (2002). "The Panoptic Role of Advertising Agencies in the Production of Consumer Culture", *Consumption, Markets and Culture*, **5**, (3), pp. 211–229.

Hackley, C. (2003a). "Divergent Representational Practices in Advertising and Consumer Research: Some Thoughts on Integration", *Qualitative Market Research: An International Journal*, **6**, (3), pp. 175–183.

Hackley, C. (2003b). *Doing Research Projects in Marketing, Management and Consumer Research*, London, Routledge.

Hackley, C. (2003c). "How Divergent Beliefs Cause Account Team Conflict", *International Journal of Advertising*, **22**, (3), pp. 313–331.

Hall, S. (1980). "Encoding/Decoding", In: Hall, S. (Ed.), *Culture, Media, Language: Working Papers in Cultural Studies 1972–79*, London, Routledge, pp. 128–138.

Hammersley, M. and Atkinson, P. (1995). *Ethnography: Principles in Practice (Second Edition)*, London, Routledge.

Hirota, J. M. (1995). "Making Product Heroes: Work in Advertising Agencies", In: Jackall, R. (Ed.), *Propaganda*, London, Macmillan Press Ltd, pp. 329–350.

Hirschman, E. C. (1989). "Role-Based Models of Advertising Creation and Production", *Journal of Advertising*, **18**, (4), pp. 42–59.

Hirschman, E. C. and Thompson, C. J. (1997). "Why Media Matter: Toward a Richer Understanding of Consumers Relationship with Advertising and Mass Media", *Journal of Advertising*, **XXVI**, (1), pp. 43–60.

Hogg, M. K. and Scoggins, B. (2001). "Telling Tales: An Ethnographic Account of Creativity in Agency-Client Relations", Paper presented at the Critical Management Studies Conference, Manchester.

Holt, D. B. (2004). *How Brands Become Icons: The Principles of Cultural Branding*, Boston, Harvard Business School Publishing Corporation.

Holt, D. B. (2005). "How Societies Desire Brands: Using Cultural Theory to Explain Brand Symbolism", Paper presented at the Dublin Institute of Technology Research Seminar Series, May 6th.

Hudson, L. A. and Ozanne, J. L. (1988). "Alternative Ways of Seeking Knowledge in Consumer Research", *Journal of Consumer Research*, **14**, (March), pp. 508–521.

Jackall, R. and Hirota, J. M. (2000). *Image Makers: Advertising, Public Relations and the Ethos of Advocacy*, Chicago, University of Chicago Press.

Jhally, S. (1987). *The Codes of Advertising: Fetishism and the Political Economy of Meaning in the Consumer Society*, New York, Routledge.

Kozinets, R. V. (2002). "Can Consumers Escape the Market? Emancipatory Illuminations from Burning Man." *Journal of Consumer Research*, **29**, (June), pp. 20–39.

Lévi-Strauss, C. (1966). *The Savage Mind*, London, Weiderfeld and Nicolson.

Lien, M. E. (1997). *Marketing and Modernity*, Oxford, Berg Publishing.

Lien, M. E. (2003). "Fame and the Ordinary: 'Authentic' Constructions of Convenience Foods", In: Dewaal Malefyt, T. and Moeran, B. (Eds.), *Advertising Cultures*, London, Berg Publishing, pp. 165–185.

Lury, C. and Warde, A. (1997). "Investments in the Imaginary Consumer: Conjectures Regarding Power, Knowledge and Advertising", In: Nava, M., Blake, A., MacRury, I. and Richards, B. (Eds.), *Buy this Book: Studies in Advertising and Consumption*, London, Routledge, pp. 87–102.

Maclaren, P. (2002). *"An Introduction to Discourse Analysis"*, Unpublished Presentation, Dublin Institute of Technology Research Seminar Series, April 6th.

Marchand, R. (1985). *Advertising: The American Dream*, Berkeley and Los Angeles, University of California Press.

Mazzarella, W. (2003). *Shovelling Smoke: Advertising and Globalization in Contemporary India*, Durham, Duke University Press.

McCracken, G. (1986). "Culture and Consumption: A Theoretical Account of the Structure and Movement of the Cultural Meaning of Consumer Goods", *Journal of Consumer Research*, **13**, (June), pp. 71–84.

McCracken, G. (1989). "Who is the Celebrity Endorser? Cultural Foundations of the Endorsement Process", *Journal of Consumer Research*, **16**, (December), pp. 310–321.

Mick, D. G. and Buhl, C. (1992). "A Meaning Based Model of Advertising Experience", *Journal of Consumer Research* **19**, (December), pp. 317–338.

Miller, D. (1997). *Capitalism: An Ethnographic Approach*, Oxford, Berg Publishing.

Moeran, B. (1996). *A Japanese Advertising Agency: An Anthropology of Media and Markets*, Surrey, Curzon Press.

Moeran, B. (2005). *The Business of Ethnography*, New York, Berg Publishing.

Nixon, S. (2003). *Advertising Cultures*, London, Sage Publications.

O'Donohoe, S. (1994). "Advertising Uses and Gratifications", *European Journal of Marketing*, **28**, (8/9), pp. 52–75.

O'Donohoe, S. (1997). "Raiding the Postmodern Pantry: Advertising Intertextuality and the Young Adult Audience", *European Journal of Marketing*, **31**, (3/4), pp. 234–253.

O'Donohoe, S. (1999). "Nationality and Negotiation of Advertising Meanings", In: Arnould, E. J. and Scott, L. M. (Eds.), *Advances in Consumer Research*, Vol. 26, Provo, UT, Association for Consumer Research, pp. 684–689.

Olsen, B. (2003). "The Revolution in Marketing Intimate Apparel: A Narrative Ethnography", In: Dewaal Malefyt, T. and Moeran, B. (Eds.), *Advertising Cultures*, Oxford, Berg Publishing, pp. 113–138.

Potter, J. (2003). "Discourse Analysis", In: Hardy, M. and Bryman, A. (Eds.), *Handbook of Data Analysis*, London, Sage, pp. 607–624.

Potter, J. and Wetherell, M. (1987). *Discourse and Social Psychology*, London, Sage Publications.

Randazzo, S. (1993). *Mythmaking on Madison Avenue*, Chicago, Probus Publishing Company.

Ritson, M. and Elliott, R. (1999). "The Social Uses of Advertising: An Ethnographic Study of Adolescent Advertising Audiences", *Journal of Consumer Research*, **26**, (December), pp. 260–277.

Ritson, M., Elliott, R. and Eccles, S. (1996). "Reframing Ikea: Commodity Signs, Consumer Creativity and The Social/Self Dialectic", In: Corfman, K. and Lynch, J. (Eds.), *Advances in Consumer Research*, Vol. 23, Provo, UT, Association for Consumer Research, pp. 127–131.

Schwartzman, H. B. (1993). *Ethnography in Organisations*, London, Sage.

Scott, L. M. (1990). "Understanding Jingles and Needledrop: A Rhetorical Approach to Music in Advertsing", *Journal of Consumer Research*, **17**, (September), pp. 223–236.

Shankar, A. (1999). "Advertising's Imbroglio", *Journal of Marketing Communications*, **5**, (1), pp. 1–15.

Sherry, J. F. J. (1987). "Advertising as a Cultural System", In: Umiker-Sebeok, J. (Ed.), *Marketing and Semiotics: New Directions in the Study of Signs for Sale*, Berlin, Mouton de Gruyter, pp. 441–461.

Soar, M. (2000). "Encoding Advertisements: Ideology and Meaning in Advertising Production", *Mass Communication and Society*, **3**, (4), pp. 415–437.

Spiggle, S. (1994). "Analysis and Interpretation of Qualitative Data in Consumer Research", *Journal of Consumer Research*, **21**, (December), pp. 491–503.

Stern, B. B. (1995). "Consumer Myths: Frye's Taxonomy and the Structural Analysis of Consumption Texts", *Journal of Consumer Research*, **22**, (September), pp. 165–185.

Taylor, S. (2001). "Locating and Conducting Discourse Analytic Research", In: Wetherell, M., Taylor, S. and Yates, S. J. (Eds.), *Discourse as Data: A Guide for Analysis*, London, Sage Publications, pp. 5–49.

Tharp, M. and Scott, L. M. (1990). "The Role of Marketing Processes in Creating Cultural Meaning", *Journal of Macromarketing*, **48**, (Fall), pp. 47–60.

Thompson, C. J. (2004). "Marketing Mythology and Discourses of Power", *Journal of Consumer Research*, **31**, (June), pp. 162–180.

Thompson, C. J. and Haytko, D. L. (1997). "Speaking of Fashion: Consumer's Uses of Fashion Discourses and the Appropriation of Countervailing Cultural Meanings", *Journal of Consumer Research*, **24**, (June), pp. 15–42.

Wetherell, M. (1998). "Positioning and Interpretive Repertoires: Conversation Analysis and Post-Structuralism in Dialogue", *Discourse and Society*, **9**, (3), pp. 387–412.

Williamson, J. (1978). *Decoding Advertisements: Ideology and Meaning in Advertising*, London, Marion Boyars Publishers Ltd.

Wood, L. A. and Kroger, R. O. (2000). *Doing Discourse Analysis: Methods for Studying Action in Talk and Text*, London, Sage Publications.

Chapter 9

DEVIN LEONARD

NIGHTMARE ON MADISON AVENUE
Media Fragmentation, Recession, Fed-Up Clients, TiVo – It's All Trouble, and the Ad Business Is Caught up in the Wake

ALTHOUGH NOT AS EXPLICITLY CRITICAL IN PERSPECTIVE as many of the other chapters in this book, this chapter nevertheless offers a useful overview of recent changes in the practices of US advertising. Originally appearing as an article in the business magazine *Fortune*, it explores the significant changes that the advertising industry, and especially advertising agencies, are experiencing in the new millennium. Leonard examines issues such as audience fragmentation and the shrinking ratings of the broadcast networks, new technologies like cell phones and DVRs, consolidation of ownership in advertising agencies, the recession of the early 2000s, and our advertising-saturated society. The author concludes that these factors have caused the culture and practice of advertising to change fundamentally, with the creative personnel losing power and prestige, while those responsible for media planning and buying have gained prestige. With this argument, this article complements the points highlighted by Joseph Turow in his later contribution to this volume.

(FORTUNE Magazine) – BBDO, ONE OF the most respected ad agencies on Madison Avenue, has had a rude awakening. The agency is famed for its hip commercials like the Pepsi Twist spot, in which aging rocker Ozzy Osbourne watches in horror as his grungy children, Jack and Kelly, are transformed into . . . Donny and Marie Osmond! Recently BBDO worked similar wonders for Chrysler. Everybody in the auto industry is talking about its ads in which a redneck car fanatic dreams of winning a drag race with the driver of a new Dodge Ram pickup equipped with a Hemi V-8 engine.

Chrysler, however, isn't being very appreciative. George Murphy, senior vice president for global brand marketing for the Chrysler Group, complains that his company is spending too much on television ads. It galls him that the price of a 30-second commercial continues to rise at a time when the broadcast networks are steadily losing their audience – and when his own marketing budget is flat because the car industry hasn't been able to raise prices for five years.

Because of that, Chrysler has been giving BBDO fits. It wants less of the agency's expensive television ads and more Internet promotions, direct mail, and events that get behinds in the seats of Chrysler vehicles. "There's definitely been erosion in the amount of money we spend on TV," Murphy confirms. The same could be said for the fees that Chrysler pays BBDO. In late May the agency eliminated 100 positions in its Detroit office.

It's a whole new world for the advertising business – and a cold one. The cost of network television ads is rising faster than most corporate marketing budgets. The Yankee Group predicts that by 2007, 20% of the nation's households will have personal video recorders like TiVo that enable viewers to skip television ads altogether. So companies are abandoning the old rules of marketing. You can't log on to the Internet without being bombarded with pop-up ads. Virgin Atlantic Airways is running magazine ads on such heavy paper that you land on them every time you flip through the publication. Burger King has given a warped twist to its "Have it your way" slogan: It created Subservient Chicken, a website where you can give orders to a garter-clad hen in a dingy motel room. Coca-Cola, Nokia, and McDonald's are quietly inserting sodas, cellular phones, and Big Macs into the videogames your children play.

You may find this new world strange and uninviting. Madison Avenue is enjoying it even less. Nearly every ad agency head repeats the same mantra: There's never been a more exciting time to be in the advertising business. That is true – but most of the thrills are the result of things they would rather not talk about.

Many of the changes cascading through the advertising agency world stem from a wave of consolidation that has swept through Madison Avenue. Five years ago nine holding companies accounted for 55% of the nation's publicly reported advertising and marketing revenues, according to media investment bank Veronis Suhler Stevenson. Since then, three of those companies have been devoured by their larger competitors. Today six companies – Omnicom, WPP, Interpublic Group, Grey Global, and France's Havas and Publicis – are responsible for 60% of the sector's revenues.

Just as this M&A binge was peaking, the business crashed headlong into the worst advertising recession since the Great Depression. Global ad spending plunged 7% to $440 billion in 2001. The agencies laid off 40,000 employees – 19% of their workforce. There was virtually no growth in ad spending over the next two years. Bernstein Research, a Wall Street firm that tracks the stock market, estimates that spending rose by only 2.8% in 2003. Things are expected to get better this year, but Bernstein says that 2004 may be the fourth year in a row when advertising company stocks underperform the S&P 500, a first for Madison Avenue.

Why is Wall Street wary? The recession brought about more change on Madison Avenue in four years than the industry has seen in four decades. Until recently many agencies pocketed 15% of the cost of the media they purchased for their clients. In the past five years big advertisers like Chrysler and Unilever have done away with commissions entirely. Instead, the vast majority of clients now pay fees based on an agency's labor costs. Worse, agencies must often negotiate not with their clients' CEOs but with procurement officials who are used to dealing with vendors of staplers and file cabinets.

All those changes have brought about a deep shift in the balance of power on Madison Avenue. For decades the industry has been dominated by the "creatives" – the self-styled hipsters with the ponytails and open-neck shirts – who came up with ideas ("Coke is it!") that were translated into television, print, radio, and billboard ads.

Beneath them toiled the media buyers, who wore suits and purchased television and radio time, magazine pages, and billboard space for clients.

Now the buyers are calling the shots. The reason is that holding companies have stripped out the buying divisions of their agencies and consolidated them into free-standing firms that use their clout to extract better media prices for clients. WPP's MindShare now handles all media buying for Unilever and American Express. Starcom MediaVest Group, a division of the Publicis Groupe, the French advertising conglomerate, does the same for Coke and Disney. Because of those deals, media buyers are providing the bulk of their parent companies' growth, while the creatives flounder.

Who will guide clients though the splintering media landscape? That's what the creatives and the buyers are fighting over now. The number of men between the ages of 18 and 34 watching prime-time television has declined 5% this season, according to Nielsen. Sixty-nine percent of U.S. magazines saw their newsstand sales slip last year, says Capell's Circulation Report. Like global warming, these developments have been predicted for years. But now they have come to pass.

The creatives say they can help clients sell diet soda and detergent in this radically changed environment because, well, that's what they've always done. The buyers accuse their creative brethren of being addicted to television and print. They say they have a much deeper understanding of the new forms of media that clients are embracing, like the Internet, video on demand, and cellular phones. But does anybody on Madison Avenue have answers as the ground shifts under their feet? Randall Rothenberg, director of intellectual capital at Booz Allen Hamilton and a columnist for *Advertising Age*, doesn't think so: "We've gone from the era of mass production, mass merchandising, and mass marketing to the era of customized products and services. Media fragmentation is atomizing audiences. The advertising industry is having a terrible time adapting."

Peter Sealey, a visiting professor of marketing at Stanford University, describes the state of Madison Avenue in starker terms. He argues that the average ad agency CEO is as blissfully unaware of the perils his industry faces as a French cavalry lieutenant in 1914. "You ask him how things are going, and he says, 'Fine. Look at the horses. You like the horses?' " says Sealey. "Meanwhile, there's a goddamn German 200 miles away building the first tank."

"I love this business," says Donny Deutsch, CEO of Deutsch Inc., a New York ad agency. "If you landed here from Mars and you looked at the elements of society — commerce, pop culture, humanity — advertising defines us more as a civilization than anything else out there. It's selling in its most grotesque obviousness. It's human manipulation. Yet it's charming. It's something we all participate in. It's what makes all the engines go. It's what allows television to exist. It's what drives people to stores."

Deutsch is probably America's best-known adman. He hosts a CNBC talk show. He has appeared on *The Apprentice*, his friend Donald Trump's reality show. Like the real estate developer, Deutsch is quick to brag about his success. Sitting in his office in lower Manhattan, his loafers up on the coffee table, the 46-year-old drops the names of clients: Johnson & Johnson, Old Navy, Mitsubishi Motors, Revlon, Expedia, and Coors. He has also made himself very rich. In 2000, Deutsch sold his agency to Interpublic in a deal valued at $265 million.

Unlike a lot of his peers, Deutsch doesn't mince words when he talks about what has happened to Madison Avenue. He says consolidation has come with a price. "A lot of the great independent spirit that has driven this industry has gone by the wayside," he says. He lashes out at his fellow agency chiefs for allowing clients to treat them like widget vendors. He fumes about media buyers who claim they understand the business better than their creative peers. "That's all bullshit," Deutsch says.

What makes Deutsch and many others on Madison Avenue especially bitter is that they remember when the industry was a wondrous place to be. Many ad agency people entered the business because they were inspired by three legends who dominated Madison Avenue in the 1960s. These men weren't just managers; they actually practiced the craft of making ads. The most famous was David Ogilvy, founder of Ogilvy & Mather, a pipe-smoking British expatriate who created the eye-patched Man in the Hathaway Shirt and Schweppes's Commander Whitehead ads. Ogilvy wrote perhaps the most renowned headline ever for an automobile ad: "At 60 miles an hour, the loudest noise in this new Rolls-Royce comes from the electric clock." His memoir, *Confessions of an Advertising Man*, sold millions.

Bill Bernbach, founder of Doyle Dane Bernbach, is equally venerated. He pounded out classic lines on his manual typewriter like "We try harder" for Avis and "You don't have to be Jewish to love Levy's" rye bread. Then there was Leo Burnett, a mythically disheveled Midwesterner who showed up at meetings with cigarette ashes on his clothes. He kept a folder on his desk labeled "Corny language" full of phrases that he said conveyed "a feeling of sodbuster honesty." He was the father of such iconic Madison Avenue characters as the Jolly Green Giant and the Marlboro Man.

These men presided over shops that cranked out ads like assembly lines. Those, of course, were the days when you could reach 90% of the country by running prime-time television commercials. So media planning was far from rocket science. A typical campaign could consist of two television commercials and a handful of magazine ads. Shelly Lazarus, now CEO of Ogilvy & Mather, joined the firm in 1971. "Most of what we were advertising at that time was directed at women," she recalls. "You had *Good Housekeeping*, *McCall's*, and *Ladies' Home Journal*. You made your selections there, you made your television commercials, and you were done."

Media buyers had little say in the process. WPP's media czar, Irwin Gotlieb, who oversees $33.7 billion in spending as CEO of GroupM, spent his early years as a buyer for the now defunct Benton & Bowles. He regularly attended meetings with his peers to discuss campaigns, and he says the creative people rarely missed a chance to put him in his place. "Typically," recalls Gotlieb, "the creative guy would lean over to me and say, 'Listen, I don't do radio. Don't you dare put any radio on the media plan!' " Gotlieb knew better than to argue. If he bought radio time, the creatives would simply "forget" to furnish the ads.

It was a strange way to do business, but Madison Avenue was a world unto itself. Perhaps the best evidence is that clients didn't compensate their agencies directly for their work – they paid a 15% commission on media purchases. So every time an ad appeared on television – and many ran for years – a cash register rang on Madison Avenue. Rosser Reeves, the late chairman of Ted Bates & Co., once bragged that the maker of Anacin spent $86.4 million running a commercial he sketched out on the back of a napkin and featuring a picture of a hammer beating inside a human head. The commercial cost Bates $8,200 to produce.

The remarkable thing is that this entire system remained in place long after Bernbach, Burnett, and Ogilvy left the stage and a new generation took over. The new CEOs – trained in finance, not copywriting – set about transforming Madison Avenue from a fen of boutiques to an industry dominated by powerful holding companies. In 1987, WPP acquired J. Walter Thompson in a hostile takeover. Two years later it devoured Ogilvy & Mather. Doyle Dane Bernbach merged with Batten Barton Durstine & Osborn (now BBDO) to form Omnicom.

The new holding companies bought public relations firms, event marketers, and Internet startups. They also bought more ad agencies. In 2000, WPP bought Young & Rubicam in a deal worth $4.7 billion. The following year Interpublic acquired True North, parent of Foote Cone & Belding, in a $2.1 billion transaction. "It was like an arms race," says *Advertising Age*'s Rothenberg.

Because of all those deals — and because of the advertising frenzy driven by the Internet bubble — annual U.S. revenues of the top seven public holding companies swelled by 44%, to $23 billion, between 1998 and 2000, according to Veronis Suhler Stevenson. Operating income soared 65%, to $2.8 billion. Their stocks performed with similar elan.

Yet ad agencies were able to continue churning out television and print ads as if it were 1965. The creatives were in control. The media buyers languished in the least desirable offices. The commission system was in its final days, but even in 2000, 21% of clients paid their agencies a percentage of media billings. It would take something cataclysmic to change Madison Avenue's insular culture, and that was not long in coming: the most horrible ad recession in more than half a century.

Ed Meyer, CEO of Grey Global Group, the industry's sixth-largest ad holding company, adores his clients. Procter & Gamble has been with Grey since the mid-1950s. Brown & Williamson Tobacco has been a client for four decades. "Once they walk in the door, they never leave," says the 77-year-old CEO proudly.

But after the ad market crashed in 2001, Meyer's clients did something that he will never entirely forgive. They brought in people from their procurement department to negotiate contracts with his company. "They don't understand our business," Meyer says bitterly.

You hear the same lament everywhere on Madison Avenue. Before the arrival of the procurement people, agency heads drew up contracts with CEOs or corporate marketing officials with whom they had strong bonds. They golfed together. They attended awards ceremonies together. The purchasing agents were a different breed. They were used to beating down suppliers of cardboard and plastic bags. They didn't care about an agency's Clio awards. They didn't want to be told about the brand-building power of a Super Bowl commercial with Britney Spears. They wanted to haggle.

For many agency heads, this was a profoundly disillusioning experience. The first thing to go was the last vestige of the commission system. The procurement people insisted on paying agencies a fee based on labor costs with a negotiated profit on top. But that was only the beginning of the discussion. Says Meyer: "The procurement people come in and literally ask, 'What is the average salary of each level of your employees? What's the agency's overhead? Do you count vacation in the overhead?' They perform massive audits, in effect."

Procurement people make no apologies. Susan Curatola, Unilever's North American director of supply management for nonproduction items, says her company pays a "significant" amount of money every year to its agencies and expects the same kind of transparency it gets from other vendors. "We simply apply the same approach to marketing," she says.

Nevertheless, some procurement people are squeezing their ad agencies in ways that their marketing department associates never would have dared. Last year DuPont's purchasing department made agencies competing for its consolidated advertising account bid against one another in a live online auction. The winner of the $70 million account was Ogilvy & Mather. Scott Nelson, DuPont's global brand manager, is quick to say that price wasn't the only deciding factor. But it was painful for some people in the advertising business to see the late David Ogilvy's agency treated like a furniture vendor.

Agencies have tried standing up to their clients' procurement departments, without much success. Donny Deutsch severed his ties with Pfizer after a dispute over how much the agency was billing the chemical company for salaries. Deutsch says his former client wanted him to reveal how much he was paying individual employees. "If agencies just refused, we could stop this," Deutsch says. "Yet agency people go, 'Okay, okay.' Then they can't figure out why they're down to a tiny margin business. It's this ridiculous cycle." (Pfizer says it requests such information only when it wants an independent auditor to make sure the company isn't being overcharged.)

"Agencies have totally lost their pricing power," says Ed Atorino, an analyst at Blaylock & Partners. Though spending began to recover in 2003, most ad companies didn't see any meaningful growth. Omnicom had organic (non-acquisition-related) revenue growth last year of 4.6%. Publicis reported organic growth of 2%. But WPP reported an anemic 0.7% increase. Interpublic had a 3.6% decline. Havas posted a drop of 5.7%.

Some of them have continued to lay people off. Interpublic, busily selling assets after losing $425 million last year, said in March that it had reduced its headcount by 3,500 positions, or 7% of its workforce. Havas said it had cut 2,011, or 11%.

There has also been widespread turnover at the top of agencies. There are new CEOs at BBDO, Young & Rubicam, J. Walter Thompson, Interpublic's McCann-Erickson, and Havas's Euro RSCG Worldwide. "These have not been the best years," sighs Ogilvy's Lazarus. "We've been though procurement. There are certain agencies where people haven't gotten bonuses or raises in years. It takes its toll."

Madison Avenue's long-suffering media buyers will look back on the recession very differently. "This is kind of the revenge of the nerds," says David Verklin, CEO of Carat North America, one of the big U.S. media-buying operations.

Indeed it is. Since the 1970s, U.S. media buyers have watched enviously as their counterparts in Europe formed freestanding companies that purchased television and radio time for clients. Their agency bosses resisted such a separation of powers. They may have looked down on their buyers, but they didn't want to lose the revenue the buyers brought in.

Then, in the late '90s, European buyers like Carat began to make inroads in the U.S. market. The response of holding companies with U.S. ad agencies was swift. In 2000, Omnicom stripped out the buying divisions of BBDO, DDB, and TWBA/Chiat/Day and merged them into the U.S. division of OMD. WPP consolidated the buying arms of J. Walter Thompson and Ogilvy & Mather into the U.S. arm of MindShare, its global media-buying operation. Leo Burnett's old shop, now called Bcom3, joined its two media-buying divisions, creating the Starcom MediaVest Group.

Media buyers offered something that every corporate procurement executive could understand: cost savings. Gillette and Unilever consolidated their media buying and planning with MindShare. McDonald's and GE opted for OMD. Pfizer and Philips chose Carat. Coke, Procter & Gamble, and Disney turned to Starcom MediaVest, which also created a special division, GM Planworks, to handle all the media planning for Detroit's largest automaker.

The buyers became the darlings of their holding companies, giving them revenue growth in the darkest hours of the recession. "In August 2002 our revenues in the U.S. started to go positive," says WPP CEO Martin Sorrell. "The strongest part of our business from this point onward was media planning and buying."

The ascension of the media buyer completely disrupted Madison Avenue's old assembly line. "We're getting to the point where the media plan is done first, and the creative is developed behind it," says Verklin. "That is a radical vision for the advertising business that would have been unheard of five years ago." He adds: "We used to be the dorks. Now we're driving the whole advertising process."

That boast unnerves the heads of traditional ad agencies, who fear they will be reduced to purely "creative" agencies. Bob Jeffrey, CEO of J. Walter Thompson, argues that clients get better campaigns when agencies such as his control both media planning and the creative side. He points out that J. Walter Thompson still does Ford's media buying and planning. Jeffrey argues that the result has been "breakthrough" ideas like the music videos on American Idol in which contestants drive Ford cars and SUVs. J. Walter Thompson also arranged for Ford vehicles to be written into the script of Fox's 24 to thwart TiVo users.

Media buyers aren't threatened in the least. They, too, are doing product placement. They are creating entire television shows. MindShare recently struck a deal with ABC to jointly produce a prime-time drama called the The Days. Its clients will have the exclusive advertising rights on the show.

Ultimately, though, everybody on Madison Avenue is wrestling with the same demons. The old forms of media on which they relied for years are rapidly losing their grip on consumers. Young men are skipping *Everybody Loves Raymond* to roam the streets as mobsters and pimps in *Grand Theft Auto: Vice City*. Standing behind those prime-time dropouts is a generation of teenagers for whom television is little more than background noise. According to a study that MindShare conducted with Arbitron, 67% of teenagers between the ages of 13 and 17 sometimes explore the Internet while watching the television. Sixty-six percent sometimes read magazines while the television is on. Fifty-six percent are instant-messaging. Thirty-four percent are also listening to the radio. That means they are bombarded with more advertising than any previous generation. But how much of it actually sticks?

The thought has clients in a panic. "The traditional marketing model is broken," Jim Stengel, Procter & Gamble's global marketing officer, told ad agency executives at an industry conference in February.

Traditional agencies cling to the hope that if they just make better ads, people won't TiVo them. "If you entertain consumers, they will seek you out," says Ken Kaess, CEO of DDB, the agency responsible for such memorable campaigns as Budweiser's "Whassup?" spots. But media buyers aren't so sure. Renetta McCann, CEO of Starcom North America, says mockingly that her creative colleagues keep pushing "that 30-second, half-a-million-dollar thing." She says that at a time when people are communicating through BlackBerries and consuming digital media on their wireless broadband-enabled laptops, ad agencies must be able to come up with something more groundbreaking.

So media buyers are taking it upon themselves to investigate the new forms of media and help clients find their way though the fragmenting media universe. Grey's MediaCom Worldwide calls consumers on their cellular phones to find out what kind of media and advertising they are exposed to at that very moment. WPP's Mindshare is distributing 20,000 PDAs that beep every 30 minutes and make similar inquiries. (Maybe if you're watching TV, surfing the Internet, instant-messaging, and listening to your iPod, you don't mind having a PDA beeping at you on the half-hour.)

These efforts are in their infancy, but the early results suggest that the transition to new media won't be easy for Madison Avenue. Alexander Schmidt-Vogel, MediaCom's CEO, points out that videogames, DVDs, iPods, mobile phones, and BlackBerries are largely ad-free media. "The amount of time people spend consuming media is growing, but the share of advertising possibilities is shrinking." Schmidt-Vogel says. He adds that in most cases, there is no way to measure the effectiveness of advertising through these new media (though Nielsen has announced that it will track consumers' exposure to product placements in videogames).

That leaves advertisers with a stark choice. They can venture forth into this strange new frontier, or they can stick with television and print, which still deliver large, if diminishing, audiences. They have generally taken the latter path. Internet ad spending grew 20% in 2003, to $7.2 billion. But it accounted for only 5% of the total $145.9 billion spent in the U.S. on ads. By contrast, spending on TV advertising was flat last year – at $45 billion.

Sumner Redstone, CEO of Viacom, CBS's parent company, likes to say that broadcast networks such as CBS are actually more valuable in an age of fragmentation. He argues that they are one of the few places that still deliver anything resembling a mass audience. There's some truth to that. Morgan Stanley analyst Richard Bilotti expects CBS to raise the prices yet again in this year's up-front market. You'd think Mindshare, Carat, and OMD might have been able to use their clout to rein in the networks. But so far they haven't had much success.

No wonder so many companies are frustrated when it comes to advertising. They may not be able to take out their grievances on the likes of Redstone, but as we've seen with Chrysler and BBDO, they sometimes take them out on their ad agencies.

Ad agency executives take comfort in the thought that things can't get any worse. But they do worry about the perception that Madison Avenue has become a depressing place to work in the past four years. Actually, it's more than a perception. Euro RSCG Worldwide recently commissioned a poll of ad agency employees and found that the majority of respondents complained that their agencies had become weaker, that people in the business weren't treated respectfully by clients, and that financial pressures made industry people "too scared to take risks."

After much deliberation, the American Association of Advertising Agencies came up with the idea of Advertising Week in New York City, an event next September intended to restore some of Madison Avenue's lost glamour. "I think one of the issues is we did a lousy job as an industry of selling ourselves," admits Kaess, the event's chairman. "It wasn't that we weren't cool. We weren't letting people know we were cool."

There will be splashy exhibits of public service advertising at Grand Central Station. Tony the Tiger will ring the opening bell at one of the city's stock exchanges. The most highly publicized event will be the induction of some of the advertising world's most cherished icons into the new Madison Avenue Walk of Fame. Who will the lucky cartoon characters be? The Jolly Green Giant? Smokey the Bear? The Keebler elves? Mr. Peanut? The public will chose from 26 nominees in a national poll conducted by USA Today and Yahoo. "We need to enjoy ourselves instead of spending all this time beating ourselves up," says Tom Carroll, CEO of the Americas TBWA/Chiat/Day.

It wouldn't hurt Madison Avenue to be a little reflective, though. So much of *Advertising Week* celebrates a vanished era when eccentric craftsmen ruled the business, media buyers knew their place, and 90% of the public watched prime-time television. Yes, that was a better time for many people in the industry. But it's gone.

It's not hard to draw parallels to the music industry. Like their Madison Avenue brethren, music industry people get misty-eyed when they look back at the era of the Beatles, the Rolling Stones, and Bob Dylan. Unfortunately, the record companies never came up with anything better. They coasted for years on revenues that rolled in when consumers replaced Dylan records with CDs. Instead of developing the same kind of enduring acts, it stamped out CDs by rap artists, few of whom were good for more than two releases. Then technology turned the world upside down. We all know what happened next.

The ad industry is in a similar position now. Is TiVo Madison Avenue's Napster? Is there some way to advertise on an iPod? It won't be easy to solve those riddles. But surely the best way for Madison Avenue to begin is to let go of the past.

Questions

1   How has power shifted in advertising agencies from creative to media buying?
2   What factors have accounted for changes in the practices of advertising?
3   What was the 15% commission system, and why has it declined?
4   How have procurement departments changed the relationship between agencies and clients?
5   What new forms of advertising do you see as complicating media buying?

Chapter 10

ELIZABETH A. SMITH AND RUTH E. MALONE

THE OUTING OF PHILIP MORRIS
Advertising Tobacco to Gay Men

THIS CASE STUDY PROFILES A MARKETING INCIDENT of the early 1990s. It details health and cultural implications stemming from a major corporation's placement of ads for an unhealthy product (cigarettes) in a medium targeted at a culturally vulnerable group (gay men). The authors highlight the different factors that "outed" Philip Morris's ad placement and made it a public issue: the eagerness of an alternative medium to attract mainstream advertising, the role of an ad agency in deciding on ad placement, and the competition of news media for exclusive stories. The chapter also focuses on the cautious nature of businesses not only when targeting a potentially controversial market, but also when responding to media attention about such targeting, especially with a product category that is also controversial. In this case, the distancing strategies that Philip Morris used in reacting to coverage said much about the socially conservative impulse of many corporations when dealing with potential controversy. The chapter also discusses the public health lessons that may be learned from this case study, especially in regards to smoking in the gay/lesbian/bisexual/transgender communities.

Numerous studies suggest that gay men have higher smoking prevalence rates than the population as a whole.[1-3] Why gay men are likelier to smoke has not been established. Hypotheses include the stresses of coming out and identity formation, depression, antigay victimization,[2] and a desire to fit into a subculture traditionally formed around gay bars, where both drinking and smoking are the norm.[4] Little previous work has explored tobacco industry influences on the gay community.

Just as it has approached other minorities,[5-7(p.336)] the tobacco industry has advertised in gay media.[8] sponsored gay community events,[9] and contributed to gay and AIDS organizations.[10,11] The normalizing effects of the tobacco industry's presence in the community may contribute to a higher smoking prevalence[12] and predispose the community to view the industry positively, support industry policy positions, and discourage tobacco control measures.[13] Advertising may have particular salience in the gay community, where it represents social validation.[14]

This study used internal tobacco industry documents and secondary historical media sources to explore the origin and reception of the first tobacco advertising in the gay press. As a "first," the campaign and events surrounding it generated discussion at the company and in the press. This historical analysis shows how the tobacco industry's approach to the gay community differs from its approach to racial minorities and suggests that tobacco control advocates have an opportunity to intervene before the relationship between the industry and the gay community becomes fully developed.

Methods

Data were collected from the Philip Morris Incorporated document. Web site (http://www.pmdocs.com/), which provides access to millions of company documents released as a result of the multistate attorneys general settlements and other cases. Between June 1, 2001, and October 1, 2001, we searched the Philip Morris Web site for documents pertaining to the industry's relationship with the gay community. We used a variety of search terms, including *gay, homosexual, queer,* and names of gay publications. We extended the searches by using names of individuals, dates, and other indexing information, in a "snowball" search strategy. Further information on document collection and searching strategies was provided previously.[15] In addition, major national newspapers and the lesbian and gay press were reviewed for the relevant period. This case study is based on review of 70 industry documents, Lexis/Nexis searches of more than 50 major newspapers, and examination of 13 lesbian and gay periodicals.

Advertising and the Gay Press

The gay press in the United States emerged in the 1950s, but it was not until the 1990s that national-circulation gay men's periodicals that appealed to mainstream advertisers were established.[16-18] One of these was *Genre,* established in 1991, which was less political and more focused on fashion and "lifestyle" than the previous generation of gay periodicals.[19] At the same time, gay marketing firms, using dubious data,[20] were "pitching" the community to advertisers by claiming that gay households had an average income up to two thirds higher than the national average.[21,22] Gay men also were reputed to have high levels of brand loyalty to companies that advertised directly to them.[23] "This is a dream market," one gay marketer said.[22]

Philip Morris Enters the Gay Market

The combination of gay self-promotion, the availability of appropriate periodicals, the increasing public awareness and acceptance of the gay community, and the desire for larger markets tempted Philip Morris to enter the market. By early 1992. Leo Burnett. Philip Morris's advertising agency, was urging the company to include the gay press in a larger campaign promoting a Benson & Hedges brand extension.[24] (A brand extension is a variation, such as low tar, king size, or soft pack, of an established brand.) A Leo Burnett media supervisor told Philip Morris that the gay community was "an area of opportunity for the brand." As "one of the first (if not the first) tobacco advertiser[s]." Philip Morris could " 'own the market' and achieve exclusivity."[24] Leo Burnett also suggested being "cautious . . . since this is . . . a brand launch" (i.e., a new product), and "the number of viable gay [publications] is limited." On Leo Burnett's recommendation, Philip Morris bought space in the October/November 1992 and December/January 1993 issues of *Genre*.[25]

Philip Morris did not expect the *Genre* advertisements to attract attention. The advertisements had no gay-specific content, and the company did not publicize them, aiming instead for a business-oriented story about how the advertising campaign would revitalize the Benson & Hedges brand. Philip Morris gave the story exclusively to Stuart Elliott, a business reporter for the *New York Times*.[26] Although Elliott was openly gay and was interested in gay marketing efforts,[21] the Philip Morris brand manager's notes[27] and Elliott's article[28] suggest that Elliott was willing to frame the story as an introduction of the brand to the business community, with no gay angle. However, the exclusive arrangement, designed to help Philip Morris control the press coverage, had the opposite effect.

The Outing of Philip Morris

Don Tuthill, the publisher of *Genre*, "outed" Philip Morris. Tuthill was thrilled to land the Philip Morris account. To publicize his accomplishment, he contacted Joanne Lipman, the advertising columnist at the *Wall Street Journal*. When Lipman asked Philip Morris to comment on its *Genre* advertising, company spokespeople declined because of the exclusive arrangement with the *Times*. "Needless to say," Philip Morris documents report, "she [Lipman] was not happy." Lipman's resulting story in the *Wall Street Journal*, headlined "Philip Morris to Push Brand in Gay Media,"[29] was, according to Philip Morris, "nasty headlined with a damaging tone that could have . . . reposition[ed] the brand."[26]

Lipman's story was picked up widely in the national media. Versions appeared in at least 7 big-city daily papers and on national and local television and radio news across the country.[30-49] This story had several elements that probably displeased Philip Morris. First, some reporters implicitly contrasted the masculine Marlboro Man with presumably effeminate gay men. The *Wall Street Journal* characterized the advertisements as "unprecedented for . . . Philip Morris, the very company behind the macho Marlboro Man."[29] NBC-TV commented that "when Philip Morris created a macho Marlboro Man, the gay man was probably not what [it] had in mind, but he is now."[42] The *New York Post*'s lead was even more jocular: "Don't look now, Marlboro Man—but you've got a brand-new gay partner."[34] *All Things Considered* treated this aspect seriously, discussing the Marlboro Man's popularity among gay men.[40]

Second, some reports suggested that the new product would be a "gay cigarette." Fox News in New York asked, "Well, just when you thought you had heard it all, how about a cigarette manufactured specifically for gays?"[44] The *New York Post*'s headline screamed, "New cigs aimed at gay smokers."[34] Most of the stories were more nuanced, claiming that the cigarette would be "targeted" to the gay community.[36,39-42,44] Some reports mentioned targeting only in Philip Morris's denial—for example, "Philip Morris denies that it is targeting any specific consumer group."[31,47,48,50]

Probably most troubling from Philip Morris's point of view, many reports brought up R.J. Reynolds' Uptown fiasco.[31,33,34,44,49] In 1989, when R.J. Reynolds' plans to market a new, high-nicotine brand called Uptown to African Americans were revealed, African American community health activists, including US Department of Health and Human Services Secretary Louis Sullivan, reacted with outrage. R.J. Reynolds dropped the brand.[51] Philip Morris could hardly have been happy to have this story rehashed in connection with its product launch.

The accusation of targeting was not entirely accurate. The impetus for advertising in *Genre* came from the advertising agency.[24,25] The agency, in turn, had been actively wooed by *Genre*.[30,52] Philip Morris had not been especially eager. Senior Vice President of Marketing David Dangoor said that there were "long discussions up the line" about the decision. Despite these reservations, Philip Morris ultimately decided that taking this "measured risk" was "the right thing to do."[53] Philip Morris apparently did no market research in the gay community before placing these advertisements, although it recognized some of the market's distinctive qualities. In 1993 the Benson & Hedges budget was slashed, but advertisements remained in *Out* and *Genre* because the space had already been purchased and was "unsuitable for other brand usage."[54]

Philip Morris took pains to emphasize that it was *not* targeting gays. The notes prepared for Michael A. Miles, chairman and chief executive officer of Philip Morris Companies Inc to use at the 1993 shareholders' meeting, suggested that he respond to questions with, "We did not develop separate advertising, nor did we attempt to position the brand specifically for gays."[55] Some gay men found this to be an effective defense. Elliott, the *Times* reporter, remarked. "It's not as though you did a special ad with two hunky guys who [had] just had sex with cigarettes in their mouths."[56]

Little evidence exists of how the story impressed the public. No visible response resembling the anti-Uptown campaigns came from either the gay community or tobacco control advocates. We could locate no newspaper articles or company documents that suggest that the exposure damaged the reputations or market share of the brand or company.

Gay Reaction

Gay leaders had a variety of reactions to the advertisements. Jerry Williams, the associate publisher of the weekly *Gay Chicago*, felt that the advertisements meant that "barriers are beginning to fall. It says 'we respect you as consumers and we want your business.' " He said he would "gladly" accept tobacco advertisements.[37] *Genre*'s Tuthill was ecstatic. "I'm just celebrating being part of the mix," he said. "We're not being excluded any longer."[30] Tuthill strongly objected to the angle of the *Wall Street Journal*'s story, which he said described "the tobacco industry . . . turning its marketing muscle on another minority." The real story, he asserted, was one of "inclusion" and of "how a conservative American company fights discrimination against homosexuals by putting its money where its mouth is."[57]

Others were more ambivalent. *The Advocate*'s editor, Jeff Yarbrough, remarked that it was difficult for gay publications to turn down advertisements because they were still "in a beggar's position, rather than a chooser's position."[40] The publisher of Chicago's *Outlines* newsmagazine said that she "might accept a cigarette ad, but balance it with equal space for a public-service message on cancer risks."[37] Another Chicago publisher of a gay periodical said that accepting cigarette advertisements "could damage [his] publication's image." He added, "To me, cigarettes kill."[37] Hal Offen, a spokesman from the Coalition of Lavender Americans on Smoking and Health—possibly the only gay tobacco control group then in existence—said, "This is a community already ravaged by addiction. We don't need the Marlboro Man to help pull the trigger."[58,59] A Lambda Legal Defense and Education Fund spokeswoman said, "I don't see how this can be construed as any kind of victory for gay rights."[34]

Philip Morris's internal account of the gay reaction appears flattering to the company but is not entirely convincing. A media relations brief recounted that Philip Morris had "fielded a variety of calls from the gay community. . . . All callers viewed [Philip Morris' advertising] as a very positive step."[60] The appreciative feedback is plausible, given the response of Tuthill and Williams and the eagerness of some segments of the gay community for commercial recognition. The company also claimed that it "saw a lot of good stories come out of the gay media praising Philip Morris."[26] This claim is not confirmed by a review of the gay press. Of 13 gay papers from across the country, only 4 had any coverage of the incident. The *San Francisco Bay Times* and the *San Francisco Sentinel* both quoted Offen. The *San Francisco Bay Times* headlined its story "Queers to Philip Morris: Drop Dead."[58,59] Two papers in Chicago also briefly covered the story.[61,62] The *Windy City Times* was the most industry-favorable, quoting Philip Morris's denial that it was "targeting" gays and mentioning market research about Benson & Hedges' popularity among gay men.[62] None of these stories praised Philip Morris.

Damage Control

Philip Morris's response to the media included 3 well-established techniques for coping with protests from racial minorities: deny, attack, and co-opt. In contrast to the company's usual emphasis on its close relationship with the community in question, however, Philip Morris chose to distance itself from the gay community (Table 10.1). As Philip Morris outlined them a few years later, the first key points to make "re: targeting minorit[ie]s" are that "Philip Morris does NOT target specific groups in society" (deny) and that "Anyone who believes that members of minority groups are more influenced by ads than [other] people is really saying that [they] are not as capable of making rational informed choices as other adults" (attack).[63]

Philip Morris made similar remarks to the media in regard to the *Genre* advertisements. The industry has frequently paid apparently independent spokespeople and front groups to represent it (co-opt), and Philip Morris made donations[68] and referred reporters who called about the *Genre* story to the Gay and Lesbian Alliance Against Defamation (GLAAD).[69]

Philip Morris had additional responses to minority group protests in its arsenal; these went unused. For example, the company liked to remind people that it had long supported the African American community by advertising in that community's publications, using African American models, hiring and promoting African Americans, and supporting institutions such as the United Negro College Fund and others "working for [civil] rights and equal opportunity because it is the right thing to do, not because of any ulterior motives."[63] Philip Morris could not have invoked any such long-standing relationship with or support for the gay community because little such support existed. In 1991, Philip Morris agreed to donate $ 1 200 000 to AIDS groups.[70–72] The company

Table 10.1 Philip Morris's Damage Control Strategies: African American Community and Gay Community

Strategy	African American Community	Gay Community
Deny targeting specific communities	"Philip Morris does NOT target specific groups in society."[63]	"We market all of our products to adult smokers, and we don't discriminate. Adult smokers includes both genders, all races and sexual preferences."[32]
Attack accusers	"Underlying the charge that . . . minorities make easy targets for marketing is the chauvinistic belief that they are incapable of making informed personal decisions for themselves."[64]	"People who have a problem with" Philip Morris's advertising in *Genre* "should really question their own levels of bigotry."[65]
Co-opt individuals or organizations	"Dr. Benjamin Hooks, former executive director of the National Association for the Advancement of Colored People, said 'critics of tobacco marketing efforts believe women and blacks are not capable of making their own free choice.' "[64]	GLAAD "has been very effective in facilitating [the] transition" of the [*Genre*] story toward "inclusion."[66]
Emphasize ties to the community	"The question shouldn't be 'why is PM advertising in the minority community?' but rather, 'where are the other major companies?' . . . PM cares enough to compete for minority business."[63]	
Distance the company from the community		"We have no plans to advertise Benson & Hedges Special Kings— or any of our other cigarette brands—in any other supposedly homosexual publications."[67]

Note. PM = Philip Morris. GLAAD = Gay and Lesbian Alliance Against Defamation.

could have used this donation as evidence of its support of the gay community. It also could have mentioned its financial contributions to GLAAD.[68]

Instead, Philip Morris spokeswoman Karen Daragan emphasized that the *Genre* advertisements were an insignificant part of the larger Benson & Hedges marketing plan, saying that the advertisements would appear in "nearly 60 other magazines" besides *Genre*.[30] The "nearly 60" figure was designed to underscore Daragan's assertion that Philip Morris marketed to all adults. Daragan also specifically mentioned *Playboy* and *Penthouse* as examples,[30] emphasizing the "heterosexuality" of the cigarette and the advertisements.

Philip Morris was especially eager to avoid any connections to gay sexuality, declining to advertise in *The Advocate* because that publication contained "sexually explicit ads."[25] At the shareholder meeting, Miles was coached to assure his audience that *Genre* "does not carry personal ads or ads for explicitly sexual products."[55] One gay publisher characterized this policy as "homophobia. They don't care about phone-sex ads in *Playboy*."[37] The company disavowed any knowledge of the gay community, telling 1 shareholder that it had "no marketing data specific to the 'homosexual market'—if such a market even exists."[73]

Denial, attack, and co-option are strategies the company used specifically to respond to accusations of target marketing. Another strategy the company used in a variety of contexts to control the flow of information was concealment. In this case, the company refused to provide a picture of the new brand or its advertising.[64] Thus, the story became one about "gay cigarettes," not Benson & Hedges.

Philip Morris's management was pleased with the company's recovery from the unwanted press coverage. Five days after the *Wall Street Journal* story, spokeswoman Daragan remarked that "the news has moved on to the much broader issue of 'inclusion' and does not mention the new cigarette by name."[69] And by early September, Senior Vice President of Marketing Dangoor concluded that the "Corporate Affairs Department did an excellent job with 'damage control.' " The initial *Wall Street Journal* article, Dangoor said, was "very unfortunate and 'unfair' "—but again, the brand was not strongly associated with the story, and "the reporting got fairer with time."[53]

Discussion

One lesson from the *Genre* incident is that tobacco control activists should disrupt the industry's tactic of concealment. Philip Morris was pleased that no pictures of the new product or its advertising reached the public and that the association between the "gay targeting" story and the new cigarette was lost. Keeping the focus on Benson & Hedges, ideally in such a way as to threaten its image or sales, might have been effective. A new product is likely the most vulnerable to any kind of negative publicity, as the Uptown episode demonstrated; activists should monitor business and advertising media closely to anticipate such introductions.

The *Genre* story also suggests that timing is a key aspect of combating concealment. Tuthill's press release came out a month before the advertisements were in print, so health advocates had time to respond. Advocates could have spent that month developing their own campaign designed for release when the advertisements appeared.

Advocates should be ready to capitalize on any attention to the tobacco industry. In this instance, Philip Morris was getting press it did not initiate with an angle that was unexpected, and an opportunity arose to build on the story. On August 15, 1992, a day after the *Genre* story broke, Doctors Ought to Care, a tobacco control advocacy group of physicians and medical students, released a batch of Philip Morris documents that focused on the company's donations to minority organizations,[74] but no link was made to the previous day's story. Doctors Ought to Care or other tobacco control activists could have made that link and potentially extended the life of both stories, as well as facilitating alliances among marginalized groups. The desire for acceptance that makes the gay community vulnerable to tobacco advertising also makes it eager to be regarded as a legitimate minority, and this opportunity could have been used to build tobacco control alliances.

The *Genre* episode also illustrates the complexity of the industry's relationships with marginalized groups. With its advertisements in *Genre*, Philip Morris was entering a lucrative new market and establishing new alliances with little investment. By not developing any gay-specific products or campaigns. Philip Morris protected itself both financially and socially. The company's only expense was for the advertisement itself, and when it was outed, the generic nature of the advertisement made the distancing strategy plausible. At the same time, by establishing itself in the vanguard of companies willing to market to gays, Philip Morris stood to gain valuable brand loyalty.

However, *Genre* was not simply waiting for Philip Morris. *The Advocate*'s Yarbrough pointed out that the gay media were beggars, not choosers, but even beggars act on their own behalf. Simply castigating Philip Morris for "targeting" ignores the publisher's decision to actively seek tobacco advertising. Tuthill did not see himself as a victim of a predatory industry: rather, he believed that he had elevated the status of the gay community by gaining support from a major corporation. Nor was Tuthill unique. As gay publications such as *Genre* became mainstream, they were more likely to get tobacco advertising and to become dependent on the revenue once they had it, and they were less likely to develop a critique of any advertiser, including the tobacco industry.[18] It was no accident that Philip Morris chose this moment to enter the gay market—and no concidence that it was welcomed.

Thus, the relationship between Philip Morris and Tuthill was a negotiation, though not one between equals. Tuthill was eager for the company's money, but Philip Morris was reluctant to be identified with gay men. And *Genre* was struggling for social acceptance and financial success, whereas the company was hungry for new markets.

This complex of factors means that public health would be well served by the development of an active gay and lesbian tobacco control movement. Objections from outsiders could be dismissed as attempts to keep gay periodicals and the gay community marginal. Health advocates would be unpersuasive if they addressed Tuthill and his ilk as mere victims, rather than acknowledging their agency. Thus, the most effective efforts would come from within the gay community, from those who share the same status and face the same choices as those accepting or courting industry support.

The time to formulate this response is now, while the relationship between the industry and the gay community is still relatively young. The contrast with the African American community makes the developmental stage of this relationship clear. Philip Morris, now The Altria Group,[75] was, and apparently still is, reluctant to identify or even be associated with the gay community. For instance, it does not publicize its contributions to gay (as opposed to AIDS) organizations such as GLAAD on its Web site (http://www.altria. com). The tobacco industry advertises to the gay community, but unlike other mainstream advertisers, it has yet to develop overtly gay-specific campaigns. The cigarette advertisements in gay magazines do not feature gay couples or symbols. Furthermore, these advertisements do not appear to be the primary support of gay periodicals. Few gay organizations are as publicly linked to the industry as GLAAD. These factors suggest that industry links to the gay community are still relatively weak, so advocates could intercede before community dependence on tobacco money becomes widespread and while public skepticism about the industry is still high.

Gay and lesbian tobacco control activists have already developed guidelines to help community organizations make the choice not to accept tobacco money.[76,77] These efforts should be nurtured by funding agencies, which could make community-level interventions a priority. Such programs should encourage activists to monitor and challenge tobacco industry support for gay media and organizations. These programs also should forge connections with tobacco control activism in other communities, and with other health activism in the gay community, such as that surrounding AIDS. The *Genre* story represents an opportunity lost, but it provides useful lessons for tobacco control in the gay community and other marginalized communities just beginning to come to the attention of the tobacco industry.

Questions

1 According to the authors, how was Philip Morris "outed" in the press?
2 How did gay leaders react to the advertisements' placement and resulting press coverage?
3 What strategies did Philip Morris use to response to media coverage of the ads?
4 What might health advocates learn from this case study about how to combat tobacco marketing?
5 How are tobacco companies still trying to market themselves?

Notes

1. Skinner WF. The prevalence and demographic predictors of illicit and licit drug use among lesbians and gay men. *Am J Public Health*. 1994;84: 1307–1310.
2. Ryan H, Wortley PM, Easton A, Pederson L, Greenwood G. Smoking among lesbians, gays, and bisexuals: a review of the literature. *Am J Prev Med*. 2001;21: 142–149.
3. Stall RD, Greenwood GL. Acree M. Paul J, Coates TJ. Cigarette smoking among gay and bisexual men. *Am J Public Health*. 1999;89: 1875–1878.
4. Harris CE. Out in life, still up in smoke? *J Gay Lesbian Med Assoc*. 1998;2: 91–92.
5. Pollay RW, Lee JS, Carter-Whitney D. Separate, but not equal: racial segmentation in cigarette advertising. *J Advertising*. 1992;21: 45–58.
6. Cummings K, Giovino G. Mendicino A. Cigarette advertising and black-white differences in brand preference. *Public Health Rep*. 1987; 102: 698–701.
7. Yerger VB. Malone RE. African American leadership groups: smoking with the enemy. *Tob Control* 2002;11: 336–45.
8. Goebel K. Lesbians and gays face tobacco targeting. *Tob Control*. 1994;3: 65–67.
9. Conkin D. Tobacco $$ for the gay community a Lucky Strike—or a cancer? *Bay Area Reporter*. December 5, 1996: 18–19.
10. Offen N. Demonstrators booted from GLAAD soiree. *Bay Area Reporter*. June 14, 2001:2.
11. Engardio JP. Outing the Marlboro Man. San *Francisco Weekly*, February 16–22. 2000: 16.
12. Tye JB. Warner KE, Clantz SA. Tobacco advertising and consumption: evidence of a causal relationship. *J Public Health Policy*. 1987;8: 492–508.
13. *Tobacco Use Among US Racial/Ethnic Minority Groups—African Americans, American Indians and Alasha Natives, Asian Americans and Pacific Islanders, and Hispanics: A Report of the Surgeon General*. Atlanta, Ga: National Center for Chronic Disease Prevention and Health Promotion, Office on Smoking and Health; 1998. Report S/N 017–001–00527–4.
14. Penaloza L. We're here, we're queer, and we're going shopping. A critical perspective on the accommodation of gays and lesbians in the US marketplace. *J Homosex*. 1996;31: 9–41.
15. Malone RE, Balbach ED. Tobacco industry documents: treasure trove or quagmire? *Tob Control*. 2000; 9: 334–338.
16. Harris D. Out of the closet, and into never-never land. *Harpers*. December 1995: 52–53.

17. Streitmatter R. *Unspeakable: The Rise of the Gay and Lesbian Press in America* Hoston, Mass: Faber & Faber; 1995.

18. Sender K. Gay readers, consumers, and a dominant gay habitus: 25 years of *The Advocate* magazine. *J Commun.* 2001;51:73–99.

19. Enrico D. Bucking trends, gay lifestyle magazine debuts. *New York Newsday.* March 21, 1991:49.

20. Fejes F, Lennon R. Defining the lesbian/gay community? Market research and the lesbian/gay press. *J Homosex.* 2000;39:25–43.

21. Elliott S. Advertisers bypass gay market. *USA Today.* July 17, 1990:B1.

22. Rigdon JE. Overcoming a deep-rooted reluctance. more firms advertise to gay community. *Wall Street Journal.* July 18, 1992:B1.

23. San Francisco Examiner. Survey shows gays have brand loyalty. *Tampa Tribune.* April 28, 1997:22.

24. Makuch M. Gay-oriented publications. 1992.03.05. Bates No. 2041794319/4320. Available at: http://www.pmdoes.com. Accessed July 16, 2001.

25. Upchurch T. Letter, 1992.06.25. Bates No. 2041794318/4322. Available at: http://www.pmdocs.com. Accessed July 11, 2001.

26. [Speech on media affairs]. 1992.09.00. Bates No. 2025893465/3471. Available at: http://www.pmdocs.com. Accessed September 12, 2001.

27. Han V. David Dangoor interview with NYT. 1992.08.12. Bates No. 2025887538/7540. Available at: http://www.pmdocs.com. Accessed September 12, 2001.

28. Elliott S. Benson & Hedges shrinks in a bid to regain growth. *New York Times.* August 27, 1992;D18.

29. Lipman J. Philip Morris to push brand in gay media 1992.08.13. Bates No. 2073723375/3376. Available at: http://www.pmdocs.com. Accessed September 13. 2001.

30. Associated Press. Philip Morris to advertise in magazine for gay men. 1992.08.13. Bates No. 2023439131. Available at: http://www.pmdocs.com. Accessed September 13, 2001.

31. Associated Press. Philip Morris sets ads in gay mag. 1992.08.14. *Philadelphia Daily News.* Bates No. 2023439126. Available at: http://www.pmdocs.com. Accessed September 25, 2001.

32. Associated Press. Cigarette giant plans its first ad campaign in gay magazine. 1992.08.14. *Detroit News.* Bates No. 2023439127. Available at: http://www.pmdocs.com. Accessed September 13, 2001.

33. Associated Press. Cigarette firm targets gay magazine for ads. 1992.08.14. *San Francisco Examiner.* Bates No. 2023439128. Available at: http://www. pmdocs.com. Accessed September 13.2001.

34. Hoffman B. New cigs aimed at gay smokers. 1992.08.14. Bates No. 2023439130. Available at: http://www.pmdocs.com. Accessed September 17. 2001.

35. MeIntyre B. Tobacco company targets gay men. *London Times.* August 15. 1992:8.

36. Scott J. Targeting gay groups a louchy issue. 1992.08.18. Bates No. 2023439139. Available at: http://www.pmdocs.com. Accessed September 13. 2001.

37. Sall I. Gay magazine gains cigarette ad—and debate. *Chicago Sun-Times.* August 18, 1992:43.

38. Video Monitoring Services of America. *Day Break.* 1992.08.13. Bates No. 2023439117. Available at: http://www.pmdocs.com. Accessed September 14, 2001.

39. Video Monitoring Services of America. *The News at Noon.* 1992.08.13. Bates No. 2023439119. Available at: http://www.pmdocs.com. Accessed September 14, 2001.

40. Video Monitoring Services of America. *All Things Considered.* 1992.08.13. Bates No. 2023439120/9121. Available at: http://www.pmdocs.com. Accessed September 14, 2001.

41. Video Monitoring Services of America. WIXS AM radio program [transcript]: 1992.08.13. Bates No. 2023439118. Available at: http://www.pmdocs.com. Accessed September 20, 2001.

42. Video Monitoring Services of America. *News at Sunrise.* 1992.08.14. Bates No. 2023439136. Available at: http://www.pmdocs.com. Accessed July 20, 2001.

43. Video Monitoring Services of America. Monitoring report Philip Morris Special Kings schedule of broadcast activity. 1992.08.14. Bates No. 2023439122/9123. Available at: http://www.pmdocs.com. Accessed September 20.2001.

44. Video Monitoring Services of America. *Good Day New York* 1992.08.17. Bates No. 2023439140/9141. Available at: http://www.pmdocs.com. Accessed July 20, 2001.

45.   Radio TV Reports. *Today* (National News) broadcast excerpt 1992.08.14. Bates No. 2023439137/9138. Available at: http://www.pmdocs.com. Accessed July 20, 2001.

46.   *Business Tonight* broadcast excerpt 1992.08.14. Bates No. 2023439134/9135. Available at: http:// www.pmdocs.com. Accessed July 20, 2001.

47.   Radio TV Reports. Headline news broadcast excerpt 1992.08.14. Bates No 2023439133. Available at: http://www.pmdocs.com. Accessed September 20. 2001.

48.   Rosato D. Cigarette ads. 1992.08.14. Bates No. 2023439129. Available at: http://www. pmdocs.com. Accessed September 13, 2001.

49.   Cigarette firm plans ads in gay magazine. 1992.08.14. Bates No. 2023439124. Available at: http://www.pmdocs.com. Accessed September 24, 2001.

50.   *Washington Post* coverage of *Genre* advertising [memo]. 1992.08.14. Bates No. 2023439125. Available at: http://www.pmdocs.com. Accessed September 14, 2001.

51.   Smith NC. Uptown, Dakota, and PowerMaster. In: Donaldson T, Gini A. eds. *Case Studies in Business Ethics*. Upper Saddle River, NJ: Prentice Hall; 1996: 53–58.

52.   Levin G. Mainstream's domino effect: liquor, fragrance, clothing advertisers ease into gay magazines. *Advertising Age*. January 18, 1993:30.

53.   Dangoor DER. Benson and Hedges Special Kings—*Genre* media coverage. 1992.09.02. Bates No. 2023439109. Available at: http://www.pmdocs.com. Accessed September 17, 2001.

54.   Schneider R. B&H Kings revised media plan. 1993.06.04. Bates No. 2044361518/1519. Available at: http://www.pmdocs.com. Accessed September 14, 2001.

55.   Annual meeting questions and answers for Michael A. Miles PM USA. 1993.01.00. Bates No. 2022989437/9448. Available at: http://www. pmdocs.com. Accessed September 14, 2001.

56.   Peterson W. NY Times interview. 1992.08.21. Bates No. 2025887508/7509. Available at: http:// www.pmdocs.com. Accessed September 12, 2001.

57.   Tuthill D. Letter from Don Tuthill to Joanne Lipman. 1992.08.17. Bates No. 2025887474/ 7475. Available at: http://www.pmdocs.com. Accessed September 13. 2001.

58.   Philip Morris targeting cigarettes to gays. *San Francisco Sentinel*. August 20, 1992:9.

59.   Avicolli Mecca T. Queers to Philip Morris: drop dead. *San Francisco Ray Times*. August 27, 1992:10.

60.   Media relations/employee communications. 1992.08.00. Bates No. 2047319345/9346. Available at: http://www.pmdocs.com. Accessed September 13, 2001.

61.   Baim T. Ad news. *Outlines* September 1992:35.

62.   Philip Morris places ad in gay magazine. *Windy City Times* August 27, 1992:10.

63.   Asbury Park Press. 1995.05.00. Bates No. 2047319798/9799. Available at: http://www. pmdocs. com. Accessed September 6, 2001.

64.   PM USA corporate affairs issues handbook. 1995.01.19. Bates No. 2044183393/3423. Available at: http://www.pmdocs.com. Accessed April 10, 2002.

65.   PM USA media affairs (920814–920821). 1992.08.21. Bates No. 2025897821/7826. Available at: http://www.pmdocs.com. Accessed September 13. 2001.

66.   Daragan K. Benson and Hedges Special Kings/ *Genre* media coverage. 1992.08.19. Bates No. 2023439110. Available at: http://www.pmdocs.com. Accessed September 17, 2001.

67.   Consumer response letter re: Genre advertising. 1992.08.21. Bates No. 2046522585/2586. Available at: http://www.pmdocs.com. Accessed September 14. 2001.

68.   Internal documents detail aggressive tobacco industry campaign. 1993.01.00. Bates No. 204789-6864/6867. Available at: http://www. pmdocs.com. Accessed November 7, 2001.

69.   Daragan K. Special Kings/*Genre* coverage. 1992.08.18. Bates No. 2023439113. Available at: http://www.pmdocs.com. Accessed September 14, 2001.

70.   Bartlett D. Q&As at 900000 and 910000 share-holders meetings. 1992.04.10. Bates No. 2023004427. Available at: http://www.pmdocs.com. Accessed September 27, 2001.

71.   Offen N, Smith EA, Malone RE. From adversary to target market: the ACT-UP boycott of Philip Morris. *Tob Control*. In press.

72.   Ramirez A. Philip Morris to increase AIDS donations. *New York Times*. May 30, 1991:D4.

73.   Parrish SC. Letter to shareholder Campos re: *Genre* advertising. 1992.08.25. Bates No. 202284-4169/4170. Available at: http://www.pmdocs. com. Accessed September 14, 2001.

74.   Babcock CR. Philip Morris donations target minority groups. *Washington Post*. August 15, 1992:A6.

75.   Smith EA. Malone RE. Altria means tobacco: Philip Morris's identity crisis. *Am J Public Health*. 2003:553–556.

76.   Drabble I., *Ethical Funding for Lesbian, Gay, Bisexual, Transgender and HIV/AIDS Community-Based Organizations: Practical Guidelines When Considering Tobacco, Alcohol, and Pharmaceutical Funding*. San Francisco, Calif: Coalition of Lavender Americans on Smoking and Health and Progressive Research and Training for Action; 2001.

77.   Gay and Lesbian Medical Association. *Healthy People 2010 Companion Document for Lesbian, Gay, Bisexual, and Transgender (LGBT) Health*. San Francisco, Calif: Gay and Lesbian Medical Association; 2001.

PART FOUR

Ads and Globalization

INTRODUCTION TO PART FOUR

LIKE MANY BUSINESSES IN AN INCREASINGLY global economy, advertising has gradually transitioned from a domestic industry to one whose arms of influence reach around the world. Although the roots of international campaigns go back to early in the twentieth century, arguably the shift to a transnational business model began in earnest in the 1980s, and today's advertising agencies and their holding companies cater to a multinational and multiethnic client base. What's more, as most media companies produce and distribute content internationally, marketers and corporations have ever more opportunities to attract consumers—and therefore influence culture—in a wide array of geographic markets.

Although the strong international presence of the advertising and media industries is perhaps not surprising, it has been the subject of great debate. Among the most significant criticisms is that local issues have been eclipsed by a commercialized, global agenda. Indigenous media systems may find themselves emphasizing advertising-friendly themes, themes often originating in the West. In addition, the ads themselves offer a celebration of consumption that may influence the value systems of local cultures. Another concern about global advertising is the issue of representation. While advertisers have long been criticized for the ways in which they portray women, children, and minority groups, they now face the additional challenge of acceptably portraying individuals and ethnic groups in cultures very different from their own.

This Part illustrates how advertisers and scholars are wrestling with these issues in a global era of marketing communication. Not only do these essays examine the influence of Western images on various nations, but they also discuss groups within these nations, including women and people of different socio-economic statuses. As you read this Part, consider the ways in which global flows of images and information may be intensifying as we move further into the twenty-first century.

Chapter 11

MAITRAYEE CHAUDHURI

GENDER AND ADVERTISEMENTS
The Rhetoric of Globalisation

ADVERTISEMENTS CAN BE CONSIDERED RICHLY VALUABLE cultural indicators. That is, they can be read for the ways in which they represent the social world and its members. Maitrayee Chaudhuri, a sociologist at the Centre for the Study of Social Systems at Jawaharlal Nehru University in New Delhi, conducts such a close analysis of Indian print advertisements, using them as a lens through which to examine the shape-shifting public discourse in contemporary India. She is particularly interested in changing gender narratives in the wake of India's globalization movement. Chaudhuri finds such narratives about the "new" Indian man and woman troublesome as they have seemingly displaced the positions occupied by the majority of India's citizens.

Introduction

This article is about advertisements and gender images, and hinges on the argument that they can be fruitfully understood as the rhetoric of India's project of globalisation. It rests on the assumption that the shift in the Indian state's economic policy in favour of globalisation has accompanied a shift in public discourse as evidenced in the media. My focus is on advertisements in the English print media—a media whose hegemonic significance cannot be wished away by its apparently inconsequential numerical strength. Because the focus is on "shift," I make frequent forays into the past for purposes of comparison. By the past I refer to the decades preceding the Indian state's far-reaching economic reforms in the latter part of the 1980s—a process commonly termed "liberalization," referring to the process of opening up the Indian market and integrating it into the global economy. This process, I argue, marks a break with the Indian state's stated sympathy with socialist ideas, with the notion of growth with equity and a public discourse on which there was near unanimity that such goals were desirable in themselves. This self-proclaimed ideology of the Indian state was a legacy of the Indian national movement, itself a rich and complex repository of ideas of which a significant part were those of socialism and distributive justice. The Indian national movement's struggle for freedom cannot therefore be simply negatively defined as an oppositional movement against British imperialism, but must be seen as a positive projection of a worldview that understood "freedom" as a commitment to political, economic, and social freedom for all sections of the people—men and women—the world over, with particular reference to the dispossessed. I would like to draw attention to this idea of "freedom," because contemporary advertisements that I analyse later also tend to articulate a vision of freedom for the Indian woman and man, but one that is very differently anchored. In emphasising the dispossessed, I do not mean to suggest that the ideology of the Indian national movement or of globalisation are ungendered, but to stress that the category of gender cannot be exclusively deployed to the exclusion of the myriad ways in which it articulates with class and the specific histories of nonwestern postcolonial societies.

I see, therefore, in the recasting of gender images in adverts, a simultaneous recreation of both a new consuming Indian "middle" class in a globalised economy and a reorientation of the salient issues taken up by the media. I emphasise that, although the explicit focus in this paper is the new normative Indian consumer who dons the glossy advertisements, a key argument is that these adverts implicitly but effectively eclipse the image of "another world" of Indian men and women—poor and battered, tribal and peasant, working class and Dalit[1]—from public discourse.[2]

Apart from the construction of a "new normative Indian man and woman," apart from the banishment of the poor and marginalised in the media in general and advertisements in particular, there has also been a shift from a widely held view in independent India that believed freedom from the commercial imperatives of sponsors would enable it to function as the fourth estate of an economically poor democracy. No newspaper or magazine today, however, can be commercially viable without advertisements.[3] Industry sources[4] show a dramatic rise in total advertising revenue. From 3,000 crore Rupees (30,000 million) in 1994–1995, it has shot up to 82,000 crores (820,000 million) in 1999–2000. Of this, 56% are from the print media and 36% from television. It is against this context that this article has been written.

Because my central contention is that there has been a shift in Indian public discourse, I will turn to history to illustrate an earlier discourse from where the shift has taken place. Indian nationalist thought was a curious mixture of disparate ideologies and world views, possible perhaps only in the tragic sites of colonized countries. Although the image of the traditional Hindu self-effacing woman was always an icon, so was the struggling Indian peasant and worker, as was the recast modern Indian woman—educated, politically aware, and yet innocent of western cultural mores. Writings of major women activists in the nationalist period opined that, unlike in the west, the Indian women's movement was supported by male reformers and nationalists. And, in contemporary times cultural nationalists have sought to portray the Indian woman as chaste, demure, and sexually sanitized, unlike her prurient western counterpart.

I have discussed elsewhere that modern Indian thought on nationalism and on the woman question was a curious agglomeration of ideas freely drawn from liberalism, socialism, and cultural revivalism (Chaudhuri, 1996). So along with conflicting gender images, there was always the attempt to represent men and women from different classes. Independent India was largely dominated by a public discourse that this body of nationalist thought had shaped. Today, some of that curious admixture of ideas on gender lingers on, and is clearly noticeable even in advertisements. It would be easy, therefore, to find images of the demure, chaste Indian woman along with the self-possessed career woman. But images of either a peasant woman or a working-class man are well-nigh impossible to discover. It is well-recognized that "society . . . requires discourse (the mapping, description and articulation of situations and processes) which by definition has the effect of annihilating and delegimitising certain views and positions while including others" (van Zoonen, 1994, p. 40). I maintain that advertisements play precisely this role of delegitimising space in public discourse for the majority of Indian men and women.

Understanding Advertisements

The focus in this article is on the text of the adverts themselves. I confine my study to select English-medium newspapers and magazines in the 1990s, a decade when India's new economic policy made its presence felt. The newspapers surveyed are *The Times of India*, its sister publication *The Economic Times, Business Standard*, and *The Hindu*. The magazines consist of women's magazines such as *Femina, The Women's Era, Savvy, The New Woman*, and the popular general weeklies like *The Sunday, The Week*, and *The Outlook*. I have been following these on a regular basis, subscribing to some and borrowing others from a local lending library that is a regular feature of middle class colonies in Delhi, often functioning from what are narrow rooms built as garages for two wheelers. I mention this because although a *Savvy* is more expensive than a *Week*, and could be therefore targeting different socio-economic segments, the daily lending rates are such that women and men can in practice read across a wide range of weeklies. I also make the point because I am *not* making a comparative analysis of advertisements that appear in different publications.[5] I am instead arguing that I discern a wider pattern despite the differences.

I attempt here to read the ideological meanings of the adverts, locating them against the concrete historical instance of liberalising India. I favour, therefore, a causal logic of determinacy, but also pay deference to the internal logic of arrangement, of internal relations, of articulations of parts within a structure. I understand advertising as "the necessary material production within which an apparently self-subsistent mode of production can alone be carried on" (Williams, 1977, pp. 92–93). The product is not separable from the act of producing (Marx, 1976, p. 1048). The analysis of adverts cannot, therefore, be separated from the economic processes of liberalisation. I take the decisive relationship between the media and monopoly capitalism as given (Murdoch & Golding 1979). Scholars have extensively dealt with this as with the impact of advertising on mass media (Curran, 1981; Williams, 1980).

This relationship between the media and adverts gets further compounded in "Third World" media, for here the issue is not just about media being profit-driven but driven by "international capitalist interests" (Reeves, 1993). The international is more often western than not, which has its own set of cultural implications for an erstwhile colonised society such as India. India has a long history of self-reliant development and fierce defence of "national sovereignty." Fears about the impact of liberalisation generally and on the media in particular persist. We thus have not only adverts but features in defense of advertisements and what they portend for a free society, now that the long years of independent India's tryst with "planned development" is over (Chaudhuri, 1998, 2000).

A concerted ideological campaign thus has to be carried out to establish the legitimacy of the new economic regime, to which advertising contributes. Adverts have been likened to myths, in that they frequently resolve social contradictions, provide models of identity, and celebrate the existing social order. As Barthes (1977) puts it, myth consists in overturning culture into nature with the quite contingent foundations of the utterance becoming Common Sense, Right Reason, the Norm and General Opinion (Barthes, 1977). That this is the way dominant ideology functions has had its share of adherents and opponents. Adherents very broadly draw their understanding, however mediated, from Marx (Marx & Engels, 1984). The suggestion that the ideas of the ruling class are the ideas of society has undergone periodic refurbishment. Gramsci (1971, p. 245) used "hegemony" to refer to the process by which general consent is actively sought for the interpretations of the ruling class. Dominant ideology becomes invisible because it is translated into common sense, appearing as the natural, apolitical state of things. Clearly, advertisements are the contemporary mediators of hegemony. In Althusserian theories of ideology the individual is interpolated by dominant ideology. Advertisements would, we can infer, act as ideological apparatuses.

Not surprisingly then, adverts have a key role to play in the ideological transformation of public discourse. And within modern advertising, gender is probably the social resource that is used most (Jhally, 1987, p. 135). The obsession is said to spring from the "signifying power" of gender. "Something that can be conveyed fleetingly in any social situation and yet something that strikes as the most basic characteristic of the individual" (Goffman, 1976, p. 7). Thus, the extremely condensed form of communication in advertising lends itself exceptionally well to an examination of cultural values, beliefs, and myths connected to gender. I argue that it also lends itself to an examination of the desirable values and practices of the normative Indian—man and woman—in a postliberalised era.

The New Generation Indian Man and Woman

The reader may understand by now that my intent is to show a shift in the dominant representation of the normative Indian, and hence, my periodic reference to the colonial past. The colonial period witnessed dramatic social transformations, region-specific histories of middle-class growth and region-specific responses of this class to articulate a modern normative Indian. Although different ideological responses contested their way through, it may not be wide of the mark to claim that they were united in their commitment to the wider Indian society—to questions of inequity and justice. Collective concern defined their notion of selfhood. If I were asked to describe the "new Indian" that adverts depict today, I would identify a typical corporate sector executive, an upwardly mobile professional who travels a great deal, works hard, and unwinds at weekends and holidays. This, I contend, would hold true for both men and women, with the difference that images of a traditional woman homemaker coexist with adverts of female high achievers, while for men images of high achievers are always at the forefront.

The entry of a large number of transnational companies at the beginning of liberalization led to a real possibility of young men and women entering the corporate sectors at salaries that their parents could not dream of even at retirement. A new work ethos entered Indian public discourse as India's middle class learned to exchange safety and security for success and upward mobility. What I am arguing is that certain changes are taking place in the ideas and ways of life of the middle class. My discussion here is nongendered to the extent that I emphasise certain new "universal" characteristics of the middle class; but in a gendered society many of these characteristics are operationalized in a gendered fashion. Thus, we have a redefining of middle-class virtues at home, with the household actively redrawn as a site of consumption. Within this context the Indian woman learns that "thrift" is no longer a virtue, and "shopping" is a legitimate pleasure (Chaudhuri, 1998), while Indian men learn that looking good is not a woman's privilege. I will focus first on the "general" impact of adverts on Indian society before moving on to gender differences in the next section.

Adverts both depict new trends and accelerate them. Adverts also obliterate other trends. This raises the contentious question of the relationship between "reality" and "representation." A central debate among feminist media scholars concerns the "distortion" theme; that the media does not represent the "real" picture of women. The epistemological basis of this transmission model of communication is twofold. One is that "there is a reality and then after the fact, our account of it" (Carey, 1989, p. 25). The second is that the role of the media in modern societies is bardic: by definition the media cannot simply "reflect" for the bard's task is primarily to render the unfamiliar into the already known, or into "common sense" (van Zoonen, 1994, p. 38).

The analysis below demonstrates how obviously adverts seek to create a branded self. My method of analysis avers that a reading of meanings from texts alone is guilty of internal fallacy, and that cognizance should be given to the author's intention. In the case of adverts the intent of the sponsor is mediated through the advert maker. Before looking into the texts of adverts themselves, therefore, it is useful to explore how the advert maker understands the emergence of the "new Indian." The "reader" is the "customer," and today the advertising industry is brainstorming about who the customer is. "What drives Sybil?" is the name for a market survey conducted by the advertising firm Lintas to study consumer profiles. "The AP Lintas universe[6] prefers to slice Indian consumers into survivors, savers, enhancers, and splurgers. The urban and rural poor are survivors, and savers are the middle classes. Enhancers are the urban upper class, and splurgers the rich" (*Brand Equity*, *The Economic Times* 16–22 June 1999).

Not all can afford to buy what the adverts seek to sell. Not all those who can afford to will buy. But they can desire and aspire to possess them and thereby be like the new Indians the adverts project. A new normative Indian is being established. I find David Chaney's observation of interest where he tries to show how "the new social form of lifestyles was coloured by some of the broader narratives of the cultural forms of consumerism" summarized under the headings of "fantasy, excess, spectacle and citizenship" (Chaney, 1994, p. 19). The first three features are reasonably self-evident. The last, citizenship, is not. Chaney's reason for using it is that he found no better way of putting the idea that mass marketing, as with other forms of mass democracy, offers the illusion of equal participation, and indeed even the glory of "national culture" without much of its substantive powers. This, I think, is a useful way of understanding advertisements and the images they extend. Most people can look at and hear adverts. Few can read adverts. Fewer still can read English adverts. The numbers that can actually possess the goods advertised are smaller still. But theoretically everyone has access to adverts, to the pleasure of looking, to desiring.

It is widely known that product advertisement has generally given way to lifestyle adverts. Hence, the language of advertisements is more about the consumer than the object to be consumed. The adverts themselves give overt profiles of the new generation. Adverts demand that the media seek an audience who are "hedonists"—who like to "experiment" and have an attitude of spending. I attempt below to identify some key features of the new Indian, but before that a few words on what it is from which the new Indian is breaking away.

Colonial societies underwent dramatic and often violent social, cultural, economic, and political changes. In response, these societies produced a whole range of social movements. A key component of these movements—reform, nationalist, radical—was a redefinition of what constituted the Indian. The dominant nationalist rhetoric suggested that the Indian be modern, rational, and rooted in India's past. His vision was embedded in a collectivist vision where the growth of the nation meant equity and justice, and a modest and low key lifestyle was a desired code in public life. The erstwhile maharajas, ostentatious displays and spectacle were not part of legitimate public discourse.

The old "new Indian" was internationalist. Nonalignment, close ties with the former socialist block, fraternity, with the nationalist struggles of Asia and Africa were creeds of public life. Here, too, internationalism meant an imagining of collective struggles of the dispossessed. It is important to make this point to distinguish the internationalist from the globe-trotting Indian.

I would like to argue that liberalization has broken down a more traditional system of marking identities within the middle class. The middle class has expanded and markings have changed. The sensualist has replaced the intellectualist paradigm. "The shift from producer to consumer capitalism has meant its disruption, which . . . has brought the transience of new styles, the introduction of a new flattening temporality and the reduction of the self to the mere politics of presentation" (Lash & Friedman, 1996, p. 18).

The New Indian is Global and Cosmopolitan

A premier builder in India makes an offer to the Nonresident Indian (NRI) that is splashed in almost all the newspapers: "Would an Elite NRI like you really need any other Residence more luxurious in India?" than "Ansals Celebrity Homes—the international class country township." Vip Skybags, with a half page picture of its luggage visible in *Outlook* and *India Today* (but not the women's magazines), writes: "He treats his export business like sport. And airport lobbies, like racing tracks." Skybag Luggage asks: "Where next? Seven wonders of the world. Five Great lakes in the States. 4 days–3 nights in Seychelles. Two semis in England. One mother-of-a-trek in the Himalayas." The advert for Mercedes-Benz, which appears in magazines (except women's magazines), says: "1. This is when he promised you his love, his hand, and a Mercedes. 2. This is when he gave you his love and his hand (pity not the Mercedes). 3. You are here now. Isn't it time?"

I have never seen an advert for Mercedes before mid-1999. Perhaps here is the contentious issue of "equality" of access, in form if not content. The relative democratization is not entirely illusory. Liberalization has led to the emergence of a much larger very rich section of the population than before. The juxtaposition of love and Mercs needs no elaboration. Significantly, the advert is addressed to the woman. The potential buyer is a man. The reason for buying—the woman.

It has been argued by some that this new Indian is cosmopolitan and unmarked by the divisions (ethnic, religious, caste) that have plagued India in the last decade or more. Some have argued that a kind of secession has taken place within Indian society whereby the middle classes, whom the market seeks, no longer have even the appearance of commitment to the larger Indian populace mired in poverty and distress. Others have sought to show that many of the "young" with an attitude of spending were among those who cheered at the demolition of the Babri Masjid (the mosque torn down by Hindu fundamentalists), and therefore, the new Indian is very much marked by class, caste, and religion. My own reading of adverts suggests that for the splurgers and enhancers, the thrust is to cultivate an image of international looks, international lifestyles. For the savers, more overt statements of cultural specificities are made. *Elle*, an up-market magazine carried on its cover page India model Sheetal Malhans who has been picked up as the face of Maybelline cosmetics. Images such as hers are truly "international," marked only by the rules of the fashion business, which are still very west-centric. When the "traditional" or "ethnicised" Indian is presented, therefore, the construct is a western one. What has become a cliched observation perhaps needs repeating in a different context. The orient is an invention of the occident.

The New Indian is Body Conscious

There is a column in almost every magazine and newspaper on health. To illustrate, "A toast to good health" has an assortment of recipes with the introductory commentary saying:

> "You are what you eat." So why not take a break from relishing fried food and oily fare that is unhealthy. Here's an assortment of low calorie salads that not only promise to keep you healthy, but also tickles your taste buds. You don't need to think twice here. So go ahead and indulge.
>
> (*New Woman*, March 1999, p. 121)

"The prospect of stretch marks may seem scary to a woman of today who is conscious of herself and her body. But today, with 'Stretch Nil' a herbal stretch mark preventive is available with the local chemist" and stretch marks "are no longer the dreadful nightmare they used to be" (*The Outlook*, May 4, 1999). The advert further mentions that "one always tends to concentrate on the baby more than oneself during pregnancy. Though this may seem the right thing to do, it is imperative the mother takes as much care of herself too." This new body consciousness cuts across gender as an article on the "slimming craze" seeks to show. "The demand of today's young men and women to keep fit and remain attractive spawned a multi-billion industry all over the world" (*The Hindu*, November 16, 1998).

A VIP luggage advert with a woman's face (three-fourths of the page) has just this line: "You don't have to be good-looking but it helps" in bold. Another of "Ever Youth; collagen and elastin"—an antiwrinkle cream—screams "STOP THAT CLOCK." This premium on youthful appearance is certainly a break in a society where age used to mean authority. I will explore the implications of the new awareness of the body in the concluding section.

The New Indian is "Free"

Advertisements have contributed to the dismantling of a public discourse where social equity was as critical as, if not more important than, growth, and have legitimised the pleasures and ethos of the free market. "Freedom," according to a caption of an American Express advert, is "knowing just how far you can go and then getting there." "It's all about living without ambiguities. Including the facts about your credit cards." Another claims: "You want more from life, because you give it your best." Both adverts have full-sized silhouettes of a young figure in a stretching-out gymnastic posture. Significantly, one of these is a man, the other a woman. Credit cards have made their presence felt in the market only in the last decade and acquired prominence in metropolitan cities in the last 5 years.

Then there is the family,[7] cycling into the sunset on the sea shore, celebrating "freedom." "I am *free* to appreciate what I have–, to look into the future–, to open new doors for my family. I am *free* because I have one of the largest financial organizations behind me" (emphasis mine). The sponsor is Hong Kong Bank, the advert visible across the selection of non-women's magazines.

The New Indian is Ethnic Not "Desi"

One feature that has been commented upon in contemporary culture has been "hybrid-ization"—the mixing and matching of styles and artifacts from different cultures and a general stylistic promiscuity and playful mixing of codes. The argument is that hegemony is passé and hybridity is the state of being. I would differ and argue that while the fashion industry's appropriation of the ethnic may be in, the Indian still cannot be just native or "desi."

In the face of competition, Amrutanjan, a traditional health care company, is going in for a complete facelift, and taking the war right to the multinational companies. "The balm is no longer being advertised as the quintessential grandma's home-treatment, or the secret recommendation of one housewife to another; the *target segment now is the hip, smarter set—the younger no-oil-in-the-hair generation*" (*Business Standard*, Wednesday January 7, 1998, emphasis mine). The American is clearly of a different order. Petal Smooth, a ladies hair shaver is "the fastest, cleanest, easiest way to remove unwanted hair" for it is "made only in the USA" and it is "*the great American way* to feminine grooming" (emphasis mine).

Gender in Advertisements

Mention of a typical Indian woman invokes set images. It is culturally loaded, filled with allusions. The dominant discourse of social reform, nationalism, and independent India's state policies explicitly sought to create a model of womanhood that was deemed authentically Indian. Much has been written on India's recasted culture, tradition, and women in the colonial period (Chaudhuri, 1993; Sangari & Vaid, 1984), and how the woman question became a site for redefining what constituted India's tradition and culture. This entire process, which was both exclusive and hegemonic, wherein a specifically upper-caste gender norm was imposed as the "Indian" norm, has been extensively documented. My purpose for referring to the past here is to underscore the fact that, while the Indian women's image was actively recast, we do not have a parallel portrayal of what the desirable Indian male ought to be. There are inferences (often contradictory) we can draw from but no deliberate exposition from the writings of Indians. What is implied is that he is "the Indian." The woman is "the Indian woman," the companiate figure but by no means the central actor. He is the upper-caste family patriarch. He is the rationalist social reformer, the nationalist with a scientific temper, the fierce cultural revivalist, desirous of the more manly virtues of the western imperial man. For the colonial rulers he was simply the effeminate babu, the groveling native or a loyal soldier from the deemed martial races (Sinha, 1997, pp. 15–16).

Although colonial descriptions of the native male are explicitly articulated, the Indian (male) account can be inferred from Indian men's recasting of the Indian woman. The reason the Indian woman has an image when the man does not is that she is the cultural emblem of the national, but he *is* the national (Chaudhuri, 1996). If colonialism ushered in an epoch of recasting of Indian femininity, liberalization, I argue, has been redefining ideas about dominant representations of Indian masculinity. I analyse below how far the new male images break with patriarchal attitudes and usher in more gender-equitable times.

What is New in the Indian Man

Liberalization has heralded a new effort to make the Indian male more like a "man," and less the "native slob." A portend of this trend is the appearance of the male in a large number of adverts. As argued earlier, there seems to be a shift from an intellectual paradigm to a sensual one, where the politics of presentation is what matters.

The New Appearance of the Indian Man

Today "male models have come a long way from the days of being props for the more popular women" (*The Week*, March 30, 1997, p. 40)

> It would be a difficult choice to make even for the beautician, considering that the market has seen an influx of male commodities. From designer underwear to men's cosmetics they are all available now. The size of the men's toiletries market is Rs 150 crore. There are shaving foams, after-shave lotions, moisturers, deodorants, eau de toilettes, colognes, hair cream, styling gels, talcum powders, shampoos and soaps.
>
> (*The Week,* March 30, 1997, p. 40)

Choice is a key word. "Ten years ago there was just Old Spice. Now you have many choices," said the deputy general manager of Menezes Cosmetics, which has 15 products like aftershaves and colognes of Blur Stratos. "The market has grown because men have realized that it is high time they looked and smelt good" (*The Week*, March 30, 1997, p. 41). Businessman Ketan Mehta agrees: if Indian men are becoming choosy it is because they have a choice that was not there earlier. "Ten years ago if I wanted a pair of suspenders even hunting I would not get a good choice" (*The Week*, March 30, 1997,

p. 40). An interesting figure of a man titled "The branded man" (*The Week*, March 30, 1997, p. 41) has an accompanying chart with arrows indicating "hair," "glass," "face," "body," "shirts," "ties," "suits," "trousers," "underwear," "belts," "socks," "shoes." Against each part we have a list of relevant brand products, for example, "socks" has "Louis Philippes, Reebok, Nike, Proline, Bata, Lacoste."

Men also feature as "catwalk kings":

> THE CONTESTANTS are topless and their polished and chiseled bodies glisten in the light. Amid loud catcalls and whistling they walk gingerly down the ramp, unnerved by the ogling and leering. They are the male beauties of India, participating in an all-male beauty contest. The leers and jeers are obviously from women. Nowadays beauty conscious men, too, are getting plenty of opportunities to exhibit themselves and have silly questions thrown at them for equally silly replies. And the women just love it.
>
> (*The Week*, May 30, 1997)

An up-market fashion magazine *Gladrags* was launched a couple of years ago and "The Gladrag Man Hunt" contest was started soon after. Maureen Wadia, the proprietor, contends that: "It's a fun context and it's also serious," for "it will make Indian men figure conscious and they should be. Why should we settle for pot bellies? We also work in offices but we take care of our figures." "They can't be sloppy and bad mannered. Etiquette is important to succeed with women or in one's job" (*The Week*, March 30, 1997, p. 40).[8]

Men, Power, and Success

Power has been men's in patriarchal societies. Power as an attribute of men may be seen as an "old" characteristic of men. My survey of adverts suggests, however, that while "power" is projected clearly as a male quality, the image of "power" that most adverts communicate is the very specific power of the successful executive in the corporate world. This is power at work, not at home. The "native" had power at home, not at work. The image here is not that of the authority exercised by the household patriarch. It is the "power" of the corporate world.[9] It is the power of achieved status, not of an ascribed one. As a men's wear advert says, "Because you know you deserve your place in the sun." The enormous possibilities that liberalization has offered to the metropolitan middle class are dramatic. This affirmation of the "self" as potentially capable of reaching high places also means an ideological distrust of those who do not go places, or go anywhere. Adverts have played an important role in bringing into parlance a language of "success" and "power." The following text of an advert selling Contessa cars is illuminating:

> We had never met before. I decided to size him up over a game of golf. But *when he pulled up his car; I knew I'd found my business partner.*
>   There was a *spring in his step*, a *firmness in his handshake* when he stepped out of his Contessa. They complement each other so well. Both of them are comfortable in the power they wield. Assertive but not arrogant. *Distinguished*, not deliberate.

> *Unflappable and in control. It is easy to know a man from his car.* So when
> you are looking for fine men, just look inside a Contessa. (emphasis mine)

The above text can be held up for closer scrutiny on two grounds. One, that there is
an overt affirmation of power as a desirable quality of men. Two, that there is an
unabashed association of the person (here male) with material objects. Descriptions of
the car and men are interchangeable. Western feminist writings have dwelt on the ways
adverts affirm traditional male qualities. My contention is that "power" and "success" as
defining attributes of malehood in India is a postliberalization phenomenon. Mention has
already been made that colonialism unleashed a process by which the Indian male had to
either masculinize himself or rest content with being the stereotypical effeminate native.
For how male can you be without power? Independent India, with its policies of growth
with equity, did little to encourage excess of any kind. Although power may have still
been an attribute, the process of democratization of "power" had clearly not taken place.
The hypothetical possibility of anybody accessing the power of a corporate executive
was absent. I randomly draw upon adverts to illustrate the deployment of the image of
"power."

"He exudes power, good looks and an ease with international corporate life style.
He is the much sought-after Organization Guru. Those who can't afford him can study
his luggage" says an ad for VIP skybag luggage. For "if Skybags in general speaks volumes
about its owner, Skybag Infiniti, one can say, speaks with the *authority* of a much sought-
after consultant" (emphasis mine). You see adverts with "him" working at the computer,
in the boardroom, at the airport. Microsoft invites the "new man" to "increase productivity at office" and also "do less work." It is noticeable that on the very next page,
Microsoft has a woman looking harassed at work with the words: "It's not a holiday you
need: It's a new office." In smaller print the words go on: "Overwhelmed by work?
Before you check out the nearest holiday spot, we suggest you check out Microsoft's
new office suite: Office 97." Could the contrasting images of the male and female
executive be accidental? As a young male professional speaks over the cellular phone,
Infosys Technological Limited enquires "A college campus? A software hot-shop? A
professionals' powerhouse?"

> When it's Denis Parkar, *clothes make more than the man*. Creations of
> mastercraftspersons, they make his future. They widen the horizon of his
> progress. And they add a whole *new power* to his personality. That's why
> when you're in one of Denis Parkar's unique line of high-class BUSINESS
> SUITS or distinctive ETHNIC OUTFITS or elegant PARTY SHIRTS,
> you're sure to stand out At home or abroad. (emphasis mine)

"The power of a perfect suit" from Bombay Dyeing "with a fall, feel and comfort
that spells luxury" shows a Caucasian-looking male dressed in a black suit. "You travel
with a purpose and we appreciate that. Ours is a hotel which speaks your language.
The *universal language of professionalism*. So take a deep breath and plunge into your
schedule. You will be surprised at how refreshing the deep end can be" reads an advert
of Oberoi Hotels (emphasis mine). The accompanying picture is again a Caucasian in
the pool.

Meet Navroze Dhondy who when he:

isn't chasing deadlines, deadlines are chasing him. Everything is wanted yesterday. Airlines meals. Late nights. Dinner diplomacy. It's difficult to cope with all this. Even more difficult for the stomach. While Navroze is fine tuning the art of crisis management, stomach management is something he delegates to Pudin Hara.

A Wipro advert, too, has the executive in a chair, phone in hand, a computer facing him, and the words: "We know how valuable your time is. That's why we have ensured that our responsive computer maintenance service is just a keystroke away from you."

Some people say pay in gold. Doors open to you. Extra hands attend to you. Ask for anything and the answer is always yes. It's amazing how the flash of BOBCARD GOLD can turn a shopping trip into an unforgettable experience. After all, it's a reflection of *financial power* that only a few possess. (emphasis mine)

The new mantra for the Indian male is power and success. He has to be rich and glamorous. He has to be at the top of his job early in life. But along with this consolidation of a western male model, we also have affirmation of gentler qualities in men. He is no brute, a point evident in a whole array of adverts sponsored to create an image of the complete man. Significantly it is the up-market male who is now attributed with softer qualities.

The Complete Man

The complete man has to be rich and successful. But to complete the persona he has to be caring, tender, and endowed with what traditionally women alone were capable of. He bathes his baby and changes the nappy. He talks to his children and worries about stains in the tablecloth. He goes for long walks in the forests. Raymond, specialists in men's wear, have been bringing out a steady string of adverts projecting the new, gentle, soft caring man. Below I cite some of the descriptions:

Indifference is out, involvement is in, hearing is out, listening is in, selling is out, relationships are in

Get real

It's-not-my-job is out, sharing is in, control is out, nurturing is in, authority is out, responsibility is in

Get real

Hierarchy is out, collaborations are in, rule models are out, role models are in, efficiency is out, effectiveness is in

Get real

What is Old in the Indian Man

The new Indian man may have acquired some new dimensions to his personality. But on the whole, he is still involved in the public world doing important things. He has no time for trivia. The cigarette industry has had a long-held practice of emphasising men's rugged nature and virile world with cigarette smoking. With the growth of the anti-tobacco movement in the west, third-world countries like India have been specially targeted. Following is the text of one such advert: "He has no room for trivia. No designer crystal. No fancy champagne, No pictures of vacations in Seychelles. Just the deep satisfaction of the world's finest smoke. For the man who has no room for trivia. A very private luxury," reads an advert for the cigarette INDIA KINGS.

He has to give his daughter away: Here is an advert with an interesting combination of the old and the new. The practice of patriliny and patrilocality within much of North Indian kinship and marriage implies that the daughter of the family has to be married out of kin and village. This departure of the bride is an emotional moment for every-body. She now no longer belongs to her natal family. She can only come when her husband's family permits it. It was part of the upper-caste Hindu male's dharma to marry her off. The advert cited below has a picture of the traditional ceremony of the daughter's departure at marriage, with the father discreetly wiping away a tear, and the words:

> Raymond Suitings
>
> Like a million fathers you knew from the moment she was born it had to happen. Like a million fathers you thought you would be prepared for it. It's okay, real men cry.

What is New in the Indian Woman

The myriad beauty contests that have sprung up all over the country reflect the way the Miss India/Miss World contests have captured the imagination of the people. My contention has been that adverts and features merge until boundaries are hard to discern. Just as Palmolive rests its advertising campaign on Miss India winners, we have features interviewing the various winners and aspirants in the media, as well as the hairdresser, the costume designer, etc. *Femina* carries a piece on "Why we need MISS AMERICA." The blurb tell us that "Jill Neimark speaks to psychologists to unravel the appeal of the Miss America Contest. We could draw some parallels here in India, too" (Neimark, 1999, p. 50).

The modern Indian woman knows how to "dare" and to "dream." NEPC Agro Foods Limited for a while brought out weekly insertions from "today's woman" ("aaj-ki-nari"). One such advert carries an athletic young girl in shorts who announces:

> I'm here again. The aaj-ki-nari. And your Sunday fitness friend. Sharing today's women's concerns for their menfolk. Ready for your weekly dose of goodness. PRESSURE CHECK. Your body is only human. Overwork, mental fatigue and undue work tensions can take their toll. Premature greying (or balding), dark circles around the eyes, insomnia are only too

common . . . You'll find that physical exercise actually takes away mental weariness . . . so a good game of shuttle or squash in the evenings is not a bad idea. How about some TM? Spare 20 minutes every day religiously for just yourself. And you'll be ready to take on the world. ALL WORK AND NO PLAY . . . If you don't have a hobby, a passion, get one . . . quick! Because a man without an absorbing extracurricular life is indeed a dull boy! Read a lot more . . . as a general rule, it takes your mind away from day-to day worries and keeps depression at bay. And while I won't say ban all late nights, smoking and social drinking, it really helps to know where to draw the line.

That's all from this aaj-ki-nari . . . this Sunday. See you same time, next week. It's a date!

Today's woman is old-fashioned enough to care and new enough to tell him what she likes. She has the standard suggestions for the overworked ambitious corporate executive. The male who is not these things is clearly a loser—a term alien to Indians even a few years ago. Alien too were ideas of space for oneself or meditation for healing.

What is Old in the Indian Woman

The Family Woman

Sushmita Sen, the first Indian woman to win the coveted Miss Universe title, was stated as reiterating the new postfeminist ideology when she said, "The essence of a woman is motherhood and teaches a man to love and care" (*The Time of India*, 16 June, 1995). The woman remains the mainstay of her family; she is the one who rears and nurtures. Not surprisingly, then, it is the woman who is targeted in adverts selling pressure cookers. The pressure cooker came into Indian housewives' lives in the 1960s and never really left it. It made cooking quicker, simpler, saved fuel, and was a more nutritious mode of cooking. It represented the Indian urban, middle-class housewife. This is one lineage with which the millennium woman has not broken. A smallish, black and white picture of a young woman with a Hawkins pressure cooker and an older woman (mother-in-law/mother) touching her arm in an expression of approval and support accompanies a text in largish print, which reads "Because my family depends on me, I depend on Hawkins." In smaller print the text goes on:

> Looking after this dear, demanding family of mine isn't easy. The children, my husband and his parents all need my time—sometimes all at once! And all of them want their food cooked just as they like it, on time, every time. Truly, I don't think I could manage without my Hawkins. It cooks so fast and never lets me down. I have had it for so many years and I have had no problems with it. It's reliable—just as I am, my husband says!

One of India's oldest manufacturers of traditional Ayurvedic medicines invokes an image of eternal Indian womanhood. Chyawanprash, a product common to India's middle-class household is "prepared the Dabur way: Authentic Ayurvedic principles matched with modern standards of hygiene and quality. A tradition helping over 25

million users build a strong immunity for more than 112 years. One day at a time."
It is not difficult to discern the parallel between the qualities of authentic Indian
womanhood and Dabur—both incorporating the best in the modern and traditional.

> Somewhere between breakfast, dinner, and history books is a subject
> called Motherhood. The story of a woman who wants to mean everything
> to everybody. Hundred questions. Million demands. No time for herself.
> No time to fall sick. Will an ordinary health tonic do the job?

Kelvinator Refrigerator asks the question. "Why do some women need the extra
room in the New 165 litre Corona Deluxe?" Below a picture of a mother, daughter/
daughter-in-law, granddaughter the answer reads "We believe it has something to do
with the extra room in their hearts."

> The joys of children, parents and grandparents all living together, are many.
> Perhaps that's why some families refuse to abandon this way of life.
> Even though houses today are becoming increasingly small.
> Which only shows that it shows that it does not necessarily take a
> larger house to accommodate a large family. It takes a large heart.
> And it's for women with such hearts that our engineers built the 165
> litre Corona Deluxe.

Women Love "Shingar"

Women's love for clothes and jewelry are part of India's folklore. An advert of a silk
shop is titled "The Ultimate Women's Paradise," while a jewelry shop claims "We
capture the fires of passion that lie in the deep of a woman's heart." Yet another sari
shop heralds women to "unravel the woman in you." While for women to beautify is in
their very essence, adverts for men celebrate men's looks but do not invoke any
"natural" reasons for doing so.

Women still save but not just money. Although up-market Indian women are visible
in the adverts, the more traditional middle-class woman is present also. Reminiscent of
an earlier era, we have a typical middle-class urban Indian woman smiling alongside a
text with a caption "Women of Today Excel Everywhere": "Women of today have a
distinct presence in every aspect of life with an inherent instinct to SAVE for safety and
security." But in another Hong Kong Bank advert the word "save" takes a twist. For now
"I save more than just money . . . I save precious time."

Conclusion

I began this article on the note that the Indian national movement and the public
discourse that independent India inherited were marked by a stated claim of social
responsibility to goals of equity, justice and "freedom." Written into the Indian constitution was a pledge to battle against discrimination on grounds of sex, caste, community, class, and tribe. Although serious gaps existed between the stated intent
towards social equity and both class and patriarchal claims on social privileges,[10] only

the very naïve would dismiss the tangible significance of the intent. Perusals of the English language print media in the last decade embolden me to claim a break, if not a discernible shift, in the dominant discourse. What comes across is the heralding of a new epoch, a celebration of a new Indian man and woman who shape their own destinies and are unabashed about their pursuit of the good life. What is conveyed also is an adroit deployment of words familiar in the earlier discourse. "Freedom" and women's "liberation" are two examples. The print media appears to have given vent to a collective feeling of the nation (read "middle class") that at last the individual (read "consumer") is *free to choose*. But it is important to recall that the language of the freedom struggle, of self-reliance and nonalignment that Indian men and women articulated in an earlier epoch also stemmed from a desire for freedom and dignity.

The crucial difference is that freedom, choice, and assertion of autonomous selfhood were earlier linked to broader issues of social justice in the collective nation (the poor and marginalised). Significantly, the onset of liberalisation has accompanied a concerted expression of the values of individualism and untrammeled selfhood. Furthermore, successful (often corporate) superwomen are too often posited as models from whom the women's movement could learn a lesson or two.[11] Accompanying this has been a questionable suggestion that the increase in male models in advertising, the practice of holding male pageants, and the presence in some adverts of a more gender-sensitive image of male-hood spell the onset of a gender-equal era. Crucially, these new discourses and gender images effectively displace the largest section of Indian men and women from the public eye.

Questions

1   What is meant by the cliché, "The orient is an invention of the occident"? How does this support Chaudhuri's larger argument?
2   Do you think the "rhetoric of globalization" that Chaudhuri describes is unique to India? Give examples of other nations/cultures that have publicly witnessed a similar transformation.
3   Although Chaudhuri focused her advertising analysis on the representations of gender, she might have used other advertising attributes to understand the rhetoric of post-globalization India. Do you agree with this statement and, if so, what factors might she have analyzed instead?

Notes

1.   Dalits have been traditionally regarded as the lowest in the caste hierarchy. Significantly, the Dalit movement in contemporary India has been very strong and has also increasingly been making its presence felt in both domestic politics and academic research.
2.   In the construction of the norm, the whole and the national have always been hegemonic and exclusive. But the dominant discourse on gender in the past had never quite so systematically excluded the poor and dispossessed. Indeed, some may argue that the working-class woman was privileged in discourse even if not in action.
3.   "Today, publications are almost mortally dependent on advertising revenue. The cover

price of publication brands move within a narrow band. While the material cost and news gathering cost of newspapers have gone up (several have folded up in the last few years), the cover price has remained stagnant. So the bottom line of any publication business can be pushed up only in advertising revenue." (Ansari Gentleman June 1999)

4. Personal interview with the Senior Economist of the Investment Information & Credit Rating Agency (ICRA).
5. I have done a more comparative analysis elsewhere (Chaudhuri 2000).
6. The Lintas advertising company conducted a market survey of target customers.
7. If the west talks of the breakup of the nuclear, in our part of the world it is the breakup of the joint family and the emergence of the nuclear family that is discussed.
8. In my field work among Asian Indian Americans I found a common complaint among the girls that the Indian man just did not know his manners. He did not know how to court a woman. A western man knew.
9. Interestingly my friends and acquaintances within the ad world and the corporate world actually mention "power" as a "high." Both men and women do so.
10. I have dealt exclusively with this tension between these two trends elsewhere (Chaudhuri 1996).
11. See Chaudhuri 2000.

References

Barthes, R. (1977). *Image, music, text*. London: Fontana.
Carey, J. (1989). *Communication as culture: Essays on media and society*. Boston, MA: Unwin Hyman.
Chaney, D. (1994). *The cultural turn*. London: Routledge.
Chaudhuri, M. (1993). *Indian women's movement: Reform and revival*. New Delhi: Radiant.
Chaudhuri, M. (1996). Citizens, workers and cultural emblems: An analysis of the first plan document. In Patricia Uberoi (Ed.), *State, social reform and sexuality* (pp. 211–235). New Delhi: Sage.
Chaudhuri, M. (1998). Print media, advertisements and the new Indian woman. *Social Action, July*, 239–252.
Chaudhuri, M. (2000). Feminism in print media. *Indian Journal of Gender Studies, September*, 263–288.
Goffman, E. (1976). *Gender advertisements*. London: The Society for the Study of Visual Communication.
Gramsci, A. (1971). *Selctions from prison notebooks*. London: Lawrence & Wishart.
Curran, J. (1981). The impact of advertising on the British mass media. *Media, Culture and Society, 3*(1), 43–69.
Jhally, S. (1987). *The codes of advertising*. London: Francis Pinter.
Lash, S., & Friedman, J. (1996). *Modernity & identity*. Oxford: Blackwell.
Marx, K. (1976). Results of the immediate process of production. In *Capital* (vol. 1). Pelican.
Marx, K., & Engels, F. (1984). The German ideology. In Karl Marx & Frederick Engels (Eds.), *The individual and society* (pp. 138–163). Moscow: Progress Publishers.
Murdoch, G., & Golding, P. (1979). Ideology and the mass media: The question of determination. In M. Barret et al. (Eds.), *Ideology and cultural production*. London: Croom Helm.
Neimark, J. (1999). Why we need Miss America. *Femina, February 1*, 50–52.
Reeves, G. (1993). *Communications in the third world*. London: Routledge.
Sangari, K., & Vaid, S. (1984). *Recasting women: Essays in colonial history*. New Delhi: Kali for Women.
Sinha, M. (1997). *Colonial masculinity: The "manly Englishman" and the "effeminate Bengali" in the late nineteenth century*. New Delhi: Kali for Women.
Williams, R. (1977). *Marxism and literature*. Oxford: Oxford University Press.
Williams, R. (1980). *Advertising, the magic system: Problems in materialism and culture* (pp. 184–191). London: Verso.
van Zoonen, L. (1994). *Feminist media studies*. London: Sage.

Newspapers and Magazines

Business Standard Wednesday January 7, 1998
The Economic Times (Brand Equity) 16–22 June 1999
Femina, February 1, 1999
Gentleman June 1999
The Hindu November 16, 1998
New Woman March 1999
Rashtriya Sahara July 1997
The Outlook, May 4, 1997
The Times of India 16 June 1995
The Week March 30, 1997
The Week May 30, 1997

Chapter 12

KATHERINE FRITH, PING SHAW, AND HONG CHENG

THE CONSTRUCTION OF BEAUTY
A Cross-Cultural Analysis of Women's Magazine Advertising

FROM *PEOPLE* MAGAZINE'S ANNUAL RANKING of the "Most Beautiful People" to the candidates on *America's Next Top Model*, to the scathing fashion critiques on celebrity blogs like Go Fug Yourself, the mass media play a crucial role in defining standards of beauty. Women's magazines, in particular, have received harsh criticism for perpetuating an unrealistic beauty ideal that privileges youth, thinness, and whiteness. Yet does this portrayal of idealized femininity translate across international borders? In this essay, communication researchers Katherine Frith, Ping Shaw, and Hong Cheng address this question by comparing depictions of beauty in women's magazine ads across Eastern and Western cultures. Although the findings reveal several marked differences in the cross-cultural construction of beauty, they also reaffirm a universal beauty standard which the authors attribute to an increasingly globalized media environment.

Each culture has a set of general beliefs about what constitutes femininity and beauty. According to Wood (1999), to be feminine in the United States is to be attractive, deferential, unaggressive, emotional, nurturing, and concerned with people and relationships. According to Hofstede (1997), in Confucian cultures, femininity is associated with virtue and modesty. The script for femininity is written into a culture and is transmitted over time through family, peers, teachers, and the media.

Likewise, beauty is a construct that varies from culture to culture and changes over time. A buxom Marilyn Monroe was the beauty ideal in the United States in the 1950s, soon to be replaced by the emaciated Twiggy of the 1960s. Whereas porcelain skin is valued in China, scarification of the skin is a beauty process in parts of Africa. Thus, the particular set of physical characteristics perceived as beautiful and desirable can vary across cultures and time periods. Advertisements offer us a unique opportunity to study the construction of beauty in a culture because advertisers are notorious for promoting a "beauty ideal" (Greer, 1999) or, as Cortese (1999) pointed out, presenting "the exemplary female prototype." Because the majority of research on images of women in advertising over the past 30 years has been conducted in the U.S. and Europe (Bordo, 1993; Courtney & Lockeretz, 1971; Gauntlett, 2002; Goffman, 1976; Kilbourne, 1987, 1999; Lafky, Duffy, Steinmaus, & Berkowitz, 1996; Richins, 1991; Soley & Kurzbad, 1986), the literature may reflect assumptions about women that are specific to Western cultures. Certain themes have dominated this literature, such as the stereotyping of women as passive and less powerful players in society, the portrayal of women as sexual objects in ads, and the cumulative effect of magazine advertising on women's self-esteem.

The purpose of this research is to compare the portrayals of beauty in women's fashion and beauty magazine advertisements from Asia and the U.S. to help understand how beauty is constructed across cultures.

Theoretical Issues

The Feminist Critique

Advertising has long been criticized by Western feminist scholars as a pervasive cultural institution that represents women in a problematic and often unacceptable way (Kates, Shaw, & Garlock, 1999). In particular, the positioning of women as sexual objects in ads has received a great deal of discussion (Jhally, 1989; Kilbourne, 1999). Although there have been numerous U.S. studies suggesting that sexual content interferes with brand name recall (Alexander & Judd, 1978; Chestnut, LaChance, & Lubitz, 1977; Horton, Lieb, & Hewitt, 1982; Richmond & Hartman, 1982; Steadman, 1969), nonetheless, attractive female bodies and sexual stimuli have historically been used in the U.S. to grab the viewer's attention and attempt to lend interest to a product or service (Frith & Mueller, 2003). According to Reichert, Lambiase, Carstarphen, and Zavoina (1999):

> In *TV Guide*, more than 35 percent of network promotional ads contain some sort of sexual reference. An analysis of Clio award-winning TV spots revealed that 29 percent contained a seductively dressed model, and 27 percent contained at least a hint of sexual suggestion. (p. 7)

The literature on sex appeal in advertising is extensive. Soley and Kurzbad (1986) compared "sex appeals" in magazine ads in the U.S. between 1964 and 1984. They found that, over time, sexual elements were becoming more visual and more overt. They concluded that female nudity and erotic content had become quite commonplace in contemporary U.S. ads. Another study of women's magazines from 1983 to 1993 showed that there was increased representation of women as sexual objects (Reichert et al., 1999). Reid and Soley (1983) found that ads with sexual content got higher visual recall/recognition scores, but the same did not apply to the verbal content.

The question most salient to this research, however, is this: Are beautiful women objectified and used in sexual ways in advertising across cultures? A number of studies have examined the portrayal of women in advertising in other societies. Comparing print advertisements from the U.S. and France, Biswas, Olsen, and Carlet (1992) reported that sex appeal was used more often in French than in U.S. advertisements. The authors interpreted this difference as being consistent with the perception that

France is sexually more liberated than the United States. In a study of women's portrayals in Chinese advertising, Cheng (1997) noted that women in Chinese television commercials wore more "demure" and less sexually suggestive clothing than did women in U.S. advertisements.

One study comparing images of women in weekly U.S. news magazines (*Time* and *Life*) to weekly Indian magazines (*India Today* and *Illustrated Weekly of India*) found very similar portrayals of women in subordinate or accessory poses among these four magazines (Griffin, Viswanath, & Schwartz, 1994). The authors concluded that many of the Western advertising conventions and poses for women were being transferred cross-culturally in conjunction with concepts like "professionalism" by Western multinational advertising agencies. In certain areas, such as the portrayal of women in predominately housewife or domestic management settings, Indian magazines far outstripped their U.S. counterparts. When comparing the use of "sexual pursuit" as a theme in advertisements (men pursuing women in an overtly sexual way), however, U.S. magazines used these portrayals three times more often than Indian magazines.

In an analysis of how Caucasian women are used in Japanese advertising, William O'Barr (1994) pointed out that Western models are posed doing things that Japanese women would never do. He says that Caucasian women are often shown being "sensual and willing" in Japanese advertising (p. 187). O'Barr suggested that this is merely mirroring the way women are portrayed in advertising in the West. Frith and Mueller (2003) showed that in conservative Asian countries like Malaysia and Indonesia, only Caucasian women are used in lingerie advertising as it would be unseemly for a local woman to be shown partially undressed.

Underlying much of the past feminist research on representation of women in advertising is the basic assumption that, within patriarchal societies, women's bodies are the object of "the male gaze" (Shields, 1990). In his seminal work on the historical significance of the female nude in Western art, John Berger (1972) explained: "[I]n the art form of the European nude, the painters and spectator-owners were usually men and the persons treated as objects, usually women" (p. 63). Much of the research on the representation of women in advertising has been anchored in Western women's experience. In her insightful essay on positionality, Fabienne Darling-Wolf (1998) described the difficulty Western feminist scholars encounter when they apply their life experiences to other cultures. She observed that there is a growing awareness within the feminist method of positionality when examining "texts positing gender oppression as the central component of all female experience" (p. 414). Thus, it is hoped that this study may help us to understand how feminine beauty ideals might manifest across cultures.

Beauty Types Research

To ascertain perceptions of women's beauty and beauty types used in advertising in contemporary U.S. culture, Solomon, Ashmore, and Longo (1992) conducted an experiment. They assembled a set of photographs of models employed by major U.S. fashion agencies and presented them to a sample of U.S. fashion magazine editors who were instructed to sort the models into piles based on similarity of looks. The results yielded relatively distinct beauty types: Classic, Feminine, Sensual, Exotic, Cute, Girl-Next-Door, Sex Kitten, and Trendy. In 1994, Englis, Solomon, and Ashmore applied the same eight beauty looks to advertisements collected from current major U.S. magazines and found the Trendy, Classic/Feminine, and Exotic/Sensual types were the most prevalent.

To date, little advertising research has attempted to look at how beauty is constructed in different cultures. In one study comparing beauty types of young girls in a Japanese version of *Seventeen* magazine to a U.S. version of the same magazine, the researchers reported that the Japanese models were typecast as "cute" and "girlish" (smiling and giggling) while the Americans girls were posed with more serious expressions, looking more defiant and independent (Maynard & Taylor, 1999).

Globalization and the Construction of Beauty

Ideally, for advertising messages to be resonant with a target audience, marketing theory holds that ads would need to reflect the social norms and cultural values of a given society (Belk, Bryce, & Pollay, 1985; Belk & Pollay, 1985; Cheng, 1994; Frith & Sengupta, 1991; Lin, 1993; Mueller, 1987). In a perfect world, we might expect that advertisements would be created by members of a particular society and consumed by members of the same society. However, globalization alters this process. Standardized campaigns can be created in the head offices of advertising agencies in the U.S. and Europe and run in foreign countries with only simple modifications such as translated headlines. Foreign branch offices of the big multinational agencies often follow Western styles when creating campaigns (Griffin, Viswanath, & Schwartz, 1994). In addition, the creative people in these branch offices have often received their training in U.S. and British universities or have interned in Western advertising agencies. The result is that the forms of representation, particularly of women, can take on a globalized or transnational look. As one Korean author put this:

> For thirty years, media have been taken to task for reproducing and reinforcing stereotyped images of women. Yet unfair representations of women in media still prevail worldwide. Sex stereotyping has been so deeply ingrained, even glorified, that the women themselves have become desensitized to their own inferior portrayal. The prospects appear even gloomier as the globalization of media progresses.
>
> (Kyung-Ja Lee, 2000, p. 86)

To better understand how women are represented in different cultures, this study uses the Englis, Solomon, and Ashmore (1994) beauty categories to examine advertisements from popular local women's fashion and beauty magazines in Singapore, Taiwan, and the U.S. The rationale for the selection of Singapore, Taiwan, and the U.S. for this study is twofold. In terms of living standards and levels of development, the three societies are comparable and therefore interesting to compare and contrast. The United States possesses a Western culture that exerts enormous influence on the rest of the world, whereas Singapore and Taiwan, both traditionally under the influence of Confucianism, are two societies representative of Eastern culture.

Although Singapore and Taiwan have many similarities, they also have some differences. Singapore has a culturally diversified society with the Chinese making up about 70% of the population, followed by about 20% Malay and 10% Indian. Taiwan is a homogeneously Chinese society. English is Singapore's official language, whereas Chinese is the mother tongue in Taiwan.

Because women's fashion and beauty magazines generally deal with beauty, it was hoped that a comparison of the advertisements in locally popular women's magazines from each of these societies would shed light on the current status of how beauty is represented in each of these cultures.

In addition to beauty types, the product category and the race of the models were analyzed. Although Cortese (1999) contended that advertisers present the exemplary female prototype in advertising regardless of product or service, other researchers (Cheng & Schweitzer, 1996; Mueller, 1987) have found a relationship between product categories and cultural values. Mueller (1987) argued that in cross-cultural research it is essential to observe the relationship between the product advertised and the appeal being made to the consumer.

Based on the literature review of women's portrayals in advertising, the following hypotheses were formulated for this study.

H1: Caucasian models will be used more often across cultures than models of other ethnic groups in women's beauty and fashion magazine advertising.

H2: The beauty types used in women's magazine advertising will differ in the U.S., Singapore, and Taiwan.

H3: The beauty types used for Caucasian models will differ from those used for Asian models.

H4: The types of products advertised in women's fashion and beauty magazines will differ across cultures.

Method

Based on the eight beauty types identified by Englis, Solomon, and Ashmore (1994), advertisements from popular fashion and beauty women's magazines in Singapore, Taiwan, and the United States were content analyzed. According to Wimmer and Dominick (2000), content analysis can aid in comparing media content to the real world. In this case, content analysis allows us to examine the portrayal of feminine identity across cultures.

To maintain comparability, the magazine types from each country were matched by format, audience demographics, local language, and circulation figures. Within the genre of women's magazines, there are various types, such as lifestyle (*Cosmopolitan*, for example), general interest (*Ladies Home Journal*), and fashion and beauty (*Vogue*). For circulation figures, we selected magazines that claimed that 80% or more of their readers were primarily local women between the ages of 20 and 35. The content for each magazine chosen was focused mainly on fashion and beauty. We also chose popular women's magazines that were published in the main local language, which was English in the U.S. and Singapore and Mandarin in Taiwan.

The women's magazines selected from Singapore were *Her World, Female*, and *Cleo*. *Female* is the second best-selling magazine in Singapore after *Her World*, with *Cleo* in third place. The latest circulation figures (2003) for *Her World* were 141,000, and for *Female* and *Cleo*, they were 83,000 and 81,000, respectively. These figures were obtained from Neilsen Research in Singapore.

Glamour, Vogue, and *Elle* are among the most popular and influential magazines in the United States that focus primarily on fashion and beauty. They were selected as the reference for a comparison with the two sets of magazines from Singapore and Taiwan. The latest circulation figures (from the second half of 2003) of these three U.S. magazines in their home country were 2,201,279 (*Glamour*), 1,192,949 (*Vogue*), and 981,117 (*Elle*). These figures were obtained from the Magazine Publishers Association.

Three of the most popular Taiwanese women's fashion and beauty magazines were chosen for this study: *Citta Bella, Jasmine*, and *Vivi*. All three magazines are published in Chinese, and the names *Jasmine* and *Vivi* are the English translations of the Chinese titles. *Citta Bella*, one of the most popular women's magazines, is published as a joint venture between a Taiwanese and a Singaporean company. The circulation figures of each of these three women's magazines are about 80,000. These figures were obtained from the magazine publishers through telephone interviews.

It is important to note that internationalization has found its way into the women's fashion and beauty magazine industry (Shaw, 1999). In each of the countries in this study, one of the top three fashion and beauty magazines is not originally a local magazine. The title *Elle* is owned by Hachette Filipacchi, a European publisher; *Cleo*, the third most widely read women's magazine in Singapore is a joint publication between an Australian publisher and a Singaporean company; and in Taiwan, the magazine *Citta Bella* is jointly published between Singaporean and Taiwanese companies.

For the purpose of this study, three issues of each magazine were chosen at random from within the 14-month period, March 2001 to April 2002. The unit of analysis was restricted to advertisements of one or more full pages containing at least one woman. The coding criteria for beauty types required that both the face and some part of the model's dress be shown in the ad. In advertisements where more than one woman was present, the largest or most dominant woman was coded. Advertisements with numerous representations of women of the same size or having no dominant main character were not included in the collection. Identical advertisements were included in the coding process because repetition is a strategy frequently used in advertising campaigns. As a result, a total of 1,236 advertisements were collected from the above-mentioned nine women's fashion and beauty magazines published in the three societies under study.

Content Categories

In the 1994 study by Englis, Solomon, and Ashmore, eight distinct content categories were identified as the most prevalent beauty types in the United States. These included Classic, Feminine, Sensual, Exotic, Cute, Girl-Next-Door, Sex Kitten, and Trendy. In order to test the reliability of these categories in an Asian context, Siew, Ching, and Tan (2001) interviewed local fashion magazine editors and advertising art directors in Singapore and conducted a content analysis of 5 years' worth of Singaporean women's magazines (1996 to 2000). These researchers found that, although the U.S. categories were viable in Singapore, one category, "Exotic," was irrelevant as it was defined by Englis et al. as "non-Caucasian." Thus, this category was excluded from the present study. Siew, Ching, and Tan also found that two other categories, Classic and Feminine, shared many general characteristics and were thus combined for the purpose of this study. Also, Cute and Girl-Next-Door shared overlapping characteristics, as did Sensual/Sex Kitten so they too were combined for this study. As a result, the coding categories for this research were Classic, Sensual/Sex Kitten, Cute/Girl-Next-Door, and Trendy.

In addition to beauty types, the models in the ads were content analyzed for race. Product categories were also analyzed (see appendix for operational definitions).

Coding

Two independent Singaporean coders, both of whom had previously lived in the U.S., carried out the coding. They were bilingual (speaking both English and Mandarin). Coders were trained using a preliminary subset of about 50 advertisements. The coders met to compare their results (Holsti, 1969). When disagreements arose, coders discussed their interpretations and a final decision was made by consensus. This process continued until both coders were comfortable with the categories. Definitions and examples of the various categories were available at all times. To establish intercoder reliability, the two coders coded the same 240 advertisements (approximately 20% of the total sample), with 80 from each country. Using Cohen's (1960) formula, the reliabilities were determined for race types ($k = .96$), beauty types ($k = .85$), and product types ($k = .94$).

Findings

As can be seen in Table 12.1, Caucasian female models were used most frequently in all three societies under study, with 91% appearing in the United States, 65% in Singapore, and 47% in Taiwan. These findings are statistically significant ($\chi^2 = 304.12$, $df = 8$, $p < 0.001$). Thus, H1 is supported. Interestingly Caucasian models appeared more often than Chinese models in both Singapore and Taiwan, two countries with predominantly Chinese populations (approximately three quarters of the population of Singapore are Chinese and almost 98% are Chinese in Taiwan).

As shown in Table 12.2, the beauty types used in the magazine advertisements did differ ($\chi^2 = 50.27$, $df = 8$, $p < 0.001$) among the U.S., Singapore, and Taiwan. Although Sexual/Sex Kitten is used more often in U.S. ads (32%) than in Singapore (19%) and Taiwanese (22%) ads, Cute/Girl Next Door is portrayed most frequently in Taiwanese ads (27%). These statistically significant differences confirm H2.

Table 12.1 Race of Models

	Singapore	Taiwan	U.S.
Chinese	111 (24%)	116 (46%)	5 (1%)
Caucasian	304 (65%)	118 (47%)	476 (91%)
Malay, Indian, Pan Asian	35 (8%)	45 (6%)	5 (1%)
Mixed races	15 (3%)	4 (1%)	9 (2%)
African-American	0	0	23 (5%)

$\chi^2 = 304.12$, $df = 8$, $p < 0.001$.

Table 12.2 Beauty Types

	Singapore	Taiwan	U.S.
Classic	249 (54%)	112 (44%)	236 (46%)
Sensual/Sex kitten	90 (19%)	56 (22%)	165 (32%)
Cute/Girl next door	72 (15%)	68 (27%)	81 (16%)
Trendy	51 (11%)	16 (6%)	27 (5%)
Other	3 (1%)	1 (1%)	9 (1%)

$\chi^2 = 50.27$, $df = 8$, $p < 0.001$.

Table 12.3 Comparison of Beauty Types for Chinese and Caucasian Models

	Chinese (n = 232)	Caucasian (n = 898)
Classic	133 (57%)	426 (47%)
Sensual/Sexy	25 (11%)	243 (27%)
Cute/Girl next door	58 (25%)	141 (16%)
Trendy	15 (6%)	77 (9%)
Other	1 (1%)	11 (1%)

$\chi^2 = 35.41$, $df = 4$, $p < 0.001$.

Although advertisements from all three countries tended to portray women in the Classic beauty type more often than other beauty types, the Sensual/Sex Kitten beauty type, which mainly relates to women's sexual attractiveness, was used more often in the U.S. than in advertisements in Singapore and Taiwan. In terms of beauty types used in the two Asian countries, the Classic beauty type was used more often in Singaporean advertisements (54%) than in Taiwanese advertisements (44%). The Trendy type was used more frequently in Singaporean (11%) than in Taiwanese (6%) advertisements. The Cute beauty type was used more often (27%) in Taiwan than in Singapore (15%).

The majority of women models in magazine ads analyzed in this study were either Chinese or Caucasian. Of the total of 1,236 ads examined, 232 ads featured Chinese models (19%) and 898 ads featured Caucasians (73%). Thus, the data on these two groups were selected for comparison.

There were significant differences in the beauty types for each race. The Classic beauty was used most frequently for both races. However, the Sensual/Sexy type was used more often (27%) with Caucasian models than with Chinese models (11%). The Cute/Girl-Next-Door type was more popular with Chinese models (25%) than with Caucasians (16%). In addition, the Trendy type was used more frequently with Caucasian models (9%) than with Chinese models (6%). These differences were statistically significant ($\chi^2 = 35.41$, $df = 4$, $p < .001$). Therefore, H3 predicting that beauty types are used differently for different races of models in women's magazine advertisements is confirmed.

Because the construction of beauty is connected to culture, it was anticipated that the beauty products advertised would be different from country to country. This was the case. There was a significant difference in the product types advertised across cultures ($\chi^2 = 168.29$, $df = 14$, $p < 0.001$). As shown in Table 12.4, the types of product advertised in women's magazines differed dramatically across cultures with beauty

Table 12.4 Product Categories

	Singapore	Taiwan	U.S.
Beauty	188 (40%)	124 (49%)	132 (25%)
Cleaning	3 (1%)	1 (1%)	1 (0%)
Clothing	118 (25%)	72 (28%)	277 (54%)
Entertainment	13 (3%)	4 (2%)	13 (2%)
Food & beverage	10 (2%)	10 (4%)	16 (3%)
Accessories	81 (17%)	25 (9%)	56 (11%)
Services	45 (10%)	5 (2%)	1 (1%)
Miscellaneous	7 (2%)	12 (5%)	22 (4%)

$\chi^2 = 168.29, df = 14, p < 0.001.$

products occupying the greatest proportion in Singapore (40%) and Taiwan (49%), whereas clothing occupied the largest proportion of ads in the U.S. (54%). Thus, H4 was supported.

Discussion

The purpose of this research was to compare the construction of beauty in women's magazines from the U.S., Singapore, and Taiwan to determine whether culture or ethnicity might play a role in how beauty is constructed in advertising. Overall, we found some similarities as well as differences. The tendency to portray women across cultures in the Classic beauty type indicates that certain aspects of beauty are more or less universal and shared by Eastern and Western cultures. It also suggests that the feminist critique of advertising for depicting women as sex objects may not be a universal phenomenon. That is, in comparing ads from Singapore, Taiwan, and the U.S., we found that Caucasian women were depicted most often in sexual portrayals across cultures. On the one hand, this may be a reflection of the more conservative Confucian cultural values held in Singapore and Taiwan, or it may be, as Fung (2000) contended, that feminist liberal philosophy has not yet been internalized by women in Asia. However, in an age of global media, where global versions of women's magazines are becoming available across cultures, researchers may wish to examine futher the ways in which various races are depicted as "beauty ideals" in global media. The findings from this study suggest that Caucasian women are being presented as sex objects in Asia while Asian models are being depicted in more demure ways.

Among the original beauty categories developed by Englis, Solomon, and Ashmore (1994), Exotic was a type excluded from this study because the definition—"ethnic looking or non-Caucasian"—seemed inappropriate at the time. However, in retrospect, the concept of an "exotic other" in Asia might very well be the Caucasian woman who displays her body in ways a Chinese model could or would not.

An alternative way of looking at these findings might be to examine some of the classic feminist arguments on representation that contend that sexuality is a form of general exchange value in Western societies (Haug, 1987). The adage, "sex sells," rings true in the West, but may not hold true in the Asian context. Traditionally, in Western art the female body has served as the object of sexual stimulation. Kuhn (1985) and

Berger (1972) have suggested that this cultural way of seeing the female form has material and historical roots.

However, displaying the female body has not been the tradition in Chinese art. In fact, traditional Chinese art often presents nature as the central focus, and human forms are often small and insignificant. Brush paintings of panoramic mountain landscapes containing very small human beings are more the norm and tend to reflect traditional Daoist beliefs in the primary importance of nature and man's place within this orderly universe. When women appear in traditional Chinese paintings, they are clothed in loose robes, and the face and hair, rather than the body, become the central focus. Thus, traditions of "gaze" may very well have developed differently in the East and the West.

Much of the literature on the representation of women in advertising is built on the feminist argument that media are patriarchal, and that in patriarchal societies, men watch women and women watch men watching women (Berger, 1972). Yet, what this research suggests is that what women think men are watching may differ across cultures. In Western societies, women may think it is mainly their bodies that get noticed by men, whereas in Asia, women may think it is their faces that are most important.

The finding that product categories differ significantly between advertising in the U.S., Singapore, and Taiwan magazines supports this contention. Beauty products that are aimed at improving women's hair, skin, and face occupied the greatest proportion of ads in Singapore (40%) and Taiwan (49%), while clothing ads occupied the largest proportion of ads in the U.S. (54%). Because marketers prefer to advertise to audiences that are particularly interested in their products, this finding again suggests that for women in the U.S. beauty is constructed in terms of "the body," and this also fits with the higher proportion of sexual beauty types found in U.S. ads. Clothing is related to the body. Wood (1999) explained that clothing is designed to call attention to women's bodies and "to make them attractive to viewers" (p. 145). Whereas across cultures the Classic beauty type does predominate, nonetheless the high proportion of clothing ads, coupled with the high proportion of Sensual and Sex Kitten beauty types (used in about 30% of the U.S. ads.), suggests that in the U.S. the body is a defining factor in beauty. In Singapore and Taiwan the defining factor seems more related to face, hair, skin (in these countries, over 40% of the ads were for beauty products). If "beauty is in the eye of the beholder," it is a cultural construct. It is possible that the beauty ideal in the U.S. is more related to body, whereas the Asian beauty ideal is more related to the face.

It is harder to explain the overuse of Caucasian models in both Singaporean (65%) and Taiwanese (47%) advertisements. The difference between the uses of Caucasian models in the two Asian countries is a matter of degree, with Singapore being more open to this practice than Taiwan. Singapore received an award from *Foreign Policy* magazine in 2000 for being the "most globalized" country in the world, and certainly, advertisers in Singapore show greater racial diversity in their ads than in either the U.S. or Taiwan. On the one hand, whereas the large proportion of Caucasian models in these two Asian countries might suggest an openness in these societies to foreign models and beauty trends, it might also lend support to theories of hegemony and cultural imperialism on the part of foreign advertisers.

The general lack of non-Caucasian models in the U.S. ads (91% of the U.S. models were Caucasian) also suggests reluctance on the part of U.S. advertisers to depict the full range of beauty types in their ads, and further suggests that even after

30 years of criticism by feminist scholars, advertisers in the U.S. still seem fixated on "whiteness."

The finding that Singaporean advertisements tend to feature the Trendy type more frequently than Taiwanese advertisements do might mirror Singapore's openness to globalization and new trends. Likewise, the higher percentage of ads for the Cute beauty type in Taiwanese ads is most probably related to their close proximity to Japan, where Maynard and Taylor (1999) have confirmed the popularity of cute, "girlish" images in female magazines.

In a nutshell, based on the findings of this study, we may conclude that the construction of beauty in women's magazine advertising does differ across cultures. However, we also observed that, increasingly, interactions between cultures in today's world have led to many cross-national and cross-cultural similarities in advertising creative strategies, including similarities seen in the traditionally different U.S. and East Asian cultures.

The significance of the research is that it brings into question some of the basic assumptions from feminist theory related to the representation of women in advertising. The consensus after years of discussion is that advertising creates unfair expectations in women because ads hold up an unattainable beauty ideal that is often related to a "desirable body shape" (Gauntlett, 2002; Greer, 1999). In fact, the fixation with body may differ from society to society. This is not to say that advertisers do not exploit women's insecurities, but what women feel insecure about will differ from culture to culture and may not always be body related. As our understanding of other cultures begins to inform our theories on representation, advertising can become a rich source of cultural and cross-cultural knowledge.

Appendix

Beauty Types

Classic: A classic elegant look, model is slightly older than average. Fair skin, feminine, glamorous, and sophisticated. Usually wears soft, demure, feminine apparel and is not heavily accessorized.

Sensual/Sex Kitten: Sexually attractive, usually wears sexy attire or revealing, tight clothes. Model can also be dressed in normal clothes but posed in an unnatural way, such as an uncomfortable, "cheesecake" pose (chest thrust forward, back arched).

Cute/Girl Next Door: Cute, casual attire, youthful appearance. Can also be outdoorsy, in a casual, active way.

Trendy: Wears faddish clothes and displays oversized accessories. Hair is tousled; there is a slight sense of chaos to this type. Can also have an "I don't give a damn" attitude.

Racial Types

Caucasian: Ethnically White in appearance. Usually American or European.

Chinese: Includes all Chinese models from Singapore, China, Taiwan, Hong Kong, and the United States. Japanese were also coded into this category because the look is primarily similar.

Malay or Indian: Darker skin, curlier hair than Chinese.

Pan-Asian: A distinct but indeterminate Asian look with some Caucasian-looking features, but the Asian heritage is more distinct than Caucasian.

African-Americans: Models with darker skin or African features.

Mixed races: An indeterminate racial type; may be partly Caucasian with some African American features or may look partly Asian, such as Indian and Chinese.

Others: Refers to Latin Americans, and other ethnically non-White models.

Product Types

This list is not inclusive and coders should use their best judgment if they find a product that is not mentioned here but is similar to the following:

Alcoholic beverages: Beer, wine, alcoholic drinks.

Beauty & personal care: Cosmetics, hair care products, skin cream, etc.

Cleaning products: Detergents, Clorox bleach, floor cleaners, etc.

Clothing: All clothing designers and manufacturers.

Entertainment & information: New movies, books, magazines, travel, internet, etc.

Food & nonalcoholic: Foods, snacks, colas, health foods.

Household appliances: TVs, VCRs, stereo equipment, etc.

Medicine: All medicines.

Personal accessories: Watches, handbags, belts, shoes, accessories, scarves, etc.

Services: Insurance and other services.

Miscellaneous: Any other products that do not fit comfortably into the above.

Questions

1   Do you think the results might have been different if the authors had compared ads within a different medium—for example, TV series or films? Why do you think women's magazines have long been considered important sites for understanding the construction of beauty?

2   A recent trend among marketers is to use "real" people in ads rather than models and celebrities; the Dove Campaign for Real Beauty (www.campaignforrealbeauty.com) is perhaps the most widely known example. Do you think this trend addresses the issues raised by the authors of this essay? What other questions/issues do these marketing campaigns raise?

3   As you will read about later, technologies are being developed that would allow you to receive an ad featuring a model who looks very much like you; your friend, meanwhile, would receive the same ad, but with a model who looks more like him or her. If this tailored marketing practice becomes widespread, how might it impact the findings of Frith, Shaw, and Cheng's analysis?

References

Alexander, W., & Judd, B. (1978). Do nudes in ads enhance brand recall? *Journal of Advertising Research*, *18*, 47–50.

Belk, R. W., Bryce, W., & Pollay, R. (1985). Materialism and individual determinism in U.S. and Japanese television advertising. In R. Lutz (Ed.), *Advances in consumer research* (pp. 568–572). Provo, UT: Association for Consumer Research.

Belk, R., & Pollay, R. (1985). Materialism and status appeal in Japanese and U.S. print advertising: A historical and cross cultural content analysis. *International Marketing Review, 2*(12), 38–47.

Berger, J. (1972). *Ways of seeing*. London: Penguin.

Biswas, A., Olsen, J. E., & Carlet, V. (1992). A comparison of print advertisements from the U.S. and France. *Journal of Advertising, 21*, 73–81.

Bordo, S. (1993). *Unbearable weights: Feminism, western culture and the body*. Berkeley: University of California.

Cheng, H. (1994). Reflections of cultural values: A content analysis of Chinese magazine advertisements from 1982 and 1992. *International Journal of Advertising, 13*, 167–183.

Cheng, H., & Schweitzer, J. C. (1996). Cultural values reflected in Chinese and U.S. television commercials. *Journal of Advertising Research, 36*, 27–45.

Cheng, H. (1997). Holding up half of the sky: A sociocultural comparison of gender role portrayals in Chinese and U.S. advertising. *International Journal of Advertising, 16*, 295–319.

Chestnut, R., La Chance, C., & Lubitz, A. (1977). The decorative female model: Sexual stimuli and the recognition of advertisements. *Journal of Advertising, 6*, 11–14.

Cohen, J. A. (1960). Coefficient for agreement of nominal scales. *Educational and Psychological Measurement, 20*, 37–46.

Cortese, A. J. (1999). *Provocateur: Images of women and minorities in advertising*. Lanham, MD: Rowman & Littlefield.

Courtney, A., & Lockeretz, S. (1971). A woman's place: An analysis of the roles portrayed by women in magazine advertisements. *Journal of Marketing, 8*, 92–95.

Darling-Wolf, F. (1998). White bodies and feminist dilemmas: On the complexity of positionality. *Journal of Communication Inquiry, 22*, 410–425.

Englis, B., Solomon, M., & Ashmore, R. (1994). Beauty before the eyes of beholders: The cultural encoding of beauty types in magazine advertising and music television. *Journal of Advertising, 23*(2), 49–63.

Frith, K. T., & Mueller, B. (2003). *Advertising and societies: Global issues*. New York: Peter Lang.

Frith, K. T., & Sengupta, S. (1991). Individualism and advertising: A cross cultural comparison. *Media Asia, 18*, 191–197.

Fung, A. (2000). Feminist philosophy and cultural representation in the Asian context. *Gazette: The International Journal of Communication Studies, 62*(2), 153–165.

Gauntlett, D. (2002). *Media, gender and identity: An introduction*. London: Routledge.

Goffman, E. (1976). *Gender advertisements*. New York: Harper & Row.

Greer, G. (1999). *The whole woman*. London: Doubleday.

Griffin, M., Viswanath, K., & Schwartz, D. (1994). Gender advertising in the U.S. and India: Exporting cultural stereotypes. *Media, Culture & Society, 16*, 487–507.

Haug, W. F. (1987). *Commodity aesthetics, ideology and culture*. New York: International General.

Hofstede, G. (1997). *Cultures and organizations: Software of the mind*. New York: McGraw-Hill.

Holsti, O. R. (1969). *Content analysis for the social sciences and humanities*. Reading, MA: Addison-Wesley.

Horton, R., Lauren L., & Hewitt, M. (1982). The effects of nudity, suggestiveness, and attractiveness on product class and brand name recall. In V. Kothari (Ed.), *Developments in marketing science* (Vol. 5, pp. 456–459). Nacogdoches, TX: Academy of Marketing Science.

Jhally, S. (1989). Advertising, gender and sex: What's wrong with a little objectification. In R. Parmentier & G. Urban (Eds.), *Working Papers and the Proceedings of the Center for Psychosocial Studies*, No. 29.

Kates, S., Shaw, G., & Garlock, G. (1999). The ever entangling web: A study of ideologies and discourses in advertising to women. *Journal of Advertising, 28*(2), 33–49.

Kilbourne, J. (1987). *Still killing us softly: Advertising's images of women* [video recording]. Cambridge, UK: Cambridge University Films.

Kilbourne, J. (1999). *Can't buy me love: How advertising changes the way we think and feel*. New York: Free Press.

Kuhn, A. (1985). *The power of the image*. Boston: Routledge & Kegan Paul.

Kyung, J. L. (2000). Country experiences: Korea. In *Changing lenses: Women's perspectives on media* (pp. 82–93). Manila, Philippines: ISIS International.

Lafky, S., Duffy, M., Steinmaus, M., & Berkowitz, D. (1996). Looking through gendered lenses: Female stereotyping in advertisements and gender role expectations. *Journalism and Mass Communications Quarterly, 73*, 379–388.

Lin, C. A. (1993). Cultural differences in message strategies: A comparison between American and Japanese TV commercials. *Journal of Advertising Research, 33*(3), 40–48.

Maynard, M., & Taylor, C. (1999). Girlish images across cultures: Analyzing Japanese versus U.S. *Seventeen* magazine ads. *Journal of Advertising, 28*(1), 39–48.

Mueller, B. (1987). Reflections of culture: An analysis of Japanese and American advertising appeals. *Journal of Advertising Research, 27*(3), 51–59.

O'Barr, W. (1994). *Culture and the ad: Exploring otherness in the world of advertising*. Boudler, CO: Westview.

Reichert, J., Lambiase, S., Carstarphen, M., & Zavoina, S. (1999). Cheesecake and beefcake: No matter how you slice it, sexual explicitness in advertising continues to increase. *Journalism and Mass Communications Quarterly, 76*(1), 7–20.

Reid, L. N., & Soley, L. (1983). Decorative models and the readership of magazine ads. *Journal of Advertising Research, 23*(2), 27–32.

Richins, M. (1991). Social comparison and the idealized images of advertising. *Journal of Consumer Research, 18*, 71–82.

Richmond, D., & Hartman, T. (1982). Sex appeal in advertising. *Journal of Advertising Research, 22*, 53–61.

Shaw, P. (1999). Internationalization of the women's magazine industry in Taiwan: Context, process and influence. *Asian Journal of Communication, 9*(2), 17–38.

Shields, V. R. (1990). Advertising visual images: Gendered ways of seeing and looking. *Journal of Communication Inquiry, 14*(2), 25–39.

Siew, F., Ching, K. S., & Tan, W. K. (2001). *Colours of beauty: Selecting and using Pan Asian, Asian and Caucasian models in Singapore women's fashion magazines*. Unpublished honors thesis. Singapore: Nanyang Technological University.

Soley, L., & Kurzbad, G. (1986). Sex in advertising: A comparison of 1964 and 1984 magazine advertisements. *Journal of Advertising, 15*(3), 46–54, 64.

Solomon, M. R., Ashmore, R., & Longo, L. C. (1992). The beauty match-up hypothesis: Congruence between types of beauty and product images in advertising. *Journal of Advertising, 21*, 23–34.

Steadman, M. (1969). How sexy illustrations affect brand recall. *Journal of Advertising Research, 9*, 15–19.

U.S. Department of Commerce (2001). *U.S. Census 2000: Profile of General Demographic Characteristics of the 2000 Census of Population and Housing*. Washington, DC: Author.

Wimmer, R. D., & Dominick, J. (2000). *Mass media research: An introduction*. Belmont, CA: Wadsworth.

Wood, J. (1999). *Communication, gender and culture* (3rd ed.). Belmont, CA: Wadsworth.

Chapter 13

ROBERT GOLDMAN AND STEPHEN PAPSON

"JUST DO IT," BUT NOT ON MY PLANET

WE LIVE IN A PHANTASMAGORIA OF CORPORATE LOGOS and brand images—think of Coca-Cola's red scrolling text, McDonald's golden arches, and Apple Inc.'s bitten macintosh. In the late 1990s, when sociology professors Robert Goldman and Stephen Papson wrote their book *Nike Culture: The Sign of the Swoosh*, the swoosh had been elevated to the ranks of internationally-recognized brand icons. Advertising tends to focus on a consumption orientation to products: millions of dollars are spent annually to associate Nike's swoosh with self-improvement messages like "Just Do It." But commodities also involve production, which typically is not addressed in advertising. When shoes are produced, they are produced in specific contexts of labor policies, industrial waste, and other costs of mass production. Nike, then, found itself criticized for the disconnect between its uplifting advertising messages and the reality of its global production processes. In this chapter from their book, the authors explain how Nike's corporate philosophy enabled the company to achieve global distinction despite mounting threats to its image, including criticisms of its overseas labor practices. As Goldman and Papson argue, "the very thing—the swoosh—that has made Nike successful in the world of consumption also acts like a magnet for negative publicity."

From Cultural Icon to Symbolic Capital

Think of the *Nike swoosh* like a piggy bank. Every time you watch a *Nike* ad that gives you viewing pleasure, or provides a moment of identification, or that encourages you to think of *Nike* as committed to something broader than its own self-interest, then you deposit a little bit of value (almost like dropping a coin in the piggy bank) into the sign. In our estimation, the *Nike swoosh* has become swollen with this kind of accumulated value to the extent that *Nike* no longer needs to name itself, but can merely show the *swoosh* symbol to brand and set apart the world of *Nike* and its imagery. "*Nike*'s marketing formula: integrate the *swoosh* into the cultural fabric of sports and harness its emotional power. The formula has proven successful, as *Nike*'s growth has coincided with the growth in sports."[1] Relying on the *swoosh* to brand its business has paid off handsomely in an annual growth rate of roughly 40% during the mid 1990s.

We have suggested that there is more than just a passing relationship between the creation of the *swoosh* as a universal cultural icon and the expansion of *Nike*'s economic capital. *Nike* is representative of a new stage of capitalist institutions rooted in the kinds of cultural economies we have been observing. Global and transnational capitalism has brought with it industries where commodities are themselves symbols.[2] No firm better fits this model than *Nike*, whose symbolic capital has acquired a huge global reach.

The primary vehicle through which *Nike* has built its cultural icon and its symbolic capital has been its advertising and sports marketing. What sets *Nike* advertising apart from others at present? In the world of television's rapid fire movement from image to image, consistent, coherent philosophies have eroded or fractured into the scattered cultural debris of images and styles. What separates *Nike* from its competitors is that it has endowed its *swoosh* symbol with the appearance that it stands for a philosophy of life.

Nike has achieved its brand preeminence in several broad stages. First, *Nike* established itself as equivalent to sports and sports culture. *Nike* has long since entrenched itself as being dedicated and committed to athletic excellence. Next *Nike* adopted a self-mocking attitude toward its own advertising. *Nike* then capitalized on the trust built up to raise a broad range of social issues like the crisis of inner-city youth that advertisers normally avoid. With *Nike*'s dominance in US markets, the next push (it has already begun) involves a global advertising strategy, which in the words of Liz Dolan, *Nike*'s former brand manager, will be based both on "a global point of view" along with "a country-by-country plan to make the brand part of the cultural fabric."[3]

In the US, the meaning of the *swoosh* stands out because so many of *Nike*'s ads acknowledge the underlying conditions of commodity relations in an often dehumanized world. Rather than repress these experiences as do the vast majority of ads, *Nike*'s sports marketing rejuvenated a middle class motivational discourse at a time when other such discourses have been discredited by the relentless hype and cynicism of television. *Nike* advertising has engaged the cultural contradictions of contemporary life in such a way that it appears to have a complex corporate personality that possesses greater authenticity than its rivals.

For almost a decade, *Nike* competed with its primary rival, *Reebok*, in what we call sign wars.[4] Sign wars take place between marketers as they try to top rival brand images but with relatively little mention of actual product benefits. With *Wieden & Kennedy* at the helm, *Nike* has thus far won its sign war battles with *Reebok*, although *Reebok* continues to counterattack. Indeed, with their "Planet *Reebok*" campaign, *Reebok* sought to counter *Nike* by constructing its own imagery of a life-world space animated by a *Reebok* philosophy. Though this campaign subsequently collapsed, *Reebok* even mimicked *Nike* by dispensing with their name proper and using only their vector icon to sign their ads. The athletic shoe market is no longer a two brand race. *Nike*'s market share has risen to 43%, while *Reebok* has dropped back to 17% and *Adidas* has risen to challenge for significant market share. Given the *swoosh*'s current dominance, *Nike* can anticipate further sign war attacks from rivals who will try to leverage the value of the *swoosh* to their own advantage. *Reebok*'s recent swipe at the successful *Nike* women's ad "If you let me play," is illustrative: "we are not waiting for anyone to *let us play*." Another recent instance of a sign war attack appeared at the end of a Shaquille O'Neal ad for *Reebok* when an imitation of *Nike*'s Little Penny puppet appears, wanting to join "Planet *Reebok*." In the next instant, Shaq "inadvertently" [wink-wink] elbows the puppet out of the picture. This is a sign wars attack pure and simple.

Reebok has not competed well against *Nike* in the area of authenticity. In the summer of 1997, the *New York Times* quoted Ruth Davis, a global product director for *Reebok* who seeks trendy celebrities to wear her shoes "and show up in the gossip rags." Her goal at the time was to put the recording sex goddesses of the moment, the Spice Girls, in *Reebok* shoes.[5] When we interviewed a *Nike* executive a few weeks later, we mentioned *Reebok*'s pursuit of the Spice Girls. She responded by pretending to clutch her throat and making a gagging gesture. Her reaction spoke not just about *Reebok*, but about the way that *Nike* envisions its own corporate identity and mission. To the *Nike* executive, the Spice Girls signified pure glamour, not authenticity. *Nike* defines itself, first and foremost, as a company that designs and markets the best products for athletes. *Nike* defines itself as the company able to tap the authenticity of sport. Here is Dan Wieden himself, reflecting upon the matter of authenticity in the body of advertising work his firm has done for *Nike*.

> The people at *Nike* taught my partner, David Kennedy, and me how to advertise – and how not to advertise. Back in 1980, when David and I first started to work on the account, *Nike* made it very clear that they hated advertising. They had developed close relationships with athletes, and they didn't want to talk to them in any phony or manipulative way. They were obsessed with authenticity, in terms of both the product and the communication. And they had a sense of what was cool.
>
> Those attitudes have guided all of *Nike*'s advertising. We try to make honest contact with the consumer, to share something that is very hip and very inside. We don't translate the inside jokes because we figure it's OK if the people who are faddish don't understand. Either you get it or you don't. It's more important for us to be true to the athletes by talking to them in a way that respects their intelligence, time, and knowledge of sports.[6]

The Image of Philosophy or the Philosophy of Image?

Many sociologists and anthropologists who study commodity culture have observed that it tends to anesthetize civic discourse and impoverish public space. Until recently we would have agreed with this. However, the growing wave of protests against *Nike* starting in 1996 regarding treatment of third world laborers seems to have shifted matters around. Might it be possible, that under shifting cultural circumstances, commercial television, sports, and advertising can actually contribute to a public sphere of discourse? During our interview with Liz Dolan in the summer of 1997, she related a conversation she had with Mark Penn, a national public opinion pollster who also works in behalf of President Clinton. Following months of criticisms in the media about the labor situation in Southeast Asia, *Nike* asked Penn to do an opinion poll for them on the subject. When Penn spoke to Dolan about the preliminary poll results he observed that *Nike* registered high awareness and familiarity scores regarding these issues. Penn added that he wished the Clinton White House could generate such interest and awareness on its issues. Dolan replied that if Clinton's concerns were placed on the sports pages, then he too might achieve this kind of expanded issue awareness. Moral and political discourse now finds itself daily woven into sports discourse.

A Land of Lost Children

Remember those "Happy Days" of youth when kids could be kids and didn't have to deal with adult problems; when kids did nothing but play. "This mythic vision of childhood still appears in Saturday morning advertising where children are shown enthusiastically playing with advertised toys. More recently, advertising has turned to another view of childhood, the child-adult. A 1994 Fuji film commercial introduced a montage of technologically sophisticated, self-aware children who "don't play kick the can any more." MCI, Microsoft, and American Express commercials replicated this look. Nike has capitalized on the sober and gray side of childhood. The self-reflexive child-adult debuted in the P.L.A.Y. campaign's look, and was evident in the "If you let me play [sports]" commercial. A comparable look reappears in a 1997 P.L.A.Y. commercial, focused on estranged children who seem to bear the weight of the world on their shoulders as they gaze directly into the camera. "We are your children" was saturated with encodings of cinema reflexivity—including black and white film, off-center framing, the look of being deep-in-serious-thought, and cold background landscapes – to signify children longing for an unalienated childhood.

> We are your children
> Your boys
> Your girls
> Your sons and daughters
> we are old for our age
> we are too fat
> can't do a pull up
> we smell
> we inhale
> we drink
> we are mothers
> we are fathers
> we are old for our age
> we have no place to play
> we have no place to play
> we want to be strong
> we want you to come out and play
> teach us to hit
> teach us to throw
> we are some children
> we are you.

Is this what is meant by a society of lost childhood? Has childhood disappeared? Or is this another instance of a panicky middle class hysterically contemplating a world where so many forces seem out of control? At the very least, this commercial invests the subject with moral drama. Nike's social imagery hints at a world where children learn to be spectators and undisciplined consumers, rather than active players. But the Nike appeal is more pointed as if bemoans the absence of adult guidance and appropriate places to play.

The Nike ad addresses the crisis of childhood but couching social criticism in cinematic codes makes it difficult to pin down the critique. Are today's parents wanting in parenting commitment? Or is it poverty with its wrenching of the family fabric that poses a significant threat to our youth? Or maybe it is television with its incessant mantra to consume that leaves youth soft in the head and the belly? Can absent parents be convinced to resume caring for their children? Here then is the crisis of childhood. Children who are unmuscled, soft and overweight, who have become jaded and cynical before their time, yearn for the return of their parents and a place to play – they yearn for a moment of innocence, the innocence of PLAY.

Consider another reading of the ad. The advertising industry has helped turn youth into a lucrative market. Advertising promotes higher levels of consumption, which necessitate higher levels of disposable income to support these purchases. Looked at this way the Nike P.L.A.Y. campaign begins to ring a little hollow, since its prestigious swoosh and its pricing practices tempt less well-to-do youth to make themselves into money-earners as soon as possible. Does turning children into brand name consumers as early as possible contribute to the erosion of childhood?

This commercial invites a variety of interpretations depending on the assumptions viewers make. Nike's appeal to parents to get more involved in their children's lives by teaching them to play might be cynically interpreted as a call to buy kids high-priced athletic shoes. Or, it might seem as a public-spirited call to volunteer ourselves and our resources to the future of America's children. As much as any ad, this one reveals the tensions between selling commodities and constructing images of public legitimacy. Embedding moral issues in the philosophy of image, no matter how well intentioned, reminds us of the perils of public discourse in the age of television. For all its moral and emotional intensity, "We are your children" frames the matter as one of choosing between hope and hopelessness, while avoiding the fundamental matter of market forces and market moralities.

Nike is one of very few contemporary corporate advertisers that has successfully constructed a recognizable philosophy. What constitutes a philosophy in the realm of television advertising? Since Western philosophy has an academic tradition, we tend to think of philosophies as grandiose encounters with metaphysical questions about Truth, Reality, Morality. Thinking of philosophy as a system of images supported by slogans and maxims seems to trivialize our inherited notions of philosophy. In the latter half of the twentieth century, both critical and conservative critiques of mass culture have decried the invasion of these simplified philosophical capsules. Writing at mid-century, Max Horkheimer and Theodor Adorno scorned the preconstituted commodity packaging of experience of any sort.[7] Imagine what they might say if they encountered the prepackaged philosophy of "Just do it" embedded, and ready for consumption, in the *swoosh* sign?

Nike has taken up its position as philosopher in campaigns ranging from the P.L.A.Y. campaign to the women's campaigns that address the meaning of everyday life. Beyond articulating a philosophy of empowerment that informs our lives, *Nike* has made its advertising a space in which to raise social questions and issues of conscience – the HIV epidemic, the plight of inner city children, the benefits of sports for young girls. These *Nike* ads touched an important chord insofar as they signified resilience and empowerment.

Perhaps it is difficult to accept that a sneaker company could become so central to public discourse. Here we must recognize how central the discourse of sport is to supporting a moral order. As commodity-driven sports aphorisms echo through American culture, they offer a fleeting sense of coherency and purpose in an otherwise increasingly fragmented social and cultural formation. Consider how many corporations participate in this discourse, as they intrusively associate their names with every aspect of sport – player of the game, bowl games, local races, starting lineups, half-time reports, points in the paint, hardest hit of the week, ad nauseam.

Because *Nike* promotes bourgeois values supported by vignettes of achievement, it appears to constitute a moral center in a media culture that otherwise seems to have none. In this sense, *Nike* television ads appear like moments of moral oasis; against the cynicism of the news (the O.J. Simpson trial), against the pornographic realism of media violence (*Top Cops*), against the hypercommercialization of other commodity signs (the *NBA* and "I love this game"), and against exaggerated sexual posturing (*Calvin Klein*). When *Nike* seems to take moral stands as in its HIV runner ad, *Nike* positions itself as standing against flashy, empty image candy in favor of the human spirit. Participation in sport is associated with morality – with learning teamwork and individual discipline, that success is associated with hard work. Still, *Nike* is perceived as having philosophical integrity not merely because it upholds the remains of bourgeois morality, but because it relentlessly irreverent about image-based posturing.

For much of the twentieth century, sport in America has been depicted as the field within which divisions and distinctions of class and race can be transcended. The ideological argument is simple: in sport, the only thing that matters is performance, achievement and playing within the rules. Today, sport is socially constructed as central to local communities, to parent–child relations, and as a prime activity for socializing youth into occupational achievers and citizens. Sport is thus positioned as an activity through which we construct our identities. When constructed as a moral force, there follows a lot of moralizing about sports with expectations that athletes maintain exemplary moral standards like priests before them. Aware that such an arena is full of hypocrisy in an era of full-contact commodification, *Nike* distinguishes acting out the principle ("Just do it") from mouthing the words. Working on the premise that consumers now seek to wear their motivational commitments and identities on their clothing, a Michael Jordan t-shirt available at *NIKETOWN* sums up this *Nike* worldview:

> *If you don't back it up with performance and hard work,*
> *talking doesn't mean a thing.*

We have argued that *Nike* has both an image of philosophy and a philosophy of image. *Nike*'s best-known photographic style idealizes the individual by mixing realism with the classicism of low angle shots and slow-motion movement shot in black and white. This isolates subjectivity from the existential conditions of time and place and reframes it as human essence. In *Nike*'s representations, signifiers of alienation plus signifiers of determination are defined as equaling transcendence. As long as one stays in the game, life has meaning. Image of philosophy and philosophy of image come together in measured *Nike* discourses such as this from a 1997 *Nike* Golf Tour ad.

> *I am not afraid to do what I want for a living.* [Pause]
> *I am down to my last $100.* [Pause]
> *I am without regrets.* [Pause]
> *Just do it.*

In *Nike*'s world, participation in the human community is defined by the will to act in accordance with our desires, and without regard to possible failure.

What happens when philosophy is reduced to a flow of images? Though simplistic and reductionist, it is democratic in the sense that an empowering philosophy becomes available to a huge number of people. When philosophy is turned into a capsule and linked to a totem-sign, it can make people feel good because they have aligned themselves with more than a run-of-the-mill product. But, of course, this makes empowerment conditional on access to disposable income as well as the relative stability of the sign and the consistency of belief embedded in it. There are various problems with this philosophy-in-a-logo approach, or what we might now refer to as ready-made praxis. First, while the consumer is now freed up to act, this philosophical system also abolishes the need for critical thought. Second, it tends to bury the relationship between biography and the socio-historical conditions within which people live. So while *Nike*'s advertising seems aimed at urging people to take responsibility for their own production of self, it cannot account for the great mass of human beings who live under conditions that deny them even this possibility. Most serious of all, the economy of signs is not stable.

Over*swoosh*ification

In a global cultural economy economic growth is contingent upon the growth of sign value. We have argued that physical labor is no longer the primary source of value in the consumer commodity. *Nike* has attached its sign to an expanding array of products and product lines in an expanding array of cultures. *Nike*'s growth seems unending. *Nike*'s sign value seemingly erupted beginning around 1986. And, in barely a decade's time, the *Nike swoosh* became a global icon.

Nike built the value of its *swoosh* by positioning itself as the company that puts athletics before commercialism. *Nike* separates itself from the pack of sporting-goods corporations by expressing this calling of sport in its slogans, advertisements, and public relations statements. Recall *Nike*'s sharp criticism of non-athletic product companies for overcommercializing the Olympics: "If a cupcake maker put its logo on an athlete that's commercialism." Via *Wieden & Kennedy, Nike* has enjoyed success tweaking the media for transforming sport into an overcommercialized enterprise.

Of course, *Nike* has played a significant role in the commercialization of sport. In *Nike*'s early days when its star was long distance runner Steve Prefontaine, *Nike* aligned itself with the rights of runners to turn professional without losing their standing with the athletic governing bodies that controlled track and field competitions. Prefontaine, and *Nike* behind him, played the role of mavericks, declaring to the track world that there would be no more deals under the table, everything now would be above board. A quarter of a century later, *Nike* has evolved into a marketing giant because it has solved more efficiently than any other in the industry the task of moving its commodities through markets. In the 1990s, *Nike* has itself pressed the boundaries, and the stakes, of commercialization into hitherto uncharted territory. After all, it was Phil Knight who signed a controversial merchandising arrangement when he aligned *Nike* with Jerry Jones and the Dallas Cowboys, America's penultimate sports commodity machine. For the price of $2.5 million annually through 2001, this deal allowed "*Nike* to paint its trademark *swoosh* on the Cowboy's stadium, develop a theme park in the stadium, and outfit all Cowboys coaches and other sideline personnel in *Nike*-made attire."[8] On other fronts, *Nike* routinely seeks exclusive financial arrangements with elite college basketball and football teams, placing the *Nike swoosh* on virtually every top team's jerseys or shoes.[9] *Nike* has been known to engage in ambush marketing to associate itself with events sponsored by competitors. Against *Adidas* and *Reebok, Nike* competes intensely for the stars of tomorrow by showering the most talented kids with free gear, thus extending commercialization down to the high school level. *Nike* employees have, on occasion, visited an inner city high school campus driving a Hummer, distributing *swoosh*-marked paraphernalia, and shooting a few hoops with the kids. "That's our target consumer, the black, urban teen," said the *Nike* representative, after giving an impromptulecture to the kids on the value of education. "It's the coolness factor – if they wear [*Nike* products], the others will follow."[10] All the activities that *Nike* decries in its ads – the bidding up of salaries, the turning of every surface into a commercial, the competition for kids' attention – *Nike* does. *Nike* is central to the commodification of sport, yet its symbol stands for the transcendent moment of sport for its own sake.

   Nike has attempted to separate itself from the taint of commercialism by adopting self-reflexive, ironic, and winking attitudes towards the subject of advertising. *Nike* advertising stands out because its ads acknowledge the penetration of commercial relations into "everyday life in the modern world."[11] *Nike* acknowledges the presence of commodification in our culture by sharing jokes about the absurdities and excesses concocted in a culture driven by money. This advertising practice of sharing an aversion to the inauthenticity of commercial life has enabled *Nike* to position itself as an ally of viewers against corporate shills and hucksters. Listen to the language of Arkansas Red in a 1997 ad as he separates the essence of basketball from the commodification of sport. His "nobody owns us" speech paints the relationships of proprietary ownership as a limiting and controlling force in sport – but it is a source of unfreedom that is forgotten as soon as real players take the court to play basketball.

> *Nobody owns us, man.*
> *When I say us, I mean ballplayers.*
> *Nobody owns us, you understand.*
> *And nobody can own basketball.*
> *There's no one person that can own this game.*
> *You can take away the* NBA.
> *So what? Take it away.*
> *You can take away endorsements*
> *So what?*
> *You can take away the logos on the shoes*
> *So what, take em all.*
> *But when you can take all that away,*
> *That Zoe,*
> *That Indiana boy,*
> *And the Street boy,*
> *You still gonna be butter!* [but-ta]

Despite the fact that surely all would agree that *Nike* is the kingpin of basketball shoe logos, this *Nike* text scoffs at the commodity form (the *NBA*, the endorsements, the logos), adopts the vernacular aesthetic of those from below, and positions itself as an appreciator – par excellence – of the Truth of Sport, all without even mentioning the *Nike* name. The Truth of Sport, according to this *Nike* text, lies in the existential joy and pleasure afforded by playing. It doesn't matter what signs appear on the shoes, because all of that is just fluff that covers the essence of basketball. If this resonates with the viewer, then there is yet another investment of authenticity onto the *swoosh*.

This *swoosh* has paid off handsomely for *Nike* profits. Today, the *swoosh* is pervasive in public spaces devoted to sports – it appears across surfaces on caps, jerseys, walls, even defining backgrounds and snowboards. *Nike* currently dominates the sign marketplace with its "*swoosh*ification" of the world. Almost every camera shot during *ESPN*'s television coverage of the 1997 *X-Games* included a colorful orange *swoosh* naming the background – naming the place. *Swoosh*ification refers to this pervasiveness.

It is ironic then that at precisely this moment of cultural domination, *Nike* becomes vulnerable because of the *swoosh*. *Swoosh*ification hints at the possibility of an impending devaluation on the *Nike swoosh*. *Nike*'s success now requires that it take seriously the threat posed by massive overexposure to the value of the *swoosh* logo. At *Nike* headquarters there is talk of "over*swoosh*ification." A self-appointed watchdog group has formed at *Nike*'s Beaverton campus, calling themselves the "*Swoosh* Integrity Committee." Their concern? Attaching the "*swoosh*" to any surface it can find, trivializes it – coffee mugs, key rings, nasal strips – and cheapens the value of the *swoosh*.[12] Recognizing the potential dilution of the *swoosh*, this internal committee focuses on maintaining the integrity of the *swoosh* by keeping it off non-sports paraphernalia. This was, of course, the danger in developing into a branded apparel company. The move from footwear to apparel has geometrically boosted the *swoosh*'s visual saturation of social spaces. In the US, any day spent in public spaces sees the *swoosh* prominently displayed on shoes, shirts, pants, socks, caps, jackets, gloves and sunglasses, not to mention the wallpapering at sporting events, or in shopping malls. It is possible to experience a sense of oversaturation. When asked about this, Liz Dolan, *Nike*'s former brand manager, indicated a need for fewer *swooshes*, not more. *Nike*'s goal, she said, is not that the *swoosh* be ubiquitous, but rather that it connotes "specialness."

The over*swoosh*ification watchdog committee will unlikely be able to solve, however, the basic dilemma that *Nike* (or any other firm in this industry) encounters in a maturing sign economy.[13] At best, it can be managed from moment to moment. Over*swoosh*ification is a metaphor for the loss of value due to oversaturation and overcommercialization. Those old capitalist demons of supply and demand have come back to haunt symbolic production in the age of mechanical reproduction.

Contested Discourses

Many of the meanings attached to the *Nike swoosh* are near and dear to us – ideals about competition and individual freedom, top performance, a universal code of morality and justice, and defiance of authority. This is what gives the *Nike* sign its value. But, the bigger *Nike* gets, the more it dominates its industry and the media, the more likely we hear of *Nike* practices that run counter to these values. The *Nike swoosh* has become a magnet for both praise and condemnation. Because *Nike* has sought to construct the appearance of a publicly spirited entity devoted to the social good, it has brought the issue of public morality front and center. How much does *Nike*'s imagery diverge from its practices? In some academic circles, this ratio between imagery and practice is the basis for what is called ideology critique. By any name, this kind of measuring stick has an important place in a democracy. However, when this type of critique is taken up in the mass media it becomes organized according to the logic of the spectacle. Thus the media have simplified the situation of shoe production in Southeast Asia to the same degree that *Nike* has abbreviated cultural issues related to authenticity, determination, social transcendence, and spiritual freedom and made them equivalent with the *Nike swoosh*. Opponents now compress all that they do not like about global capitalism and inscribe it on the *Nike swoosh*. With highly compacted and potent symbolizations comes a new form of symbolic politics.

Building sign value by positioning oneself as a moral presence necessitates that one's own practices be above reproach. But, *Nike* is a global corporation that competes in a world capitalist economic system where there are winners and losers: those who are paid highly and those who are paid poorly. The logic of capital demands that profit be squeezed from every part of the production/exchange process. As *Nike*'s sign value grows, the gap between *Nike*'s moral/commercial rhetoric and the world of real social relations becomes increasingly apparent because the media that carry, and cultivate, the system of signs, recognize that a celebrity sign — just as much as a celebrity figure — carries instant news value. Updating the folk adage of an earlier epoch, we now realize that "those who live by the Sign also die by the Sign."

Looking for contradictions, ironies, and moments of hypocrisy that can be turned into a story angle, the media lurks and pounces at every opportunity. *Nike* is now vulnerable precisely because the *swoosh* is so inflated with cultural value. Political action groups, mainstream TV programming such as *Prime Time* or *60 Minutes*, and sports writers now find a ready target in the *Nike swoosh*. And as the tides of spectacle politics turn, it has grown ever more fashionable to engage in *Nike* bashing. "The anti-*Nike* backlash is not just about the company's labor record. It's also a reaction to the global reach of the *Nike* brand, the wall-to-wall ubiquity of its corporate moniker."[14]

Oversupply leads to devaluation every time. In this climate, *Nike* has been challenged by those claiming a higher moral ground. And these moral attacks have come from almost every angle. It might be useful for a moment to revisit some of the public relations headaches that have surfaced in recent years as *Nike* evolved into a "ubiquitous" global presence.

In the late 1980s and early 1990s *Nike* found itself the subject of nagging criticism for culturally and economically exploiting the inner-city black community and not reinvesting in it. For instance, over the years there has surfaced and resurfaced what amounts to an urban folk legend about kids who kill other kids for overpriced sneakers. In the early 1990s, Jesse Jackson and Operation PUSH made headlines when they accused *Nike* of not providing sufficient employment opportunities for minority workers. And, when *Nike* ran a series of TV ads with Spike Lee addressing questions of racism, critics assailed the ads, arguing that they "smack[ed] of opportunism and hypocrisy."[15]

Starting with the embarrassing revelation that Pakistani child labor was stitching soccer balls, *Nike* was in the news week after week during 1996 and 1997. This was not the first time that *Nike*'s production practices in Asia had been rendered visible. In 1992, Nena Baker of *The Oregonian* wrote an exposé on "The Hidden Hands of *Nike*."[16] But there was not yet the necessary cultural atmosphere to give resonance to the story. *Nike*'s sign value was not yet pervasive enough. However, when charges of poor wages and working conditions in Indonesia and Vietnam resurfaced in 1996, followed by rippling waves of media coverage of an incident involving Vietnamese assembly workers beaten with a shoe by a Korean floor manager in a *Nike*-affiliated factory, public attention stayed focused on *Nike*. To try to blunt the criticism, *Nike* hired Andrew Young, former UN Ambassador and mayor of Atlanta, in February 1997, to investigate its factories and evaluate its *Code of Conduct* for relations with third-world producers.

> As an advocate of human rights, I am involved because *Nike* has expressed its determination to be a leader for positive corporate change. Their commitment can result in growth and opportunity for the communities around the world where they operate.[17]

Still, the string of bad press continued as 10,000 Indonesian workers struck in a *Nike* factory "just days after *Nike* put its name to a groundbreaking anti-sweatshop pact between labor, human rights groups and apparel-makers."[18] Days later a violent rampage took place among these workers in Jakarta as protesters burned cars and ransacked offices, while 3000 workers in a Vietnam factory struck over wages.[19] As the public relations quagmire deepened, almost anything seemed to get thrown into the mix. Even in the realm of signification, *Nike* found itself under attack when the Council on American-Islamic Relations demanded a public apology from *Nike* for a shoe logo on the Air Bakin' model intended to signify a flame that instead resembled the word "Allah" in the Arabic script.[20]

To address the labor issues raised by its critics, *Nike* has engaged a series of studies and audits. After the Andrew Young report proved less persuasive with its critics than *Nike* might have hoped because of its methodology and because it did not address the wage issue, *Nike* contracted with an MBA team from Dartmouth's Tuck School to study wages and living conditions in Asia. The research reported by the Dartmouth group found that "*Nike* factory workers in Southeast Asia help support their families and have discretionary income" left over after meeting basic needs to both consume and save.[21] Just weeks later an activist group leaked an environmental safety audit that *Ernst & Young* had done on a Vietnamese factory that produces shoes for *Nike*. The leaked report indicated problems with noise and solvent pollution (toluene, a carcinogenic ingredient in the adhesive used). Critics saw the document as further evidence that *Nike* failed to take care of the well being of workers. *Nike*'s spokesperson replied by rhetorically asking how many other firms take the initiative to do internal environmental audits, and argued that the audit was yet another indicator that *Nike* was dedicated to responsibly locating and correcting problems. But the charges and countercharges continue as questions about the methodology of the *Nike* sponsored reports have been raised.[22]

These critiques of *Nike* take two general paths. One set of criticisms mentioned above addresses production practices and the contradictions of global capitalism, but without naming the latter. In behalf of poor youth on both sides of the planet, anti-*Nike* protests in November 1997 linked the price of athletic shoes in the inner city to wage rates in Asia as a matter of morality, not legality.

> Dozens of young people from 11 settlement houses around the city are planning to dump their old *Nikes* at the store to protest what they say is the shoe company's double exploitation of the poor. They are part of a growing movement that has criticized *Nike* for failing to pay workers in Asian factories a living wage – about $3 a day in Indonesia, for example – while charging style-setting urban teen-agers upwards of $100 for the shoes.

"*Nike* is making billions of dollars in America off you guys," said Mike Gitelson, a social worker who helped start the protest. "Let's get this straight, *Nike* is doing nothing illegal. For us, it is a moral question. You can't make that much money off us and refuse to give your people enough money to live on."[23]

A second set of concerns usually pivot around cultural challenges to *Nike*'s legitimation advertising. Advertising strategies that had previously drawn public acclaim for *Nike*, began to elicit boos as well. Even *Nike*'s tribute to Jackie Robinson in an ad on the fiftieth anniversary of his breaking the "color barrier" in professional baseball became a contested discourse. The *Nike* commercial crafted a sequence of shots of baseball players present and past, who each, in turn, thank Jackie Robinson for opening up major league baseball to black athletes. Sewn together as a visual poem voiced with sincere affect. *Nike*'s ad took on the reverential tone of a liturgical prayer:

> *for letting me be the player I always wanted to be*
> *for letting me compete against the very best*
> *for letting fathers and sons realize their dreams*
> *for Reggie Jackson's 3 home runs*
> *for Ernie Banks playing too*
> *for Roberto Clemente throwing to third*
> *for Hank Aaron's 715*
> *for my 21 years in the major's*
> *for the chance to play in October*
> *for the joys of stealing home*
> *for all us that never got to play*
> *for enduring every taunt*
> *and not lashing but in hate*
> *for standing up with dignity*
> *for standing up*
> *for opening our eyes*
> *for the power of an entire race.*
> *Thanks, Jackie*
> *Thanks, Jackie*
> *Thank you*
> *Thank you*
> *Thank you Jackie Robinson*
> *Thank you*

The litany was signed with the *swoosh*. In conjunction with the campaign. *Nike* donated $350,000 toward scholarship awarded by the Jackie Robinson Foundation. This drew praise from Robinson's widow and daughter. "You must understand, Phil Knight was the chairman of our dinner," said Sharon Robinson. "They had a connection to the Jackie Robinson Foundation that has been going on all year, even before that. We don't see it as exploitative at all. It's a beautiful commercial."[24]

But, sportswriters cried hypocrisy at *Nike* for running this commercial tribute to Jackie Robinson as a way of "insinuating" itself into great moments of sports history with which it had nothing to do. Suddenly, sports writers were playing the role of deconstructionists and ideology critics, challenging the way in which *Nike* advertisements seek to build the value of its image by investing it with authentic significance, in this case drawn from the memory of Jackie Robinson, a heroic American icon. The sportswriters didn't just deconstruct, they did so for the purpose of assigning an alternative sign value to *Nike*, that of a dark empire driven by the "greedy" Phil Knight.[25]

> Consider a recent commercial featuring black baseball stars thanking Jackie Robinson for breaking the color line. It is a touching tribute, grainy film footage mixed with heartfelt messages. It looks like some philanthropic foundation put it together. But when the moment peaks, and your heart is open, what's the last thing you see? *A Nike swoosh*. Same way you see a *Nike swoosh* after those Tiger Woods commercials, in which the children of the world – all races, mind you – dream of being Tiger You'll notice these ads do not try to sell you shoes or clothing – which are, after all, what *Nike* makes. But that should be your first warning. By its founder's admission, *Nike* is no longer in the shoe business; it's in the image business. It wants you to feel a certain way. It wants you and your kids to desire the *swoosh* subliminally, under the skin, without even knowing why. Call it planned addiction. First, *Nike* wants your mind. Then it takes your wallet.[26]

We might ordinarily expect to find stories about the global economy on the front pages, but we don't because news reporters have naturalized capitalism as the economy, not as one historical method of organizing an economy. And yet, we often find reports that question the morality of applying the logic of capital to the domain of sports. But why? Why has semiotic and moral critique become the bailiwick of sportswriters? To compete in the global cultural economy corporations must produce culture (signs) as well as commodities. One approach to investing commodities with cultural value has been to draw on the meaning of sports in people's lives. By investing commodities with moral purpose – and particularly with moral purpose that draws on the meaningfulness of sport – *Nike* has unintentionally made it incumbent on sportswriters to defend and protect their moral turf from profanation.

The *Swoosh* and its Contradictions

The story we have tried to tell treats *Nike*'s construction of the *swoosh* as the hub of a complex set of cultural contradictions. While *Nike* attempts to continually add value to its symbol by controlling its meaning and ensuring its pervasiveness, other participants have brought their own agenda to this negotiated space. When *Press for Change* or *Campaign for Labor Rights* bring unacceptable work place practices into the light of public discourse, the sign value of the *swoosh* may become tarnished. For them, the disparity between advertising images and production processes reflects the disparity between the lives of those in the core and those in the periphery. And when sportswriters condemn *Nike* for bringing the "image business" into the world of sports, corrupting youth by engaging them in "planned addiction," we see the contested terrain shift to *Nike*'s own image and its position in a system of cultural production.

One of the interesting sidelights to the media coverage of "the *Nike* controversy" as the press put it, has been how other companies disappear from view. Where are *Reebok*, *Adidas*, and *Fila* in these stories about production practices? Media criticism rarely identifies, and it certainly never inflates, the root logic of Capital, or the structure of the global economy. Instead, criticism on television and in the newspapers flows out of the gap between representation and practice. When *Nike* celebrates athletic activity as self-affirming, liberating, empowering, and transcendental, and by representational equivalence attaches itself to its own promotions in order to swell its sign value, *Nike* practices become a ready target because its advertising has made the *swoosh* so very visible, and so loaded it with significance. In other words, the very thing – the *swoosh* – that has made *Nike* successful in the world of consumption also acts like a magnet for negative publicity.

Strange as it may seem, an important institutional space for the public culture of a global system of capitalism has fallen to advertising. In this space, corporations construct motifs that depict globalization with imagery of liberalism, multiculturalism, and universal humanism.[27] *Nike* speaks the language of universal rights, concern for children, transcendence over the categories of age, race, gender, disability or any social stereotype. As moral philosophy, its images speak out against racism, sexism, and ageism *Nike's* imagery celebrates sport athletic activity, and play as universally rewarding categories. Playing makes for healthier, more productive citizens, and better self-actualized human beings. However, no matter what its imagery suggests, *Nike*, like any other capitalist firm, must operate within the relationships and constraints of competitive capitalist marketplaces. No matter how many P.L.A.Y. commercials *Nike* runs on TV, there will still be haunting images of production practices in Pakistan, Indonesia, and Vietnam. And as the world grows more unified, it becomes increasingly difficult to suppress entirely those gaps between image and practice, between humanism and capitalism, between moral philosophy and the bottom line of corporate profit growth.

When *Nike* engages issues of personal transcendence, race, gender and class in the public arena, it positions itself as a corporation with a sense of what is ethical, and not just what is expedient. But in a cynical commodity world, this kind of communication is automatically suspect. When idealism is expressed in commercial messages and transformed into a multi-billion dollar global industry, contradictions will surface. *Nike's* engagement in public discourse comes at a price – the expectation that it make itself accountable to a higher standard than that ordinarily practiced in a capitalist world. This is a virtual impossibility since the capitalist firm must do its business in a capitalist world.[28] "Just do it" may be an empowering slogan but it is no match for the imperatives of capitalist institutions. And sure enough, in December 1997, *Nike* dumped its established "Just do it" slogan in favor of a supposedly more enabling slogan, "I can." Perhaps the shift was pursued to avoid the trap of letting one's public imagery get stale, perhaps it was a response to slower than expected sales, declining future orders, a buildup of inventory, a steadily slipping stock price, and the continuing stream of public criticism that leveraged familiarity with the "Just do it" slogan into anti-*Nike* campaign slogans.

In what we have called an economy of sign value, brand logos like the *swoosh* have become subject to an accelerated tempo of competition in image markets. When cultural meanings are turned into commodities that can be attached to other commodities for the purpose of making them stand out, all the old rules of currencies and commodities come into play. Symbols like the *swoosh* become vulnerable to oversaturation and an accelerated rate of value burnout. We have discussed in some detail how *Nike* has positioned itself as irreverent and rebellious to try to offset these tendencies by appearing to value authenticity over the manipulativeness of the marketplace. We have also seen how difficult it is to maintain this dual commitment to sincerity and irreverence when the material world keeps impinging. To do so demands that advertisers find ways to make their images relevant and to do so in an already saturated commercial environment requires taking risks – raising issues that commercials have previously avoided because they touch on the sphere of public debate. Compounding this, like any other firm that seeks to play in this global consumer economy, *Nike* must concern itself with how to balance over*swoosh*ification against the fear that other competitors will take over part of its sign space. *Nike* faces a self-contradictory image environment that is coming to haunt all firms that wish to play in this global system. Who would have ever dreamt that commercial slogans could give rise to something much larger?

Questions

1   Writing in 1998, Goldman and Papson argue, "Nike is one of the very few contemporary corporate advertisers that has successfully constructed a recognizable philosophy." Is this still the case?

2   In this essay, the authors describe how Nike faced the threat of "overswooshification," which they describe as "oversaturation and overcommercialization." Do you think Nike indeed became overswooshified? What other products and brands have become unpopular in light of their own ubiquity?

3   The authors explain how in the mid-1990s, Nike positioned itself as an ethically conscious company. Today, many companies have launched socially responsible campaigns, including the Gap RED campaign and those brands that support Breast Cancer Awareness. On what grounds have such campaigns been criticized?

Notes and References

1.   Jeff Jensen, "Marketer of the year: *Nike* honored: ubiquitous *swoosh* illustrates how brand represents not just shoes but all of sports," *Advertising Age*, December 16, 1996, p. 1.
2.   See Scott Lash and John Urry, *Economies of Signs and Space* (Sage, London, 1994).
3.   Cited in Jensen, "Marketer of the year: *Nike* honored," p. 1.
4.   See Robert Goldman and Stephen Papson, *Sign Wars* (Guilford, New York, 1996).
5.   Jennifer Steinhauer. "*Nike* is in a league of its own, with no big rival, it calls the shots in athletic shoes," *The New York Times*, June 7 1997, p. 21.
6.   Dan Wieden, "A sense of cool: *Nike*'s theory of advertising," *Harvard Business Review*, July/August 1992, p. 97ff.
7.   Max Horkeliner and Theodor W. Adorno, "The culture industry," *Dialectic of Enlightenment*, translated by John Cunning (Allen Lane, London, 1973), pp. 120–67.
8.   Richard Sandomit, "Dollars and Dallas: league of their own?" *The New York Times*, September 24 1995, pp. 1, 13.
9.   Jeff Manning, "*Nike* Inc. *swooshes* into deal at Ohio State," *The Oregonian*, December 30 1995, pp. B7, B8.
10. Jeff Manning, "Guerrilla marketing: the other final four," *The Oregonian*, April 3 1995, p. A1.

11. The phrase is from Henri Lefebvre's, *Everyday Life in the Modern World* (Harper & Row, New York, 1971).

12. Putting the sign (the *swoosh*) on an object deemed to have little corresponding value, the value of the sign suffers.

13. See Goldman and Papson, *Sign Wars*.

14. Josh Peit, "Alas, poor *Nike*: the real reason *Nike* is the most reviled company in the galaxy," *The Willamette Week*, November 5, 1997, pp. 20–24, 26, 28.

15. "When shove came to PUSH. (PUSH demands jobs for blacks at *Nike*)," *The Economist* 316 (September 22 1990), p. 28, Cyndee Miller, "Advertisers promote racial harmony; *Nike* criticized," *Marketing News*, July 6 1992, p. 1.

16. Nena Baker, "The hidden hands of *Nike*," *The Oregonian*, August 9 1992, pp. A1, A10–11.

17. "*Nike* hires Andrew Young's group to evaluate its code of conduct," *The Oregonian*, February 25 1997, p. C1.

18. Jeff Manning, "*Nike* strikers in Indonesia back on job," *The Oregonian*, April 24 1997, pp. E1, E2.

19. Jim Hill, "*Nike* plant shuts after worker protest," *The Oregonian*, April 27 1997, pp. 21, 512.

20. "Muslims demand apology for *Nike* logo," *San Antonio Express News*, April 10 1997, p. 2E. Samanthi Levine "Recall or no, *Nike* shoe still available," *The Oregonian*, June 27 1997, pp. C1, C2.

21. "Study *Nike* pay more than adequate," *The Oregonian*, October 17 1997, pp. C1, C3.

22. Jeff Manning, "Audit *Nike* factory workers at risk," *The Oregonian*, November 8 1997, p. B., Dara O'Rourke, "Smoke from a hired gun a critique of *Nike*'s labor and environmental auditing in Vietnam as performed by Ernst & Young," unpublished paper under the auspices of the Transnational Resource and Action Center (TRAC) San Francisco, California, www.corpwatch.org. November 10 1997.

23. David Gonzales, "Youthful foes go toe to toe with *Nike*," *The New York Times*, September 27 1997.

24. Ken Rosenihal, "*Nike* ad may be self-serving, but end does justify means," *Baltimore Sun*, April 14 1997, p. 1C.

25. At the shrill end of these indictments was a piece by Joal D. Joseph, "Horrid business practices enrich *Nike*; Shoe company's fortunes come from exploitation of workers in Third World countries," *The Fresno Bee*, June 30 1996, p. 55. His condemnation began, "Phil Knight is the godfather of the *Nike* Mafia."

26. Mitch Albom, "Mind your money because *Nike* has designs on both," *Pittsburgh Post-Gazette*, June 14 1997, p. B3. See also, Tom Archdeacon. "For *NIKE*, it's about shoes," *Dayton Daily News*, April 6 1997, p. 1D.

27. Within this system of images, *Nike* stands for participation in the global community through sports, *Benetton* through political awareness, *Microsoft* through imagination synergized by its software, *IBM* through technological power, *Coca-Cola* through the celebration of harmony, the *Body Shop* through ecological and global concern. Corporate signs of global unification construct images of global citizenship, multicultural respect, and social and environmental concern. Such advertising encourages consumers to view themselves as citizens of the world, while the corporations appear as a unifying force in a world otherwise experienced as increasingly fragmented and conflictual.

28. For a recent account of the political-economic circumstances of producing shoes in the South Asian region of the global capitalist economy see Jeff Manning's series in *The Oregonian* in November 1997. Manning's "Tracks across the globe" consisted of three instalments: "Day 1: *Nike*'s Asian machine goes on trial," November 9, pp. A1, A14–15; "Day 2; poverty's legions flock to *Nike*," November 10, pp. A1, A6–A7; and "Day 3: *Nike* steps into political minefield," November 11, pp. A1, A6–A7. See also William Greider, *One World, Ready or Not: The Manic Logic of Global Capitalism* (Simon & Schuster, New York, 1997).

PART FIVE

Ads and Cultural Meaning

INTRODUCTION TO PART FIVE

IF WE LOOK AT ALL OF THE MEDIA CONTENT distributed throughout our culture, a lot of different content types, or genres, can be found. News, self-improvement, detective fiction, romance stories, domestic comedies, superhero adventures, and many others are common genres of our popular culture. But perhaps the most prevalent media genre is the advertisement. If a viewer watches an hour of ad-supported TV, then at least one-fourth—and often one-third—of that time is devoted to TV commercials. Magazines and newspapers typically devote over 50 percent of their content to ads. Websites may feature multiple ad forms; many outdoor settings are cluttered with billboards, and some media—such as the yellow pages phonebook, catalogs, infomercials, and home shopping channels—are 100 percent advertising.

Advertising, then, is a dominant symbol system in our culture. Although the advertisers' number one goal is to sell their branded product, these advertisements contain other messages beyond this selling goal. The need to grab our attention, to differentiate one marketing demographic from another, and to add relevant meaning to a brand, often leads to the creation of meaning that goes beyond selling. Advertisements tell stories—and these stories have morals about what is good and bad, what particular social groups are like, and what humans should attend to and even covet. As such, the meaning in advertising often involves issues of social power: how are different groups and issues portrayed in advertising, and what are the implications for how different audiences might understand, and value, these groups or issues?

The readings in this Part focus on such cultural meanings in advertising. The first two contributions in this Part are broader in their approach and their authors are known for, if not their defenses of advertising, then at least their beliefs that many critics of advertising overemphasize its cultural dangers. Twitchell, for example, posits that advertising and communication about brands are modern cultural storytelling forms, frequently building commonalities between consumer groups attracted to the values associated with a brand. Schudson also broadly explores the potential power and limitations of advertising as a symbolic system and how it may focus on certain values over others, although he does not believe that advertising creates and imposes new values out of whole cloth. The last two readings focus on specific meanings about race and gender in advertising and highlight the often-problematic nature of such meanings. Watts and Orbe examine the contradictory meanings about race and male friendship in the very popular Budweiser "Whassup" campaign from the early 2000s. Goodman focuses on how young Latina and Caucasian women interpret and incorporate in their lives messages of thinness and body appearance in popular media targeted at women, including advertising.

Chapter 14

JAMES B. TWITCHELL

REFLECTIONS AND REVIEWS
An English Teacher Looks at Branding

THIS PIECE WAS ORIGINALLY WRITTEN for advertising researchers, published in *Journal of Consumer Research*. Coming from a background in English literature, Twitchell offers a literary look at ads and brands which he argues is not unlike literature or enduring myths of a culture, and in fact may be more relevant to modern life. Like great literature, he argues, advertising creates emotional meanings through the stories they tell in attaching values to brands. We also differentiate advertisements by different genres (a greeting card commercial is different from a beer commercial), and many of the trademarked brand characters found in ads resonate with long-established mythic forms (Green Giant, Keebler Elves).

Twitchell reflects on how advertising and brands, in an observation similar to that of Raymond Williams, attributes broader cultural meaning to things. As such, brands are often presented as having magical or religious implications. And because in advertising the successful consumer of a brand is the beneficiary of these different magic powers, brands also construct different images of human agency. According to ads, a Chevy truck consumer has different abilities because of her embrace of that brand compared to a Lexus consumer.

About 15 years ago I was teaching a survey course in Romantic poetry, and some student asked why the course was a requirement for graduation. I explained the importance of cultural literacy as a goal of school-based education.

To show them how common knowledge worked, I said that at the end of the nineteenth century almost any literate person could fill in the blank in this sentence: "My heart leaps up when I behold a [blank] in the sky." Who today can fill in that missing blank? My students stared blankly, just as I would have done at their age. Well, I puffed, the missing word is "rainbow," and it is an important line from Wordsworth, and an important line in English Romanticism, and an important line in Christian culture. So there, you little philistines! Take that!

No matter. They just sat there. This was not going to change their lives. However, *my* life was about to change. It happened in a heartbeat. From the back row a kid who always wore a baseball hat backward erupted: "My heart leaps up, Professor Twitchell, when I behold golden arches in the sky." The class howled in glee. Touché.

If having a culture means sharing stories. Baseballcap was saying, here it is. Come and get it. OK, it is a culture not centered on a covenant with God but with a meat patty; still, you get the point. He never said another word that semester. He did not have to. In the never-ending battle between instructor and pupil, Baseballcap had scored a technical knockout.

A Brand is a Cultural Story, Well, Kind of . . .

Baseballcap's culture is built on a commercial variant of storytelling called branding. While I realize that to readers of the *Journal of Consumer Research* a brand means many different things—most of them quite sophisticated—to me a brand is simply a story attached to a manufactured object. As you remember from Lit 101, stories are fictions filled with character, plot, points of view, and an implied purpose called a meaning. Early stories announced this purpose with an attached moral, as with Aesop's *Fables* or biblical parables. Often, however, the purpose of a story is to generate a feeling or emotional response in the listener. Such stories usually rise to some kind of climax. Almost everyone can recall an Edgar Allan Poe story (*The Pit and the Pendulum*, *The Tell-Tale Heart*, *The Fall of the House of Usher*, . . .) simply in terms of the sensation. While stories can start in any number of places, they usually end by delivering that emotional punch. Sometimes they start ab ovo, sometimes in media res, and sometimes they even go backward, but the key to appreciating stories is often overlooked: stories often carry emotions as meaning. In a sense, we learn how to think and feel by hearing stories.

One of the traits of a good story is that it can easily get concentrated into just a sentence or two—the gist. One of the reasons that study guides like Monarch or Cliff Notes are the staple of every schoolboy (and the bane of every instructor) is that powerful stories often have easily expressed kernels, hyperconcentrated plots. Lousy stories are unfocused. They have no center. Good ones often whirl around a small nucleus.

What of these: a young man unwittingly slays his father and marries his mother. A Moorish prince is tormented by suspicions of his white bride's infidelity. A cur-mudgeonly old skinflint is humanized by a trio of apparitions on Christmas Eve. A staid gentleman scientist performs an experiment on himself that turns him into a libidinous monster. An ordinary man wakes up one morning to discover that he has been trans-formed into a cockroach. A savvy lad rafts down a river with a black slave. An obsessed man chases a whale while his crew suffers.

In academic lingo, the ability of a story to be expressed in a single kernel is called a holophrasm. It reduces sentences to a word, for example, or complex ideas to a nubbin. Oddly enough, great art tends to be holophrastic. So too with great brands. The brand gathers its power because it concentrates what is called in adspeak "ownership."

As opposed to the high-art story that usually is stabilized in print, the brand story is fluid. Often this story can occur visually, which demonstrates the power of a logo. We all know the golden arches, the Texaco star, Lucky Strike bull's-eye, Shell's shell, the Holiday Inn sign, the Playboy bunny, Nike's swoosh, the CBS eye, the Red Cross, or the

Rolls Royce swooping woman. Sometimes we find the kernel inside a tune. Remember the percolating sound of Maxwell House coffee, Coke's "I'd Like to Teach the World to Sing," McDonald's "You Deserve a Break Today," the Cable News Network war music, the Teabury shuffle, or a cat food's "Meow, Meow, Meow" song?

Sometimes the kernel will be colored. Not only do we know the difference between Pepsi blue and Coke red, we know Pepsi blue is not Tiffany blue, Kleenex blue, or IBM blue, and Coke red is not Marlboro red, which is not Heinz red or Budweiser red. We know the difference between Hertz yellow, Kodak yellow, Sunoco yellow, and Caterpillar yellow, between Heineken green and John Deere green. We know Hershey's brown makes sense, while UPS's brown really makes no sense. One is brown of chocolate while the other is brown of . . . well, that is the problem.

Often brand kernels often reside in identification characters whose generating story is elsewhere. Here we can really appreciate how close brand narratives are to folktales. Consider these brand stories simply in terms of their provenances. We recognize the archetypes as they migrate from Greek mythology like Hermes carrying flowers for FTD, from folklore like the Keebler elves living in the Hollow Tree, from cartoon town like Poppin' Fresh (the Pillsbury Doughboy), from the world of half-human/half cartoon like Ronald McDonald, from our human world like the Marlboro man, from animals made human like Charlie the Tuna, or from the natural world like the Exxon tiger.

The Concept of Genre

Because literary stories are so various we have developed a rather sophisticated system for classification based on affect. What emotion do they promise? For instance, if you want to cry, you read stories called sentimental romances. If you want the hair on the nape of your neck to be lifted, you pick up a horror story from a tradition called the gothic. This phenomenon of stories fitting into emotion-delivering formats is called "genre."

In the modern world of commercial storytelling we have developed the same kind of story variation but have not yet developed an understanding of brand genres. So we know what a beer ad feels like, we know the hushed confidentiality of feminine product advertising, we recognize the way that luxury cars are displayed, and we know the music that accompanies chewing gum or chocolate candy. We are so sophisticated about advertising genres that we know the difference between Coke and Pepsi advertising, or between McDonald's and Burger Chef, between Levi's and Diesel, Nike and Adidas. We do not know ingredient differences, but we know genre differences. What we lack, and what we will no doubt develop over the next generations, is a critical apparatus that lets us appreciate conformity and variation in commercial speech as we can now in art speech.

The reason why we have been so slow to appreciate a culture based on commercial storytelling is obvious. It happened so quickly! And it happened with (ugh!) things. Essentially what has happened to stories is that they have jumped loose of individual storytellers and became part of a global cacophony used to distinguish machine-made products. These sagas are now being told everywhere, on every surface, at all times of the day. For this explosion in storytelling to occur—what people in advertising refer to as "clutter" (rather like a doctor shooting up a patient with adrenaline and then complaining that he will not quiet down)—a number of innovations in narrative had to happen. Oddly enough, two of these storytelling developments happened in the high-art period called Romanticism. And so, since that is what I am supposed to be teaching, let's take a look.

How Did Brands Get to Be Narratives?

To understand how stories got attached to manufactured things—branding—we need to appreciate two seemingly unrelated cultural transformations that occurred during the nineteenth century. These crucial shifts in perception are (1) the common accept-ance of the pathetic fallacy and (2) the rise of impressionism as a narrative and pictorial device. From a marketing point of view, both innovations transformed not just how stories got told but how the audience could actively participate in the consumption of, first, fictions, and secondarily, material goods. These techniques made modern branding not just possible but inevitable.

Here, oddly enough, the Romantic poets lent a hand. One of the legacies of Romanticism was not that it made feeling into an epistemology (you know it is right because it feels right) but that the poets also made the startling contention that inanimate things and nonhuman life share feeling. The universe is sentient. Admittedly, this is often proffered as a way to shock, but it soon becomes a way to inform and expand consciousness. Even rocks, said Samuel Taylor Coleridge, have feelings. Here is just a bit of the feeling phenomenon as expressed by William Wordsworth in a lyrical ballad called "Lines Written in Early Spring" (Van Doren 2002, pp. 75–76). Unlikely as it may be, the process he limns at the end of the eighteenth century is at the heart of commercial branding.

> I heard a thousand blended notes,
> While in a grove I sate reclined,
> In that sweet mood when pleasant thoughts
> Bring sad thoughts to the mind.
>
> To her fair works did Nature link
> The human soul that through me ran:
> And much it grieved my heart to think
> What man has made of man.
>
> Through primrose tufts, in that green bower,
> The periwinkle trailed its wreaths:
> And 'tis my faith that every flower
> Enjoys the air it breathes.
>
> The birds around me hopped and played,
> Their thoughts I cannot measure:
> But the least motion which they made
> It seemed a thrill of pleasure.
>
> The budding twigs spread out their fan,
> To catch the breezy air:

And I must think, do all I can,
That there was pleasure there.

If this belief from heaven be sent,
If such be Nature's holy plan.
Have I not reason to lament
What man has made of man?

When Wordsworth states that he believes that flowers enjoy the air, that the birds have thoughts, and that the budding twigs sense pleasure, he is willingly and almost belligerently threatening the concept of rational knowing. This unarticulated paradigm of evaluation—what was called the "Great Chain of Being" in Elizabethan times—essentially orders the values of life for a culture. With the exception of the burst of Romanticism about the time of the French Revolution, it usually excludes sentience from the natural world. Flowers do not have joy, twigs cannot sense pleasure, and birds most certainly do not think.

But Wordsworth did not go far enough. Other poets did. And in so doing they ushered in one of the truly radical shifts in temper, known by the art-historical term "impressionism." While this shift is best seen in oil painting later in the century, we can glimpse it in poetry. Remember Keats's "Ode on a Grecian Urn" from high school days (Barnard 1988, pp. 344–46)? Of course not. In the poem the speaker looks at an ancient urn and starts asking questions of it. First, he wants to know what story is being told on the urn. Young lovers are imaged in frozen pursuit, and he wonders who they are and how they feel. Next, Keats walks around the urn and sees the scene of a priest leading a heifer to some kind of sacrifice. He wonders what religious ceremony is being enacted. Here is his mental interrogatory:

Who are these coming to the sacrifice?
To what green altar, O mysterious priest.
Lead'st thou that heifer lowing at the skies,
And all her silken flanks with garlands drest?
What little town by river or sea-shore,
Or mountain-built with peaceful citadel,
Is emptied of its folk, this pious morn?
And, little town, thy streets for evermore
Will silent be: and not a soul, to tell
Why thou art desolate, can e'er return.

Keats is now asking for information that is not on the urn. If the little town were on the urn, he would know if it was up in the hills or down by the seashore. He is starting to animate the urn and give it human characteristics, rather as Wordsworth did with nature when he attributed feeling to birds and flowers. Keats is essentially treating the object like something/someone which/who can respond to his questioning—a thing that can tell a story. He is treating it, in other words, in a singularly modern way—like a brand.

In the final stanza, all the stops are removed, and Keats out-Wordsworths Wordsworth. Here are the lines:

> O Attic shape! fair attitude! with brede
> Of marble men and maidens overwrought,
> With forest branches and the trodden weed:
> Thou, silent form! dost tease us out of thought
> As doth eternity: Cold Pastoral!
>
> When old age shall this generation waste,
> Thou shalt remain, in midst of other woe
> Than ours, a friend to man, to whom thou say'st,
> "Beauty is truth, truth beauty,—that is all
> Ye know on earth, and all ye need to know."

Any schoolboy appreciates what is going on, at least what appears to be going on. Keats seems to be hearing what the urn is saying. In other words, it talks! And, far more importantly, it seems to say something rather profound although it is enigmatic. But who cares? It is the shock of reciprocity that is startling.

The Pathetic Fallacy Is the Truth of Branding

Why are we not shocked by the Neon ad (Fig. 14.1)? Why don't we immediately shut this kind of communication down? Why does it draw us closer to the car? By the same token, why do we countenance such creatures as Poppin' Fresh, the Pillsbury Dough-boy, Mr. Clean, Aunt Jemima, Tony the Tiger, or the Tidy Bowl man who lives in the toilet? Clearly something has happened between Keats and modern advertising. What-ever it is, the process entails all these factors: (1) the storytelling necessity of separating fungible products be they Grecian urns or Wedgwood pottery, (2) the humanizing of the material world in much the same way the Impressionists humanized the natural world, and (3) the willingness to move back and forth between one's self and a work of artistic or commercial creation, suspending judgment, in hopes of building some kind of relationship.

Colin Campbell, an English sociologist who studies consumption, argues that indeed something happened to the Western imagination in the early nineteenth century to make the application of stories to inanimate objects possible (Campbell 1989). He contends that we essentially stopped rationalizing and started dreaming. After all, that is what Romanticism was all about, the end of the Age of Reason. And, as the objects of our dreams became material not ethereal, we started to spiritualize the secular, to give the stuff of getting and spending a transcendental affect. Ultimately, that is what the Industrial Revolution was finally all about—not just making things, but making meaning for things.

Seen from this point of view, the Industrial Revolution did not suddenly make us want things and the stories that went along with them. The Industrial Revolution was the result of our materialism, not the cause of it. But we do not always know what we want. If we knew what things meant, then we could choose things on the basis of some inner need. But we do not know. So, in a sense, we are not materialistic enough! That is why stories-brands can get in between us and the objects. We desperately want mean-ing, things cannot supply it, and so we install it. That is why branding (and Romantic poetry) works.

Figure 14.1 Neon car ad.

Such an irony, Colin Campbell admits, that Romanticism, the putative enemy of material consumption, should have paved the way for the marketing of excess stuff by foregrounding the life of sensation, privileging the process of daydreaming, and encouraging the attribution of spiritual yearning to the nonreligious world. In splitting the personality into active and contemplative and praising the latter, in foregrounding fiction and reneging on reason, in making impulse and emotion acceptable, in valuing loitering and drifting, and in encouraging solipsism and the rise of the individual response, the enemies of getting and spending made the Industrial Revolution of getting and spending possible. Technology may have provided the machines, but the Romantic poets loaded the software.

Where We Are Now

The process is still unfolding. Clearly something has happened between my earlier view of cultural literacy (the rainbow) and Baseballcap's (the golden arches). At a simplistic level we have, it seems, exchanged knowledge of history and science (a knowledge of book learning) for knowledge of products and how such products interlock to form coherent social patterns (a knowledge of brands). Where narratives used to cluster around abstract concepts like nationalism, ancestry, history, art, and afterlife, the dominant modern stories cluster around such stuff as cigarettes, sugar water, beer, and car tires. Think of it: even the simplest things like meat patties, coffee, denim, sneakers, gasoline, water, credit cards, television networks, batteries, and airplanes have deep drum-rolling stories behind them. The stories are linked into cycles, some lasting for generations, some changing every few months.

In a sense, brand stories have become modern sagas. While a saga is a format usually associated with frozen families huddled around a campfire in Scandinavia telling stories about swords and monsters, it might be productive to let it thaw a bit and consider the saga in the context of commercial branding. In so doing we provide both a recognized pedigree and a context in which to understand how we talk about manufactured things.

Since the traditional saga is transmitted orally, the story picks up and discards subplots and characters as it is being continually reformed for new audiences. In fact, the real saga format is interactive. In lit-crit jargon, it is called "dialogic." The saga is formed of give and take between audience and storyteller in which the audience clearly participates in the choice of subplots. Rather like telling your kids a good-night tale where the kids say, "Tell us Little Red Riding Hood but this time really describe the wolf's teeth," so the sagameister cocks an ear in the telling. Hence all the variants. The process is rather like an advertising campaign in which there is a continual shuffling of idioms. Think of the Absolut campaign, the Energizer Bunny's endless adventures, or Coke's shuffling of claims.

Generations ago we knew where we were by bloodline ancestry, by religious affiliation, by marriage partner, by similar lines on the vita, by job description, by club, and by accent. Today we know where we are by what saga we are consuming. So we move through choice of car, designer suit, handbag, or vacation spot as we move through stages of life. Saga stories convey social place and purpose; they are attached to shifting objects, and we learn to understand them finger-snap fast. Here is a throwaway line from the BBC sitcom *Absolutely Fabulous* that illustrates how compressed our knowledge has become. Edwina receives a gift of earrings from her daughter. "Are they Lacroix?" Edwina asks eagerly. "Do you like them?" asks her daughter. "I do if they're Lacroix," replies Edwina. The brandsaga does the work not just of characterization but also of worldview.

Brands as Gated Communities

Brands are not just the new Esperanto, they are the new emotional triggers and social markers. Edwina knows that. So does Baseballcap. What matters is what is not matter. What marks the modern world is that certain brand fictions have been able to generate a deep and almost instantaneous bond between consumers. We speak of brand families of manufactured objects, never really appreciating that such families may well extend into the human sphere—the true brand extension. We use the term "brand loyalty" without appreciating the power of what such affiliation really means.

We all know from the way that certain automobile owners wave at each other solely on the basis of the brand of car they drive (e.g., Saab), how certain computer users form chat groups that extend friendship beyond simple discussion of shared equipment or operating systems (e.g., Apple or Linux), how the alumni of certain schools seem to bond even if they were not in the same class (Dartmouth College), and even how dog owners will cross busy streets to chat with someone with the same breed, but we do not know exactly what to make of this meaning.

While we may recognize cult-community status woven around such disparate brandsagas as the Mazda Miata, Krispy Kreme donuts, Zippo lighters, Jeeps, Tupperware, various cigars and wines, to say nothing of the entire communities created by designer-label clothing like Hilfiger, Gucci, Armani, and Ralph Lauren, we do not know where these stories are taking us. Often even a simple product can attain such status solely on the basis of seeming exclusivity. Remember how Coors beer used to be the magical brand in the 1970s, even starring in a movie in which Burt Reynolds risked life and limb to transport it to Atlanta? Or what Nike running shoes used to be like?

Often ownership is self-consciously fetishized as with Harley Davidson. As has been pointed out, any brand that encourages its acolytes to literally transfer the logo onto their body as a tattoo, any brand that has believers using the owner's manual as a Bible for marriage ceremonies, any brand that has pilgrimage celebrations like the various Bike Weeks, any brand that has a version of the Ford pickup truck fitted out with a cargo bed specially designed to coddle the bike, well, whatever that brand is, it is getting almost religious.

Brands as Religious Stories

If you listen to the language of marketing you will often hear revelations of this process of sanctification via consumption. You will hear words like "brand soul" and "brand icon." This may be more than self-serving gobbledygook. We are now, it seems to me, in the process of spiritualizing commercial brands. After all, that is what luxury is all about. Luxe consumption is becoming sacred with certain almost teleological brands. Whatever it was that had our medieval forefathers believing that this relic was the knucklebone of a saint and that it had mystical power is still operating in the land of deluxe. How else to explain something so irrational as Evian water, a Dior purse, or a Martha Stewart rolling pin?

High-end brands mimic the promise of religious metaphors and analogies. Transient materialism. Secular epiphany. Yes, brand owners talk about the soul of their brands, brand aura, and of their brands as icons, to be sure. By this they mean that their brands have a symbolic, almost a religious significance, which goes way beyond their worth as products. The key thing is to worship them, not in any formal church sense but in a marketplace sense. Can brand advertising then be considered a kind of mantra, in which the repetition of the brand has an incantational power? Might this partially explain the shocking revelation some years ago that street kids were literally killing each other for their shoes or sports jackets?

If you look at the stories we share, I mean really share—so much so that we cannot even remember how we learned about them—you will see something rather startling. These stories invariably have deep roots in mythology. Take the cartoon characters or identification characters of commercial products, for instance. The Jolly Green Giant seems a mimic of the giant of lore, the Pillsbury Doughboy seems the perpetual jester, Tony the Tiger is the affable lion, characters in advertisements for light beer seem to be pranksters of various kinds while performers in sneaker ads are like Olympian heroes,

Harley Davidson users are portrayed as eternal outlaws, blue jeans wearers are often going-where-none-have-gone-before explorers, the Marlboro man invokes the independent outsider, Betty Crocker the archetypical good mother, and so on. Brand-sagas, while shallow, are usually drawn from the preliterate or the preprint world. All right, they may not be the hero with a thousand faces, but they are from the same family.

Of course we fetishize the world with a brand mythology. How else could we endure it? Could it be that brands are becoming the necessary iconic equipment used to cross liminal space, like the transition between adolescence and adulthood, from single to married, from nonfamily to reproductive, from job to retirement, from condemned to saved? Are they now doing the social work of organized religion? Why should we think that rituals, tribes, rites of passage, incantations, and other such terms of cultural transition should not also apply to us? Do we not also desire to transcend the material world and experience satisfaction of life by consuming material stuff?

And that, it seems to me, is the future of commercial brands and why Baseballcap got it right. The narratives of stuff, the fictions surrounding machine-made objects, are providing the cultural literacy necessary to form community. As with other stories, brandsagas are inclusive and exclusive. What separates our modern sense of community from others that have come before is that the ability to enter these communities depends not on lucky birth, skin color, religious affiliation, or a host of other attributes usually installed at birth but a desire to consume both objects and their fictions. I have glossed over the obvious problems of such a culture (clearly, it is wasteful and intellectually shallow for starters), but it may prove to be more fair and democratic than what has come before. Who knows? But this is a question that much of the world currently seems intent on deciding.

Questions

1   How do the concepts of genre and narrative relate to brands?
2   How does the author argue that the Romantic Movement encouraged/led to the concept of branding?
3   How do brands serve as gated communities and religious stories?
4   What advertisements do you see as shared cultural symbols in your particular "gated community" of consumers?

References

Barnard, John, ed. (1988), *John Keats: The Complete Poems*, 3d ed., London: Penguin Classics.
Campbell, Colin (1989), *The Romantic Ethic and the Spirit of Modern Consumerism*, Oxford: Blackwell.
Van Doren, Mark, ed. (2002), *Selected Poetry of William Wordsworth*, New York: Modern Library Classics.

Chapter 15

MICHAEL SCHUDSON

ADVERTISING AS CAPITALIST REALISM

THIS CHAPTER IS FROM MICHAEL SCHUDSON'S BOOK from the 1980s, *Advertising, The Uneasy Persuasion*. In that book, he argues that advertising's social and cultural influence is "dubious" and often overstated by its critics. In this well-known chapter, which appears near the end of that book, he looks at advertising's potential influence as a capitalistic value system. His metaphor, "capitalist realism," is drawn from the concept of socialist realism, a form of official state art of the Soviet Union designed to idealize life under that regime. Schudson asks, "does advertising serve the same function under capitalism?," even if it is not officially state sanctioned in the same way.

Schudson's skepticism about the power of advertising is evident in this chapter. He argues that advertising is an abstraction of life that selectively offers certain cultural values over others, but also argues that we often are dismissive of advertising's messages. He is unconvinced by comparisons of modern advertising to religion, but also recognizes some commonalities between the two cultural systems. He concludes, though, that advertising as a larger symbolic system may have some long-term effects that reinforce capitalism, especially in the absence of an equally pervasive presence of competing value systems.

Advertising, as the early agency Lord and Thomas put it, is "salesmanship in print." It is just that simple, just that complex. Understanding advertising entails understanding the difference between personal and printed or broadcast communication; the differences entailed in the "decontextualization" of thought and feeling that systems of mass communication make possible. With the invention of writing in human history, anthropologist Jack Goody observes, "Speech is no longer tied to an occasion: it becomes timeless. Nor is it attached to a person; on paper, it becomes more abstract, more depersonalized."[1] For Goody, this opens the way to science, to the growth of criticism, and to a more tolerant attitude toward one's own frame of reference. But the same forces that enable people to see themselves as individuals independent of social and traditional contexts make people susceptible to the appeals of mass media, including advertising. This is an openness or susceptibility qualitatively different from the householder's vulnerability to the direct sales pitch. Among other things, it connects the consumer not only to an item for sale and a person selling it but to an invisible, yet present, audience of others attuned to the same item for sale and the same symbols used to promote it. The advertisement, like the sales talk, links a seller to a buyer. Unlike the sales talk, it connects the buyer to an assemblage of buyers through words and pictures available to all of them and tailored to no one of them. Advertising is part of the establishment and reflection of a common symbolic culture.

Advertising, whether or not it sells cars or chocolate, surrounds us and enters into us, so that when we speak we may speak in or with reference to the language of advertising and when we see we may see through schemata that advertising has made salient for us. Whether advertising is, as David Potter claimed, the distinctive institution of an affluent society,[2] or, as Mason Griff wrote, the "central institution of mass society,"[3] can at this point be legitimately doubted. At the same time, it is a distinctive and central *symbolic* structure. And, strictly as symbol, the power of advertising may be considerable. Advertising may shape our sense of values even under conditions where it does not greatly corrupt our buying habits. I want now to take up the position of the UNESCO MacBride Commission (and many others) that advertising "tends to promote attitudes and life-styles which extol acquisition and consumption at the expense of other values."[4]

The Concept of Capitalist Realism

When a person places a classified ad or when a department store announces a January white sale, the intention is to sell goods. In the classifieds, this usually means a unique transaction – a particular house is for sale, a particular job is available, a particular used car is offered. When the given item is sold, the ad is discontinued. With the department store, the situation is less individualized. The store wants to attract customers not only to the linens department but to the store in general and not only in January but always. Still, the ad does relatively little to attract customers except to announce what goods it has to sell at what price. This may be an effort to make a store-loyal customer as well as to sell the product. But the main task is to identify the product, plainly, and to announce its price, breathlessly.

National consumer goods advertising differs sharply from this model of advertising. The connection between ad and sale, so direct in classified ads, or between ad and customer contact, reasonably direct in the January white Sale ad, is very remote in the national consumer-goods ad. It is indirect in both space and time. The commercial for Coca-Cola or Alka-Seltzer does not say how the customer can buy the advertised product; it does not typically announce a phone number to call or a place to shop. It takes for granted the consumer's shopping skills and it assumes the successful distribution of the product to retail stores. In time, it does not presume a quick response of customers to its efforts. It does not presume that the consumers it wants to reach will see any given showing of the ad or, seeing it, quickly respond by buying. It is a general reminder or reinforcer, not an urgent appeal to go out and buy. What the ad says or pictures, then, is obliged to be relatively placeless and relatively timeless. National consumer-goods advertising is highly abstracted and self-contained. Where particular places are shown, they are generally flattened – a car, for instance, displayed in front of the Capitol building in Washington, does not connect the car to a particular place but to a familiar image of a place, photographed from the most familiar head-on spot. What is shown is more recognizable as a postcard than as physical space. A 1980 VW ad airbrushed out the statue of Ulysses S. Grant when it shot an ad in front of the Capitol because "only a small piece of it was sticking above the car. It looked confusing, so we took it out.[5] Particular times are almost never identified in magazine and television advertising, though timeless occasions are – the birthday party, the New Year's party, the weekend.

Similarly, the people pictured in magazine ads or television commercials are abstract people. This is not to say they are fictive characters. In a play or television series, actors generally portray particular people with particular names who, in the fictive universe they occupy, exist in a set of relations with other fictional characters and have a range of meanings within that world. An advertisement is not like this, it does not construct a fully fictive world. The actor or model does not play a particular person but a social type or a demographic category. A television actress, for instance, will be asked to audition for commercials that call for a "twenty-six to thirty-five-year-old P&G housewife." She is not supposed to represent a twenty-six-year-old or a thirty-year-old or a thirty-five-year-old but a "twenty-six–thirty-five-year-old" housewife, the sort likely to buy Procter & Gamble products. The age range from twenty-six to thirty-five corresponds not so much to a physical type as to a presumed social type with predictable consumer patterns. It is a demographic grouping used for market research. An actress seeking a role in a television commercial is expected to have two wardrobes ready for auditions, standard and "upscale." She is to represent either the middle-American housewife or the affluent American housewife, but never a particular person.[6]

There are apparent exceptions to this rule of abstractness but they themselves are instructive. Think, for instance, of the Polaroid camera commercials (of about 1977–82) in which James Garner apparently speaks as James Garner. But does he? After all, he is not really married to Mariette Hartley, the actress who plays his wife in the commercial. They are playing a couple (indeed, they are playing a couple playing). Some kind of fiction is being created. It is a fiction that rests for success on viewers knowing a lot about James Garner. But the television audience knows little or nothing about James Garner, the person. Garner does not play himself, the person, nor does he play a particular fictive character. Instead, he plays what I would call the generalized James Garner role, the type for which James Garner is always cast – handsome, gentle, bumbling, endearing, a combination of Bret Maverick from "Maverick" and Jim Rockford from "The Rockford Files."

Similarly, Robert Young did not play himself in the Sanka coffee ads where he identified himself as Robert Young. He played the generalized Robert Young character, a combination of his role as Jim Anderson in the television series "Father Knows Best" and his title role in "Marcus Welby, M.D.," quintessentially cheerful, moderate, mature, and full of good sense.[7] Even in many straightforward testimonial ads, the person played is not the actor or athlete as a human being but the actor or athlete flattened into a celebrity, a person, in Daniel Boorstin's nice phrase, "known for his well-knownness."[8]

Television stars who do commercials, ostensibly in their own names, invariably present their television personalities, not their own. When American Express sought to emphasize that their traveler's checks offered travelers security, they "looked for a spokesman perceived by the public as an authority on crime." Thus the choice of Karl Malden; not because he is Karl Malden, but because he once was Lt. Mike Stone in "The Streets of San Francisco." Similarly, Bill Cosby was used in Jello Pudding commercials because he had established himself in so many programs for children and was in a position to remind mothers that children like Jello.[9]

The task of the television personalities in commercials is to *appear*, suggesting and pulling back into well-established characters. The viewing audience will do the rest. Thus, established fictional characters may be as successful as well-known personalities. Old Lonely, the Maytag repairman, has done commercials for two decades and so has Mr. Whipple for Charmin; Madge the Manicurist (for Palmolive dishwashing liquid), Speedy Alka-Seltzer, and the Hamm's beer bear have been on and off the air for a generation. For the unknown actor, doing a television commercial presents an odd challenge. It is a kind of anti-acting. As one actress, Linda Stratton, put it: "You have to pull back into yourself, rather than project like on the stage. It's an entirely different technique that must be learned."[10]

This flat, abstract world of the advertisement is part of a deliberate effort to connect specific products in people's imaginations with certain demographic groupings or needs or occasions. Sometimes, in an effort not to exclude any potential customers from identifying with the product, advertisers choose not to show *any* people in their ads. For a generation from the 1930s into the 1950s, Guinness stout did not show people drinking in their ads: "This policy of non-identification was deliberate. It was argued that if Guinness was a drink for everyone, to identify it with a particular section of the market would be to limit its appeal."[11] In other cases, market research or good hunches or common sense identifies the specific population group most likely to consume the advertised product in quantity. Then an abstract representation of that group will be pictured in the ad.

Thus, abstraction is essential to the aesthetic and intention of contemporary national consumer-goods advertising. It does not represent reality nor does it build a fully fictive world. It exists, instead, on its own plane of reality, a plane I will call capitalist realism. By this term, I mean to label a set of aesthetic conventions, but I mean also to link them to the political economy whose values they celebrate and promote.

This is a different intention from that of Erving Goffman who notes some of the same features of advertisements and refers to them as "commercial realism."[12] For Goffman, commercial realism is "the standard transformation employed in contemporary ads," the particular kind of public portraiture advertising uses. Goffman suggests that commercial realism differs in two respects from the way people present themselves in actual life. In real life, according to Goffman, human activity is highly ritualized. People act out and live in social ideals, presenting to the world stereotyped pictures of themselves. In advertising, this is even more true; advertising is "hyper-ritualization." Second, advertising is *edited*. In both life and advertising, people present social ideals. But, in life, people are "stuck with a considerable amount of dull footage." People cannot edit their behavior enough to provide a purely ritualized social ideal. In commercial realism, editing is thorough and the social ideal is thereby portrayed as completely as possible.[13] Goffman's position is helpful but it is limited to characterizing the conventions of commercial art rather than trying also to link them to their cultural role in advanced capitalist societies. Of course, that may not be a task one can ultimately master, but I think it is worth attempting.

I can make what I mean by capitalist realism more clear by comparing it to socialist realism, the term from which, obviously, I have derived it. Socialist realism is official, state-sanctioned and state-governed art as practiced in the Soviet Union. As the First Soviet Writers' Congress defined it in 1934, socialist realism is an art obliged to present a "correct historically concrete representation of reality in its revolutionary development" and to do so in a form that will educate "the working masses in the spirit of socialism."[14] In practice, this means that artists and writers must meet certain aesthetic and moral demands. In theory, these demands are all in the service of a kind of realism. Socialist realist art must be faithful to life – but in certain prescribed ways:

1. Art should picture reality in simplified and typified ways so that it communicates effectively to the masses.
2. Art should picture life, but not as it is so much as life as it should become, life worth emulating.
3. Art should picture reality not in its individuality but only as it reveals larger social significance.
4. Art should picture reality as progress toward the future and so represent social struggles positively. It should carry an air of optimism.
5. Art should focus on contemporary life, creating pleasing images of new social phenomena, revealing and endorsing new features of society and thus aiding the masses in assimilating them.[15]

Without getting into a study of Soviet art, it should be apparent that the parallels are strong between what socialist realism is designed to do and what advertising in capitalist society intends to do, at least, national advertising for consumer goods. One could easily say that advertising tries to present a "correct historically concrete representation of reality in its capitalist development." What I will suggest in the next few pages is that American advertising, like socialist realist art, simplifies and typifies. It does not claim to picture reality as it is but reality as it should be – life and lives worth emulating. It is always photography or drama or discourse with a message – rarely picturing individuals, it shows people only as incarnations of larger social categories. It always assumes that there is progress. It is thoroughly optimistic, providing for any troubles that it identifies a solution in a particular product or style of life. It focuses, of course, on the new, and if it shows some signs of respect for tradition, this is only to help in the assimilation of some new commercial creation.

I do not want to suggest that magazine and television advertisements are always "realistic" in any conventional sense. Often commercials seek realism, but sometimes the aesthetic mode is surrealism, especially in ads for products, like perfume, closely connected in the culture to dream, fantasy, and desire. Sometimes the ad is in the mode of comedy or farce. The Federal Express television commercials with a Federal Express employee talking at a superhumanly rapid clip offer an example of this sort. Television commercials may picture ordinary citizens playing themselves – a self-consciously realistic style, or they may have well-known actors in consumer roles, or they may have little-known actors playing consumers, or they may do without actors altogether and use animation. Most of these forms are well enough established to generate parodies of them in other commercials. Not all of these forms employ the usual conventions of dramatic realism, but all of them tend toward the kind of abstractness I have outlined. They are set out of time and out of space. In most cases, real or surreal, sentimental or comic, straight or camp, they present simplified social scenes that show the world "as it should be," they picture people as representatives of larger social categories, and they seek an accommodation with whatever is new or newly marketable.

At present, efforts at a kind of realism or even super-realism dominate the making of advertisements, even in ads that are not, in dramatic form, realistic. For instance, there is a vogue for actors who do not look like actors. Karl Malden (for American Express Co.) and Robert Morley (for British Airways) are actors with character rather than beauty, "real-people actors." Robert Meury, copy chief at Backer & Spielvogel says, "We've been using celebrities in our Miller Lite spots from the start. But never just any celebrity – and never just any context. We make sure our stars are guys you'd enjoy having a beer with. And the locations we film in are always real bars. We even let our celebrities have a hand in the copy – the more involvement the better. After all, it isn't a performance we're after; we just want our spots to feel *real*." Joe Sedelmaier, one of the most successful and original directors of commercials, on location in Los Angeles to cast a commercial for the Del Taco fast food chain, complained, "It is impossible to cast in L.A. Everyone looks plastic."[16] The whole American Express campaign, "Don't leave home without it," plays with the idea of celebrity, featuring famous people who are not visually well known. This inverts the conventions of celebrity advertising and induces the viewer to participate in the ad as in a guessing game.

The choice of "real" actors and real settings is matched by a move toward graininess rather than slickness in the film itself. There is also a move toward a kind of "documentary" style in television commercials that major advertisers, including Xerox Corp., Miles Laboratories Inc. (Alka-Seltzer), The Stroh Brewery Co., and General Motors Corp., favor. This "open camera" approach relies less on storyboard preparation of a commercial, more on what may happen spontaneously when the film is rolling. In 1983 Whitehall Laboratories (Anacin) initiated a kind of super- or hyper-realism in its television advertising.[17]

Of course, "real" is a cultural construct. The makers of commercials do not want what is real but, what will seem real on film. Artificial rain is better than "God's rain" because it shows up better on film or tape. Seeking sites for the filming of the "Reach Out and Touch Someone" commercials, N. W. Ayer's staff sought not just actual homes but homes that would look real. By that, they meant homes that would look stereo-typical, homes that would be consistent with a type they sought to picture as representa-tive. Nothing in the commercial should distract the viewer. Nothing should lead the audience to criticize, to say, "That doesn't look real." So each piece of furniture had to be consistent with the overall image of the house even if, in fact, few houses are like the one depicted. In commercial production, there is a passionate, obsessive attention to making every detail look "right."[18]

If anything, advertising looks more real than it should. As Barbara Rosenblum writes in her study of professional photography, advertising photography uses "crisp focus" to create "a dense and busily detailed surface. Light is used in conjunction with focus to create a hypertactile effect. Things look real; in fact, almost too real." The surface is "overaccented," she says, and this "keeps the viewer's interest up front, in the foreground or middleground."[19] The rich, cinematic, often crowded detail in magazine ads and television commercials is most unlike the simple, bold wall posters of China or the Soviet Union and very unlike America's own social realist art of the thirties. The aesthetic sensibility is very different. The emotional intensity is very different, too; socialist realism is emotionally overextended, tugging toward inspiration, while capitalist realism is either cool, relishing understatement because it relies on common understanding with its audience, or sentimental, appealing openly to basic human feelings it is certain are already in place. There is no drawing out or up. The effort is to do with art what a former Foote, Cone & Belding creative chief urged his employees to do in writing copy for the consumer: "Talk to him in a way that gets him nodding in agreement before you try to sell him something."[20] The similarity between advertising and socialist realism is that both forms subordinate everything to a message that romanticizes the present or the potential of the present. If the visual aesthetic of socialist realism is designed to dignify the simplicity of human labor in the service of the state, the aesthetic of capitalist realism – without a masterplan of purposes – glorifies the pleasures and freedoms of consumer choice in defense of the virtues of private life and material ambitions.

Is Advertising State Art?

Advertising is not an official, state art.[21] There is no rulebook from an ad writers' congress. The government provides no positive guidance for advertising. It does provide some limitations on what advertisers may say. The Federal Trade Commission regulates advertising, avowedly in the interest of promoting full and fair information in the marketplace. The courts have some authority over advertising, too, though the tendency in recent decisions has been to deny it, extending First Amendment protection to "commercial speech." The government registers and protects patents and trademarks and thus encourages new product innovation and, by extension, the advertising that accompanies it. The government provides direct and indirect subsidies of advertising, not least of all by being a major advertiser itself in military recruiting and other areas.[22] What is official about advertising, if anything, is not that it is to a limited degree government regulated or government subsidized but that the government tacitly gives approval and support, along with the rest of society, to *unofficial* expression.

It would be playing with words to speak of advertising as "official" art. But to do so offers some interesting clarification. For instance, in the conflict over the 1980 Moscow Olympics in the wake of the Soviet invasion of Afghanistan, commentators of all political stripes deplored the fact that the Soviets intended to use the Olympics for "propaganda" purposes, to promote the communist way of life. Of course, Moscow intended exactly that. But how different is this from the way Americans used the 1980 Winter Olympics in Lake Placid? What is, the sum of advertising for Minolta Corp., General Foods Corp. (Maxwell House), Texas Instruments Inc., Levi Strauss & Co., and the American Broadcasting Company if not efforts to advance the "American" or "capitalist" way of life?[23]

But only occasionally do advertisements invoke a sense of the nation as a whole, as in Olympics sponsorship or in a slogan like, "America is turning Seven-Up." Only occasionally do commercials make direct reference to American political ideals – Franklin Roosevelt brought the New Deal, John Kennedy the New Frontier, and Procter & Gamble brings to menstruating women "New Freedom." Reference to the nation as a whole is probably more common in American advertising than in European advertising. A British advertising executive, David Bernstein, has observed that American ads talk more about "America" than British ads speak of "Britain." In slogans like, "America shops for values at Sears" or "Helping insure the American way of life,"

advertising directly assimilates to its marketing goal the promotion of patriotic sentiment.[24] Still, most ads do not explicitly draw attention to the American polity but focus
on homely toothpastes, cat foods, laundry detergents, and canned beers. If these ads are
not strictly "official," can it be said nonetheless that they are advertisements for "capitalism" or the "American way of life"?

Taken collectively, these ads do articulate some of the operative values of American
capitalism. As Soviet art idealizes the producer, American art idealizes the consumer;
their tractor in the fields is matched by our home entertainment center in the den. Our
advertising is clearly different from the univocal, centrally organized, and tightly controlled Soviet propaganda efforts. But it, too, is socially sanctioned and omnipresent. To
engage in an elaborate analysis of advertising content is not my intention here. It seems
clear enough that advertisements often point to middle-class material comfort as an
enviable condition. It is also clear that advertisements reproduce and even sometimes
exaggerate long-standing social inequalities. Black people are still largely invisible in
advertising. Women are depicted as subordinate to men, childlike in both their charm
and their dependence. All ideals and values are called into the service of and subordin-
ated to the purchase of goods and the attainment of a materially satisfying style of life.[25]

One study nicely reveals a larger theme. Brigitte Jordan and Kathleen Bryant
examined five hundred magazine advertisements in which couples were pictured. They
drew their samples from popular magazines, women's magazines, men's magazines, and
general circulation periodicals. They found, as one would expect, that the couples are
almost always portrayed as happy, often happy in their intimacy. Couples are shown
having fun, being affectionate, expressing sexuality, or demonstrating commitment to
each other. There are no old, poor, sick, or unattractive couples in the ads. However the
couples are pictured, they are invariably attentive to each other. As Jordan and Bryant
argue, couples in life often are doing different things, even when they are together;
there is regularly "mutual inattentiveness in the company of each other." Not so, in
advertising. The authors found only six ads out of five hundred in which the couples
were not shown in "explicit mutual reference."[26]

This suggests, again, that typification and idealization are the modes by which
advertisements are produced. There is no intention of capturing life as it "really" is, but
there is every intention of portraying social ideals, representing as normative those
relatively rare moments of specialness, bliss, or dreamlike satisfaction. What kind of
satisfaction is pictured may vary widely – it may be sexual, it may be familial, it may be
the expression of social values like the long-term commitment of a husband and wife to
each other. It may be the values of male friendship at a bar or on a fishing trip, the
intimacy of parent and child relations expressed in a telephone call or in a mother-
daughter conversation that revolves around a commercial product. One Coca-Cola
commercial I saw screened at a convention of advertisers showed a boy running in a
field. It cut to the farmyard where two attractive people, obviously mother and father,
were standing by the barn. They open the barn doors and the camera goes back to the
boy running faster. Back to the barn, a pony is brought out. The happy faces of the
parents – sharing, by the way, a Coke. The boy, surprise and joy on his face, coming
closer. The parents, smiling at each other, drinking a Coke, perhaps tears in their eyes.
The boy, joyous, hugging the pony. The proud parents. The boy, looking lovingly at his
Mom and Dad. The parents, looking at each other. At the boy. And that was all. It was
beautifully done. It brought the hint of tears to my own eyes and it evoked great
enthusiasm in the auditorium. The advertisement does not so much invent social values

or ideals of its own as it borrows, usurps, or exploits what advertisers take to be prevailing social values. It then reminds us of beautiful moments in our own lives or it pictures magical moments we would like to experience.

There is little one would want to call "capitalist" in these moments. Indeed, if capitalism is a system promoting private ownership, these ads are oddly anticapitalist or noncapitalist, honoring traditions of social solidarity like family, kinship, and friendship that at least in principle are in conflict with the logic of the market. What is capitalist is that these values are put to work to sell goods, invoked in the service of the market-place. And what is also distinctively capitalist is that the satisfactions portrayed are invariably private, even if they are familial or social; they do not invoke public or collective values. They offer a public portraiture of ideals and values consistent with the promotion of a social order in which people are encouraged to think of themselves and their private worlds. Think of how hollow public service announcements generally sound. They, too, invoke values that matter to people. But they do not have the all-important frame that encompasses product advertising; they do not end in a sales pitch. Advertisements normally are complete only if there is, explicitly or implicitly, a call to the viewer or reader to take a small, do-able action well within his or her experience. The public service announcements ask for a sacrifice or gift, if they ask for anything. People are capable of sacrifice and of giving, but the television announcement that asks for sacrifice seems incongruous.[27]

The Functions of a Pervasive Art Form

If advertising is not an official or state art, it is nonetheless clearly *art*. The development of painting, photography, and prints in the fine arts has been intimately intertwined with the development of commercial art for a century. While few American writers have joined Malcolm Cowley in exclaiming that literature "should borrow a little punch and confidence from American business,"[28] artists and photographers from Toulouse-Lautrec on have frequently done commercial art or been influenced by it. The difference between fashion photography and photography as art is subtle, if it exists at all, and certainly the techniques and innovations in fashion photography influence photography as fine art as often as the other way around. In recent years, television commercial techniques have influenced film and commercial directors have become makers of feature films.[29]

Needless to say, most advertising is dull and conventional, as creative workers in the business are the first to point out. But there is no question that advertising shapes aesthetic tastes, and at least occasionally educates the eye in ways serious artists can applaud. Critics quick to attack the "desires" advertising promotes are apt not to notice, or having noticed, to reject, the visual tastes advertising shapes. One can gaze, as literary historian Leo Spitzer observed, "with disinterested enjoyment" at an advertisement whose claims for its product do not seem the least bit credible. Advertising "may offer a fulfillment of the *aesthetic* desires of modern humanity."[30] In a study of children's attitudes toward television commercials, Thomas Robertson and John Rossiter found a sharp decline in the extent to which children trust commercials, from first grade to third grade to fifth. But when asked if they *liked* commercials, the decline was less severe.[31] Even cultivated and critical adults, if honest, will acknowledge very often a certain "liking" or aesthetic appeal in ads they may in other respects find offensive.

It is important to acknowledge, then, that advertising is art – and is often more successful aesthetically than commercially. (In a 1981 survey of what television commercials people find the "most outstanding," a third of the people who selected Kodak ads praised James Garner and Mariette Hartley for their roles. In fact, Garner and Hartley appeared in Polaroid commercials – aesthetically successful without leaving as strong a commercial impression as the sponsor might have wished.)[32] We collect it. Old candy and coffee tins, old Coke signs, old tourist brochures, these are our antiques, our collected unconscious. But if advertising is art, the question remains: What does art do? What does art that is intended to do something do? What does art do, especially art as pervasive and penetrating as advertising in the contemporary United States?

As obvious as this question seems to be, its formulation is not yet satisfactory. Does advertising turn people into consumers? Does it create needs and desires? Or does it rest for its minimal plausibility on exactly the world its critics (and some of its proponents) claim it is creating? Take, for instance, James Duesenberry's theory of consumer behavior, which he derives from the simple assumptions that (1) people see goods around them superior to what they own and (2) that people believe high-quality goods are desirable and important. Surely advertising reinforces the belief that high-quality goods are desirable and important and surely it leads people to see representations of superior goods around them but it does not seem reasonable to imagine that advertising had much to do with creating these conditions in the first place. Duesenberry takes the belief in the worth of superior goods to lie deep in American culture:

> In a fundamental sense the basic source of the drive toward higher consumption is to be found in the character of our culture. A rising standard of living is one of the major goals of our society. Much of our public policy is directed toward this end. Societies are compared with one another on the basis of the size of their incomes. In the individual sphere people do not expect to live as their parents did, but more comfortably and conveniently. The consumption pattern of the moment is conceived of not as part of a way of life, but only as a temporary adjustment to circumstances. We expect to take the first available chance to change the pattern.[33]

That sounds like a world advertising would love to create, if it could. But it also sounds like the world Tocqueville described in 1830, well before advertising was much more than long gray lists of patent medicine notices in the newspapers. It sounds as much like a world likely to invent modern advertising as a world that modern advertising would like to invent.

Then What Does Advertising Do?

Advertising might be said to lead people to a belief in something. Advertising may make people believe they are inadequate without Product X and that Product X will satisfactorily manage their inadequacies. More likely, it may remind them of inadequacies they have already felt and may lead them, once at least, to try a new product that just might help, even though they are well aware that it probably will not. Alternatively, advertising may lead people to believe generally in the efficacy of manufactured consumer goods for handling all sorts of ills, medical or social or political, even if a given ad fails to persuade that a given product is efficacious. There is the question of belief in a small sense – do people put faith in the explicit claims of advertisements, change their attitudes toward advertised goods, and go out and buy them? And there is the question of belief in a larger sense – do the assumptions and attitudes implicit in advertising become the assumptions and attitudes of the people surrounded by ads, whether or not they actually buy the advertised goods?

Social critics have argued that the greatest danger of advertising may be that it creates belief in the larger sense. It has been common coin of advertising critics that advertising is a kind of religion. This goes back at least to James Rorty who wrote of the religious power of advertising, holding that "advertising becomes a body of doctrine."[34] Ann Douglas has written that advertising is "the only faith of a secularized consumer society."[35] In more measured tones, Leo Spitzer relates advertising to the "preaching mentality" in Protestantism and says that advertising "has taken over the role of the teacher of morals." The advertiser, "like the preacher" must constantly remind the backslider of "his real advantage" and "must 'create the demand' for the better."[36]

Others have observed that many leading advertisers were the children of ministers or grew up in strict, religious households.[37] The trouble with these remarks, and others like them, is that they fail to establish what kind of belief, if any, people actually have in advertisements. And they fail to observe that advertising is quintessentially part of the profane, not the sacred, world. Marghanita Laski has observed of British television that neither religious programs nor royal occasions are interrupted or closely juxtaposed to commercial messages. This is true, though to a lesser degree, with American television – the more sacred the subject, the less the profanity of advertising is allowed to intrude. If it does intrude, the advertiser takes special pains to provide unusually dignified and restrained commercials. If the advertiser fails to make such an adjustment, as in the commercial sponsorship of a docudrama on the Holocaust in 1980, public outrage follows.[38]

So I am not persuaded by the "advertising is religion" metaphor, on the face of it. But the problem with seeing advertising as religion goes still deeper: advertising may be more powerful the less people believe in it, the less it is an acknowledged creed. This idea can be formulated in several ways. Northrop Frye has argued that advertisements, like other propaganda, "stun and demoralize the critical consciousness with statements too absurd or extreme to be dealt with seriously by it." Advertisements thus wrest from people "not necessarily acceptance, but dependence on their versions of reality." Frye continues:

> Advertising implies an economy which has some independence from the political structure, and as long as this independence exists, advertising can be taken as a kind of ironic game. Like other forms of irony, it says what it does not wholly mean, but nobody is obliged to believe its statements literally. Hence it creates an illusion of detachment and mental superiority even when one is obeying its exhortations.[39]

Literary critics have been more sensitive than social scientists to the possibility that communications do not mean what they say – and that this may be the very center of their power. There has rarely been room for the study of irony in social science but irony is a key element in literary studies. Leo Spitzer, like Frye, observes that ads do not ask to be taken literally. In a Sunkist oranges ad he analyzed, he found that the ad "transports the listener into a world of Arcadian beauty, but with no insistence that this world really exists." The ad pictures "an Arcady of material prosperity," but Spitzer holds that the spectator "is equipped with his own criteria, and subtracts automatically from the pictures of felicity and luxury which smile at him from the billboards."[40]

According to Spitzer, people are detached in relation to advertising. They feel detached, disillusioned, and forcibly reminded of the tension between life as it is lived and life as it is pictured. This is a characteristic attitude toward precious or baroque art. In this attitude, no condemnation of the excess of the art is necessary because one is so firmly anchored in the matter-of-fact reality that contradicts it.

For Spitzer, people are genuinely detached in relation to advertising. They view it from an aesthetic distance. For Frye, in contrast, people have only "an illusion of detachment." For Frye, it is precisely the belief people have that they *are* detached that makes the power of advertising all the more insidious. Advertising may create attitudes and inclinations even when it does not inspire belief, it succeeds in creating attitudes because it does not make the mistake of *asking* for belief.

This corresponds to the argument of a leading market researcher, Herbert Krugman, of General Electric Co. research. He holds that the special power of television advertising is that the ads interest us so little, not that they appeal to us so much. Television engages the audience in "low-involvement learning." Krugman's argument is that the evidence in psychology on the learning and memorization of nonsense syllables or other trivial terms is very much like the results in market research on the recall of television commercials. He draws from this the suggestion that the two kinds of learning may be psychologically the same, a "learning without involvement." In such learning, people are not "persuaded" of something. Nor do their attitudes change. But there is a kind of "sleeper" effect. While viewers are not persuaded, they do alter the structure of their perceptions about a product, shifting "the relative salience of attributes" in the advertised brand. Nothing follows from this until the consumer arrives at the supermarket, ready to make a purchase. Here, at the behavioral level, the real change occurs:

> . . . the purchase situation is the catalyst that reassembles or brings out all
> the potentials for shifts in salience that have accumulated up to that point.
> The product or package is then suddenly seen in a new, "somehow different" light although nothing verbalizable may have changed *up to that
> point.*[41]

Consumers in front of the television screen are relatively unwary. They take ads to be trivial or transparent or both. What Krugman suggests is that precisely this attitude enables the ad to be successful. Were consumers convinced of the importance of ads, they would bring into play an array of "perceptual defenses" as they do in situations of persuasion regarding important matters.

Any understanding of advertising in American culture must come to grips with the ironic game it plays with us and we play with it. If there are signs that Americans bow to the gods of advertising, there are equally indications that people find the gods ridiculous. It is part of the popular culture that advertisements are silly. Taking potshots at commercials has been a mainstay of *Mad* magazine and of stand-up comedians for decades. When Lonesome Rhodes meets Marsha Coulihan, station manager for a country radio station, in Budd Schulberg's story, "Your Arkansas Traveler," he says to her:

"You must be a mighty smart little gal to be handlin' this here raddio station all by yourself." She replies: "My good man, I am able to read without laughing out loud any commercial that is placed before me. I am able to pick out a group of records and point to the guy in the control room each time I want him to play one. And that is how you run a rural radio station."[42]

If advertising is the faith of a secular society, it is a faith that inspires remarkably little professed devotion. If it is a body of doctrine, it is odd that so few followers would affirm the doctrine to be true, let alone inspired. Christopher Lasch has seen this problem. He argues that the trouble with the mass media is not that they purvey untruths but that "the rise of mass media makes the categories of truth and falsehood irrelevant to an evaluation of their influence. Truth has given way to credibility, facts to statements that sound authoritative without conveying any authoritative information."[43] But this analysis will not do for the problem of advertising. People are not confused about the importance of truth and falsity in their daily lives. It is just that they do not regularly apply judgments of truth to advertisements. Their relationship to advertisements is not a matter of evidence, truth, belief, or even credibility.

Then what is it? Whether Krugman's formulation is right or wrong, his view at least leads us to ask more pointedly what kind of belief or nonbelief people have in relation to advertising. Again, this is in some sense a question about religion. The form of the question of whether or not people believe advertising messages is like the question of whether or not people believe in and are affected by religious teachings. On the latter question, anthropologist Melford Spiro has distinguished five levels at which people may "learn" an ideology:

1. Most weakly, they may *learn about* an ideological concept.
2. They may learn about and *understand* the concept.
3. They may *believe* the concept to be true or right.
4. The concept may become salient to them and inform their "behavioral environment" – that is, they may not only believe the concept but organize their lives contingent on that belief.
5. They may internalize the belief so that it is not only cognitively salient but motivationally important. It not only guides but instigates action.[44]

Tests of the effectiveness of advertising are most often test of "recall"; ads are judged by the market researchers to be "effective" if they have established Level I belief, learning about a concept. Advertisers, of course, are more interested in Levels 4 and 5, although their ability to measure success at these levels is modest. Most theories of advertising assume that the stages of belief are successive, that consumers must go through Level 1 before Level 2, Level 2 before Level 3, and so on. What Krugman argues and what Northrop Frye can be taken to be saying, is that one can reach Level 4 without ever passing through Level 3. The voices of advertising may inform a person's "behavioral environment" without inspiring belief at any time or at any fundamental level. The stages are not sequential. One is independent from the next.

"What characterizes the so-called advanced societies," Roland Barthes wrote, "is that they today consume images and no longer, like those of the past, beliefs; they are therefore more liberal, less fanatical, but also more 'false' (less 'authentic')."[45] Barthes is right about the present but very likely exaggerates the break from the past. A few years ago I saw a wonderful exhibit at the Museum of Traditional and Popular Arts in

Paris, dealing with religion in rural France in the nineteenth century. The exhibit demonstrated that religious imagery was omnipresent in the French countryside. There were paintings, crucifixes, saints, and Bible verses adorning the most humble objects – plates, spoons, cabinets, religious articles of all sorts, especially holiday objects, lithographs for the living room wall, greeting cards, illustrated books, board games for children, pillowcases, marriage contracts, painted furniture for children, paper dolls, carved and painted signs for religious processions, and so forth. Of course, the largest architectural monuments in most towns were the churches, presiding over life crises and the visual landscape alike. And, as French historian Georges Duby has argued, the grandeur of church architecture was intended as a form of "visual propaganda."[46]

None of this necessarily made the ordinary French peasant a believing Christian. There were pagan rites in nineteenth-century rural France, as there are still today. Nor, I expect, did this mass-mediated reinforcement of Christian culture make the peasant ignore the venality of the church as an institution or the sins of its local representatives.

Still, the Church self-consciously used imagery to uplift its followers and potential followers, and there was no comparable suffusion of the countryside by other systems of ideas, ideals, dreams, and images. When one thought of salvation or, more modestly, searched for meanings for making sense of life, there was primarily the materials of the Church to work with. It has been said that languages do not differ in what they can express but in what they can *express easily*.[47] It is the same with pervasive or official art: it brings some images and expressions quickly to mind and makes others relatively unavailable. However blatant the content of the art, its consequences remain more subtle. Works of art, in general, anthropologist Clifford Geertz has written, do not in the first instance "celebrate social structure or forward useful doctrine. They materialize a way of experiencing; bring a particular cast of mind into the world of objects, where men can look at it."[48] Art, he says, does not create the material culture nor serve as a primary force shaping experience. The experience is already there. The art is a commentary on it. The public does not require the experience it already has but a statement or reflection on it: "What it needs is an object rich enough to see it in; rich enough, even, to, in seeing it, deepen it."[49]

Capitalist realist art, like socialist realism, more often flattens than deepens experience. Here I judge the art and not the way of life it promotes. Jack Kerouac may deepen our experience of the road and the automobile, but the advertising agencies for General Motors and Ford typically flatten and thin our experience of the same objects. This need not be so. The AT&T "Reach Out and Touch Someone" commercials for long-distance telephone calling sentimentalize an experience that genuinely has or can have a sentimental element. If these ads do not deepen the experience they at least articulate it in satisfying ways.

There is another side to the coin: if an ad successfully romanticizes a moment, it provides a model of sentiment that one's own more varied and complicated experience cannot live up to. Most of our phone calls, even with loved ones, are boring or routine. When art romanticizes the exotic or the exalted, it does not call our own experience into question, but when it begins to take everyday life as the subject of its idealization, it creates for the audience a new relationship to art. The audience can judge the art against its own experience and can thereby know that the art idealizes and falsifies. At the same time, the art enchants and tantalizes the audience with the possibility that it is *not* false. If it can play on this ambiguity, art becomes less an imitation of life and turns life into a disappointing approximation of art.

The issue is not that advertising art materializes or "images" certain *experiences* but, as Geertz says, a *way* of *experiencing*. The concern with advertising is that this way of experiencing – a consumer way of life – does not do justice to the best that the human being has to offer and, indeed, entraps people in exploitative and self-defeating activity. But what can it really mean to say that art materializes a way of experience? What does that do? Why should a social system *care* to materialize its way of experiencing? The individual artists, writers, and actors who put the ads together do not feel this need. They frequently have a hard time taking their work seriously or finding it expressive of anything at all they care about.

Think of a smaller social system, a two-person social system, a marriage. Imagine it to be a good marriage, where love is expressed daily in a vast array of shared experiences, shared dreams, shared tasks and moments. In this ideal marriage, the couple continually make and remake their love. Then why, in this marriage, would anything be amiss if the two people did not say to each other, "I love you"? Why, in a relationship of such obviously enacted love, should it seem necessary to say out loud, "I love you"?

Because, I think, making the present audible and making the implicit explicit is necessary to engage and renew a whole train of commitments, responsibilities, and possibilities. "I love you" does not create what is not present. Nor does it seal what is present. But it must be spoken and respoken. It is necessary speech because people need to see in pictures or hear in words even what they already know as deeply as they know anything, *especially* what they know as deeply as they know anything. Words are actions.

This is also true in large social systems. Advertising is capitalism's way of saying "I love you" to itself.

The analogy, of course, is not perfect and I do not mean to jump from marriage to market with unqualified abandon. But in social systems writ large – and not just capitalism but all social systems – there are efforts both individual and collective to turn experience into words, pictures, and doctrines. Once created, these manifestations have consequences. They become molds for thought and feeling, if one takes a deterministic metaphor, or they become "equipment for living" if one prefers a more voluntaristic model or – to borrow from Max Weber and choose a metaphor somewhere in the middle, they serve as switchmen on the tracks of history. In the case of advertising, people do not necessarily "believe" in the values that advertisements present. Nor need they believe for a market economy to survive and prosper. People need simply get used to, or get used to not getting used to, the institutional structures that govern their lives. Advertising does not make people believe in capitalist institutions or even in consumer values, but so long as alternative articulations of values are relatively hard to locate in the culture, capitalist realist art will have some power.

Of course, alternative values *are* available in American culture. In some artistic, intellectual, and ethnic enclaves, one can encounter premises and principles that directly challenge capitalism and the expansion of the market to all phases of life. In contrast, the mainstream news and entertainment media operate within a relatively circumscribed range of values. But even in this narrower discourse, there is often criticism of consumer values or of the excesses of a consumer society. I came upon attacks on materialism, suburbia, conformity, and advertising in the 1950s as a student in social studies classes in a public junior high school and high school. Only a few years ago, people spoke contemptuously of the "me generation" and President Jimmy Carter diagnosed a national "crisis of confidence," opining that "we've discovered that owning things and consuming things does not satisfy our longing for meaning."[50] Recent lampooning of "Preppies" and "Yuppies" (young, upwardly-mobile professionals) betrays anxiety about, if also accommodation to, consumption as a way of life. So I do not suggest that advertisements have a monopoly in the symbolic marketplace, Still, no other cultural form is as accessible to children; no other form confronts visitors and immigrants to our society (and migrants from one part of society to another) so forcefully, and probably only professional sports surpasses advertising as a source of visual and verbal clichés, aphorisms, and proverbs. Advertising has a special cultural power.

The pictures of life that ads parade before consumers are familiar, scenes of life as in some sense we know it or would like to know it. Advertisements pick up and represent values already in the culture. But these values, however deep or widespread, are not the only ones people have or aspire to, and the pervasiveness of advertising makes us forget this. Advertising picks up some of the things that people hold dear and re-presents them to people as *all* of what they value, assuring them that the sponsor is the patron of common ideals. That is what capitalist realist art, like other pervasive symbolic systems, does. Recall again that languages differ not in what they can express but in what they can express *easily*. This is also true in the languages of art, ideology, and propaganda. It is the kind of small difference that makes a world of difference and helps construct and maintain different worlds.

Questions

1   What are the characteristics of socialist realism, and how is advertising a capitalist equivalent?
2   In what ways do advertisements attempt to construct realism?
3   Why does the author believe that advertising is not exactly a modern religion?
4   How does the author believe that advertising might ultimately affect us?
5   Ultimately, what are the other modern value systems that you feel compete with advertising?

Notes

1.   Jack Goody, Domestication of the Savage Mind (Cambridge: Cambridge University Press, 1977), p. 44.
2.   David Potter, People of Plenty (Chicago: University of Chicago Press, 1954).
3.   Mason Griff, "Advertising: the Central Institution of Mass Society," Diogenes no. 68 (Winter 1969): 120–37.
4.   International Commission for the Study of Communication Problems (MacBride Commission), Many Voices, One World (London: Kogan Page, 1980), p. 110.
5.   "A Vanishing Statue of Ulysses S. Grant," Washington Post Magazine, February 3, 1980, p. 4.
6.   Personal Interview with a Hollywood actress, 1981. Quentin Schultze argues that advertising is "acultural." He writes, "Advertising directed at distant audiences and created by professional symbol brokers shows no respect for culture that has been seasoned over time and cultivated in geographic space. Advertising is not simply false consciousness; it is

acultural." This is not quite so – it is middle-class culture, homogenized, yes, with regional and ethnic wrinkles smoothed out, but middle class nonetheless. See Quentin Schultze, "Advertising, Culture, and Economic Interest," Communication Research 8 (July 1981): 377.

7.   Gerald Miller, creative director for Young & Rubincam, told the Los Angeles Times that Robert Young was the choice as Sanka spokesman because "he represents deliberate, mature, seasoned advice." Nancy Yoshihara, "Advertising Success? It's in the Stars," Los Angeles Times, February 12, 1981, p. 12.

8.   Daniel Boorstin, The Image (New York: Atheneum, 1962: Harper Colophon, 1964), p. 57.

9.   Ainsworth Howard, "More Than Just a Passing Fancy," Advertising Age 50 (July 30, 1979): S-2 and Nancy Yoshihara, "Advertising Success? It's in the Stars," Los Angeles Times, February 12, 1981, p. 1. The abstractness of product spokespersons was challenged when Pat Boone agreed in an FTC consent decree to be held personally responsible for failure of the acne medication he endorsed, Acne-Statin, to give satisfaction. He also agreed to make reasonable efforts to verify the claims of any products he would endorse in the future. The world of celebrity endorsers was briefly shaken, but the FTC did not seek consumer refunds for Acne-Statin and the Boone case, settled in the spring of 1978, seems already ancient history. See "FTC Says Star Responsible for Endorsement," Advertising Age, May 15, 1978, p. 1. Martin Esslin has also observed the relative abstractness of "real people" in television commercials. See The Age of Television (San Francisco: W. H. Freeman, 1982), p. 50.

10. On fictional characters in commercials, see Lawrence Ingrassia, "Marketing: As Mr. Whippe Shows, Ad Stars Can Bring Long-Term Sales Gains," Wall Street Journal, March 10, 1981, pp. 1, 16.

11. F.G. Wigglesworth, "The Evolution of Guiness Advertising," Journal of Advertising History 3 (March 1980): 16.

13. Erving Goffman, Gender Advertisements (New York: Harper and Row, 1976), p. 15.

13. Ibid., pp. 15, 84.

14. Quoted in Aleksandr Fadyev, "Socialist Realism," in Encyclopedia of World Literature in the Twentieth Century (New York: Frederick Ungar, 1971), vol, 3, p. 299.

15. See articles on "social realism" by Gero von Wilpert and Aleksandr Fadyev in Encyclopedia of World Literature in the Twentieth Century (New York: Frederick Ungar, 1971), vol, 3, p. 298–301. See also Caradog v. Janes, Soviet Socialist Realism: Origins of a Theory (London: Macmillan, 1973), pp. 90–93. My own list of five features of socialist realism abstracts from these works. See also Abram Tertz, On Socialist Realism (New York: Vintage Books, 1960). Leo Bogart, Strategy in Advertising (New York: Harcourt, Brace and World, 1967), pp. 6–7, discusses advertising as propaganda and compares it to Soviet propaganda.

16. Lynn Hirschberg, "When You Absolutely, Positively Want the Best," Esquire 100 (August 1983): 55. For the material on the current vogue for realism in commericals, see Karen Thorsen, "Wives to celebrities: Search for au naturel," Advertising Age, July 21, 1980, pp. S-8,S-9, S-16. But see also T.J. Jackson Lears, "Some Versions of Fantasy: Toward a Cultural History of American Advertising, 1880–1930," Prospects 9(1984) which cites ad men's concern for realism in advertising in the first decade of this century.

17. Bill Abrams, "Marketing: Anacin's New, Intense TV Ads Try to Avoid 'Sanitized' Look," Wall Street Journal, October 13, 1983, p. 31.

18. See especially Michael Arlen, Thirty Seconds (Harmondsworth, England: Penguin Books, 1981).

19. Barbara Rosenblum, Photographers at Work (New York: Holmes and Meier, 1978), p. 16.

20. John O'Toole, The Trouble with Advertising (New York: Chelsea House, 1981), P. 89.

21. Raymond Williams, "The Magic System," New Left Review, no. 4 (July–August 1960) holds that advertising is "in a sense, the official art of modern capitalist society" (p. 27). His essay is expanded as "Advertising: The Magic System" and included in Raynod Williams, Problems with Materialism and Culture (London: Verso Editions, 1980), pp. 170–95.

22. See the FTC's statement of philosophy and policy, Consumer Information Remedies (Washington, D.C.: U.S. Government Printing Office, 1979). On court decisions regarding "commercial speech," see especially Virginia State Board of Pharmacy v. Virginia Citizens Consumer Council, 425 U.S. 746 (1976) and Bates v. State Bar of Arizona, 433 U.S. 350 (1977). These and other recent cases substantially undo Valentine v. Chrestensen, 316 U.S. 52 (1942) which established that commercial speech does not qualify for First Amendment

protection. See Jerome A. Barron and C. Thomas Dienes, Handbook of Free Speech and Free Press (Boston: Little, Brown, 1979), pp. 155–88. While the United States itself is not a dominant buyer of advertising space, direct government advertising can be an important issue, as it is in Canada. There the government is the leading advertiser in the country, spending $58 million a year. The American government, in comparison, spent $173 million on advertising in 1981, but this made it only the twenty-fourth largest American advertiser. The Canadian ads are generally reminders of "what your government is doing for you" and have drawn public criticism. Peggy Berkowitz, "Government Is Top Advertiser in Canada, Angering Its Critics," Wall Street Journal, March 4, 1982, p. 29. In the American situation, government support of advertising takes place in a variety of ways, including subsidies to election campaigns that help finance political advertising, U.S. Department of Agriculture subsidies for advertising individual commodities, and very importantly preferential postal rates for magazines and newspapers – indirectly a subsidy of advertising itself. Murray L. Weidenbaurn and Linda L. Rockwood discuss the ways in which the government subsidizes advertising in "Government as a Promoter and Subsidizer of Advertising," in The Political Economy of Advertising, ed. David G. Tuerck (Washington, D.C.: American Enterprise Institute, 1978), pp. 41–60.

Advertising has also received some support from the government during war time and has substantially improved its reputation with the public and potential critics by turning its energies to support of war efforts in both World War I and World War II. See Daniel Pope, "The Development of National Advertising, 1865–1920" (Ph.D. diss., Columbia University, 1973), pp. 331–33, on World War I and Frank Fox, Madison Avenue Goes to War: The Strange Military Career of American Advertising 1941–45 (Provo, Utah: Brigham Young University Press, Charles E. Merrill monograph series, 1975) on World War II.

23.   This is not to mention more nationalistic outbursts like the paperback book by the New York Times staff, Miracle on Ice, advertised under a banner headline, "How We Beat the Russians," New York Times, March 2, 1980, p. 57. On the use of the Olympics to promote private industry, see Marilyn Chase, "Firms Find Sponsoring Team for 1980 Games Is Good Way to Compete," Wall Street Journal, April 13, 1979, p. 1; and Roy J. Harris, Jr., "U.S. Athletes' Training Gains as Private Giving Lifts Budget for Games," Wall Street Journal, September 9, 1983, p. 1.

24.   David Bernstein, "U.S. Advertising as Seen in the U. K.," lecture at Advertising Age "Advertising Week" convention, Chicago, Ill., August, 1979. See also the send-up of "American-ness" in commercials in Ellis Weiner, "Patriotic Spot (60 secs.)," New Yorker, June 30, 1980, p. 31.

25.   See, for instance, on women, Erving Coffman, Gender Advertisements (New York: Harper & Row, 1976); Gaye Tuchman, Arlene Kaplan Daniels, and James Benet, Hearth and Home: Images of Women in the Mass Media (New York: Oxford University Press, 1978); on blacks, see the literature review in George Comstock, et. al., Television and Human Behavior (New York: Columbia University Press, 1978), pp. 35–39.

26.   Brigitte Jordan and Kathleen Bryant, "The Advertised Couple: The Portrayal of the Couple and their Relationship in Popular Magazine Advertisements," paper presented at the Popular Culture Association and American Culture Association meetings, Pittsburgh, Penn., April 28, 1979. Forthcoming in Journal of Popular Culture 17 (1984).

27.   Public service announcements (PSA's) produced by the Advertising Council have been criticized as thinly veiled advertisements for capitalism. See Richard Ohmann, "An Agency for All Social Ills," Cyrano's Journal I (Fall 1982): 36–37 and the companion article, by William Lutz, "The Gospel According to the Advertising Council," pp. 10–11, in the same issue. Also see Bruce Howard, "The Advertising Council: Selling Lies," Ramparts 13 (December 1974–January 1975): 25–26, 29–32 and David L. Paletz, Roberta E. Pearson, and Donald L. Willis, Politics in Public Service Advertising on Television (New York: Praeger, 1977).

28.   Cowley is cited in David E. Shi, "Advertising and the Literary Imagination During the Jazz Age," Journal of American Culture 2 (Summer 1979): 172.

29.   See John Barnicoat, A Concise History of Posters (New York: Oxford University Press), on the intertwining of art history and advertising history. On commercial directors moving to

feature films, see Patrick Goldstein, "Leech Has Knack for Commercials," Los Angeles Times, September 9, 1983, p. VI-1.

30. Leo Spitzer, "American Advertising Explained as Popular Art," Essays on English and American Literature (Princeton: Princeton University Press, 1962), p. 265n22 and p. 249n2. Of course, advertising may be ugly as well as attractive and tasteless as well as an educator of tastes. This has been an issue especially in outdoor advertising. In the nineteenth century, when advertisers were less constrained than they are today, they covered rocks and cliffs and trees with their announcements. Niagara Falls and Yellowstone became backdrops to patent medicine advertisements painted directly on the rock formations. The New York Tribune in 1876 complained that scenery had become "obscenery." A wave of protest led to changes in advertising practice at the end of the nineteenth century, but outdoor signs and billboards are still often defacements of cherished landscapes. On the nineteenth century, see James Harvey Young, Toadstool Millionaires (Princeton: Princeton University Press, 1961), p. 123. See also Ronald Berman, "Origins of the Art of Advertising," Journal of Aesthetic Education (Fall 1983): 61–69.

31. Thomas Robertson and John Rossiter, "Children and Commercial Persuasion: An Attribution Theory Analysis," Journal of Consumer Research 1 (June 1974): 17.

32. Bill Abrams, "The 1981 TV Advertisements That People Remember Most," Wall Street Journal, February 25, 1982, p. 29.

33. James S. Duesenberry, Income, Saving, and the Theory of Consumer Behavior. (Cambridge: Harvard Economic Study No. 87, 1949; New York: Oxford University Press, 1967), p. 26.

34. James Rorty, Our Master's Voice (New York: John Day, 1934, Arno Press, reprint, 1976), p. 16.

35. Ann Douglas, The Feminization of American Culture (New York: Alfred A. Knopf, 1977), p. 80.

36. Spitzer, "American Advertising," p. 273.

37. Daniel Pope, "The Development of National Advertising, 1865–1920" (Ph.D. diss., Columbia University, 1973), p. 320. See also a book just published as this volume goes to press: Stephen Fox, The Mirror Makers: A History of American Advertising and Its Creators (New York: William Morrow, 1984).

38. Marghanita Laski, "Advertising: Sacred and Profane," Twentieth Century 165 (February 1959): 118–29. On ads sponsoring "Holocaust," see Marvin Kitman, "Ads Disrupting Holocaust," in The Commercial Connection, ed. John W. Wright (New York: Delta Books, 1979), pp. 262–454.

39. Northrop Frye, The Modern Century (Toronto: Oxford University Press, 1967), p. 26. See also Frye's remarks on consumer skepticism of advertising in The Educated Imagination (Indianapolis: Indiana University Press, 1964), p. 138, where he writes, "Our reaction to advertising is really a form of literary criticism."

40. Spitzer, "American Advertising," p. 264 and p. 265n22.

41. Herbert E. Krugman, "The Impact of Television Advertising: Learning Without Involvement," Public Opinion Quarterly 29 (1965): 161. See also John C. Maloney, "Curiosity versus Disbelief in Advertising," Journal of Advertising Research 2 (June 1962): 2–6.

42. Budd Schulberg, Some Faces in the Crowd (New York: Random House, 1953).

43. Christopher Lasch, The Culture of Narcissism (New York: W. W. Norton, 1978), p. 74.

44. Melford Spiro, "Buddhism and Economic Action in Burma," American Anthropologist 68 (October 1966): 1163.

45. Roland Barthes, Camera Lucida (New York: Hill and Wang, 1981), p. 119.

46. Georges Duby, The Age of the Cathedrals: Art and Society, 980–1420 (Chicago: University of Chicago Press, 1981), p. 135.

47. "Languages differ not so much as to what can be said in them, but rather as to what it is relatively easy to say in them." Charles Hackett, "Chinese vs. English: An Exploration of the Whorfian Hypothesis," in Language in Culture, ed. H. Hoijer (Chicago: University of Chicago Press, 1954), p. 122.

48. Clifford Geertz, "Art as a Cultural System," MLN 91 (1976): 1478.

49. Ibid., p. 1483.

50. "Transcript of President's Address to Country on Energy Problems," New York Times, July 16, 1979, p. A-10.

Chapter 16

ERIC KING WATTS AND MARK P. ORBE

THE SPECTACULAR CONSUMPTION OF "TRUE" AFRICAN AMERICAN CULTURE
"Whassup" with the Budweiser Guys?

THIS CHAPTER FOCUSES ON ONE PARTICULARLY popular ad campaign that debuted during the Superbowl: the Budweiser "Whassup" campaign, featuring a small group of African American male friends. This ad campaign so struck the public imagination that it expanded beyond its original 30-second commercial form and became, for a time, a spectacular part of the larger popular culture. The commercial actors appeared on talk shows; "Whassup" became a catch phrase; parodies of the ad appeared on the Internet. But why was it so popular, and was it popular for different reasons to different groups? Using a combination of production analysis, analysis of the ad's content, and focus groups of audiences with different ethnicities, Watts and Orbe try to unpack the mixed meanings and appeals of the campaign. They argue that, in this ad, two seemingly conflicting social values collide: the celebration of the "universal value" of male bonding versus a hip, edgy but perhaps ultimately distancing depiction of African American culture for mainstream white culture.

The authors find much that is admirable in the ad itself, including the portrayal of close black male friendship and the black males as active "watchers," rather than the ones being watched. However, they also find that there are some stereotypical characteristics of black males in the ad as well, including the portrayal of black males as behaving in a comically exaggerated manner with overly broad emotional displays. The focus groups, they argue, also revealed different interpretations of the ads that tended to be defined along racial lines, with views differing about whether the ad campaign was primarily targeted at African Americans, or instead at "everyone," which may have been understood by white participants as white culture.

Charles Stone, III, must have felt as though he had gone to sleep and awoken in Oz. It was three short years ago that he captured on film candid moments among three of his friends, edited them into an engrossing and visually stunning short film called "True," and used it as a video resumé. Stone was "floored" when Anheuser-Busch asked him to translate his film into a 60-second commercial spot for Budweiser beer (McCarthy, 2000, p. 8B). Stone was equally surprised when, out of respect for "realism," he was allowed to cast those same friends from the short film for the commercial. It must have seemed even more surreal to be in Cannes during the summer of 2000 to accept the advertising world's version of the "Oscar," the Grand Prix and Golden Lion, and to hear his friends' greeting, now the world's most famous catchphrase, bouncing off café walls and rippling along the beaches—"Whassup?!" It must have been bizarre to witness the usually stodgy Cannes judges joyfully exchanging the greeting in international accents—especially since the advertising elite admits to a cultivated distaste for the popular (McCarthy, 2000). This admission, however, didn't hurt the market value of the Budweiser "True" commercials one bit. To understand why this is so, one must explore the nature of spectacular consumption.

Let us begin our journey by considering this odd commentary offered up by *Advertising Age*'s ad review staff after Stone's commercial aired during the 2000 Superbowl: "A bunch of friends, all black, greet each other with exaggerated 'Wuzuppppppppp?' salutations that sound like retching. [Our] staff, the single whitest enclave outside of Latvia, doesn't quite get it but suspects it is very funny . . ." (Garfield, 2000b, p. 4). But, what's so mysterious? These guys simply greet each other—over and over—with what has been described as a "verbal high-five" (Farhi, 2000, p. C1). Also of interest is the fact that *USA Today*'s Admeter rated the commercial as the Superbowl's most popular; and so let us turn the question on its axis: if *Advertising Age* is correct and the humor is baffling, why is it so popular? After all, the ad is about four friends sitting around doing "nothin'[but] watching the game, having a Bud"? How is it that a series of commercials about four African American friends can be simultaneously "pretty out there," incomprehensible, and yet enjoy such massive appeal so as to become Budweiser's hottest ad campaign ever? (Adande, 2000, p. D1).

The pop culture craze associated with the "Whassup?!" guys leaves some observers dumbfounded and amazed. But others chalk up the frenzy to either the universality of male bonding or to white America's continued fascination with black expression. On the one hand, the commercials' appeal is associated with these ads' depiction of a classic and commonly inarticulate male-bonding ritual. From this perspective, the secret to their popularity lies in their utter *familiarity*. On the other hand, their appeal is linked to the notion that the ads are "weird," "oddball," "strange," "funky," and "True"; that is, "authentically" black. In other words, their appeal is also predicated upon their *unfamiliarity*.

Due to its parsimony, this dichotomy between the universal and the distinctive is misleading. If we perceive the ads as "universal" expressions of masculine communal norms, they speak in a single, unproblematic voice. They say, in essence, "I love you, man!" This time, the men just *happen* to be black. Thus, through a projection of "positive realism" (Cassidy & Katula, 1995), the "Whassup?!" ads testify to increased diversity in television commercials and to African American male affection. Understood in this manner, the American ideal of human universalism is affirmed through a display of black fraternal care made familiar. Indeed, according to David English, an Anheuser-Busch vice-president, the "universal" appeal of the short film allowed him to look "past the color of the guys to the situation of guys being guys, and the communication between friends" (Heller, 2000, p. 11). Hence, in attempts to explain the soaring market value of these ads, Anheuser-Busch spokespersons often reference their "universality"—that is, their colorlessness. But, since the ads are also described as "cool" and "edgy," and the "Whassup?!" guys are widely perceived as the hippest group of friends on TV, they signify a pleasure principle orienting white consumption of blackness (hooks, 1992). And so, it has occurred to us that this dichotomy between the universal and the distinctive conceals a strategy. That is, references to the ads' "universal" qualities obscure the way in which blackness can be made to behave in accordance with the American ideology of universalism. By encouraging viewers to "celebrate" blackness conceived in terms of *sameness*, the ad campaign deflects attention away from the ways in which blackness as *otherness* is annexed and appropriated as commodity and hides from view the fact that American culture exhibits a profound *ambivalence* toward "authentic" blackness (Entman & Rojecki, 2000).

This essay seeks to explore this ambivalence as it is reproduced and displayed through Budweiser's "Whassup?!" ad campaign. We argue that the ad campaign constitutes and administers cultural "authenticity" as a market value. From the perspective of spectacular consumption, the intensity of the pleasure of consuming the other is directly (and paradoxically) related to the replication and magnification of "authentic" difference. Moreover, the logic of spectacular consumption compels us to pay attention to how the act of consumption transforms the relation between the consumer and the consumed. We contend that as the market economy seeks to regulate and integrate "authentic" difference, white American ambivalence toward blackness is paradoxically both assuaged by its "universality" and heightened by its distinctiveness. This conflicted set of impulses and feelings can be witnessed in the commercials, disclosed in corporate strategy, and observed in focus group interviews. Hence, this essay proceeds in three stages: first, we explicate what we mean by spectacular consumption, relating it to the commodification of the "Whassup?!" guys. Second, we provide an interpretation of the original commercial so as to show how white American ambivalence concerning race is inscribed in the ad. Third, we discuss the results of focus group interviews that were used to gain insight into "consumer" perceptions of the ads. We conclude with some observations about the on-going development of the "Whassup" line of commercials and the racial ambivalence they promote.

Spectacular Consumption and the Reproduction of the "Authentic"

Treating the spectacle as a rhetorical construction, David E. Procter focuses his critical attention on how a spectacle as an "event" can be called forth by rhetors seeking to build community (1990, p. 118). Drawing from the work of Murray Edelman, Thomas B. Farrell and others, Procter posits the concept of a "dynamic spectacle" as requiring "a fusion of material event with the symbolic construction of that event and with audience needs" (1990, p. 119). From this perspective, the spectacle is a choreographed happening like a celebration or memorial that brings together the interpretive materials for rhetorical *praxis*. As Procter's analysis demonstrates, the critic is charged with the task of determining how rhetoric transformed the material event into a spectacle and how the spectacle builds community. Our understanding of spectacle both converges with and diverges from this account. We share Procter's concern with the constructed nature of spectacle and the capacity of interested persons to shape it. In particular, we find useful Procter's understanding of spectacle as a mediated phenomenon that transforms persons' lived reality. However, we do not conceive of spectacle as an event or as a happening, with a clearly defined beginning, middle, and an end; here, the spectacle is a *condition*—a characteristic of our collective being. It must, therefore, be understood ontologically as well as rhetorically.

Guy Debord (1983), in *Society of the Spectacle*, explains that as social systems shift from industrial to post-industrial economies they also undergo ontological change. Rather than being organized around the exchange of goods based upon actual use values, the spectacle establishes mass consumption as a way of life. When sign value replaces use value as the foundation of being in this fashion, human beings need no longer be concerned with discovering the essence of *Dasein*, for the "true" nature of one's being is up for grabs; it can be fabricated through *appearances* (Best & Kellner, 1997; Ewen, 1988). In the society of the spectacle, even facets of one's very body can be manufactured in keeping with the latest trend. Importantly, as Jean Baudrillard (1984) has forewarned, a society's capacity to replicate and manipulate forms of public culture forces upon all of us a virtual supersedure of the life world by the signifiers that previously represented it. By destabilizing the ways through which we ascribe meaning and value to our experiences, the spectacle mediates our understanding of the world through a distribution of commercialized signs. Although this process may not be conspiratorial (Hall, 1995), it is hardly random; the economics of the spectacle lead to the orchestration of meaning and value so as to realize the "moment when the commodity has attained the total occupation of social life" (Debord, 1983, p. 13). As the spectacle structures both work and play, diverse aspects of life are made significant inasmuch as they can be made marketable. Thus, these processes magnify—that is, make spectacular—previously private worlds and the persons who inhabit them.

Spectacular consumption is, thus, structured in a fashion different from traditional spectacle; its rhetorics respond to cultural variables in diverse patterns oriented by the logic of sign value. A key rhetorical resource in the economy of spectacular consumption, then, is the paradoxical tension between the "different" and the widely available. On the one hand, the pleasure of consuming otherness is advanced by the Other's uniqueness. On the other hand, in a mass consumer culture, commodity value rises to a sufficient level only when the Other undergoes massive replication: "In a hyperreal culture, things are conceived from the point of view of *reproducibility*, as we come to think something is *real* only insofar as it exists as a serialized commodity, as able to be bought and sold, as able to be made into a novel or a movie" (Best & Kellner, 1997, p. 102, emphasis added). The consuming rhetoric of the spectacle thus promotes a contradiction as it seeks strategically to reproduce on a massive scale the singularity associated with the "authentic." And yet these attempts persist because the market value of such reproductions escalates as long as the "aura" of "authenticity" can be maintained (Benjamin, 1984).

Clearly, cultural difference provides a particularly valuable resource for spectacular consumption. The differences found among cultures provide a resource of the new and the unfamiliar that is particularly valuable because those differences can be projected as "authentic" even as they are commercially manufactured. In the case of the Budweiser ads, public consumption of the ads triggers an overvaluation and fabrication of black bodies in living spaces represented as "real life." Spectacular consumption, then, describes the process by which the material and symbolic relations among the culture industry, the life worlds of persons, and the ontological status of cultural forms are transformed in terms generated by public consumption (Watts, 1997).

The successful masking of the fact that the "Whassup?!" guys are "ontologically eroded" as cultural forms (Best & Kellner, 1997, p. 102), thus, extends beyond the texts of the ads themselves to a series of related texts that together constitute the on-going production of spectacle. The "aura" of the "True" ads is itself replicated through corporate strategy linking public opinion, corporate discourse, and testimony from the "Whassup?!" guys themselves. Our understanding of "reality" is mediated through a matrix of imagery in the spectacle.

One key dimension of these appeals is the way the "universal" dimensions of the commercials enhance the "aura" of "authenticity" by making explicit claims to "real life." "Whassup?!" is called a "common guy greeting," (Farhi, 2000, p. C1) and "Whassup?!" enthusiasts identify how the ads are said to reflect "the essence of what [men] do on Sunday afternoons" (Adande, 2000, p. D1). According to Bob Scarpelli, the creative director of the advertising agency responsible for the campaign, this doing nothing is labeled a "common experience" that "resonate[s]" because men can say, " 'That's me and my buddies.' " Although there is a gender gap with the ads, and men like them more, many women nonetheless chime in by remarking " 'That's my husband, my boyfriend or my brother' " (McCarthy, 2000a, p. 3B). Anheuser-Busch frequently cites marketing research that explains the ads' "cross-over appeal" in terms of "universal" friendship and "about being with your buddies" (McCarthy, 2000D, p. 6B).

Discussing the fact that the target audience for this campaign was originally composed of "Everymen" (Garfield, 2000a, p. 2), meaning mostly white men, "Whassup?!" ad promoters like Anheuser-Busch V.P. Bob Lachky refer to focus group reviews where "predominately Anglo" crowds report that each of the ads " 'is a colorless thing. . . .' " (Adande, 2000, p. D1). Similarly, after the first of the ads garnered the Cannes top prize, *Advertising Age* explained the accolade by saying that "America saw [the ad] not as an inside-black-culture joke but [as] a universal expression of eloquent male inarticulateness" (Garfield, 2000a, p. 2). The point that we are making here is that these statements posit as *prima facie* evidence for the existence of a colorblind society the fact that white folks *claim* identification with black (mediated) experiences. This claim seems reasonable and perhaps even promising when one understands that it is premised upon the captivating depiction of black male affection and camaraderie among real life friends. Commenting in the *Washington Post*, one observer writes that the ads "provide a glimpse into a private world of four men at leisure. The joy each man expresses in greeting and being greeted by his longtime friends is infectious, universal and, it seems, genuine" (Farhi, 2000, p. C2). This display is important given the fact that television advertising rarely shows black affection (Entman & Rojecki, 2000; hooks, 1992).

In spectacular consumption the linkages among the spheres of social life, the culture industry, and public consumption allow dynamic discursive and pragmatic interplays of influence; corporate appeals to universalism thus encourage backing from the "Whassup?!" guys as they recount their real life affections for an insatiable media. For example, Charles Stone has repeatedly testified to the ads' "universal message of male bonding" (McCarthy, 2000B, p. 2B) by describing how the whole thing got started: " 'That's really how we talk to each other. We used to call each other on the phone 15 years ago, during our college years, and that was our greeting. People say it seems real to them. It *is* real' " (Farhi, 2000, p. C2, emphasis added). " 'It really wasn't acting,' " remarks Paul Williams, the "Whassup?!" guy with the big hair. " 'It was us being us' " (Adande, 2000, p. 2). Scott Brooks, who plays and is "Dookie" in the ads, agrees: "You can't fake that kind of chemistry,' " he remarked during a promotional tour in St. Louis. "We're really friends' " (McCarthy, 2000d, p. 7B). It is important to acknowledge that these messages arise out of bona fide and caring relationships among the men.

This appeal to a putatively universal experience of male bonding is a conflicted one, however, because it is made through black men in a white dominated culture, wherein the "universal" has long been portrayed in terms of whiteness. Thus, it is the very assertion of the "Whassup?!" crew inhabiting an "authentic" (black) life world that helps warrant the ads' presumed transcendence of blackness for white viewers. We do not want nor need to become involved in a debate over whether Western humanism actually allows for such transcendence. We mean only to demonstrate that there exists a discursive tension between appeals to colorlessness and appeals to black cultural distinctiveness. This discursive stress becomes most acute as we explore the contours and shapes of cultural "authenticity." Anheuser-Busch now boasts that the ads enjoy mass appeal by virtue of their essential colorlessness; it did not, however, begin conceiving of the ads with this virtue in mind. Originally, Anheuser-Busch wanted a "multicultural cast" (Farhi, 2000, p. C1). This sort of marketing strategy has rightly been understood as *color-conscious* because it arises out of a concern that an all-black cast would alienate predominately white audiences (Entman & Rojecki, 2000; Jhally, 1995). Additionally, Stone's argument about casting his friends was assented to by Anheuser-Busch because its ad agency, DDB World Wide, was equally concerned with keeping it "real." Similarly, early in the campaign's genesis, Stone thought that the conservative tendencies of the DDB would be placated if he altered the tagline, "True," to read "Right." A vice president of Anheuser-Busch asked that he change it back to the more desirable "slang" term saying that " 'True is cool' " (McCarthy, 2000c, p. 9B).

Hence we can see that despite the "universality" of the "Whassup?!" guys' life world, Anheuser-Busch and its ad agency paid close attention to how black culture should be shaped for consumption. The many media references to how "Whassup?!" is now the "coolest way to say hello" (McCarthy, 2000d, p. 6B) and the "hip greeting of choice" (McCarthy, 2000c, p. 8B) testify to the fact that African American cultural forms are still the standard bearer of pop cultural fashion. Elijah Anderson argues that the commercials represent something "very specific to black people" (in Farhi, 2000, C3). Similarly, Michael Dyson believes that they convey the notion that "black vernacular" can be mass marketed without being white washed (in Heller, 2000, p. 11). Indeed, "authentic" blackness is *more* valuable to spectacular consumption than representations of blackness as sameness precisely *because* it is more anxiety producing.

The energy created within the interstices of spectacular consumption arises in part out of the desire for white folk to reconstitute their identities through acts of black consumption (hooks, 1992). To this end, the 1990s seemed to have normalized the market appropriation of black styles. " 'When they write the history of popular culture in the 20th century,' " comments MTV's Chris Connelly, " 'they can sum it up in one sentence which is, white kids wanting to be as cool as black kids' " (in Graham, 2000, p. D9.) This desire is undeniable, but as hooks so perceptively points out, white folk do not want to *become* black (1992). The discursive spaces of white privilege must be maintained even as the consumption of blackness intensifies. Spectacular consumption as a critical lens brings into focus how the energy from this dialectic is harnessed by the replication of specific features of the "authentic."

Budweiser ad executives want the funkiness and edginess of the "Whassup?!" campaign to become characteristics associated with Budweiser. The strategy is premised on the logic that Bud is a "colloquial beer" and fits in with the signs of the Other (Farhi, 2000, C2). There are corporate and legal means to enable such identification. For example, Anheuser-Busch has trademarked the term "Whassup?!" for its exclusive market use (McGuire, 2000). Moreover, unlike the African American life world out of which it comes, where its intonation and its spelling vary among its particular usages, Budweiser has suggested a proper pronunciation for "Whassup?!" and has copyrighted an "official spelling . . . w-h-a-s-s-u-p, although there's an optional p on the end" (Adande, 2000, p. 2). These technical measures are significant, but they cannot overcome a fundamental problem with consumption. That is, the "image-system of the marketplace reflects our desire and dreams, yet we have only the pleasure of the images to sustain us in our actual experience with goods" (Jhally, 1995, p. 80). This is so if we conceive of Budweiser beer as the good being consumed. This is not the case in spectacular consumption, however, where the "Whassup?!" guys themselves constitute the product. "And no one is better at making a complete, integrated promotional effort than Anheuser-Busch; they've gotten every ounce of publicity out of this that can be gotten" (McGuire, 2000, p. E1).

During a 10-day promotional tour during the summer of 2000, Scott Brooks, Paul Williams, and Fred Thomas completed their transformations from product spokespersons to products—the "Whassup?!" guys. Bouncing from one Budweiser-sponsored media event to another, one reporter noted a pattern in the form of a question: "how many times do they estimate that they stick their tongues out in a given promotional day?" (McGuire, 2000, p. E1). This question can be modified and multiplied to illuminate the operations of hyperreality. How often does one have to repeat one's background and display on cue one's genuine affection for the other guys to maintain the "aura"? How can such an "aura" even be cultivated through scripted "spontaneity"? How will the "Whassup?!" guys stay "True" to black expression given the contention made by Russell Rickford of Drexel University that "once a phrase has become mainstream, black folks stop using it and go on to something else"? (McGuire, 2000, p. E1). Although the ad campaign may have already reached its saturation point, spectacular consumption compels the continued replication of value and handsomely rewards its replicants. Charles Stone, III, is now a hot directing commodity who has a movie deal, a contract with Anheuser-Busch for more commercials, and who gets meetings with actors like Dustin Hoffman. There is also a lot of talk about a possible sitcom or movie deal for the friends. At any rate, their "Q-rating," a TV recognizability quotient, is so high that Brooks, once a bouncer in Philadelphia, was forced to quit his job. Also, Williams, a typically out-of-work actor, has been able to sift through scripts and pay his rent for an entire year (McGuire, 2000, E2).

This media buzz translates into the sort of "talk value" (McCarthy, 2000b, p. 2B) that is partly responsible for convincing the Cannes officials to put aside their misgivings concerning the ads' popularity in the face of the "Whassup?!" guys' spectacularity (Garfield, 2000a). In other words, the public consumption of the ads and the actors is constitutive of a commitment to replicating image value. This commitment compels industry brokers like the Cannes folks to shift their values away from rewarding artistic accomplishment in advertising and toward recognizing ads "that work," ads that sustain spectacular consumption (McCarthy, 2000b, p. 2B). It also helps generate conflicted discursive performances that, through a critical reading of the first "True" ad, further reveal how white ambivalence helps mold public displays of "authentic" blackness.

"Watching the Game, Having a Bud": An Exploration of Competing Strategies and Visions of "True" Consumption

The Budweiser "True" commercial offers a setting in which gender and cultural per-formances are conditioned by sports and spectatorship; "masculinity" and "blackness" emerge as key themes in this world where men lounge in front of televisions and make seemingly inconsequential conversation. Although the repose of these men is casual, even languid, there is quite a bit of action going on. This is so despite the fact that Stone is "laid back" on the couch transfixed by the game on TV; he and his friends appear in this ad as both observers and players of a spectacular "game." As actors in a commercial the fact that they are being watched cannot be denied, but their performances display a heightened sense of awareness of the politics and character of the white (consumptive) gaze. And so, the ad testifies to competing visions; the "True" commercial demonstrates a form of self-reflexivity that focuses our attention on how the "Whassup?!" guys play a game in which they recognize (that is, see) the ways that their "play" is overvalued as "authentic" cultural performance. The significance of these competing visions comes into view as we integrate a textual analysis with a critical lens that takes into consider-ation how spectacular consumption is constitutive of images that mediate "real life" social relations. The "True" ad emerges as a conflicted statement on how cultural commodities in the spectacle are made self-conscious—that is, made aware of how their appearance can maximize their market potential. In order to keep track of all of this seeing and being seen, let's begin with the opening scene.

Charles Stone sets the mood and tone for the first act of this three-part drama. Clutching a beer bottle and stretching out on a sofa he stares vacantly into the lights of a TV; we faintly hear the color commentary of a game. Unlike advertisements where the sports fanatic is caught up in the ecstasy and agony of the sporting event, Stone is nearly catatonic, not invested in the sporting event, but tuned in nevertheless to the ritualistic character of masculine spectatorship. Put simply, Stone seems nearly perfect as the Sunday afternoon "couch potato."

The telephone rings. Stone, without diverting his gaze, answers the phone: "Hello."

The camera cuts to Paul Williams who signals for us both a departure from how TV advertising depicts conventional male-bonding rituals oriented around sports spectator-ship and an *intensification* of the mood and tone established by Stone. As we have already noted, Williams was not initially considered for his own part in the ad because Stone was told to find actors to make up an ethnic rainbow. Since such a cast would have been "diverse," the cast would not only collectively signify the ideal of American integration but it would also allow white viewers to "identify with fellow whites, and resonate to their on-screen relationships with each other" (Entman & Rojecki, 2000, p. 167). Williams is, therefore, a violation of this ad strategy precisely because his speech and his look mark him as other in a world of mainstream marketing. Compared to Stone's conservative style, Williams's Afro signifies "exoticism." On the other hand, Williams wholly identifies with Stone's tone and mood, endorsing a performance that testifies both to the timelessness of the ritual and the character of their relationship. Williams and Stone are watching the same game and having the same beer; their shared interest in the game does not testify to its importance, but rather it reinforces the significance of *being there for one another* during the game. Male bonding transmutes into black male affection as Williams and Stone demonstrate their interpersonal comfort and communal linguistic styles.

Williams: "Ay, who, whassup?"
Stone: "Nothin', B, watchin' the game, havin' a Bud. Whassup wit'chu?"
Williams: "Nothin', watchin' the game, havin' a Bud."
Stone: "True, true."

This dialogue punctuates the episode, signaling its end, and announces the following act. Fred Thomas enters the scene and greets Stone exuberantly. "Whassup?!" With flaring nostrils and wagging tongue, Stone mirrors Thomas's performance. Williams asks Stone, "yo, who's that" and Stone directs Thomas to "yo, pick up the phone." Williams, Thomas, and Stone share a joyful and comical verbal hug that ripples outward and embraces Scott "Dookie" Brooks. Stone's editing creates a visual montage of gleeful faces and a kind of musical tribute to the group expression as each man's voice contributes to a shrilling chorus. As a display of black masculine affection, the scene represents brotherly responsibility. As Williams asks about Thomas and as Thomas wonders "where's Dookie?," viewers bear witness to black men acknowledging their need and care for the well-being of other black men.

This mutual affection is nonetheless potentially troubling to white audience members. Ever since the importation of African slaves, black solidarity has been constituted as a threat to white power. Rather than being a detriment to white readings of the commercial, however, this well-spring of angst provides a potent commercial resource, specifically a resource for humor. At the heart of humor is the release of repression, the release of repressed hostility in particular (Gruner, 1997). As a corporate sign of control and regulation, "Whassup?!" thus signifies the comic relief of white angst.

It is precisely the affective display that is historically troubling to white consumption and most subject to being made pleasurable and docile by the operations of spectacular consumption (hooks, 1992; Madhubuti, 1990; West, 1994). During this second act, the greeting balloons into a full-blown caricature of itself and, thus, seems to fit within a tradition of clowning and buffoonery (Franklin, 2000). The "Whassup?!" guys play a role that is, in part, constitutive of white ambivalence toward "true" blackness. Entman and Rojecki (2000) argue that 21st century white attitudes find comfort in imagining racial comity because it affirms American ideals regarding our capacity to all get along. But racial comity can easily be turned into racial hostility if whites are confronted with portrayals of race that challenge the presumption of white privilege or articulate the presence of widespread racism (Entman & Rojecki, 2000). Since the presumption of white privilege is tacitly maintained through the promotion of black fragmentation (Lusane, 1994; Allen, 1990), black community functions as a menace to white supremacy. And so, illustrations of black communalism are shaped at the outset so that the anxiety and fear aroused in white viewers can supercharge the consumption of black humor or black sex. Thus, the "aura" of "authenticity" that envelops the familial relations among the men functions like lightning in a bottle—a brilliant danger. White spectators have their fears initially triggered by "authentic" blackness, only to have them strategically vented by this self-parody of black community. Attuned in this way, we can now hear the nervous laughter of the *Advertising Age* staff that "doesn't quite get it but suspects [that is, *hopes*] it is very funny . . ." (Garfield, 2000, p. 4).

This comic display is, therefore, paradoxical. As a "play" in the game, it points to the impossibility of replicating black cultural "authenticity" even as it relies on its presumed aura. It gives the lie to claims of authenticity as the "Whassup?!" guys distort their real life expression—making it "untrue"—for the benefit of the white gaze.

Rather than be "real" for a white audience, the "Whassup?!" guys are asked to play a game that is predicated on hyperreality and hyperbolic black acting. Moreover, since Scott Brooks has described the performance as "exaggerated," this play is understood as such by the "Whassup?!" guys themselves (Heller, 2000, p. 11). But this observation brings up another related insight. If the second act is a self-conscious play during the game of spectacular consumption, the other two acts (the third mirrors the first) can be understood as the "Whassup?!" guys attempt to remain "True." That is, they are representative of how the friends see themselves and a dramatization of their collective understanding of how one makes the "game" work for you. Indeed, Stone's script tells us as much.

In the first and third acts, Stone and Williams are concerned with their collective participation in a spectator ritual. The scenes are centered on the black masculine gaze and cool pose (Majors & Billson, 1992). Stone and Williams testify to the fact that they are not just objects under surveillance here, but rather they are engaged in subjective (subversive?) acts of observation and consumption. Specifically, they are *watching* the game, *having* a Bud." In the opening and closing acts of this commercial, the tagline "true" signifies the shared understanding of how to self-promote and shape-shift for the purposes of "having a Bud," of taking advantage of Budweiser's desire for (and fear of) their blackness and in the process, maximizing their own market value. The second act is a festive and troubling demonstration of just such a shared strategy, framed not by individualism, but communalism. The colorful exchange among the friends displays a joy that can still be seen and heard despite the deformations, contortions, and amplifications.

It is true that spectacular consumption *precedes* even the first act and therefore always already makes demands on the "Whassup?!" guys. From this perspective we can appreciate how previously private enclaves and persons can be colonized and transformed into sources for spectacular consumption. We should not be surprised that these operations convert and multiply "Whassup?!" into a series of commercialized signs that perhaps no longer say anything important concerning black culture but are nearly self-referential, standing for little more than their own market value. But the spectacular consumption of the "Whassup?!" guys brings up yet another concern. White imitation of black life alters the character of social relations among real folks. Not only is the appropriation of black styles profitable, the potential for racial hostility—a function of white ambivalence—is preserved and cultivated by stylish diversions (Kennedy, 2000).

Spectacular consumption functions as a capacitor for such ambivalence, seizing its energies and releasing them in planned microbursts directed at stimulating more consumption. White ambivalence toward blackness is, thus, replicated alongside consumable "blackness." And although this operation nears the character of *simulacra*, we can feel its effects in our everyday real world as black folk are told to "lighten up," or when one's refusal to "play the fool" provokes racial enmity. It may also be the case that "authentic" black affection emerges, however fleetingly, as an expression that is potentially redistributed among a wider circle of friends and communities as "True." But this is a question best left in abeyance until we explore how "real" folks consume these images.

Focus Group Insights: Diverse Perspectives on Similar Themes

Thus far, we have explicated how spectacular consumption provides insight into the commodification of the "Whassup?!" guys and have provided a textual analysis of the original commercial. Throughout these discussions, we have made reference to the various ways that the marketing potential of the commercials seems to be a function of the perceived "authenticity" of the "Whassup?!" guys. Consequently, we facilitated a number of focus group discussions to gain insight into one general research question: How are "Whassup?!" ads consumed by different viewers? As can be seen in the following section, accessing divergent perspectives in this manner proved invaluable in strengthening our current critical analysis. In order to gain insight into the various ways that television consumers interacted with the "Whassup?!" commercials, we conducted a series of discussions with undergraduate students at a large, Midwestern university.

Specifically, we drew from one 300-level communication class whose content focused on issues related to race and culture. A total of thirty-seven people were involved in this aspect of our analysis. These persons were diverse in terms of their race-ethnicity (17 African Americans, 11 European Americans, 3 Asian Americans, 3 Hispanic/Latino Americans, and 3 individuals who identify as biracial) and gender (24 women and 13 men). Thirty six of the participants were 18 to 24 years of age.

Our focus group discussions included several steps. First, all thirty-seven participants were shown four of the "Whassup?!" commercials featuring the "Whassup?!" guys in different settings. Participants were then asked to write down their responses to a number of questions, including: what was your initial reaction to these commercials (either now or at an earlier time)?; is the reaction the same for all of the commercials, or do they vary from commercial to commercial?; and who do you think the target audience is for these commercials? Then, two spoofs of the "Whassup?!" commercials featuring "Superheroes" and "Grandmas" were shown. These spoofs were not produced by DDBO or Anheuser-Busch, but we thought they might help give depth to our understanding of audience responses to the advertisements. Again, participants were asked to record how, if at all, their perceptions of these commercials were different than the previous ones viewed. In addition, each person was asked to express their opinions about the apparent marketing strategy behind the series of "Whassup?!" ads.

During a subsequent session, the thirty-seven participants were randomly divided into seven small (5–6 person) groups to discuss their reactions to the commercials. Following these brief 10-minute discussions, a larger 30-minute discussion of all participants was facilitated in order to clarify and extend those insights that were included in the written responses. This larger discussion was unstructured in that participants were simply asked to share some of their perceptions of the commercials as discussed via their individual comments and the small group discussions.

Our thematic analysis of the written and oral comments provided by the focus group participants was guided by three criteria outlined by Owens (1984): repetition, recurrence, and forcefulness. As such, the texts generated via the written comments and larger group discussions were reviewed for preliminary themes. Subsequently, eight preliminary themes were reviewed until a smaller number of core themes emerged that we believe captured the essence of the participants' comments. Through this interpretative reduction process, three specific thematic insights that enhance our critical analysis of the "Whassup?!" guys were identified. Each of these is explicated in the remaining sections of this essay.

Relating to the "Experience"

Almost without exception, the participants found the "Whassup?!" ads to be highly creative, unique, and entertaining. In fact, bursts of audible laughter filled the room while the commercials were being shown. Initial written descriptions, as well as subsequent group discussions, displayed a general consensus that the "Whassup?!" guys had "hit a comedic nerve" with mass audiences. However, a deeper level of scrutiny in terms of why participants felt the ads were so funny reveals some interesting patterns.

Analysis of written responses provides insight into differences between non-African Americans and African Americans. Nearly every African American woman and man perceived the "Whassup?!" commercials as targeted at young African Americans in general, and young African American males in particular. Several commented specifically on the use of an all-black cast, while others pointed to the ways in which the ads featured "the common language of black men." Without question, African Americans responded favorably to the ads because of the "authentic" ways in which black culture was represented. The black students tended to conclude that most non-African Americans would not relate to the content of the commercials. One African American explained in no uncertain terms that:

> This ad, in particular, is [targeted] at young Black men. The reason [why I say this] is because of the language and the style of the commercial . . . these are not things that a man 35+ would do or phrases that a man 35+ would use. They are things that young Black men do.

What the African American participants did not anticipate, however, were the powerful ways in which non-African Americans also identified with the depiction of the "Whassup?!" guys. For example, only one European American commented on how the ad targeted the African American community:

> I've never seen these commercials before, but I've heard so much about them. I think that Budweiser is trying to appeal to the African American community because it has been known in the past as sort of a "hill-billy, ol' boy brew." These commercials bring BUD out of being just a "white man's beer" . . . Trust me, I used to cocktail waitress—it is!!!

It is significant that out of all of the European, Latino, and Asian American participants she was the *only* non-African American to perceive the "Whassup?!" guys as targeting the black community. Contrary to African American perceptions, nearly all other racial/ethnic group members perceived the ad as representative of male life experiences. Reflecting on our earlier discussion of how "authenticity" functions, it became apparent that non-African American men related to the images of "guys"—not necessarily "Whassup?!" guys—doing "guy things." One European American man shared that:

> [I] had seen the commercials before and found [them] highly comical because I could relate to the experience of having a beer and watching a game with my friends acting silly . . . The target audience of the commercial is clearly men in their early-late twenties.

By and large, non-African Americans focused on the "universal" nature of male bonding and sports. One Asian American male agreed that the target audience was "anyone from the ages of 18–30 who drink beer," but added, "yes, the 'what's up' guys are all black, but I don't think that blacks are the target audience because everyone loves those commercials." European American women were also quick to point out the lack of cultural specificity in the behaviors of the "Whassup?!" guys. The quotation below is representative of several similar comments.

> I had never seen those actual commercials but I had heard about them . . . all of my male friends acted like the men on the video a lot last year. My initial reaction is that it was just a bunch of burly men (weird) . . . Guys always have an inside joke or way of showing off to their buddies.

The contrast between how different racial/ethnic groups perceived the target audience of the "Whassup?!" commercials is of particular significance given Anheuser-Busch's explicit objective to create a campaign that would be appealing to predominately white audiences. How, then, was it also able to sell the "Whassup?!" guys to African American audiences who yearned for media displays of black culture? The basic principles related to spectacular consumption provide a schemata that makes available answers to this lingering question. As explicated in the next thematic section, we argue that marketing strategists are able, ironically, to negotiate such tensions by emphasizing the cultural "authenticity" of the "Whassup?!" guys.

(Re-)Emphasizing Cultural Authenticity

As stated earlier, responses to the initial "Whassup?!" ads were overwhelmingly positive. However, when participants were asked to comment on their perceptions of two spoof commercials, their reactions were quite varied and significantly different than those based on the initial ads. Specifically, many commented on how the ads "didn't make sense." "I really don't know what the intent of these two commercials were," shared one biracial woman. Some, but certainly not all, of the African American participants felt that the change in actors reflected a different target audience. This makes sense given that the general consensus was that the initial ads that featured the "Whassup?!" guys were targeted at young African Americans. Many didn't know how to perceive the spoof ads: "These characters don't fit the voices. The voices are very African American; the faces on the screen are very WHITE." However, one African American articulated how the ad did, in fact, continue to target African Americans. She concluded that these two ads "were a cool, creative way to target blacks . . . I still believe the intent is to attract African Americans by subliminally making fun of Whites."

In comparison, non-African Americans saw these ads as extensions of earlier "Whassup?!" commercials. One European American woman described the spoofs as:

> . . . really funny! They are different because you've got these "white" people trying to be "black" . . . That's the perception I got anyway. I also think that that's why they were so funny—because it was outrageous in that you never should see that.

Another European American woman extended these comments and implicated associations of stereotypical behaviors and subsequently connected them to the perceived target audience:

> They are funny because they took two groups: Superhero cartoons and elderly white women who don't normally talk LOUD and made them do the same dialogue. Neither of the two groups were the target audience: The target audience remained the same.

As had the African American participants, several of these European Americans understood how these parodies extended earlier attempts to make use of the "authentic" to attract a large audience. Interestingly, it appears that non-African Americans continue to identify with the "universal" appeal of the "Whassup?!" guys in direct relation to seeing how absurd it could be when "uncool" people try to imitate them. In other words, "we" (those of us who are "cool") can continue to relate—or even strengthen our relationship—to the "Whassup?!" guys because of the perceived distinction between "us" and those who are spoofed.

Several key ideas emerge as central to the way the spoofs reinforce the original advertisements. First, from the perspective of non-African Americans, the spoof ads appear to strengthen the "universal" appeal of the "Whassup?!" guys; this is accomplished by featuring the absurdity of attempting to reproduce its "aura" with different faces and in different settings. Second, for African American viewers the spoof ads strengthen the "authentic" nature of the "Whassup?!" guys for a very similar reason: the ads hint that white (unhip) characters can't "really" imitate black culture. As described earlier, one of the basic tenets associated with spectacular consumption is that the pleasure of consuming otherness is advanced by the Other's uniqueness. Perhaps these spoof ads help to re-establish the unique nature of the "Whassup?!" guys by parodying attempts to serialize the authentic. This point is best captured in another spoof ad that was never aired but is available at the *adcritic.com* website where it frequently is listed in the top ten. This commercial features a group of young European American friends who attempt to use "Whassup?!" as a means to display their "coolness" at a summer gathering. Despite their continued efforts, though, they are never able to capture correctly the authentic greeting. Again, this spoof enhances the "Whassup?!" aura by illustrating that the coolness associated with it, and with black culture generally, is virtually impossible to replicate. In this way, the commodity value of the image that is already "owned" increases by virtue of its "uniqueness."

An Unconsciousness of Commodification

The final questions posed to participants in our focus groups related to their perceptions of the marketing strategies that manufactured the "Whassup?!" ads. Most participants felt that the advertising campaign was highly effective, with African Americans focusing on the inclusion of the black community, and non-African Americans applauding the use of "humor [that could be] enjoyed across racial barriers." Across racial and ethnic groups, however, several participants questioned what the "Whassup?!" ads had to do with selling beer. One African American woman commented that "the strategy was humorous and attention-getting, but the product could have been emphasized more." What seemed to be just below the level of consciousness for some participants was the idea that the "product" was not the beer, but the "authenticity" of the "Whassup?!" guys. This critical understanding, however, was not lost on all participants. Several participants discussed the increased exposure that the company got in light of the commercials' popularity and effective use of humor in associating their product with the "in-crowd." In fact, one Korean/American woman applauded Anheuser-Busch's marketing creativity:

> Budweiser knows how to capture their audience's attention by using humor. I think [the ads] are effective because they're catchy and people are always talking about their commercials. As to how much beer they sell, I'm not sure because I don't drink; however, I think because people think the commercials are cool, they might think their beer is too.

While some participants made this connection, only one person talked specifically about the historical pattern of the dominant culture co-opting black cultural artifacts for profit. Consequently, comments that focused on the "Whassup?!" guys (e.g., "they are hilarious!!!") were few; more significant attention was paid to the "genius" of Anheuser-Busch. In this regard, it was the corporate marketing team—and not the "Whassup?!" guys—that was given most of the "credit" for the success of the ads. One African American woman, for instance, praised "the folks at BUD [for] using an every-day phrase for some and turn[ing] it into a million dollar commercial." Comments lauding Anheuser-Busch's ability to use humor to market their products were consistent. Interestingly, the "Whassup?!" guys—despite the central role that Charles Stone played in the development of the ads—were seen as pawns strategically deployed by corporate culture. Consistent with the operations of spectacular consumption, the focus groups believed that the "authenticity" of the "Whassup?!" guys was at once "real" and manufactured for mass consumption.

One final point of critical analysis crystallizes the powerful ways in which the "Whassup?!" guys were commodified by mass mediated marketing. Within his written responses, one biracial man (Filipino/European American) described his reaction to the ads in relation to a previous Budweiser advertising campaign:

> I've seen these ["Whassup?!"] ads before. My initial response to these was that they were pretty funny. When I see them now, I still can't help but laugh. These ad wizards at Budweiser out-did themselves this time. I love these guys—a lot better than the frogs. The marketing strategy is GENIUS. I am a Bud man. It is the King of Beers. They've won my vote.

This comment is especially didactic as it unwittingly brings to the surface the paradox of spectacular consumption. The commodification of the "Whassup?!" guys is perceived from the perspective of other Budweiser fabrications. The realization that, philosophically speaking, a fabrication cannot be "authentic" in the way that the focus groups articulated is discouraged by the simultaneous replication of the "aura." This contradiction can be apparently maintained, in part, because "real life" social relations are themselves always already mediated in the spectacle.

Conclusions

Throughout this essay we have argued that the "Whassup?!" ad campaign is constitutive of an ambivalence in the white imagination regarding "authentic" blackness. Idealism concerning racial comity interpenetrates racial pessimism in such a way as to produce discursive tensions within cultural artifacts that seek to sell "race." In the "Whassup?!" campaign, this stress is actualized within the discursive contours of "authenticity." In terms of denoting "universalism" or "sameness," the ad campaign is perceived as delivering a male-bonding ritual with which "everyman" can identify. Conversely, "authenticity" also implicates distinctive black style and culture. The "True" ads explicitly reference a notion of realism that holds in tension differences associated with how spectators see the "authentic" as either colorless or colorful. Moreover, we contend that the operations of spectacular consumption replicate and amplify this ambivalence because the anxiety inscribed in it enhances the market value of black imagery.

Our focus group analysis demonstrates how white consumers overtly recognize the "universal" character of the "authentic" masculine ritual while tacitly appreciating the ads as (black) ultra-hip. We posit that this cultural dissociation is a sign of how the white imagination appropriates blackness as commodity while denying such appropriation. Blackness here intensifies the pleasure of "eating the other" (hooks 1992, p. 21) and brokers an escalation of the commodity value of the "Whassup?!" guys. Such "pleasure" is a symptom of ambivalence. But also white ambivalence toward "true" blackness forces a *suppression* of the character of such consumption precisely because its conscious recognition would turn the white gaze upon itself. That is, white consumers would be compelled to interrogate the reasons why consuming Otherness as a historically cultivated taste is predicated on white supremacy. Since this sort of public deliberation may reduce the angst white people experience when faced with blackness, spectacular consumption seeks to prefabricate the conditions in which such denial is an effect of public consumption itself. This is why the replication of white ambivalence toward blackness becomes a central facet of these consumptive processes. Endorsing the "universality" of "colorless" male bonding pays tribute to American idealism about race relations but it cannot (and is not meant to) displace the significance of distinctive black culture. In the white imagination, such a tribute is replicated just as carefully and consumed just as voraciously as the "authentic" blackness that it obscures.

Our textual analysis of the original "Whassup?!" commercial demonstrated how the ad is made up of competing consumptive impulses. Stone's script is itself a strategic response to the operations through which he and his friends were being commodified. The ad vectors in two directions at once; it satiates and mollifies white desires and fears regarding "real" black brotherhood by turning the greeting into a cartoon version of itself. It also gestures toward a site of cultural integrity beyond the shouts and shrills of the corporate sign of "Whassup?!" In the first and third acts of the commerical, Stone and Williams "have a Bud" and observe how the spectacular game is played. Their subjective and consumptive acts help reshape the conditions of their commodification because they serve as a narrative frame for the second hyperbolic scene. Understood from this perspective, the ad begins and ends with a commentary on how to "keep it real" while playing the "game."

The game continues. While there have been several interesting "Whassup?!" spin offs, the "True" ad that appeared during the 2001 Superbowl critically dramatizes the problem that spectacular consumption poses for critics who seek to conceive of "reality" and "power" in conventional terms. As a replica of the original commercial, the ad reintroduces us to notions of cultural authenticity and surveillance. This ad, however, features two white guys and their brown friend and represents the inversion of cultural cool.

The phone rings. "Brett," looking rather stiff while watching TV, answers the phone:

> "This is Brett."
>
> "What are you doing?"
>
> "What are *you* doing?"
>
> "Just watching the market recap, drinking an import."
>
> "That is correct. That is correct!"

A knowing audience is immediately clued into the fact that this conversation is "lame" and even strange compared to the familiar rhythm of the "Whassup?!" guys. Indeed, the fact that these new friends are drinking imported beer signifies a kind of *foreignness*. "Chad" (who is brown) enters carrying a tennis racket and exclaims "what are you doing?" and "Brett" directs him to "pick up the cordless." The friends exchange their cumbersome greeting with comedic gusto. Despite the fact that the scene is silly, we would like to note some serious implications. Viewers who are knowledgeable about "Whassup?!" cool are encouraged to ridicule the "What are you doing" guys. Although signifying economic privilege, they are marginalized as un-hip (and, perhaps, un-American) "wannabes." Moreover, the "What are you doing" guys seem unaware that their cultural performance is out of fashion. At the end of the commercial, Fred Thomas and Paul Williams are shown having a Bud and watching the "wannabes" on TV. Here, the ad characterizes the black male gaze as central and authoritative as the "Whassup?!" guys look at each other with facial expressions that say, "these guys can't be for real"; their capacity to sit in judgment over the "wannabes" places "authentic" black culture in a position of cultural commodity privilege. But popular culture domin-ance is not the only significant issue. While the "Whassup?!" guys are watching their imitators fail, the "What are you doing" guys are keeping an eye on fluctuations in the value of consumer culture in general; they are "watching the market recap."

Such competing visions of "authenticity" and power are provocative; in spectacular consumption, "real" cultural value is produced through both perspectives. An audience familiar with the "Whassup?!" guys can share in their repose even as it identifies with the "What are you doing" guys' focus on capital investment. Critics are encouraged to see that the ad, in part, represents the notion that spectacular consumption itself is cool. After all, as arbiters of good taste the "Whassup?!" guys are transfixed by the other guys' spectacle. Thus, their consumptive habits stand in for ours and culminate in increased market value for "authentic" black culture and any of its manufactured opposites. This process is also paradoxical because it relies on the notion of cultural essentialism (like "true" blackness) even as cultural boundaries become more permeable and lived experi-ences become more malleable.

But this dialectic brings up the character of white American ambivalence once again. The "Whassup?!" guys' consumptive gaze is energized by representing the "What are you doing" guys as "inauthentic" and "foreign" laughing stocks. In so doing, however, the ad constitutes "authentic" blackness as authoritative and, thus, perpetuates the threat. So, not only does the ad's humor help to alleviate such angst, but the ad seems to mediate this danger by placing the "What are you doing" guys' economic power over against the cultural allure of the "Whassup?!" guys. The discursive space of white capitalist power (despite the fact that "Chad" is brown) is tacitly maintained by the reproduction of this ambivalence.

The schemata of spectacular consumption not only allows us to explore how image value is manufactured and magnified, but also to perceive how persons and life worlds are transformed in terms of values generated by their public consumption. Hence, the critic is steered away from an overemphasis on forms of autonomy, individual or cultural; such autonomy is not wholly denied, but symbolic forms are understood as constitutive of substances and of relations that are shaped by the character of public consumption. From this perspective, the culture industry does not dictate forms of consumption; nor does an agent determine her own image; they are both altered by the ways that forms are consumed. The relations among the industry, the life worlds of persons, and cultural forms cannot be adequately understood as characterized by *exchanges* of meaning and value; they are more precisely meaning and value *transfusions*. And so, we contend that the "True" character of the "authentic" in the land of spectacular consumption is neither an ontological given nor a semiotic project. Rather, it is a decentralized and localized achievement based only in part on one's lived experience, now understood as a function of how ways of life are commodified and consumed.

Questions

1   How does the "Whassup?!" campaign mix both familiarity and unfamiliarity?
2   What do the authors argue are the three narrative parts of the original advertisement in the campaign in terms of its construction of African American males?
3   How did Caucasians and People of Color differ in their interpretations of the ads' appeal and construction of meaning?
4   Why did the researchers show parodies of the "Whassup?!" campaign to the focus groups?
5   Are there other ads where portrayals of race seem to be contradictory?

References

Adande, J. A. (2000, January 31). Couch potatoes capture a mood. *Los Angeles Times*, D1.

Allen, R.L. (1990). *Black awakening in capitalist America*. Trenton, NJ: Africa World Press.

Baudrillard, J. (1984). The precession of simulacra. In Wallis, B. (Ed.), *Art after modernism* (pp. 253–281). New York: The Contemporary Art Museum.

Benjamin, W. (1984). The author as producer. In Wallis, B. (Ed.), *Art after modernism* (pp. 297–310). New York: The Contemporary Art Museum.

Best, S. & Kellner, D. (1997). *The postmodern turn*. New York: Guilford Press.

Cassidy, M. & Katula, R. (1995). The black experience in advertising: an interview with Thomas J. Burrell. In Dines, G. & Humez, J.M. (Eds.), *Gender, race, and class in media* (pp. 93–98). Thousand Oaks, Ca.: Sage Publications.

Debord, G. (1983). *Society of the spectacle*. Detroit: Black and Red Press.

Entman, R. & Rojecki, A. (2000). *The black image in the white mind: Media and race in America*. Chicago: University of Chicago Press.

Ewen, S. (1988). *All consuming images: The politics of style in contemporary culture*. New York: Basic Books, Inc.

Farhi, P. (2000, March 14). Whassup? Glad you asked; Budweiser's ads tap into male bonding rituals. *Washington Post*, C1.

Franklin, C. (2000, June 1). Letter to the Editors. *Advertising Age*, 6.

Garfield, B. (2000a, June). Budweiser has all Cannes asking whasssuppppp? *Advertising Age*. Available: www.advertisingage/adreview.com.

Garfield, B. (2000b, January). Superbowl ad standout? Whatever.com. *Advertising Age*. Available: www.advertisingage/adreview.com.

Gruner, C. R. (1997). *The game of humor: A comprehensive theory of why we laugh*. New Brunswick, NJ: Transaction Publishers.

Hall, S. (1995). The whites of their eyes: Racist Ideologies in the media. In Dines, G. & Humez, J.M. (Eds.), *Gender, race, and class in media* (pp. 18–22). Thousand Oaks, Ca.: Sage Publications.

Heller, K. (2000, March 19). "Whassup?" A new career, Budweiser ads turn four black friends into major pop icons. *Houston Chronicle*, 11.

hooks, b. (1992). *Black looks: Race and representation*. Boston: South End Press.

Jhally, S. (1995). Image-based culture: Advertising and popular culture. In Dines, G. & Humez, J.M. (Eds.), *Gender, race, and class in media* (pp. 77–87). Thousand Oaks, Ca.: Sage Publications.

Kennedy, D. (2000). Marketing Goods, marketing images: The Impact of advertising on race. *Arizona State Law Journal, 32*, 615.

Lusane, C. (1994). *African Americans at the crossroads: The restructuring of black leadership and the 1992 elections*. Boston: South End Press.

Madhubuti, H.R. (1990). *Black men: Obsolete, single, dangerous?* Chicago: Third World Press.

Majors, R. (1992). *Cool pose: The dilemmas of black manhood in America*. New York: Lexington Books.

McGuire, J.M. (2000, June 28). Whassupp?! You ask? *St. Louis Post-Dispatch*, E1.

Owen, W. (1984). Interpretive themes in relational communication. *Quarterly Journal of Speech, 70*, 274–287.

Procter, D.E. (1990). The dynamic spectacle: Transforming experience into social forms of community. *Querterly Journal of Speech, 76*, 117–133.

Watts, E.K. (1997). An exploration of spectacular consumption: Gangsta rap as cultural commodity. *Communication Studies, 48*, 42–58.

West, C. (1994). *Race matters*. New York: Vintage Books.

Chapter 17

J. ROBYN GOODMAN

FLABLESS IS FABULOUS

How Latina and Anglo Women Read and
Incorporate the Excessively Thin Body Ideal
into Everyday Experience

SIMILAR TO THE PREVIOUS CHAPTER, this chapter also uses focus
groups to understand about how meaning is generated from commercial culture.
In this case, the gendered body image in media—thinness—is studied. Many scholars
have concluded that males and females are portrayed differently in advertising, with
women especially being subjected to unrealistically thin and sexualized portrayals. This
study asks how young women understand such images. The focus groups were comprised of three groups of female college students: an all-Caucasian group, an
all-Latina group, and a mixed group. Applying Stuart Hall's concepts of preferred,
negotiated and oppositional interpretations of media messages, the author argues that,
on at least some issues, the Latinas in the groups tended to have a more oppositional,
or critical, view of mediated images of thin bodies, and critiqued the thinness ideal as
unhealthy. They discussed their awareness of thinness as a white cultural norm, as
well as their own non-participation in the dominant culture. The Latina participants
also discussed the specific cultural norms in Latino culture, like the role of food, which
again mitigate the influence of desiring thin body types.

Despite this, the chapter also notes that most women interviewed had more of a negotiated relationship to thinness and the commercial media's role in perpetuating that
body image. Participants recognized, for example, that media images of thinness were
highly constructed (such as airbrushing, atypically thin models and the extreme
behaviors needed to be that thin). However, many of the young women interviewed still
admitted that they want to be thin. In fact, many of the participants noted that they
viewed thinness as a source of personal power. With these points, the chapter highlights
the often contradictory effects that commercial media may have upon media audiences
beyond the message of "buy this product."

> I learned about womanhood from fashion magazines, Madison Avenue
> and Hollywood. [Indeed,] magazine articles, television commercials,
> lunchroom conversation, gymnastics coaches and write-ups on models
> had saturated me with diet savvy. Once I decided to lose weight, I quickly
> turned expert. . . . Over the next five years, I devoted my life to losing my
> weight. Society applauded my shrinking. Pound after pound the applause
> continued.[1]

Anorexia, along with other eating disorders, has steadily become more prevalent among
women during the past thirty years.[2] Of the estimated five to ten million suffering from
anorexia, bulimia, or compulsive overeating, 90 percent to 95 percent are women,
especially college women.[3] Recent studies argue that between 5 percent and 20 percent
of all college students suffer from an eating disorder.[4] An additional 12 percent to 33
percent of noneating-disordered women occasionally control their weight through
vomiting, diuretics, and laxatives.[5]

Although combinations of biological, psychological, familial, and sociological factors may precipitate eating disorders,[6] many researchers view sociocultural influences,
particularly the excessively thin body ideal for women, as the major contributor to the
rise in eating disorders.[7] They point to constant media depictions of excessively thin,
female models[8] who weigh 23 percent less than the average woman and fit the established weight criteria for anorexia.[9]

The ubiquity of media images of excessively thin women may be said to create an
environment of disordered-eating messages for women to internalize, providing disordered bodies with which to compare themselves.[10] Previous studies have found relationships between media images of thin women and women's poor body image and
eating disorders.[11] However, the majority of women do not develop such disorders, so
the mediated ideal does not affect all women equally.

Most studies, furthermore, assume women of color are more capable of resisting
dominant standards of beauty than Anglo women.[12] Yet evidence suggests the mediated
ideal does adversely influence some women of color, so it is unclear how women of color
negotiate thinness messages.[13] This study, then, uses focus group interviews of college
women to compare Anglo and Latina participants' readings of the mediated ideal.

In examining women's negotiations of the mediated ideal, this study draws on
literature that stresses audience interpretations of media texts.[14] The study also assumes
that media representations influence individuals' relationships to the dominant class,
cultivating ideas, norms, and values to form a common worldview serving the dominant
class' needs.[15] Images of excessively thin women in the media presumably curb wom-
en's power—by making them obsess over their weight and weakening their minds and
bodies through self-imposed semi-starvation.[16]

Because the media are the main information source about social processes and
images and self-presentation, women are likely to attend to and use media images as
guides for their attitudes and behaviors.[17] These thin images, then, supposedly define
women as the dominant class' subjects by offering thinness as the ideal state of women's
bodies. Any other body shape becomes aberrant. Women who attain excessive thinness
gain social and economic rewards, which reinforces the desire to be thin.[18] However,
individuals read media texts on the basis of socially formed conventions and codes and
different cultural experiences, so their readings do not always correspond to the belief
that excessive thinness is natural and desirable.[19]

Literature Review

Past research demonstrates that the female body in media portrayals has become increasingly thin during the past several decades.[20] For example, Garner et al. and Wiseman et al. studied the height, weight, and body measurements of *Playboy* center-folds from 1958–1978 and 1979–1988, respectively.[21] Both found the yearly mean weight of *Playboy* centerfolds was significantly less than population means. The media also encourage a thinner standard for women than for men.[22] Silverstein et al. found 69 percent of female characters on television were thin compared to 17.5 percent of men.[23] Andersen and DiDomenico found ten times as many dieting messages in ads and articles from popular women's magazines as popular men's magazines.[24]

Effects research shows significant relationships between exposure to thin, female images in magazines and television and anorexia, bulimia, drive for thinness, body dissatisfaction, lowered self-esteem, anger, depression, hostility, body anxiety, shame, and endorsement of the thin ideal.[25] Anglos seem to have slightly greater body dissatisfaction than Latinas but equal levels of disordered eating and dieting.[26] However, several studies have found Latina acculturation level driving the variables;[27] Chamorro and Flores-Ortiz found second-generation Mexican-Americans had the highest levels of disordered eating and acculturation among first- through fifth-generation Mexican-Americans.[28]

Several researchers have found girls and women idealize thin bodies, cite media models as influences on body satisfaction, and aspire to emulate the ideal.[29] Yet these same women criticize the ideal as unattainable and call for more diverse bodies in the media.[30] The present study addresses this seeming contradiction by illuminating how women negotiate these messages.

Method

Study's Background

Focus groups were conducted during a one-week period in March 2000. The author served as the moderator; two Anglos and one Filipino assisted. Latina and Anglo women who were 18- to 24-year-old U.S. residents and attended a large, southwestern university were recruited from a predominantly freshman dormitory; an all women's dormitory; an advertising research class; advertisements posted in the main library; and a Latina sorority. They received dinner and $10 for participating.

Consistent with the goal of theoretical saturation, focus groups were added until little new information was obtained.[31] Three groups were needed (a total of 24 partici-pants), which is typical for theoretical saturation.[32] One consisted of 6 white females who were mostly upper middle class. A second comprised 12 members of a Latina sorority (1 lower, 4 lower-middle, 5 middle, 2 upper-middle class). The third group included 1 lower-middle-class Latina, 3 middle-class Anglos, 1 upper-middle-class Latina, 1 upper-middle-class Anglo.

All 24 women said mass media were an integral part of their daily routines. The women watched approximately two hours of television daily. Both Latina and Anglo women watched *Friends, Oprah,* and *Dawson's Creek.* The Anglo women watched the *Simpsons* and *Felicity* more often, whereas the Latina women watched more daytime soap operas and MTV. The majority also read at least one magazine a week, particularly *Cosmopolitan* and *Glamour*. *Latina* and *Hispanic* magazines were popular with Latina women, too.

Constant Comparison

Using Glaser and Strauss' four-stage constant comparison method,[33] each statement was coded into as many categories as possible.[34] Categories and properties were integrated by comparing statements with category attributes[35] in order to integrate the various categories into a more unified whole and "make some related theoretical sense of each comparison."[36] Then the list of categories was reduced, based on the theory's boundaries and theoretical saturation.[37]

Analysis

Ideal Femininity in Magazines

The women described the current ideal body shape in fashion magazines as "thin and tall" (Anglo), "big breasts" (Anglo), "anorexic" (Latina), and "skinny with muscles like Jennifer Aniston" (Latina). All the women, regardless of race, perceived the ideal as extremely thin, even anorexic. A few noted the ideal as having toned yet skinny muscles and/or large breasts. Many denied that a thin woman could naturally have large breasts.

Perceptions of the Thinness Ideal

Anglo women noted the schism between perceptions and actions regarding the ideal. One said that "everyone says it's gross, but they still strive toward it." Another said that "everybody condemns it, but at the same time wants to be skinnier and feel that they have to be perfect." Their perceptions indicate they learned the rules for femininity from the media and society,[38] but their perceptions were negotiated. They perceived excessive thinness as "sick looking," but they still desired it.

In contrast, few of the Latina women referred to this split between what they perceived and how they acted. They tended to criticize the ideal as lacking feminine curves and as "unhealthy." One Latina said that models were "sick looking" and looked "like they haven't eaten." Another said they did not "look feminine because they don't have breasts and stuff." Their more oppositional reading of excessive thinness in mainstream media apparently had two sources. First, they realized the thin ideal was a manifestation of the dominant group, of which they would never be a part. For example, one Latina said: "I think that people who belong to a non-Anglo ethnic group have less stress on them than other women because they know they won't be the ideal. Regardless of their weight, they don't have that skin color. . . . Regardless of weight, their face is angular, so they don't revolve around the ideal."

Second, the Latina women said they grew up around bigger women, food played a central role in their culture, and Hispanic men tended to like bigger women. Their cultural ideal was further reflected in Hispanic magazines. One woman noted that the women were "thicker" in *Latina* compared to *Cosmo*. Another Latina said: "I grew up reading Spanish magazines in Mexico and a lot of people [in the media] are thin but have hips or they're not as muscular. They have a big behind like Jennifer Lopez used to have. That's the average or the ideal in those magazines."

Yet the Latina women were not impervious to the mediated ideal. A few admitted that they or their friends wanted to emulate the ideal. For example, one Latina said she wanted to be "really skinny like a girl in *Cosmo*. I think it's horrible and so degrading to women, but honestly, I just want to look like that." Their dual beliefs in the dominant cultural messages of excessive thinness and the Hispanic cultural messages of a full-figured ideal show their need to negotiate between the two cultures in their everyday lives.

Fit Not Flabby

Despite different perceptions on the thinness ideal in the media, Latina and Anglo women emphasized that the ideal body had nothing to do with weight or size. A Latina noted the ideal body was toned "so you can wear something tight and not have a roll line." An Anglo said: "I don't want gravity doing anything. I would be perfectly happy gaining five pounds if it were all muscle" and "my thighs don't jiggle." All groups discussed the desire to develop muscles rather than lose weight. Their discourse revealed that "toning" was an acceptable action, but not weight loss. They also described their ideal as a "normal" body, which was "shapely," not excessively thin. Yet their idea of "shapely" was slender, albeit muscular. A Latina said she liked Tyra Banks, because she's "more voluptuous" than most models. An Anglo suggested that the ideal should be a little more realistic, like Cindy Crawford as opposed to people like Ally McBeal.

According to Bordo,[39] the media disseminate two ideals—the excessively thin ideal and the flab-free, muscular ideal. Although the two seem different, they "are united in battle against a common enemy: the soft, the loose, unsolid, excess flesh. It is perfectly permissible in our culture to have substantial weight and bulk—so long as it is tightly managed."[40] Both the Latina and Anglo women, then, have a dominant reading of mediated female images. They desire the flab-free, tightly controlled body they see in the media.[41]

This desire for and belief in the tightly controlled body also emerged in the Anglo women's conversation about flab in the media. One Anglo woman noted that in the James Bond movie *You Only Live Twice*, the "girl had a somewhat flabby tummy." However, she questioned her own criticism of the character because "she looked really good" and was "*a Bond* girl." Asked why she initially thought the "Bond girl" was flabby, she said, "Because now you wouldn't see a Bond girl with an ounce of fat on her." Other Anglo women expressed similar ambiguity. These women saw the flab-free ideal as being a media creation yet still found it desirable, normal, and ideal.

> ANGLO: Every once in a while you'll see where they forgot to retouch an area, or you'll see in a magazine a girl with a fat roll or something. And you're like gross, and then you think about it and are like that's a totally normal girl.

Negotiating Media's Reality

All the women criticized the thin mediated ideal because of the models' sacrifices to attain it and the lack of realism in the models' media images. The women shared stories they had heard about the models' sacrifices for achieving the ideal body, such as laxative abuse and substance abuse. A Latina said she heard four models will share one hamburger.

Furthermore, the women continually reiterated that media models were unrealistic. An Anglo said: "Even in the most average of people, even the most athletic or attractive never fit that [media] ideal." A Latina said the unrealistic, unattainable ideal meant "we all have to have perfect breasts and a perfect butt." Their views of these unrealistic mediated ideals were rooted in their awareness of media techniques used to create feminine perfection such as airbrushing, removing inches and loose skin, and bodily enhancement. They recalled specific cases of photo manipulation, for example, a story on *E!* about a female model whose ankle was drastically thinned in a Tommy Hilfiger ad. Recalling an *Oprah* show discussion of a 17-year-old cover model, airbrushed to look perfect, a Latina called airbrushing a 17-year-old girl "ridiculous."

The discourses on the models' sacrifices for the ideal and the ideal's lack of realism helped establish the differences between themselves (reality) and the ideal (fantasy) and why the media ideal is unattainable for a normal, "real" woman. Their interpretation of these images was a way to resist the belief that any woman can achieve ideal thinness if she practices self-control.[42]

According to Freedman, female beauty in the media "is packaged and peddled as an illusion that anyone can cultivate."[43] Indeed, some women's beliefs conformed to the dominant ideology's emphasis on the egalitarian nature of thinness[44]—all women can be beautiful because thinness is the only requirement.[45] A few saw thinness as attainable. For example, an Anglo said that while some beauty trends were "off-the-wall," thinness is attainable: "You might not be thin right now but give me two months and I can look like the models, too."

These contradictions in many women's readings of ideal female bodies in the media—unrealistic yet attainable—can be explained within the context of the post-modern world. According to Bordo,[46] women know that the images are artificial: "But, in the era of the 'hyperreal' (as Baudrillard calls it), such 'knowledge' is faded and frayed . . . unable to cast a shadow of doubt over the dazzling, compelling, authoritative images themselves."[47] So even if women know these images are contrived, many will still pursue the illusory reality.

Media Effects on Body Image

Regardless of their inconsistent readings of thinness messages in the media, most said the mediated ideal negatively affected their and their friends' body image.

> LATINA: [The constant portrayal of thin media models] kind of backfires because there are super skinny girls that look at the pictures and think they're still fat. It's ridiculous. You're below average to begin with. They think they're fat compared to a 16-year-old.

> LATINA: They [media models] influenced me a lot. Like, I was very much

why can't I look like that. A lot of my friends had eating disorders. It was
like a trend.

Because the mediated ideal did prompt some of these women and their friends to
lose weight, the mediated ideal was activated through what Stacey[48] calls identificatory
practices. Identificatory practices are based on resemblance, in which the viewer recognizes points of similarity between herself and an image, and often transforms herself to
become the image.[49] In others, the mediated ideal produced a self-critical gaze and a
deep sense of body dissatisfaction.

Many Anglo women and a few Latina women felt that the mediated ideal affected
them daily, given that they frequently thought about and cried over their bodies.

> ANGLO: It doesn't run my life, but I do honestly think about my weight
> a lot. Like one day I'll eat a lot and I'll feel like I can't do that and go
> work out. I guess when you're a naturally skinny person it is hard to
> understand it.

> ANGLO: I think about it a lot more than I'd like to admit. I would love to
> be that [thin], but I don't know if I don't have the will power or if I'm just
> [voice trails off]. Some days I would love to have that body, and some days
> I'm just perfectly happy.

Such persistent thoughts of their bodies reflect how the thinness ideology not
only teaches women "the standards currently worshipped as ideal" but to equate "self-
worth with appearance."[50] A theme underlying many of the women's statements is
diminished self-worth when they cannot achieve the ideal ("I never get that perfect
body") or act in ways that thwart the ideal ("eating a lot"). Second, these statements
reflect the women's shame and confusion when they do not fit the ideal.[51] One
woman felt compelled to exercise and to deny herself pleasure to alleviate the shame
of eating.

Media as a Socializing Agent

As agents of socialization, media influence women.[52] The media contribute to learning
and adoption of norms and behavioral expectations by showing symbolic rewards and
punishments for particular attitudes and behaviors.[53] Because people desire social
rewards, they integrate the norms and behaviors that bring the greatest rewards.
Because the media consistently depict thin women receiving social rewards such as
acceptance, love, and success,[54] women are likely to strive for thinness.

The women clearly recognized this socializing process. One Anglo woman said
women are "really impressionable when we're younger." She added: "Now we don't
think about it because those impressions are already in us. Maybe we don't look at each
of the models and consciously think, oh, I want to be like her, but maybe that is what we
actually do." Another Anglo described women as conditioned by media to want to be
thin; if more "plus-size" models were in the media, she said, "we'd get accustomed to
seeing them."

These women's recognition of their socialization into the thinness ideology denies
the media's (or any other public institution's) unilateral ability to produce a false

consciousness in the public. However, much of the Anglo women's conversations revealed that they have incorporated the thinness ideology into their everyday views of life and were not conscious of this incorporation. One Anglo woman described seeing a "really big girl" running full speed at the gym. She added: "The back of her legs were like all cellulite. I couldn't help myself in saying I wonder if she just started working out or I wonder why she's so big if she's running like that."

Even though Anglo women did not recognize or denied cultural and media socialization, most of the women saw some degree of agency in dealing with media's potentially harmful effects.

> LATINA: It's a lot of society, too, because our society seems to create
> women as beauty objects. Granted the media influence people, but you
> have your own ideas.

Most denied that people must "buy into" thinness as ideal. They were able to oppose the dominant readings of thinness in media and possibly create a divergent view. Unfortunately for many of the women, the lure of the "toned" ideal and society's positive view of a thin, taut body overpowered their agency.

Pleasure Not Necessarily Pain

Despite the fact that the women saw the mediated ideal producing negative influences, they found pleasure and escape in viewing the glamorous images. An Anglo said she reads magazines because "it's escape" and "these people are glamorous." A Latina said, "If you want to watch TV or look at magazines, you don't want to look at everybody else. You want to look at the more glamorous, unrealistic, a different portrayal than you see everyday."

Both groups of women are describing what Stacey calls identificatory fantasy.[55] Identificatory fantasies establish excessively thin media models as the "other," and the viewers gain pleasure in objectifying the "other."[56] Differentiating between themselves and the media model, these women derive pleasure from the model's glamour and unattainability, their temporary access to the model's world, and from their objectification of the model.[57]

The Privileged Body is the Media's Ideal

Latina and Anglo women were aware of the judgments and associations people make based on body size, even for children. They said people accord thin women positive social characteristics and overweight women negative social characteristics. A Latina put the contrast starkly: "Obesity is seen as lethargic. Skinny girls are seen as they can get-the-job-done kind of mentality. They're both just stereotypes."

Moreover, the women said overweight females were treated as social outcasts for their nonconformance to the ideal. One Anglo said of her obese, 9-year-old niece: "It is a social factor because nobody wants to be with the little, fat girl. . . . Her life is that much harder because everybody judges her on her weight." Another Anglo said that, as someone who had been overweight by forty to fifty pounds, she realized the prejudice against heavy people: "You look at a[n overweight] girl and automatically think she's lazy."

The women's discourses about their and their family's battles with weight and society's images of them support the contention that beauty—and thus thinness—is rewarded in women.[58] Such weight-based judgments in this culture are often based on American values of self-help, self-denial, and self-control.[59] Because fat violates self-control and self-denial, society may blame and shun the individual.[60] Society often assumes overweight individuals are lazy because they cannot control their appetite.[61] On the other hand, having the toned, thin body connotes that one cares for oneself and has the "correct" attitude in regards to self-control and self-denial.[62] Thus, those with the "correct" attitude receive favorable judgments and are assumed to be successful, competent, and in control.[63]

Thinness and Attention

Latina and Anglo women understood that people pay attention to thin women.

> LATINA: They [thin women] get more positive attention. It's horrible and sad, but the media created that kind of mentality for some people. You would get more positive attention with job interviews, waitressing, and stuff.

> ANGLO: What's celebrity, who's photographed, what's something impressive is a beautiful woman and not a talented woman or an ambitious woman. It's a beautiful woman, period. And if that's what you're aspiring to be and you look at who is rewarded, that is what is rewarded, so that's what we strive to be.

Such comments suggest that these women realize the importance of beauty in U.S. culture. The beautiful (thin) woman receives positive attention. The Anglo woman's comment reveals her knowledge that society values women for their looks, not their deeds, and that beauty is her most highly valued commodity.[64] As she states, many women strive to be thin and beautiful so they can receive social rewards. Thus, many of these women are enculturated into the dominant ideology but not as cultural dupes. They are aware of why they are following the ideology but see no other choice if they want to receive social rewards.

Career and the Thin Body

Every woman in this study was acutely aware that thinness was a route to economic success.[65] For example, an Anglo said: "[Some of my friends saw] their moms were in the work-place needing to be thin to get the promotion and needing to be thin to go to that interview." The media, they said, reinforced beliefs that women need slender bodies to get good jobs and attain economic success. A Latina discussed a *20/20* segment in which two different women—one thin and one obese—applied for a job. Despite equivalent credentials, the interviewer immediately favored the thinner woman.

Attracting Men

Although neither Latina nor Anglo women listed ability to attract men as an advantage of thinness, many agreed that men are attracted to thin women. A Latina said men "will not talk to you if you are not thin." The women attributed men's desire for a thin woman to media socialization. As one Latina explained, "Just like we want to be thin because of the magazines, men get caught up in the ideal, too. If they don't go for it, there must be something wrong with them." Their comments underscore their sense that media help condition the male gaze to find female thinness attractive by depicting thin women in a positive manner.[66] The media also help condition men to view "possessing" the mediated ideal as a designation of social status.[67]

In addition, all agreed the mediated ideal created false expectations in men, with one Anglo saying that some men she knows "have this poster of these really skinny, pretty girls in their room," but deny her claim that the image is touched up and believe "no, it's real." Their anecdotes also reflect a belief in consumer societies that the right products lead to self-transformation.[68] One Latina who had worked at Victoria's Secret recalled men coming in with the catalogue saying, "I want my wife to wear that." "It's like they have the idea that their wife is going to magically turn into a double-D," she said.

Power and Control

Finally, thinness was said to provide women, particularly the Anglo women, a sense of power and control. These women felt empowered by their mastery over their bodies and by people's response to their mastery. As one Anglo stated, "You can tell when you look good and when you don't by how people respond to you." Another Anglo said, "Your body is your first impression. It's like your power tool. If you walk into a room and people stare at you, it gives you a sense of power, a sense of control that you get when you're like, look I've done this to myself or I look this good. It's a really addicting feeling."

The thinness ideology in the media employs control and mastery as common themes.[69] These women recognized that the thin body connotes power, will, and mastery, which the American culture values.[70] Hence, they feel power and control in achieving thinness. Second, women's power is structured in a vertical hierarchy based on their attainment of desirable physical attributes such as thinness.[71] To increase one's power, one has to be thinner than her competition. Both men and women are pressured into bodily control, but society provides men alternative avenues besides dieting.[72]

What Women Do for the Mediated Ideal

The rewards thin women accrue compelled many women and their friends to follow the thinness ideology. Latina and Anglo women's pursuit of thinness involved, among others mechanisms, laxatives, Ipecac, Metabolife, smoking, chewing gum, diet pills, and exercise. An Anglo recalled high school friends who took speed for weeks before prom. She herself drank and smoked during high school, so her stomach would hurt enough not to eat.

However, an important difference emerged in how Latina and Anglo women discussed dieting. Whereas the Anglo women talked about it in terms of cultural and social pressures, the Latina women discussed it more in terms of health. A Latina explained that diabetes runs in Hispanics, so many dieted to prevent diabetes. Another Latina woman described losing weight to increase sports stamina (although she also referred to being able to wear "something where your stomach shows and it not being an issue").

Diet Savvy

As a whole, these women were diet savvy, whether they dieted or not. They knew the specifics of the Atkin's protein diet and the cabbage soup diet.[73] Yet they noted that many girls and women ignore the health risks associated with dieting. One Anglo said women know dieting is terrible, "but they do it just for this week and then it just keeps on happening and happening."

Furthermore, they said media help women ignore the health warnings. First, media constantly disseminate dieting tips. An Anglo noted the number of television shows focusing on dieting. Another discussed how magazines support dieting: "One of the little blurbs is going to say something about dieting. Lose fifteen pounds in a month or one way to firm your abs. That touches women and grabs them." Although the media discuss the dangers of dieting, they create a side-show atmosphere with their depictions of those who had horrible dieting experiences as "freaks of nature."[74] By establishing them as freaks, the "normal" woman can ignore the health risks.

Discussion

The Latina and Anglo women's discourses were complex, shaded, and sometimes contradictory. In general, their attitudes and beliefs were negotiated and at times oppositional, albeit at varying levels. The women's flabless, muscular body ideal matched one of the mediated ideals, but they criticized the sacrifices models make to attain the ideal and the lack of realism in media images. Many compared themselves to the mediated ideal and had incorporated the dominant thinness ideology into their everyday views of femininity. However, they were equally aware of the media as a socializing force and felt they could deal with the ideal's negative effects. Many found the images pleasureable even though these images provoked body dissatisfaction.

Despite their negotiated attitudes, most of their behaviors followed the mediated ideal. Most Anglo women and many Latina women dieted and exercised to become "healthier," but their definition of health included removing unwanted flab and toning their bodies, consistent with the dominant ideology. More Anglo women (and fewer Latinas) reported extreme behaviors such as restrictive eating or excessive exercise.

The women's discourses also illuminated why most of these women's behaviors often followed the mediated ideal despite their attitudinal resistance. They were aware of and desired the economic and social rewards that thinness produces. Further, they were aware of others' acceptance of the ideal and understood that others often judge them by the ideal. Even when these women were critical of the ideal, they felt pressure to strive for thinness, given the social and economic consequences.

Many said achieving thinness provided them a sense of power: an underlying thread in their discourses was that bodily self-control was their primary means to exert control in the social world.[75] Latina women's discourses belied the belief that women of color do not suffer from the effects of the thinness norm and are better able to resist dominant standards of beauty. Similar to their Anglo counterparts, they chose a body ideal that corresponded to the flabless, muscular mediated ideal: some said the mediated ideal negatively influenced their self-image. They also were aware of the positive judgments, attention, and economic successes received when conforming to the mediated ideal. Both Latina and Anglo women pursued the mediated ideal through diet and exercise, although the Latina women more often cast this in terms of health rather than weight loss. Indeed, Hispanic culture provided many Latinas with an alternative lens on thinness. They were more critical of the mediated ideal, knowing that their physical differences excluded them from attaining the ideal and that their culture and Hispanic men appreciated a more voluptuous female form.

Although Grogan says women aspire to be thin regardless of their criticisms of the ideal,[76] the internalization of the thinness ideal is not a simple, linear process but a highly negotiated and complex process occurring over the long term. Women's attitudes and beliefs did not always correspond to the dominant equation of beauty and excessive thinness. They were more critical as they matured and, if they had high self-esteem, were exposed to an alternative feminine ideal, or had friends or family critical of the ideology. Although they desired a flabless, muscular body, the Latina women found greater social acceptance of a larger, curvier figure in their community and media, and many were satisfied with a heavier body. One extremely thin Latina said she wanted to be larger. Meanwhile, Anglo women's desire to be thin was mediated by their families' and friends' beliefs and actions and their individual focus on appearance.

However, their negotiated attitudes gave way to hegemonic behaviors to varying degrees. Those who were already thin and found achievement in other realms did not pursue the ideal to the same degree. In general, the results showed that the negative influence of thin images in the media on women tends to be a consequence of long-term exposure that naturalizes thinness, thereby shaping their attitudes, beliefs, and behaviors to varying degrees. The women's discourses suggest that without the media audience's critical engagement with the thinness ideology and without the audience's resistance to behaviors consistent with the ideology, there was limited hope of curbing the oppressiveness of the thinness ideology.

These results should be considered, however, in light of the women's youth and education. Many of these women said that, prior to coming to college, they did not know the power of the media and the techniques for producing a false ideal. Future research should be conducted with other races and age groups to see how African-American and Asian women, adolescent girls, and older women negotiate the thinness messages and how women's negotiations change over time.

Questions

1   What are some contextual reasons why Latina women may have been more resistant to media messages about thinness?

2   What were some main ways that Latina women and Anglo women were similar in their responses to mediated thinness? How were they different?

3   In what ways did "negotiated" readings of media images and their effects reveal contradictions about how the participants both questioned and accepted the thinness ideal?

4   How do you feel body images in advertisements affect your own sense of self? Do you feel body attractiveness is a source of social influence?

Notes

1. Abra Fortune Chernik, "The Body Politic," in *Listen Up: Voices From the Next Feminist Generation*, ed. Barbara Findelen (Seattle, WA: Seal Press. Chernik, 1995), 76.
2. Kristen Harrison and Joanne Cantor, "The Relationship Between Media Consumption and Eating Disorders," *Journal of Communication* 47 (spring 1997): 40–66.
3. Kim Hubbard, Anne-Marie O'Neill, and Christina Cheakalos, "Out of Control: Weight-obsessed, Stressed-out Coeds Are Increasingly Falling Prey to Eating Disorders," *People*, (12 April 1999): 52–69; Naomi Wolf, *The Beauty Myth: How Images of Beauty Are Used Against Women* (New York: Doubleday, 1991); Jill S. Zimmerman, "An Image to Heal," *Humanist* 57 (January-February 1997): 20–26.
4. James E. Brody, "Shots Fired in War on Eating Disorders," *Austin American-Statesman*, 2 February 1996, sec. F, p. 1,7; Hubbard, O'Neill, and Cheakalos, "Out of Control."
5. Susan Bordo, *Unbearable Weight: Feminism, Western Culture, and The Body* (Berkley, CA: University of California Press, 1993); available from the World Wide Web: www.nedic.on.ca
6. *What Causes Eating Disorders* [online]. Anorexia Nervosa and Related Eating Disorders, Inc. [cited 10–19–99]. Available from the World Wide Web: http://www.anred.com/causes.html.
7. Eric Stice, Erika Schupak-Neuberg, Heather E. Shaw, and Richard I. Stein, "Relation of Media Exposure to Eating Disorder Symptomatology: An Examination of Mediating Mechanisms," *Journal of Abnormal Psychology* 103 (4, 1994): 836–40; Marika Tiggermann and Amanda S. Pickering, "Role of Television in Adolescent Women's Body Dissatisfaction and Drive for Thinness," *International Journal of Eating Disorders* 20(2, 1996): 199–203; Glenn Waller and Julie Shaw, "The Media Influence on Eating Problems," in *Why Women? Gender Issues and Eating Disorders*, ed. Bridget Dolan and Inez Gitzinger (Atlantic Highlands, NJ: The Athlone Press, 1994): 44–54.
8. Stice et al., "Relation of Media Exposure"; Waller and Shaw, "The Media Influence."
9. Colleen Thompson, *Society and Eating Disorders*, 1996 [online]. [cited 7 September 1999]. Available from the World Wide Web: http:// www.mirror-mirror.org/society.htm; Kathryn J. Zerbe, *The Body Betrayed: Women, Eating Disorders and Treatment* (Washington, DC: American Psychiatric Press, 1993); Wolf, *The Beauty Myth*.
10. Chernik, "The Body Politic"; Bordo, *Unbearable Weight*.
11. e.g., Harrison and Cantor, "Relationship Between Media Consumption"; Sherry L. Turner, Heather Hamilton, Meija Jacobs, Laurie M. Angood, and Deanne Hovde Dwyer, "The Influence of Fashion Magazines on the Body Image Satisfaction of College Women: An Exploratory Analysis," *Adolescence* 32 (127, 1997): 603–614; Stice et al., "Relation of Media Exposure"; Lori M. Irving, "Mirror Images: Effect of the Standard of Beauty on the Self-and Body-Esteem of Women Exhibiting Varying Levels of Bulimic Symptoms," *Journal of Social and Clinical Psychology* 9 (2, 1990): 230–42.
12. Bordo, *Unbearable Weight*; Becky Thompson, *A Hunger So Wide and So Deep: American Women Speak Out on Eating Problems* (Minneapolis, MN: University of Minnesota Press, 1994).
13. Thompson, *A Hunger So Wide and So Deep*; Helen Malson, *The Thin Woman: Feminism. Post-Structuralism and the Social Psychology of Anorexia Nervosa* (London & New York: Routledge, 1998).
14. Jon Cruz and Justin Lewis, *Viewing, Reading, Listening: Audiences and Cultural Receptions* (Boulder, CO: Westview Press, 1994); David Morley, *Television, Audiences & Cultural Studies* (New York: Routledge, 1992); Antonio Gramsci, *Selections From the Prison Notebooks* (London: Lawrence and Wishart, 1971); Shaun Moores, *Interpreting Audiences: The Ethnography of Media Consumption* (Thousand Oaks, CA: Sage Publications, 1993).
15. C. von Feilitzen, "Media Violence: Four Research Perspectives," in *Approaches to Audiences: A Reader*, ed. Roger Dickinson, Ramaswami Harindranath, and Olga Linne (London & New

York: Oxford University Press, Inc., 1998): 88–103; Gramsci, *Selections From the Prison Notebooks*; Moores, *Interpreting Audiences*.

16.   Wolf, *The Beauty Myth*; Rita J. Freedman, *Beauty Bound* (Lexington, MA: Lexington Books, 1986); Sarah Grogan, *Body Images: Understanding Body Dissatisfaction in Men, Women, and Children* (New York: Routledge, 1999); Bordo, *Unbearable Weight*.

17.   G. Murdock, "Mass Communication and the Construction of Meaning," in *Approaches to Audiences: A Reader*, ed. Dickingson, Harindranath, and Linne, 205–217, 206.

18.   Susan Orbach, *Hunger Strike: The Anorectic's Struggle as a Metaphor for the Age* (London: Penguin, 1993); Roberta Pollack Seid, "Too 'Close to the Bone': The Historical Context for Women's Obsession with Slenderness," in *Feminist Perspectives on Eating Disorders*, ed. Patricia Fallon, Melanie A. Katzman, and Susan C. Wooley (New York: The Guilford Press, 1994): 3–18.

19.   Gramsci, *Selections From the Prison Notebooks*; Stuart Hall, "Encoding/decoding," in *Culture, Media, Language*, ed. Stuart Hall (London: Hutchinson, 1980): 128–38; von Feilitzen, "Media Violence"; John Fiske, "Television: Polysemy and Popularity," in *Approaches to Audiences: A Reader*, ed. Dickingson, Harindranath, and Linne, 194–204; Janice A. Radway, *Reading the Romance: Women, Patriarchy and Popular Literature* (London: Verso Books, 1984).

20.   Brett Silverstein, Lauren Perdue, Barbara Peterson, and Eileen Kelly, "The Role of the Mass Media in Promoting a Thin Standard of Bodily Attractiveness for Women," *Sex Roles* 14 (9–10, 1986): 519–32; Claire V. Wiseman, James J. Gray, James E. Mosimann, and Anthony H. Ahrens, "Cultural Expectations for Thinness in Women: An Update," *International Journal of Eating Disorders* 11 (1, 1992): 85–89; David M. Garner, Paul E. Garfinkel, Donald Schwartz, and Michael Thompson, "Cultural Expectations of Thinness in Women," *Psychological Reports* 47 (1980): 483–91.

21.   Garner et al., "Cultural Expectations"; Wiseman et al., "Cultural Expectations: Update."

22.   Carol J. Nemeroff, Richard I. Stein, Nancy S. Diehl, and Karen M. Smilack, "From the Cleavers to the Clintons: role choices and body orientation as reflected in magazine article content," *International Journal of Eating Disorders* 16 (2, 1994): 167–77; Silverstein et al., "The Role of the Mass Media"; Arnold E. Andersen and L. DiDomenico, "Diet vs. shape content in popular male and female magazines: A dose-response relationship to the incidence of eating disorder?" *International Journal of Eating Disorder* 11 (3, 1992): 283–87.

23.   Silverstein et al., "The Role of the Mass Media."

24.   Andersen and DiDomenico, "Diet vs. shape content."

25.   Leora Pinhas, Brenda B. Toner, Alisha Ali, Paul E. Garfinkel, and Noreen Stuckless, "The Effects of the Ideal of Female Beauty on Mood and Body Satisfaction," *International Journal of Eating Disorders* 25 (2, 1999): 223–26; Harrison and Cantor, "Relationship Between Media Consumption"; Stice et al., "Relation of Media Exposure"; Irving, "Mirror Images"; Eric Stice and Heather E. Shaw, "Adverse Effects of the Media Portrayed Thin-Ideal on Women and Linkages to Bulimic Symptomatology," *Journal of Social and Clinical Psychology* 13 (3, 1994): 288–308; Renee A. Botta, "Television Images and Adolescent Girls' Body Image Disturbance," *Journal of Communication* 49 (2, 1999): 22–41.

26.   James Rosen and Janet Gross, "Prevalence of Weight Reducing and Weight Gaining in Adolescent Girls and Boys," *Health Psychology* 6 (2, 1987): 131–47; Andres J. Pumariega, "Acculturation and Eating Attitudes in Adolescent Girls: A Comparative and Correlational Study," *Journal of American Academy of Child and Adolescent Psychiatry* 25 (2, 1986): 276–79; Madeleine Altabe, "Ethnicity and body image: Quantitative and qualitative analysis." *International Journal of Eating Disorder* 23 (2, 1998): 153–59.

27.   Rebecca Chamorro and Yvette Flores-Ortiz, "Acculturation and disordered eating patterns among Mexican American women," *International Journal of Eating Disorder* 28 (1, 2000): 125–29; Pumariega, "Acculturation and Eating Attitudes."

28.   Chamorro and Flores-Ortiz, "Acculturation and disordered eating patterns."

29.   Grogan, *Body Images*; Malson, *The Thin Woman*; M. Gigi Durham, "Girls, Media, and the Negotiation of Sexuality: A Study of Race, Class, and Gender in Adolescent Peer Groups," *Journalism & Mass Communication Quarterly* 76 (summer 1999): 193–216; Lisa L. Duke, "Black in a Blonde World: Race and Girls' Interpretations of the Feminine Ideal in Teen Magazines," *Journalism & Mass Communication Quarterly* 77 (summer 2000): 367–95.

30.   Grogan, *Body Images*.

31. Richard A. Krueger, *Focus Groups: A Practical Guide for Applied Research* (Newbury Park, CA: Sage, 1988), 54.

32. David L. Morgan, *Focus Groups as Qualitative Research*, 2d ed. (Thousand Oaks, CA: Sage, 1997.

33. Barney G. Glaser and Anselm L. Strauss, *The Discovery of Grounded Theory: Strategies for Qualitative Research* (Chicago: Aldine Atherton, 1967).

34. Thomas R. Lindlof, *Qualitative Communication Research Methods* (Thousand Oaks, CA: Sage, 1995); Krueger, *Focus Groups*.

35. Glaser and Strauss, *The Discovery of Grounded Theory*, 108.

36. Glaser and Strauss, *The Discovery of Grounded Theory*, 109.

37. Glaser and Strauss, *The Discovery of Grounded Theory*; Lindlof, *Qualitative Communication Research Methods*.

38. Bordo, *Unbearable Weight*.

39. Bordo, *Unbearable Weight*.

40. Bordo, *Unbearable Weight*, 191.

41. Bordo, *Unbearable Weight*.

42. Bordo, *Unbearable Weight*.

43. Freedman, *Beauty Bound*, 5.

44. Roberta P. Seid, *Never Too Thin: Why Women Are at War with Their Bodies* (New York: Prentice Hall Press, 1989).

45. Seid, "Too 'Close to the Bone.' "

46. Bordo, *Unbearable Weight*.

47. Bordo, *Unbearable Weight*, 104.

48. Jackie Stacey, "Feminine Fascinations: Forms of Identification in Star-Audience Relations" in *Feminist Film Theory: A Reader*, ed. Sue Thornham (New York: New York University Press, 1999), 196–209.

49. Stacey, "Feminine Fascinations."

50. Freedman, *Beauty Bound*, 25.

51. Thompson, *A Hunger So Wide and So Deep*.

52. Marjorie Ferguson, *Forever Feminine: Women's Magazines and the Cult of Femininity* (Aldershot, Hants: Gower, 1983).

53. Albert Bandura, *Social Learning Theory* (Englewood Cliffs, NJ: Prentice-Hall, 1977).

54. Seid, *Never Too Thin*; Bordo, *Unbearable Weight*.

55. Stacey, "Feminine Fascinations."

56. Laura Mulvey, "Visual Pleasure and Narrative Cinema" in *Feminist Film Theory: A Reader*, ed. Sue Thornham (New York: New York University Press, 1999), 58–69.

57. Stacey, "Feminine Fascinations"; Mulvey, "Visual Pleasure and Narrative Cinema."

58. Orbach, *Hunger Strike*.

59. Grogan, *Body Images*; Freedman, *Beauty Bound*.

60. Seid, "Too 'Close to the Bone.' "

61. Freedman, *Beauty Bound*.

62. Bordo, *Unbearable Weight*.

63. Bordo, *Unbearable Weight*; Grogan, *Body Images*.

64. Freedman, *Beauty Bound*, 24.

65. Orbach, *Hunger Strike*; Seid, "Too 'Close to the Bone.' "

66. O. W. Wooley, "And Man Created 'Woman': Representations of Women's Bodies in Western Culture," in *Feminist Perspectives on Eating Disorders*, ed. Patricia Fallon, Melanie A. Katzman, and Susan C. Wooley (New York: The Guilford Press, 1994): 19–43.

67. Bordo, *Unbearable Weight*.

68. Ellen McCracken, *Decoding Women's Magazines: From Mademoiselle to Ms.* (New York: St. Martin's Press, 1993); Jean Kilbourne, "Still Killing Us Softly: Advertising and the Obsession with Thinness," in *Feminist Perspectives on Eating Disorders*, ed. Patricia Fallon, Melanie A. Katzman, and Susan C. Wooley (New York: The Guilford Press, 1994), 395–418; Bordo, *Unbearable Weight*.

69. Bordo, *Unbearable Weight*.

70. Bordo, *Unbearable Weight*.

71. Ferguson, *Forever Feminine*; Wolf, *The Beauty Myth*.

72.   Waller and Shaw, "The Media Influence," 48.
73.   It takes more calories to digest the soup than the soup actually provides.
74.   Bordo, *Unbearable Weight*.
75.   Bordo, *Unbearable Weight*; Waller and Shaw, "The Media Influence on Eating Problems," 44–54.
76.   Grogan, *Body Images*.

PART SIX

Ads and Politics

INTRODUCTION TO PART SIX

MUCH OF THE WORK IN THIS BOOK DEALS WITH Politics with a capital "P." In this case, Politics is a synonym for social power. Issues of ideology and hegemony, then, are political in this sense. But the practices of politics, with a small "p," are also relevant to advertising and consumer culture. By politics in this second sense it is meant the specific mechanisms of government and democracy. As modern citizens, then, we know that material products are not the only things sold in ads, but so are political policies, political ideas, and of course politicians themselves. This Part asks: In what ways do politics and politicians use advertising, and to what extent have they become brands themselves?

The three chapters in this Part focus on advertising and small "p" politics. Dickinson in his contribution looks at how citizenship was used as a commodified value to connect to branded products in ads immediately after the events of September 11, 2001. As he argues, consumption was framed as a necessary and patriotic activity for good citizens in the post-9/11 world. The other two chapters review many of the trends about the role of advertising in the political campaign process. Hardy's chapter surveys key themes in the role of traditional media advertising—including one peculiar form, the negative ad—in the campaign process. Vargas explores the increasingly wide use of newer digital media, especially the Internet, as politicians exploit and adjust to these recent technologies to court voters during the election process.

Chapter 18

GREG DICKINSON

SELLING DEMOCRACY
Consumer Culture and Citizenship in the Wake of September 11

D ICKINSON EXPLORES HOW ADVERTISING ATTEMPTS TO estab-
lish connections between two very different concepts: consumption and citizenship.
He notes that in modern US culture there has been an historical link in public discourse between citizenship and consumerism, including advertising messages during
the Cold War that contrasted purported abundant American consumer choice with
restrictive Communist societies.

   Given the tragic and unique situation facing marketers, especially those in New York,
after September 11, he argues that ads for products after 9/11 "constituted," or
rhetorically created, a particular type of citizen: the citizen whose patriotic duty was
to consume in a post-9/11 world. In this case, then, the "problem" that advertising
tried to solve was "do not let the terrorists win," and the solution to defeating
them was to reinvigorate consumption behavior. Ads went through different stages
in this post-9/11 linkage, going from the commemorative to the philanthropic to
finally blatantly associating themes of security and safety—both sources of great
anxiety at that time—to consumption. He concludes that equating citizenship with
consumption, as these post-9/11 ads did, may undermine other forms of democratic
participation.

   Right now we are all Americans.
         (Allianz Group advertisement, September 16, 2001, p. 45)

   As rhetoric is a mode of knowing, it must include some kind of aesthetic
   knowledge; as a practical art, it will be likely to include the aesthetic sense
   that registers how the world is both mundane and sublime, a world of both
   economy and awe, technique and terror.

                                         (Hariman, 1998, p. 16)

On September 16, 2001, Kmart bought a full-page advertisement in the *New York Times* in which the page is filled with an image of the United States Flag. At the bottom of the page is an explanation: "Instructions for use: Remove from newspaper. Place in window. **Embrace Freedom**" (Kmart, 2001, p. B3). In small print, Kmart identified itself as the sponsor of the advertisement: "from the over 250,000 Kmart associates" (Kmart, 2001, p. B3). Although the advertisement makes no direct mention of the attacks of September 11, 2001, the image is clearly a response to the crisis. Appearing on Sunday immediately following the attacks, this advertisement serves as a nearly ideal example of the ways corporations responded to the material and symbolic attack on the United States.

As a response to the attacks of September 11, 2001, the Kmart advertisement works precisely between the sublime and the mundane of which Hariman (1998) wrote. The attacks and the subsequent collapse of the World Trade Center were terrorizing and fearsome. The event was "sublime." Yet, as Hariman (1998) pointed out, the practical arts of rhetoric and democratic governing work by weaving awe-inspiring sublimity with the crafty intelligence of the mundane and everyday. In its very banality (a newsprint flag taped to a window), the Kmart advertisement reweaves the sublime into the practical, the everyday, and the mundane.

This advertisement does not do this work by itself; instead it is part of a larger historical discourse mobilized in particular ways following the attack. This discourse urges Americans to enact their citizenship through consumption. Advertisers faced particular difficulties in confronting the post-September 11 environment. Shopping in the context of the life altering, mortal attack seemed a banal and selfish action. Selling seemed in even worse taste. Television networks, for instance, provided round-the-clock coverage of the disaster uninterrupted by advertisements. At the same time, consumption was and is crucial to maintaining the health of advertisers specifically and the economy more generally, a point eventually acknowledged explicitly in buy-American and travel more campaigns. How corporations responded to the attacks was crucial to not offending taste while keeping the dollars flowing.

In attacking the World Trade Center, the terrorists aimed their assault not simply at official U.S. interests (the attack on the Pentagon is more clearly an attack on the United States as a political entity), but directed their concerns at commercial globalization. Barber (1995) in his influential book *McWorld vs. Jihad* argues that a fundamental characteristic of contemporary global culture is the conflict between the universalization of Western capitalism (a capitalism that is identified most deeply with the United States, Brennan, 1997) and the resistance to this universalization as grounded in race, ethnicity, and/or religion. Transnational corporations—the protagonists of McWorld—serve as a reasonable target for the frustrations of the people struggling against the homogenizing forces of Western capitalism (Barber, 1995; Baudot, 2001; Brennan, 1997; Callinicos, 2001; Hardt & Negri, 2000; Ritzer, 1998).

In the first month after September 11, corporate marketers used advertisements to make two specific rhetorical claims. First, they created identification between themselves and America such that the health of corporations was congruent with the health of the nation. Second, they suggested that enacting consumption was a central mode of enacting citizenship and patriotism. In this article, I outline the theory of constitutive rhetoric, which serves as a theoretical framework for critical analysis of the advertisements. I also trace the emergence of the citizen consumer in 19th and 20th century discourse. Using these theoretical and historical frameworks, I then demonstrate that the advertisements under analysis (re)constitute the audience as citizen consumers, showing how the advertisements proffer consumption as a primary means for responding to the attacks of September 11.

Constituting the Citizen Consumer

The traditional view of the relation between rhetoric and audience suggests that audiences and rhetors exist prior to the rhetorical act (Charland, 1987). These audiences are more or less conscious of their position as audiences and, as such, make rational, conscious decisions about the arguments the rhetor makes. The rhetor, like the audience, is also conscious of her/his position as rhetor and strategically constructs arguments designed to appeal to the audience. Aristotle's (1991) definition of rhetoric as the "ability, in each particular case, to see the available means of persuasion" (p. 36) encodes this rationalistic form of rhetoric.

Rhetorical and critical theory in the twentieth and twenty-first centuries finds this conceptualization of the rhetoric/audience relationship unsatisfactory. Perhaps most prominent in shifting this rhetoric/audience relationship is Burke's (1969) move to include identification as a crucial term in rhetorical theory. In the *Rhetoric of Motives*, Burke (1969) argues that persuasion underestimates the ways rhetoric functions, often at an unconscious level, to create identification or connections between individuals. Rhetoric as identification functions far more globally than does rhetoric as persuasion and often does the prior work of creating the groups to which persuasive messages can then be directed.

Charland (1987) in his germinal essay "Constitutive Rhetoric" takes up Burke's notion of identification and the emphasis on rhetoric's ability to create audiences. "Theories of rhetoric as persuasion," Charland writes, "cannot account for the audiences that rhetoric addresses" (p. 134). Charland argues that becoming a subject (i.e., an audience member) is to take up a position in the discourse. This "taking up" is not, however, entirely or even mostly voluntary. When individuals enter a rhetorical situation and acknowledge or recognize the rhetorical address, they become the audience member the text calls forth. However, as Charland points out, this hailing is not a one-time action, but is constantly repeated. "This rhetoric of identification is ongoing, not restricted to one hailing, but usually part of a rhetoric of socialization. Thus, one must already be part of the audience of a rhetorical situation in which persuasion could occur" (p. 138). Each rhetorical act draws on preexisting discursive positions and, in addressing the audience, recreates those positions. Rhetoric as constitutive both creates and recreates the audience itself. The rhetoric of post-September 11 advertisements demonstrates that the constitution of the audience of the citizen-consumer is processual and ongoing. Drawing on pre-September 11 images of the citizen consumer, the advertisements immediately following the attacks work to reconstitute Americans as citizen-consumers. Tracing the pre-September 11 history of the constitution of the citizen consumer becomes crucial to understanding the post-September 11 reaction.

Citizen Consumers

Over the last 125 years, consumer culture has become a crucial way for individuals to enact their public citizenship in Europe and the United States. By the 1880s a robust consumer sphere vied with the public sphere as a site of public and civic action (de Grazia, 1996). The development of consumer culture represented a deep break with earlier forms of capitalism as economic activity shifted from production—in the home and in small shops—to the consumption of mass-produced goods (Altman, 1990). Mass media texts urging consumption (Marchand, 1985; Pumphrey, 1987) encouraged this shift. Altman (1990), for example, explores the Better Homes in America campaign that was intimately linked with the women's general interest magazine *The Delineator*. The magazine collaborated with Secretary of Commerce Herbert Hoover to urge both homeownership and consumption of newly created, mass-produced household goods like washing machines. The discourse of the Better Homes in America campaign combined consumption and patriotism in powerfully persuasive ways. Altman (1990) noted, for example, an advertisement for Western Lumber Company quoting Herbert Hoover as asserting that the family and the family home are central to civilizations. This advertisement draws together the discourses of consumption with the authority of government discourse to persuasively connect consumption and civic engagement.

In this way, advertisers used political language as one means of understanding and justifying consumption. During the Depression, advertisers turned to the language of politics to legitimate their own activities and to describe products and consumers (McGovern, 1998). This language of politics sought to turn consumption into a political practice, equating consumer choice with voting, freedom, and the exercise of civic responsibility. As McGovern (1998) writes, "in metaphors equating consumers with citizens and purchasing with voting, admen portrayed consumption as the true exercise of the individual's civic role and public identity; consumption as the ritual means of affirming one's nationality as an American" (p. 42). By the end of the Depression, advertising succeeded in securing two crucial and interrelated connections: first that consumption serves as a central mode of citizenship, and second that being a good consumer and a good American are fundamentally connected.

Not only did advertisers and marketers connect consumption and citizenship, the government officials increasingly looked to consumerism as an important form of enfranchisement. The state supported consumerism through policymaking that created a post-World War I "world where mass consumption not only shaped the economy, but also altered the political realm, becoming a new vehicle for delivering the traditional American promises of democracy and egalitarianism" (Cohen, 1998, p. 111). As Cohen (1998) argues, many New Dealers saw empowerment of consumers as one way of enhancing civic roles of common people while at the same time maintaining free enterprise. Official Washington language began to equate democracy and American nationalism with consumer goods and consumer possibilities (Lipsitz, 1998, p. 142). By the 1950s connecting consumption to democracy shifted under the weight of the cold war. Consumer capitalism offered the means of creating an egalitarian society and, thus, became a way to "beat the Soviets at their own game of creating a classless society" (Cohen, 2003, p. 125). President Eisenhower asserted that consumer capitalism could help win the cold war, declaring "war upon [the Soviet Union] in the peaceful field of trade" (cited in Cohen, 2003, p. 127).

This discourse connecting consumer choice to democratic freedom remained robust in the 1990s and the new century before the attacks of September 11, 2001. As Barber (1995) writes,

> Political agnostics, they [capitalistic markets] nonetheless borrow and warp political ideas and political terms. . . . Brand choice and, within brands, item choice (Crest Blue and Crest Regular), have been widely taken to constitute the essence of freedom in market societies and have even been sold to "new democracies" as such.
>
> (p. 72)

This language of consumer/democratic choice remains coherent prior to the September 11 attacks. For example on September 13, 2000, just less than a year before the attacks on the World Trade Center, LG (2000) advertised a new wireless service that is "dedicated to life, liberty & the pursuit of joy" (p. A14). Taking on the language of the Declaration of Independence, the advertisement suggests that using a cellular phone can serve as at least one mode for practicing the fundamental rights inherent in citizenship. A similar argument is offered in a full-page Dell (2000) computer advertisement published the following Sunday. The advertisement reads: "Free speech, free press, free DVD. [Only in America]" (p. Y9). What should be clear, then, is that consumption and the language of citizenship have become intertwined over the last 150 years.

The Constituting Text

McGee (1990) argues that in postmodernity texts are fragmentary. The critic must construct a meaningful text out of the nearly limitless fragments available. In constructing the "text" for this critical analysis, I investigated every advertisement published in the *New York Times* for the 3 months immediately following the attacks of September 11, 2001.[1] The *New York Times* was particularly important for the ways it simultaneously served New Yorkers and a national readership as one of three "large, nationally influential newspapers" (Dennis et al., 1992, p. 59).[2] The *New York Times* served then as an ideal site for companies to address local, national, and even international audiences in the days following the attacks.

From this group of advertisements, I selected ones that in visual or verbal content addressed or responded to the attacks, 246 fulfilled the criteria for analysis. Of these 246 advertisements, nearly half (n = 122) were full-page advertisements and of these full-page advertisements, just over half (n = 64) were placed in the first section (section A) of the paper.[3] The number and prominence of the advertisements suggest their importance to the corporate advertisers placing them and the perceived visibility the advertisements would have to readers. In comparing the selected advertisements to advertisements from the same time the previous year it became clear that themes developed in the post-September 11 advertisements were unique even as they drew on the visual and verbal themes of consumer citizenship. The advertisements I have selected, taken together, make a rhetorically compelling image of the citizen consumer, an image that, as suggested in the conclusion, is found other textual fragments, in particular fragments of the political rhetoric in the immediate post-September 11 moment.[4] Constructing a "text" out of these advertisements allows insight into the ways this particular discourse strives to settle identity in an unsettled moment.

Nationalizing Consumption

In the month after September 11, corporations used advertisements to create identification between themselves and Americans and, using this identification, urged Americans to see consumption as powerful means for enacting patriotism in a post-September 11 world. Crucial in making these arguments was their order. The advertisements began by creating identification between corporations and the nation. In creating this identification, corporations came to look like citizens. The advertisements began to connect consumption to patriotism—and thus citizenship—by urging consumers to give generously to relief efforts. Urging charitable contributions served as a rhetorical link to asserting consumption as a crucial practice in support of the nation. This final move most fully recreates the audience as citizen consumers.

The Corporation as Citizen

The first response by advertisers to September 11 appeared on September 12. These first advertisements set the tone visually and verbally for the ways companies would initially respond to tragedy. Although there are a number of design characteristics common to many of these early advertisements (e.g., they express sympathy and support for the families and friends of the victims, they emphasize the logos and names of the companies buying the advertisements, they are very visually simple) what is essential for this argument is the way the advertisements nationalize companies by identifying them with the United States.

A small advertisement for Best Buy (2001) coalesces many of the rhetorical strategies typical of advertisements run immediately following September 11. "As you weep, we weep/ As you pray, we pray/ As you endure/ we will endure" (p. B14). Visually the advertisement is very simple, just elegantly typed verse surrounded by white space and centered over a small Best Buy logo. Taking this advertisement as representative I explore its rhetorical workings and then begin to think about the differences encoded in some of its companion advertisements.

Perhaps most striking about this advertisement is that it does not advertise any particular product or service. In one sense, this absence is not conspicuous. Indeed, if the advertisement had at once addressed the tragedy *and* explicitly tried to sell DVD players, the company would have been subject to accusations of poor taste. Every advertisement that addressed September 11 in the first 4 days after the tragedy made the choice to focus on the tragedy, not selling. This choice signals a crucial distinction between these advertisements and those before September 11 that use patriotic language. In advertisements placed before the attacks, patriotic language would be directly connected to purchasing a particular product or service (as in the advertisements for LG wireless services and Dell computers). After September 11, the advertisements eliminated direct selling, focusing exclusively on creating a comforting identification among corporation, audience, and nation.

In the Best Buy (2001) advertisement, identification is created through the use of the pronouns "you" and "we." "As *you* weep, *we* weep [italics added]" (p. B14). "You" always includes an individual addressed, but it can either suggest a single individual or a collectively addressed group. Both seem to be at work here. Because this advertisement appears in the *New York Times*, there is a real sense in which the you is the individual reader. At the same time, within both the context of mass media where numerous people will read the same newspaper and the same advertisements and in which the tragedy is not individual but collective, you is also collective. Within the rhetorical context of a tragedy that is being named as an attack on America, you is not only read as the collective of *New York Times* readers but as individual Americans.

The "we" in the advertisement allows Best Buy to take on an identity that is not limited to selling television sets. Instead, this company is personified: It weeps and prays just as does the individual reader and Americans as a whole. Thus, whereas the we/you language works as division between audience and rhetor, our common weeping and the praying creates a more fundamental identification that is, in Burke's (1969) words, compensatory to division. In this way, Best Buy becomes as American as you. This personalizing and nationalizing of the company is cemented in the final two lines of the verse: "As you endure/we will endure" (Best Buy, 2001, p. B14). The advertisement equates the endurance of Americans and America with the company, as Best Buy's future becomes a sign of the enduring of the country.

This Best Buy advertisement typifies advertisements from this early post-September 11 period. Use of "we," "us," and "you," the expression of sorrow and sympathy; the creation of the relationship among organization, employees, and citizens runs across nearly all the advertisements of these first three days (see, for example, ABC Carpet and Home, 2001; Bailey Banks and Biddle, 2001; Cartier, 2001; ExxonMobil, 2001; Kreis Collection, 2001; Macy's, 2001; Tiffany and Company, 2001a; Verizon Wireless, 2001a: Vitamin Shoppe, 2001). Each of these advertisements assiduously avoids selling any product or service, yet each asserts connections to the audience and the nation. As a group, these advertisements provide the language for beginning to think about the relationship between corporate organizations, the tragedy, and the nation.

This nationalization of brands is more visually explicit in another set of advertisements that adds a visual element beyond the white space, type, and logo thematic explored above. The Saks Fifth Avenue advertisement of September 13 is the first to make connections among brand, flag, and September 11. In this small advertisement, a waving U.S. flag is captioned "with sadness" (Saks Fifth Avenue, 2001, p. B3). The Saks logo appears in the bottom third of the advertisement. This advertisement resembles previous Saks advertisements that had run for some time in the *New York Times* but in place of jewelry or clothing waves the flag. By using the flag, Saks eliminates any ambiguity found in the Best Buy advertisement, openly connecting brand and national identity. The advertisement creates a second rhetorical effect, one that becomes much more explicit in the days to come. This effect entails the commodification of the flag and, thus, the commodification of the signs of national identity. The flag is placed in the exact spot in the advertisement usually reserved for the product for sale, which portrays the flag as commodity and suggests that buying the flag may be a way of enacting one's national identity. Just as importantly, it implies that selling the flag is an appropriate way of being a good corporate and national citizen. Saks becomes a purveyor of the signs of nationalism and in so doing takes on the mantle of national identity. Perhaps the most obvious example of this use of the flag as nationalizing move is the full-page advertisement run by Kmart discussed above. Kmart provides the mode by which the practice of freedom is possible. And, just in case the reader has forgotten how the flag really looks, the advertisement's fine print that reads "this side up," reminds us which side is up. Saks Fifth Avenue and Kmart are only two of the many corporations that use the U.S. flag in their advertisements (see, for example, Brown Harris Stevens, 2001;

Carlyle, 2001; Classic Sofa, 2001; Cushman and Wakefield, 2001; Garden State Volvo, 2001; Lord and Taylor, 2001; Manhattan Auto Group, 2001; Mercedes-Benz Greenwich, 2001; New York Times Company, 2001; Paul Miller Family, 2001; Staples, 2001).

A final thematic is ubiquitous in the first 4 publishing days after September 11. Financial companies, many of which had offices in the World Trade Center towers, produced advertisements designed to reassure clients that the companies are still able to manage client resources. The first of these, an advertisement by Morgan Stanley, appeared on September 13. It is a full-page advertisement, which, although bigger than the Best Buy advertisement, draws on the same visual resources. It is composed of simple type centered in white space. However, rather than being a poetic attempt to express condolences, it is an open letter from the chair of Morgan Stanley, Philip J. Purcell. The advertisement begins with a statement of condolences for those lost and proclaims the victims innocent and part of what will be "one of the most tragic events in American history" (Morgan Stanley, 2001, p. B3). The advertisement strives to restore client confidence in the financial institutions that anchor New York. After expressing sorrow for the events, the advertisement states:

> Thanks to our network of over 60,000 people throughout the world, including those in New York City, our assets and all of our clients' assets are completely safe. And we are ready to begin again as soon as the markets reopen.
>
> We are a company built on strength. Strength of resources. But even more important, strength of character.
>
> We are a company that will never forget the extraordinary value of human life.
>
> (Morgan Stanley, 2001, p. B3)

This is the first post-September 11 advertisement to directly address the tragedy in a way that connects the attacks and business interests. Financial companies bore the brunt of the attack because they formed a significant number of the tenants in the World Trade Center towers. The attack struck the center of globalized financial networks. Within this context, globalized financial companies had a particular burden in responding. The attack raised questions about the security of the global financial networks as well as the security of individual accounts.

This advertisement directly addressed these concerns. The advertisement promises reassurance that no financial resources have been lost, and that more money can be made soon. In short, the attackers, in spite of their spectacular momentary success, will enjoy no long-term success in disabling the global system they have attacked. Supporting, investing in, committing to Morgan Stanley is a way of resisting the attacks. Again, the themes of the Morgan Stanley advertisement are not idiosyncratic, but instead run across numerous advertisements in these first 4 days (American Express, 2001; Insignia, 2001; JP Morgan Chase, 2001; Macy's, 2001; Merrill Lynch, 2001; Target/Mervyn's/Marshall Field's, 2001). We see 4 days after the attacks the first attempts to reconnect corporate culture with patriotism and, through patriotism, citizenship. This connection between the corporation and citizenship lays the rhetorical groundwork for identifying consumption with civic duty, a connection that was strengthened in the following days.

Citizenship as Charitable Giving

Having worked to nationalize themselves, corporations then turned to the work of getting individuals back to buying. Appeals to charitable giving linked the early nationalizing advertisements and later advertisements that promoted consumption. The first of these advertisements was run by the New York Times Company. In this advertisement the company announced the opening of a new fund the 9/11 Neediest Fund (New York Times Company, 2001). Other corporations quickly took up charity as a way of responding to the crisis. On September 16, Sears ran an advertisement urging support of the American Red Cross through donations of money and blood. Money could be donated at any Sears store or through the Sears Web site. Further, Sears (2001) itself "donated $1 million in immediate support of relief efforts" (p. 41). Two pages later appeared an advertisement run by The Home Depot (2001).

> At The Home Depot, we want to take back something we said.
>
> Recently, we've been suggesting that you bring your tax rebate to The Home Depot and spend it with us. In light of last Tuesday's tragic events, we want to take that suggestion back and make another one.
>
> Bring your 2001 tax rebate, and even more if you can, to The Home Depot and donate it to the United Way's September 11th Fund to aid families affected by the terrorist attacks. . . .
>
> We can get back to building our own house soon enough. Right now it's time to help our neighbors.
>
> (p. 43)

This advertisement directly addresses the ways consumption and the tragedy go together. The advertisement suggests that this is the wrong time to spend money on oneself. Instead, the money ought be donated to survivors and victims. This sentiment expresses the difficulties advertisers faced as they hoped to return customers to buying. While the advertisement urged individuals to *not* buy goods in the store, it also strove to create goodwill for the The Home Depot in hopes that consumers would return to buy later. Advertisements by GM and Staples on September 16th, Verizon and Fleet on the 17th, Bank of America on the 18th, and AOL Time Warner on the 19th promote these themes. In each case, the advertisements urge donations to particular private, non-profit corporations and, in some cases like that of Sears, trumpet their own donations to the relief (AOL Time Warner, 2001; Bank of America, 2001; Fleet, 2001; GM, 2001a; Staples, 2001; Verizon Wireless, 2001b).

On the 19th, however, a new variation appeared that linked consumption and civic responsibility. For the first time, consumer practices are asserted as one way of responding appropriately to the tragedy. Morrell and Company sponsored an advertisement promoting a charity wine auction to be held on December 8, 2001. Wineries, wine growers, wine shippers, and private parties were urged to donate wines for the auction, the proceeds of which were designated for the New York Police and Fire Widows and Children's Benefit Fund. Donating and buying wines in the auction served as a "direct" response to September 11 (Morrell and Company, 2001). On the 20th this move to connect consumption to citizenship was taken one step further, as retailer David Yurman (2001) advertised that 15% of sales would be donated to the Silver Shield Foundation.

Seven days after the attacks, consumers are offered the possibility of responding to the tragedy through consumption. Indeed, the logic suggests that consumers ought to spend as much as possible because spending more leads to greater donations. Similarly, East Harbor Chinese and Japanese Restaurant promised to donate the proceeds of 3 days of business and Stuart and Frankle, a brokerage firm, planned to donate all the commissions earned in a single day to the New York Times 9/11 Neediest Fund (East Harbor Chinese and Japanese Restaurant, 2001; Stuart and Frankle, 2001). These advertisements, then, begin to link consumption with citizenship through the intermediary of charitable giving.

Citizenship as Consumption

Advertising the donation of proceeds or portions of proceeds to various charitable organizations directly connected consumption with citizenship without the intermediary of charitable deeds. Ford entered this new territory first, with a full-page advertisement published September 22. "Ford Drives America" reads the headline (Ford, 2001, p. A26). "In light of these challenging times, we at Ford want to do our part to help move America forward" (Ford, 2001, p. A26). The very next day, GM unveiled a print advertising campaign that explicitly worked the relationship between consumption and citizenship. An advertisement headlined "Keep America Rolling" argued that buying and selling cars was crucial to the new, post-September 11 world.

> On September 11, the world as we knew it came to an end.
> We sat glued to our televisions, watching events unfold that shook us to our very core. And suddenly, the little things that had previously divided us seemed wholly insignificant.
> Now it's time to move forward. For years, the auto industry has played a crucial role in our economy. General Motors takes that responsibility seriously.
> We think it's important to keep workers working, and for the economy to keep rolling along. It won't be easy. But nothing important ever is.
> (GM, 2001b, p. A47)

This advertisement identifies GM as an American company, intimately linking the fate of the company with the fate of the country. It starts the identification as many other advertisements do with liberal use of the first person plural ("the world as we knew it," "*We* sat glued to *our* televisions [italics added]," "the little things that had previously divided *us*").

Second, the advertisement identifies the automobile industry as "crucial" to the U.S. economy. This central role creates a responsibility that GM "takes seriously." The profit motive central to GM becomes a "serious" matter in maintaining U.S. interests. The interests of GM and the interests of the nation are now one and the same. GM identifies itself not only with the nation but also with the consumer and constitutes the reader of the advertisement as a consumer-citizen. The last paragraph of the advertisement reads: "This may very well be the most serious crisis our nation has ever faced. In this time of terrible adversity, let's stand together. And keep America rolling" (2001b, p. A47). As GM and consumers—both central citizens of the United States—face this crisis, they can do so by doing what they have always done: building and buying cars, and in so doing, keeping America "rolling."

This emphasis on consumption as civic action in advertisements is reinforced in the style section of the Sunday *New York Times* 10 days after the attacks. In a three-quarter-page layout, the paper displays eight products that demonstrate patriotism and good taste, most of which utilize the flag or stars as a prominent design feature. Ellen Tien (2001), designer of the page, justifies the display this way:

> The recovery effort must include shopping, Mayor Rudolph W. Giuliani has been telling New Yorkers. Spend money to support local business. Even before he issued his plea, retailers were scrambling for products to be sold in cooperation with relief groups. Manufacturers and retailers of the items featured here have pledged to donate a portion of the sales to rescue workers and families of victims of the World Trade Center disaster. Which means the civic-minded can now buy a little guilt-free pleasure.
>
> (p. ST3)

This layout brings together all the themes in making consumption a civic action. Buying and wearing images of the flag became one way of being patriotic. This patriotism is enhanced by the fact that a portion of the proceeds from the purchases is donated to relief efforts. Buying a star-encrusted dog collar then allows the consumer to enact, display, and perform civic duty. As the dog wears the collar, the owner declares her/his patriotism while financially supporting the victims of the tragedy. The "civic-minded" can have pleasure, style, and civility all in one simple purchase. Not surprisingly, immediately below this display is a Tiffany advertisement displaying a U.S. flag made of jewels and precious stones (Tiffany, 2001b).

It is crucial to recognize the interpenetration of editorial, political, and advertising content of this layout. The page functions as an unpaid advertisement for the products displayed. A *New York Times* journalist chose the products and justified the display by repeating Giuliani's assertion that New York City residents ought to return to consumption. In the face of one of the most costly attacks on the U.S. in history, citizenship has been equated with consumer action.

As Charland (1987) argues, subject positions are never finalized and fully secured. Under the pressures of particular historical moments, subjectivities are open to change or are in need of resecuring. The attacks of September 11 raised the chaos of life to a flash point, reminding U.S. Americans that the nation's borders were not as secure as desired and that an accepted way of life was more fragile than imagined. Into this chaos, advertisements proffered a stabilizing and familiar position of citizen consumer, a position that allowed individuals to return to business as usual, not so much as a way of ignoring or covering over the tragedy but as a directly effective response to the threat the terrorists posed. The purpose of these advertisements, then, is not directly logical or even persuasive. They are less concerned with selling particular products and more concerned with creating particular subject positions and articulating one way of stabilizing daily living within the chaos of life (Whitson & Poulakos, 1993).

The contemporary corporation was primed to proffer these responses. As the historical overview above suggests, consumption and citizenship were already deeply linked. What is more, contemporary research by business and organization scholars asserts that creating an image of an organization through storytelling and careful image management creates value for the organization. Contemporary business and organization scholars write explicitly about these images as aesthetic (Mouritsen, 2000) and designed to create identification among the organization and its various "stakeholders" (Albert & Whetten, 1985; Dowling, 2001; Larsen, 2000). Mouritsen (2000) argues that the expressive corporation creates intellectual capital that

> is grounded in a form of aesthetic reflexivity, where the conventionally coherent grand scheme of organizational development is supplanted by the localized, step-by-step "unmediated mediation" of the problems of the day. In other words, the grand cognitive scheme of planned strategy is replaced by localized small schemes of empowerment.
>
> (pp. 224–225)

The advertisements investigated here are precisely about the aesthetic creation of identification among the organization, its employees, its customers, and the nation. Indeed it is striking how seldom the advertisements—especially in the first few days—work to sell any product or service. Instead, what is at stake in the advertisements is the relationship of the organization to the chaos and anxiety of the immediate post-attack days.

In the first month after September 11, corporations used advertisements to make two specific rhetorical claims. They created identification between themselves and America, such that the health of the corporation was part of the health of the nation. Having created this identification, the advertisements turned to the (re)constitution of the audience as citizen consumers. In resecuring this subject position, advertisers argued that it was citizens' patriotic duty to return to the stores, the dealerships, and the airways. This connection was not just made, however, by the companies. The *New York Times* involved itself in this debate through its editorial content that emphasized patriotic fashion for sale.

"Get down to Disney World"

This construction of citizens as consumers was so profound and so thorough that it permeated rhetoric at the highest reaches of our public discourse. President George W. Bush (2001a), speaking in Chicago, 15 days after the attacks, takes up this appeal for consumer citizenship. Standing between the CEOs of American Airlines and United Airlines (the companies whose planes were used for the attacks), Bush says, "I think it's interesting that on one side, we see American; on the other side it says United. Because that's what we are—America is united." The move from the company names to the patriotic claim is easy. The corporate names draw on the well of patriotism for their own rhetorical force, and did so long before the events of September 11. Bush is drawing on the related legacy from the New Deal of connecting national and corporate interests.

But Bush goes further, arguing that flying in airplanes is a crucial way of standing against terrorism. "You stand against terror by flying the airplanes. . . . We will not surrender our freedom to travel . . . we will not surrender our freedoms in America," Bush (2001a) asserts. Bush, in this speech, associates our freedom to fly with fundamental U.S. freedoms, equivalent to freedom of speech, association, or religious practice. Yet, as Bush expands on this freedom he does not argue for the importance of travel in creating political or civic association, instead freedom to travel is most strongly associated with business and tourism. Bush (2001a) urges citizens to fly in order to "do your business around the country. Fly and enjoy America's great destination spots. Get down to Disney World in Florida. Take your families and enjoy life, the way we want it to be enjoyed." Thus, Bush suggested that it is our patriotic duty to visit the great image of America and the great American image of the world, Disney World. And it is our duty to enjoy life with our families. In flying to Disney World, we will be standing up to terrorism, demonstrating that although the terrorists may think they have "struck our soul, [they] haven't touched it" (Bush, 2001a). The soul of citizenship, then, rests in doing business, buying cars, and visiting the happiest place on Earth. Nearly 2 months after the attacks, Bush again asserted that resistance to terrorism and the enactment of citizenship rested on these consumerist activities of buying and selling.

> People are going about their daily lives, working and shopping and playing, worshiping at churches and synagogues and mosques, going to movies and to baseball games. Life in America is going forward—and as the 4th-grader who wrote me knew, that is the ultimate repudiation of terrorism.
>
> (Bush, 2001b, p. 100)

Enjoying life, shopping, and playing, filling leisure time by visiting theme parks, buying jewel-studded flags and star-spangled dog accessories serve as the props for contemporary citizenship and are the surest signs the terrorists have not won. This vision is an *image* of citizenship that U.S. corporations tried to sell in the month after the tragedy. And indeed, if these advertisements and the President are to be believed, back to the business of consumption is precisely back to the business of the nation. None of this image of citizenship as consumption should be particularly surprising. The trajectory of citizenship over the last 100 years leads us in a nearly direct line to a point where consumer capitalism serves as citizenship, where private rather than collective actions, decisions, and commitments are at the forefront of politics (Barber, 1995; Berlant, 1997).

Perhaps just as important are the ways the discourse of freedom and patriotism as consumption is paired with what Bullock (2003) called a political discourse of aggressive law enforcement. At the very moment when George W. Bush and corporate advertisers were urging a return to consumption, Bush, Attorney General John Ashcroft, and other government officials were arguing for reinvigorated policing. Although the new emphasis on "law enforcement" endangers a set of civil liberties only recently won, these activities are justified as necessary for the preservation of the American way of life (Bullock, 2003). Placing the foregoing analysis of commercial discourse beside the political discourse of renewed policing suggests that the freedoms preserved include the freedom to buy and sell. In the baldest formulation, then, Americans are asked to compromise or even substitute one set of freedoms (those we might call civil) for the assurance of another set (those we might call consumptive).

This choice of freedoms might make sense in a globalized world. As Held (1995) argues, we live in a world in which

> international order is structured by agencies, organizations, associations and companies over which citizens have minimum, if any, control, and in regard to which they have little basis to signal (dis)agreement; and . . . both routine and extraordinary decisions taken by representatives of

nations and nation-states profoundly affect not only their citizens but also the citizens of other nation-states.

(pp. 135–136)

In this globalized context, "democracy" is exceptionally difficult to define. Corporations, invested in this international, globalized order, recognize the desire of citizens to have some effective voice in the order. They proffer consumer choice as one mode of having democratic control, an offer seconded by governmental spokespeople including the president. Meanwhile, renewed and vigorous law enforcement within the U.S. and military incursions in foreign lands serve as securing counterbalances to the democratic choice offered by corporations.

These advertisements then work to constitute the audience and corporations as "citizen consumers" (Cohen, 1998, p. 111), and democratic choice as consumer choice. Marrying political activity with economic activity, the advertisements work hard to bolster the economy and generate consumer confidence not simply for the purpose of profit making, but instead as a fundamental civic duty. "Business as usual," the United Airlines advertisement reads. "Yesterday, a cliché. Today, a principle" (United, 2001, p. A25). As the advertisement makes clear, the business of buying and selling is about more than profits and losses. It is also about nationality, patriotism, and civic duty. The advertisements—combining the sublimity of the terror with the banality of "business of usual"—create stability and order out of a world violently torn asunder. Constituting the audience as citizen consumers offers individuals shopping, flying, and visits to Disneyland as powerfully mundane modes of responding to the awfulness of the unleashed terror.

Questions

1   What are the two rhetorical claims that corporate marketers made in their ads after 9/11?
2   What were common characteristics of ads in the *New York Times* *immediately* after 9/11?
3   What key transitional role did philanthropy and charity play in early 9/11 ads?
4   What was the reason that President Bush gave for why people should travel? What does the author argue could have been an alternative reason?
5   How have advertisements referenced other social crises (like Hurricane Katrina or the Iraq War)?

Notes

1.   Although I read advertisements for three months, it became clear that the crucial time period for corporations was the six weeks following the attacks. Thus all the advertisements I studied came from this period.
2.   Although advertisers chose a range of outlets for their messages, my reading of the *Los Angeles Times, Washington Post, Rocky Mountain News*, and *Denver Post* for this exact time period suggests that no newspaper was as important for corporations in communicating in an immediate and daily way to their audiences.

3.   Another 44 advertisements were at least quarter page or larger. Thus over 166 of the 246 (or about two-thirds) advertisements fill at least one-fourth of the total page.

4.   In an attempt to see what differences appeared in pre- and post-September 11, 2001, advertising. I investigated *New York Times* advertisements from September 11–October 11, 2000. Advertisements during this period that addressed politics and citizenship were primarily for political interest groups and addressed specifically political issues (see, Alliance for Better Campaigns, 2000: Campaign for America's Choice, 2000: People for the American Way, 2000: Save our Environment Coalition, 2000).

References

ABC Carpet and Home. (2001, September 14). [Advertisement]. *New York Times*, late edition, p. B6.

Albert, S., & Whetten, D. A. (1985). Organizational identity. *Research in Organizational Behavior, 7,* 263–295.

Alianz Group. (2001, September 16). [Advertisement]. *New York Times Magazine*, late edition, p. 45.

Alliance for Better Campaigns. (2000, September 15), [Advertisement], *New York Times*, late edition, p. A35.

Altman K. E. (1990). Consuming ideology: The Better Home in America campaign. *Critical Studies in Mass Communication, 7,* 286–307.

American Express. (2001, September 14). [Advertisement]. *New York Times*, late edition, p. C5.

AOL Time Warner. (2001, September 19). [Advertisement]. *New York Times*, late edition, p. A19.

Aristotle. (1991). *On rhetoric.* (G. A. Kennedy, Trans.). New York: Oxford University Press.

Bailey Banks and Biddle. (2001, September 14). [Advertisement]. *New York Times*, late edition, p. B2.

Bank of America, (2001, September 18). [Advertisement]. *New York Times*, late edition, p. A21.

Barber, B. R. (1995). *McWorld vs. Jihad.* New York: Times Books.

Baudot, J., (Ed.). (2001). *Building a world community: Globalisation and the common good.* Seattle: University of Washington Press.

Berlant, L. (1997). *The queen of America goes to Washington city: Essays on sex and citizenship.* Durham. NC: Duke University Press.

Best Buy, (2001, September 2001). [Advertisement]. *New York Times*, late edition, p. B14.

Brennan, T. (1997). *At home in the world: Cosmopolitanism now.* Cambridge: Harvard University Press.

Brown Harris Stevens. (2001, September 16), [Advertisement]. *New York Times*, p. RE4.

Bullock, D. (2003, November). *Taking liberties: John Ashcroft and the new rhetoric of law enforcement.* Paper presented at the meeting of the National Communication Association, Miami Beach. F1.

Burke, K. (1969). *A rhetoric of motives.* Berkeley: University of California Press.

Bush, G. W. (2001a, September 27). *Get On Board.* Retrieved May 18, 2002, from http://white-house.gov/ new/releases/2001/09/print/20010927–1.html

Bush, G. W. (2001b). Homeland security. *Vital Speeches of the Day, 68,* 98–101.

Callinicos, A. (2001). *Against the third way: An anti-capitalist critique.* Malden, MA: Blackwell Publishers.

Campaign for America's Choice. (2000, September 15). [Advertisement]. *New York Times*, p. A21.

Carlyle, (2001, September 16). [Advertisement]. *New York Times*, late edition, p. A26.

Cartier. (2001, September 14). [Advertisement]. *New York Times*, late edition, p. B2.

Charland, M. (1987). Constitutive rhetoric: The case of the *Peuple Québécois. Quarterly Journal of Speech, 73,* 133–150.

Classic Sofa, (2001, September 13). [Advertisement]. *New York Times*, late edition, p. F3.

Cohen, L. (1998). The new deal state and the making of citizen consumers. In S. Strasser, C. McGovern, & M. Judt (Eds.). *Getting and spending: European and American consumer societies in the twentieth century* (pp. 111–125). New York: Cambridge University Press.

Cohen, L. (2003). *A consumers' republic: The politics of mass consumption in postwar America.* New York: Alfred A. Knopf.

Cushman and Wakefield. (2001, September 16). [Advertisement]. *New York Times*, late edition, p. 37.

David Yurman, (2001, September 20). [Advertisement]. *New York Times*, late edition, p. A4.

Dell. (2000, September 17), [Advertisement]. *New York Times*, national edition, p. Y9.

Dennis, E. F., Pavlik, M., Rachlin, J., Smillie, S., Stebenne. D., & Thalmier, M. (1992). *Covering the presidential primaries*. New York: Freedom Forum Media Studies Center.

de Grazia, V. (1996). Empowering women as citizen-consumers. In V. de Grazia with E. Furlough (Eds.), *The sex of things: Gender and consumption in historical perspective* (pp. 273–286). Berkeley: University of California Press.

Dowling, G. (2001). *Creating corporate reputations: Identity, image and performance*. Oxford, UK: Oxford University Press.

East Harbor Chinese and Japanese Restaurant. (2001, September 20). [Advertisement]. *New York Times*, p. A25.

ExxonMobil. (2001, September 13). [Advertisement]. *New York Times*, late edition, p. A27.

Fleet. (2001, September 17). [Advertisement]. *New York Times*, late edition, p. B11.

Ford. (2001, September 22). [Advertisement]. *New York Times*, late edition, p. A26.

Garden State Volvo. (2001, September 16). [Advertisement]. *New York Times*, late edition, p. AU12.

GM. (2001a, September 16). [Advertisement], *New York Times Magazine*, late edition, p. 52.

GM. (2001b, September 23). [Advertisement], *New York Times*, late edition, p. A47.

Hardt, M., & Negri, A. (2000). *Empire*. Cambridge. MA: Harvard University Press.

Hariman, R. (1998). Terrible beauty and mundane detail: Aesthetic knowledge in the practice of everyday life. *Argumentation and Advocacy, 35*, 10–18.

Held, D. (1995). *Democracy and the global order: From the modern state to cosmopolitan governance*. Stanford, CA: Stanford University Press.

The Home Depot. (2001, September 16). [Advertisement], *New York Times Magazine*, late edition. p. 43.

Insignia. (2001, September 14). [Advertisement], *New York Times*, late edition, p. C7.

JP Morgan Chase. (2001, September 14). [Advertisement], *New York Times*, late edition, p. C16.

Kmart. (2001, September 16). [Advertisement]. *New York Times*, p. B3.

Kreis Collection. (2001, September 14). [Advertisement]. *New York Times*, late edition. p. B4.

Larsen, M. H. (2000). Managing the corporate story. In M. Schultz. M. J. Hatch, & M. H. Larsen (Eds.), *The expressive organization: Linking identity, reputation, and the corporate brand* (pp. 196–207). Oxford. UK: Oxford University Press.

Lipsitz, G. (1998). Consumer spending as state project: Yesterday's solutions and today's problems. In S. Strasser, C. McGovern, & M. Judt (Eds.), *Getting and spending: European and American consumer societies in the twentieth century* (pp. 127–147). New York: Cambridge University Press.

LG. (2000, September 13). [Advertisement]. *New York Times*, late edition, p. A14.

Lord and Taylor. (2001, September 16). [Advertisement]. *New York Times Magazine*. Sunday. p. 31.

Macy's. (2001, September 13). [Advertisement]. *New York Times*, late edition, p. B5.

Manhattan Auto Group. (2001, September 16). [Advertisement]. *New York Times*, late edition, p. AU16.

Marchand, R. (1985). *Advertising the American dream: Making way for modernity*. Berkeley: University of California Press.

McGee, M. C. (1990). Text, context, and the fragmentation of contemporary culture. *Western Journal of Communication, 54*, 274–289.

McGovern, C. (1998). Consumption and citizenship in the United States, 1900–1940. In S. Strasser, C. McGovern. & M. Judt (Eds.), *Getting and spending: European and American consumer societies in the twentieth century* (pp. 37–58). New York: Cambridge University Press.

Mercedes-Benz Greenwich. (2001. September 16). [Advertisement]. *New York Times*, late edition, p. AU5.

Merrill Lynch. (2001, September 14). [Advertisement]. *New York Times*, late edition, p. C3.

Morgan Stanley. (2001, September 13). [Advertisement]. *New York Times*, late edition, p. B3.

Morrell and Company. (2001, September 19). [Advertisement]. *New York Times*, late edition, p. F7.

Mouritsen, J. (2000). Valuing expressive organizations: Intellectual capital and the visualization of value creation. In M. Schultz, M.J. Hatch, & M. H. Larsen (Eds.), *The expressive organization: Linking identity, reputation, and the corporate brand* (pp. 208–229). Oxford, UK: Oxford University Press.

New York Times Company. (2001, September 15). [Advertisement]. *New York Times*, late edition, p. A24.

Paul Miller Family. (2001. September 16). [Advertisement]. *New York Times*, late edition, p. AU13.

People for the American Way. (2000, September 15). [Advertisement]. *New York Times*, late edition, p. A33.

Pumphrey, M. (1987). The flapper, the housewife and the making of modernity. *Cultural Studies, 1*, 179–194.

Ritzer, G. (1998). *The McDonaldization thesis: Explorations and extensions*. Thousand Oaks. CA: Sage.

Saks Fifth Avenue. (2001, September 13). [Advertisement]. *New York Times*, late edition, p. B3.

Save our Environment Coalition. (2000, September 15). [Advertisement]. *New York Times*, p. A21.

Sears. (2001, September 16). [Advertisement]. *New York Times Magazine*, late edition, p. 41.

Staples. (2001, September 16). [Advertisement]. *New York Times*, late edition, p. BU15.

Stuart and Frankel. (2001, September 20). [Advertisement]. *New York Times*, late edition, p. C16.

Target/Mervyn's/Marshall Field's. (2001, September 14). [Advertisement]. *New York Times*, late edition, p. C8.

Tien, F. (2001, September 23). Pulse. *New York Times*, late edition, p. ST3.

Tiffany and Company. (2001a, September 14). [Advertisement]. *New York Times*, late edition, p. B3.

Tiffany and Company. (2001b, September 23). [Advertisement]. *New York Times*, late edition, p. ST3.

United. (2001, October 4). [Advertisement]. *New York Times*, late edition, p. A25.

Verizon Wireless. (2001a, September 14). [Advertisement]. *New York Times*, late edition, p. A28.

Verizon Wireless. (2001b, September 17). [Advertisement]. *New York Times*, late edition, p. A16.

Vitamin Shoppe. (2001, September 13). [Advertisement]. *New York Times*, late edition, p. B13.

Whitson, S., & Poulakos, J. (1993). Nietzsche and the aesthetics of rhetoric. *Quarterly Journal of Speech, 79*, 131–145.

Chapter 19

BRUCE W. HARDY

POLITICAL ADVERTISING IN
US PRESIDENTIAL CAMPAIGNS
Messages, Targeting, and Effects

HARDY OFFERS A SUMMARY OF THE ROLE OF ADVERTISING in the campaign process for US presidential candidates. He discusses the advantages to politicians of using advertising versus other forms of publicity, including news coverage. He also examines the reasons politicians have gravitated toward attack ads, a form of communication that can be misleading. One theme in this and the following chapter is that trends in political advertising parallel trends in product advertising. One such trend, as the author notes, is how political ads are targeting very narrow voting blocks.

The second half of the chapter explores the effectiveness of political advertisements. In this section, Hardy presents the results of an original analysis using survey data and ad placement patterns. He demonstrates that political advertising can have a significant effect upon the outcome of an election.

Introduction

In 1796, during the first contested US presidential election, Republican handbills that vilified Federalist John Adams as an aristocrat and a monarchist were nailed to posts and doors of houses. In 1828, "the coffin handbills" were distributed by Andrew Jackson's opponents attacking "Old Hickory" for ruthlessly executing six soldiers, including a Baptist minister, for deserting their posts after the Battle of New Orleans. The handbill stated that the men had finished serving their tour and thought they could go home. Handbills—printed pamphlets intended for wide distribution—were some of the first forms of political advertising in contested presidential elections in the United States.

Today, of course, handbills have given way to more technically advanced channels for getting candidate messages out to the voting public. Political advertising on television has dominated campaign activity in the US ever since Ben Duffy, of the BBDO ad agency, took over as media advisor for Eisenhower's successful presidential bid. The 1952 presidential campaign between Democratic Adlai Stevenson and Republican Dwight Eisenhower was the first to feature television advertising; in fact, television exceeded radio in ad spending (Jamieson, 1996, p. 41). The successful Republicans reportedly spent between $800,000 and $1.5 million on their spots; greatly outspending the Democrats' $77,000 ad budget (Jamieson, 1996). However, the Stevenson campaign outspent the Republicans on television airtime for delivery of speeches as the Democratic candidate did not embrace filming scripted advertisements as Ike had.

The major role of television spots in US presidential campaigns is illustrated by the 2004 presidential campaign, when the candidates and conventions combined to spend over a billion dollars (Federal Election Commission, 2005) with more than $600 million of this spent on advertising (TNS Media Intelligence, 2004). Newer technologies like the Internet and mobile digital devices have also been utilized by presidential candidates' campaigns as viable channels in which to get their messages out to potential voters.

There are two main reasons why advertising plays such a major role in the strategy of a political campaign. First, campaigns completely control their message in political advertisements. During high-profile elections, such as the US presidential election, front-running candidates receive a large amount of media coverage. Unlike news coverage, debates, or other forms of mediated political communication, campaign messages in advertisements are not subject to immediate interpretation, vetting, and filtering by a media analyst or organization. In recent years, however, independent organizations, such as FactCheck.org, have devoted great energy into checking the veracity of claims made in political ads. In low-profile campaigns, or for lower-tier candidates in high-profile campaigns, political advertisements are important because they can be used to introduce a candidate to the public, much like a new product is introduced to consumers. Due to the press's reliance on "horse-race" campaign coverage that focuses on strategy and politicking (Cappella & Jamieson, 1996; 1997; Jamieson, 1992; Patterson, 1993; 2002) most media attention is paid to the front-running candidates of the two major parties and less attention is paid to lower-tier candidates during the primaries or third-party candidates during the general election. In 1992, third-party candidate Ross Perot, candidate for the Reform Party, used thirty-minute "infomercials" to make up for the lack of mainstream media exposure.

The second reason for a major role of advertising is the fact that campaigns can more precisely target specific audiences to receive their messages. Relying on national and local news to get your message to voters does not guarantee that certain desirable sub-populations of voters will actually be reached. Furthermore, blanketing the entire nation with television spots is money ill spent by a campaign because certain votes are more important than others as a result of the US electoral process.

Campaigns are motivated to focus on voters from a small set of specific states—"the battleground states." Battleground states in US presidential elections are states where one major party does not enjoy overwhelming support and each candidate of the two major parties has a chance of winning the electoral votes of the state. While New York and California are primarily Democratic states and Texas and South Carolina are primarily Republican, the major parties share support in states like Ohio, Pennsylvania, and Florida. These battleground states are important because they present the best opportunity to gain electoral votes as most states (except for Maine and Nebraska) have a "winner take all" system. Since candidates ignore the popular vote and focus on electoral votes, candidates also ignore states that they believe that they will easily win or states that they know they will lose. Therefore, the majority of advertisements are in media markets found in and around battleground states.

In addition, the two-party system that has long dominated US politics has made party identification an accessible heuristic for people to use in vote decisions. A heuristic is an "educated guess" or a "rule of thumb" that citizens can use to simplify voting decisions. For example, citizens can rely on party identification because they may believe that if a candidate is a member of the same party as they are the candidate must share their positions on issues. Around two-thirds of voting age Americans identify themselves as either Republican or Democrat with each party being, roughly, of equivalent size. Very rarely will these citizens cross party lines when casting a ballot. This leaves less than a third of the voting-age population that does not identify with a specific political party and makes them targets for the political campaigns because they are deemed persuadable. In US presidential elections a relatively small portion of citizens is of real interest to campaign advertising strategists.

Control Over the Message—Attacks and Deception

Although political advertisements very rarely explicitly lie, deceptive claims and attacks dominate advertising messages in politics, so much so that former Senator Tom Daschle called negative advertising "the crack cocaine of politics"[1] Unlike advertising a new cereal or shampoo, political advertisements are embedded in a market where there are, for the most part, only two choices—a Republican or a Democrat. Having only one main competitor lends itself to attack messages—or negative advertising. The "cola wars" during the 1980s between Pepsi and Coca-Cola and, more recently, the "beer wars" between Miller Lite and Bud Light illustrate this point as advertisements from these companies feature negative attacks on their competitors. However, failing the "Pepsi Challenge" or having a "taste referee" throw a penalty flag when someone picks the competitor's beer is mild compared to the attacks often featured in political advertisements. As Jamieson noted, the rhetoric surrounding political campaigns has become more vitriolic, increasingly moving from "game metaphors" to "war metaphors" (Jamieson, 1992).

Political advertisements are often deceptive or misleading because campaigns are inherently contests over competing viewpoints that, in ads, may be presented as straight facts. For example, the claim made during the 2004 presidential election that Democratic candidate "John Kerry *betrayed* his country by testifying against the Vietnam War before the Senate Foreign Relations Committee upon his return home," is a statement of opinion. Some citizens might believe that any critique of America during a time of war is an act of disloyalty, while other citizens might believe that it is an act of citizen duty (Hardy, Jamieson, & Winneg, 2008). The fact that John Kerry is a Democratic Senator from Massachusetts who served in Vietnam and testified before the Foreign Relations Committee is not, however, a matter of opinion; it is an uncontested fact that can be supported by accepted sources for information. In between matters of opinion and uncontested facts are "contested facts" which form the basis for many messages in political advertisements, typically reflecting the world views of Republicans and Democrats.

The level and effectiveness of ad deception result from the communication environment established by US presidential campaigns, the cognitive capacity of average citizens, and the argument structure of political advertisements. During a high-profile political campaign the sheer amount of information may be overwhelming for many citizens to comprehend. This combined with the effort required to obtain and maintain high levels of knowledge on the candidates' issue stances lead many citizens to infer a candidate issue stance based on the use of heuristics or cognitive shortcuts rather than firmly held knowledge (Popkin, 1994; Lupia & McCubbins, 1998). Heuristics, of course, cannot compensate for a lack of knowledge if they prompt erroneous inferences. Political campaigns are often characterized by misleading claims that try to capitalize on voters' use of heuristics (see Jackson & Jamieson, 2004). For example, during the 2004 election, the commonly held heuristic that Republicans are more likely to cut social programs than Democrats led voters to accept the Democrats' claim that President George W. Bush would actually cut Social Security for those now receiving it. The heuristic that Democrats are weak on defense and national security led the public to believe the Republican claim that Democratic candidate John Kerry voted for cuts in intelligence after September 11th as a senator (Jamieson & Hardy, 2007). Both claims were false.

Political advertisements are often enthymemes. An enthymeme is a type of argument structure that omits certain facts and premises of the argument and capitalizes on the capacity of humans to construct complete narratives out of incomplete information. Messages in political advertisements invite audiences to fill in the missing information. As mentioned above, the information that audiences bring to the messages is often based on heuristics instead of held factual knowledge; enthymemes may exploit this tendency

A now famous example of a political advertisement that invited audiences to fill in the blanks is the controversial Daisy ad from the Lyndon Johnson campaign against Barry Goldwater in 1964. This ad opens with a young girl plucking and counting pedals from a daisy. As she gets to number nine a count-down in a Cape-Canaveral voice fades in and overtakes the audio track. The camera zooms into the little girl's face and suddenly a mushroom cloud overtakes the screen. At this point Lyndon Johnson's voice is heard: "These are the stakes. To make a world in which all of God's children can live, or to go into the dark. We must love each other or die."

In the Daisy ad, Barry Goldwater, his policy stances, his character, or anything remotely related to the Republican candidate is never explicitly mentioned. Yet the Republican campaign called "foul play" when the ad was aired—and it was only aired once. The Republicans knew that this ad would lead viewers to believe that Barry Goldwater, if elected president, would cause nuclear war. The ad never tells the viewer that Goldwater would cause a nuclear war; the viewer fills in this information with their already held preconceptions of the candidates. Johnston's campaign consistently characterized Goldwater as an extremist and unfit for office during the Cold War and in the nuclear age throughout the campaign.

Despite its unstated premises, this advertisement is one of the most famous attack ads in history. The backlash was intense and the Goldwater campaign demanded that it be withdrawn. The Goldwater campaign filed a complaint with the Fair Campaign Practices Committee that stated "This horror-type commercial is designed to arouse basic emotions and has no place in campaign. I demand you call on the President to halt this smear attack on a United States Senator and the candidate for the Republican Party for the Presidency" (c.f. Jamieson, 1996, p. 200). The "smear attack," again, never even mentioned Goldwater's name or showed his picture.

For a more recent example, let's turn to the 2004 campaign. One of the misleading claims made in a television ad focused on Democratic candidate John F. Kerry's proposal to cut intelligence funding (i.e., funding for the CIA, FBI, and other law enforcement agencies) in 1994 and 1995. Titled "Wolves," the ad for incumbent President George W. Bush implied that Kerry proposed these cuts after September 11th. The ad obscured the fact that influential Republicans had supported the same cuts as well. (For a detailed analysis of the claims in the ad visit FactCheck.org.[2]) Made in spring of 2004, the Bush camp waited until the end of October to release it after focus groups revealed the ad to be highly effective. The advertisement's visuals featured a pack of wolves in a forest eyeing the camera preparing to attack:

> **Announcer:** In an increasingly dangerous world . . . Even after the first
> terrorist attack on America . . . John Kerry and the liberals in Congress
> voted to slash America's intelligence operations. By 6 billion dollars . . .
> Cuts so deep they would have weakened America's defenses. And weak-
> ness attracts those who are waiting to do America harm.

After the airing of "Wolves," NBC's *Today* show featured a panel of undecided voters and their reactions to the ad. Some of the panelists thought that it was powerful. Panelist Anthony explained: "Just the way they portrayed the—deep music, trying to give a serious note to it. It kind of catches your attention. You're think [sic] where are the wolves coming in? And it's kind of putting you in a position where you don't want to be preyed on." Other panelists were not as moved. Panelist Steve commented, "All it does is ratchet up fear in everybody, and sir, reminds them of all of the things that they need to worry about."[3]

Factcheck.org director Brooks Jackson also joined the show to explain why this ad is misleading. Jackson pointed out that the ad refers to the first World Trade Center Attack in 1993, that the cut was not $6 billion, and that it was less than four percent of intelligence spending at the time. Panelist Michael responds, "It's a slick marketing package. It happens real quick where they talk about—the $6 billion, but right away you think 9–11."[4]

As part of the the 2004 National Annenberg Election Survey (NAES), the Annenberg Public Policy Center (APPC) conducted a survey of a random sample of 3,400 citizens to assess the extent to which they believed deceptive claims made by, or on behalf of, the Bush and Kerry campaigns. Respondents rated the accuracy of 41 claims made by the major party campaigns in 2004, claims also checked for accuracy by FactCheck.org, a project of the APPC. The survey found that, on average, respondents could correctly identify the truthfulness of only 42 percent of the claims—a failing grade by any standard (Jamieson & Hardy, 2007). This is problematic as misguided beliefs lead to misguided voting.

Control Over Targeting

The main goal of political advertising is to maximize votes for a candidate. To do this a campaign needs to locate the pool of potential voters that can influence an election outcome in their favor, not only in terms of geographic location but also in terms of socio-political demographic sub-populations.

Targeting audiences based on geographic location is generally simpler during primaries than the general election. Because of the state-centric nature of the primary system all ad buys are local instead of national. However, even for the general election, national ad buys are not only expensive but also inefficient as their reach is spread equally across all media markets, battleground states, and non-battleground states. Therefore, during the general election, campaigns focus on states where the electoral votes could go either to a Democrat or a Republican.

Within specific states, campaigns' advertising strategists are also interested in targeting certain types of people. Audiences for television shows systematically vary on key demographic variables such as age, education, race, and gender and campaigns buy air time around shows with audiences that match the demographic make-up of voters that the candidate is trying to persuade. This is very similar to niche targeting of consumer products (see Turow, 1997, 2006).

In his book, *Ad Wars*, West (2005) stated that, besides demographic considerations, "there are turnout considerations. Candidates want to target citizens who are sympathetic and *likely* to vote" (p. 27, emphasis added). Candidates do not want to target citizens who are politically apathetic and do not vote. Therefore, many political ads are aired around news broadcasts with the belief that those interested in the news are more likely to be politically active.

In the last decade there have been great technical advancements in identifying target audiences by political campaigns. During the 2004 election, the Bush campaign relied on a targeting tactic called "LifeTargeting" which predicted "with 90 percent certainty how [an individual] would vote" (Sosnik, Dowd, & Fournier, 2006, p. 35). This type of targeting combines information from political-party voter lists, consumer data compiled by data mining companies, and in-house polls to identify the "political/ lifestyle DNA" of individual voters. For example, "If John Doe earned $150,000, drove a Porsche, subscribed to a golf magazine, paid National Rifle Association dues, *and told a Bush pollster* he was a pro-tax cut conservative who backed President Bush's war against terrorism, the Bush team figured that anybody with similar lifestyle tastes would hold similar political views" (Sosnik, Dowd, & Fournier, 2006, p. 36). The use of consumer data to create political profiles of individual voters is relatively new in political campaigns. The Kerry camp had nothing comparable in 2004 and according to Sosnik, Dowd, and Fournier (2006), older techniques could not predict vote intention "with even 60 percent certainty" (p. 38). Additionally, LifeTargeting allowed them to identify more specific sub-populations of interest that are much more complex than targeting based on gender and age. For example, in the state of Michigan, during the 2004 campaign, the Bush campaign:

> [I]dentified 101,200 politically moderate, middle-class voters whose No.1 issue was terrorism. They were roughly in the same stage of life and had similar lifestyles. Though they were more likely to come from union households and therefore sure to be targeted by Kerry, most of them supported Bush's reelection. The Bush team labeled them Terrorism Moderates.
>
> (p. 36)

Since the 2004 presidential election, micro-targeting techniques are becoming more and more prevalent in political campaigns. In fact, New York City Mayor and multi-billionaire Michael Bloomberg secretly polled across the US and mined consumer data to create political profiles of citizens in order to determine if he should enter the 2008 presidential race as a third-party candidate (Associated Press, 2008). Consumer data-mining combined with other advanced micro-targeting techniques will soon be the norm in targeting audiences for political advertising.

A campaign's control of message and control of targeting makes political advertising a very important communication tool during a bid for the presidency. Yet political advertising is a relatively small part of the communication environment during a presidential election. Mainstream broadcast and cable news, interpersonal discussion among citizens, grassroots mobilization and interpersonal contact with campaign volunteers, political talk radio, partisan media, and the ever-growing amount of user-generated—some objective and some partisan—media on the internet are also important. There are also viral emails and anonymous postcards that are spread across the nation vilifying candidates, push-polling, and robo-callers. Traditional political advertising is in competition with a large variety of other communication. Therefore, a question that must be asked is: How influential are political advertisements during presidential campaigns?

The Influence of Political Advertising

Unfortunately, separating out a generalized political ad effect from other campaign communication effect is extremely difficult. Furthermore, the interplay between the varying contextual environments in which political advertisements are aired and differences in messages and production values in ads makes it much more complicated to develop generalized theories of the influence of political advertisements. At best, political communication scholars can zero in on a specific ad, or sets of ads, aired at a specific time during a specific campaign and make inferences on the influence of those advertisements on voting decisions and election outcomes.

The influence of political advertising needs to be examined at both the individual level—i.e. does political advertising influence the opinions and actions of individual citizens?—and at the aggregate level—i.e. does political advertising influence election outcomes? At first it may seem intuitive that if advertisements influence individuals then they must influence election outcomes. Yet the presidential campaigns of the major parties are often equally strong in skill and resources and the impact of advertisements that come from both sides may actually cancel each other out (Zaller, 1992). Each individual ad may have specific influences on certain groups of people, and this influence is likely to be short-lived, but when taken together the total effect of all advertisements from both parties on an election outcome may be limited.

Despite this, political advertising can have a detectable influence at the individual and at the aggregate level. The evidence at the individual level comes from an illustrative analysis I conducted using data from the 2004 National Annenberg Election Study (NAES). Evidence for the influence of political advertising on an election outcome is provided by reviewing the analyses conducted by Johnston, Hagen and Jamieson (2004) using data from the 2000 NAES.

The Individual Level Influence of Political Advertising

The following illustration examines the differences in assessments, during the 2004 general election, of both incumbent President George W. Bush and Democratic challenger John Kerry on the character trait "strong leader" by voters in battleground states and non-battleground states to assess the impact of political advertising.

For the following illustration I analyze data from the 2004 National Annenberg Election Study (NAES). The NAES contains responses from 81,422 adults interviewed by phone from October 7, 2003 through November 16, 2004. The NAES was conducted on a daily schedule with an average of 207.2 completed interviews per day. In this chapter, I examine a segment of the NAES that spans July 1, 2004 through November 1, 2004 and includes 36,912 respondents. This time frame starts when Kerry announced Senator John Edwards as his running mate in early July (July 6, 2004) and ends a day before Election Day (November 2, 2004). During this time, all respondents were asked on a 1–10 scale to apply different phrases to the two candidates; one of these phrases was "strong leader." Respondents that did not provide an answer or "did not know" were coded as missing data.[5]

To assess respondents' assessment of the candidates as a "strong leader," and how that changes over time, I first aggregate the data by calculating an average of the individual responses of each day (Kenski, 2004). This allows for the creation of a data-point for each day and allows for the graphical visualization of the data across time.[6]

The Natural Experiments in US Presidential Campaigns

As outlined above, the US electoral process has the outcome that all votes are not of equal weight. Battleground states give candidates a greater opportunity to win electoral votes than states where the majority of the population supports one party. Therefore campaigns are becoming "natural experiments" for researchers interested in campaign effects because candidates focus on the battleground states. Referring to the 2000 election, Johnston, Hagen, and Jamieson (2004) stated, "[T]hese states were somewhat of a microcosm of the country as a whole, and this made the campaign into a natural experiment: One set of voters got the ad and visit 'treatment' the others did not" (p. 66).

Figure 19.1 shows the five-day moving averages of the ratings of the candidates on the trait "strong leader" in all states. As can be seen, Bush consistently received higher ratings on this trait than Kerry. However, in the beginning of August 2004 the lines of the figure almost converge. A plausible explanation is that this convergence is the result of the Democratic convention that took place during the last week of July. After the first week in August 2004, however, Bush and Kerry diverge on the trait strong leader with Bush consistently beating him throughout the rest of the campaign.

Is this an advertising effect? The first step in answering this question is to compare the ratings of the candidates as strong leader across battleground and non-battleground states. Figure 19.2 details the average ratings of Bush and Kerry as strong leader in battleground states. The most noticeable divergence appears in the second week of August 2004 and continues with Bush trumping Kerry throughout. Figure 19.3 shows the average rating of the non-battleground states.[7] A similar divergence appears after the beginning of September 2004. Likewise, this is most likely the outcome of the GOP

Figure 19.1 Evaluations of George W. Bush and John Kerry as strong leader.

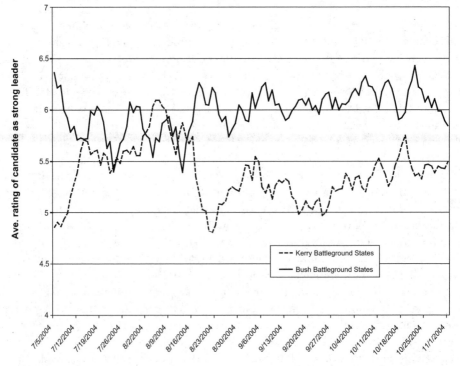

Figure 19.2 Evaluations of George W. Bush and John Kerry as strong leader—battle-ground states.

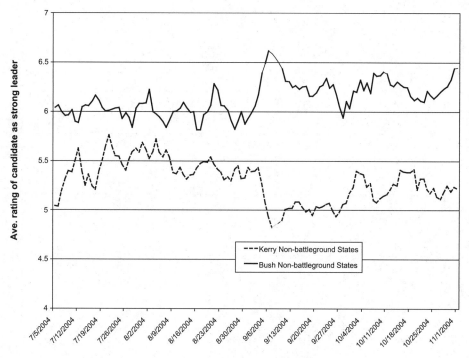

Figure 19.3 Evaluations of George W. Bush and John Kerry as strong leader—non-battleground states.

Convention that was highlighted by speeches from Arnold Schwarzenegger and Laura Bush and a fiery attack on the Democrats by fellow Democrat Zell Miller.

To further examine the divergence in the second week of August, I plotted the difference between the strong leader ratings of Bush and Kerry. As Figure 19.4 shows, in the non-battleground states Bush's lead over Kerry on this trait is relatively stable. On the other hand, in the battleground states, we see a dip in the first part of August 2004—Kerry shows an advantage on this trait—followed by a relatively large increase by Bush.

To empirically test if this jump in Bush's rating as strong leader is statistically significant, I compared the average ratings of Bush as strong leader before and after the mid-August jump by battleground versus non-battleground states. I did the same for the rating of Kerry as strong leader. To do this I partitioned the data into two independent samples. The first sample was from August 3, 2004 to August 13, 2004, and the second sample from August 14, 2004 to August 24, 2004. The samples are 10-day time frames before and after the point when the difference between assessments of Bush and Kerry as a strong leader was at its lowest—the August 13, 2004 value of Figure 19.4.

Table 19.1 shows that for both candidates, statistically significant differences in ratings across the two samples only occur in the battleground states. Due to the "natural experiment" of US presidential elections, the battleground states got the advertising "treatment" and the non-battleground states did not. At its simplest interpretation, something is happening in these states that did not happen in the non-battleground states.

These analyses are limited in that they only show that there are differences. What

Figure 19.4 Difference between Bush and Kerry "Strong Leader" rating by battleground and non-battleground states for August 2004.

Table 19.1 Differences in Mean Rating of Bush and Kerry as Strong Leader by Beginning of August and mid-August.

	Sample 1 8/03–8/13/04 $n = 3,003$	Sample 2 8/14–8/24/04 $n = 3,207$	Mean Difference (absolute value)	T – Statistic
Bush as Strong Leader				
Battleground states	5.70	6.12	.427	2.265*
Non-battleground states	5.94	6.02	.071	.558
Kerry as Strong Leader				
Battleground states	5.90	5.10	.807	4.436**
Non-battleground states	5.46	5.39	.067	.557

causes these differences? Political advertising? The average cost per day of all political television advertisement during the twenty days used in these analyses was nearly $94,000 for battleground states and $12,000 for non-battleground states. Given the large disparity in the money spent on ads in battleground versus non-battleground states, it is plausible that the difference in ratings of the candidates as a strong leader is an effect of political advertising. To shed light on the possible impact of political advertising I examined the ads released during the beginning month of August, 2004

The most obvious advertisements released during this time that would explain the decrease in Kerry's ratings as a strong leader is the first Swift Boat Veterans for Truth

(SBVT)[8] advertisement. This advertisement was aired from August 6, 2004 through August 13, 2004 in media markets of battleground states such as Charleston, West Virginia and Youngstown, Ohio. This advertisement, titled "Any Question," explicitly attacked Kerry's leadership ability. The advertisement contained comments from men who served with Kerry during the Vietnam War. These comments included, "John Kerry betrayed the men and women he served with in Vietnam" and "he lacks the capacity to lead."

Directly after, the Bush campaign released an advertisement titled "Solemn Duty" that aired August 11, 2004 to August 20, 2004. Similar to the SBVT advertisement, this ad was aired in media markets of battleground states from Miami, Florida to Albuquerque, New Mexico. The advertisement shows George W. Bush sitting next to First Lady, Laura Bush in a living room setting:

> **Bush:** My solemn duty is to lead our nation, to protect ourselves. You can't imagine the great agony of a mom or a dad having to make the decision about which child to pick up first on September the 11th. We cannot hesitate; we cannot yield; we must do everything in our power to bring an enemy to justice before they hurt us again.

I argue that these two advertisements, in part, caused the jump in Bush's rating and the decline in Kerry's rating as a strong leader. The first sentence of the Bush advertisement states that leading the nation is Bush's solemn duty then followed by a reflection of September 11, making terrorism salient and thus leading individuals living in battleground states—states in which the advertisement aired—to have higher rating of Bush as a strong leader—especially against terrorism. This advertisement in combination with the SBVT advertisement—which attacked Kerry as a strong leader and also aired in battleground states—led to the sharp divergence between Bush and Kerry regarding this trait during the month of August.

Looking at competing political advertisements during this time, the Kerry campaign and the Democratic National Convention only attacked Bush for his tax plan. The Democrats did not air any advertisements that mentioned leadership for Kerry or Bush. Therefore, in the ad wars there were no messages that competed against the message that Bush was a strong leader and Kerry was not. If there were competing messages from the Kerry campaign the influence of the SBVT and the Bush camp might not have been as dramatic. As Bush campaign media consultant Mark McKinnon noted, "As you rewind the campaign, one of the things that's gotten a lot of analysis was [the Kerry's campaign] failure to respond quickly and aggressively" (Interview, 2005). This might have been the decisive moment in the campaign.

However, the results outlined here are not 100 percent conclusive. For instance, during this month, both candidates were campaigning in the battleground states. In fact, in the beginning of August, 2004, the candidates held campaign events a half-mile away of each other in Davenport, Iowa (Candidates Cross Paths, 2004). It is possible that this campaigning could have an unaccounted influence on these results.

In addition, this illustration details the impact of specific political advertisements on respondents' assessment of the candidates' leadership qualities during a specific time period. This illustration does not tell us at all if the SBVT, or the Bush ad, influenced the outcome of the 2004 election. Mapping such short-term individual level effects of political advertisements to election outcome is extremely difficult. For evidence supporting a political advertising effect on an election outcome let's turn to the work of Johnston, Hagen, and Jamison (2004) in the following section.

The Aggregate Level Influence of Political Advertisements

Political campaigns and political advertisements are designed to win elections. Yet, the actual utility in achieving this goal is questionable as some scholars suggest that campaigns may only have a very small, or even zero, effect on individual voting behavior and election outcomes (Campbell, 2000; Holbrook, 1996). Before the 2000 US presidential election, political science was dominated by economic forecasting of election outcomes (e.g. Kramer, 1971): if the economy is good the incumbent party keeps the White House, if the economy is bad citizens vote for change. The main assumption among political scientists was simply that campaigns do not matter in election outcomes. For decades, scholars of US presidential elections have acknowledged that "fundamentals" like social forces—i.e., parental influence—predispose partisan identification which, in turn, dictates citizens' decisions when electing a president. The early Columbia and Michigan voting studies (e.g., Berelson, Lazarsfeld, & McPhee, 1954; Campbell, Converse, Miller & Stokes, 1960; Katz & Lazarsfeld, 1955) suggested that campaign communication played a very limited role in vote choice. If campaigns mattered at all, it was to highlight to voters their own preferences. Gelman and King (1993) argued that campaigns serve an informing function that fosters "enlighten preferences." These researchers argued that because the importance of fundamentals gain strength as a campaign progresses, the campaign must highlight these fundamentals to voters. Their study was an attempt to explain why early "trial-heat" and "horse race" poll results appear to be all over the map when forecasting models so accurately predict the final outcomes. In past elections, the polls reported by the major news outlets during the general election showed a close race between major party candidates, while forecasting models based on past economic conditions and incumbent party approval accurately predicted election outcomes before the presidential campaigns gained full force.

However, the 2000 campaign brought economic forecasting models into question (see the special issue of *PS: Political Science and Politics,* 2001, Vol. 34, Issue 1). How could Vice President Al Gore lose during a good economy? How could George W. Bush lose the popular vote yet still find himself in the White House? Most forecasting models put Al Gore as the winner with a comfortable margin. Johnston, Hagen, and Jamieson (2004) attributed the 2000 election outcome to the campaign and, more specifically, to political advertising. Consider the concluding paragraph of their book:

> The typical forecast placed Gore some eight points ahead of George W. Bush. Our own data indicate that in late September Gore's margin was about where the forecasts said it should be, eight points. In most elections, this would have seemed insurmountable. Campbell's (2000) review of postwar elections suggests that Gore would lose ground but, given the late date of this eight point lead, still win decisively. What no account predicted is that a lead of eight points would disappear overnight. The inference is obvious: the election was close because the campaign made it so.

Johnston, Hagen and Jamieson presented the 2000 campaign in three distinct stages. The first stage showed Gore enjoying a lead with an average share of the two-party vote of 53.7 percent which was just below the median predicted share from published economic forecasting models. The second stage showed Gore's share of the two-party vote plunge 14 points. The final stage showed the two candidates neck-and-neck. In fact, in the last seventeen days of the election Bush led eight days and Gore led nine.

The downfall of Gore, Johnston et al. argue, was the direct outcome from attacks on Gore's character: a combination of Republican political advertisements mixed with a set of news stories about Al Gore making up a story about how his mother-in-law's prescriptions cost more than his dog's. These researchers argued that the interplay between political advertisements and news stories that attacked Gore's character diminished his share of the vote and ultimately cost him the election. This is a major claim that counters much of the political science literature on the impact of political advertisements on vote decisions.

In the end, Gore won the popular vote but not the electoral vote and the presidency. Johnston, Hagen and Jamieson argue that Bush outspent Gore on advertising in the "battleground" states but Gore was more successful in getting his message—attacking Bush on his social security plan—across broadcast news. Their book details how each candidate profited when ad spending was greater than the competitor. During the last week of the campaign Bush gained 4 percentage points of the two-party share in the battleground states because he outspent Gore—for every 5 ads that Bush ran, Gore only ran 2. In non-battleground states, where no ads were aired, Gore gained on favorable network news coverage. In sum, substantial political adverting effects influenced the outcome of the election.

In the few weeks before Election Day, Gore gained across the nation because the mainstream news media picked up on his social security message. Voters in non-battleground states were being persuaded to vote for the vice president. Yet this momentum was slowed in the battleground states because of Bush's ad buys; affording Bush the electoral votes from some of these important states. In the end, according to Johnston, Hagen, and Jamieson (2004), political advertising in a few select states by the Bush campaign explains why Bush won the presidential election but not the popular vote.

Conclusion

Political advertising plays a major role in the strategy of a political campaign because of the control that campaign strategist hold over the message in ads and the targeting of audiences. Using enthymematic arguments that invite audiences to apply heuristics and pre-held perceptions of the candidates to fill in the blanks of the incomplete narrative of a 30-second spot, advertising strategists can promote claims that might deviate from the truth, but yet maximize votes. Advanced techniques in audience targeting afford campaigns the ability to pin-point persuadable voters that may be influenced by such advertising messages. In addition to outlining these two main characteristics that separate political advertising from other forms of political communication, this chapter provided evidence that suggest that political advertising can not only influence short-term public opinion, but can also influence the outcomes of elections.

This chapter focused mainly on advertisements that conform to the tradition 30-second televised spot. The nature of consumer advertising is ever changing (see Turow, 2006) and political advertising will follow suit. As stated above, making generalized statements on the influence of political advertising is extremely difficult and will only become more difficult because of the continual technological advances in production, targeting, and distribution of candidate messages.

Questions

1   Why has political advertising become such an important aspect of modern presidential campaigning?
2   What factors encourage the use of deceptive/misleading attack ads by presidential candidates?
3   What were the characteristics and legacy of the famous "Daisy" ad?
4   How and why have politicians used targeting in their advertising?
5   What evidence do we have that political advertising works?
6   What are the specific strategies used in recent campaign ads?

Notes

1. Quote taken from a column by George Will, "The First Amendment on Trial," *Washington Post*, Nov. 29, 2002.
2. "Would Kerry Throw us to the Wolves? A Misleading Bush Ad Criticizes Kerry for Proposal to Cut Intelligence Spending—A Decade Ago, By 4% When Some Republicans Also Proposed Cuts" (October 23, 2004).
3. "A Panel of Undecided Voters Weigh in on Political Ads and Their Effectiveness; Brooks Jackson of FactCheck.org Gives the Facts on the Issues mentioned in the Ads" (October 27, 2004, 07:00 AM ET), *Today*, NBC.
4. Ibid.
5. Descriptive statistics for these variables: George W. Bush: $N = 24,081$; $M = 6.10$; $SD = 3.41$; John Kerry: $N = 22,638$; $M = 5.31$; $SD = 3.21$.
6. The segment of the NAES that I am analyzing does include July 4, 2004 and no interviews were conducted on this national holiday. Following Kenski's (2004) advice, the missing data were imputed by taking the average of the days surrounding the missing date. Because daily cross-sections are subject to random sampling variation, real shifts are "scarcely detectable through the uninteresting day-to-day fluctuations induced by sampling error" (Johnston et al. 1992, 26). Therefore, we pooled the data across days to "smooth" out the random variation. Throughout this study, I employ a 5-day prior moving average, i.e., any particular day's value is an averaged of values of that day and the preceding four days.
7. The 2004 battleground states were Colorado, Florida, Iowa, Michigan, Minnesota, Nevada, New Hampshire, New Mexico, Ohio, Oregon, Pennsylvania, Wisconsin, and West Virginia.
8. The SBVT is a "527 group" which is a tax-exempt organization that is created to influence nominations and elections. Such groups are independent of the political parties and are not subject to regulation by the Federal Election Commission.

References

Associated Press *'Bloomberg Gathering Data to Gauge Support'*: MSNBC, January 9, 2008, http://www.msnbc.msn.com/id/22577977/.

Berelson, B., Lazarsfeld, P. F., & McPhee, W. N. (1954). *Voting: A study of opinion formation in presidential campaigns.* Chicago: University of Chicago Press.

Campbell, A., Converse, P. E., Miller, W. E., & Stokes, D. E. (1960). *The American Voter.* New York: John Wiley.

Campbell, J. E. (1996). *The American campaign: U.S. presidential campaigns and the national vote.* College Station, TX: Texas A&M University Press.

Candidates Cross Paths in Key Battleground State (2004, August 4). *Online News Hour.* Accessed online (October 29, 2005): http://www.pbs.org/newshour/updates/iowa_08-04-04.html.

Cappella, J. N., & Jamieson, K. H. (1996). News frames, political cynicism, and media cynicism. *The Annals of the American Academy of Political and Social Science, 546,* 71–85.

Cappella, J. N., & Jamieson, K. H. (1997). *Spiral of cynicism: The press and the public good.* Oxford: Oxford University Press.

Federal Election Commission (2005, March). *RECORD, 31, 3.*

Gelman, A., & King, G. (1993). Why are American presidential polls so variable when votes are so predictable? *British Journal of Political Science, 23,* 409–451.

Hardy, B, W., Jamieson, K. H., & Winneg, K. (2008). Wired to fact: The utility of the internet in identifying deception during the 2004 US presidential campaign. In A. Chadwick and P. Howard (Eds.), *Routledge Handbook of Internet Politics* (pp. 131–143). London: Routledge Press.

Holbrook, T. M. (1996). *Do campaigns matter?* Thousand Oaks, CA: Sage.

Interview with Mark McKinnon (2005, April 12). *Frontline.* Access online (October 30, 2005): http://www.pbs.org/wgbh/pages/frontline/shows/architect/interviews//mckinnon.html

Jamieson, K. H. (1992). *Dirty politics: Deception, distraction, and democracy.* New York: Oxford University Press.

Jamieson, K. H. (1996). *Packaging the presidency: A history and criticism of presidential campaign advertising.* Oxford: Oxford University Press.

Jamieson, K. H., & Hardy, B. W. (2007). Unmasking deception: The capacity, disposition, and challenges facing the press. In D. Graber, D. McQuail, & P. Norris (Eds.), *The politics of news: The news of politics* (2nd edition) (pp. 117–138). Washington, DC: CQ Press.

Johnston, R., Blais, A., Brady H. E. & Crête, J. (1992). *Letting the people decide: Dynamics of a Canadian election.* Stanford: Stanford University Press.

Johnston, R., Hagen, M. G., & Jamieson, K. H. (2004). *The 2000 presidential election and the foundation of party politics.* Cambridge: Cambridge University Press.

Kenski, K. (2004). Visualizing data across the campaign. In D. Romer, K. Kenski, P. Waldman, C. Adasiewicz, & K. H. Jamieson (Eds.), *Capturing campaign dynamics: The National Annenberg Election Survey.* Oxford: Oxford University Press.

Kramer, G. H. (1971). Short-term fluctuations in U.S. Voting behavior, 1896–1964. *American Political Science Review, 65,* 131–143.

Lupia, A., & McCubbins, M. D. (1998). *The democratic dilemma: Can citizens learn what they need to know?* New York: Cambridge University Press.

Patterson, T. E. (1993). *Out of order: How the decline of political parties and the growing power of the news media undermine the American way of life.* New York: Knopf.

Popkin, S. L. (1994). *The reasoning voter: Communication and persuasion in presidential campaigns* (2nd edition). Chicago, IL: University of Chicago Press.

Sosnik, M. J., Dowd, M. J., & Fournier, R. (2006). *Applebee's America.* New York: Simon & Schuster.

TNS Media Intelligence (2004, November 1). U.S. political advertising spending reaches $1.45 billion. Accessed online (October 26, 2005): http://www.tns-mi.com/news/11012004.htm.

Turow, J. (1997). *Breaking up America: Advertising and the new media world.* Chicago: The University of Chicago Press.

Turow, J. (2006). *Niche envy: Marketing discrimination in the digital age.* Cambridge, MA: MIT Press.

West, D. M. (2005). *Air wars: Television advertising in election campaigns, 1952–2004* (4th edition). Washington, D.C.: CQ Press.

Zaller, J. R. (1992). *The nature and origins of mass opinion.* Cambridge: Cambridge University Press.

Chapter 20

JOSE ANTONIO VARGAS

CAMPAIGN.USA

With the Internet comes a
New Political "Clickocracy"

I N THIS ENTRY, VARGAS SURVEYS THE CHANGES to political
campaigns that the Internet has triggered. These changes include elements that
politicians were glad to exploit, including the fundraising potential that credit-card
accepting websites offer and the publicity advantages of official and unofficial
pro-candidate sites. On the other hand, the ease of creation and distribution of images
and soundbites, as well as the 24-hour instantaneous news cycle of the Internet, means
that political candidates also cannot control their persuasive message with the same
tried and true techniques of the past. Opponents can create "mashups" of inconsistent
statements and circulate them widely on distribution sites such as YouTube. Camera
phones make it easy to capture a politician's misstatements during even semi-private
moments. No doubt we will continue to see the campaign process change as it adjusts
to this also-changing new media environment.

We saw it coming.

Just as MySpace and Facebook change the way we communicate, just as YouTube alters
the way we entertain ourselves, just as eBay and iTunes modify the way we shop, the
Internet is transforming the way we engage with this never-ending presidential
campaign.

Like it or not, we now belong to a clickocracy—one nation under Google, with video
and e-mail for all.

Want to find a candidate's position on home foreclosures?

In the past we scoured the newspaper or found the phone number for campaign
headquarters and placed a call. Now we Google "John McCain," "Barack Obama" or
"Hillary Clinton" and drown in the information flood.

Want to give money to a candidate?

These days all it takes is a credit card and three clicks—once on the home page, then on the "donate" button, then on "submit." That's much easier than writing a check and making sure you have the right address to mail it to, and certainly more accessible and egalitarian than attending a black-tie fundraiser at the Capital Hilton. No wonder, then, that Clinton and Obama collectively raised $75 million online in February, roughly $2.5 million a day. If politics is money, there's a new bank in town.

Want to create an anti-Obama Facebook group or a pro-McCain video?

Who's going to stop you?

This interactive medium is rebooting the first three words of the 220-year-old U.S. Constitution for the 21st century.

Online, "We the people . . ." takes on a whole new meaning.

There are some who question the impact or the value of the new online politics. Andrew Keen, author of "The Cult of the Amateur" and critic of the YouTubing, Facebooking, Wikipedia-ing masses, says the Internet's role in the campaign is "mostly hype, personality-driven, the 'American Idol'-ization of politics."

If the Internet is indeed having "great impact," Keen reasons, Ron Paul, the Republican Party's Internet rock star, would have won the nomination. Obama, who's greatly benefited from his online popularity, "would have been successful without the help of the Internet anyway," he says.

Then Keen slips back to his general assessment of the medium. "The problem with the Internet is it's the opposite of nuance," he says. "It's media with a hammer."

Keen, however, is in the minority.

For many, the Internet has ushered in an irreversible and seemingly seismic shift—not only for voters but also for candidates. Sure, the Web, like TV, has its limitations. A campaign's online strategy can't single-handedly win an election any more than its TV ads can. Still, the Web's impact has been profound. For instance, running a serious campaign means raising a serious amount of money. Without the Web, the relatively unknown Obama would have been unable to mount such a strong challenge to the more prominent Clinton. Nearly 60 percent of the $193 million that Obama has raised so far in his campaign—about $112 million—came from online contributions, with 90 percent of them in amounts of $100 or less.

"What we're watching is an evolution away from Washington's control, away from the power that big money and big donors used to have a monopoly on," says Tom Daschle, a South Dakota Democrat and former Senate majority leader.

Adds Richard Viguerie, often called the "funding father" of the modern conservative movement for his effective use of direct mail: "The establishment, the power structure, the Karl Roves, are losing control of the process. There's a new center of power developing."

Nothing rattles a campaign more than losing control of its message.

Campaigns are centralized, hierarchal, top-down operations. Everything's timed, choreographed. Staffers stay on message.

That goes against the very nature of the Web, where hijacking a candidate's message and spreading it around is easily done with the help of YouTube, a few rudimentary video editing skills and an e-mail list.

There are examples galore, and here's one of the first: On Jan. 9, 2007, a YouTube mash-up of Mitt Romney declaring his earlier support for abortion and gay rights—positions he later renounced—went viral.

Less than 10 hours later, his staff countered with a video reiterating Romney's current positions. But the damage had been done, and it reverberated from then on. Type "Romney" and "flip flop" into the search engine on YouTube and some 180 videos pop up.

Steve Grove, head of news and politics at YouTube, says it's one thing for a voter to read about Romney's earlier views on abortion in a newspaper article or watch a 30-second sound bite on the evening news. It's quite another to watch a video of a younger Romney, in a five-minute video titled "The Real Romney?," state, "I believe that abortion should be safe and legal in this country."

To Joe Trippi, who pioneered Howard Dean's insurgent online campaign in 2003, this is "the beauty and also the curse of the Web. . . . Like it or not, an army of people are working for you or against you." A veteran of past presidential campaigns—he worked for Sen. Edward Kennedy, former vice president Walter Mondale and former congressman Richard Gephardt—Trippi says the hardest thing for him to learn was to cede control.

This is a tension within every campaign, says Micah Sifry, co-founder of TechPresident, a bipartisan group blog that tracks how candidates are campaigning online. Though Sifry has been impressed with Obama's Web strategy—"again and again, we've seen how well they've married online enthusiasm with on-the-ground mobilization," he says—Sifry asserts that Obama's Internet team erred early on. Last spring, it sought control of a MySpace page that carried Obama's name but was independently created by an Obama supporter. "The campaign should have let the supporter control his page," Sifry says.

That lapse, however, is nothing compared with the wariness that many Republican candidates have about the Web.

Michael Turk, who led President Bush's online strategy in 2004 and recently worked as a consultant for Fred Thompson, says many Republicans still think of the Web as "an expensive brochure, like a slick direct mail." McCain's site, for instance, "is definitely an extension of the broadcast, send-receive model," he says. "The overwhelming majority of space on his home page is all about McCain, and not about how real people can get involved." But the candidate's campaign has made some improvements. "They've opened up comments on the site," Turk observes.

Another example concerned the YouTube debate. After the Democratic CNN/YouTube debate last year in which the public, including a talking snowman concerned about global warming, uploaded questions to CNN producers, most of the GOP contenders were slow to accept the invitation for their turn. "I think the presidency ought to be held at a higher level than having to answer questions from a snowman," Romney told the Manchester (N.H.) Union Leader. Pressured by young, Web-savvy conservatives who said the YouTube snub was a mistake (and who created the site SavetheDebate.com), all the candidates eventually agreed to the format.

Mindy Finn, another veteran of the Bush campaign, worked for Turk four years ago and headed Romney's online strategy until he dropped out in February.

"For campaigns, losing control also means letting candidates show more of their real personalities. A candidate is not going to be 'on' all the time, unless he or she is a really good actor. A candidate has to be himself or herself," Finn says. "In this new online era, everyone's watching, and if you're not being yourself, chances are you'll slip. And someone, somewhere, will blog about it, or upload it on YouTube."

Kathleen Hall Jamieson, a professor at the University of Pennsylvania and a chronicler of presidential races for more than 40 years, says the Internet "has the capacity to immerse people in the everyday minutiae of a campaign like no other medium before it." The problem with TV news, especially on cable, is that it distributes a message that many in the audience don't want to get, Jamieson says. Online, where we choose to sign up for a campaign's e-mail list, we're more inclined not only to read the e-mails we receive but also forward them to friends and relatives. Same goes for YouTube. A viewer makes a conscious decision to click on a video, says Jamieson, who points out a recent disconnect between what pundits are talking about in the 24-hour cable news cycle and what people are watching online.

After Obama's speech on race, cable news anchors repeatedly replayed sound bites from the Rev. Jeremiah Wright's sermons, which were uploaded on YouTube and linked on countless blogs. Videos of Obama's 37-minute speech, however, surpassed those clips in views. So far, Obama's speech has been viewed more than 4 million times, making it the most viewed video uploaded by a presidential candidate yet on the site.

Remember the axiom, driven by the rise of TV, that politics is theater? Candidates are actors in front of a camera and we're in the audience? All that's changing. Now everyone can be an actor and be in the audience.

"In the past there was only a passive relationship between the producer and the audience. But the audience has also become the producer. That's very empowering—and a huge change," says Jamieson.

"There's a dark side to this, of course. Voters can only read and watch and interact with everything they agree with, creating a hyper-partisan and largely uninformed electorate. But there's also a bright side where an informed and engaged electorate can participate in discussions that are relevant to the political process. Which way we'll eventually go, we'll have to see."

While Internet usage is still unevenly distributed—and older, reliable voters still primarily rely on broadcast media and newspapers to keep abreast of politics—as a whole we're getting more information about the campaigns online than we did in 2004, says Lee Rainie, director of the Pew Internet & American Life Project. A Pew survey released in January said that nearly a quarter of Americans say they regularly learn something about the campaign from the Internet. That figure is 42 percent among voters under 30, a historically unreliable voting bloc that has surprised pollsters by turning out in record numbers during the Democratic primaries.

When dial-up was the norm and AOL reigned supreme, the caption on a now famous New Yorker cartoon read: "On the Internet, no one knows you're a dog."

Thirteen years and a lifetime later online, not only do we know the name of the person behind the computer, he'll also show us his YouTube channel—and talk endlessly about why he supports his candidate.

Nathaniel Morris, a senior at Osbourn Park High School in Manassas, has fallen hard for Clinton. Not only has he donated $50 to her online, his YouTube channel is a shrine to the former first lady. The page's wallpaper reads "Hillary" and most of the 16 videos he's uploaded, including a three-minute mash-up set to the music of the metal rock band Shiny Toy Guns, are pro-Clinton.

"I've compared her positions with Obama and McCain and Edwards online. I watched clips of her debate performances on YouTube. I went to a rally in Manassas and volunteered for the campaign," says the 18-year-old, who waits tables at Romano's Macaroni Grill.

"Being a young Clinton supporter is not exactly the cool thing to be at school. Most of my friends are for Obama," Morris says. His mom, Lea, voted for Obama. His dad, Russell, leans toward McCain. "But I didn't want to just jump on a bandwagon."

So what about Ron Paul?

No Republican candidate—not Romney, not Rudy Giuliani, not Mike Huckabee—came close to his popularity on YouTube, Facebook and MySpace, the online social networking trifecta. He had more MeetUp groups than any candidate, including Obama. For some time "Ron Paul," ahead of "iPhone" and "Paris Hilton," was the most searched term on Technorati, which offers a real-time glimpse of the blogosphere.

But it was his online fundraising prowess that most impressed—and downright baffled—his opponents and the media. He raised more than $4 million on Nov. 5, then another $6 million on Dec. 16. Of the $36 million he raised throughout his campaign, $32 million came from the Internet. That's $5 million more than what Dean, last cycle's online phenomenon, raised during his candidacy.

That money allowed him to expand the number of campaign staffers from minuscule to modest. But the votes didn't follow. Though Paul earned 10 percent of the vote in Iowa and finished second (albeit with tiny totals) in Montana and Nevada, in many states he only got between 3 and 8 percent of the vote.

So when Paul bowed out of the race last month, the temptation was to conclude that this Internet thing can only do so much.

But take another look:

Although Paul is a 10-term congressman from Texas, he was virtually unknown nationally before this race. Yet by March 6, when Paul announced via a seven-minute video that he was dropping out, the 72-year-old made it further than anyone thought he would. He bested Giuliani, the onetime front-runner for the nomination. He beat conservative darling/former senator/movie-TV star Fred Thompson. He did way better than Sen. Sam Brownback, or Rep. Duncan Hunter, or former governor Jim Gilmore.

For Ron Paul, the Internet did more than enough.

Questions

1   How does the Internet shift control over messages during a political campaign?
2   How does the 24-hour news cycle of the Internet influence the public face of political candidates?
3   How does the Internet encourage "hyper-partisan" politics?
4   In what ways do you use the Internet to gather—or send—political information?

PART SEVEN

Advertising and the Active Citizen

INTRODUCTION TO PART SEVEN

CONSIDER, FOR A MOMENT, THE TERM *citizen-consumer*. How does your responsibility as a citizen relate to your role as a consumer? Perhaps you are having a hard time answering this question because you never thought that there was much overlap between these individual terms. Maybe you even think of them as paradoxical. Yet throughout much of the 20th century, many individuals felt that their roles in the civic world and in the marketplace were inseparable. Consumer rights movements are a form of activism in this sense. In fact, the American civil rights movement was marked by victories in the commercial sphere, including equal access to a consumer society.[1]

As you will read about in the first essay in this Part, many citizens spearheaded advocacy movements during the 1960s and 1970s in hopes of improving regulation and fair practices in the commercial sphere. This includes health and safety codes and warning labels that are still in use today. The other two essays in this Part focus on contemporary forms of activism, including grassroots movements and, more controversially, organized media "pranks."

Although the Internet is discussed only briefly in these essays, it is no doubt shaping the course of anti-corporate activism in the 21st century. As you read, consider both the strengths and limits of the advocacy approaches discussed; how these practices have changed and are changing in light of new technologies; and how you understand your own responsibilities as a citizen-consumer.

Note

1. Cohen, L. (2003). *A consumer's republic: The politics of mass consumption in postwar America*. New York: Knopf.

Chapter 21

GARY CROSS

A NEW CONSUMERISM, 1960–1980

AFTER EMERGING VICTORIOUS FROM THE SECOND WORLD WAR, America experienced a period of unprecedented economic growth, which laid the foundation for a culture of consumption. Yet by the early 1960s, many scholars and citizens began to criticize the spirit of abundance that marked the previous decade. This essay, excerpted from Gary Cross's book *An All-Consuming Century: Why Commercialism Won in Modern America*, explores this critical consumer movement as it developed during the 1960s and 1970s. Cross, a cultural historian and distinguished professor at The Pennsylvania State University, illustrates how this "new consumerism" involved critiques of both the culture of materialism and the advertising industry that fueled it. This era also witnessed a surging consumer rights movement. Although later sections in this book explore the limitations of this movement and the degree to which it was co-opted by the advertising industry, the reverberations of the movement can still be felt in the form of significant environmental, safety, finance, and health regulations, and foreshadowed the later trends explored by Christine Harold and Naomi Klein in the chapters that follow.

By the early 1960s, a consensus had emerged around managed growth. Presidential economic advisers James Tobin and Walter Heller openly embraced the Keynesian doctrine that government was obliged to maintain high wages and rising consumer demand. This policy, they believed, should be acceptable even to conservatives because it neither required a redistribution of wealth nor threatened private property.[1] High wages meant high profits when everyone assumed the duty to spend. Classes converged and ideology disappeared, noted sociologist Harold Wilensky, thanks to the mass production/mass consumption machine. Mainstream sociologist Seymour Martin Lipset's declaration sums up this optimistic view: "the fundamental problems of the industrial revolution have been solved." Daniel Bell saw an "end of ideology" where questions of adjustments rather than principles would absorb future policy makers. Even business leaders embraced President Johnson's Great Society social programs as the price for affluence. Government spending oiled a well-constructed economic machine – making it work better by adjusting consumer demand when needed and by bringing the poor into the system through education and a helping hand.[2]

In sharp contrast to the old ideal of a republic of thrift, the continuous expansion of personal desire was the foundation of an apparently frictionless economic democracy. Economist George Katona declared, "It is precisely the wanting and striving for improvements in private living standards that forms the solid basis of American prosperity. Only if the so-called private opulence increases still further can we hope to overcome public poverty."[3] The key was aspiration, not the mere meeting of needs. The driving force was not in leveling but in stimulating wants.[4]

Where there was aspiration, there was advertising. Marketing professor Steuart Britt offered a conventional defense of advertising in 1960. Of course, ads sold stuff Americans did not need. All people really require is a cave and a fire, but advertising informed them of the new and improved. Without it, Americans would still be content with the old and inferior. Britt admitted that consumer choice led to waste and trivia, "but the alternative of government regulation is far worse." In any case, the consumer is "sovereign." More and more goods chased the discretionary dollars of spenders, requiring aggressive advertising to get an audience. And consumers were demanding and fickle. Britt reminded readers that 80–90 percent of new product ideas never got to market and that scarcely 4 percent of these survived more than two years. Ads were necessary in a system of self-service shopping and were far cheaper than the old system of pushy sales staff.[5]

These ideas were the stock in trade of advertising and marketing courses in American business schools. Nevertheless, they began to be challenged by the late 1950s. Senator Estes Kefauver proposed a Department of the Consumer in the cabinet, convinced that the market alone could not protect consumers' interests. Politicians saw a better educated and more affluent public demanding safer and higher quality products. They noted also that consumers were frustrated by their difficulty in determining true credit costs or making knowledgeable comparisons between similar products.[6] As Senator Warren Magnuson put it, the self-regulation of business had become inadequate due to the "recent explosion in consumer buying and credit and the changing conditions in technology and marketing." Consumer exploitation had replaced labor exploitation as the central problem of modern society, and consumers needed friends in government.[7]

At the core of this critique was an attack on advertising. Vance Packard's *Hidden Persuaders* revived the idea popularized by F. J. Schlink and Stuart Chase in the 1920s that business manipulated consumers into buying goods they really did not need. Packard exposed a new trend in advertising called motivational research, which used depth psychology to sell goods by appealing to the desire for status and self-indulgence and by preying on feelings of personal inadequacy. Packard's critique was no lament by a marginal intellectual. His book became a major best-seller. Even advertisers were worried about their public image,[8] and with good reason. In 1958, TV quiz-show scandals involving sponsors who fed answers to popular contestants to raise ratings added to a growing discontent with hard-sell TV ads and commercial manipulation.[9]

Reporting on fraud against consumers became a minor industry in the 1960s. For example, Sidney Margolius warned Americans about loan sharks, unnecessary car repairs, home improvement scams, and overpriced insurance. He attacked the food industry for converting "inexpensive ingredients into costly processed foods." Prices for heavily advertised breakfast cereals rose twice as fast as those of other foods, even though they were often of little nutritional value. Ads and labeling were often deceptive. Honey Comb cereal, for example, had more salt than honey on it. Lack of standards in packaging made comparisons of volume and prices impossible, Margolius complained. Advertising efforts to make meaningless distinctions between different brands of detergents and toothpaste only drove up prices.[10] Even the sacred cow of 1950s consumerism, the car, was under attack. From 1957, declining sales told auto makers that the planned obsolescence of the annual model change and the resulting excesses of fins and chrome were no longer working. The car industry had obviously favored fashion over utilitarian improvements. That certainly was Ralph Nader's point in *Unsafe at Any Speed: The Designed-in Dangers in the American Automobile* (1965). The young consumer advocate argued that rising numbers of car injuries resulted not from more collisions per se but from lack of seat belts, cushioning, and other safety devices in American cars.[11]

Many consumer advocates like Margolius took a distinctly patronizing tone when they warned that the poor were wasting their welfare payments on overpriced food and clothing. At the same time, the middle class kept up an artificial standard of living only with "moonlighting husbands, working wives and some remarkable and often lifelong juggling of debts." The consumer, hoodwinked by clever cheats and too vain and insecure to stand up to the flimflam, needed the advice of experts and the protection of government.[12]

Other critics went beyond this notion of the "benighted consumer." Ralph Nader argued that corporate influence over regulatory agencies and monopolistic pricing were as important as deceptive merchandising. Only in a freely competitive economy would producers be forced to respond to consumers. At the same time, Nader favored public-supported legal assistance to the poor so that they could defend their interests against finance companies, landlords, and car dealers. Consumers needed protection from the industry that had not yet been "toilet trained" and continued to dump dangerous chemicals into the water supply and the air.[13]

Nader's advocacy of consumer rights dovetailed with a wide-ranging critique of unrestrained growth and its impact on the environment. Awareness of the problem had been growing for years. As early as 1943, the boom town of Los Angeles experienced its first bout with "smog," dust mixed with industrial and automobile emissions. Other new byproducts of postwar consumption included pollution from DDT (used first as a pesticide in 1939), detergents (which began replacing soap in 1946), and plastics. In 1965, power outages in New York brought home how dependent Americans had become on a complex and imperfect energy/power system. Ground-water contamination from storage tanks, hazardous waste sites, and land-fills was becoming a major problem by the 1960s.[14]

In response, a new kind of environmentalism emerged that went beyond advocating resource and wilderness management – thinking that had dominated the conservationism of the Progressive era. The new environmentalists proposed a systematic critique of economic growth. Setting the tone of this analysis were Fairfield Osborn's *Our Plundered Planet* (1948) and *The Limits of the Earth* (1953). In these books, Osborn attacked the common view that modern technology had eliminated the need to preserve resources and nature's equilibrium. He insisted that Americans had to abandon the comforting faith that growth could overcome all human problems: "the goal of humanitarianism is not the quantity but the quality of living. If we evade the choice, the inevitable looms ahead of us – even sterner forces will make the decision for us. We cannot delay or evade. For now, as we look, we can see the limits of the earth."[15]

Rachel Carson's *Silent Spring* (1962) shared this urgency in its indictment of the indiscriminate use of pesticides: "Future historians may well be amazed by our distorted sense of proportion. How could intelligent beings seek to control a few unwanted species by a method that contaminated the entire environment and brought the threat of disease and death even to their own kind?" Chemicals that polluted air and water supplies affected the entire food chain – and all for the sake of "perfect" vegetables and the suburban demand "that crabgrass must go at whatever cost."[16] Carson's program was modest (she advocated using natural pests rather than chemicals), but she also raised questions about the ecological costs of the consumer culture.

Others went much further. Paul Ehrlich's *The Population Bomb* (1968) was a hard-hitting attack on population growth, another critical component of prosperity. The "economics of the 1960s are dead," he insisted. Affluence was a party that has come to an end. "In the 1970s the world will undergo famines," and the United States, the greatest consumer, could not stand in isolation. In an apocalyptic tone common for the era, Ehrlich insisted that Americans must reduce family size immediately. The central problem was easy to see: "too many cars, too many factories, too much detergent . . . all can be traced easily to *too many people*." While some environmentalists questioned his emphasis on population (over pollution) controls, Ehrlich's prescription surely was a frontal attack on the growth ethic. He wanted a tax policy to discourage large families (even proposing a tax on diaper services) and he suggested that enlightened people mock and openly condemn couples with three or more children as foolish and selfish.[17]

Still more germane to this growing concern about the effect of growth was the attack on excessive use of scarce resources. Vance Packard's *The Waste Makers* (1960) complained that American's economic miracle in the 1950s was based on the "throw-away spirit" and planned obsolescence. He argued that manufacturers designed cars and appliances to have ever shorter life expectancies and to become undesirable long before they were worn out. By 1956, cars were scrapped three years earlier than they were in the late 1940s. Moreover, the car and furniture industries copied that old trick of the women's fashion business by using changes in color, style, and material to make products indispensable one season and anathema the next. According to Packard, manu-facturers facing stagnant markets used these tactics to create an "artificial demand." The long-term cost was the exhaustion of scarce resources.[18]

An even more powerful warning of resource shortages was the Club of Rome's *The Limits to Growth* (1972). This manifesto boldly claimed that "The basic behavior mode of the world system is exponential growth of population and capital, followed by collapse." Using mathematical calculations to predict population change and resource use, this book anticipated global shortages in essential raw materials, pollution, and starvation by 2100 unless zero population and limited growth were achieved.[19] E. F. Schumacher's *Small Is Beautiful* (1973) did not engage in such dire predictions, but flatly rejected the social costs of growth: "The cultivation and expansion of needs is the antithesis of wisdom. It is also the antithesis of freedom and peace." Unlimited development of consumer markets not only destroyed "non-renewable goods" but also devastated com-munities and meaningful work by encouraging centralized production over local crafts. People must take precedence over goods, insisted Schumacher, even cheap and plentiful goods.[20]

The consumer rights and environmental movements had a similar response to the consumerism of the 1950s, an appeal to fairness and prudence. With important exceptions, their solutions tended to be pragmatic, requiring legislative reform or specific, if voluntary, behavioral changes. A different kind of critique came from a disenchantment with the culture of the 1950s and its containment of individual expression.

This revolt against the conformity and "materialism" of the suburban populuxe was associated with the Bohemian or beatnik, but it was hardly invented by these social outcasts. In the late 1950s, the threat of mass consumer society to individual creativity was an oft-repeated refrain in the pages of *Life, Time*, and even *Readers' Digest*. Affluence had produced feelings of guilt. Americans brought up in the Depression were disquieted by signs that creature comforts had made the young soft (and they did not refrain from lecturing their offspring on this theme). The push-button age had made children lazy and flabby, perhaps too decadent to prevail against the Red Hordes. And the success of the Russian Sputnik over the American space program in 1957 seemed to prove the point. Americans brought up on the virtues of thrift and making do resisted the blandishments of hucksters and motivational research's pleas to spend freely. Many also began to question the price of the populuxe – jobs that male providers often secretly hated and expectations that female homemakers find fulfillment in shiny kitchen floors and well-equipped children.[21]

Especially troubling was how merchandisers seemed to threaten vaunted values of individual sufficiency. Again Packard's best-selling books struck a nerve. In *Status Seekers* and *Hidden Persuaders*, he lamented how Americans were taking their clues from the advertising and entertainment media rather than from themselves. The new affluence did not create a classless society. Instead, it produced a mass of insecure individuals each trying to define and display themselves through their goods. Packard despaired at how the modern home with its pseudocolonial decor appealed to status rather than practicality or the "real" lives of its owners. His solutions were ascetic, prudent, and most of all individualistic. Abandoning the status game and being true to oneself alone would bring "self-respect, serenity, and individual fulfillment."[22] In many ways, Packard was only updating the turn-of-the-century ideas of Thorstein Veblen, but with a twist: he attacked not the filthy rich "leisure class" but the aspiring working and lower middle classes. His views echoed the popular song "Little Boxes," which mocked the tract houses of postwar wage earners that were constructed of "ticky tacky" and made their inhabitants "all come out the same." This was as much a put-down of the populuxe culture of the wage earner as an attack upon consumer conformity.

A common assumption in this critique of consumerism was that wage earners were no longer exploited by their employers and economic inequality. Rather, in the words of the influential German emigré, Herbert Marcuse, many workers had become "happy slaves" duped by the belief "that the system delivers the goods." The true exploitation for Marcuse was in confining gratifications to the consumer culture, "which, in satisfying [the consumer's] needs, perpetuates his servitude." Workers' longing for speed boats and flashy cars enslaved them to meaningless jobs. By the late 1960s, Marcuse found hope for liberation only among the "young middle-class intelligentsia, and among the ghetto black populations," who either had discovered the emptiness of affluence or were excluded from, and thus not duped by, the commodity system.[23]

Few Americans had read or understood this German philosopher. Still, he gave abstract expression to ideas that gained wide currency. As early as 1957, Norman Mailer argued for resistance to "slow death by conformity." In a classic "Beat" manifesto, Mailer put the issue simply, "one is Hip or one is Square." And to be the "white

Negro," apart from the oppressive world of middle-class respectability, was the only way to be free. In his 1961 essay, "The Bomb in the Brooks Brothers Suit," David McReynolds saw an emerging middle-class rebellion against the confining life of the consumer culture. The revolutionaries were no longer from the working class ("Old Sam Gompers' dinner pail is full"). Rather, the modern rebel was the educated, if insecure, white-collar employee who could see from experience the madness of Madison Avenue.[24] This understanding of "revolution" was at the heart of the counterculture when it was adopted by middle-class youths in the 1960s.

It is not entirely fair to interpret the counterculture of the late 1960s and early 1970s as the logical outgrowth of these critiques of consumer culture. Certainly Packard did not see the connection (given his commitment to a self-denying individualism), and even Marcuse was critical of the ease by which notions of personal liberation were "co-opted" by money makers who peddled drug accessories and hard rock music. But that culture of youth did draw upon the critique of conformity and the idealization of the authentic self.

Charles Reich's countercultural manifesto, The Greening of America, faithfully reflected that youth movement by indicting the "system" without repeating the older call for simplicity. The socioeconomic order destroyed individuality, not by naked economic or physical oppression but by enslaving wage earners while satisfying their false wants as consumers. Reich's solution was not to resurrect a rugged frontier individualism (as Packard suggested) or to cultivate the arts (as some conservative critics and even Marcuse advised). Rather, his answer came from the contradictions of the consumer culture itself: "In trying to sell more and more commodities by the use of [real] needs, advertising cannot help but raise the intensity of the needs themselves." Ads, for example, appealed to the desire for status and thus made people want dignity. This made revolutionaries out of the "satisfied" middle class (at least the young), whose vision was expanded by the ultimate inability of affluence to deliver on its promises. This required no radical break with a culture of expanding desires. On the contrary, affluence led to "Consciousness III," a new willingness to experience adventure, sex, nature, physical activity, and an inner life that had been contained by the domestic consumerism of the 1950s.[25]

As many have noted, the hippies' free love and drug culture of the mid-1960s was a "democratic" version of the Beats' Bohemian tradition of the late 1950s. Not only had many of the hippies grown up with such classical critiques of middle-class culture as Paul Goodman's Growing Up Absurd, J. D. Salinger's Catcher in the Rye, and even Mad Magazine, but some had even read Beat primers like Jack Kerouac's On the Road and Allen Ginsberg's Howl.[26] Still, in January 1967, the hippies took a new path when they rejected the Beats' coffeehouse and personal odyssey for the mass "Human Be-In," a free-flowing event in San Francisco involving thousands in rock music, poetry, and theatrical happenings in the open air. As self-appointed countercultural leader Jerry Rubin recalled, "all the tribes [were] getting together doing their own thing." Rubin saw this event as a beginning of a new community, free from the old hierarchies and hypocrisies of the 1950s. The Beats' austere individualism disappeared, but the critique of conformity did not.[27]

The new youth culture repudiated the "happy slave's" trade-off of repressive and meaningless work for the right to join the consumer society. A 1966 Newsweek survey of college seniors found only 31 percent were seriously considering careers in business, while 74 percent felt business was a "dog eat dog" world. A Fortune study found that money making appealed to few students, and many criticized the conformity and lack of personal fulfillment in business.[28] The basis of this attack on the consumer culture was a quest for self-expression. The "trip," be it with drugs, politics, or whatever, was a personal adventure – a protest against the confinement of affluence. As Reich insisted, a "Consciousness III person will not study law to help society, if law is not what he wants to do with his life." Or as Rubin put it, "Our message: Don't grow up. Growing up means giving up your dreams."[29] All this may have been irresponsible, a denial of duty to family, community, and country, possible only in a rich country where youths could afford to forget that they would soon have obligations. Nevertheless, it was also an extraordinary rejection of a culture that identified "delivering the goods" to the masses with freedom. Even more, it was a refusal to confine desire within the circle of work and the home.

Together, the consumer rights, environmental, and countercultural movements offered a serious critique of the consumerist consensus of the 1950s. This led to wide-ranging attacks on unrestrained markets, attempts to reduce controls, and even challenges to cultural norms. Yet by the end of the 1970s, not only were political challenges to the consumer market largely marginalized, but the cultural attack on consumerism had proven to be ephemeral and even a boon to a new kind of individualistic consumerism.

Questions

1   Identify some contemporary examples of consumer rights activism.
2   Which of the issues discussed in this essay—including cultural, ethical, and environmental concerns about consumer culture—are most prevalent today?
3   "In the late 1950s, the threat of mass consumer society to individual creativity was an oft-repeated refrain in the pages of *Life, Time,* and even *Readers' Digest."* Explain whether or not mainstream media of today still take this viewpoint.

Notes

1.   Jim Heath, *John F. Kennedy and the Business Community* (Chicago: University of Chicago Press, 1969), 118–120; Richard Barber, "The New Partnership," *New Republic* 23(Aug. 13, 1966): 22.
2.   Harold Wilensky, "Mass Culture and Mass Society," *American Sociological Review* 29(April 1964): 173–197; S. M. Lipset, "The End of Ideology," in Chaim Waxman, ed., *The End of Ideology Debate* (New York: Funk & Wagnalls, 1968), 73; Daniel Bell, *End of Ideology: On the Exhaustion of Political Ideas in the Fifties* (Glencoe, Ill.: Free Press, 1960), ch. 1. See Paul Blumberg, *Inequality in an Age of Decline* (New York: Oxford University Press, 1980), ch. 1 for more on the theory of class convergence.
3.   George Katona, *The Mass Consumption Society* (New York: McGraw-Hill, 1964), 50–53, 65; Bell, *End of Ideology,* 38. Note also Daniel Horowitz, "The Emigré as Celebrant of American Consumer Culture," in Susan Strasser, ed., *Getting and Spending: European and American Consumer Societies in the Twentieth Century* (Washington, D.C.: Cambridge University Press,

1998), 149–166. John Rae's history of American automobility combines a similar effort to equate democracy with mass ownership of this mobile durable good and to condemn critics for elitism. J. Rae, *The Road and the Car in America* (Cambridge: MIT Press, 1971). Similar views are in Peter Passell and Leonard Ross, *The Retreat from Riches: Affluence and Its Enemies* (New York: Viking, 1973).

4.   Katona, *The Mass Consumption Society*, 3, 9; George Katona et al., *Aspiration and Affluence: Comparative Studies in the United States and Western Europe* (New York: McGraw-Hill, 1971), 12, 11, 15.

5.   Steuart Britt, *The Spenders: Where and Why Your Money Goes* (New York: McGraw-Hill, 1960), 31, 37–40, 65, 66, 117, 151.

6.   Lucy Black Creighton, *Pretenders to the Throne: The Consumer Movement in the United States* (Lexington, Mass.: Lexington Books, 1976), 33; Barbara Murray, *Consumerism: The Eternal Triangle* (Pacific Palisades, Calif.: Goodyear, 1973), 16–55.

7.   Warren Magnuson and Jean Carper, *The Dark Side of the Marketplace: The Plight of the American Consumer* (Englewood Cliffs, N.J.: Prentice-Hall, 1968), ix, 59.

8.   Vance Packard, *Hidden Persuaders* (New York: David McKay, 1957), 19, 25, 59, 117; Daniel Horowitz, *Vance Packard and American Social Criticism* (Chapel Hill: University of North Carolina Press, 1994), 133.

9.   David Vogel, *Fluctuating Fortunes: The Political Power of Business in America* (New York: Basic, 1988), 31.

10. Sidney Margolius, *The Innocent Consumer vs. the Exploiters* (New York: Trident, 1967), 1, 6, 7, 11, 107, 113; S. Margolius, *The Responsible Consumer*, Public Affairs Pamphlet No. 453 (Sept. 1970): 1, 3, 4. See also David Caplovitz, *The Poor Pay More: Consumer Practices of Low-Income Families* (New York: Free Press, 1963) and Hillel Black, *Buy Now, Pay Later* (New York: Morrow, 1961), 6, 105.

11. Ralph Nader, *Unsafe at Any Speed: The Designed-in Dangers in the American Automobile* (New York: Grossman, 1965). See also John Jerome, *Death of the Automobile* (New York: Norton, 1972); Emma Rothschild, *Paradise Lost: The Decline of the Automobile Industrial Age* (New York: Random House, 1973); David Gartman, *Auto Opium: A Social History of American Automobile Design* (London: Routledge, 1994), ch. 7.

12. Margolius, *The Innocent Consumer vs. the Exploiters*, 113.

13. Ralph Nader, "A Citizens' Guide to the American Economy," in Ralph Nader, ed., *The Consumer and Corporate Accountability* (New York: Harcourt Brace Jovanovich, 1973), 4–18, 51; Ralph Nader, "The Great American Gyp," in Murray, *Consumerism*, 39–51; and Creighton, *Pretenders to the Throne*, ch. 5.

14. Kendall Bailes, *Environmental History: Critical Issues in Comparative Perspective* (Lanham, Md.: University Press of America, 1985); Victor Scheffer, *The Shaping of Environmentalism in America* (Seattle: University of Washington Press, 1991); J. M. Petulla, *American Environmental History* (Columbus, Ohio: Merrill, 1988).

15. Fairfield Osborn, *The Limits of the Earth* (Boston: Little, Brown, 1953), 226.

16. Rachel Carson, *Silent Spring* (New York: Houghton Mifflin, 1962), 19, 16, 17, 161.

17. Paul Ehrlich, *The Population Bomb* (New York: Ballantine, 1968), 20–21, 60, 67, 129, 137, 185–187.

18. Vance Packard, *The Waste Makers* (New York: David McKay, 1960), 36, 69, 85, 93.

19. Donella Meadows, *The Limits to Growth* (New York: Universe Books, 1972), 127. Jeremy Rifkin, *Entropy, A New World View* (New York: Bantam, 1981), 248–254 saw the dissipation of energy as the ultimate meaning of consumer culture.

20. E. F. Schumacher, *Small Is Beautiful: A Study of Economics as if People Mattered* (London: Blond & Briggs, 1973), 19, 29, 55, 166. Note also Gary Snyder's *Turtle Island* (New York: New Directions, 1974), 91–100, which finds mass consumption the source of conflict, envy, and the breakup of community. For Snyder, a spiritual renewal, not government, was necessary to surmount the causes of consumerism.

21. Thomas Frank, *The Conquest of Cool* (Chicago: University of Chicago Press, 1997), 59, ch. 1; Barbara Ehrenreich, *Fear of Falling: The Inner Life of the Middle Class* (New York: HarperCollins, 1990), 32–36.

22. Packard, *Hidden Persuaders*, 5, 59, 201, 236; V. Packard, *The Status Seekers* (New York: David McKay, 1961), 200, 220, 314, 318. See also Horowitz, *Vance Packard*, ch. 6.

23. Herbert Marcuse, *One-Dimensional Society* (Boston: Beacon, 1964), 84, 57, 72–73; H. Marcuse, *An Essay on Liberation* (Boston: Beacon, 1969), 4, 51; H. Marcuse, *Counterrevolution and Revolt* (Boston: Beacon, 1972), 14.

24. Norman Mailer, "The White Negro: Superficial Reflections on the Hipster," (1957) in his book of essays, *Advertisements for Myself* (New York: Putnam, 1959), 339; David McReynolds, *We Have Been Invaded by the 21st Century* (New York: Praeger, 1970), 94, 98.

25. Charles Reich, *The Greening of America* (New York: Random House, 1970), 192, 194, 196, 222, 152–153; Theodore Roszak, *The Making of a Counter Culture* (Garden City, N.Y.: Doubleday, 1969), 9, 49, 65.

26. Note Michael Harrington's view of the hippie movement as a democratization of Bohemia made into banality. "We Few, We Happy Few, We Bohemians," *Esquire* (Aug. 1972): 164; Leonard Wolf, *Voices from the Love Generation* (Boston: Little, Brown, 1968), xxi.

27. Jerry Rubin, *Do It: Scenarios of a Revolution* (New York: Ballantine, 1970), 55; Bruce Pollack, *When Music Mattered: Rock in the 1960s* (New York: Holt, Rinehart, and Winston, 1984), 181–182; Edward Morgan, *The 60s Experience: Hard Lessons About Modern America* (Philadelphia: Temple University Press, 1991), 178–201.

28. Gordon Fish, "Students in Business: What Do They Think About It: Why?" *Vital Issues* (March 1969):1; "The Private World of the Class of '66," *Fortune* (Feb. 1966):130.

29. Reich, *The Greening of America*, 231; Rubin, *Do It*, 87.

Chapter 22

CHRISTINE HAROLD

PRANKING RHETORIC
"Culture Jamming" as Media Activism

ON CHRISTMAS MORNING OF 1989, hundreds of little girls who had asked Santa Claus for a Teen Talk Barbie received quite a surprise: the "voice" of the doll had been replaced by that of G.I. Joe, who grunted through Barbie's painted lips, "Eat lead, Cobra!" Perhaps not surprisingly, the incident received widespread media attention. Yet this incident was no accident; rather, it was a media prank orchestrated by a group known as the Barbie Liberation Organization, which sought to "correct the problem of gender-based stereotyping in children's toys." Christine Harold, a faculty member at the University of Washington, describes this and other instances of "culture jamming" in the essay that follows. Culture jamming is an activist movement that aims to "undermine the marketing rhetoric of multinational corporations," most visibly through hoaxes involving the media and advertising industries. Harold considers media pranking to be an especially effective form of culture jamming for it works within the system that it seeks to protest. She contrasts the strategy of "pranking" with other forms of culture jamming, specifically parodies and "opt-out" movements like "Buy-Nothing Day," which she views as less effective.

> "Pranks aren't reactive like acts of revenge. They don't punish, they provoke. . . . Revenge is a science, pranking is an art."
> (Reverend Al, of the Cacophony Society pranking group, quoted in Branwyn, 1997, p. 277)

> "Illusion is a revolutionary weapon."
> (Burroughs, 1998, p. 284)

In late 2003, *Adbusters*, the activist magazine known for its parodic "subvertisements" and scathing critiques of consumer culture, launched its most ambitious anti-branding campaign yet. Its "Blackspot" sneaker, an unassuming black canvas shoe, with a large white spot where one would expect a corporate logo, is intended to "uncool" sportswear giant Nike by offering an ethically produced alternative to the Nike swoosh. The magazine's first goal is to challenge Nike's controversial CEO by way of a full-page ad in *The New York Times* declaring:

> Phil Knight had a dream. He'd sell shoes. He'd sell dreams. He'd get rich. He'd use sweatshops if he had to. Then along came the new shoe. Plain. Simple. Cheap. Fair. Designed for only one thing. Kicking Phil's ass. The Unswoosher.
>
> (Blackspot website, 2004)

Adbusters is also encouraging its readers to help spread the "Blackspot virus" by graffiti-ing black spots on Niketown windows and displays across the U.S. and Canada. Although it remains to be seen whether the campaign will, as *Adbusters* hopes, "set a precedent that will revolutionize capitalism" (Blackspot, 2004), to date well over 200 independent shoe stores and 4000 individuals have placed orders for the shoes, and Blackspot was featured in *The New York Times Magazine*'s special "Year in Ideas" issue as one of the "best ideas of 2003."

    Adbusters is at the forefront of an insurgent political movement known loosely as "culture jamming." This movement seeks to undermine the marketing rhetoric of multinational corporations, specifically through such practices as media hoaxing, corporate sabotage, billboard "liberation," and trademark infringement. Ad parodies, popularized through magazines such as *Adbusters* and *Stay Free!* and countless websites, are by far the most prevalent of culture jamming strategies. Ad parodies attempting to serve as rhetorical x-rays, revealing the "true logic" of advertising, are a common way for so-called "subvertisers" to talk back to the multimedia spectacle of corporate marketing. An *Adbusters* parody of Calvin Klein's "heroin chic" ads of the mid-1990s, for example, features a female model hunched over a toilet, vomiting, presumably to maintain her waifish figure. The ad tells viewers that women are dissatisfied with their own bodies because "the beauty industry is the beast." In another, Joe Chemo, a cancer-ridden cartoon camel, derides the infamous Joe Camel campaign and a Tommy Hilfiger spoof depicts his customers as sheep, wanting only to "follow the flock." The Gap's infamous appropriation of the likenesses of counter-culture heroes Jack Kerouac and James Dean to sell khaki pants inspired a similar response from the adbusting community. To the Gap's claim that "Kerouac wore khakis," a group of Australian subvertisers responded with the likeness of another 20th century icon who wore khakis as well—Adolf Hitler. As such, Gap khakis were recoded as a means not to rugged individuality but genocidal totalitarianism—the conformist impulse writ large.

    Ad parodies such as these might be categorized as a strategy of rhetorical sabotage, an attempt to impede the machinery of marketing. *Adbusters*' own "culture jammer's manifesto," for example, declares: "We will jam the pop-culture marketers and bring their image factory to a sudden, shuddering halt" (Lasn, 1999, p. 128). The industrial imagery here is telling. It invokes the most traditional target of sabotage—the factory. Historically, sabotage, or monkey-wrenching, has been a dominant oppositional response to industrial power. The word "sabotage," according to Merriam-Webster's dictionary (1993), emerged in Europe around 1910, at the height of the industrial revolution. Indeed, it is a term that is inextricably linked to industrial capitalism. The first definition of sabotage offered in Webster's is the "destruction of an employer's property or the hindering of manufacturing by discontented workers." Webster's explains that the word comes from "sabot," the name for the wooden shoes worn in many European countries in the 19th century. "Saboter," then, meant "to clatter with sabots" or to "botch," presumably by throwing one's wooden shoes into the machinery. "Sabotage" means literally to "clog" with one's clogs.

I suggest that while the advertising sabotage articulated by *Adbusters* is not without some rhetorical value, it does little to address the rhetoric of contemporary market- ing—a mode of power that is quite happy to oblige subversive rhetoric and shocking imagery. Indeed, parody and irony are the dominant motifs of many successful mass- marketing campaigns. Through a kind of nudge-and-wink knowingness, Madison Avenue culture jammers make every effort to subvert traditional advertising tropes— selling, as cultural critic Thomas Frank (1997) has put it, edgy brands as tickets to the rhetorical "lynching" of consumerism. As Fredric Jameson (1991) has famously argued, the cultural logic that accompanies this era of late capitalism is defined by a codification of the eccentric modernist styles of resistance. For example, contemporary advertising is teeming with the language of revolution. But, as Jameson points out, these flagrantly rebellious styles "ostentatiously deviate from a norm which then reasserts itself, in a not necessarily unfriendly way, by a systematic mimicry of their willful eccentricities" (1991, p. 16). In other words, parody becomes one of many social codes—codes that are as available to the capitalist as they are to the artist—and, as such "finds itself without vocation" (p. 16) as a rhetoric of protest in late capitalism.

Further, I want to suggest that despite its deconstructive sensibility, parody, an example of what Mikhail Bakhtin (1984) would describe as turning the world upside down, perpetuates a commitment to rhetorical binaries—the hierarchical form it supposedly wants to upset. The frustration expressed by *Adbusters*' readers (if the magazine's often scathing letters section is any indication) implies that being told what is best for them is no more welcome coming from *Adbusters* than it is coming from advertisers. This may be, in part, because the parodic form neglects what literary theorist Jeffrey Nealon (1993, p. 30) calls the "crucial operation" of deconstruction, *reinscribing* oppositions—for example, health/sickness or authenticity/conformity— back into a larger textual field. Hence parody, as negative critique, is not up to the task of undermining the parodist's own purchase on the Truth as it maintains both a hierarchy of language and the protestor's role as revealer. Parody derides the *content* of what it sees as oppressive rhetoric, but fails to attend to its *patterns*.

In this essay, I explore the rhetorical strategies of an alternative sort of culture jammer—the prankster—who resists less through negating and opposing dominant rhetorics than by playfully and provocatively folding existing cultural forms in on themselves. The prankster performs an art of rhetorical jujitsu, in an effort to redirect the resources of commercial media toward new ends. In what follows, I first detail the theoretical frame through which I engage the political art of culture jamming including why, specifically, the prankster's ethic may offer a more compelling response than parody to contemporary cultural and economic forces. Second, in an effort to explore pranking in action I offer three contemporary case studies of radical and mainstream efforts to hijack popular media forms: the culture jamming collective ®™ark (pro- nounced "artmark"); the San Francisco-based Biotic Baking Brigade; and the American Legacy Foundation's INFKT Truth campaign. Finally, I conclude by suggesting that although pranking strategies do perform the Aristotelian notion of exploiting available means, for them to be fully imagined as rhetoric, rhetoric itself may have to be somewhat recalibrated in its role as a mass-mediated political art. As I will discuss, although culture jamming should not be seen as a replacement for more traditional modes of civic engagement, the playful and disruptive strategies of the prankster have much to offer social justice movements in the so-called "post-industrial" era.

Intensifying Media Forms: A Theory of Culture Jamming

The term "culture jamming" is based on the CB slang word "jamming" in which one disrupts existing transmissions. It usually implies an interruption, a sabotage, hoax, prank, banditry, or blockage of what are seen as the monolithic power structures governing cultural life. Like Umberto Eco's "semiological guerrillas" (1986, p. 135), culture jammers seek to "introduce noise into the signal" that might otherwise obliterate alternatives to it (Dery, 1993). Culture jamming is usually described as a kind of "glutting" of the system; it is an amping up of contradictory rhetorical messages in an effort to engender a qualitative change. In this sense, jamming need not be seen only as a damming, or a stopping of corporate media, as *Adbusters*' monkey-wrenching imagery implies. Rather, it may be more useful to consider jamming as an artful proliferation of messages, a rhetorical process of intervention and invention, which challenges the ability of corporate discourses to make meaning in predictable ways.

Many contemporary culture jammers describe themselves as political heirs to the Situationists, a group of avant-garde artists that flourished in 1950s and 1960s Europe. The Situationists were committed to detouring pre-existing political and commercial rhetorics in an effort to subvert and reclaim them. For the Situationists, led by *Society of the Spectacle* author Guy Debord, everyday life was being overrun by the Spectacle, a novel mode of social domination in which the industrial age's coercive manual labor was replaced by capitalism's deceitful promise of fulfillment through entertainment and consumption. Their main strategy, *détournement*, was an effort to "devalue the currency of the Spectacle" (Lasn, 1999, p. 108) that they claimed had kidnapped authentic life. Examples include everything from rewording conversations between popular comic strip characters, to reworking the sign on a storefront, to making subversive collages out of familiar commercial and government images. *Détournement* can be translated as "detour" or "diversion" but other, more subtle meanings in the French include "hijacking," "embezzlement," "corruption," and "misappropriation" (Sadler, 1999). Although many ad parodists, such as those at *Adbusters*, see themselves as carrying the revolutionary mantle of the Situationists, Debord and his comrades were decidedly opposed to parody as an effective rhetorical strategy, because it maintained, rather than unsettled, audiences' purchase on truth.

As I have mentioned, a major limitation of the adbuster's reliance on parody as a revelatory device is that this device has been enthusiastically embraced by marketers as well. This insistence on revealing a hidden truth also becomes a problem for other reasons. Such an insistence disallows a forceful response to what it faces because it can only *react*. It is a rhetoric that resentfully tells its audience "Things are not as they should be" without affirming possible alternatives. Saying no is itself an often satisfying alternative, but it is hardly one on which to build a lasting political movement.

The no-sayer is, in essence, yoked in a dialectic tug of war with the rhetoric it negates. *Adbusters*' Blackspot sneaker campaign, for example, may be more proactive than its subvertisements (*Adbusters* is, for example, proposing to build a "clean" factory in China should the campaign succeed), but the rhetorical message is similar. It is mobilized, first and foremost, by a desire to "kick Phil's ass." Second, then, because the no-sayer has not challenged the essential form of the binary, one can never negate adequately by its own, dialectical standards. A rhetoric that is defined by negation must always encounter more boundaries that must be overcome. More transgression is always required, which inevitably produces more cynicism and resentment. Certainly, saying no is sometimes a crucial political strategy. However, I suggest that asceticism may not be an effective intervention into the scintillating world of consumer culture; and ironically, by ardently pursuing the authentic realm "out there," one plays one's role as consumer in the fullest possible sense, endlessly chasing after something just beyond reach.

Finally—and most crucial for the discussion of pranking that follows—whereas parody may have significant impact in certain rhetorical situations, it should not be seen as a transhistorical category that is inherently subversive; primarily because capitalism itself is not a transhistorical system. It is constantly taking new shapes and producing different kinds of effects. A specific conversation between two theorists of contemporary capitalism, Michel Foucault and Gilles Deleuze, offers a productive model through which to conceptualize the political practices of culture jamming (Deleuze, 1990). Foucault and Deleuze conceived contemporary capitalism as undergoing a shift from *disciplinarity* to *control*. Under disciplinary societies, most famously theorized by Foucault, previously feudalist modes of production were brought together, organized, and confined in order to maximize efficiency and profit. Disciplinary societies operate primarily through the confinement and atomization of individuals (for example, through the familiar models of the prison, the classroom, or the factory). This was the mode of power most appropriate to a Fordist world in which assembly-line style production was the most efficient way for capital to expand. Fordism required a certain level of *standardization* to function. Workers were more or less interchangeable and labor practices were repeated with as little variation as possible. Concurrently, the advertising industry emerged to standardize the consumers who would make up the markets for these newly mass produced products.

Deleuze pursues Foucault's acknowledgement late in his career that the West is now undergoing a transformation from the disciplinarity necessary for an industrial economy to a service economy organized, in part, through the increased control of consumer desires. Control societies do not operate through the confinement and silencing of individuals but "through continuous control and communication" (1990, p. 174). That is, people are not denied access to information and knowledges but are granted ever greater access to them through the opening up of technologies and the hybridization of institutions. However, what might appear as new freedoms also enable business to increasingly modulate every aspect of life. I suggest that the proliferation of the rhetoric of consumerism, in part, marks this shift from discipline to control. Because of this emerging shift from disciplinarity (which spotlights the political rhetoric of the nation-state) to control (which increasingly relies on the visual rhetoric of the market), the opportunities for political protest have shifted as well.

At least two modes of intervention or resistance emerge out of and in response to the logics of disciplinarity and control—sabotage and appropriation. I loosely affiliate sabotage with disciplinarity and appropriation with control. However, I want to be careful, here, to complicate any neat distinction between the two. Although appropriation may be increasing in the face of greater control, both strategies continue to function in response to similar problems through deploying different tools. As Deleuze has suggested, disciplinarity does not disappear with the emergence of control. Control is an intensification, rather than a replacement, of discipline.

Media pranksters, an increasingly active type of consumer activist, prefer affirmation and appropriation to opposition and sabotage. Whereas the culture jammer as saboteur opposes commercialism through revelatory rhetoric such as parody, pranksters can be seen as comedians, as playful explorers of the commercial media landscape. In the third essay of *On the Genealogy of Morals*, Nietzsche (1989) argues that the ascetic ideal, that resentful no-saying of the first order, "has at present only *one* kind of real enemy capable of *harming* it: the comedians of this ideal—for they arouse mistrust of it" (p. 160). Unlike the ascetic, the comedian is not interested in revenge or "bringing the people to consciousness" as if she can use her comedy to expose the truth or push the limits of power until they reveal their true logic. These are the goals of the parodist, not the comedian. To reveal, one must stand in a familiar place and know just what is behind the spectacular curtain. In contrast, the comedian is something of a surfer with no firm, knowable ground on which to stand. Rather, she learns to navigate a force that is already in motion and will continue to be in motion long after she has passed. Whereas parodists attempt to change things in the name of a presupposed value, comedians diagnose a specific situation, and try something to see what responses they can provoke.

Legendary New York performance artist and media hoaxer Joey Skaggs has been provoking people for over three decades. Since 1966, Skaggs has been putting people on, using the news media's own insatiable appetite for sensational images as his canvas. Skaggs says of his work:

> I had concepts that I thought would make a statement. *I was using the media as a medium.* Rather than sticking with oil paint, the media became my medium; I got involved with the phenomenon of the media and communication as my art.
>
> (Vale & Juno, p. 36, emphasis mine)

Skaggs's most famous and widely disseminated "image event" (DeLuca, 1999) was his 1976 "Cathouse for Dogs," a phony doggie brothel in a makeshift storefront where one could supposedly have one's dog sexually "serviced." To begin, Skaggs simply issued press releases and ran the following advertisement in the *Village Voice*:

CATHOUSE FOR DOGS

> Featuring a savory selection of hot bitches. From pedigree (Fifi, the French Poodle) to mutts (Lady the Tramp). Handler and vet on duty. Stud and photo service available. No weirdos, please. Dogs only. By appointment. Call 254-7878.

On the face of it this silly prank hardly seems the kind of thing that would garner much reaction save from a few perverts or curious thrill-seekers. However, Skaggs's "Cathouse for Dogs" received more attention than even he imagined. Several New York television stations sent camera crews, the *Soho News* ran a piece, and the ASPCA, the Bureau of Animal Affairs and the NYPD vice squad, as well as the Mayor's office, all campaigned to put Skaggs out of business.

His greatest exposure, though, came by way of an *ABC News* interview. With little more than some footage of mating dogs and an interview with Skaggs, ABC produced a standard "wrap-around" news piece—interview-footage-interview—and aired it in a larger story about animal abuse. Skaggs's hoax quickly spread, earning him international media attention as well as a lawsuit from the ASPCA. Skaggs is careful to point out that his production was purely rhetorical:

> I didn't want customers—it was never my intent to defraud or deceive people for money. Deceit—yes, fraud—no. . . . An artist is much different from a con-man. I am a con-man, but I'm a con-fidence, con-ceptual, con-artist. That's different.
>
> (Vale & Juno, 1987, p. 40)

Artistic intentions aside, that year, Skaggs was subpoenaed by the Attorney General's office for "illegally running a cathouse for dogs" (Vale & Juno, 1987, p. 40). Meanwhile, ABC's documentary piece featuring Skaggs's cathouse was nominated for an Emmy as "best news broadcast of the year" (pp. 40–41)! Facing criminal charges, Skaggs publicly revealed his cathouse as a hoax. Facing professional humiliation, the ABC journalists never retracted their story, despite Skaggs's revelation.

Skaggs's hoax illustrates an important characteristic of the media. It functions, in his words, as something of a "telephone game" in which meaning and content mutate with each repetition:

> In this day and age, with electronic telecommunications instantaneously darting around the globe and people feeding off everyone else's network of nerve endings, a misspelled word or a misplaced exclamation mark can totally change what is being said. And it's almost impossible to determine where the accidental change came from. And that's on a mild level. It's even *intentionally* done. Governments are doing it, corporations are doing it. Individuals within the media itself are doing it, and people like myself are doing it to make sociopolitical commentaries [about the irresponsibility of the news media].
>
> (Vale & Juno, 1987, pp. 40–41)

As Skaggs suggests, his strategy is not uniquely his own, the domain only of the political subversive. Rather, he observes that unpredictable differentiation is an unavoidable effect as texts are disseminated across the mediascape. Messages and images mutate as they migrate through the vast variety of media outlets, until questions of source and original intent cease to matter. As he notes, governments and corporations often sponsor disinformation campaigns, using the media to start rumors or deflect the public's attention from potential scandals. Indeed, thanks to ABC's professional constraints, Skaggs's cathouse for dogs remains on the record as historical "fact."

Skaggs's cathouse for dogs event—as well as his many others, which included a "celebrity sperm bank" and a Thanksgiving world hunger performance piece—is noteworthy because it exemplifies pranking as a strategic mode of engagement with commercial media and consumer culture in general. Skaggs's project clearly functions as a prank in its most familiar sense: a trick, a practical joke, or a mischievous act. This is a prank in the mundane sense of tying a classmate's shoelaces together under the desk, or short-sheeting a bed. A prank affords the prankster a certain "gotcha!" pleasure at having pulled one over on an unsuspecting party. But, more importantly for our purposes here, Joey Skaggs's prank—as well as the others I will discuss shortly—also illustrates two alternative senses of the word:

(1)   In Middle English, to prank was to add a stylistic flourish as to one's dress: to deck, or adorn as in "to dress, or deck in a gay, bright, or showy manner; to decorate; to deck oneself *out*, dress oneself *up*."

(2)   Prank can also mean a fold, or a "pleat, as in the figurative sense of 'wrinkle'" (Vale & Juno, 1987, preface, page not enumerated).

These alternative senses of prank are imperative for this discussion of culture jamming. In neither alternative is a prank an act of dialectical opposition. In the first alternative sense, as in to "deck in a showy manner," a prank is a *stylistic exaggeration*. It is a kind of *layering up* of adornment in a conspicuous way that produces some sort of qualitative change. Prank, in this sense, is an augmentation of dominant modes of communication that interrupts their conventional patterns. In the second alternative sense, a prank is a wrinkle, or a fold. Like a fold, a prank can render a qualitative change by turning and doubling a material or text. This qualitative change is produced not through the addition of novelty, but through reconfiguration of the object itself. For analytical purposes, let us continue to stretch and layer the meaning of prank to include a folding over of mass-mediated rhetoric. Dominant texts are wrinkled, they are folded, they ravel and unravel as a result of these stylistic layerings. In the case studies that follow, I will play with these alternative senses of prank—adornment and folding—in an attempt to describe the rhetorical possibilities of media pranking.

While we are playing with definitions, however, let us consider another: I propose an alternative sense of jamming itself. Ultimately, if marketing is, as Deleuze suggests, "now the instrument of social control" (1990, p. 181), then perhaps activists must better learn to play and manipulate that instrument. Rather than approach jamming as simply a monkey-wrenching or opposition to marketing rhetoric, as the activists at *Adbusters* might have it, perhaps activists might approach it as well-trained musicians do music—as a familiar field on which to improvise, interpret, and experiment.

Earlier, I discussed the etymological roots of sabotage (literally, throwing one's clogs into the machinery) in the industrial revolution. This is a response to a disciplinary model of power that ad parodists continue to practice, despite the waning of the factory as both the symbolic and material engine of the contemporary marketplace. However, in what is little more than a side note in its definition of sabotage, *Webster's* states that, in addition to referring to wooden shoes, "sabot" also denotes "a thrust transmitting carrier," or a kind of "launching tube." This second definition provides a compelling alternative sense of the concept of sabotage. As we have seen, in its monkey-wrenching version, sabotage implies destruction or the stopping and hindering of flows through the introduction of an outside element. Put simply, it is a clogging. However, in the word's second sense, as a launching tube, sabotage also implies a channeling, or a transmission of energy or resources through a conduit. This implies that resistance can also enable and direct energy flows rather than merely thwart them. With this in mind, one's rhetorical tools need not come from outside at all, as an oppositional model might insist. Further, as the invocation of tube and carrier implies, and as we have seen from the previous examples of culture jamming, sabotage is not a chaotic, shapeless, anarchic practice, but one that is restrained and shaped by the machinery from which it emerges;

without the transmitting carrier, no thrust. In other words, constraints can be seen as immanent to those flows that seek to transform them.

Jamming, in this second, interpretive sense, requires both practice and knowledge of one's instrument as well as a dynamic exchange among a community of agents. Jamming, although it often implies a free-form chaos, requires knowledgeable and disciplined players to work. Recall, for example, Joey Skaggs's description of the work he put into his cathouse for dogs. He painstakingly set up an image event that would appeal to the needs of the televisual news media. He employed the strategies of a television producer in an effort to fold the medium over on itself. As Skaggs suggests, the broadcast media itself is his canvas. And Skaggs knows the contours of his canvas well:

> First there's the hook, when I do the performance; next, I document the process of miscommunication, or how the media twists the content and meaning of the message; finally, I talk about the serious issues underlying the performance piece. The media often trivialize the third stage by saying "Oh, he's a hoaxter, he has an ego problem, he wants attention, etc."
> (quoted in Frauenfelder & Branwyn, 1995, pp. 40–41)

Skaggs's strategies do not oppose dominant modes of power; they utilize them. As he suggests, "You're already being pranked every day. If you think *I'm* the prankster, you are sadly mistaken" (p. 41).

To jam as a musician does is to interpret an existing text. I do not mean here, interpret as in trying to make one word correspond directly to its equivalent as one does when translating a text from one language to another, where the interpreter is obliged to make the translation as correct as possible. Rather, I mean interpret in its sense as appropriation, as when a group of jazz musicians appropriate an existing piece of music, or a set of chord progressions and, in doing so, produce a new interpretation. This interpretation does not necessarily correspond to anything outside itself. It does not fail or succeed at representing an original. However, it does contain familiar textual residues. Jamming as appropriation, in these ways, differs from jamming as sabotage.

Pranking as Rhetorical Appropriation

This section focuses on three contemporary examples of media pranking. The first two, the Barbie Liberation Organization and the Biotic Baking Brigade, typify much pranking activism: both are protean collections of activists temporarily stealing the limelight of the mainstream organizations or leaders they target. Both can easily be categorized as engaging in guerrilla media strategies in the terms described above. The third example, the American Legacy Foundation's Truth campaign, an official organization's attempt to thwart teen smoking, maintains a guerrilla aesthetic and ethic but differs from the others in terms of its scope and resources. Unlike the other examples, which operate on shoestring budgets and the media savvy of activists, the Truth campaign is well funded by court-ordered tobacco industry dollars. It is the result of a successful hybrid of traditional legal advocacy and a deployment of the comedic sensibility of the prankster.

Hacking Gender: ®™ark and The Barbie Liberation Organization

In 1989, a group of culture jammers known only as the Barbie Liberation Organization (BLO) pranked the infamously litigious Mattel Corporation through its most prized brand: Barbie. Barbie and Hasbro, Inc.'s military action figure G. I. Joe are notorious for reinforcing unrealistic, even dangerous, gender stereotypes. But, for the BLO, Mattel's Teen Talk Barbie proved to be the last straw. The doll, enhanced with a computer chip "voice box," was programmed to giggle random phrases when a button on her back was pressed. Mattel's chosen phrases included: "Math class is tough!"; "I love shopping!"; and "Will we ever have enough clothes?" (*Culture Jammer's Encyclopedia*). In response, the Manhattan-based BLO organized a prank that continues to generate discussion on feminist and culture jamming websites. Taking advantage of the mechanical similarities between Teen Talk Barbie and her male counterpart Talking Duke G. I. Joe, the BLO purchased hundreds of each doll from local stores, took them home and switched their voice chips. At the height of the Christmas shopping season, they returned the dolls to stores so they could be resold to unknowing shoppers. When children opened their toys on Christmas morning, instead of Barbie chirping cheerful affirmations of American girlishness she growled, in the butch voice of G. I. Joe: "Eat lead, Cobra!"; "Dead men tell no lies!"; and "Vengeance is mine!" Meanwhile, Joe exclaimed: "Let's plan our dream wedding!"

The rhetorical message of the Great Barbie Hack may be somewhat obvious. The sheer dissonance created by hearing gender inappropriate voices and sentiments may have made absurd otherwise normalized gender norms. As one BLO operative put it: "Our goal is to reveal and correct the problem of gender-based stereotyping in children's toys" (quoted in Greenberg, 1994, para. 5). Another told *The New York Times*: "We are trying to make a statement about the way toys can encourage negative behavior in children, particularly given rising acts of violence and sexism" (Dery, 1994, para. 5). Political goals aside, the dolls have become something of a collector's item. As another BLO member jokingly told National Public Radio's Scott Simon, the BLO is good for business:

> Nobody wants to return [the dolls] . . . We think that our program of putting them back on the shelves [benefits] everyone: The storekeepers make money twice, we stimulate the economy, the consumer gets a better product and our message gets heard.
>
> (Dery, 1994, para. 9)

It also may have confused and upset children on Christmas morning. But not seven-year-old Zachariah Zelin who received one of the altered G. I. Joes. When asked "whether he wanted Santa to take back the feminine Joe, he responded sharply 'No way. I love him. I like everything about him' " reports one Associated Press writer (Greenberg, 1994, para. 13).

What was truly inspired about the BLO was their media savvy. Each "hacked" doll had a sticker on its back urging recipients "Call your local TV news," ensuring television journalists would have real disgruntled families to interview for their reports (*Culture Jammer's Encyclopedia*). Further, the group later utilized the new medium of the Internet to disseminate detailed instructions on how to perform such hacks, complete with pictures and diagrams, enabling others to perpetuate the practice. The BLO claims to have inspired similar hacks in Canada, France, and England. Finally, using a strategy increasingly popular with media activists, the BLO produced its own pre-packaged news pieces to be distributed to content-hungry local television stations. The video documentaries showed doll hackers at work, "post-op" Barbies and Joes, and interviews with BLO members explaining their project. The videos were sent out to television stations complete with press releases explaining what BLO had done and why.

When reporters asked the toy manufacturers for their reaction, one Hasbro, Inc., spokesman simply called the attack "ridiculous." Another was amused, but non-plussed: "This will move us to have a good laugh and go on making more G. I. Joes. Barbie dolls and G. I. Joes are part of American culture." Mattel officials downplayed the attack, saying they had received no complaints from consumers (Greenberg, 1994, para. 10).

The BLO was the first and most prominent culture jamming project funded by ®™ark, something of a culture jamming clearing house that has modeled itself after a corporation. Although its actual numbers are somewhat ambiguous, according to the group's website:

> ®™ark is a brokerage that benefits from "limited liability" just like any other corporation; using this principle, ®™ark supports the sabotage (informative alteration) of corporate products, from dolls and children's learning tools to electronic action games, by channelling funds from investors to workers for specific projects grouped into "mutual funds."
> (®™ark website, Frequently Asked Questions, para. 7)

®™ark exploits rather than condemns a corporate luxury that rankles many culture jammers—a corporation's ability to skirt certain legal restrictions that individuals are obliged to heed. As a private corporation, the group enables activists and investors to participate in illegal product tampering without much personal risk. As the group describes its mission: "®™ark is indeed just a corporation, and it benefits from corporate protections, but unlike other corporations, its 'bottom line' is to improve culture, rather than its own pocketbook; it seeks *cultural* profit, not financial" (®™ark website, Frequently Asked Questions, para. 8).

®™ark spokesperson Ray Thomas argues that many people still think of power in "the old terms"—that is, government power. His group seeks to make explicit the increasing power of corporations: "They are so adaptable, and they're so organic that it's hard to speak of any one corporation as the enemy. It's more the system that allows tremendous abuse" (*How to make trouble*, December 7, 1998). Rather than attempting to dismantle the corporate power system, Thomas and the other activists at ®™ark exploit it; they observe the "adaptable" and "organic" nature of corporations and approach it as fertile soil for rhetorical and political appropriation. As one Australian journalist notes, ®™ark has "cleverly aped the structures and jargons of a financial institution, even down to a smarmingly corporate-sounding promotional video" (*How to make trouble*, December 7, 1998). Opening with warnings from Abraham Lincoln about unfettered corporate power, the aforementioned video—"Bringing it to You!"—offers viewers a history of the corporation and rehearses ®™ark's style of corporate sabotage. In the spirit of pranking as I want to conceive it here, ®™ark folds and augments the corporate model in a way that offers new dimensions for rhetorical invention.

Pie Crimes and Misdemeanors: The Biotic Baking Brigade

In 1998, Nobel prize-winning economist Milton Friedman (along with conservative California governor Pete Wilson, multi-millionaire Steve Forbes, and former Secretary of State under Ronald Reagan, George Schultz) was attending a conference on the benefits of privatizing public education. As Friedman was greeting well-wishers, a young man emerged from the crowd, exclaiming "Mr. Friedman, it's a good day to pie!" and heaved a coconut crème pie into the face of the famous Chicago-school economist. With that, the Biotic Baking Brigade (BBB) executed the first of what would be many successful missions: publicly delivering pies to "pompous people." Since its inception, BBB victims have included Microsoft founder Bill Gates, CEO of genetic engineering giant Monsanto Robert Shapiro, Chevron CEO Kenneth Derr, San Francisco Mayor Willie Brown, and World Trade Organization Chief, Renato Ruggiero.

When reporting the public pieing of Mayor Willie Brown (who had just mandated a city-wide sweep of the homeless), a confused San Francisco anchorman asked: "Is it funny? Is it some kind of statement? A physical assault?" (*The Pie's the Limit*, 1999). The BBB is consistently ready with pointed answers for journalists asking the inevitable question—"Why?" In the case of Milton Friedman, for example, BBB "special agent" Christian Parenti says:

> Milton Friedman is the chief architect of neo-liberal economics. [His] particular brand of economics further allows multi-national corporations to rape the land, to plunder social systems . . . to prevent any type of popular resistance to occur. So, even though Milton Friedman may seem like a strange target, like just some fuddy-duddy old geek, the man is like a purveyor of an ideological poison that is central to the kinds of policies and politics that are threatening the health of the planet and threatening the interests of common people all over the planet.
>
> (*The Pie's the Limit*, 1999)

A pie in the face of Milton Friedman becomes what rhetoricians would call a *synechdoche*; it is an easy visual short hand for a whole host of grievances against globalization's prevailing economic ideology.

The BBB's Rahula Janowski explains the logic behind the group's choice of "weapon": "Pie is an example that you don't have to revere someone just because they're more powerful than you . . . Pie is the great equalizer. How wealthy and powerful are you with pie dripping off your face?" Janowski points out that many CEOs and other powerful people do not often put themselves in situations where they hear dissent. So the BBB seeks them out in public fora, often where the target is giving a speech in some controlled, formal environment:

> It's a message of "we know who you are and we don't agree with what you're doing." And it also puts a face on that dissent. Here's this person and they're willing to come right up and put the pie in your face. Like, "we *really* don't like what you're doing."
>
> (*The Pie's the Limit*, 1999)

Importantly, the face that gets disseminated throughout the mediascape is not that of an angry protestor, as is often the case, but the often well-known face of a captain of industry. The face of Bill Gates is a familiar image for evening news audiences; however, after being pranked by the BBB, its ability to convey authority and influence is moment-arily disenabled.

Although their message is clearly one that opposes the ideologies and practices of their targets—genetic engineering, neo-liberal economics, clear cutting of the redwoods, or corporate monopolies—their tactic of choice, pie-throwing, expresses that opposition in such a way that makes it difficult for targets to respond or audiences to understand in traditional ways. As one BBB agent, Rosie Rosebud explains: "A clown, a comedian, is someone who can laugh at themselves, they can laugh at society, and their rulers" (*The Pie's the Limit*, 1999). The BBB's rhetoric, when its agents speak to reporters, is clearly oppositional in nature, but it is their comedic posture and creation of spectacular images that get them the interviews in the first place.

The BBB understands well how to get its agenda into newspapers and television broadcasts. Unlike *Adbusters*, the BBB does not remain resentfully on the outside, denied access to what DeLuca and Peeples (2002) call the "public screen" by the commercial media. Instead, they hijack events that are already orchestrated for television—public speeches, rallies, meet-and-greets, and so on. They know that the image of a famous politician or captain of industry getting a pie in the face is so striking, the image-hungry media cannot help but cover it. Bill Gates with lemon meringue dripping from his nose *will* make the five-o'clock news. Unlike its more ascetic counterparts, the BBB does not condemn the news; it makes it by cooking up tasty images for the Spectacle to consume. As San Francisco prankster Mark Pauline puts it in another context:

> The media can never deny coverage to a good spectacle. No matter how ridiculous, absurd, insane or illogical something is, if it achieves a certain identity as a spectacle, the media has to deal with it. They have no choice. They're hamstrung by their own needs, to the extent that they're like a puppet in the face of such events.
>
> (Vale & Juno, 1987, p. 14)

Again, BBB agents are always on-hand to offer journalists a quick interpretive sound bite, such as "Monsanto CEO Robert Shapiro is the Pinochet of the food world [so] he's gotten his just desserts!" But the image of the powerful being pied says more than a spoken message ever could. As Janowski explains: "The American public under-stands the impact of the message that is put forth by a pie. I mean, I think of the Three Stooges. Think of the Marx Brothers. It's *very, very plain* what's happening when a pie is delivered" (*The Pie's the Limit*, 1999). A pie in the face becomes a powerful rhetorical symbol that requires little explanation. Agent "Salmonberry" puts it most succinctly: "I think the history of pie-throwing shows that it's a form of visual *Esperanto*. It's a universal language. Everyone understands the pie in the face. [It's about] taking their spectacle and just spinning it around. It allows people to have a laugh at the expense of the rich and powerful and otherwise unaccountable" (*The Pie's the Limit*, 1999). The BBB, then, mobilizes two familiar but dissonant visuals—a sober public speaker and a pie in the face—and by joining them, produces a kind of political jujitsu, using the power of the broadcast media toward its own ends.

To ensure its images make the news, the BBB sends its own camera operators on missions. In some cases, as with the pieing of Chevron CEO Kenneth Derr, the news media cannot be counted on to capture the moment on video. Like the Barbie Liberation Organization, the Biotic Baking Brigade happily provides budget-strapped local news stations with ready-made video packages, complete with interviews and images. This is a strategy often used by corporate advertisers hoping to create a "buzz" around a new product. Advertisers regularly offer pre-produced marketing stunts packaged as news features (known in the PR world as "video press releases"), which local news stations can easily queue up for broadcast. Result: free content for the station and free advertising for the corporation. Media pranksters like those in the BLO or the BBB just borrow that strategy, turning the media's love of images over on itself, creating a venue for issues that the commercial media often ignore. Further, BBB agents, despite their somewhat militant politics, are always clean cut, articulate, and wear a sly smile. Hence, they are not easily dismissed as militant hippie radicals creating anarchy. They realize that they, too, must look the part for broadcast television if they are to gain access to it. As BBB agents are always sure to tell reporters, civil disobedience is "as American as apple pie."[1]

INFKT Truth: Pranking Big Tobacco

One of the most successful models of media pranking comes in the form of an institutionally sanctioned public service campaign: the American Legacy Foundation's "INFKT Truth" campaign. Funded with more than $100 million of tobacco money per annum (Arnold faces anti-smoking challenge, 2002) after the 1998 "master settlement" agreement between tobacco companies and 46 states, the impeccably produced television, print, radio, and web campaign distinguished by a bright orange background and the cyber-style font and graphics popular in rave and gaming culture, Truth seeks to mobilize young people against Big Tobacco. As its use of the phonetic device "INFKT" implies, the Truth campaign encourages young people to infect their peers with knowledge about how the tobacco industry markets to children.

Unlike Nancy Reagan's "Just say no" campaign that was, by most accounts, a dismal failure in the 1980s, Truth invites young people to assume a subversive posture that is far more active than just impotently saying no to tobacco. An underlying assumption of INFKT Truth is that Nike's provocation to "just do it" has proven far more compelling to young people than Reagan's message of abstinence could ever be. In an article about teen anti-smoking campaigns, one Scottish newspaper sarcastically asks: "Would you embrace a drug-free lifestyle on the advice of an emaciated former actress with concrete hair and a designer clothes habit many times more expensive than the average teenager's dope habit?" (Harris, 1996, p. 14). Whereas the "just say no" admonishment came from the First Lady, an unmistakable symbol of the establishment, the Truth campaign takes seriously young people's anti-authoritarian attitudes and positions itself with them. Rather than asking teenagers to correct their own individual behavior, Truth encourages a critical analysis of tobacco as an industry.

Before the American Legacy Foundation launched its Truth campaign in 2000, the most prominent voice against underage smoking was the tobacco industry itself, forced by a series of courtroom battles to sponsor anti-smoking public service announcements. At first blush, these tobacco-sponsored announcements seemed well-intentioned, but their rhetoric was so out of touch with the tropes of so-called "Generation Y" that they seem purposefully ineffective. Take, for example, tobacco giant Lorillard's "Tobacco is

Wacko (if you're a teen)" campaign that supposedly sought to discourage kids from picking up the habit. First, let us assume that for most of today's teens and "tweens" as the market has so cleverly labeled pre-adolescents, "wacko" is probably not on the slang radar. More importantly, Lorillard neglects the fact that being "outside the box," "on the edge," "Xtreme" or, okay, even slightly "wacko" is exactly what is understood as cool for today's kids. Other advertisers pursuing the volatile teen market have known this for some time. Although even the most cursory analysis of market-produced rebellion shows that kids are encouraged to rebel symbolically in a mass produced way—by purchasing the latest "edgy" product – kids at least want to feel that they are choosing not to run with the herd when buying this or that brand of widget.

On the face of it, then, it might seem that Lorillard misses what proves effective with the youth market when it states that it is wacko (read: edgy) to smoke cigarettes. Although it hopelessly fudges the vernacular of today's teens, it perpetuates the aura that makes smoking so sexy to kids in the first place. Smoking is what distinguishes you from the pack. It is what makes you a rebel. In this light, Lorillard's choice of the outdated "wacko" is clearly not misguided at all. In fact, it is most likely that the company's court-ordered anti-smoking campaign was ineffective by design. As one anti-tobacco website puts it:

> The tobacco industry favors only measures that are known not to work well and may even be counter-productive—such as age-related restrictions, retailer schemes, exhortation from parents and teachers, and "finger wagging" messages that smoking is only for grown ups. These methods deflect attention away from the industry, are difficult to enforce, and present cigarettes as a "forbidden fruit" reserved for adults – exactly what most young people aspire to be!
>
> (*Exposing the truth*, para. 6)

Indeed, the outdated choice of "wacko" makes the "Don't Smoke" message all the more unhip, which leaves tobacco products untainted by any odor of unfashionability. In all, the tobacco industry spent a lot of money to tell kids that more than anything else its product makes you a rebel, which is precisely the message sent by every other successful youth marketer.

In contrast, the Truth campaign does not just tell kids not to smoke. In fact finger-waving messages never appear in its literature or imagery at all. Instead, Truth encourages young people to become culture jammers, or pranksters, themselves, and even provides them with the tools to do it. The Truth campaign is successful because it maximizes a truism in contemporary marketing: kids want to feel like they are "sticking it to the man" even if "the man" provides them the tools with which to do so. One of the group's slogans makes its non-conformist posture clear: "Join Truth now! But, don't think of it as 'joining' something." Whereas the tobacco industry's pseudo-attempt to curb teen smoking continues to afford the smoker the rebellious subject position, Truth flips that equation. In the Truth campaign, the non-smoking teen is the rebel, and tobacco executives, rather than parents and teachers, represent "the man." By rehearsing a series of pranks instigated by ordinary teenagers, Truth offers kids a new mode of agency in relation to tobacco advertising. It is an agency that is born of engaged mischief and hip rebellion rather than no-saying and abstention.

For example, one series of magazine ads provides kids with an incredibly simple way to become anti-tobacco activists. In several popular teen magazines, the group took out double-page spreads featuring Truth's trademark orange background and bold white letters. One spread read, "CIGARETTE SMOKE HAS ARSENIC," and the other, "AMMONIA IS ADDED TO CIGARETTES." On the following page is a picture of bookstores, magazine stands, and grocery store checkouts with magazines opened to these Truth "billboards". The demonstrative ads urge readers to "Spread the knowledge. Infect truth." Not only does Truth provide mini billboards inside teen magazines, it shows contexts in which those billboards might be displayed. In doing so, it provides young people with a quick and easy way to protest, to feel as if they are committing a subversive act, however small and temporary.

In another magazine campaign, Truth provides stickers in the shape of blank conversation bubbles as in a comic strip. Next to the free stickers is a picture of a Marlboro Man advertisement "augmented" by one of the stickers. In this case, someone has written: "When I get tired of counting cow patties, I like to count the 4,000 chemicals in cigarette smoke." The bubbles are outlined in the familiar Truth orange but are otherwise just blank slates, ready for kids to contribute their own messages to the vast sea of advertising. In short, it demonstrates an easy way for kids to hijack the advertisements that so saturate their landscape. As tobacco giant R. J. Reynolds itself is aware, the visual vocabulary of comic books appeals to kids. In a 1973 memo on how to better market its Camel cigarettes to young people, an R. J. Reynolds executive wrote "Comic strip type copy might get a much higher readership among younger people than any other type of copy" (*Tobacco Facts*). The company put this wisdom to use years later in its controversial Joe Camel campaign. In response, Truth launched its bubble campaign, folding Tobacco's enthusiasm for the rhetorical power of comic book imagery over on itself and, in doing so, allowing kids to participate in the construction of a new narrative.

The Truth bubble campaign borrows a common mode of *détournement* employed by the Situationists who often revised the dialogue in popular comic strips as a venue for their own subversive messages. As Situationist Reneé Viénet (1981, p. 214) argued, "comic strips are the only truly popular literature of our century" and as such were a potentially powerful vehicle for rhetorical intervention. The Situationists hijacked existing comics, but they also borrowed the familiar dialogue bubbles that had become part of the popular vernacular as vehicles for revision in other venues. Viénet writes: "it is also possible to detourn *any* advertising billboards – particularly those in subway corridors, which form remarkable sequences – by pasting over pre-prepared placards" (p. 214). Anticipating terminology popular with contemporary culture jammers, he described the practice as "guerrilla media" warfare (p. 214). In this spirit, the Truth campaign, in effect, trains young people to practice their own brand of Situationism, by confiscating a small space from commercial advertising and using it as a site for rhetorical invention. The goal to reclaim public space from the increasing "contamination" of commercial messages is shared by many culture jammers—billboard liberators, graffiti artists, and hackers, for example—but these practices usually require a criminal act, defacing private property. The Truth bubble strategy is no different in that it is, in effect, encouraging young people to vandalize a corporation's property. But, unlike other culture jammers who readily embrace their role as cultural guerrillas, Truth's suggested hijack is noteworthy in that it comes from a government-regulated organization working with legally granted tobacco money.

The content of the Truth campaign's rhetoric is not fundamentally different from the *Adbusters* strategy of negative critique. What differentiates the two is the form of their rhetorical strategy. Unlike the magazine's Joe Camel parody, Joe Chemo, which critiques cigarette smoking and the ads that promote it, Truth unabashedly appropriates the rhetorical tropes of branding; it taps into the language of the market. Its signature color orange, its use of white asterisk pop-ups to connote a virus spreading, and its digital font are consistent in its magazine, television, and Internet campaigns. In effect, Truth is an excellent example of good brand management. The current INFKT Truth campaign experiments with a mode of rhetoric that is not grounded in the proclamations of any individual speaking subject. It promotes a kind of word-of-mouth dissemination of arguments against the tobacco industry. As such, it capitalizes on what may be two favorite pastimes of many teens: rebellion and gossip.

Conclusion: Pranking Rhetoric in the Commercial Mediascape

The title of this essay, "pranking rhetoric," was carefully chosen. On one hand, it names a category of rhetorical action: pranking. On the other, it articulates an underlying premise of this analysis. That is, in order to consider pranking as rhetoric, rhetoric itself must be, well, pranked. And, here, I mean prank in all its forms: to trick, but also to fold, and to adorn. The practices discussed in this essay – pranks, hoaxes, *détourne-ments*—are not explicitly persuasive, if we understand persuasion as a targeted change in meaning structures. As I have suggested, they do not necessarily rely on that "aha!" moment when an audience becomes conscious of some new insight. Also, their effectiveness does not depend on the ethos or charisma of a specific rhetor. Hence, they fall outside the expectations of what conventionally qualifies as effective rhetoric. Clear arguments do often follow pranks – as in the Biotic Baking Brigade's critique of neo-liberal economics – but those arguments are translations of pranks. They do not account for the power of the pranks themselves. One might even argue that such translations dilute the rhetorical power pranks have to confuse and provoke. In other words, attaching an explicit argument, making a prank make sense, may undermine what is unique about pranking's signifying rhetoric in the first place.

The mass-mediated pranks and hoaxes discussed here do not oppose traditional notions of rhetoric, but they do repattern them in interesting ways. Media pranksters undermine the proprietary authority of rhetoric by hijacking its sanctioned venues, as does the Biotic Baking Brigade. Hoaxes challenge rhetoric's relationship to truth (either the art's "misuse" as a tool for propaganda, or its "correct use" in revealing facts to audiences), because they produce rhetorical effects that have little to do with facts or evidence, as in Joey Skaggs's cathouse for dogs. In general, pranking has the potential to unravel rhetoric's continued reliance on individual auteurs (be they presidents or pro-testors) because a prank's source is often impossible to locate and, ultimately, irrelevant to its political impacts.

Traditionally, communication has largely been conceived in industrial, Fordist terms. Arguments are systematically and rationally assembled. Messages move teleo-logically toward an end product—persuasion. Perhaps the strategies of pranking and branding (its commercial counterpart) may have something to teach communication scholars. As North America moves into an economy driven as much by information and marketing as the production of tangible goods, it becomes all the more crucial that communication scholars attend to the battles being waged over commercialization. A basic tenet of both the marketing and prankster world is that ideas and innovations spread less like widgets coming off an assembly line than like viruses in an ecosystem (see, for the most prominent example, Rushkoff, 1996). Indeed, viruses *communicate* diseases, yet they cannot be said to possess intentions nor progress teleologically, as a factory model might imply.

Vale and Juno (1987), in *Pranks!*, their edited collection of interviews with political pranksters, acknowledge that pranking can often be funny, even trivial. However, they remind us that pranks can also pose a "direct challenge to all verbal and behavioral *routines*, and [undermine] the sovereign authority of words, language, visual images, and social conventions in general" (Vale & Juno, 1987, preface, page not enumerated). Contemporary commercial culture depends upon consumers having somewhat routinized responses to words and images; however, these responses need not be completely homogenous. Indeed, it is the protean, polysemic nature of brands that allows them to be disseminated globally, across individuals and cultures. For example, Nike's swoosh may signify "self-discipline" to one person, and "liberty" to another; and it is likely that the Nike corporation does not much care how people interpret it as long as they keep buying Nike products. This is the viral power of the brand—its ability to provoke through sheer replication of form.

Pranking—as intensification, augmentation, folding – is conceptually and practically quite different from how we often consider rhetorics of protest. Pranking is often comedic, but not in a satirical, derisive sense that prescribes a "correct" political position. It takes the logic of branding seriously. As the famous rallying cry of Nike CEO Phil Knight—"Brands! Not products!" – illustrates, successful brands are not limited to a closed system of representation. The swoosh has the capacity to signify much more than sneakers, or even products, and that is just the way Nike wants it. Nike understands that in an age where the factory has largely been moved overseas, it is now in the business of producing something much more profitable than sportswear: its product is seductive imagery and the loyal consumers it attracts.

As I have argued throughout, pranking repatterns commercial rhetoric less by protesting a disciplinary mode of power (clogging the machinery of the image factory) than by strategically augmenting and utilizing the precious resources the contemporary media ecology affords. In doing so, pranksters, those comedians of the commercial media landscape, make manifest Michel Foucault's (1983) observation that one need not be sad to be militant. Rather than using political action to discredit a line of thought (as the parodist might have it), Foucault urges us to "use political practice as an *intensifier* of thought, and analysis as a multiplier of the forms and domains for the intervention of political action" (1983, p. xii).[2] Culture jamming multiplies the tools of intervention for contemporary media and consumer activists. It does so by embracing the viral character of communication, a quality long understood by marketers. So-called "cool hunters," for example, employ the tools of anthropologists who engage in "diffusion research" to determine how ideas spread through cultures. These marketers, like their anthropologist counterparts, have learned that people tend to adopt messages less in response to rational arguments than through exposure and example (Gladwell, 1997). Activists with a prankster ethic, such as those promoting the INFKT Truth campaign, capitalize on this capacity of ideas to multiply and disseminate like viruses. Further, although *Adbusters'* campaign to spread the Blackspot virus may still promote oppositional content, its embrace of the viral form indicates the group's advertising savvy. Tellingly, the magazine's focus on advertising parodies has waned in recent years.

It is important to note that the opportunities offered by culture jamming should not be seen as supplanting other, more traditional modes of engagement that continue to produce powerful rhetorical and political effects. Culture jamming—largely a response to consumerism and corporate power – may not be as productive in rhetorical situations that call for legal or policy interventions, for example. Further, culture jamming may be an effective strategy for engaging corporations who rely heavily on positive public relations, but may do little in the face of those which benefit from working beneath the public's radar. For these reasons, it may be most helpful to take seriously culture jamming, and pranking in particular, as important components of rhetorical hybrids, collections of tools that activists and scholars can utilize when intervening in the complex world of commercial discourse.

Finally, whereas ad parodies and satire offer up alternative interpretations of marketing rhetoric, pranks potentially upset the obligation of rhetoric to *represent* at all. Pranks intensify the polysemic quality of the signs on which marketing campaigns rely. They exacerbate the slippage in the signification process in such a way that polysemy may no longer serve the corporate author's effort to spread its ultimate message: buy! As Vale and Juno write, pranks

> attack the fundamental mechanisms of a society in which all social/verbal intercourse functions as a means toward a future *consumer exchange*, either of goods or experience. It is possible to view *every* "entertainment" experience marketed today either as an act of consumption, a prelude to an act of consumption, or both.
>
> (1987, preface, page not enumerated)

In response to the increasing rhetorical prominence of marketers, who Deleuze (1990) describes as "the arrogant breed who are our masters," pranks enact his insistence that "We've got to hijack speech. Creating has always been something different from communicating. The key thing may be to create vacuoles of non-communication, circuit breakers, so we can elude control" (p. 175). In this sense, pranks – precisely because they border on the non-sensical – reconfigure the very structures of meaning and production on which corporate media and advertising depend. Pranking—by layering and folding the rhetorical field – addresses the *patterns* of power rather than its *contents*. It does so by taking its cue, in part, from the incredible success of commercial rhetoric to infect contemporary culture.

Questions

1   Which of the pranks that Harold describes do you think was most effective? Explain why.
2   What are some of the strengths of and limits to "culture jamming"?
3   Harold notes that "culture jamming should not be seen as a replacement for more traditional modes of civic engagement." What modes of engagement do you think she is referring to? Do you agree with this statement?

Notes

1.   The phrase is reminiscent of Black Panther leader Huey Newton's famous phrase: "Violence is as American as cherry pie."
2.   In his preface, Foucault is interpreting the themes of Gilles Deleuze and Felix Guattari (2000).

References

®™*ark*. Retrieved January 27, 2004, from: http: //www.rtmark.com/faq.html.

Arnold faces anti-smoking challenges. (2002, January). *Adweek*, p. 1.

Bakhtin, M. M. (1984). *Rabelais and his world* (H. Iswolsky, Trans.). Bloomington, IN: Indiana University Press.

Blackspot. Retrieved January 21, 2004, from http://www.blackspotsneaker.org/sneaker.html.

Branwyn, G. (1997). *Jamming the media: A citizen's guide*. San Francisco: Chronicle Books.

Burroughs, W. S. (1998). Word virus. In J. Grauerholz & I. Silverberg (Eds.), *Electronic revolution* (pp. 294–313). New York: Grove Press.

Culture jammer's encyclopedia. Retrieved January 25, 2004, from http://www.sniggle.net/barbie.php.

Deleuze, G. (1990). *Negotiations*. New York: Columbia University Press.

Deleuze, G., & Guattari, F. (2000). *Anti-Oedipus: Capitalism and schizophrenia*. Minneapolis: University of Minnesota Press.

DeLuca, K. M. (1999). *Image politics: The new rhetoric of environmental activism*. New York: Guilford Press.

DeLuca, K., & Peeples, J. (2002, June). From public sphere to public screen: democracy, activism, and the "violence" of Seattle. *Critical Studies in Media Communication, 19*, 125–151.

Dery, M. (1993). *Culture jamming: Hacking, slashing and sniping in the empire of the signs*. Westfield, NJ: Open Pamphlet Series.

Dery, M. (1994). *Hacking Barbie's voice box:"Vengeance is mine!"* Retrieved January 25, 2004, from http://www.levity.com/markdery/barbie.html.

Eco, U. (1986). *Travels in hyperreality*. New York: Harcourt Brace Jovanovich.

The ethical sneaker. (2003, December 14). *The New York Times Magazine*, p. 64.

Exposing the truth: Tobacco industry "anti-tobacco" youth programs. Retrieved January 21, 2004, from http://www.essentialaction.org/tobacco/aofm/0103. Published March 2001.

Frank, T. (1997). Why Johnny can't dissent. In T. Frank & M. Weiland, (Eds.), *Commodify your dissent: Salvos from the Baffler*. New York: Norton.

Frauenfelder, S., & Branwyn, K. (Eds.). (1995). *The happy mutant handbook*. New York: Riverhead Books.

Gladwell, M. (1997, March 17). The coolhunt. *The New Yorker*. Retrieved January 25, 2004, from http://www.gladwell.com/1997/1997_03_17_a_cool.htm.

Greenberg, B. (1994, Spring). The BLO—Barbie liberation organization—strikes. *The Unit Circle Magazine*. Retrieved January 21, 2004, from http://www.etext.org/Zines/UnitCircle/uc3/page10.html.

Hacking Barbie with the Barbie Liberation Organization. Retrieved January 21, 2004 from http://www.brillomag.net/No1/blo.htm.

Harris, G. (1996, January 16). Just say no to the preaching and scaremongering. *The Scotsman*, 14.

How to make trouble and influence. *The Australian Broadcasting Corporation*. Retrieved January 21, 2004 from http://www.abc.net.au/arts/headspace/rn/bbing/trouble/b.htm.

Jameson, F. (1991). *Postmodernism: Or, the cultural logic of late capitalism*. Durham: Duke University Press.

Lasn, K. (1999). *Culture jam: The uncooling of America*™. New York: Eagle Brook.

Merriam-Webster's collegiate dictionary. (10th ed.). (1993). Springfield, MA: Merriam-Webster.

Nealon, J. T. (1993). *Double reading: Postmodernism after deconstruction*. New York: Cornell University Press.

Nietzsche, F. (1989). *On the genealogy of morals and Ecce Homo* (W. Kaufmann, Trans.). New York: Vintage.

The pie's the limit!: A documentary on the global pasty uprising. (1999). Video recording. San Francisco: Whispered Media.

Rushkoff, D. (1996). *Media virus!* New York: Ballantine Books.

Sadler, S. (1999). *The situationist city.* Cambridge: MIT Press.

Tobacco facts. Retrieved January 21, 2004, from http://www.tobaccofacts.org/ozone/o2z-howthey-seeyou.html.

Vale, V., & Juno, A. (Eds.). (1987). *Pranks!* San Francisco: RE/Search.

Viénet, R. (1981). The situationists and the new forms of action against politics and art. In K. Knabb (Ed.), *The situationist international anthology* (pp. 213–216). Berkeley: Bureau of Public Secrets.

Chapter 23

NAOMI KLEIN

LOCAL FOREIGN POLICY
Students and Communities Join the Fray

IS THERE ANY HOPE FOR ORDINARY CITIZENS to rally against corporate brand behemoths like PepsiCo, McDonald's, and Nike? Writer-activist Naomi Klein seems to think so. In the following piece, Klein suggests the potential for anticorporate activism at the school, university, and community levels. To make her point, she highlights a number of successful cases of "brand backlash," where organizations have protested the labor practices of those corporations that seek to sponsor them (for example, Nike-sponsored sports uniforms or Coca-Cola brand beverages in school lunchrooms). This essay is excerpted from Klein's award-winning book *No Logo: Taking Aim at the Brand Bullies*, which introduces some thought-provoking concerns about corporate branding.

> Pretty soon we'll have to do our own offshore drilling.
> Berkeley, California, city councilor Polly Armstrong on her council's decision to
> outlaw municipal gasoline purchases from all the major oil companies

"Okay. I need people on each door. Let's go!" shouted Sean Hayes in the distinctive clipped baritone of a high-school basketball coach, which, as it happens, he is. "Let's go!" Coach Hayes bellowed again, clapping his meaty hands loud enough for the sound to bounce off the walls of the huge gymnasium of St. Mary's Secondary School in Pickering, Ontario (a town best known for its proximity to a nuclear power plant of questionable quality).

Hayes had invited me to participate in the school's first "Sweatshop Fashion Show," an event he began planning when he discovered that the basketball team's made-in-Indonesia Nike sneakers had likely been manufactured under sweatshop conditions. He's an unapologetic jock with a conscience and, together with a handful of do-gooder students, had organized today's event to get the other two thousand kids at St. Mary's to think about the clothes they wear in terms beyond "cool" or "lame."

The plan was simple: as student models decked out in logowear strutted down a makeshift runway, another student off to the side would read a prepared narration about the lives of the Third World workers who made the gear. The students would quickly follow that with scenes from *Mickey Mouse Goes to Haiti* and a skit about how teenagers often feel "unloved, unwanted, unacceptable and unpopular if you do not have the right clothes." My part would come at the end, when I was to give a short speech about my research in export processing zones, and then facilitate a question-and-answer period. It sounded straightforward enough.

While we were waiting for the bell to ring and the students to stream in, Hayes turned to me and said, with a forced smile: "I hope the kids actually hear the message and don't think it's just a regular fashion show." Having read the students' prepared narration I couldn't help thinking that his concern sounded, frankly, paranoid. True, fashion shows have become such a high-school stalwart that they now rival car washes as the prom fundraiser of choice. But did Hayes actually think his students were so heartless that they could listen to testimony about starvation wages and physical abuse and expect that the clothing in question would be on sale at a discount after the assembly? Just then, a couple of teenage boys poked their heads in the door and checked out the frantic preparations. "Yo, guys," one of them said. "I'm guessing fashion show – this should be a joke." Coach Hayes looked nervous.

As two thousand students piled onto the bleachers, the room came alive with the giddiness that accompanies all mass reprieves from class, whether for school plays, AIDS education lectures, teachers' strikes or fire alarms. A quick scan of the room turned up no logos on these kids, but that was definitely not by choice. St. Mary's is a Catholic school and the students wear uniforms – bland affairs that they were nonetheless working for all they were worth. It's hard to make gray flannel slacks and acrylic navy sweaters look like gangsta gear but the guys were doing their best, wearing their pants pulled down halfway to their knees with patterned boxer shorts bunched over their belts. The girls were pushing the envelope too, pairing their drab tunics with platform loafers and black lipstick.

As it turned out, Coach Hayes's concerns were well founded. As the hip-hop started playing and the first kids bounded down the runway in Nike shoes and workout wear, the assembly broke into cheers and applause. The moment the young woman saddled with reading the earnest voice-over began, "Welcome to the world of Nike . . ." she was drowned out by hoots and whistles. It didn't take much to figure out that they weren't cheering for her but rather at the mere mention of the word Nike – everyone's favorite celebrity brand.

Waiting for my cue, I was ready to flee the modern teenage world forever, but after some booming threats from Coach Hayes, the crowd finally quieted down. My speech was at least not booed and the discussion that followed was among the liveliest I've ever witnessed. The first question (as at all Sweatshop 101 events) was "What brands are sweatshop-free?" – Adidas? they asked. Reebok? The Gap? I told the St. Mary's students that shopping for an exploitation-free wardrobe at the mall is next to impossible, given the way all the large brands produce. The best way to make a difference, I told them, is to stay informed by surfing the Net, and by letting companies know what you think by writing letters and asking lots of questions at the store. The St. Mary's kids were deeply skeptical of this non-answer. "Look, I don't have time to be some kind of major political activist every time I go to the mall," one girl said, right hand planted firmly on right hip. "Just tell me what kind of shoes are okay to buy, okay?"

Another girl, who looked about sixteen, sashayed to the microphone. "I'd just like to say that this is capitalism, okay, and people are allowed to make money and if you don't like it maybe you're just jealous."

The hands shot up in response. "No, *I'd* just like to say that you are totally screwed up and just because everyone is doing something doesn't mean it's right—you've got to stand up for what you believe in instead of just standing in front of the mirror trying to look good!"

After watching thousands of Ricki and Oprah episodes, these kids take to the talk-show format as naturally as Elizabeth Dole. Just as they had cheered for Nike moments before, the students now cheered for each other – dog-pound style, with lots of "you-go-girls." Moments before the bell for next period, Coach Hayes made time for one last question. A boy in saggy slacks sauntered across the gym holding his standard-issue navy blue sweater away from his lanky body with two fingers, as if he detected a foul odor. Then, he slouched down to the mike and said, in an impeccable teenage monotone, "Umm, Coach Hayes, if working conditions are so bad in Indonesia, then why do we have to wear these uniforms? We buy thousands of these things and it says right here that they are 'Made in Indonesia.' I'd just like to know, how do you know they weren't made in sweatshops?"

The auditorium exploded. It was a serious burn. Another student rushed to the mike and suggested that the students should try to find out who makes their uniforms, a project for which there was no shortage of volunteers. When I left St. Mary's that day, the school had its work cut out for it.

There's no denying that the motivation behind the St. Mary's students' new-found concern over Indonesian labor conditions was that they had just discovered a high-minded excuse to refuse to wear their lame-ass uniforms – not an entirely selfless concern. But even if it was inadvertent, they had also stumbled across one of the most powerful levers being used to pry reform out of seemingly amoral multinational corporations.

When high schools, universities, places of worship, unions, city councils and other levels of government apply ethical standards to their bulk purchasing decisions, it takes anticorporate campaigning a significant step beyond the mostly symbolic warfare of adbusting and superstore protesting. Such community institutions are not only collections of individual consumers, they are also consumers themselves – and powerful ones at that. Thousands of schools like St. Mary's ordering thousands of uniforms each – it adds up to a lot of uniforms. They also buy sports equipment for their teams, food for their cafeterias and drinks for their vending machines. Municipal governments buy uniforms for their police forces, gas for their garbage trucks and computers for their offices; and they also invest their pension funds on the stock market. Universities, for their part, select telecommunications companies for their Internet portals, use banks to hold their money and invest endowments that can represent billions of dollars. And, of course, they are also increasingly involved in direct sponsorship arrangements with corporations. Most important, bulk institutional purchases and sponsorship deals are among the most sought after contracts in the marketplace, and corporations are forever trying to outbid one another to land them.

What all these business arrangements have in common is that they exist at a distinctive intersection between civic life (ostensibly governed by principles of "public good") and the corporate profit-making motive. When corporations sponsor an event on a university campus or sign a deal with a municipal government, they cross an important line between private and public space—a line that is not part of a consumer's interaction with a corporation as an individual shopper. We don't expect morality at the mall but, to some extent, we do still expect it in our public spaces—in our schools, national parks and municipal playgrounds.

So while it may be cold comfort to some, there is a positive side effect of the fact that, increasingly, private corporations are staking a claim to these public spaces. Over the past four years, there has been a collective realization among many public, civic and religious institutions that having a multinational corporation as a guest in your house – whether as a supplier or a sponsor – presents an important political opportunity. With their huge buying power, public and non-profit institutions can exert real public-interest pressure on otherwise freewheeling private corporations. This is nowhere more true than in the schools and universities.

Students Teach the Brands a Lesson

As we have already seen, soft-drink, sneaker and fast-food companies have been forging a flurry of exclusive logo allegiances with high schools, colleges and universities. Like the Olympic games, many universities have "official" airlines, banks, long-distance carriers and computer suppliers. For the sponsoring companies, these exclusive arrangements offer opportunities to foster warm and fuzzy logo loyalties during those formative college years – not to mention a chance to pick up some quasi-academic legitimacy. (Being the official supplier of a top-flight university sounds almost as if a panel of tenured professors got together and scientifically determined that Coke Is It! or Our Fries Are Crispier! For some lucky corporations, it can be like getting an honorary degree.)

However, these same corporations have at times discovered that there can be an unanticipated downside to these "partnerships": that the sense of ownership that goes along with sponsoring is not always the kind of passive consumer allegiance that the companies had bargained for. In a climate of mounting concern about corporate ethics, students are finding that a great way to grab the attention of aloof multinationals is to kick up a fuss about the extracurricular activities of their university's official brand – whether Coke, Pepsi, Nike, McDonald's, Starbucks or Northern Telecom. Rather than simply complaining about amorphous "corporatization," young activists have begun to use their status as sought-after sponsorees to retaliate against forces they considered invasive on their campuses to begin with. In this volatile context, a particularly aggressive sponsorship deal can act as a political catalyst, instigating wide-ranging debate on everything from unfair labor conditions to trading with dictators. Just ask Pepsi.

Pepsi . . . has been at the forefront of the drive to purchase students as a captive market. Its exclusive vending arrangements have paved the way for copycat deals, and fast-food outlets owned by PepsiCo were among the first to establish a presence in high schools and on university campuses in North America. One of Pepsi's first campus vending deals was with Ottawa's Carleton University in 1993. Since marketing on campus was still somewhat jarring back then, many students were immediately resentful at being forced into this tacit product endorsement, and were determined not to give their official drink a warm welcome. Members of the university's chapter of the Public Interest and Research Group — a network of campus social-justice organizations stretching across North America known as PIRGs — discovered that PepsiCo was producing and selling its soft drinks in Burma, the brutal dictatorship now called Myanmar. The Carleton students weren't sure how to deal with the information, so they posted a notice about Pepsi's involvement in Burma on a few on-line bulletin boards that covered student issues. Gradually, other universities where Pepsi was the official drink started requesting more information. Pretty soon, the Ottawa group had developed and distributed hundreds of "campus action kits," with pamphlets, petitions, and "Gotta Boycott" and "Pepsi, Stuff It" stickers. "How can you help free Burma?" one pamphlet asks. "Pressure schools to terminate food or beverage contracts selling PepsiCo products until it leaves Burma."

Many students did just that. As a result, in April 1996 Harvard rejected a proposed $1 million vending deal with Pepsi, citing the company's Burma holdings. Stanford University cost Pepsi an estimated $800,000 when a petition signed by two thousand students blocked the construction of a PepsiCo-owned Taco Bell restaurant. The stakes were even higher in Britain where campus soft-drink contracts are coordinated centrally through the National Union of Students' services wing. "Pepsi had just beat out Coke for the contract," recalls Guy Hughes, a campaigner with the London-based group Third World First. "Pepsi was being sold in eight hundred student unions across the U.K., so we used the consortium as a lever to pressure Pepsi. When [the student union] met with the company, one factor for Pepsi was that the boycott had become international."[1]

Aung San Suu Kyi, the leader of Burma's opposition party that was elected to power in 1990, only to be prevented from taking office by the military, has offered encouragement to this nascent movement. In 1997, in a speech read by her husband (who has since died) at the American University in Washington, D.C., she singled out students in the call to put pressure on multinational corporations that are invested in Burma. "Please use your liberty to promote ours," she said. "Take a principled stand against companies which are doing business with the military regime of Burma."[2]

After the campus boycotts made it into *The New York Times*, Pepsi sold its shares in a controversial Burmese bottling plant whose owner, Thien Tun, had publicly called for Suu Kyi's democracy movement to be "ostracized and crushed." Student activists, however, dismissed the move as a "paper shuffle" because Pepsi products were still being sold and produced in Burma. Finally, facing continued pressure, Pepsi announced its "total disengagement" from Burma on January 24, 1997. When Zar Ni, the coordinator of the American student movement, heard the news, he sent an E-mail out on the Free Burma Coalition listserve: "We finally tied the Pepsi Animal down! We did it!! We all did it!!! . . . We now KNOW we have the grassroots power to yank one of the most powerful corporations in the world."

If there is a moral to this story, it is that Pepsi's drive to capture the campus market landed the company at the center of a debate in which it had no desire to participate. It wanted university students to be its poster children — its real live Generation Next — but instead, the students turned the tables and made Pepsi the poster corporation for their campus Free Burma movement. Sein Win, a leader in exile of Burma's elected National League for Democracy, observed that "PepsiCo very much takes care of its image. It wanted to press the drink's image as 'the taste of a young generation,' so when the young generation participates in boycotts, it hurts the effort."[3] Simon Billenness, an ethical investment specialist who spearheaded the Burma campaign, is more blunt: "Pepsi," he says, "was under siege from its own target market."[4] And Reid Cooper, coordinator of the Carleton University campaign, notes that without Pepsi's thirst for campus branding, Burma's plight might never have become an issue on campuses. "Pepsi tried to go into the schools," he tells me in an interview, "and from there it was spontaneous combustion."

Not surprisingly, the Pepsi victory has emboldened the Free Burma campaign on the campuses. The students have adopted the slogan "Burma: South Africa of the Nineties" and claim to be "The largest human rights campaign in cyberspace."[5] Today, more than one hundred colleges and twenty high schools around the world are part of the Free Burma Coalition. The extent to which the country's liberty has become a student cause célèbre became apparent when, in August 1998, eighteen foreign activists – most of them university students – were arrested in Rangoon for handing out leaflets expressing support for Burma's democracy movement. Not surprisingly, the event caught the attention of the international media. The court sentenced the activists to five years of hard labor, but at the last minute deported them instead of imprisoning them.

Other student campaigns have focused on different corporations and different dictators. With Pepsi out of Burma, attention began to shift on campuses to Coca-Cola's investments in Nigeria. At Kent State University and other schools where Coke won the campus cola war, students argued that Coke's high-profile presence in Nigeria offered an air of legitimacy to the country's illegitimate military regime (which, at the time, was still in power). Once again, the issue of Nigerian human rights might never have reached much beyond KSU's Amnesty International Club, but because Coke and the school had entered into a sponsorship-style arrangement, the campaign took off and students began shouting that their university had blood on its hands.

There have also been a number of food fights, most of them related to McDonald's expanding presence on college campuses. In 1997, the British National Union of Students entered into an agreement with McDonald's to distribute "privilege cards" to all undergraduates in the U.K. When students showed the card, they got a free cheeseburger every time they ordered a Big Mac, fries and drink. But campus environmentalists opposed the deal, forcing the student association to bow out of the marketing alliance in March 1998. In providing its reasons for the change of heart, the association cited the company's "anti-union practices, exploitation of employees, its contribution to the destruction of the environment, animal cruelty and the promotion of unhealthy food products"—all carefully worded references to the McLibel judge's findings.[6]

As the brand backlash spreads, students are beginning to question not only sponsorship arrangements with the likes of McDonald's and Pepsi, but also the less flashy partnerships that their universities have with the private sector. Whether it's bankers on the board of governors, corporate-endowed professorships or the naming of campus buildings after benefactors, all are facing scrutiny from a more economically politicized student body. British students have stepped up a campaign to pressure their universities to stop accepting grant money from the oil industry, and in British Columbia, the University of Victoria Senate voted in November 1998 to refuse scholarship money from Shell. This agenda of corporate resistance is gradually becoming more structured, as students from across North America come together at annual conferences such as the 1997 "Democracy Teach-In: Campus Democracy vs. Corporate Control" at the University of Chicago, where they attend seminars like "Research: For People or Profit?" "Investigating Your Campus" and "What Is a Corporation and Why Is There a Problem?" In June 1999, student activists again came together, this time in Toledo, Ohio, in the newly formed Student Alliance to Reform Corporations. The purpose of the gathering was to launch a national campaign to force universities to invest their money only with companies that respect human rights and do not degrade the environment.

It should come as no surprise that by far the most controversial campus-corporate partnerships have been ones involving that most controversial of companies: Nike. Since the shoe industry's use of sweatshop labor became common knowledge, the deals that Nike had signed with hundreds of athletic departments in universities have become among the most contentious issues on campuses today, with "Ban the Swoosh" buttons rivaling women's symbols as the undergraduate accessory of choice. And in what Nike must see as the ultimate slap in the face, college campuses where the company has paid out millions of dollars to sponsor sports teams (University of North Carolina, Duke University, Stanford, Penn State and Arizona State, to name just a few) have become the hottest spots of the international anti-Nike campaign. According to the Campaign for Labor Rights, "These contracts, which are a center-piece of Nike marketing, have now turned into a public relations nightmare for the company. Nike's aggressive campus marketing has now been forced into a defensive posture."[7]

   At the University of Arizona, students attempted to get their university president to reconsider the school's endorsement of Nike products by delivering a pile of old Nike shoes to his office (followed by cameras from two local television stations). According to a student organizer, James Tracy, "each pair of shoes had a tale of Nike's abuse attached to them for the president to consider."[8] At Stanford University, similar protests greeted the athletic department's decision to sign a four-year, $5 million contract with Nike. In fact, bashing Nike has become such a popular sport on campus that at Florida State University – a major jock college – a group of students built an anti-Nike float for the 1997 homecoming parade.

   Most of these universities are locked into multiyear sponsorship deals with Nike, but at the University of California at Irvine, students went after the company when its contract with the women's basketball team was up for renewal. Faced with mounting pressure from the student body, the school's athletic department decided to switch to Converse. On another campus, soccer coach Kim Keady was unable to persuade his employer, St. John's University, to stop forcing its team to use Nike gear. So, in the summer of 1998, he quit his job as assistant coach in protest.[9]

   University of North Carolina student Marion Traub-Werner explains the appeal of this new movement: "Obviously there's the labor issue. But we're also concerned about Nike's intrusion into our campus culture. The swoosh is everywhere – in addition to all the uniforms, it's on the game schedules, it's on all the posters and it dominates the clothing section in the campus store."[10] Like no other company, Nike has branded this generation, and so if students now have the chance to brand Nike as an exploiter – well, the chance is too good to pass up.

The Real Brand U

While many campuses are busily taking on the brand-name interlopers, others are realizing that their universities are themselves brand names. Ivy League universities, and colleges with all-star sports teams, have extensive clothing lines, several of which rival the market share of many commercial designers. They also share many of the same labor problems. In 1998, the UNITE garment workers union published a report on the BJ&B factory in an export processing zone in the Dominican Republic. Workers at BJ&B, one of the world's largest manufacturers of baseball hats, embroider the school logos and crests of at least nine large American universities, including Cornell, Duke, Georgetown, Harvard and University of Michigan. The conditions at BJ&B were signature free-trade-zone ones: long hours of forced overtime, fierce union busting (including layoffs of organizers), short-term contracts, paychecks insufficient to feed a family, pregnancy tests, sexual harassment, abusive management, unsafe drinking water and huge markups (while the hats sold, on average, for $19.95, workers saw only 8 cents of that).[11] And of course, most of the workers were young women, a fact that was brought home when the union sponsored a trip to the U.S. for two former employees of the factory: nineteen-year-old Kenia Rodriguez and twenty-year-old Roselio Reyes. The two workers visited many of the universities whose logos they used to stitch on caps, speaking to gatherings of students who were exactly their age. "In the name of the 2,050 workers in this factory, and the people in this town, we ask for your support," Reyes said to an audience of students at the University of Illinois.[12]

These revelations about factory conditions were hardly surprising. College licensing is big business, and the players — Fruit of the Loom, Champion, Russell — have all shifted to contract factories with the rest of the garment industry, and make liberal use of free-trade zones around the world. In the U.S., the licensing of college names is a $2.5 billion annual industry, much of it brokered through the Collegiate Licensing Company. Duke University alone sells around $25 million worth of clothing associated with its winning basketball team every year. To meet the demand, it has seven hundred licensees who contract to hundreds of plants in the U.S. and in ten other countries.[13]

Because of Duke's leading role as a campus apparel manufacturer, a group of activists decided to turn the school into a model of ethical manufacturing — not only for other schools, but for the scandal-racked garment industry as a whole. In March 1998, Duke University unveiled a landmark policy requiring that all companies making T-shirts, baseball hats and sweatshirts bearing the "Duke" name agree to a set of clear labor standards. The code required that contractors pay the legal minimum wage, maintain safe working conditions and allow workers to form unions, no matter where the factories were located. What makes the policy more substantial than most other codes in the garment sector is that it requires factories to undergo inspections from independent monitors — a provision that sent Nike and Shell screaming from the negotiating table, despite overwhelming evidence that their stated standards are being disregarded on the ground. Brown University followed two months later with a tough code of its own.

Tico Almeida, a senior at Duke University, explains that many students have a powerful reaction when they learn about the workers who produce their team clothing in free-trade zones. "You have two groups of people, roughly the same age, who are getting such different experiences out of the same institutions," he says. And once again, says David Tannenbaum, an undergraduate at Princeton, the logo (this time a school logo) provides the global link. "While the workers are making our clothes thousands of miles away, in other ways we're close to it – we're wearing these clothes every day."[14]

The summer after the Duke and Brown codes were passed was filled with activity. In July, anti-sweatshop organizers from campuses across the country gathered in New York and organized themselves into a coalition, United Students Against Sweatshops. In August, a delegation of eight students, including Tico Almeida, went on a fact-finding mission to free-trade zones in Nicaragua, El Salvador and Honduras. Almeida told me he was hoping to find Duke sweatshirts because he had seen the "Made in Honduras" tag on clothing sold on his campus. But he soon discovered what most people do when they visit free-trade zones: that a potent combination of secrecy, deferred responsibility and militarism forms a protective barricade around much of the global garment industry. "It was like taking random stabs in the dark," he recalls.

When classes resumed in September 1998 and the student travelers were back on campus, the issue of sweatshop labor exploded into what *The New York Times* described as "the biggest surge in campus activism in nearly two decades."[15] At Duke, Georgetown, Wisconsin, North Carolina, Arizona, Michigan, Princeton, Stanford, Harvard, Brown, Cornell and University of California at Berkeley there were conferences, teach-ins, protests and sit-ins – some lasting three and four days. At Yale University, students held a "knit-in." All the demonstrations led to agreements from school administrators to demand higher labor standards from the companies that manufacture their wares.

This fast-growing movement has a somewhat unlikely rallying cry: "Corporate disclosure." The central demand is for the companies that produce college-affiliated clothing to hand over the names and addresses of all their factories around the world and open themselves up to monitoring. Who makes your school clothing, the students say, should not be a mystery. They argue that with the garment industry being the global, contracted-out maze that it is, the onus must be on companies to prove their goods *aren't* made in sweatshops – not on investigative activists to prove that they are. The students are also pushing for their schools to demand that contractors pay a "living wage," as opposed to the legal minimum wage. By May 1999, at least four administrations had agreed in principle to push their suppliers on the living-wage issue. There is no agreement about how to turn those well-meaning commitments into real changes in the export factories. Everyone involved in the anti-sweatshop movement does agree, however, that even getting issues like disclosure and a living wage on the negotiating table with manufacturers represents a major victory, one that has eluded campaigners for many years.

In a smaller but equally precedent-setting initiative, Archbishop Theodore McCarrick announced in October 1997 that his Newark, New Jersey, archdiocese would become a "no sweat" zone. The initiative includes introducing an anti-sweatshop curriculum into all 185 Catholic schools in the area, identifying the manufacturers of all their school uniforms and monitoring them to make sure the clothes are being produced under fair labor conditions – just as the students at St. Mary's in Pickering, Ontario, decided to do.

All in all, students have picked up the gauntlet on the sweatshop issue with an enthusiasm that has taken the aging labor movement by storm. United Students Against Sweatshops, after only one year in existence, claimed chapters on a hundred U.S.

campuses and a sister network in Canada. Free the Children, young Craig Kielburger's Toronto-based anti-child-labor organization (he was the thirteen-year-old who challenged the Canadian prime minister to review child-labor practices in India) has meanwhile gained strength in high schools and grade schools around the world. Charles Kernaghan, with his "outing" of Kathie Lee Gifford and Mickey Mouse, may have started this wave of labor organizing, but by the end of the 1998–99 academic year, he knew he was no longer driving it. In a letter to the United Students Against Sweatshops, he wrote: "Right now it is your student movement which is leading the way and carrying the heaviest weight in the struggle to end sweatshop abuses and child labor. Your effectiveness is forcing the companies to respond."[16]

Times have changed. As William Cahn writes in his history of the Lawrence Mill sweatshop strike of 1912, "Nearby Harvard University allowed students credit for their midterm examinations if they agreed to serve in the militia against the strikers. 'Insolent, well-fed Harvard men,' the *New York Call* reported, 'parade up and down, their rifles loaded . . . their bayonets glittering.' "[17] Today, students are squarely on the other side of sweatshop labor disputes: as the target market for everything from Guess jeans to Nike soccer balls and Duke-embossed baseball hats, young people are taking the sweatshop issue personally.

Questions

1   How does the type of activism that Klein writes about compare with the practice of "culture jamming" described by Christine Harold? Which do you think is more effective?

2   Provide examples of anti-corporate campaigns or movements that you have learned about through the Internet. In what context did you hear about these movements? How did they encourage participation?

Notes

1. Personal interview.
2. G. Kramer, "Suu Kyi Urges U.S. Boycott," Associated Press, 27 January 1997.
3. Farhan Haq, "Burma-Finance: Oil company digs in heels despite Rangoon's record," Inter Press Service, 4 February 1997.
4. "Pepsi, Burma, Take 2: Pepsi Responds to Aims of Target Audience," Dow Jones News Service, 27 January 1997.
5. Free Burma Coalition Web site.
6. "NUS Withdraws from McDonald's 'Privilege Card' Scheme," McLibel Support Campaign press release, 14 April 1998.
7. "Nike Campaign Strategy, Part 1," *Labor Alerts*, 14 January 1998.
8. "Reports on Nike Demos," *Labor Alerts*, 21 April 1998.
9. Verena Dobnik, "Anti-Sweatshop Protesters March up Fifth Avenue," Associated Press, 6 March 1999.
10. Feit, "Stepping on Nike's Toes."
11. "Was Your School's Cap Made in This Sweatshop? A UNITE Report on Campus Caps Made by BJ&B in the Dominican Republic," released 13 April 1998.

12. "Dominican Republic Workers Urge University of Illinois to Demand Humane Factory Conditions," *Daily Illini*, 24 April 1998.
13. Steven Greenhouse, "Duke to Adopt a Code to Prevent Apparel from Being Made in Sweatshops," *New York Times*, 8 March 1998.
14. Steven Greenhouse, "Activism Surges at Campuses Nationwide, and Labor Is at Issue," *New York Times*, 29 March 1999.
15. Ibid.
16. "An Open Letter to the Students," by Charles Kernaghan, undated.
17. William Cahn, *Lawrence 1912: The Bread & Roses Strike* (New York: The Pilgrim Press, 1977), 174.

PART EIGHT

Ads and the Future

INTRODUCTION TO PART EIGHT

THE FIRST DECADE OF THE TWENTY-FIRST CENTURY has witnessed a remarkable transformation in the ways in which advertisers reach out to potential consumers. Indeed, you are probably quite familiar with some of the new and emergent strategies that marketers are relying on to "break through the clutter," an industry phrase that reflects the challenge of standing out in a ubiquitous advertising environment. Ads that were formerly enclosed within the boundaries of media now appear virtually everywhere. Television commercials that used to be developed by a team of creative experts are now being produced and edited by "real people"—the commercial version of User Generated Content—and attracting significant buzz in the process. And the tradition of product *placement* has been replaced by product *integration*, where a branded good or service becomes the centerpiece of a TV program or movie script.

Changes in technology, particularly the rise of the Internet and mobile communication, are no doubt fueling these shifts in advertising. Yet the implications of the twenty-first-century marketing landscape are more than technological. The trends described above also raise pressing social questions. For example, what are the societal and environmental costs of a world in which ads infiltrate every "nook and cranny" of public life? Is there hope for an objective media system in an age when the division between advertising and editorial matter is blurring? Should we believe the claims of advertising and media producers that "the consumer is king"? Finally, what price do we pay for information that is increasingly customized to our interests?

The four essays in this Part examine these questions through various industrial and normative lenses. Each of them is concerned with the ever more commercial nature of our society, and each of them draws provocative—and at times troubling—conclusions. Hopefully this selection of writings will encourage you to take seriously the changes in our contemporary cultural and media systems and to understand the potential implications for yourself, your community, and the world in which you live.

Reflect also on the forms of consumer activism explored in the previous Part as you read about what scholars say are some possible roads down the advertising and consumer future, and how we may influence what roads are taken.

Chapter 24

MARK ANDREJEVIC

THE WORK OF BEING WATCHED
Interactive Media and the Exploitation of Self-Disclosure

MORE THAN TWO DECADES HAVE PASSED since communication researchers began to consider the ways in which television audiences perform labor. According to one widely cited theory, audiences perform "the work of watching" by viewing the commercials that are embedded in television programs.[1] In this article, communication researcher Mark Andrejevic suggests that audiences in today's interactive media environment also engage in "the work of being watched." That is, by trading their personal information for customized offers, audiences provide an invaluable source of labor for corporations: market research. To Andrejevic, this system is based on a power imbalance between those "who control the means of surveillance" and audience members. It thus raises broader questions about the "democratic" potential of Internet communication.

During the halcyon days of the high-tech economy—at the dawn of the new millennium—an entrepreneurial-minded former employee of the AirTouch corporation decided to change his name to DotComGuy and live his life on-line. For the former Mitch Maddox (a.k.a. DotComGuy) the decision was more than just a life-style decision; it was a business decision. By living his life in front of 25 cameras installed in his house and yard, DotComGuy hoped to demonstrate the benefits of e-commerce, ordering everything he needed on-line so that he wouldn't have to leave his home for a year. As an on-line advertisement for e-commerce—an entrepreneurial Truman Burbank–DotComGuy hoped to turn his Website into a for-profit corporation that would generate enough money to support his handlers and earn him a $98,000 paycheck for his year-long stint in the DotCompound.

The plan started swimmingly—Dot-ComGuy's stunt resulted in media coverage that drew sponsors and captured the attention of viewers, who generated more than a million hits a day for his Website during its first few months (personal interview with Mitch Maddox, Sept. 16, 2000). By the end of the year, the euphoria over the on-line economy had been replaced by a healthy dose of skepticism, and as the NASDAQ headed south, so did DotComGuy's fortunes. On New Year's Day 2001, DotComGuy left the compound behind and forfeited his $98,000 payday, keeping as payment only those products that the company had purchased or received for promotional purposes (Copeland, 2001). DotComGuy's venture may have failed as a business enterprise, but it succeeded in drawing attention to an important aspect of the emerging online economy: the productivity of comprehensive surveillance.

DotComGuy understood that while he was in the DotCompound, he was *working* 24-hours-a-day. Even when he was sleeping, the image of Maddox tucked into bed in his Dallas home was surrounded with banner ads and the names of sponsors, some of which were posted on the walls of his house. It was for the work he was performing by subjecting himself to online surveillance that DotComGuy was to receive his $98,000 payday. That he failed to turn a profit doesn't alter the economic fact upon which his entrepreneurial venture was based: that the emerging online economy increasingly seeks to exploit the work of being watched. DotComGuy may have failed to capitalize on this labor as an entrepreneur, but major corporations continue to attempt to exploit the economic potential of this labor on a much larger scale.

Some 15 years ago, Jhally and Livant (1986), inspired by the work of Dallas Smythe (1977; 1981), argued that communication theory needed to take seriously the notion that audiences were working when they were watching television. This paper seeks to develop their argument a bit further—to update it, as it were, for an era of new-media interactivity—by highlighting the emerging significance of the work not just of watching, but of *being* watched. The two complement each other, insofar as the development of interactive media allows for the rationalization of viewing and consumption in general, thanks to devices like interactive television that watch us while we watch. In the era of "reality" TV, wherein networks are winning ratings battles by enlisting people to submit their lives to comprehensive scrutiny, the claim that being watched is a form of value-generating labor ought not to be a particularly surprising one. We are not just facing a world in which a few select members of the audience are entering the celebrity ranks and cashing in on their 15 minutes of fame, but one in which non-celebrities—the remaining viewers—are being recruited to participate in the labor of being watched to an unprecedented degree by subjecting the details of their daily lives to increasingly pervasive and comprehensive forms of high-tech monitoring. Their viewing habits, their shopping habits, even their whereabouts are subject not just to monitoring but to inclusion in detailed marketing databases, thanks to the advent of computer-based forms of interactive media. This observation has become a commonplace in the popular literature on new media and has generated plenty of discussion on the fate of personal privacy in the on-line economy (see, for example, Garfinkel, 2000; Rosen, 2000; Whitaker, 1999). The consensus seems to be that the development of interactive media and of computer processing and storage power enable the increasing economic exploitation of comprehensive forms of consumer monitoring. In response, organizations like the Electronic Privacy Information Center (EPIC) have organized to advocate for consumer privacy rights and protection from creeping corporate surveillance.

The drawback of much of the discussion about privacy, as authors including Lyon (1994) and Gandy (1993) have suggested, is that the attempt to defend privacy rights has a disconcerting tendency to work as much in the interest of the corporations doing the monitoring as in that of the individuals being monitored. The development of demographic databases relies heavily on the protection accorded to private property, since these databases are profitable in large part because the information they contain is proprietary. As Lyon (1994) puts it, "Privacy grows from the same modern soil as surveillance, which is another reason for doubting its efficacy as a tool of counter-surveillance" (p. 21).

As an alternative to the popular portrayal of the proliferation of corporate surveillance in terms of the incredible shrinking private sphere, this essay suggests an approach influenced by the concerns of political economy and the analysis of disciplinary panopticism. Conceived as a form of labor, the work of being watched can be critiqued in terms of power and differential access to both the means of surveillance and the benefits derived from their deployment. The operative question is not whether a particular conception of privacy has been violated but, rather: what are the relations that underwrite entry into a relationship of surveillance, and who profits from the work of being watched? Such an analysis draws its inspiration from Robins and Webster's (1999) assessment of the Information Revolution as "a matter of differential (and unequal) access to, and control over, information resources" (p. 91). Gandy (1993), quoting Klaus Lenk, cuts to the heart of the matter:

> The real issue at stake is not personal privacy, which is an ill-defined concept, greatly varying according to the cultural context. It is power gains of bureaucracies, both private and public, at the expense of individuals and the non-organized sectors of society. (p. 52)

Foucault's (1975/1977) discussion of disciplinary surveillance offers an approach to the question of power that seems particularly relevant to the development of the online economy since it focuses not so much on the repressive force of panopticism, but its productive deployment. The potential of the online economy that has recently attracted so much speculation—both financial and cultural—is predicated in large part on the anticipated productivity of generalized network surveillance. The power in question is not the static domination of a sovereign Big Brother, but that of a self-stimulating incitement to productivity: the multiplication of desiring subjects and subjects' desires in accordance with the rationalization of consumption. In this context, the production of ever more refined and detailed categories of desiring subjectivities serves, as Butler's (1997) analysis suggests, as a site for the reiteration of existing conditions and relations of power.

The starting point for an analysis of surveillance as exploitation is the assertion that just as workplace monitoring contributes to the rationalization of production, so on-line surveillance contributes to the rationalization of consumption. The attempt to extend the monitoring reach of corporate managers via the internet serves to compel personal disclosure by replacing non-monitored forms of consumption with monitored interactive transactions. The following sections attempt to trace the outlines of the process whereby the work of being watched comes to serve as a means of rationalizing not just what Jhally and Livant (1986) call the work of watching, but the process of on-line consumption in general. The goal is to offer an alternative approach to the debate over on-line privacy in the era of new-media interactivity. Not only is the privacy defense aligned with the process it ostensibly contests, but, practically speaking, it has failed to provide effective resistance to encroaching surveillance. Indeed, opponents of corporate surveillance seem unable to provide a compelling rationale for privacy protection in an era when consumers remain surprisingly willing to surrender increasingly comprehensive forms of personal information in response to offers of convenience and customization.

Perhaps some awareness of the way in which the new "transparency" exacerbates informational asymmetries and power imbalances, serving as a form of marketplace discipline, might provide stronger grounds for a critique of the proliferation of corporate surveillance. Such a critique might also help challenge the promotion of interactive technologies (and the forms of consumption and production they facilitate) as inherently democratic and empowering. This essay seeks to provide one starting point for such a challenge by exploring how the promise of interactivity functions as an invitation to engage in the work of being watched. The remaining sections of the essay trace the development of the productive role of surveillance from its deployment in the workplace to its extension into the realm of online consumption, drawing on the example of interactive TV, especially TiVo, to illustrate the importance of interactive media to the rationalization of e-commerce.

Productive Surveillance

The productivity of surveillance, for the purposes of this article, can be understood as being always parasitic upon another form of labor. For example, Braverman's (1974) discussion of the pioneering work of Frederick Taylor in developing a system of workplace rationalization in the late 19th and early 20th centuries highlights the reliance of what Taylor called "scientific management" upon comprehensive forms of workplace monitoring. Taylor's description of how he succeeded in dramatically increasing the productivity of steel workers starts off with a description of the role of surveillance in deciding which workers would be targeted. Managers observed the entire workforce for four days before choosing several workers upon whom to focus their efforts: "A careful study was then made of each of these men. We looked up their history as far back as practicable and thorough inquiries were made as to the character, habits, and the ambition of each of them" (Taylor, as quoted in Braverman, 1974, p. 104). The selected worker's training consisted in his being supervised by a manager who observed his every action, timing him with a stopwatch, and dictating the laborer's actions down to the most specific detail. The result of all this monitoring and managing was that the productivity of the day laborer, whom Taylor refers to in his case study as "Schmidt," almost quadrupled. The activity of being watched wasn't productive on its own, but coupled with another form of labor, it helped multiply the latter's productivity. Over time, the recognition of the productivity of surveillance helped to institutionalize the rationalization of production based on ever more detailed forms of workplace monitoring, including Gilbreth's famous time and motion studies.

Among those who write about surveillance, Foucault (1975/1977; 1976/1978) has powerfully thematized its productive aspect, which all too often gets short shrift in the critical literature on surveillance. For example, Giddens's (1981) discussion of the police power of the surveillance state, as well as the various discussions of disciplinary surveillance offered by Norris and Armstrong (1999), Lyon (1994), and Gandy (1993), retain strong overtones of what Foucault describes as the insistence in the West on "seeing the power it exercises as juridical and negative rather than technical and positive" (1980, p. 121). This tendency is also reflected in the public debate over online privacy, which centers on the "invasion" of privacy and the oppressive surveillance capacity of the state. The emphasis is upon the ways in which disciplinary surveillance creates "docile bodies" and not upon the more suggestive aspect of Foucault's analysis: the spiraling cycle of productivity incited by disciplinary regimes: the fact that docile bodies are not rendered inert, but stimulated. As Foucault puts it in *Discipline and Punish* (1975/1977): "Let us say that discipline is the unitary technique by which the body is reduced as a 'political' force at the least cost and maximized as a useful force" (p. 221). Docility and pacification are certainly among the goals of discipline, but the real power of surveillance is a relentlessly productive and stimulating one:

> The Panopticon . . . has a role of amplification; although it arranges power, although it is intended to make it more economic and effective, it does so not for power itself . . . its aim is to strengthen the social forces—to increase production, to develop the economy . . . to increase and multiply.
>
> (1977, p. 208)

This power—and not the sterile juridical "repressive" gaze of Big Brother—is what attracts the interest and the capital of the online economy.

In contemporary terms, productive disciplinary power stimulates the proliferation of desiring subjectivities through the multiplication of consumption categories: the endless sub-categorization and specification of individualized sets of tastes and preferences. Recording and measuring, specifying and naming, these are the current watchwords of the marketing industry, which doesn't "set boundaries" for consumption, but extends its various forms, "pursuing them to lines of indefinite penetration" (Foucault 1976/1978, p. 47). For example, the proponents of mass customization (Negroponte, 1995; Pine, 1993; Gates 1996) imagine the possibilities of specifying desire ever more narrowly based not just on consumers' past preferences and socio-economic backgrounds, but on the details of the moment: location, the time of day, the weather. As in the case of sexuality, the elaboration and proliferation of desire are achieved through subjection to a discursive regime of self-disclosure whose contemporary cultural manifestations include not just the mania for interactivity, but the confessional culture of a talk show nation, and, most recently, the ethos of willing submission to comprehensive surveillance associated with the booming reality TV trend.

The power of Foucault's approach is that it extends its consideration of the productive role of panoptic surveillance beyond the realm of the workplace. The accumulation of bodies—their organization and deployment not just within the factory walls, but in the "privacy" of homes and bedrooms—is a necessary corollary to the accumulation of capital (and vice versa). As Foucault puts it, capitalism "would not be possible without the controlled insertion of bodies into the machinery of production and the adjustment of the phenomena of population to economic processes" (1975/1977, p. 141). Disciplinary surveillance does not just underwrite subjection to the proliferation of desire, it also—and not incidentally—enhances economic productivity.

Foucault's account of the productive role of desire thus provides a useful rejoinder to those who engage in what Schiller (1988) describes as a "Sisyphean attempt to distinguish productive from unproductive labor in terms of a hypostasized set of productive activities" (p. 36). The information economy—including that designed to stimulate consumption via the accumulation, manipulation, and deployment of information derived from consumer surveillance—is economically productive, and the labor associated with it can be identified by its status as a value-generating activity. The stimulation and rationalization of consumer desire are a practical corollary to the rationalization of production proper. As Harvey (1999), following Marx, puts it, "production and consumption relate to each other so that 'each of them creates the other in completing itself, and creates itself as the other' " (p. 80). For example, as historians, marketers, and social critics alike have recognized (Marchand, 1985; Sloan, 1963; Robins & Webster, 1999), the development of consumer society required techniques for stimulating consumption to keep pace with the increasing volume and variety of products made available by the technological and managerial advances associated with the industrial revolution. These techniques went far beyond management of the workplace proper, and relied upon detailed monitoring of consumer habits and lifestyles. Gathering this information was the work of market researchers and advertisers—work that is becoming increasingly important in the era of niche markets and customized products and services. Interactive technologies, as the business world has come to recognize (Mougayar, 1998), allow for much of this work to be offloaded onto consumers, who increasingly provide detailed information about themselves as they consume. The economic value of this information means not just that it can be bought and sold, but that consumers are often compensated for their participation in producing it.

Rationalizing the Work of Watching

Jhally and Livant (1986) describe another form of labor for which consumers are "paid": the work of watching. Building on their approach, this section takes the argument a step further by exploring the way in which the work of *being watched* contributes to the rationalization of the work of watching. Jhally and Livant's analysis is straightforward: audiences perform work by viewing advertising in exchange for "payment" in the form of programming content. The viewing of advertising is productive because it helps "speed up the selling of commodities, their circulation from production to consumption. . . . Through advertising, the rapid consumption of commodities cuts down on circulation and storage costs for industrial capital" (p. 125). In these terms, watching advertising might be understood as an activity in which, as Harvey (1999) puts it, the process of consumption completes itself in the process of production.

For the purposes of a consideration of the labor of *being* watched, the crucial point made by Jhally and Livant (1986) is that the goal of media management is to rationalize the work of watching—to "make the audience watch harder" (p. 133), just as Taylor made Schmidt quadruple his daily productivity. One strategy for rationalization is niche marketing, which Jhally and Livant describe as "the specification and fractionation of the audience" that leads to "a form of 'concentrated viewing' in which there is (from the point of view of advertisers) little wasted watching" (p. 133). As in the case of Schmidt, what is needed is detailed information about the audience labor force: both its background and its behavior. The commodification of this information has already been institutionalized as the secondary market in ratings, whose growth accompanied that of the electronic mass media. The labor of *being* watched goes hand-in-hand with the work of watching: viewers are monitored so advertisers can be ensured that this work is being done as efficiently as possible. Ratings, in this context, are informational commodities that generate value because they help to rationalize the viewing process. They become what Mosco (1996), following Meehan, describes as "cybernetic" commodities: "feedback" commodities produced through consumption or interaction (p. 151).

Within the context of the mass media, the labor of being watched faced certain limitations, both structural and cultural. Watching advertising may be a form of work, according to Jhally and Livant, but it does not take place within a centralized space that would allow broadcasters to stand over viewers with a stopwatch, as in the case of the scientific management of the factory labor force. Indeed, a certain expectation of privacy outside the workplace is one of the hurdles that those who would rationalize the work of being watched need to overcome. The fact that we accept surveillance more readily in the workplace is a function of the characteristic spatio-temporal differentiation associated with wage labor in modernity, according to Giddens (1981): "Two opposed modes of time-consciousness, 'working time' and 'one's own' or 'free time', become basic divisions within the phenomenal experience of the day" (p. 137). Surveillance, within this schema, is associated with time that is not free, but which is subject to the asymmetrical power relations of the workplace, underwritten by the workers' subordination to those who control the space of production.

The productive potential of the labor of being watched is further limited by the structure of the mass media, which are only capable of exploiting the logic of market fractionation up to a point. It is desirable to isolate an affluent demographic, but to continue to subdivide the audience beyond a certain point would be counter-productive, not least because the existing technology is not well-suited to individualized programming. At the same time, detailed monitoring has tended to be relatively costly and has relied to a large extent on the consent of the monitored. Thus, the television industry has, until recently, contented itself with the relatively small sample offered by the Nielsen ratings, rather than attempting more detailed and comprehensive approaches to managing the work of watching. However, the advent of interactive, networked forms of content delivery promises to overcome these limitations and to develop the potential of the work of being watched to its fullest.

Interactive Surveillance in the Digital Enclosure

The emerging model of the on-line economy is explicitly based on the strategy for rationalizing and disciplining the labor of viewing—and of consumption in general—so as to make it more productive. The goal is to replace mass marketing and production with customized programming, products, and marketing. In the business literature (Mougayar, 1998; Pine, 1993), this paradigm is described as "mass customization": the ability to produce mass quantities of products that are, at the same time, custom-tailored to niche markets and, at the extreme, to specific individuals. Described as the advent of flexible production in response to increasingly volatile market conditions, mass customization represents the enhanced capacity of interactive technology to exploit the productive potential of market segmentation. Viewed as a strategy for promoting consumption, niche marketing is not a demand-driven phenomenon, instigated by the sudden, inexplicable volatility of consumer preferences, but rather, as Harvey (1990) suggests, a supply-side response to the saturation of the mass market.

In the media market, as well as in other segments of the economy, the promise of interactive communication technologies is to surpass the structural limitations that prevented the exploitation of increasingly compact market niches. If the advent of cable television allowed for market segmentation up to a point, the development of digital delivery allows for its extension down to the level of the individual viewer. Bill Gates

(1996), for example, anticipates a world in which not just the timing and choice of programs will be customized, but in which the content and the advertising can be adapted to viewer preferences, allowing individuals to choose the type of ending they want, the setting of the movie, and even the stars (who can be "customized" thanks to digitization). Similarly, customized advertising would ensure that every ad is tailored to the demographics of its recipient. A similar logic could be extended to products other than media programming. For example, computerization, according to Gates (1996), will allow "Increasing numbers of products—from shoes to chairs, from newspapers and magazines to music albums" to be "created on the spot to match the exact specifications of a particular person" (p. 188). Half a decade after Gates made these predictions, *Wired* magazine, in its April, 2001 "Megatrends" issue declared "personal fabrication on demand" to be one of the top emerging trends of the new millennium (p. 172).

The attempt to develop increasingly customized programming and products foregrounds the economic importance of what might be described as the 21st century digital confessional: an incitement to self-disclosure as a form of self-expression and individuation. Interactive (cybernetic) media promote this self-disclosure insofar as they offer the potential to integrate the labor of watching with that of *being* watched. The cybernetic economy thus anticipates the productivity of a digital form of disciplinary panopticism, predicated not just on the monitoring gaze, but on the vast array of digital data made available by interactive and convergent communication technologies.

The accumulation of detailed demographic information allows not only for the customization of products and programming, but also for customized pricing. Whereas mass production was reliant on the aggregation of individual demand curves, customization allows for the dis-aggregation of demand curves, and thus for the possibility that producers can extract some of the "surplus" previously realized by consumers. Amazon.com's recent experiments in "variable pricing" anticipated this dis-aggregation by attempting to charge customers different prices for the same product, based on demographic information gleaned on-line from purchasers' "cookies" (Grossman, 2000).

Digital Enclosure

The current deployment of the Internet for e-commerce may be viewed as an attempt to achieve in the realm of consumption what the enclosure movement achieved in the realm of production: an inducement to enter into a relationship of surveillance-based rationalization. The process of digital enclosure can be defined, in these terms, as the process whereby activities formerly carried out beyond the monitoring capacity of the Internet are enfolded into its virtual space. The process is still very much in its early stages, but is heavily underwritten by investments in new media technologies (Schiller, 1999) and by the enthusiastic and breathless predictions of cyber-futurists that continue to make their way into the mass media. Lester (2001) notes that entrance into what I call the digital enclosure is often voluntary (at least for the moment), but he coins an interesting term to suggest that consumers are compelled to go on-line for an increasing array of transactions by "the tyranny of convenience" (p. 28). The current trend suggests that over time, alternatives to this "tyranny" may be increasingly foreclosed. The result is that consumption and leisure behaviors will increasingly migrate into virtual spaces where they can double as a form of commodity-generating labor. If the latest work of a popular author or musical group is available *only* on-line, consumers are compelled to enter a virtual space within which very detailed forms of surveillance can take place. Electronic databases can keep track not only of who is reading or listening to what, but when and where.

The exploitation of the labor of being watched is thus crucially reliant upon public acceptance of the penetration of digital surveillance into the realm of "free" time. That this acceptance may not be immediately forthcoming is reflected in surveys like the 1999 *Wall Street Journal*-NBC poll cited by Lester (2001) for its finding that "privacy is the issue that concerns Americans most about the twenty-first century, ahead of over-population, racial tensions, and global warming" (p. 27). Lawmakers have recognized the importance to the digital economy of assuaging these concerns and are attempting to pass legislation to ensure consumers a certain degree of "privacy protection" (Labaton, 2000, p. A1). The problem with such legislation from a business standpoint, and perhaps one of the reason it tends to get bogged down in committees, is that it threatens to dry up the flow of surveillance-generated information that is the life-blood of the economy it ostensibly enables.

The more promising approach, from a corporate perspective, has been to attempt to reposition surveillance as a form of consumer control. The popular reception of the Internet as a means of democratizing mediated interaction and surpassing the one-way, top-down mass media certainly works in favor of this attempt. Thus, the claims of the cyber-celebrants, such as George Gilder's (1994) oft-cited prediction that "The force of microelectronics will blow apart all the monopolies, hierarchies, pyramids, and power grids of established industrial society" (p. 180) line up neatly with the corporate prom-ise that the interactive digital market is "a customer's paradise," presumably because the "customer is in control" (Mougayar, 1998, p. 176). Casting the net slightly wider, it is worth investigating the extent to which the celebration of the progressive potential of interactivity in some strands of media theory helps to promote the advantages of entry into the digital enclosure. The more we view this enclosure as a site for the potential revitalization of community (Rheingold, 1993) and democracy (Brady, 1998; Kellner, 1999), the more inviting it appears. Similarly, as Robins and Webster (1999) suggest, the celebration of the information age as a post-industrial resolution to the depredations of industrial society helps background the fundamental continuity of the "information era" with the exploitative relations of industrial capitalism. My intent is not to dismiss the progressive potential of interactive media outright, but rather to note how neatly their uncritical promotion lines up with the interests of those who would deploy the interactive capability of new media to exploit the work of being watched.

In short, the promise of the "revolutionary" potential of new media bears a marked similarity to the deployment of the supposedly subversive potential of sex that Foucault (1976/1978) outlines in his discussion of the "repressive hypothesis." When, for example, the *New York Times* informs its readers that the advent of interactive digital television is "the beginning of the end of another socialistic force in American life: the mass market" (Lewis, 2000), it contributes to the deployment of what might be called "the mass society repressive hypothesis." The latter underwrites the ostensibly sub-versive potential of interactivity even as it stimulates the productivity of consumer labor. The most familiar version of this hypothesis suggests that mass production worked to stifle the forms of individuation and self-expression that will be fostered in the upcoming digital revolution: that the incitement to divulge our consumption-related behavior (and what else is there, from a marketing perspective?) paradoxically represents a subversion of the totalitarian, homogenizing forces of the mass market. As in the case of the deployment of the repressive hypothesis, the promised subversion turns out to be an incitement to multiply the very forms of self-disclosure that serve the disciplinary regime they purportedly subvert. As Marchand (1985) suggests, the promise of individuation—of the self-overcoming of mass homogeneity—was a strategy of the regime of mass society *from its inception*. Mass society's ostensible self-overcoming becomes a ruse for the incitement to self-disclosure crucial to the rationalization of what undoubtedly remains a form of mass consumption.

The Example of TiVo

Recent developments in television technology can perhaps provide a more concrete example of how the work of being watched is deployed to rationalize the work of watching. The emergence of digital VCR technology, including TiVo, ReplayTV, and Microsoft's Ultimate TV, anticipates the way in which the digital enclosure overcomes the limitations of the mass media while enhancing their productivity. The rudimentary data generated by Nielsen Media Research, based on a sample of some 5,000 homes, may have been good enough for the standardized advertising fare offered by pre-interactive television, but it clearly cannot provide the information necessary to custom-tailor advertising to the 105 million households with television sets in the United States. As Daryl Simm, the former head of worldwide media programming for Procter & Gamble, and the current head of media at the Omnicom conglomerate recently put it,

> The measurement we use today is very crude. . . . It's an average measurement of the number of viewers watching an individual program that does not even measure the commercial break. When you think about improvements in measuring viewing habits, you think not about incremental changes but great leaps.
>
> (Lewis, 2000, p. 41)

The developers of digital VCR technology are looking to make that leap. For home viewers, digital VCRs offer several advantages over their analog ancestors: they can record several shows at the same time; they store dozens of hours of programming which can be retrieved at a moment's notice; and they automatically record programs in response to keyword requests. From the advertisers' perspective, digital VCRs offer a highly detailed form of demographic monitoring. As a rather celebratory piece about TiVo in *The New York Times* put it,

> While the viewer watched television, the box would watch the viewer. It would record the owner's viewing habits in a way that TV viewing habits have never been recorded. . . . Over time, the box would come to know what the viewer liked maybe even better than the viewer himself.
>
> (Lewis, 2000, p. 38)

Even as it retrieves programming for viewers, the digital VCR doubles as a monitoring device in the service of the system's operators, creating a detailed "time and motion study" of viewing habits that can be sold to advertisers and producers. In the panoptic register, the digital VCR becomes an automated consumption confessional: an incitement to divulge the most intimate details of one's viewing habits.

In this respect, the digital VCR represents a preliminary attempt to bring the activity of television viewing within the monitoring reach of the digital enclosure. The enticement to consumers is that of convenience and customization (perhaps even self-expression). As Lewis (2000) puts it, "Over time, the viewer would create, in essence, his own private television channel, stored on a hard drive in the black box, tailored with great precision to his interests" (p. 38). There is a degree of truth to the claim of convenience: devices like TiVo will allow viewers to more easily store and record those programs they want to watch. This is, perhaps, the compensation viewers receive in exchange for providing detailed information about their viewing habits. They will also be able to skip through commercials in 30-second intervals, but this advantage is being rendered obsolete by the integration of advertising content into the program itself (Elliott, 2000).

Drawing on the promotional strategy of the digital economy, celebrants of the new technology have adopted the "revolutionary" promise that new media will transfer control to viewers and consumers as a means of promoting their products. One of the early advertising spots for TiVo, for example, featured two bouncers throwing a network executive through his plate glass window, enacting the dethroning of centralized corporate control. This image corresponds with the description in *The New York Times* of TiVo as a challenge to the mass market and top-down, centralized planning. According to this account, when viewed through the lens of the new "freedom" that TiVo ostensibly offers consumers, "The entire history of commercial television suddenly appears to have been a Stalinist plot erected, as it has been, on force from above rather than choice from below" (Lewis, 2000, p. 41). This retelling of history promotes interactive technologies as one more force bringing about what Shapiro (1999) calls "the control revolution," whereby "new technology is allowing individuals to take power from large institutions such as government, corporations, and the media. To an unprecedented degree, we can decide what news and information we're exposed to" (p. xi).

Disturbingly, this perspective is not unique to mainstream news outlets and business-oriented futurism, as evidenced by the fact that *Adbusters*, the "hip," alternative magazine of media criticism and culture jamming, hailed TiVo as a technology that "struck true fear into the hearts of the transnational bosses," because it "sticks it to every broadcast advertiser" (Flood, 2001, p. 17). The *Adbusters* article goes on to claim that TiVo is among those new-media technologies that herald "something revolutionary. Something almost purely democratic. Something essentially non-commercial, driven not by price but by value. At long last, the people—could it be true?—would have control of what they wanted to hear and see" (2001, p. 17). In this portrayal of the revolutionary promise of the new technology, the champions of subversive chic close ranks with their ostensible foes: neo-liberal propagandists like Wriston (1992) and Gilder (1994).

Perhaps not surprisingly—given the anticipated role of TiVo in allowing for comprehensive demographic monitoring—the "transnational bosses" aren't quivering in their boots. Rather, they have been investing whole-heartedly in the technology that will purportedly undermine their fiefdom. In 1999, Time Warner, Disney, NBC and CBS invested a combined total of more than $100 million in digital VCR technology (Lewis, 2000, pp. 40–41). Either the prognosticators of democratic utopia are overly optimistic or the "transnational bosses" of industry are working overtime against their own interests. History, combined with the market potential of interactive monitoring, tends to side with the bosses against the revolutionary promise. This tendency is not inherent in the technology itself, which, as Lessig (1999) points out, lends itself to diverse uses depending on how it is configured and deployed. Rather it is a reflection of the imperatives of the decisions we make about how to use those technologies and upon the pressures exerted by those in a position to develop and implement the Internet of the future. The increasing privatization of the network infrastructure combined with the recent spate of merger activity designed to exploit the commercial potential of the Internet suggests those applications that promise to be commercially successful (economically profitable) will likely take top priority.

All of which should come as no surprise to those familiar with the history of electronic media in the United States—a history that has largely been the story of technological developments adapted to commercial ends. Often, as the critical history compiled by Solomon and McChesney (1993) suggests, this story has followed a pattern whereby non-commercial and community-oriented users are displaced by commercial applications as the medium is developed over time. Despite the claims of those who herald the subversive potential of the Internet—whether in the realm of theory or popular culture—there is little evidence to suggest the Internet will enact a radical departure from this pattern. On the contrary, applications originally heralded as subversive of centralized corporate control, such as Napster and Freenet, are already being tailored to serve commercial purposes. If it is not difficult to imagine how interactive media could help promote more democratic forms of mediated communication, it is even easier to envision their role in allowing for ever more sophisticated techniques for the exploitation of the work of being watched.

Whether or not TiVo and its competitors are ultimately successful, they are helping to forge the commercial paradigm of interactive media as a means of inducing viewers to watch more efficiently. Subscribers to TiVo—or to the next generation of interactive television—will help lead the way into a digital enclosure wherein the work of watching can be as closely monitored as was the manual labor overseen by Frederick Taylor. The compilation of detailed demographic profiles of viewers will be facilitated by computer storage and retrieval techniques so as to ensure "wasted" watching will be kept to a minimum. The celebrants of mass customization envision this will take place in two ways: first, advertising will be tailored to match the demographics of each household and, eventually, of individual viewers; second, the line between content and advertising will continue to blur to the point of extinction.

If, as Gates (1996) suggests, every item of clothing, every location, and every product in a television show can—within the context of an interactive medium— double as both an advertising appeal and a clickable purchase point, *all* viewing counts as work in the sense outlined by Jhally and Livant (1986). Indeed, all activity of virtually any kind that can be monitored within this enclosure becomes work, as in the example of Mitch Maddox's DotCompound. In the case of interactive television, the added convenience of customization may well work to maximize not just the relative time devoted to the work of watching, but overall viewing time. The Replay Corporation has already found that "its customers watch, on average, three hours more television each week than they did before they got the box" (Lewis, 2000, p. 40).

The model of interactive television is generalizable to an increasing variety of activities that take place within the digital enclosure—and, to the extent that monitoring is involved, more and more activities seem to fall under the umbrella of consumption. The work of being watched can, in other words, help to rationalize the entire spectrum of consumption-related activities that have traditionally taken place beyond the monitoring gaze of the workplace. The general outlines of a commercial model for interactive media can thus be gleaned from the example of TiVo. Its main components are: customization (the disaggregation of demand curves, the direct linkage between a specific act of production and a targeted act of consumption), interactivity (the ability to monitor consumers in the act of consumption), off-loading labor to consumers (who perform the work of generating their own demographic information), and the development of an on-going relationship with consumers (that allows for the exploitation of demographic information gathered over time).

Perhaps not surprisingly, several elements of this business model can be discerned in the development of a recent, supposedly subversive media technology: that of the music file-sharing utility Napster. As *Wired* magazine recently noted in a short aside to its celebratory coverage of the revolutionary potential of "peer-to-peer" networking, Napster represents a forward-looking business model for the on-line economy: "the system keeps customer relationships in-house, but outsources the lion's share of infrastructure back to a captive audience. It's . . . clear that a better music-industry strategy would be not to ban Napster's technology, but to make it their own" (Kuptz, 2000, p. 236). The German publishing giant Bertelsmann, with a major presence in the recording industry, clearly agrees, as evidenced by its decision to enter into a partnership with Napster. This arrangement should not be viewed as an aberration or a "sellout" on the part of Napster—whose ostensible assault on the record industry was not a subversion of market logic per se, but one more example of the "creative destruction" that Schumpeter (1947) famously attributed to the process of capitalist development: the replacement of an older business paradigm by a newer one.

Like TiVo, Napster-style technology allows for the comprehensive documentation of on-line consumption: it enables not only the monitoring of music selections downloaded by users, but, potentially, the retrieval of their entire on-line music inventory. It may well offer companies like Bertelsmann the ability to peer into subscribers' virtual CD-cabinets and eventually to catalogue their actual listening habits in order to market to them more effectively. Just as TiVo offloads the work of market research to consumers who add to their profile of preferences with every program they select, Napster potentially offloads this work to users who share files on-line. Moreover, as the *Wired* article notes, the Napster model also offloads infrastructure to consumers, whose home computers become the repository for the music files traded on-line. Napster technology makes possible the future envisioned by Gates (1996), wherein subscribers will be able to download music to portable digital devices and to pay according to how often they plan to listen to an individual track. In this respect the future of online music and television delivery envisioned by the industry represents the application of mediated interactivity to the emerging paradigm of surveillance-based customization. The result is the promise that consumers will be able to perform the work of being watched with even greater efficiency.

Conclusion

Rumors of the death of privacy in the 21st century have been greatly exaggerated. The increasingly important role of on-line surveillance in the digital economy should be constructed not as the disappearance of privacy per se, but as a shift in control over personal information from individuals to *private* corporations. The information in question—behavioral habits, consumption preferences, and so on—is emphatically not being publicized. It is, rather, being aggregated into proprietary commodities, whose economic value is dependent, at least in part, upon the fact that they are privately owned. Such commodities are integral to the exploitation of customized markets and the administration of the "flexible" mode of production associated with mass customization. Making markets more efficient, according to this model, means surpassing the paradigm of the mass market and its associated inefficiencies, including the cost of gathering demographic information, of storing inventory, and of attempting to sell a mass-produced product at a standardized price. Interactive media combined with the development of computer memory and processing speed allow for the comprehensive forms of surveillance crucial to the scientific management of consumption within the digital enclosure.

Like the factory workers of the early 20th century, the consumers of the early 21st century will be subjected to more sophisticated monitoring techniques and their attendant forms of productive discipline. The intended result is the stimulation of the forces of consumption—the indirect complement of the enhanced productivity associated with network technology. If the effort expended in shopping feels more and more like labor, if we find ourselves negotiating ever more complex sets of choices that require more sophisticated forms of technological literacy, the digital economy is poised to harness the productive power of that labor through the potential of interactivity.

At the same time, it is worth pointing out the potentially productive contradiction at the heart of the promise of the digital "revolution". If indeed its promise is predicated on the subversion of the very forms of market control it serves, this promise invokes a moment of critique. This is the flip side of Foucault's assertion of the subject as the site of the reiteration of conditions of power. It is the critical moment heralded by Butler's (1997) assertion that "Where conditions of subordination make possible the assumption of power, the power assumed remains tied to those conditions, but in an ambivalent way" (p. 13). Subjection/subjectification suggests that the conditions of power are not reproduced "automatically" but can be contested by the very forms of subjectivity they produce. From this perspective, it is telling that in the celebratory discourse of the digital revolution, centralized forms of market control are re-presented as homologous with their former opponent: totalitarian, centralized planning. Intriguing avenues for resistance open up in an era when the *New York Times* can liken the television network system to Stalinism. Such critiques might do well to start with the premises appealed to by the digital revolution: that there is a need for greater shared control of the economic and political processes that shape our lives in an age of seemingly dramatic technological transformation. Even if the promise of interactivity as a form of de-centralization and shared control fails to be realized (as is suggested by the flurry of record-breaking merger activity in recent years), its implicit assessment of the shortcomings of mass society serves as a potential purchase point for a critique of the very rationalization it enables. In this respect, the realization that the promise of interactivity bases its appeal on perceived forms of exploitation (that ought to be overcome) lines up with Foucault's observation that where there is power, there is also, always, the potential for resistance.

Of central interest from a critical perspective, therefore, is the extent to which the marketers of the digital revolution continue to base its appeal upon the interpellation of an "active," empowered consumer. As consumers start to realize that their activity feels more like labor (filling out online surveys, taking the time to "design" customized products and services) and less like empowerment, it is likely that the explicit appeal to shared control will be replaced by the emerging trend toward automated, autonomous forms of "convenient" monitoring. This is the direction anticipated by futurists like Negroponte (1995) and the planners behind the MIT "Project Oxygen," whose goal is to make computers as invisible and ubiquitous as air. Their approach represents a retreat from the version of the "active" consumer associated with explicitly participatory forms of data gathering that characterized some of the early experiments in interactivity (the "design your own sneaker" or "write a review of this book" approach). Instead, the goal is the proliferation of an increasingly invisible, automated, and autonomous network. The agency of the active consumer is displaced onto what Negroponte (1995) calls "the digital butler." Interactivity will likely be increasingly reformulated as inter-*passivity* insofar as the goal is to make the monitoring process as unobtrusive as possible. The call to "action" will be displaced onto the ubiquitous technology, whose autonomy is designed to replace that of the consumer/viewer. Perhaps an early incarnation of this unobtrusive form of monitoring is the browser "cookie." Designed to increase convenience by allowing a site to remember a particular visitor so that customized settings don't have to be reconfigured, the "cookie" doubles as a digital butler for marketers, providing detailed browsing information about online consumers. It is hard not to imagine that the same would be true of other forms of digital butlers, whose allegiance remains rather more ambiguous than Negroponte implies. As these services become increasingly invisible and fade into the background, the increasingly monitored and transparent consumer comes to the fore.

In the face of the emergence of increasingly ubiquitous and invisible forms of monitoring, the appeal to privacy is often enlisted as a form of resistance. This type of resistance is rendered problematic by the fact that what is taking place—despite the recurring claim that the end of privacy is upon us—is the extensive *appropriation* of personal information. More information than ever before is being privatized as it is collected and aggregated so that it can be re-sold as a commodity or incorporated into the development of customized commodities. The enclosure and monopolization of this information reinforce power asymmetries in two ways: by concentrating control over the resources available for the production of subjects' desires and desiring subjects, and by the imposition of a comprehensive panoptic regime. The digital enclosure has the potential to become what Giddens (1981), following Goffman, terms a "total institution." The good news, perhaps, is that once the red-herring of the "death" of privacy is debunked, the enclosure of personal information can be properly addressed as a form of exploitation predicated on unequal access to the means of data collection, storage, and manipulation. A discussion of surveillance might then be couched in terms of conditions of power that compel entry into the digital enclosure and submission to comprehensive monitoring as a means of stimulating and rationalizing consumption. The way in which the promise of participation is deployed as an incentive to submit to the work of being watched might be further illuminated by the extension of models of "concertive control" (Papa, Auwal, & Singh, 1997; Tompkins & Cheney, 1985) to the realm of consumer labor. Additionally, such a discussion would necessarily address the questions of who controls the means of surveillance and to what ends, how this power is reproduced through subjection to interactive monitoring, who benefits from the work of being watched, and who is compelled to surrender control over personal information in exchange for a minimum "wage" of convenience or customization. For too long, the discussion of mediated interactivity has tended to assume that as long as the Internet allowed unfettered interactivity, questions of network control and ownership were rendered moot by the revolutionary potential of the technology itself. Perhaps it is not too much to hope that an understanding of the relation of interactivity to disciplinary surveillance and, thus, to the labor of being watched might work to counter the unwonted euphoria of the utopian cyber-determinists and to refocus the question of the fate of collective control over personal information. Otherwise, we may all find ourselves toiling productively away in the DotCompound, narrowcasting the rhythms of our daily lives to an ever smaller and more exclusive audience of private corporations.

Questions

1   How does Andrejevic justify his claim that "being watched" is a form of labor? Do you agree with his viewpoint?
2   What activities do you engage in that might be considered forms of labor?
3   How would Andrejevic incorporate social networking sites like MySpace and Facebook into his discussion?

Note

1.   Jhally, S., & Livant, B. (1986). Watching as working: The valorization of audience consciousness. *Journal of Communication, 36*(3), 124–43.

References

Bedell, D. (2000, March 2). FTC to survey e-commerce sites on how they use customers' data. *The Dallas Morning News*, p. 1F.

Braverman, H. (1974). *Labor and monopoly capital*. New York: Monthly Review Press.

Bryan, C. (1998). Electronic democracy and the civic networking movement. In R. Tsagarousianou, D. Tambini, & C. Bryan (Eds.), *Cyberdemocracy: Technology, cities, and civic networks* (pp. 1–17). London: Routledge.

Butler, J. (1997). *The psychic life of power*. Palo Alto: Stanford University Press.

Choney, S. (2001, March 27). Juno may not charge, but it's no free lunch. *The San Diego Union-Tribune*, p. 2.

Copeland, L. (2001, Jan. 3). For DotComGuy, the end of the online line. *The Washington Post*, p. C2.

Elliott, S. (2000, Oct. 13). TiVo teams up with the Omnicom Group to tell the world about digital video recorder. *The New York Times*, p. C4.

Flood, H. (2001, March/April). Linux, TiVo, Napster . . . information wants to be free. You got a problem with that? *Adbusters*, No. 34, 17.

Foucault, M. (1976/1977). *Discipline and punish: The birth of the prison* (A. Sheridan, Trans.). New York: Vintage Books.

Foucault, M. (1976/1978). *The history of sexuality: An introduction* (Vol. I) (R. Hurley, Trans.). New York: Vintage Books.

Foucault, M. (1980). *The Foucault reader* (P. Rabinow, Ed.). New York: Pantheon Books.

Gandy, O. (1993). *The panoptic sort: A political economy of personal information*. Boulder, CO: Westview.

Garfinkel, S. (2000). *Database nation: The death of privacy in the 21ˢᵗ century*. Cambridge: O'Reilly.

Gates, B. (1996). *The road ahead*. New York: Penguin.

Giddens, A. (1981). *A contemporary critique of historical materialism*. Berkeley: University of California Press.

Gilder, G. (1994). *Life after television: The coming transformation of media and American life*. New York: Norton.

Grossman, W. (2000, Oct. 26). Shock of the new for Amazon customers. *The Daily Telegraph* (London), p. 70.

Harvey, D. (1990). *The condition of postmodernity*. Cambridge: Blackwell.

Harvey, D. (1999). *The limits to capital*. London: Verso.

Jhally, S., & Livant, B. (1986). Watching as working: The valorization of audience consciousness. *Journal of Communication, 36*, 124–143.

Kellner, D. (1999). Globalisation from below? Toward a radical democratic technopolitics. *Angelaki, 4*, 101–111.

Kuptz, J. (2000, October). Independence array. *Wired*, 236–237.

Labaton, S. (2000, May 20). U.S. is said to seek new law to bolster privacy on Internet. *New York Times*, p. A1.

Lessig, L. (1999). *Code: And other laws of cyberspace*. New York: Basic Books.

Lester, T. (2001, March). The reinvention of privacy. *The Atlantic Monthly*, 27–39.

Lewis, M. (2000, Aug. 13). Boombox. *The New York Times Magazine*, 36–67.

Lyon, D. (1994). *The electronic eye: The rise of surveillance society*. Minneapolis: University of Minneapolis Press.

Marchand, R. (1985). *Advertising the American dream: Making way for modernity, 1920–1940*. Berkeley: University of California Press.

Mosco, V. (1996). *The political economy of communication*. London: Sage.

Mougayar, W. (1998). *Opening digital markets*. New York: McGraw-Hill.

Negroponte, N. (1995). *Being digital*. New York: Alfred A. Knopf.

Norris, C., and Armstrong, G. (1999). *The maximum surveillance society: The rise of CCTV*. Oxford: Berg.

Papa, M. J., Auwal, M. A., & Singhal, A. (1997, September). Organizing for social change within concertive control systems: Member identification, empowerment, and the masking of discipline. *Communication Monographs, 64*, 219–249.

Pine, J. (1993). *Mass customization: The new frontier in business competition*. Cambridge, MA: Harvard University Press.

Rheingold, H. (1993). *Virtual community*. Reading, MA: Addison-Wesley.

Robins, K., & Webster, F. (1999). *Times of the technoculture: From the information society to the virtual life*. London: Routledge.

Rosen, J. (2000). *The unwanted gaze: The destruction of privacy in America*. New York: Random House.

Schiller, D. (1988). How to think about information. In V. Mosco & J. Wasko (Eds.), *The Political Economy of Information* (pp. 27–43). Madison: University of Wisconsin Press.

Schiller, D. (1999). *Digital capitalism*. Cambridge, MA: The MIT Press.

Schumpeter, J. (1947). *Capitalism, socialism, and democracy*. New York: Harper & Brothers.

Shapiro, A. (1999). *The control revolution: How the Internet is putting individuals in charge and changing the world we know*. New York: PublicAffairs.

Sloan, A. (1963). *My years with General Motors*. Garden City, NY: Doubleday.

Smythe, D. (1981). *Dependency road: Communications, capitalism, consciousness, and Canada*. Toronto: Ablex.

Smythe, D. (1977). Communications: Blindspot of western Marxism. *Canadian Journal of Political and Social Theory, 1*, 1–27.

Tompkins, P. K., & Cheney, G. (1985). Communication and unobtrusive control in contemporary organizations. In R.D. McPhee & P.K. Tompkins (Eds.), *Organizational communication: Traditional themes and new directions* (pp. 179–210). Newbury Park, CA: Sage.

Whitaker, R. (1999). *The end of privacy: How total surveillance is becoming a reality*. New York: New Press.

Wriston, W. (1992). *The twilight of sovereignty: How the information revolution is transforming our world*. New York: Scribner.

Chapter 25

JOSEPH TUROW

ADVERTISERS AND AUDIENCE AUTONOMY AT THE END OF TELEVISION

AMONG THE NARRATIVES CIRCULATING ABOUT the digital media environment is that new technologies have shifted control from media producers to audiences. Yet Joseph Turow, one of the editors of this book, contends that this "rhetoric of audience autonomy" is not necessarily a twenty-first-century phenomenon. Indeed, marketers have long been concerned about the power of audiences to tune out advertisers—both literally (with remote controls and DVRs) and metaphorically (by ignoring ads). Today, however, advertisers are turning to new marketing techniques in hopes of better managing consumer control. Perhaps the most profound strategy is database marketing, a development which foregrounds concerns about identity, privacy, and the way marketers construct audiences and the social world.

A hallmark of discussions about the end of television and the new media rising in its stead is the idea that audiences are more independent than ever from the power of advertisers. The reason, say many executives and some academics, is that people now have the ability to use technology to evade TV and web commercials, to use the internet to read impartial critiques of products, and to use multiple vehicles to create their own audiovisual news and entertainment outside the commercial-media orbit. In a 2006 keynote address to the Association of National Advertisers convention, the C.E.O. of Procter and Gamble not only agreed that in the emerging era "the power is with the consumer," he concluded that as a result advertisers must for the first time "let go" of the notion that they rather than consumers control the shaping of their brands' images.[1]

This essay argues that despite the rhetoric of audience autonomy, and typical of the history of advertiser–consumer relations, marketers are working aggressively with major media firms to maintain and even extend their influence over ad-viewing experiences and brand consciousness. While it is an open question whether and how much marketers will be able to control their audiences' perspectives about their products, their 21st century attempts to do it are having profound implications for the evolving structure of audiovisual media and for consumers' relation to the retail environment.

Writing in 1991 about the US television industry, Ien Ang emphasized that in order to get their work done successfully executives need to take steps to believe they can control their audience.[2] She described a tension-filled process rife with concerns that audiences might not view what the TV executives and their ad-industry sponsors had spent so much money to prepare. To the sponsors, of course, the major objective centered on leading the audience to view 15- and 30-second commercial messages; the shows were just an excuse to get the viewers there.

What Ang didn't note is that the television industry is merely the latest location of this challenge. Marketers have probably always been irked by the power that intended audience members hold to not pay attention to—and even dismiss the value of—the marketers' ads, especially when the ads pay for content or activities that the consumers value. In the early 20th century, for example, the editor of the *Ladies Home Journal* felt compelled to imply to readers that they should respect the presence of ads as part of an implicit contract with the reader to supply a desirable magazine at a low price. "The fact must never be forgotten," he wrote, "that no magazine in the United States could give what it is giving to the reader each month if it were not for the revenue which the advertiser brings to the magazine."[3]

Advertisers felt the same tension, and implied the same contract, in the broadcast radio industry. By 1930 radio advertising evidently irked enough people that the radio-technology pioneer Lee DeForrest could write seriously in *Radio News* about how a wireless remote control might be developed with which "the long-suffering radio user" could "instantly assassinate the advertising announcer and allow the set to resume its musical outpourings when the story of the tooth-paste or furniture sales-man is terminated."[4] No such device was sold commercially, though, and a chronicler generally sympathetic to the advertising industry asserted that radio listeners under-stood the implicit contract: They "tolerated, if they did not enjoy the enforced intru-sions [by advertisers] as inevitable, seeing it as the price they had to pay for heady pleasures."[5] Discussions in the marketing trade press from the 1940s onward suggest that advertisers and media executives made the same attribution regarding television's audiences.

But radio and television executives, along with their advertising counterparts, understood that having the audience tolerate the "contract" was not enough. They needed to carry out the twin job of getting people's attention and impelling them to buy. Stories in and out of the trade press noted that people talked, visited the kitchen or used the bathroom during commercial breaks. Ad agencies consequently saw garnering people's attention through compelling ads in compelling programs as one of their primary challenges. They judged whether their choices of programs to sponsor were successful through a ratings system that in television was monopolized by the Nielsen company. With rare exceptions, Nielsen provided data for viewers' tuning in of shows, not specifically of commercials within the shows. To judge whether ads were persuasive, advertisers turned to Daniel Starch, who in the early decades of the 20th century pioneered ways of measuring the readership of a print advertisement. Ad practitioners carried the notion over to radio and television. In the absence of proving a direct relationship between commercial and purchase, "recall" became a surrogate for a commercial's success. Copywriters and art directors made high recall an important value in a commercial's creation. And in their attempts to get good recall and encourage purchasing, ad executives helped fund a science of desire that drew on instinct psychology, Freudian analysis, motivation research, brain studies, and other attempts to understand consumption and persuasion.

Television executives saw it as their major task to help advertisers draw and keep attractive audiences, as determined by the Nielsen company's ratings. Exactly what "attractive audiences" meant, and how to draw and keep them, were ideas that changed over the decades in network and local TV. Network television typically led the way, and the evening schedule was its highest priced (and highest stakes) arena for implementing audience-attracting ideas. In the 1950s era of full sponsorship, network executives saw their role mainly as encouraging Americans to buy TV sets and collecting sponsors that would select and mount the most appealing shows possible. By the 1960s, however, advertisers were showing an interest in purchasing slots within several shows, not fully-sponsoring programs, and the heads of CBS, NBC and ABC were determined to control the relationship among programs in their prime time schedules. The goal was to bring as many viewers as possible to the start of the period (7:30pm Eastern and Pacific) and then to array shows in such a way as to keep or increase that audience size through prime time's end at 11pm.

Carrying out this goal were network programming directors. They quickly became celebrities, known on Madison Avenue and in the popular press by their ability to choose successful series. The word was that the best of the executives (Mike Dann, Fred Silverman, Brandon Tartikoff) had special talents for intuiting what Americans would like; Silverman, for example, was widely hailed as "the man with the golden gut."[6] For their part, the network mavens took pains to convince advertisers that beyond intuition they were developing systematic survey and program-analyzing techniques to guide the choice of shows as well as tactics such as least objectionable programs, lead-ins, lead-outs and hammocking to array the programs for optimal audience flow through the prime time schedule.

By the 1960s, television and advertising executives, academics, and members of the public shared a construction of TV as fundamentally a box with a screen in the home that provides viewers with numbered channels from which flowed various genres of programming.[7] The programming goals—and the related strategies and tactics—changed over the decades as advertisers' audience objectives changed. Nielsen's decision in the late 1960s to regularly include age in its ratings reports dovetailed with advertisers' interest in going beyond considering only audience size in deciding where to put their TV dollars. It was the beginning of a gradual ramp-up in TV advertisers' desire to choose their network TV viewers by a variety of characteristics. Advertisers considered this approach particularly important beginning the 1980s as cable and satellite technologies multiplied the number of channels most Americans received in the 1980s. With broadcast audiences declining as viewers fragmented across dozens of channels, ad executives needed increasing specificity about viewers to justify placing their TV ads in one or another network. By the late 1990s Nielsen reports routinely included age, gender, race, Hispanic ethnicity, and levels of income. For network programming directors of the 1990s, the multiplication of networks, advertisers' interest in segmentation, and the routine use of the remote control channel changer meant that several of the old programming strategies would not work as well as in the past. Soft-pedaling audience flow in the late 1990s, NBC urged viewers to make time for individual series, a practice dubbed "appointment television." Madison Avenue seemed to think it worked—that in the new environment the right audiences could be made to pay attention to the right ads—and other networks copied it.

Then came TiVo. For many media and marketing executives the appearance of the digital video recorder marked the beginning of the end of television as they had known it. Essentially a computer with a large hard drive, the DVR (also called a PVR—personal video recorder) acted like a video cassette recorder in enabling its owners to record programs and view them at other times. Unlike a VCR, the technology marketed to the public by TiVo and other firms was connected to an updatable guide that made finding programs across more than one hundred channels easy. Also unlike a VCR, in some versions made by ReplayTV (and in "hacked" versions of TiVo) it allowed viewers to skip ahead 30 seconds at a time without at all viewing what was skipped. That, advertisers knew, would be commercials. In fact, ReplayTV used its PVR's facility for skipping over commercials as a selling point in its early ads.

Those who said the fear of DVRs was exaggerated pointed out that sales figures were rather small. One trade article in 2002 called the DVR "a technology in search of a business model."[8] Others disagreed strongly. They pointed out that the sales rate of branded DVRs was increasing and that home satellite firms and cable systems were beginning to integrate unbranded versions into set-top boxes. They noted TiVo's admission that 60 percent to 70 percent of people watching via its technology were skipping commercials. And they admonished that whatever accommodation advertisers would make with DVR firms, it would undercut the by-then-traditional approach of mounting 15- or 30- second commercials within shows.

Jamie Kellner, CEO of Turner Broadcasting, railed against DVRs in ways that echoed media and marketing executives' traditional fear of losing control over the ability to guide the audience to commercials. In 2004 he told the magazine *Cable World* that DVR users were "stealing" television by skipping commercials. To him the contract between advertisers and TV audiences was quite real. "[As a viewer,] Your contract with the network when you get the show is you're going to watch the spots," he said. "Otherwise you couldn't get the show on an ad-supported basis. Any time you skip a commercial or watch the button you're actually stealing the programming." When his interviewer asked him "What if you have to go to the bathroom or get up to get a Coke," Kellner responded: "I guess there's a certain amount of tolerance for going to the bathroom. But if you formalize it and you create a device that skips certain second increments, you've got that for only one reason, unless you go to the bathroom for 30 seconds. They've done that just to make it easy for someone to skip a commercial."[9]

The concern that Kellner and other TV executives had around DVRs ran deeper than viewers' ability to skip commercials. It reflected a broader worry that digital devices that would remake television to give consumers the kind of control over what and when they watched that was already emerging on the internet. To some TV executives, this ability threatened to upend the routines of predictable scheduling and advertising placement that had become the verities upon which commercial US television was based. To make matters worse, at the same time belief in ratings—those arbiters of 20th century advertising decision making—began to crumble. Basic questions about Nielsen television data raised the troubling question of whether young men had really abandoned traditional television for video games and the web or whether the data that suggest they had done so was wrong. Nielsen's discovery that the young men had returned did little to quell the suspicion among television and advertising executives that the ratings company was using outmoded methods to explore an audience it didn't understand in a territory it didn't know. Even more fundamental, the lack of granularity in the Nielsen reports—their inability to divide viewers into multifarious niches based on demographics, lifestyles, and buying habits—meant that the ratings could not be helpful to marketers in their increasingly urgent use of information repositories about individuals and their households to evaluate whether they wanted certain types of people as customers and to target them via certain media and certain ads.

With the worry that consumers could really push away ads better than ever before, that consumers were increasingly turning to the internet and other digital media, that they were often poaching TV materials without their associated commercials, and that TV ratings might not be useful to truly revealing the extent of that, some major marketers did pause rhetorically to assure everyone that they applauded consumers' creative new media habits. At the same time, though, they began to change their own advertising patterns so as to ensure as much as possible that they could follow, and influence, the consumers they wanted to reach wherever they went. Broadly speaking, three strategies had emerged by 2007: product integration and cross-promotion across a variety of media platforms, including television; channeling so-called "user generated content" into a commercial context that could enhance product integration and cross promotion; and the cultivation of an environment of acceptability for database marketing so that marketers can identify the individuals they particularly want to target for promotional and user-generated relationships.

An early version of the first strategy was "product placement," the act of trading or buying an item's position within media content. The practice can be traced back to at least the silent movies and became a frenzied TV phenomenon in the wake of marketers' first concerns about DVRs. Rather quickly, however, marketers realized that simply inserting a mention or item in part of a program would rarely get them far in demonstrating the item or building its personality. While a next step involved integrating the item or service into the TV action (producer Mark Burnett's *The Apprentice* was the poster program for this activity on NBC), ad executives soon concluded that this approach too was self-limiting in an era where their target consumer's attention was fleeting and often far from particular programs and even from the traditional TV set. Marketers' current strategy is therefore to create a mix of advertising and product integration that provocatively piques the interest of the target audience so that they visit the marketer's website to see more, share the ideas about it virally via the web and across a variety of media platforms, including television. The Super Bowl provides the optimal service for advertisers looking to use television as one element in a multimedia promotion. In the mid-2000s, the season-ending football match is still a place on sponsored network TV to find young adult men in huge numbers. Rather than adopting the pre-TiVo goal of aiming thirty second commercials at them with the hope that the ads will enhance brand identities and sales, recent Super Bowl advertisers have seen the game commercial as a way to engage the audience weeks before its airing and far after it. The website naming company Godaddy.com, for example, has cultivated a reputation for creating Super Bowl commercials that network executives consider unacceptably sexual. In the months before the event it whips up young-adult interest in the commercials it is trying to get past the censors, and it uses the steamy spot that the network accepted to drive the core audience to its website where they can see ones that did not make it through, enjoy racier versions of the accepted one, and learn about the company. "We can't get across what we do in a 30-second spot," noted the company's

CEO "so we have to run a spot that is polarizing enough to get people to come to our website to see more."[10]

Anheuser-Busch, the largest Superbowl advertiser, took an even more drastic tack. Apart from encouraging discussion about its spots in the weeks prior to the CBS show, the beermaker used its in-game commercials to kick off Bud.TV, what can only be described as a clear acknowledgement that the end of traditional TV is at hand for the company's core twentysomething consumers. "What cable and satellite were to the last generation, digital is to this generation," said A-B's vice present of global media. Pitching the site as full-service entertainment network on the web, the company promised to limit product placement drastically and instead offer up a place where Bud drinkers could find collegial entertainment that would generate buzz offline and on. "What they're offering up is bigger than integration," opined an executive from the marketing communication giant Omnicom. Its branded entertainment arm was involved in the project. He explained: "They're offering up a destination, a community for their audience, and I think that's even a bigger idea than placing products in shows."[11]

Part of the marketers' goal of creating a website highly trafficked by its target audience relates to the second strategy for a post-television world: channeling their target audience's creativity into the firms' commercial orbits in ways that will enhance their identification with company products. User-generated content is a term that characterizes the digital video, blogging, podcasting, mobile phone photography, software and wikis that millions of people are creating as technologies of production and distribution become more accessible and affordable than in previous decades. Wikipedia says the term "came into the mainstream in 2005," but a Nexis search of *Advertising Age* reveals that it was already on the marketers' radar in 2000 as a way to bring people closer to companies.[12] The popular press celebrated Facebook, YouTube, MySpace and similar social media sites as the incarnation of (in Wikipedia's words) "collaboration, skill-building and discovery" by "end-users as opposed to traditional media producers, licensed broadcasters, and production companies." Marketers, for their part, saw the phenomenon as a way to bond consumers to them by giving them the incentive, and sometimes even the tools, to create advertisements about them. While some advertisers sneered—one suggested that user-generated commercials involved the inmates taking over the asylum—many others mounted multimedia ad-making contests with prizes and fame as the rewards. The 2007 Super Bowl gave these activities a particularly high profile, as Frito Lay, General Motors, and the National Football League ran consumer generated ads that had been chosen from thousands of nominations. In addition, all three firms pumped hoopla around the submissions and the final selection that linked the user-generated strategy to the one involving cross-promotion. Television emerged as one node in a multichannel extravaganza that focused on generating excitement in young male adults.

If the first two strategies represent marketers' attempts to regain their powerful footing *vis à vis* consumers in the post-television era, they do it knowing that down the road is their holy grail of leverage: database marketing. Advertising and media executives see the internet, now the most interactive of electronic media, as a test bed for gathering and analyzing information about the audience in the interest of better persuading them. The recipe involves attempting to take charge by attempting to inculcate a strong sense of brand trust while gathering information with which to decide whether and how a customer is worth engaging in customized digital relationships. Six interrelated activities form the heart of the logic: screening consumers for appropriateness, interacting with them electronically, targeted tracking of them, data mining, mass customization of advertising messages, and the cultivation of relationships based on the knowledge gained.

The collection of data, their analysis, and the implementation of messages based on them are still in its relative infancy on the web, but this is moving forward according to an industrial logic that marketing and media executives repeat often: To get consumers to pay attention to commercial messages, marketers must know as much as possible about them and interact with them whenever and wherever they can convince consumers to find them relevant. As a result, cable companies are experimenting with commercials that change based on the data the firm collects about the household and its members. Internet-protocol-television executives talk about streaming customized ads and even programs based upon the niches that sponsors would like to reach. Mobile phone companies are deciding how deeply, and when, they should turn over their internet "decks" to direct marketers who would know the location of people being reached. And outdoor advertising companies are planning a reality in which database-driven, location-based communication between billboards, PDAs, and phones are an everyday event.

Much of these targeted messages are focused on influencing the behavior of customers when they enter stores, virtual or physical. One of the most important marketing developments of the early 21st century is the movement of database-driven media to the center of the retailing experience. The supermarket has for a few decades been a carnival of media vehicles such as mats, audio services, multiple video screens and shelf coupons. These festooneries remain, but they are now overlaid with digital communication experiments that aim to track customers as they move through the stores and offer discounts based on shopping histories. Clothing stores and electronics retailers are likewise tracking customers and customizing offers online and off. The logic and importance of customer identification to competitive strategy are so vital that consultants talk seriously about encouraging desirable customers to identify themselves biometrically (through eye scans or fingerprints) so that the store's pricing environment might be customized to match their interests.

Executives insist that these activities are needed to give their desirable customers what they want or they will go elsewhere. Discussions at industry meetings and in the trade press also underscore the future importance that executives place on consumer databases to present different types of people with appropriately different depictions of their brands in media and retail surroundings. Although the rhetoric of customer autonomy does underlie all these activities, the actions by marketing and media executives reflect a grim determination to manage consumer power rather than merely allow it to bloom untamed. Irrespective of how much they succeed in doing it, the database-driven strategies they have chosen are profoundly reshaping the media landscape. The audiovisual presentation of news, entertainment and advertising certainly has a place in this emerging world, but it must be conceptualized quite differently from the domestic box that we call "television." The activities raise critical questions about how audience-tailored news, entertainment, and advertising will reshape shared storytelling in the coming century. Seen through a marketing perspective, "the end of television" points to socially challenging vistas ahead.

Questions

1   What does Turow mean by the "rhetoric of audience autonomy?" How might this apply to other media, besides television?
2   How might advertisers benefit from the idea that, as the Procter and Gamble CEO stated, "The power is with the consumer"?
3   Compare Turow's perspective on database marketing with Mark Andrejevic's discussion of the interactive economy. How are their arguments similar? How do they differ?

Notes

1. A.G. Lafley, quoted in Matthew Creamer, "ANA Confab offers Up More Than Tee Times," *Advertising Age*, October 9, 2006, p. 1.
2. Ien Ang, *Desperately Seeking the Audience* (London: Routledge, 1991).
3. James Playsted Wood, *The Story of Advertising* (New York: Ronald, 1958), p. 405.
4. Lee DeForrest, "Dr. DeForrest Designs the Anti-Ad," *Radio News*, September 1930, pp. 215, 285.
5. Wood, p. 411.
6. See, for example, Phil Klier, "Highbrow or Low, TV Programmer Could Spot a Hit," *Atlanta Journal-Constitution*, August 28, 1997, p. 1D.
7. A good analysis of this construction of television is by Raymond Williams, *Television: Technology and Cultural Form* (New York: Schocken, 1975).
8. Bradley Johnson, "TiVo, ReplayTV View for Uncertain Prize," *Advertising Age*, November 4, 2002, p. 42.
9. Staci D. Kramer, "Content's King," *Cable World*," April 29, 2004.
10. Bob Parsons, quoted in Bruce Horovitz, "Marketers Set Up a Screen Play," *USA Today*, February 2, 2007, p. 1B.
11. Gail Schiller, Bud.TV Hops to it With Originals," *Hollywood Reporter*, February 2, 2007.
12. "User-generated Content," Wikipedia (http://en.wikipedia.org/wiki/User-Generated_Content), accessed on February 5, 2007; and Patricia Riedman, "Dot-com slump crimps marketing," *Advertising Age*, May 29, 2000, p. 66.

Chapter 26

GARY RUSKIN AND JULIET SCHOR

EVERY NOOK AND CRANNY
The Dangerous Spread of Commercialized Culture

YOU HAVE LIKELY NOTICED THAT ADS TODAY appear in some highly unlikely places—scrolled across sidewalks, on screens at the gas station, and even stamped on eggs at the supermarket! The fact that commercial culture has oozed into every "nook and cranny" has Gary Ruskin, Executive Director of Commercial Alert, and Juliet Schor, a professor of sociology at Boston College and author of *Born to Buy!*, alarmed. In this article from the *Multinational Monitor*, a non-profit magazine that analyzes corporate activity, the authors criticize the ways in which advertising has infiltrated such public institutions as the media, education, government, and religious systems. Such a ubiquitous environment of advertising, they argue, has had significant social ramifications—ranging from the spread of the obesity epidemic to environmental damage to a corporate-controlled public agenda.

In December 2004, many people in Washington D.C. paused to absorb the meaning in the lighting of the National Christmas Tree, at the White House Ellipse. At that event, President George W. Bush reflected that the "love and gifts" of Christmas were "signs and symbols of even a greater love and gift that came on a holy night."

But these signs weren't the only ones on display. Perhaps it was not surprising that the illumination was sponsored by MCI, which, as MCI WorldCom, committed one of the largest corporate frauds in history. Such public displays of commercialism have become commonplace in the United States.

The rise of commercialism is an artifact of the growth of corporate power. It began as part of a political and ideological response by corporations to wage pressures, rising social expenditures, and the successes of the environmental and consumer movements in the late 1960s and early 1970s. Corporations fostered the anti-tax movement and support for corporate welfare, which helped create funding crises in state and local governments and schools, and made them more willing to carry commercial advertising. They promoted "free market" ideology, privatization and consumerism, while denigrating the public sphere. In the late 1970s, Mobil Oil began its decades-long advertising on the New York Times op-ed page, one example of a larger corporate effort to reverse a precipitous decline in public approval of corporations. They also became adept at manipulating the campaign finance system, and weaknesses in the federal bribery statute, to procure influence in governments at all levels.

Perhaps most importantly, the commercialization of government and culture and the growing importance of material acquisition and consumer lifestyles were hastened by the co-optation of potentially countervailing institutions, such as churches (papal visits have been sponsored by Pepsi, Federal Express and Mercedes-Benz), governments, schools, universities and nongovernmental organizations.

While advertising has long been an element in the circus of U.S. life, not until recently has it been recognized as having political or social merit. For nearly two centuries, advertising (lawyers call it commercial speech) was not protected by the U.S. Constitution. The U.S. Supreme Court ruled in 1942 that states could regulate commercial speech at will. But in 1976, the Court granted constitutional protection to commercial speech. Corporations have used this new right of speech to proliferate advertising into nearly every nook and cranny of life.

Entering the Schoolhouse

During most of the twentieth century, there was little advertising in schools. That changed in 1989, when Chris Whittle's Channel One enticed schools to accept advertising, by offering to loan TV sets to classrooms. Each school day, Channel One features at least two minutes of ads, and 10 minutes of news, fluff, banter and quizzes. The program is shown to about 8 million children in 12,000 schools.

Soda, candy and fast food companies soon learned Channel One's lesson of using financial incentives to gain access to schoolchildren. By 2000, 94 percent of high schools allowed the sale of soda, and 72 percent allowed sale of chocolate candy. Energy, candy, personal care products, even automobile manufacturers have entered the classroom with "sponsored educational materials," that is, ads in the guise of free "curricula."

Until recently, corporate incursion in schools has mainly gone under the radar. However, the rise of childhood obesity has engendered stiff political opposition to junk food marketing, and in the last three years, coalitions of progressives, conservatives and public health groups have made headway. The State of California has banned the sale of soda in elementary, middle and junior high schools. In Maine, soda and candy suppliers have removed their products from vending machines in all schools. Arkansas banned candy and soda vending machines in elementary schools. Los Angeles, Chicago and New York have city-wide bans on the sale of soda in schools. Channel One was expelled from the Nashville public schools in the 2002–3 school year, and will be removed from Seattle in early 2005. Thanks to activist pressure, a company called ZapMe! which placed computers in thousands of schools to advertise and extract data from students, was removed from all schools across the country.

Ad Creep and Spam Culture

Advertisers have long relied on 30 second TV spots to deliver messages to mass audiences. During the 1990s, the impact of these ads began to drop off, in part because viewers simply clicked to different programs during ads. In response, many advertisers began to place ads elsewhere, leading to "ad creep"—the spread of ads throughout social space and cultural institutions. Whole new marketing sub specialties developed, such as "place based" advertising, which coerces captive viewers to watch video ads. Examples include ads before movies, ads on buses and trains in cities (Chicago, Milwaukee and Orlando), and CNN's Airport channel. Video ads are also now common on ATMs, gas pumps, in convenience stores and doctors' offices.

Another form of ad creep is "product placement," in which advertisers pay to have their product included in movies, TV shows, museum exhibits, or other forms of media and culture. Product placement is thought to be more effective than the traditional 30 second ad because it sneaks by the viewer's critical faculties. Product placement has recently occurred in novels, and children's books. Some U.S. TV programs (American Idol, The Restaurant, The Apprentice) and movies (Minority Report, Cellular) are so full of product placement than they resemble infomercials. By contrast, many European nations, such as Austria, Germany, Norway and the United Kingdom, ban or sharply restrict product placement on television.

Commercial use of the Internet was forbidden as recently as the early 1990s, and the first spam wasn't sent until 1994. But the marketing industry quickly penetrated this sphere as well, and now 70 percent of all e-mail is spam, according to the spam filter firm Postini Inc. Pop-ups, pop-unders and ad ware have become major annoyances for Internet users. Telemarketing became so unpopular that the corporate-friendly Federal Trade Commission established a National Do Not Call Registry, which has brought relief from telemarketing calls to 64 million households.

Even major cultural institutions have been harnessed by the advertising industry. During 2001–2002, the Smithsonian Institution, perhaps the most important U.S. cultural institution, established the General Motors Hall of Transportation and the Lockheed Martin Imax Theater. Following public opposition and Congressional action, the commercialization of the Smithsonian has largely been halted. In 2000, the Library of Congress hosted a giant celebration for Coca-Cola, essentially converting the nation's most important library into a prop to sell soda pop.

Targeting Kids

For a time, institutions of childhood were relatively uncommercialized, as adults subscribed to the notion of childhood innocence, and the need to keep children from the "profane" commercial world. But what was once a trickle of advertising to children has become a flood. Corporations spend about $15 billion marketing to children in the United States each year, and by the mid-1990s, the average child was exposed to 40,000 TV ads annually.

Children have few legal protections from corporate marketers in the United States. This contrasts strongly to the European Union, which has enacted restrictions. Norway and Sweden have banned television advertising to children under 12 years of age; in Italy, advertising during TV cartoons is illegal, and toy advertising is illegal in

Greece between 7 AM and 11 PM. Advertising before and after children's programs is banned in Austria.

COMMERCIALIZED CONVERSATION

Conversation among family and friends may be the last refuge from commercialism. Not surprisingly, marketers have sought to exploit personal relationships, through the contrivance of word-of-mouth "buzz." Specialized "buzz marketing" firms and projects have arisen during the last five years. Proctor & Gamble has set up a buzz marketing shop called Tremor, which has enlisted about 280,000 teenagers as a free sales force under its control, and they are now launching a spin-off called Tremor Moms.

(G.R. & J.S.)

Government Brought to You by . . .

As fiscal crises have descended upon local governments, they have turned to advertisers as a revenue source. This trend began inauspiciously in Buffalo, New York in 1995 when Pratt & Lambert, a local paint company, purchased the right to call itself the city's official paint. The next year the company was bought by Sherwin Williams, which closed the local factory and eliminated its 200 jobs.

In 1997, Ocean City, Maryland signed an exclusive marketing deal to make Coca-Cola the city's official drink, and other cities have followed with similar deals with Coke or Pepsi. Even mighty New York City has succumbed, signing a $166 million exclusive marketing deal with Snapple, after which some critics dubbed it the "Big Snapple."

At the United Nations, UNICEF made a stir in 2002 when it announced that it would "team up" with McDonald's, the world's largest fast food company, to promote "McDonald's World Children's Day" in celebration of the anniversary of the United Nations' adoption of the Convention on the Rights of the Child. Public health and children's advocates across the globe protested, prompting UNICEF to decline participation in later years.

Another victory for the anti-commercialism forces, perhaps the most significant, came in 2004, when the World Health Organization's Framework Convention on Tobacco Control became legally binding. The treaty commits nations to prohibit tobacco advertising to the extent their constitutions allow it.

Impacts

Because the phenomenon of commercialism has become so ubiquitous, it is not surprising that its effects are as well. Perhaps most alarming has been the epidemic of marketing-related diseases afflicting people in the United States, and especially children, such as obesity, type 2 diabetes and smoking-related illnesses. Each day, about 2,000 U.S. children begin to smoke, and about one-third of them will die from tobacco-related illnesses. Children are inundated with advertising for high calorie junk food and fast food, and, predictably, 15 percent of U.S. children aged 6 to 19 are now overweight.

Excessive commercialism is also creating a more materialistic populace. In 2003, the annual UCLA survey of incoming college freshmen found that the number of students who said it was a very important or essential life goal to "develop a meaningful philosophy of life" fell to an all time low of 39 percent, while succeeding financially has increased to a 13-year high, at 74 percent. High involvement in consumer culture has been shown (by Schor) to be a significant cause of depression, anxiety, low self-esteem and psychosomatic complaints in children, findings which parallel similar studies of materialism among teens and adults. Other impacts are more intangible. A 2004 poll by Yankelovich Partners found that 61 percent of the U.S. public "feel that the amount of marketing and advertising is out of control," and 65 percent "feel constantly bombarded with too much advertising and marketing." Is advertising diminishing our sense of general well being? Perhaps.

The purpose of most commercial advertising to increase demand for a product. As John Kenneth Galbraith noted 40 years ago, the macro effect of advertising is to artificially boost the demand for private goods, thereby reducing the "demand" or support for unadvertised, public goods. The predictable result has been the backlash to taxes, and reduced provision of public goods and services.

This imbalance also affects the natural environment. The additional consumption created by the estimated $265 billion that the advertising industry spent in 2004 also yielded more pollution, natural resource destruction, carbon dioxide emissions and global warming.

Finally, advertising has also contributed to a narrowing of the public discourse, as advertising-driven media grow ever more timid. Sometimes it seems as if we live in an echo chamber, a place where corporations speak and everyone else listens.

Governments at all levels have failed to address these impacts. That may be because the most insidious effect of commercialism is to undermine government integrity. As governments adopt commercial values, and are integrated into corporate marketing, they develop conflicts of interest that make them less likely to take stands against commercialism.

Disgust among Yourselves

As corporations consolidate their control over governments and culture, we don't expect an outright reversal of commercialization in the near future.

That's true despite considerable public sentiment for more limits and regulations on advertising and marketing. However, as commercialism grows more intrusive, public distaste for it will likely increase, as will political support for restricting it. In the long run, we believe this hopeful trend will gather strength.

In the not-too-distant future, the significance of the lighting of the National Christmas Tree may no longer be overshadowed by public relations efforts to create goodwill for corporate wrongdoers.

Questions

1   How does the argument about the "narrowing of public discourse" relate to articles you read in previous Parts? How does it differ?
2   Although the authors seem to suggest advertisers are responsible for an obesity epidemic, those in the industry have responded that families and the government should take responsibility for health issues. Where do you stand on this issue and why?
3   Ruskin and Schor conclude by suggesting the role of the public in changing our commercial culture. Do you agree with their position?

Chapter 27

SUT JHALLY

ADVERTISING AT THE EDGE OF THE APOCALYPSE[*]

S UT JHALLY, A PROFESSOR OF COMMUNICATION at the University of
Massachusetts, has dedicated his career to examining the role of advertisers in
shaping our sense of the social world. As founder and Executive Director of the non-
profit Media Education Foundation, he has spearheaded numerous projects aimed at
educating people about our concentrated system of media ownership. He has also written extensively on the social implications of a consumerist culture, and in this provocative essay, he argues that our advertising system has the potential to "[destroy] the
world as we know it." The argument he makes is a striking one: the advertising industry has done tremendous damage to our environment by suggesting that the path to
happiness is paved with the unending acquisition of consumer goods. As you read this
essay, think about the recent steps that are being taken to reverse environmental
damage—and how far they go in addressing the problems Jhally raises.

Colonizing Culture

Karl Marx, the pre-eminent analyst of 19th century industrial capitalism, wrote in
1867, in the very opening lines of *Capital* that: "The wealth of societies in which the
capitalist mode of production prevails appears as an 'immense collection of commodities'." (Marx 1976, p.125) In seeking to initially distinguish his object of analysis from
preceding societies, Marx referred to the way the society showed itself on a surface level
and highlighted a *quantitative* dimension—the number of objects that humans interacted with in everyday life.

  Indeed, no other society in history has been able to match the immense productive
output of industrial capitalism. This feature colors the way in which the society presents
itself – the way it *appears*. Objects are everywhere in capitalism. In this sense, capitalism is truly a revolutionary society, dramatically altering the very landscape of social
life, in a way no other form of social organization had been able to achieve in such a

short period of time. (In *The Communist Manifesto* Marx and Engels would coin the famous phrase "all that is solid melts into air" to highlight capitalism's unique dynamism.) It is this that strikes Marx as distinctive as he observes 19th century London. The starting point of his own critique therefore is not what he believes is the dominating agent of the society, *capital*, nor is it what he believes creates the value and wealth, *labor* – instead it is the *commodity*. From this surface appearance Marx then proceeds to peel away the outer skin of the society and to penetrate to the underlying essential structure that lies in the "hidden abode" of production.

It is not enough of course to only produce the "immense collection of commodities" – they must also be *sold*, so that further investment in production is feasible. Once produced commodities must go through the circuit of distribution, exchange and consumption, so that profit can be returned to the owners of capital and value can be "realized" again in a money form. If the circuit is not completed the system would collapse into stagnation and depression. Capitalism therefore has to ensure the sale of commodities on *pain of death*. In that sense the problem of capitalism is not mass production (which has been solved) but is instead the *problem of consumption*. That is why from the early years of this century it is more accurate to use the label "the consumer culture" to describe the western industrial market societies.

So central is consumption to its survival and growth that at the end of the 19th century industrial capitalism invented a unique new institution – the advertising industry – to ensure that the "immense accumulation of commodities" are converted back into a money form. The function of this new industry would be to recruit the best creative talent of the society and to create a culture in which desire and identity would be fused with commodities – to make the dead world of things come alive with human and social possibilities (what Marx would prophetically call the "fetishism of commodities"). And indeed there has never been a propaganda effort to match the effort of advertising in the 20th century. More thought, effort, creativity, time, and attention to detail has gone into the selling of the immense collection of commodities than any other campaign in human history to change public consciousness. One indication of this is simply the amount of money that has been exponentially expended on this effort. Today, in the United States alone, over $175 billion a year is spent to sell us things. This concentration of effort is unprecedented.

It should not be surprising that something this central and with so much being expended on it should become an important presence in social life. Indeed, commercial interests intent on maximizing the consumption of the immense collection of commodities have colonized more and more of the spaces of our culture. For instance, almost the entire media system (television and print) has been developed as a delivery system for marketers – its prime function is to produce audiences for sale to advertisers. Both the advertisements it carries, as well as the editorial matter that acts as a support for it, celebrate the consumer society. The movie system, at one time outside the direct influence of the broader marketing system, is now fully integrated into it through the strategies of licensing, tie-ins and product placements. The prime function of many Hollywood films today is to aid in the selling of the immense collection of commodities. As public funds are drained from the non-commercial cultural sector, art galleries, museums and symphonies bid for corporate sponsorship. Even those institutions thought to be outside of the market are being sucked in. High schools now sell the sides of their buses, the spaces of their hallways and the classroom time of their students to hawkers of candy bars, soft drinks and jeans. In New York City, sponsors are being sought for public playgrounds. In the contemporary world everything is sponsored by someone. The latest plans of Space Marketing Inc. call for rockets to deliver mile-wide mylar billboards to compete with the sun and the moon for the attention of the earth's population.

With advertising messages on everything from fruit on supermarket shelves, to urinals, and to literally the space beneath our feet (Bamboo lingerie conducted a spray-paint pavement campaign in Manhattan telling consumers that "from here it looks likes you could use some new underwear"), it should not be surprising that many commentators now identify the realm of culture as simply an *adjunct* to the system of production and consumption.

Indeed so overwhelming has the commercial colonization of our culture become that it has created its own problems for marketers who now worry about how to ensure that their *individual* message stands out from the "clutter" and the "noise" of this busy environment. In that sense the main competition for marketers is not simply other brands in their product type, but all the other advertisers who are competing for the attention of an increasingly cynical audience which is doing all it can to avoid ads. In a strange paradox, as advertising takes over more and more space in the culture the job of the individual advertisers becomes much more difficult. Therefore even greater care and resources are poured into the creation of commercial messages – much greater care than the surrounding editorial matter designed to capture the attention of the audience. Indeed if we wanted to compare national television commercials to something equivalent, it would the biggest budget movie blockbusters. Second by second, it costs more to produce the average network ad than a movie like *Jurassic Park*.

The twin results of these developments are that advertising is everywhere and huge amounts of money and creativity are expended upon them.

If Marx were writing today I believe that not only would he be struck by the presence of even more objects, but also by the ever-present "discourse through and about objects" that permeates the spaces of our public and private domains. (see Leiss et al 1990 p. 1) This commercial discourse is the *ground* on which we live, the *space* in which we learn to think, the *lens* through which we come to understand the world that surrounds us. In seeking to understand where we are headed as a society, an adequate analysis of this commercial environment is essential.

Seeking this understanding will involve clarifying what we mean by the power and effectiveness of ads, and of being able to pose the right question. For too long debate has been concentrated around the issue of whether ad campaigns create demand for a particular product. If you are Pepsi Cola, or Ford, or Anheuser Busch, then it may be the right question for your interests. But, if you are interested in the social power of advertising – the impact of advertising on society – then that is the wrong question.

The right question would ask about the *cultural* role of advertising, not its marketing role. Culture is the place and space where a society tells stories about itself, where values are articulated and expressed, where notions of good and evil, of morality and immorality, are defined. In our culture it is the stories of advertising that dominate the spaces that mediate this function. If human beings are essentially a storytelling species, then to study advertising is to examine the central storytelling mechanism of our society. The correct question to ask from this perspective, is not whether particular ads sell the products they are hawking, but what are the consistent stories that advertising spins as a whole about what is important in the world, about how to behave, about what is good and bad. Indeed, it is to ask what *values* does advertising consistently push.

Happiness

Every society has to tell a story about happiness, about how individuals can see themselves and feel both subjectively and objectively good. The cultural system of advertising gives a very specific answer to that question for our society. *The way to happiness and satisfaction is through the consumption of objects through the market place.* Commodities will make us happy. (Leiss 1976 p. 4) In one very important sense that is the consistent and explicit message of every single message within the system of market communication.

Neither the fact of advertising's colonization of the horizons of imagination or the pushing of a story about the centrality of goods to human satisfaction should surprise us. The immense collection of goods have to be consumed (and even more goods produced) and the story that is used to ensure this function is to equate goods with happiness. Insiders to the system have recognized this obvious fact for many years. Retail analyst Victor Liebow said, just after the second world war

> Our enormously productive economy . . . demands that we make consumption our way of life, that we convert the buying and the selling of goods into rituals, that we seek our spiritual satisfaction, our ego satisfaction in commodities . . . We need things consumed, burned up, worn out, replaced, and discarded at an ever increasing rate.
>
> (in Durning 1991 p. 153)

So economic growth is justified not simply on the basis that it will provide employment (after all a host of alternative non-productive activities could also provide that) but because it will give us access to more things that will make us happy. This rationale for the existing system of ever-increasing production is told by advertising in the most compelling form possible. In fact it is this story, that human satisfaction is intimately connected to the provisions of the market, to economic growth, that is the major motivating force for social change as we start the 21st century.

The social upheavals of eastern Europe were pushed by this vision. As Gloria Steinem described the East German transformation: "First we have a revolution then we go shopping." (in Ehrenreich 1990 p.46) The attractions of this vision in the Third World are not difficult to discern. When your reality is empty stomachs and empty shelves, no wonder the marketplace appears as the panacea for your problems. When your reality is hunger and despair it should not be surprising that the seductive images of desire and abundance emanating from the advertising system should be so influential in thinking about social and economic policy. Indeed not only happiness but political freedom itself is made possible by access to the immense collection of commodities. These are very powerful stories that equate happiness and freedom with consumption – and advertising is the main propaganda arm of this view.

The question that we need to pose at this stage (that is almost never asked) is, "Is it true?" Does happiness come from material things? Do we get happier as a society as we get richer, as our standard of living increases, as we have more access to the immense collection of objects? Obviously these are complex issues, but the general answer to these questions is "no." (See Leiss et al 1990 Chapter 10 for a fuller discussion of these issues.)

In a series of surveys conducted in the United States starting in 1945 (labeled "the

rs sought to examine the link between material wealth and
'uded that, when examined both cross-culturally as well
'e is a very *weak* correlation. Why should this be so?
ss more closely the conclusions appear to be less
jective might suggest. In another series of surveys (the
were asked about the kinds of things that are important
constitute a good quality of life. The findings of this line
the elements of satisfaction were divided up into social values
s) and material values (economic security and success) the former
ter in terms of importance. What people say they really want out of life
ny and control of life; good self-esteem; warm family relationships; tension-
.eisure time; close and intimate friends; as well as romance and love. This is not to
say that material values are not important. They form a necessary component of a
good quality of life. But above a certain level of poverty and comfort, material things
stop giving us the kind of satisfaction that the magical world of advertising insists they
can deliver.

These conclusions point to one of the great ironies of the market system. The
market is good at providing those things that can be bought and sold and it pushed
us – via advertising – in that direction. But the real sources of happiness – social
relationships – are outside the capability of the marketplace to provide. The marketplace cannot provide love, it cannot provide real friendships, it cannot provide sociability. It can provide other material things and services – but they are not what makes us
happy.

The advertising industry has known this since at least the 1920s and in fact has
stopped trying to sell us things based on their material qualities alone. If we examine the
advertising of the end of the 19th and first years of the 20th century, we would see that
advertising talked a lot about the properties of commodities – what they did, how well
they did it, etc.. But starting in the 1920s advertising shifts to talking about the
relationship of objects to the social life of people. It starts to connect commodities (the
things they have to sell) with the powerful images of a deeply desired social life that
people say they want.

No wonder then that advertising is so attractive to us, so powerful, so seductive.
What it offers us are images of the real sources of human happiness – family life,
romance and love, sexuality and pleasure, friendship and sociability, leisure and relaxation, independence and control of life. That is why advertising is so powerful, that is
what is real about it. The cruel illusion of advertising however is in the way that it links
those qualities to a place that by definition cannot provide it – the market and the
immense collection of commodities. The falsity of advertising is not in the *appeals* it
makes (which are very real) but in the *answers* it provides. We want love and friendship
and sexuality – and advertising points the way to it through objects.

To reject or criticize advertising as false and manipulative misses the point. Ad
executive Jerry Goodis puts it this way: "Advertising doesn't mirror how people are
acting but how they are dreaming." (in Nelson 1983) It taps into our real emotions and
repackages them back to us connected to the world of things. What advertising really
reflects in that sense is the *dreamlife* of the culture. Even saying this however simplifies a
deeper process because advertisers do more than mirror our dreamlife – they help to
create it. They *translate* our desires (for love, for family, for friendship, for adventure,
for sex) into our dreams. Advertising is like a fantasy factory, taking our desire for

human social contact and reconceiving it, reconceptualizing it, connecting it with the world of commodities and then translating into a form that can be communicated.

The great irony is that as advertising does this it draws us further away from what really has the capacity to satisfy us (meaningful human contact and relationships) to what does not (material things). In that sense advertising *reduces* our capacity to become happy by pushing us, cajoling us, to carry on in the direction of things. If we really wanted to create a world that reflected our desires then the consumer culture would not be it. It would look very different – a society that stressed and built the institutions that would foster social relationships, rather than endless material accumulation.

Advertising's role in channeling us in these fruitless directions is profound. In one sense, its function is analagous to the drug pusher on the street corner. As we try and break our addiction to things it is there, constantly offering us another "hit." By persistently pushing the idea of the good life being connected to products, and by colonizing every nook and cranny of the culture where alternative ideas could be raised, advertising is an important part of the creation of what Tibor Scitovsky (1976) calls "the joyless economy." The great political challenge that emerges from this analysis is how to connect our real desires to a truly human world, rather than the dead world of the "immense collection of commodities."

"There is No Such Thing as 'Society' "

A culture dominated by commercial messages that tells individuals that the way to happiness is through consuming objects bought in the marketplace gives a very particular answer to the question of "what is society?" – what is it that binds us together in some kind of collective way, what concerns or interests do we share? In fact, Margaret Thatcher, the former Conservative British Prime Minister, gave the most succinct answer to this question from the viewpoint of the market. In perhaps her most (in)famous quote she announced: "There is no such thing as 'society'. There are just individuals and their families." According to Mrs. Thatcher, there is nothing solid we can call society – no group values, no collective interests – society is just a bunch of individuals acting on their own.

Indeed this is precisely how advertising talks to us. It addresses us not as members of society talking about collective issues, but as *individuals*. It talks about our individual needs and desires. It does not talk about those things we have to negotiate *collectively*, such as poverty, healthcare, housing and the homeless, the environment, etc.

The market appeals to the worst in us (greed, selfishness) and discourages what is the best about us (compassion, caring, and generosity).

Again this should not surprise us. In those societies where the marketplace dominates then what will be stressed is what the marketplace can deliver – and advertising is the main voice of the marketplace – so discussions of collective issues are pushed to the margins of the culture. They are not there in the center of the main system of communication that exists in the society. It is no accident that politically the market vision associated with neo-conservatives has come to dominate at exactly that time when advertising has been pushing the same values into every available space in the culture. The widespread disillusionment with "government" (and hence with thinking about issues in a collective manner) has found extremely fertile ground in the fields of commercial culture.

Unfortunately, we are now in a situation, both globally and domestically, where solutions to pressing nuclear and environmental problems will have to take a *collective* form. The marketplace cannot deal with the problems that face us at the turn of the millenium. For example it cannot deal with the threat of nuclear extermination that is still with us in the post-Cold War age. It cannot deal with global warming, the erosion of the ozone layer, or the depletion of our non-renewable resources. The effects of the way we do "business" are no longer localized, they are now global, and we will have to have international and collective ways of dealing with them. Individual action will not be enough. As the environmentalist slogan puts it "we *all* live downstream now."

Domestically, how do we find a way to tackle issues such as the nightmares of our inner cities, the ravages of poverty, the neglect of healthcare for the most vulnerable section of the population? How can we find a way to talk realistically and passionately of such problems within a culture where the central message is "don't worry, be happy?" As Barbara Ehrenreich says:

> Television commercials offer solutions to hundreds of problems we didn't even know we had – from "morning mouth" to shampoo build-up – but nowhere in the consumer culture do we find anyone offering us such mundane necessities as affordable health insurance, childcare, housing, or higher education. The flip side of the consumer spectacle . . . is the starved and impoverished public sector. We have Teenage Mutant Ninja Turtles, but no way to feed and educate the one-fifth of American children who are growing up in poverty. We have dozens of varieties of breakfast cereal, and no help for the hungry.
>
> (Ehrenreich 1990 p.47)

In that sense, advertising systematically relegates discussion of key societal issues to the peripheries of the culture and talks in powerful ways instead of individual desire, fantasy, pleasure and comfort.

Partly this is because of advertising's *monopolization* of cultural life. There is no space left for different types of discussion, no space at the center of the society where alternative values could be expressed. But it is also connected to the failure of those who care about collective issues to create alternative visions that can compete in any way with the commercial vision. The major alternatives offered to date have been a gray and dismal *stateism*. This occurred not only in the western societies but also in the former so called "socialist" societies of eastern Europe. These repressive societies never found a way to connect to people in any kind of pleasurable way, relegating issues of pleasure and individual expression to the non-essential and distracting aspects of social life. This indeed was the core of the failure of Communism in Eastern Europe. As Ehrenreich reminds us, not only was it unable to deliver the material goods, but it was unable to create a fully human "ideological retort to the powerful seductive messages of the capitalist consumer culture." (Ehrenreich 1990 p.47) The problems are no less severe domestically.

> Everything enticing and appealing is located in the (thoroughly private) consumer spectacle. In contrast, the public sector looms as a realm devoid of erotic promise – the home of the IRS, the DMV, and other irritating, intrusive bureaucracies. Thus, though everyone wants national health

insurance, and parental leave, few are moved to wage political struggles for them. "Necessity" is not enough; we may have to find a way to glamorize the possibility of an activist public sector, and to glamorize the possibility of public activism.

(Ehrenreich 1990 p.47)

The imperative task for those who want to stress a different set of values is to make the struggle for social change fun and sexy. By that I do not mean that we have to use images of sexuality, but that we have to find a way of thinking about the struggle against poverty, against homelessness, for healthcare and child-care, to protect the environment, in terms of *pleasure and fun and happiness*.

To make this glamorization of collective issues possible will require that the present commercial monopoly of the channels of communication be broken in favor of a more democratic access where difficult discussion of important and relevant issues may be possible. While the situation may appear hopeless we should remind ourselves of how important capitalism deems its monopoly of the imagination to be. The campaigns of successive United States governments against the Cuban revolution, and the obsession of our national security state with the Sandinista revolution in Nicaragua in the 1980s, demonstrate the importance that capitalism places on smashing the alternative model. Even as the United States government continues to support the most vicious, barbarous, brutal and murderous regimes around the world, it takes explicit aim at those governments that have tried to redistribute wealth to the most needy — who have been prioritized collective values over the values of selfishness and greed. The monopoly of the vision is vital and capitalism knows it.

The End of the World as We Know It

The consumer vision that is pushed by advertising and which is conquering the world is based fundamentally, as I argued before, on a notion of *economic growth*. Growth requires resources (both raw materials and energy) and there is a broad consensus among environmental scholars that the earth cannot sustain past levels of expansion based upon resource-intensive modes of economic activity, especially as more and more nations struggle to join the feeding trough.

The environmental crisis is complex and multilayered, cutting across both production and consumption issues. For instance just in terms of resource depletion, we know that we are rapidly exhausting what the earth can offer and that if the present growth and consumption trends continued unchecked, the limits to growth on the planet will be reached sometime within the next century. Industrial production uses up resources and energy at a rate that had never before even been imagined. Since 1950 the world's population has used up more of the earth's resources than all the generations that came before. (Durning 1991 p.157) In 50 years we have matched the use of thousands of years. The west and especially Americans have used the most of these resources so we have a special responsibility for the approaching crisis. In another hundred years we will have exhausted the planet.

But even more than that, we will have done irreparable damage to the environment on which we depend for everything. As environmental activist Barry Commoner says:

The environment makes up a huge, enormously complex living machine that forms a thin dynamic layer on the earth's surface, and every human activity depends on the integrity and proper functioning of this machine . . . This machine is our biological capital, the basic apparatus on which our total productivity depends. If we destroy it, our most advanced technology will become useless and any economic and political system that depends on it will flounder. The environmental crisis is a signal of the approaching catastrophe.

(Commoner 1971 p.16–17)

The clearest indication of the way in which we produce is having an effect on the ecosphere of the planet is the depletion of the ozone layer, which has dramatically increased the amount of ultraviolet radiation that is damaging or lethal to many life forms on the planet. In 1985 scientists discovered the existence of a huge hole in the ozone layer over the South Pole that is the size of the United States illustrating how the activities of humans are changing the very make-up of the earth. In his book *The End of Nature* Bill McKibben reminds us that "we have done this ourselves . . . . by driving our cars, building our factories, cutting down our forests, turning on air conditioners." (1989 p.45) He writes that the history of the world is full of the most incredible events that changed the way we lived, but they are all dwarfed by what we have accomplished in the last 50 years.

Man's efforts, even at their mightiest, were tiny compared with the size of the planet – the Roman Empire meant nothing to the Arctic or the Amazon. But now, the way of life of one part of the world in one half-century is altering every inch and every hour of the globe.

(1989 p.46)

The situation is so bad that the scientific community is desperately trying to get the attention of the rest of us to wake up to the danger. The Union of Concerned Scientists (representing 1700 of the world's leading scientists, including a majority of Nobel laureates in the sciences) recently issued this appeal:

Human beings and the natural world are on a collision course. Human activities inflict harsh and irreversible damage on the environment and on critical resources. If not checked, many of our current practices put at serious risk the future that we wish for human society and the plant and animal kingdoms, and may so alter the living world that it will be unable to sustain life in the manner we know. Fundamental changes are urgent if we are to avoid the collision our present course will bring.

It is important to avoid the prediction of immediate catastrophe. We have already done a lot of damage but the real environmental crisis will not hit until some time in the middle of the next century. However to avoid that catastrophe we have to take action *now*. We have to put in place the steps that will save us in 70 years time.

The metaphor that best describes the task before us is of an oil tanker heading for a crash on the shore. Because of its momentum and size, to avoid crashing, the oil tanker has to start turning well before it reaches the coast, anticipating its own momentum. If it starts turning too late it will smash into the coast. That is where the consumer society is right now. We have to make fundamental changes in the way we organize ourselves, in what we stress in our economy, if want to avoid the catastrophe in 70 years time. We have to take action *now*.

In that sense the present generation has a unique responsibility in human history. It is literally up to us to save the world, to make the changes we need to make. If we do not, we will be in barbarism and savagery towards each other in 70 years time. We have to make short-term sacifices. We have to give up our our non-essential appliances. We especially have to rethink our relationship to the car. We have to make *real* changes — not just recycling but fundamental changes in how we live and produce. And we cannot do this individually, we have to do it collectively. We have to find the political will somehow to do this—and we may even be dead when its real effects will be felt. The vital issue is "how do we identify with that generation in the next century?" As the political philosopher Robert Heilbroner says:

> A crucial problem for the world of the future will be a concern for generations to come. Where will such concern arise? . . . Contemporary industrial man, his appetite for the present whetted by the values of a high-consumption society and his attitude toward the future influenced by the prevailing canons of self-concern, has but a limited motivation to form such bonds. There are many who would sacrifice much for their children; fewer would do so for their grandchildren.
>
> (Heilbroner 1980 pp. 134–5)

Forming such bonds will be made even more difficult within our current context that stresses individual (not social) needs and the immediate situation (not the long-term). The advertising system will form *the ground* on which we think about the future of the human race, and there is nothing there that should give us any hope for the development of such a perspective. The time-frame of advertising is very short-term. It does not encourage us to think beyond the immediacy of present sensual experience. Indeed it may well be the case that as the advertising environment gets more and more crowded, with more and more of what advertisers label as "noise" threatening to drown out individual messages, the appeal will be made to levels of experience that cut through clutter, appealing immediately and deeply to very emotional states. Striking emotional imagery that grabs the "gut" instantly leaves no room for thinking about anything. Sexual imagery, especially in the age of AIDS where sex is being connected to death, will need to become even more powerful and immediate, to overcome any possible negative associations — indeed to remove us from the world of connotation and meaning construed cognitively. The value of a collective social future is one that does not, and will not, find expression within our commercially dominated culture. Indeed the prevailing values provide no incentive to develop bonds with future generations and there is a real sense of nihilism and despair about the future, and a closing of ranks against the outside.

Imagining a Different Future

Over a 100 years ago, Marx observed that there were two directions that capitalism could take: towards a democratic "socialism" or towards a brutal "barbarism." Both long-term and recent evidence would seem to indicate that the latter is where we are headed, unless alternative values quickly come to the fore.

Many people thought that the environmental crisis would be the linchpin for the lessening of international tensions as we recognized our interdependence and our collective security and future. But as the Persian Gulf War made clear, the New World Order will be based upon a struggle for scarce resources. Before the propaganda rationale shifted to the "struggle for freedom and democracy," George Bush reminded the American people that the troops were being dispatched to the Gulf to protect the resources that make possible "our way of life". An automobile culture and commodity-based culture such as ours is reliant upon sources of cheap oil. And if the cost of that is 100,000 dead Iraquis, well so be it. In such a scenario the peoples of the Third World will be seen as enemies who are making unreasonable claims on "our" resources. The future and the Third World can wait. Our commercial dominated cultural discourse reminds us powerfully every day, we need *ours* and we need it *now*. In that sense the Gulf War is a preview of what is to come. As the world runs out of resources, the most powerful military sources will use that might to ensure access.

The destructive aspects of capitalism (its short-term nature, its denial of collective values, its stress on the material life), are starting to be recognized by some people who have made their fortunes through the market. The billionaire turned philanthropist George Soros (1997) talks about what he calls "the capitalist threat" – and culturally speaking, advertising is the main voice of that threat. To the extent that it pushes us towards material things for satisfaction and away from the construction of social relationships, it pushes us down the road to increased economic production that is driving the coming environmental catastrophe. To the extent that it talks about our individual and private needs, it pushes discussion about collective issues to the margins. To the extent that it talks about the present only, it makes thinking about the future difficult. To the extent that it does all these things, then advertising becomes one of the major obstacles to our survival as a species.

Getting out of this situation, coming up with new ways to look at the world, will require enormous work, and one response may just be to enjoy the end of the world – one last great fling, the party to end all parties. The alternative response, to change the situation, to work for humane, collective long-term values, will require an effort of the most immense kind.

And there is evidence to be hopeful about the results of such an attempt. It is important to stress that creating and maintaining the present structure of the consumer culture takes enormous work and effort. The reason consumer ways of looking at the world predominate is because there are billions of dollars being spent on it every single day. The consumer culture is not simply erected and then forgotten. It has to be held in place by the activities of the ad industry, and increasingly the activities of the public relations industry. Capitalism has to try really hard to convince us about the value of the commercial vision. In some senses consumer capitalism is a house of cards, held together in a fragile way by immense effort, and it could just as soon melt away as hold together. It will depend if there are viable alternatives that will motivate people to believe in a different future, if there are other ideas as pleasurable, as powerful, as fun, as passionate with which people can identify.

I am reminded here of the work of Antonio Gramsci who coined the famous phrase, "pessimism of the intellect, optimism of the will." "Pessimism of the intellect" means recognizing the reality of our present circumstances, analyzing the vast forces arrayed against us, but insisting on the possibilities and the moral desirability of social change – that is "the optimism of the will," believing in human values that will be the inspiration for us to struggle for our survival

I do not want to be too Pollyanaish about the possibilities of social change. It is not just collective values that need to be struggled for, but collective values that recognize individual rights and individual creativity. There are many *repressive* collective movements already in existence – from our own home-grown Christian fundamentalists to the Islamic zealots of the Taliban in Afghanistan. The task is not easy. It means balancing and integrating different views of the world. As Ehrenreich writes:

> Can we envision a society which values – not "collectivity" with its dreary implications of conformity – but what I can only think to call *conviviality*, which could, potentially, be built right into the social infrastructure with opportunities, at all levels for rewarding, democratic participation? Can we envision a society that does not dismiss individualism, but truly values individual creative expression – including dissidence, debate, non-conformity, artistic experimentation, and in the larger sense, adventure . . . the project remains what it has always been: to replace the consumer culture with a genuinely *human* culture.
>
> (Ehrenreich 1990 p.47)

The stakes are simply too high for us not to deal with the real and pressing problems that face us as a species – finding a progressive and humane collective solution to the global crisis and ensuring for our children and future generations a world fit for truly human habitation.

Questions

1   How does Jhally defend his position that "our survival as a species is dependent upon minimizing the threat of advertising"? Do you agree with his line of argument?

2   In recent years, many marketers have launched green—or environmentally safe—products and brands. Do you think this trend addresses the concerns of this essay? How might Jhally respond to these marketers?

3   "If human beings are essentially a storytelling species, then to study advertising is to examine the central storytelling mechanism of our society." Come up with a short list of popular advertising campaigns today and identity what stories they tell of contemporary society.

Note

*   Some of the ideas in this chapter have been presented by myself before in "Commercial Culture, Collective Values, and the Future" (*Texas Law Review* Vol 71 No 4, 1993) and the videotape *Advertising and the End of the World* (Media Education Foundation, Northampton, MA, 1998).

428 SUT JHALLY

References

Commoner, Barry (1971) *The Closing Circle; nature, man and technology*. Knopf, New York.
Durning, Alan (1991) "Asking How Much is Enough" in Lester Brown et al. *State of the World 1991*. Norton, New York.
Ehrenreich, Barbara (1990) "Laden with Lard," *ZETA*, July/Aug.
Heilbroner, Robert (1980) *An Inquiry into the Human Prospect: Updated and Reconsidered for the 1980s*. Norton, New York.
Leiss, William (1976) *The Limits to Satisfaction*. Marion Boyars, London.
Leiss, William, Stephen Kline and Sut Jhally (1990) *Social Communication in Advertising* (second edition). Routledge, New York.
Marx, Karl (1976) *Capital* (Vol 1), tr. B. Brewster. Penguin, London.
McKibben, Bill (1989) *The End of Nature*. Randon House, New York.
Nelson, Joyce (1983) "As the Brain Tunes Out, the TV Admen Tune In," *Globe and Mail*.
Scitovsky, Tibor (1976) *The Joyless Economy*. Oxford University Press, New York.
Soros, George (1997) "The Capitalist Threat," *The Atlantic Monthly*, February.

Index

ABC 114, 122–3, 156, 353–4, 404
Absolutely Fabulous 234
abstraction 238–40, 241–2
active consumer 398–9
activism: anti-corporate 7, 369–79; civil
    rights 337; consumer rights 340–1,
    342–3; economic censorship 100–2;
    environmentalism *see* environmentalism;
    pranking 7, 348–68; tobacco control
    166–7
ad creep 412
Adams, J. 312
Adbusters 350, 364, 395; Blackspot sneaker
    348–9, 351–2, 365
addiction 421
Adidas 208
adornment 355
Advertest Research 63–4, 65
Advertisement Tax 16
advertisers: economic censorship 92–3,
    104–5, 105–6; and the female consumer
    60–2; models of communication 99–100
advertising 13–24; and the cultural and social
    world 134–5; defining 2–4; development
    16–20; history 14–16; system 20–4
advertising acceptability departments 103
advertising agencies 131; creative perspective
    133–49; recent changes in the industry 6,
    150–8
advertising recession 151, 154

advertising revenue 77, 92; children's TV
    114; India 176
Advertising Week 157–8
advertorials 96
African Americans 162; Budweiser 'Whassup'
    campaign and African American culture 7,
    256–74; Nike and 216, 218–19; Philip
    Morris and 163, 164
air travel 306–7
airbrushing 280
All in the Family 101
Allen, W.T. 42–3
Almeida, T. 376, 377
Altman, K.E. 298
AMA 86
Amazon 392
American Airlines 306
American Association of Advertising Agencies
    157
American Council on Science and Health 88
American Express 239–40
American Legacy Foundation 'INFKT Truth'
    campaign 356, 361–4
American Society for Thrift 33
American Telephone and Telegraph (AT&T)
    29–30; Information Department 43, 46–9;
    public relations 38–53
American Tobacco Company 87
Americans for Responsible Television 101
Ancient Forests: Rage Over Trees 101

Andersen, A.E. 277
Andrews, B.R. 32
Ang, I. 403
Anglo women 275–90
Anheuser-Busch 256–7, 260, 261–2, 407
animation 116
Annenberg Public Policy Center (APPC) 316
anti-corporate activism 7, 369–79
appearance 183–4, 189
appliances 18
appointment television 404
appropriation 352–3
Arizona, University of 375
'Arkansas Red' (J. Allen) 214
Arnold, T. 93
art 20, 24; advertising as pervasive art form
    245–6; capitalist realism 237–55; Chinese
    202; socialist realism 241, 242; state art
    241, 243–5
art directors 137–46
Ashcroft, J. 307
Ashmore, R. 195–6, 197
'Ask Imhotep' 123–4
Atorino, E. 155
attack: damage control strategy 163, 164, 165;
    political advertising 314–16, 325
attractiveness 284
attention 283
audience: labor and surveillance 385–401;
    rhetoric and 297; TV 402–9
audience research 63–4
authenticity: Budweiser 'Whassup' campaign
    258–62, 264–5, 268–9, 271–3; Nike and
    209, 218–19; speculative consumption and
    the reproduction of the authentic 258–62

Baker, C.E. 97, 98, 104, 106
Baker, N. 216
Barber, B.R. 296, 298–9
Barbie Liberation Organization (BLO) 348,
    356, 357–8
Barnouw, E. 81
Barry, C.C. 69
Barthes, R. 32, 178, 249
bathrooms 33
Batten, Barton, Durstine and Osborn (BBDO)
    87, 150–1
battleground states 313–14, 319–22, 323, 325
'battling' metaphor 140–1
Baughman, J.L. 62
Beat culture 344
beauty, construction of 193–206

beauty types 195–6, 197, 198–9, 199–200,
    201, 203
Beckerman, D.M. 93
Beecham's 18
belief 246–7, 249; circuits of 136
Bell Companies 41; see also American
    Telephone and Telegraph (AT&T)
Bell and Howell Company 81
Bell System 41
Benetton 102–3
Bennett, J.G. 76–7
Benson and Hedges 160–1, 162
Berger, J. 195
Bergreen, L. 70
Bernbach, B. 153
Bernstein, D. 243–4
Bernstein, S. 98
Bernstein Research 151
Bertelsmann 397
Best Buy 300–1
Better Homes in America campaign 298
Billenness, S. 374
Biotic Baking Brigade (BBB) 356, 359–61
Biswas, A. 194–5
BJ&B 376
Blackspot sneakers campaign 348–9, 351–2
blame 98–100
Bloomberg, M. 318
Bobcard Gold 186
Boddy, W. 62
body: female and the construction of beauty
    201–2, 203; media effects on body image
    280–1; New Indian and body
    consciousness 181; women and excessive
    thinness 275–90
Bordo, S. 279
Bourdieu, P. 143
boycotts 101, 104–5
Brandreth, Dr 76–7
brands 13–14; literary approach to branding
    227–36; student anti-corporate activism
    372–5
Braverman, H. 388
Bretz, R. 63
bricoleurs 145
Britt, S. 340
Bronstein, C. 71
Brooks, J. 84
Brooks, S. 260, 262, 264, 265
Brown, T. 102–3
Brown, W. 359
Brown University 376

Brown and Williamson Tobacco Corporation
    80, 88–9
Bryant, K. 244
Bud.TV 407
Budd, M. 112
Budweiser 'Whassup' campaign 7, 256–74
Buffalo, New York 413
bugs 111
bulk institutional purchases 371
bumpers (program separators) 111, 115,
    122–3
Burger King 151
Burke, K. 297
Burma 373–4
Burnett, L. 153
Bush, G. 34, 426
Bush, G.W. 306–7, 410; 2000 presidential
    campaign 324–5; 2004 presidential
    campaign 315, 316, 319–23
Butler, J. 398
buzz marketing 413

cable television 404
Cahn, W. 378
California, University of 375
Calvin Klein 349
Camel News Caravan 79
Campbell, C. 232–3
candy 411
capitalism 7, 21, 220, 416–17, 423, 425–6
capitalist realism 237–55; concept 238–43
car industry 304, 341
career 283
Carlet, V. 194–5
Carleton University, Ottawa 372–3
Carlyle, T. 18
Carson, R. 342
Carstarphen, M. 195
Carter, B. 92
Cartoon Network 114, 124
cathouse for dogs 353–4
CDs 158
celebrities 239–40, 242
Center for the Study of Commercialism (CSC)
    99, 106
Chamorro, R. 277
Chaney, D. 179
Channel One 411
channel surfing 120–1
charitable giving 303–4
Charland, M. 297
Charlotte Observer 88

Chayefsky, P. 81
Cheng, H. 195
childhood 210–11
children 413–14; targeting 412–13; see also
    schools
children's television 110–27
Children's Television Act 1990 114–15
Chinese art 202
Ching, K.S. 198–9
Chipso 30
choice 183–4
Christian Leaders for Responsible Television
    (CLeaR-TV) 100
Chrysler 150–1
Chyanwanprash 188–9
cigarettes see tobacco
circle of communication model 99–100
circuits of belief 136
citizen consumers 297–9
citizenship 179; as charitable giving 303–4; as
    consumption 304–6; consumption and
    after September 11 295–311; corporations
    as citizens 300–2
civil rights movement 337
class, social 64; Indian middle class 178–82
classified ads 14, 15, 16, 238
clients, and control of creative process 143–4
Clinton, H. 332
clothing, and anti-corporate activism 7,
    369–79
Club of Rome 342
CNN 330
Coalition of Lavender Americans on Smoking
    and Health 163
Coca-Cola 244–5, 374, 412
Cohen, L. 298
cold war 298
collective values 421–7
college newspapers 103
Collegiate Licensing Company 376
Collins, R.K.L. 91, 106
colonial societies 178, 180
colonization of culture 416–18
color 32–3
color-consciousness 261
Colorado coal miners' strike 39
Columbia Broadcasting Systems (CBS) 65,
    395, 404
comedians 353
comedies, television 62
comic strips 363
commercial realism 240

commercial television 62
commercialism 410–15; colonization of culture 416–18; of sport 213–15
commission system 153, 154
commodification, unconsciousness of 269–70
commodities 416–17
commodity flow 110–27; construct 111–13; inter-channel 120–1; intra-channel 116–20; synergistic 121–4
Commoner, B. 423–4
communication: circle of communication model 99–100; top-down model 99
communism 422
community: anti-corporate activism 7, 369–79; brands as gated communities 234–5
comparative shopping 85
competing strategies 263–5
complete man 186
concealment 165
Concerned Citizens for Quality Television 101
condom advertising 103
Consciousness III 344–5
conservative consumer groups 100–1
consolidation 151, 153–4
constant comparison method 278
Constitution 411; First Amendment 97, 105, 106, 243
constitutive rhetoric 297–9
consumer culture 4–5; critiques of 34–5; in historical perspective 25–37
consumer durables 61
consumer rights activism 340–1, 342–3
consumerism, 'new' 339–47
consumers 21–4; female 60–2; models of communication 99–100; voice 100–2
consumption: and citizenship after September 11 295–311; citizenship as 304–6; nationalizing 300–6; theory of consumer behaviour 246
content: economic censorship 91–109; media content and advertising 76–90
content analysis: advertising after September 11 299–308; Budweiser 'Whassup' campaign 263–5; women's magazines 197–203
Contessa cars 184–5
contested discourses 215–19
contradictions, cultural 219–21
control: clients and the creative process 143–4; disciplinarity and 352–3; thin body and 284

convenience 25, 29–31
conviviality 427
'cookie' 399
cooking shows 66
cool hunters 365
Cooper, R. 374
co-option 163, 164, 165
copytesting 142–3
copywriters 137–46
Corner, J. 112
corporate disclosure 377
corporate greed 44
corporations: anti-corporate activism 7, 369–79; as citizens 300–2; power 358, 410–11
corruption 77; subtle 78–9
Cosby, B. 240
cosmopolitanism 180–1
Council on American-Islamic Relations 217
counterculture 344–5
couples 244
Craig, R.L. 94, 98
Craig, S. 112
creative workers: and media buyers 151–2; perspective of 133–49
credit cards 182
Creel, G. 39–40
Cronin, A.M. 136
Cuban revolution 423
cultural discourse 138–40
cultural icon 207–9
cultural intermediaries 135–6, 140
cultural signifiers 140
cultural world 134–5
culture jamming 348–68; theory of 351–6
Curatola, S. 154

Dabur 188–9
Daisy ad 315–16
Dallas Cowboys 213
damage control strategies 163–5
Dangoor, D. 162, 165
Danilova, A. 68
Daragan, K. 164, 165
Darling-Wolf, F. 195
Daschle, T. 329
database marketing 406, 407–8
Dauenspeck, R.D. 69
daughters, marriage of 187
David Yurman 303
Davis, R. 209
Days, The 156

daytime television 59–75
DDB World Wide 261
deaths from smoking 85–9
Debord, G. 259, 351
deception 314–16, 340–1
DeForrest, L. 403
Deleuze, G. 352, 366
Delineator, The 298
Dell 299
demand 339–40
democracy 22, 97; consumer culture
    and citizenship after September 11
    295–311
denial 163, 164, 165
Denis Parkar clothing 185
department stores 238
Depression 298
Derr, K. 359, 360
detachment 248
détournement 351, 363
Deutsch, D. 152–3, 155
DiDomenico, L. 277
dieting 284–5
Digimon 117–18, 120
digital butler 399
digital enclosure 392–4, 399; interactive
    surveillance in 391–2
digital VCR technology 394–7, 405–6
discipline 352–3, 389
disclosure, corporate 377
discourse analysis 137–44
Disney 114, 121, 122–3, 395
Disney World 307
distancing strategy 163–5
distinctiveness, universalism and 257–8
distortion 179
Doctors Ought to Care 165
Dolan, L. 208, 215
dolls, 'hacked' 348, 357–8
domestic sphere 27, 61–2
dominant ideology 178
Dominican Republic 376
DotComGuy (M. Maddox) 385–6
Douglas, S.J. 61, 62
Dowd, M.J. 317
drama 81
Du Mont 63, 64
Duesenberry, J. 246
Duke University 376
duplicate products 29–30
DuPont 154–5
Durning, A. 423

East Harbor Chinese and Japanese Restaurant
    304
Eastern Europe 422
eating disorders 276
e-commerce 385–6
economic censorship 91–109; regulating
    98–106
economic forecasting models 324
economic growth 339–40, 341–2, 343, 419,
    423
Editor and Publisher 88
editorials 82–3, 103
education of the public 45, 50
Ehrenreich, B. 422–3, 427
Ehrlich, P. 342
Eisenhower, D. 313
electric signs 18, 19
Electronic Privacy Information Center (EPIC)
    386
Elliott, S. 161, 162
Ellsworth, J.T. 41–2, 43, 49
empowerment 398–9
Englis, B. 195–6, 197
English, D. 257
enlightened self-interest 50
enthymemes 315–16
environmentalism 35, 341–3; global
    environmental problems 414, 422, 423–5
Esquire 82
ethnicity 182; African Americans see African
    Americans; construction of beauty 199,
    200, 201, 202–3, 203–4; and female body
    thinness 275–90
ethnography 133, 137–44
European Union 412–13
everyday objects 28
Ewen, S. 62
experience 250–1; relating to 267–8

factories 27
Fair Campaign Practices Committee 315
Faludi, S. 71
family 187, 188–9
fashion 31–3, 84
Federal Commission on Industrial Relations
    39, 40
Federal Communications Commission (FCC)
    79, 80, 88, 106
Federal Trade Commission 105, 243
'feeding the brain' 138–40
feeling: inanimate objects and 230–2; stories
    and 228

feminism 34, 194–5
femininity 193; ideal in magazines 278
'fighting' metaphor 140–1
films *see* movies
financial companies 302
Finn, M. 331
First Amendment 97, 105, 106, 243
Fish, F.P. 41
fitness 279
flabbiness 279
flag, US 296, 301, 305
Flores-Ortiz, Y. 277
Florida State University 375
'fluff' 83
fly-posting 18
focus groups 266–70, 277–86
folding 355
food 84; early advertising of patent foods 18
Food and Drug Administration 105
Ford 31, 93, 304
Fordism 352
Fortier, Mr 47
Foucault, M. 136, 352, 365, 387, 388–9, 393
Fournier, R. 317
Fox Network 103; Kids Network 114, 117, 118
fragmentation, media 156–7
France 250
Francis, A. 68
Frank, B. 104
fraud, against consumers 340–1
Free Burma Coalition 374
Free the Children 378
free press 102
free speech 96, 97–8
freedom 176, 182, 190, 419; convenience and 30; of the media 102–3
Freenet 396
Friedan, B. 59–60, 62
Friedman, J. 180
Friedman, M. 359
Frigidaire 30
Frito Lay 407
Frye, N. 247, 248
Funk and Wagnalls 83

G.I. Joe 348, 357–8
Galbraith, J.K. 414
game metaphor 140–1
Gap 349
Garner, D.M. 277
Garner, J. 239, 246

Garry Moore Show, The 65
gated communities, brands as 234–5
Gates, B. 359, 360, 391–2, 397
Gay and Lesbian Alliance Against Defamation (GLAAD) 163, 164, 166
gay and lesbian tobacco control movement 166–7
gay press, advertising tobacco in 159–70
Geertz, C. 250, 251
Gelman, A. 324
General Electric 30
General Motors (GM) 30, 93, 304, 407
gender 7; and advertising 175–92; stereotypes and Barbie Liberation Organization 357–8
genre 229–30
Genre 160–7
Giddens, A. 388, 391
Gilder, G. 393
Giuliani, R. 305, 332
Gladrags 184
Glance, S. 88
globalization 296; and the construction of beauty 196–7; gender and adverts in India 175–92
Godaddy.com 406
Godey's Lady Book 82
Goffman, E. 178, 240
Goldwater, B. 315–16
Goodis, J. 420
Goody, J. 237
Gordon, J. 119–20
Gore, A. 324–5
Gotlieb, I. 153
Gould, J. 69
government restrictions 105–6
Gramsci, A. 426
'Great Chain of Being' 231
Griffin, M. 195
Grove, S. 330
Guinness 240
Gulf War 426

'hacked' dolls 348, 357–8
Hackley, C. 136
Hagen, M.G. 324–5
Hall, E.K. 46
Halverstadt, A.N. 79, 80
handbills 18, 312
happiness 419–21
happiness surveys 419–20
Haralovich, M.B. 61–2

Hariman, R. 295, 296
Harley Davidson 235
Harper's 82
Hartley, M. 239, 246
Hartman, P. 93
Hartmann, S.M. 61
Harvard University 373, 378
Harvey, D. 390
Havas 155
Hawkins pressure cookers 188
Hayes, S. 369, 370
Head, S.W. 66
health 181; marketing related diseases
    413–14; media coverage of smoking and
    85–9
hegemony 178
Heilbroner, R. 425
Held, D. 307–8
Heller, W. 339
heuristics 314, 315
hippies 344
Hirota, J.M. 135
history: of advertising 14–16; historical
    perspective on consumer culture 25–37
hit lists 93
hoaxes 353–5, 364
Hofstede, G. 193
holding companies 152, 153–4
holophrasm 228–9
Home 59, 60, 67–70; response to and its
    demise 69–70
Home Depot, The 303
homemaking 61–2, 62–3, 65–70
homosexuality 105; advertising tobacco to gay
    men 159–70
Hoover, H. 298
Horton, D. 63
household, and the industrial order 26–7
Houston Chronicle 85, 97
Hudson Vitamin Products 87
Hughes, G. 373
'Human Be-In' 344
hybridization 182

I Remember Mama 62
ideal body shape 275–90; perceptions of
    278–80; privilege and 282–4; what women
    do to attain 284–5
idealization 244–5
identification: post-September 11 advertising
    300–1, 306; rhetoric as 297
identificatory fantasies 282

identificatory practices 281
ideology: dominant 178; levels of 'learning' an
    ideology 249; of science 141–3; system of
    2–3, 5
ideology critique 215–19
image: gaps between image and practice 220;
    of philosophy and philosophy of image
    209–13
immigrants 44
impressionism 230, 231–2
India 175–92
India Kings 187
industrial barons 51
industrial order 26–7
Industrial Revolution 16, 21, 232
'INFKT Truth' campaign 356, 361–4
Information Revolution 387
infotainment 77
integral ads 113
intelligence gathering 49
interactive media 385–401
inter-channel commodity flow 120–1
intergenerational responsibility 425
internationalism 180–1
Internet 71; database marketing 407–8;
    DotComGuy 385–6; impact on political
    campaigns 328–33; inter-media
    commodity flow 123–4; spam 412;
    surveillance 387, 391–4, 396, 399
interpretation 356
interpretative repertoires 137–44
Interpublic 154, 155
intra-channel commodity flow 116–20
irony 247–9
iVillage 71
Ivory Soap 32, 78

J. Walter Thompson 156
Jackson, A. 312
Jackson, J. 216
Jameson, F. 350
Jamieson, K.H. 324–5, 331
Janowski, R. 359, 360
Jeffrey, B. 156
Jello Pudding 240
Jhally, S. 386, 390–1
Joe Chemo 364
Johnson, L.B. 315–16
Johnson, S. 15–16
Johnston, R. 324–5
Jordan, B. 244
Jovan fragrance 102

Juno, A. 365, 366

Kaess, K. 156, 157
Kansas City 42
Kate Smith Hour, The 64, 65, 67
Katona, G. 340
Keady, K. 375
Keats, J. 231–2
Keen, A. 329
Kefauver, E. 340
Kellner, J. 405
Kelvinator Refrigerator 189
Ken 82
Kent State University 374
Kernaghan, C. 378
Kerry, J. 314, 315, 316, 319–23
Kids WB 114, 117, 119, 123–4
Kielburger, C. 378
King, G. 324
Kipling, R. 93–4
Kleinfeld, N.R. 93
Kmart 296, 301
Knight, P. 213, 218, 219, 349, 365
Kramer, R. 98
Krugman, H. 248
Kunkel, D. 119
Kushell, L. 71
Kyrk, H. 32
Kyung, J.L. 196

labor issues *see* sweatshop labor
Ladies Home Journal 403
Lambiase, S. 194
Lancet, The 85–6
Lasch, C. 249
Lash, S. 180
Laski, M. 247
Latina women 275–90
laughter 117
laundry products 30
law enforcement 307–8
Law and Order 92
Lawrence Mill sweatshop strike 378
Lazarus, S. 153, 155
leadership, strong 319–24
learning: levels of 'learning' an ideology 249;
    low involvement and without involvement
    248
Lee, I.L. 39–40
Lee, S. 216
Leiss, W. 64
Lenk, K. 387

Leo Burnett agency 160–1
Lester, T. 392, 393
Levi-Strauss, C. 145
Lewis, D.J. 49
Lewis, M. 394, 395
LG 299
liberalization 175, 177, 180, 183, 190
Library of Congress 412
licensed characters 113–14, 117–18
Liebow, V. 419
Lien, M.E. 145
lifestyle ads 180
LifeTargeting 317
Lifetime 71
Linkreum, R. 69
Lipman, J. 94, 161
Lipovetsky, G. 31, 32
Lippmann, W. 44
Lipset, S.M. 339
Lipsitz, G. 61, 62
Livant, B. 386, 390–1
living end credits 110
living wage 377
local governments: anti-corporate activism
    371–2; commercialism 413
Lorillard 361–2
low-involvement learning 248
Ludlow Massacre 39
Lynd, H.M. 33
Lynd, R.S. 33
Lyon, D. 387

Macy's 95, 97
Maddox, M. (DotComGuy) 385–6
magazine advertising (on TV) 67
magazine format (TV) 63, 67–70
magazines: content and advertising 82–3,
    87–8; economic censorship 93, 93–4,
    95–6; gender and adverts in India 175–92;
    Truth campaign 362–3; women's *see*
    women's magazines
magic system 20–4
Magnuson, W. 340
Mahler, R. 93
Mailer, N. 343
Malden, K. 240, 242
male bonding 257, 260–1, 263–4
male gaze 195
Malhans, S. 181
Marchand, R. 32, 67, 394
Marcuse, H. 343, 344
Margolius, S. 340–1

Mark, K. 416–17, 425
market 28–9
market basket surveys 85
Married . . . With Children 105
Marshall, J. 68
mass consumption 32
mass customization 389, 391–2, 396
mass production 27–8
mass society repressive hypothesis 393–4
materialism 13, 20, 232–3, 414
Mattel Corporation 357, 358
May, E.T. 61
McCain, J. 330
McCann, R. 156
McCarrick, T. 377
McChesney, R.W. 70
McCracken, G. 134
McDonald's 374; World Children's Day 413
McFadyen, R.W. 65
McGovern, C. 298
MCI 410
McIlrath, M. 119
McKibben, B. 424
McKinnon, M. 323
McNulty, J. 104–5
McReynolds, D. 344
media: content and advertising 76–90;
    economic censorship 93–7, 102–3, 105–6;
    effects on body image 280–1; female body
    and realism 280; fragmentation 156–7;
    models of communication 99–100;
    socializing agent 281–2
media buyers 152, 155–6
media pranking 7, 348–68
media support system 3–4, 5
medicines 15, 17, 18
men: advertising cigarettes to gay men
    159–70; Indian print media 183–7
Mercedes-Benz 180
mergers and acquisitions 151, 153–4
Meury, R. 242
Meyer, E. 154
MGM 85
Mickey Mouse Club 113
Microsoft 185
middle class, Indian 178–82
Mills, T. 67, 69
Milwaukee 42
MindShare 4, 152, 155, 156
Missouri and Kansas Telephone Company 42
Mobil Oil 411
Modern Medicine 83

Modleski, T. 112
Montagu, A. 68
Montgomery Ward company 33
Moody's Magazine 47
Morgan Stanley 302
Morley, R. 242
Morrell and Company 303
Morris, N. 332
Moscow Olympics (1980) 243
Mother Jones 87
motivational research 340
Mouritsen, J. 306
movies 417; reviews 85
multiple content forms 117–18
Murphy, G. 150, 151
music industry 158, 397
myth 178; branding and mythology 229,
    235–6

Nader, R. 341
Napster 396, 397
narrative 228–36
Nast, C. 82
National Annenberg Election Study (NAES)
    316, 319
National Association of Radio and Television
    Broadcasters (NARTB) 66
National Broadcasting Corporation (NBC) 65,
    79, 97, 395, 404; *Home* 59, 60, 67–70;
    Today 316
National Christmas Tree lighting ceremony
    410
National Coalition on Television Violence
    (NCTV) 100–1
National Do Not Call Registry 412
National Football League 407
National Union of Students (UK) 373, 374
natural experiments 319–24
need, satisfaction of 22–3
negative advertising 314–16, 325
Negroponte, N. 399
Nelson, S. 155
neo-conservatism 421
Neon car advert 232, 233
NEPC Agro Foods 187–8
network programming directors 404
'new consumerism' 339–47
New Deal 298
'New Indians' 178–82
New Jersey archdiocese 377
New York City 413
New York Herald 76–7

New York Times 83, 95, 97; advertising after September 11th 296, 299–308; feature on products demonstrating patriotism 305

New York Times Company 83, 303

New York Times Index 86

New Yorker, The 102–3

News Corporation 114

news-books 14–15

newspapers 51; content and advertising 83–5, 86, 88; economic censorship 93, 93–4, 95–6; gender and adverts in India 175–92; history of advertising 14–17, 18–19

Newsweek 87

Ni, Z. 373

Nicaragua 423

Nickelodeon 114

Nielsen Company 403, 404, 405–6

Nietzsche, F. 353

Nigeria 374

Nightingales 101

Nike 6, 349, 365; advertising and Nike's production processes 207–22; cultural contradictions 219–21; labor issues 209, 216–18, 369, 375

nuclear weapons 422

Nurses Association 101

Obama, B. 329, 330, 331

O'Barr, W. 195

Oberoi Hotels 185

obesity and overweight 282–3, 413–14

obsolescence 25, 342; as a marketing tool 31–2

Ocean City, Maryland 413

Offen, H. 163

Ogilvy, D. 153

oil 426

Okay Mother 64

Olsen, J.E. 194–5

Olympic Games 243

OMD 155

Omnicom 154, 155

O'Neil, R.N. 93

Operation PUSH 216

optimism of the will 426–7

Osborn, F. 341–2

Oxygen 71

ozone layer depletion 424

Packard, V. 340, 342, 343, 344

Pajama Party 71

panopticon 136

Parenti, C. 359

Paris Museum of Traditional and Popular Arts 249–50

Parks, B. 69

parodies: culture jamming 349, 350, 351–2; spoof 'Whassup' ads 266, 268–9

party identification 314

pathetic fallacy 230, 232–3

patriotism 300–8

Paul, R. 329, 332

Pauline, M. 360

Pears 18

Penn, M. 209–10

Pepsi 372–4

Pepsi Twist 150

Perot, R. 313

'personality' items 19

pessimism of the intellect 426–7

pesticides 342

Pew Internet and American Life Project 331

Pfizer 155

pharmaceutical firms 83

Philip Morris 159–70; damage control strategies 163–5

philosophy 209–13

phone rates 45

phonograph 63

photography 242, 245

Piccoli, S. 93

pie-throwing 359–61

Pinkham, R.A.H. 68

placards 18

play 210–11

pleasure 282

Pokémon 117, 121

Polaroid 239, 246

political advertising 312–27; aggregate level influence 324–5; individual level influence 319–24; influence of 318–25; *see also* presidential campaigns

political fundraising 328–9, 332

Pool, H.W. 47

population growth 342

Posner, V. 98

posters 18

Potter, J. 137

power: Budweiser 'Whassup' campaign 272–3; children's TV and power differences between sources and audiences 125; corporations 358, 410–11; female thinness and 284; interactive media and 398–400; men, success and 184–6;

relationship between advertising creatives and client 143–4

pranking 7, 348–68; as rhetorical appropriation 356–64

Prefontaine, S. 213

presidential campaigns: impact of the Internet 328–33; role of advertising 312–27

price customization 392

prime time 81

print media: advertising and content 82–3; economic censorship 93, 93–4, 94–5; gender and adverts in India 175–92; see also magazines, newspapers

Printer's Ink 88

privacy 386–7, 387–8, 393, 399

private sphere 27, 61–2

privilege 282–4

privilege cards 374

Procter, D.E. 258

Procter and Gamble (P&G) 4, 30, 78, 79–80, 93, 413

procurement departments 154–5

product integration and cross-promotion 406–7

product placement 406, 412

productivity 388–90

products: safety and environmental standards 105–6; types and content analysis of women's magazines 199, 200–1, 202, 204

program characters 118–20

program-length commercials 115

program promotions 115

program separators (bumpers) 111, 115, 122–3

Project Oxygen 399

Prose, F. 71, 72

Prudential Insurance 80

public opinion 47–9

public relations 19–20; development in AT&T 38–53

public service announcements (PSAs) 245; children's TV 115, 119–20, 124

public sphere 27, 51

Publicis 155

Publicity Bureau 41–3

Puckric, K. 71

Pudin Hara 185–6

puffery 15, 16, 17–18

quality of life surveys 420

Quintessence 102

R.J. Reynolds 162, 363

RTMark 357–8

radio 60–1, 62, 63, 403; advertising and content 78–81

Radio Shack 93

Rainie, L. 331

Ramirez, A. 93

ratings, TV 404, 405–6

rationalization 389–91

Raymond Suitings 187

Reader's Digest 83

Reader's Digest 83, 87

Reader's Digest Association 83

Reagan, N. 361

real estate 84

realism: advertising as capitalist realism 237–55; female body in the media 280

reality, and representation 179

reassurance 302

recall 249, 403–4

recession, advertising 151, 154

Redstone, S. 157

Reebok 208–9

Reeves, R. 153

regulation 98–106

Reich, C. 344, 345

Reichert, J. 194

relating to an experience 267–8

religion 247, 249–50; brands as religious stories 235–6

Replay Corporation 396

ReplayTV 394, 405

representation, reality and 179

repressive hypothesis 393–4

reproducibility 259

research 142–3

resource depletion 423

resource scarcity 342, 426

Reyes, R. 376

rhetoric 297; constitutive 297–9; pranking rhetoric 356–66

risk 142–3

'roadblocks' 121

Robertson, B. 66

Robertson, T. 245

Robins, K. 387, 393

Robinson, J. 218–19

Rockefeller, J.D. 39, 43, 50

Rodriguez, K. 376

Roe vs Wade 97

Rogers, Mrs H.J. 69

Rogers, W. 76

Romanticism 230–2, 232–3
Romney, M. 330, 331
Roosevelt, T. 50
Roots 81
Rosebud, R. 360
Rosenblum, B. 242
Ross, E.A. 51
Rossiter, J. 245
Rothenberg, R. 152
Rubin, J. 344, 345
Ruggiero, J. 359

sabotage 349–50, 352–3, 355–6
sagas 234
Saks Fifth Avenue 301
Sandburg, C. 39
Sandinista revolution 423
sandwich boards 18, 19
Sanka coffee 239
Satterfield, D. 68
satellite television 404
Saturday Night Live 93
Scarpelli, B. 260
Schiller, D. 389
Schmidt-Vogel, A. 157
Schofield, A. 61
Schonberger, E. 87
schools: advertising in 411; anti-corporate
    activism 369–72, 377
Schumacher, E.F. 342
Schwartz, D. 195
science, ideology of 141–3
scientific management 388
Scott, L.M. 134
Sealey, P. 152
Sears 303
Securities Exchange Commission 105
Sedelmaier, J. 242
segue ads 113
Sein Win 373–4
Seiter, E. 116, 125
self-censorship 97
self-improvement 71
selling atmosphere 81–2
Sen, S. 188
sensitized concepts 115
September 11 attacks, consumption after 7,
    295–311
sex appeal 194–5
Shapiro, A. 395
Shapiro, R. 359, 360
shared textual elements 116–17

shopping programs 66
Shortway, R. 83
Siew, F. 198–9
Sifry, M. 330
sign wars 208–9
Silverman, F. 404
Silverman, J. 97
Silverstein, B. 277
Simm, D. 394
Singapore 196–203
Situationists 351, 363
Skaggs, J. 353–5, 356
Skybag luggage 185
Smith, B.R. 103
Smith, H.K. 88
Smith, R.C. 87
Smithsonian Institution 412
smoking *see* tobacco
Smokurb 87
soap operas 60, 63
soaps 28
Soar, M. 135–6
social change, need for 423–7
social discourse 138–40
social justice 34
social media sites 407
social organization 22
social problems 422–3
Social Research 64
social systems 251
social world 134–5
socialism 21; socialist societies in Eastern
    Europe 422
socialist realism 241, 242
socialization 281–2
society 421–3
Society for Checking the Abuses of Public
    Advertising (SCAPA) 19
soda pop 411
'Solemn Duty' ad 323
Soley, L.C. 94, 98
Solomon, M. 195–6, 197
Soros, G. 426
Sorrell, M. 156
Sosnik, M.J. 317
sounds 116–17
Space Marketing Inc. 418
spam 412
spectacle, the 259, 351
spectacular consumption 256–74; and the
    reproduction of the authentic 258–62
Spice Girls 209

Spigel, L. 63, 68
Spiro, M. 249
Spitzer, L. 247–8
sponsorship 411, 417–18; anti-corporate activism 371–2, 372–3, 374–5; children's TV 113; Nike 213–15
sport: commercialization of 213–15; Nike advertising 208, 211–12, 213–15
squeezed credits 110
St John's University 375
St Mary's Secondary School, Pickering, Ohio 369–71
Stacey, J. 281, 282
Stamp Duty 16, 18
Standard Oil 39
standardization 27–8, 33, 352
Stanford University 373, 375
Starch, D. 403
Starcom MediaVest Group 152, 155
Stasheff, E. 62–3
state art 241, 243–5
stateism 422
Steinem, G. 93
Steinman, C. 112
Stengel, J. 156
Sterling Drugs 64
Stevenson, A. 313
Stone, C. 256–7, 260, 261, 262, 263–4, 265
stories 228–36
Stratton, L. 240
Stroh Brewery 101
strong leadership 319–24
Stuart and Frankle 304
Student Alliance to Reform Corporations 375
students' anti-corporate activism 7, 369–79
study guides 228
stylistic exaggeration 355
subordination 398
success 184–6
Sullivan, Mr 47
Sun Kyi, Aung San 373
Super Bowl 257, 406–7
supermarkets 408
surveillance 385–401
Sweatshop Fashion Show 369–71
sweatshop labor: Nike 209, 216–18, 369, 375; student activism 369–71, 375, 376–8
Swift Boat Veterans for Truth (SBVT) 322–3
Swoosh Integrity Committee 215
swooshification 215; see also Nike
symbolic capital 207–9

synechdoche 359
synergistic commodity flow 121–4
systems: advertising as magic system 20–4; interconnected systems of ideology and media support 2–4, 5; social systems 251

Taiwan 196–203
Tan, W.K. 198–9
Tannenbaum, D. 377
Tarde, G. 48, 51
targeting: children 412–13; perceptions of target audience of 'Whassup' campaign 267–8; political advertising 316–18
Taylor, F.W. 388
Teen Talk Barbie 348, 357–8
teenage smoking 356, 361–4
telemarketing 412
telephone operators 45
telephone rates 45
telephones 41–51
Telerep 93
television (TV) 150–1, 248, 412; advertising and content 78–81, 88; audience 402–9; capitalist realism 239–40, 241–2; children's TV 110–27; economic censorship 92–3, 94–5; presidential campaigns 313, 315–16, 318–26; women and early daytime TV industry 59–75
television flow 111–12
television personalities 239–40, 242
terrorist attacks, advertising after 7, 295–311
Texas, University of 103
textual elements, shared 116–17
Tharp, M. 134
Thatcher, M. 421
thinness, body 275–90
Third World First 373
Thomas, F. 262, 264, 272
Thomas, R. 358
thrift 33
Tien, E. 305
Tierney, T.F. 29
time: saving 29; surveillance and 391
Time 87
Time Warner 114, 121, 123, 395
TiVo 151, 394–7, 405
tobacco 413; advertising to gay men 159–70; advertising and media content 85–9; pranking against tobacco companies 356, 361–4

Tobacco Institute 86
Tobin, J. 339
Today 316
Today Show, The 67
Tonight Show, The 67
top-down model of communication 99
Tortorici, P. 101
toy industry 113–14; pranking against 348, 356, 357–8
Tracy, J. 375
Traub-Werner, M. 375
Tremor 413
Trippi, J. 330
Trout, J. 100
truth 249
Truth campaign 356, 361–4
Turk, M. 330
Tuthill, D. 161, 162, 166
two-way communication 40

unconsciousness of commodification 269–70
UNESCO MacBride Commission 238
UNICEF 413
Union of Concerned Scientists 424
UNITE 376
United Airlines 306, 308
United Kingdom Billposters Association 18, 19
United States (US): flag 296, 301, 305; presidential campaigns *see* presidential campaigns; women's magazines compared with Singapore and Taiwan 196–203
United Students Against Sweatshops 377–8
universal service 46
universalism 260–1, 271; and distinctiveness 257–8
universities 371–8
Uptown 162
user-generated content 406, 407

Vail, T.N. 40–1, 43–7, 47–8, 49–50, 50–1
Vale, V. 365, 366
values: alternative to capitalism 251–2; collective 421–7; promoted by advertising 244–5, 418–21
Veblen, T. 33, 34, 343
Viacom 114, 121
video press releases 360–1
Viénet, R. 363
Viguerie, R. 329
viral communication 365

Virgin Atlantic Airways 151
Verklin, D. 155, 156
Viswanath, K. 195
Vogue 82–3

WABD 63, 64
Washington Star 85
Webster, F. 387, 393
Week, The 183–4
West, D.M. 317
Wetherell, M. 137
'Whassup' campaign 7, 256–74
'What are you doing' advert 271–3
Whelan, E. 87–8
Whitehall Laboratories 80
Wieden, D. 209
Wildmon, D. 100
Williams, J. 162
Williams, P. 260, 262, 263–4, 265, 272
Williams, R. 111–12
Willis, P. 82
Wipro 186
Wired 392
Wiseman, C.V. 277
Wolf, D. 92, 93
'Wolves' ad 316
women: advertisers and the female consumer 60–2; and early daytime TV industry 59–75; excessive thinness 275–90; Indian print media 182–3, 187–9
women's magazines 87–8; and the construction of beauty 193–206; India 175–92
Wood, J. 193
Wordsworth, W. 230–1
work: audience labor and surveillance 385–401; sweatshop labor *see* sweatshop labor; women and 61
working conditions 45
workplace monitoring 388, 391
World Children's Day 413
World Health Organization (WHO) 86; Framework Convention on Tobacco Control 413
World Trade Center 296, 302
WorldCom 410
WPP 153–4, 155
Wright, J. 331

Yarbrough, J. 162, 166
Yeaman, A. 89
Young, A. 217

Young, R. 239
Your Television Shopper 66
YouTube 330–1

ZapMel 411
Zavoina, S. 194
Zoonen, L. van 177